Communication Systems Modelling and Simulation

Using MATLAB® and Simulink®

Communication Systems Modelling and Simulation

Using MATLAB® and Simulink®

K C Raveendranathan

Professor and Head

Department of Electronics & Communication Engineering

Government Engineering College Barton Hill

Thiruvananthapuram 695 035

Universities Press

UNIVERSITIES PRESS (INDIA) PRIVATE LIMITED

Registered Office
3-6-747/1/A & 3-6-754/1, Himayatnagar, Hyderabad 500 029 (A.P.), India
E-mail: info@universitiespress.com; Web: www.universitiespress.com

Distributed by
Orient Blackswan Private Limited

Registered Office
3-6-752 Himayatnagar, Hyderabad 500 029 (A.P.), India

Other Offices
Bangalore / Bhopal / Bhubaneshwar / Chandigarh / Chennai / Ernakulam / Guwahati
Hyderabad / Jaipur / Kolkata / Lucknow / Mumbai / New Delhi / Noida / Patna

First published 2011

ISBN 978 81 7371 722 2

Typeset in Life BT 10/12 *by*
OSDATA, Hyderabad 500 049

Printed at
Printline Printers
Hyderabad 500 029

Published by
Universities Press (India) Private Limited
3-6-747/1/A & 3-6-754/1, Himayatnagar
Hyderabad 500 029 (A.P.), India

To
my daughters
Anuja and Aabha

Contents

Preface

Signals and systems, communication theory, control systems, analog communication, digital communication and digital signal processing can be taught more effectively with a high level computer programming language. Of all computer languages, MATLAB® is the preferred language of the technical computing fraternity. MATLAB is very user-friendly and has a fast learning curve. It is can be used as the backbone of simulations, thereby reinforcing the concepts taught in the above courses.

For several years, while teaching undergraduate students various courses in communications systems, the author had felt the need of a book which would provide the theoretical background as well as the practical know-how of modelling and simulating systems with ease. *Communications Systems Modelling and Simulation Using MATLAB and Simulink* was the result.

The style adapted in the entire text is quite straight-forward: first the concepts are presented in a lucid and clear-cut manner. This is followed by appropriate simulations in MATLAB/Simulink. Relevant MATLAB source code is given whenever it is used to illustrate a point. All the programmes given in the text have been tested on MATLAB kernel version 7.10 (Release R2010a) and are almost bug-free. However, they would also work well with a lower version, such as 7.0 (Release 14).

The book starts with a brief introduction to computer simulation. The elementary concepts in systems simulation are discussed in Chapter 1. Various types of simulations are also considered. Important performance measures and major simulation tools are also discussed. The second chapter starts with a brief introduction to MATLAB programming for system simulation. We also consider several free-ware alternatives to MATLAB like Octave, and Scilab. It is hoped that the student/teacher will effectively use this material as a starting point in programming in MATLAB, and soon graduate to system level programming, making use of any of the books mentioned in *Further Reading*.

The third chapter is entirely devoted to system simulation techniques using Simulink ®. The real power of a GUI-based tool like Simulink is introduced with several examples. The concept of signals and systems is clearly brought out in Chapter 4. Several examples are given with the help of MATLAB plots. Analog and discrete time signals are clearly discussed. The signal processing toolbox in MATLAB is introduced for this purpose. In

Chapter 5, we discuss simulation of analog modulation systems. The chapter starts with the basic concepts of modulation and its need and merits. It goes on to discuss amplitude modulation (AM). Simulation of angle modulation is the topic of discussion in Chapter 6. The mathematical equation for FM and PM waves are derived and Bessel functions are introduced. The interrelationship between FM and PM are carefully brought in. Simulation of FM and PM generation is done for typical input waveforms like square waveforms and triangular waveforms. Digital modulation schemes like ASK, FSK and PSK are discussed in Chapter 7. Chapter 8 deals with probability and random processes. It is assumed that students have a basic knowledge of probability concepts. Advanced concepts like random variables and random processes, statistical independence, autocorrelation and cross-correlation functions and covariance are explained. A number of probability density/mass functions are introduced with the help of their mathematical models. Corresponding 2-D plots are obtained using MATLAB.

Several graded examples are given throughout the text. The book contains a number of figures and tables which make the discussion more clear and lucid. A bibliography is appended at the end of each chapter, which would be of some assistance to the advanced learner. The reader is encouraged to look for errors that might have crept in, and communicate the same to the author through e-mail at ravi@gecbh.ac.in.

Acknowledgements

The author would like to place on record his immense thanks to his students, faculty colleagues, and the reviewers who have contributed considerably to the successful completion of this book. This project is supported by The MathWorksTM Inc. under their Book Program for Authors. Special thanks to Mrs B S Ramya of The MathWorks India Office Bangalore; Ms Naomi Fernandez, the Book Program coordinator at The MathWorks Inc., USA; and Ms Meg Vulliez and Ms Dana Wright of The MathWorks Inc., USA for providing all the software licenses so promptly. Thanks are also due to the publishers for taking up this project and completing it in a short time. The constructive suggestions made by the reviewers are thankfully acknowledged. The author would also like to appreciate the moral support rendered by his wife Sobha and daughters Anuja and Aabha during the entire period he spent preparing the manuscript.

K.C.Raveendranathan

1

Introduction to Systems, Models and Simulations

Soon after computers conquered the technology landscape, system simulation emerged as an efficient tool to model, simulate and solve real world engineering problems. Through the work of engineers, applied mathematicians, and physicists over the years, theoreticians discovered an uncanny ability at the core of computer simulation: it could potentially solve any system of physical phenomena through a set of partial differential equations (PDEs)—equations which could describe all sorts of physics such as fluid motion, electromagnetic fields, and structural mechanics. In essence, the theoreticians realised that computer simulation could translate these well-known mathematical objects and in turn the physical phenomena, into a computationally equivalent digital format.

A model is a simplified representation of a system at some particular point in time or space created to promote a better understanding of the real system. A simulation is the manipulation of a model in such a way that it operates on compressed time or space, thus enabling one to perceive interactions that would not otherwise be apparent because of their separation in time or space. Modelling and simulation together form a discipline for developing a level of understanding of the interaction of the parts of a system, and of the system as a whole. The level of understanding which may be developed through this discipline is seldom achievable through any other discipline.

Simulation, in other words, is the process of realising the model of a real or imagined system and conducting experiments with that model. Thus, computer simulations can represent real or imaginary situations. They allow users to study or try things that would be difficult or impossible to do in real life. Simulation attempts to predict aspects of the behaviour of some system by creating an approximate (mathematical) model of it. Computers provide an ideal environment for building simulations. Simulations have many uses, including the following:

- Businesses use simulations to develop and optimise processes since they can lower risks associated with critical decisions.
- Engineers use simulations to prototype and test designs.

- Researchers use simulations to validate hypotheses.

In a broader sense, computing can be viewed as simulation because computer programs resemble the domains to which they are applied. Simulations are particularly useful when a real life process

- is too dangerous,
- takes too long to complete,
- is too quick to study or
- is too expensive to create.

The intention of this book is to study modelling and simulation of various real world electrical engineering problems using the computational tool MATLAB®, which is a highly inherently parallel high level language and Simulink®. We will consider the most important concepts in modelling and simulations in this chapter.

1.1 Systems Simulation: The Shortest Route to Applications

Advancements in computing power, availability of personal computer based modelling and simulation, and efficient computational methodology have helped sophisticated prescriptive simulation modelling such as optimisation to pursue investigations in systems analysis, design, and control processes that were previously beyond the reach of modellers and decision makers.

1.1.1 Introduction

Computer system users, administrators, and designers usually have a goal of highest performance at lowest cost. Modelling and simulation of the system design trade-off is good preparation for design and engineering decisions in real world jobs. In this book, we will study computer systems modelling and simulation using MATLAB and Simulink. But before we start, we need to have a proper knowledge of both the techniques of simulation modelling and the simulated systems themselves.

In addition to its use as a tool to better understand and optimise performance and/or reliability of systems, simulation is also extensively used to verify the correctness of designs. Most, if not all, digital integrated circuits manufactured today are first extensively simulated before they are manufactured to identify and correct design errors. Simulation of the product early in the design cycle is important because the cost of repairing mistakes detected later in the product life cycle increases dramatically the later it is detected. Another important application of simulation is in developing "Virtual environments", for example, for training. Similar to the holodeck in the popular science-fiction television programme *Star Trek*, simulations generate dynamic environments with which users can interact "as if they were really there". Such simulations are used extensively today to train military personnel for battlefield situations, at a fraction of the cost of running exercises involving real tanks, aircraft, and so on.

Dynamic modelling in organisations is the collective ability to understand the implications of change over time. This skill lies at the heart of successful strategic decision process. The availability of effective visual modelling and simulation enables the analyst and the decision maker to boost their dynamic decision making by rehearsing strategy which would avoid hidden pitfalls.

1.1.2 Computer Simulation

System simulation is the mimicking of the operation of a real system, such as the day-to-day operation of a bank, or the value of a stock portfolio over a time period, or the running of an assembly line in a factory, or the staff assignment of a hospital or a security company, in a computer. Instead of building extensive mathematical models with the help of experts, readily available simulation software has made it possible for non-experts, who are managers but not programmers to model and analyse the operation of a real system.

A system simulation can also be defined as the execution of a model, represented by a computer program that gives information about the system being investigated. The simulation approach of analysing a model is opposed to the analytical approach, where the method of analysing the system is purely theoretical. As this approach is more reliable, simulation provides gives more flexibility and convenience. The activities of the model consist of events which are activated at certain points in time. In this way, they affect the overall state of the system. The points in time that an event is activated are randomised, so there is no need for input from outside the system. Events exist autonomously and they are discrete so nothing happens between the execution of two events. The *SIMSCRIPT* provides a process-based approach of writing a simulation program. With this approach, the components of the program consist of entities which combine several related events into one process.

In the field of simulation, the concept of "principle of computational equivalence" has beneficial implications for the decision maker. Simulated experimentation accelerates and replaces effectively the "wait and see" anxieties in discovering new insight and explanations of future behaviour of the real system. With the integration of artificial intelligence, agents and other modelling techniques, simulation has become an effective and appropriate decision support for managers.

1.2 Modelling and Simulation

Simulation, in general terms, is pretending that one is dealing with a real thing while really working with an imitation. In operations research, the imitation is a computer model of the simulated reality. A flight simulator on a personal computer is also a computer model of some aspects of the flight: it shows on the screen, the controls and what the "pilot" (the person who operates it) is supposed to see from the "cockpit" (his seat).

One can list several reasons for resorting to computer simulations.

1. The cost of the experiment by simulation works out to be cheaper. To fly a simulator is safer and cheaper than the real airplane. For precisely this reason, models are used in industry, commerce, and military: it is very costly, dangerous and often impossible to make experiments with real systems. Provided that models are adequate descriptions of reality (they are valid), experimenting with them can save money, suffering and even time.

2. Simulations are more appropriate means to study a *dynamically changing system*. Systems that change with time, such as a gas station where cars come and go (called dynamic systems) and involve randomness, render themselves easily to a simulation study. Modelling complex dynamic systems theoretically need too many simplifications and the emerging models may, therefore, not be valid. Simulation does not require that many simplifying assumptions, making it the only tool feasible even in the absence of randomness.

3. Simulations can easily be done based on the mathematical model of the system. For example, we may describe the behaviour of a gas station graphically by plotting the number of cars in the station; the state of the system. Every time a car arrives, the graph increases by one unit, while a departing car causes the graph to drop one unit. This graph (called sample path), can be obtained from observing a real station. But it can also be artificially constructed. Simulation consists of such artificial construction and the analysis of the resulting sample path (or more sample paths in more complex cases).

1.3 Types of Simulations

The etymology of simulations is very versatile. We need to consider the following types of simulations.

- Discrete event simulation
- Continuous simulation
- Steady state simulation
- Random event simulation
- Social simulation
- Web enabled simulation
- Parallel and distributed simulation

1.3.1 Discrete Event Simulation

The sample path in the case of the gas station consisted of only horizontal and vertical lines, as car arrivals and departures occurred at distinct points of time, which we will refer to as events. Between any two consecutive events, nothing happens—the graph is horizontal. When the number of events are finite, we call the simulation a *discrete event simulation*. Discrete event simulation (DES) is very suitable for implementation in a digital computer.

1.3.2 Continuous Simulation

In some systems, the state changes all the time, not just at the time of some discrete event. For example, the water level in a reservoir with a given inflow and outflow may change all the time. In such cases, *continuous simulation* is more appropriate, although discrete event simulation can serve as an approximation.

1.3.3 Steady State Simulation

Unlike in queueing theory where steady state results for some models are easily obtainable, steady state simulation is not an easy task. The opposite is true for obtaining results for the transient period (i.e., the warm-up period).

To gather steady state simulation output requires statistical assurance that the simulation model has reached the steady state. The main difficulty is in obtaining independent simulation runs excluding the transient period. The two techniques commonly used for steady state simulation are the *method of batch means*, and the *method of independent replication*.

The two methods are similar in performance—they depend on the magnitude of the traffic intensity. The other available technique is the *regenerative method*, which is mostly used for its theoretically nice properties. However it is rarely applied in actual simulation for obtaining steady state numerical results.

1.3.4 Random Event simulation

Quite often than not, real world events are *random* events and statistical models are more appropriate to study them. A simple example could be building a simulation of a gas station with a single pump served by a single service man. Assume that the arrival of cars as well their service times are random. At first we will identify the following:

- *States* number of cars waiting for service and number of cars served at any moment,
- *Events* arrival of cars, start of service, end of service,
- *Entities* these are the cars,
- *Queue* the queue of cars in front of the pump, waiting for service,
- *Random realisations* inter-arrival times, service times, and
- *Distributions* we shall assume exponential distributions for both the inter-arrival time and the service time.

At event of entity arrival, create next arrival. If the server is free, send entity for start of service. Otherwise, it joins the queue. At event of service start, the server becomes occupied. Schedule the end of service for this entity. At event of service end, the server becomes free. If entities are waiting in queue, remove the first entity from the queue; and send it for start of service.

We have not yet fully formulated the problem. Some initiation is still required, for example, the creation of the first arrival. Lastly, the above *flow chart* is translated into code. This is easy with an appropriate library which has sub-routines for creation, scheduling, proper timing of events, queue manipulations, random variate generation and statistics collection. Besides the above, the program should record the number of cars in the system before and after every change, together with the length of each event.

1.3.5 Social Simulation

Social scientists have always constructed models of social phenomena. Simulation is an important method for modelling social and economic processes. In particular, it provides a "middle way" between the richness of discursive theorising and rigorous but restrictive mathematical models. There are different types of computer simulation and their applications for social scientific problems.

Faster hardware and improved software have made building complex simulations easier. Computer simulation methods can be effective for the development of theories as well as for prediction. For example, macro-economic models have been used to simulate future changes in the economy; and simulations have been used in psychology to study cognitive mechanisms.

1.3.6 Web Enabled Simulation

Web based simulation is quickly emerging as an area of significant interest for both simulation researchers and simulation practitioners. This interest in web based simulation is a natural outgrowth of the proliferation of the World Wide Web (WWW) and its attendant technologies, e.g. HTML, HTTP, CGI and so on. The ensuing popularity and reliance upon computer simulation as a problem solving and decision support systems tool have fostered web enabled simulation.

The emergence of the network friendly programming language, Java, and of distributed object technologies like the common object request broker architecture (CORBA) and the object linking and embedding/component object model (OLE/COM) have had particularly decisive effects on the state of simulation practice.

1.3.7 Parallel and Distributed Simulation

The increasing size of systems and designs requires more efficient simulation strategies to accelerate the simulation process. Parallel and distributed simulation approaches seem to be a promising approach in this direction. Current topics under extensive research are the following.

- Synchronisation, scheduling, memory management, randomised and reactive/adaptive algorithms, partitioning and load balancing.
- Synchronisation in multi-user distributed simulation, virtual reality environments, high level architecture (HLA) [1] and inter-operability.
- System modelling for parallel simulation, specification, re-use of models/code, and parallelising existing simulations.
- Language and implementation issues, models of parallel simulation, execution environments, and libraries.
- Theoretical and empirical studies, prediction and analysis, cost models, benchmarks, and comparative studies.
- Computer architectures, VLSI, telecommunication networks, manufacturing, dynamic systems, and biological/social systems.
- Web based distributed simulation such as multimedia and real time applications, fault tolerance, implementation issues, use of Java, and CORBA.

1.4 Discrete Event Systems (DES)

Discrete event systems (DES) are dynamic systems which evolve in time by the occurrence of events at possibly irregular time intervals. They are in abundance in real world applications. Examples include traffic systems, flexible manufacturing systems, computer communications systems, production lines, coherent lifetime systems, and flow networks. Most of these systems can be modelled in terms of discrete events whose occurrence causes the system to change from one state to another. In designing, analysing and operating such complex systems, one is interested not only in performance evaluation but also in sensitivity analysis and optimisation.

A typical stochastic system has a large number of control parameters that can have a significant impact on the performance of the system. To establish a basic knowledge of the behaviour of a system when the input parameter values are changed and to estimate the relative importance of the input parameters, *sensitivity analysis* applies small changes to the nominal values of input parameters. For systems simulation, variations of the input parameter values cannot be made infinitely small. The sensitivity of the performance measure with respect to an input parameter is therefore defined as a (partial) derivative.

Sensitivity analysis is concerned with evaluating sensitivities (gradients, Hessian, etc.) of performance measures with respect to the parameters of interest. It helps to make design and operational decisions, and plays a pivotal role in identifying the most significant system parameters, as well as sub-systems that may result in bottlenecks.

The major steps involved in discrete event simulation are the following:

1. *Problem formulation* Identify controllable and uncontrollable inputs. Identify the

[1] HLA, in the context of simulation, is a distributed computer simulation standard.

constraints on the decision variables. Define the measure of system performance and an objective function. Develop a preliminary model structure to interrelate the inputs and the measure of performance.

2. *Data collection and analysis* Regardless of the method used to collect the data, the decision of how much to collect is a trade-off between cost and accuracy.
3. *Simulation model development* Acquiring sufficient understanding of the system to develop an appropriate conceptual, logical and then simulation model is one of the most difficult tasks in simulation analysis.
4. *Model validation, verification and calibration* In general, verification focuses on the internal consistency of a model, while validation is concerned with the correspondence between the model and reality. The term "validation" is applied to those processes which seek to determine whether or not a simulation is correct with respect to the "real" system. More prosaically, validation is concerned with the question, "Are we building the right system?". Verification, on the other hand, seeks to answer the question, "Are we building the system right?" Verification checks that the implementation of the simulation model (program) corresponds to the model. Validation checks that the model corresponds to reality. Calibration checks that the data generated by the simulation matches real (observed) data.
   - *Validation* The process of comparing the model's output with the behaviour of the phenomenon. In other words: comparing model execution to reality (physical or otherwise)
   - *Verification* The process of comparing the computer code with the model to ensure that the code is a correct implementation of the model.
   - *Calibration* The process of parameter estimation for a model. Calibration is the tweaking/tuning of existing parameters and usually does not involve the introduction of new ones which change the model structure. In the context of optimisation, calibration is an optimisation procedure involved in system identification or during experimental design.
5. *Input and output analysis* Discrete-event simulation models typically have stochastic components that mimic the probabilistic nature of the system under consideration. Successful input modelling requires a close match between the input model and the true underlying probabilistic mechanism associated with the system. The input data analysis is to model an element (e.g., arrival process, service times) in a discrete event simulation given a data set collected on the element of interest. At this stage, intensive error checking on the input data, including external, policy, random and deterministic variables, is performed. System simulation experiment is done to learn about its behaviour. Careful planning, or designing, of simulation experiments is generally a great help, saving time and effort by providing efficient ways to estimate the effects of changes

in the model's inputs on its outputs. Statistical experimental design methods are mostly used for simulation experiments.

6. *Performance evaluation and what-if analysis* The "what-if" analysis is at the very heart of simulation models.
7. *Sensitivity estimation* Users must be provided with affordable techniques to analyse the sensitivity of a model if they are to understand which relationships are meaningful in complicated models.
8. *Optimisation* Traditional optimisation techniques require gradient estimation. As with sensitivity analysis, the current approach for optimisation requires intensive simulation to construct an approximate surface response function. Incorporating gradient estimation techniques into convergent algorithms, such as Robbins–Monroe type algorithms for optimisation purposes have been considered.
9. *Gradient estimation applications* There are a number of applications which measure sensitivity information, (i.e., the gradient, Hessian, etc.), local information, structural properties, response surface generation, goal-seeking problem, optimisation, what-if problem, and meta-modelling.
10. *Report generating* Report generation is a critical link in the communication process between the model and the end user.

1.5 Determination of Time to Reach Steady State

There are several methods to estimate the long-term performance measure of a system, such as batch means, independent replications and the regenerative method. Batch means is a method of estimating the steady-state characteristic from a single-run simulation. The single run is partitioned into equal size batches large enough for estimates obtained from different batches to be approximately independent. It is important to ensure that the bias due to initial conditions is removed to achieve at least a covariance stationary waiting time process. An obvious remedy is to run the simulation for a period large enough to remove the effect of the initial bias. During this transient period, no attempt should be made to record the output of the simulation. The results during this period are rejected. At the end of this transient period, the waiting time of customers are collected for analysis. The practical question is, "How long should the transient period, p be?" Abate and Whitt provided a relatively simple and closed form expression for the time required (t_p) for an $M/M/1/$ queue system (with traffic intensity r) starting at the origin (empty) to reach and remain within 100% of the steady state limit as follows:[2]

$$t_p(r) = 2C(r)\frac{\ln\left\{\frac{1}{(1-p)(1+2C(r))}\right\}}{(1-r)^2} \tag{1.1}$$

[2] Although this result was developed for $M/M/1$ queues, it has already been established that it can serve as an approximation for more general, i.e., $GI/G/1$ queues.

where

$$C(r) = \frac{2 + r + (r^2 + 4r)^{1/2}}{4}. \tag{1.2}$$

1.6 Determination of the Desirable Number of Trials

The two widely used methods for experimentation on simulation models are *method of batch means*, and *independent replications*. Intuitively, one may say the method of independent replication is superior in producing a statistically "good" estimate of the system's performance measure. In fact, not one method is superior in all cases—it all depends on the traffic intensity r.

After deciding what method is more suitable, the main question is determining the number of runs or trials. That is, at the planning stage of a simulation, investigation into the number of simulation runs (n) is critical.

The confidence level of simulation output drawn from a set of simulation runs depends on the size of the data set. The larger the number of runs, the higher is the associated confidence. However, more simulation runs also require more effort and resources for large systems. Thus, the main goal must be in finding the smallest number of simulation runs that will provide the desirable confidence. *When the statistics for calculating the number of simulation trials is not available from existing database, a pilot simulation is needed.*

1.7 Selection of Simulation Software

The vast amount of simulation software available can be overwhelming for new users. The following list contains only a random sample of software in market today, and it is no way exhaustive.

- ACSL
- APROS
- ARTIFEX
- Arena
- AutoMod
- C++SIM
- CSIM
- Call$im
- Flexsim 3D
- CommSim
- SRML
- SPICE
- SUGAR
- Scicos
- SimPy
- MIMIC
- FluidFlow
- GPSS
- Gepasi
- JavSim
- MJX
- MedModel
- Mesquite
- Multiverse
- NETWORK
- OPNET Modeler
- POSES++
- Simulat8
- Powersim
- QUEST
- REAL
- SHIFT
- SIMPLE++
- SIMSCRIPT
- SLAM
- SMPL
- SimBank
- SimPlusPlus
- TIERRA
- Witness
- SIMNON
- EICASLAB
- NetSim
- Javasim
- Simulink®
- SimElectronics®
- SimEvents®
- Stateflow®

- ModelSim®
- CircuitLogix
- ASCEND
- Mathematica®.
- Visual Modelling
- *Z*
- VisSim
- Simula.

There are several things that make a simulation package ideal. Some are properties of the package, such as support, reactivity to bug notification, interface, etc. Some are properties of the user, such as their needs, their level of expertise, and so on. For these reasons, asking which is the best package is not relevant. The first question to ask is, for what purpose one needs the software—whether it is meant for education, teaching, student projects or research.

The answer to the question, *"What are the important aspects to look for in a package?"* depends on specific applications. However some general criteria are the following.

- Input facilities
- Processing that allows some programming
- Optimisation capability
- Output facilities
- Environment including training and support services
- Input–output statistical data analysis capability
- Cost factor

1.8 High Performance Simulation Tools

High performance computing has grown largely in scale with Moore's law. As hundreds of millions—and soon to be billions—of transistors crowd onto processor chips, they support computing devices of more and more complexity. Predicting the performance of these machines often requires sophisticated software programs to model them. Performance simulators—software programs typically written in a high-level language such as C or C++ —enable exploration of design alternatives for future high performance computers.

Performance modelling and analysis are now integral to the design flow of modern computing systems, especially for high-performance microprocessors. Designers begin by developing performance models of the target architecture, followed by its actual logic design—also called register transfer language, or RTL. Circuit designers convert the logic specification into circuits, and layout engineers eventually position the circuits on the processor floor plan. For very complex designs, such a design process can take as long as seven years. Of course, the process involves close interactions between the steps. The performance model, in particular, is refined as logic, and circuit designers feed back better timing estimates for different hardware components of the target architecture. Thus, the performance model's fidelity to the target architecture is often key to the success of the architecture itself.

Additionally, the performance model must run atleast faster than the RTL; otherwise, developers might as well obtain performance estimates from the logic blocks themselves.

Experience shows that performance models usually run several orders of magnitude faster than RTL.

The increased complexity of target architectures and applications has made performance modelling a daunting task. Microarchitecture pipelines have extended from five to 20 stages to exploit increasing levels of parallelism. This trend will continue as Web server and database markets require both fine-grained multithreading embedded in aggressive pipelines and coarse-grained multiprocessing spanning multiple processors. Such multithreading and multiprocessing architectures are even being done on chip, exemplified by Intel's hyperthreaded architectures, IBM's Power4, and Hewlett-Packard's Mako processor.

Estimating system performance for several scenarios via simulation generally requires a separate simulation run for each scenario. In some very special cases, such as the exponential density $f(y; v) = ve^{-vy}$, one can obtain the perturbed estimate using perturbation analysis directly as follows. One generates the random variate Y by using the inverse transformation:

$$Y_i = \frac{1}{v} \ln\left(\frac{1}{U_i}\right) \tag{1.3}$$

where $\ln$ is the natural logarithm and U_i is a random number distributed uniformly in $[0, 1]$. In the case of perturbed v, the counterpart realisation using the same U_i is

$$Y_i = \frac{1}{v + dv} \ln\left(\frac{1}{U_i}\right). \tag{1.4}$$

Clearly, this single run approach is limited, since the inverse transformation is not always available in closed form.

Thus, one of the real benefits of modelling and simulation is its ability to accomplish a time and space compression between the inter-relationships within a system. This brings into view the results of interactions that would normally escape us because they are not closely related in time and space. Thus, modelling and simulation can provide a way of understanding dynamic complexity.

Understanding the performance of distributed computing, network servers, and parallel applications on the new generation of processors requires studying how they interact with the system architecture and the operating system. Unfortunately, performance models that can evaluate system architectures and operating systems have evolved into extremely complex and gigantic software projects.

There are several performance simulators—*Rsim, Simics, SimpleScalar*, and *Asim*—that address different aspects of the complexities encountered in performance simulation.

Performance simulation is a research topic of long-standing importance and it comprises a vast amount of literature. The simplest technique for optimising the performance of a simulation is the random selection of some points in the search region for estimating the performance measure. In this technique, one usually fixes the number of simulation runs and takes the smallest (or largest) estimated performance measure as the optimum. This method is useful in combination with other techniques to create a multi-start process for global optimisation. The most effective technique to overcome local optimality for discrete optimisation is the Tabu Search technique. In general, probabilistic search techniques, as a class, offer several advantages over other optimisation techniques based on gradients. In the random search technique, the objective function can be non-smooth or even have discontinuities. The search program is simple to implement on a computer, and it often shows good convergence characteristics in noisy environments. More importantly, it can offer a global solution in a multi-modal problem, if the technique is employed in the global sense.

1.9 Conclusion

A system is understood to be an entity which maintains its existence through the interaction of its parts. A model is a simplified representation of the actual system created to promote understanding. Whether a model is good or not depends on the extent to which it promotes understanding. Since all models are simplifications of reality there is always a trade-off as to what level of detail is included in the model. If too little detail is included in the model, one runs the risk of missing relevant interactions and the resultant model does not promote understanding. If too much detail is included in the model, the model may become overly complicated and actually preclude the development of understanding. One simply cannot develop models in the context of the entire universe.

A simulation generally refers to a computerised version of the model which is run over time to study the implications of the defined interactions. Simulations are generally iterative in there development. One develops a model, simulates it, learns from the simulation, revises the model, and continues the iterations until an adequate level of understanding is developed.

With the growing incidence of computer modelling and simulation, the scope of the simulation domain must be extended to include much more than traditional optimisation techniques. Optimisation techniques for simulation must also account specifically for the randomness inherent in estimating the performance measure and satisfying the constraints of stochastic systems. We have discussed the most widely used simulation techniques that can be effectively integrated into a simulation model. We have also described techniques for post-solution analysis with the aim of theoretical unification with the existing techniques.

General comparisons among different techniques in terms of bias, variance, and computational complexity are not possible. However, a few studies rely on real computer simulations to compare different techniques in terms of accuracy and number of iterations. Total computational effort for reduction in both the bias and variance of the estimate depends on the computational budget allocated for a simulation optimisation. No single technique works effectively and/or efficiently in all cases.

Further Reading

1. Bossel, H. *Modelling and Simulation*. A. K. Peters Publishers. 1994.
2. Fishman, G. *Discrete Event Simulation: Modelling, Programming and Analysis*. Berlin: Springer-Verlag. 2001.
3. Klee, Harold. *Simulation of Dynamic Systems with MATLAB and Simulink*. New York: CRC Press. 2007.
4. Law, Averill M. and W. David Kelton. *Simulation Modelling and Analysis*, 3rd Edition. McGraw-Hill 2000.
5. Liu, J.S. *Monte Carlo Strategies in Scientific Computing*. New York: Springer. 2001.
6. Ross, Sheldon M. *Simulation*, 4th Edition. Academic Press. 2008.
7. Rubinstein, R. and B. Melamed. *Modern Simulation and Modelling*. Wiley. 1998.

2

Introduction to Programming in MATLAB

In this chapter we will introduce the basic concepts in the MATLAB® programming environment. It should be noted that MATLAB is the *defacto language of the technical computing community*, the world over. Most of the modern day communication systems simulation is done with the help of this powerful high level language. MATLAB provides an interactive programming environment with hundreds of built-in functions for technical computations, graphics, and animation. The built-in functions provide excellent tools for linear algebra, data analysis, signal processing, optimisation, numerical solution of ordinary differential equations (ODEs), quadrature and many other types of scientific computations. There are several functions for 2-D and 3-D graphics and for animation. Both professional (commercial) and student versions of MATLAB are available.

2.1 Introduction to MATLAB

MATLAB stands for *MATrix LABoratory*. It is a high performance numerical computation and visualisation language. MATLAB is supported by almost all operating systems platforms. In the 1960s and 1970s, before the appearance of personal computers, complex and large-scale calculations were done on large mainframes using code primarily developed with FORTRAN[1]. As a number of related large sub-routines were developed for specific computational purposes, they were organised into public domain packages and distributed for free. MATLAB was originally created as a front end for one of these, the LINPACK package—a group of routines for working with matrices and linear algebra by the University of New Mexico and Stanford University. The primary developer, Professor Cleve Moler (Figure 2.1) at the University of New Mexico, eventually founded The MathWorks™, Inc., to further develop and market the product in a commercial setting. From the original MATLAB, a high powered suite of applications has evolved.

[1] FORTRAN is an acronym for FORmula TRANslator

Figure 2.1 Cleve B. Moler (1939 –): The numerical analyst who developed MATLAB

The language is interpreter based and the commands are executed line by line by the MATLAB interpreter. However compilers are available for later versions. The currently available (latest) version, R2010a, was released in March 2010. The MATLAB R2010a suite features the newest kernel, MATLAB 7.10. It is largely backward compatible with recent MATLAB versions, but there are some slight changes. The MathWorks, Inc. now is on a semi-annual cycle of releasing updates of MATLAB and its various auxiliaries in March and September.

The reason why MATLAB is so useful for signal processing is that it was not designed specifically for signal processing but for mathematics. An important feature of MATLAB is that it is optimised for matrix operations. Matrix operations are very conveniently handled in MATLAB, with the same ease as scalars. This will become very evident as we go further. MATLAB is considered to be the most suited programming language for communication system modelling and simulation.

2.2 Basic Features of MATLAB

The fundamental data type in MATLAB is an array. Dimensioning is not necessary. Vectors (of size $1 \times N$ or $N \times 1$) are the next simpler data type. Two types of formats are available for integers—short and long. The short integer represents the integers in 16 bits and long integer in 32 bits. Strings/structures are another data type. MATLAB is optimised for array/vector processing. Certain features of C/C++ (for example, inheritance and operator overloading) is carried over in MATLAB too. MATLAB has a very rich repertoire of built-in mathematical/logical functions. Users are free to enhance this list of functions. A collection of special functions is available as toolboxes. Communication engineering students may find the following toolboxes most suitable for their courses.

- Signal Processing Toolbox
- Communications Toolbox
- Simulink Control Design
- Control System Toolbox
- Simulink
- Neural Network Toolbox

- Fuzzy Logic Toolbox
- Communications Blockset
- Symbolic Math Toolbox
- Signal Processing Blockset
- RF Blockset
- Statistics Toolbox

A typical MATLAB default desktop (in version 6.1 onwards) is illustrated in Figure 2.2.

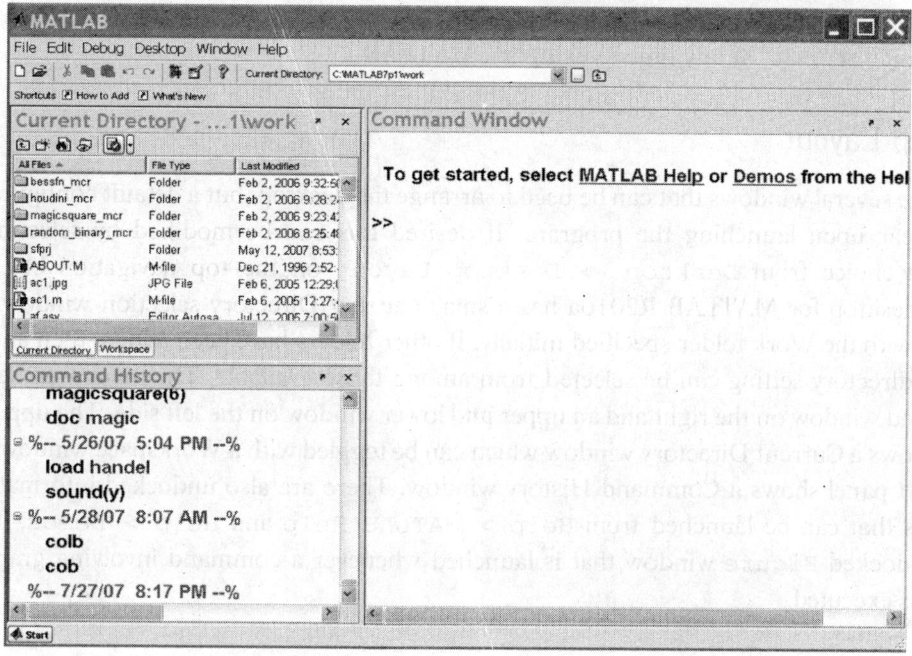

Figure 2.2 Typical MATLAB default desktop

MATLAB provides an external interface to run Fortran and C/C++ programs within it. One can write and save MATLAB programs in M-files, which have the extension .m, for example, "sample.m". We can use the editor/debugger built into MATLAB to create M-files. MATLAB uses two types of M-files: *script files* and *function files*. A *script file* contains a sequence of MATLAB commands, and is very useful when you need to use many commands for a particular application. As script files contain MATLAB commands, they are also called *command files*. We can execute the script file at the command window prompt by typing its name without the extension .m.

2.2.1 Starting MATLAB

To start MATLAB on a MS Windows® system, double-click on the MATLAB icon or select MATLAB from the start menu. One will then see the MATLAB Desktop as shown in

Figure 2.2. The Desktop manages the Command window and a Help browser, as well as other tools.

We use the Command window to communicate with the MATLAB program by typing instructions of various types called *commands, functions,* and *statements*. MATLAB displays the prompt (>>) to indicate that it is ready to receive instructions.

Type "quit" or "exit" at any time to exit from MATLAB.

Desktop Layout

There are several windows that can be used to arrange the desktop, but a default configuration will appear upon launching the program. If desired this can be modified by selecting an alternate choice from `Desktop -> Desktop Layout` on the top navigation bar. The default desktop for MATLAB R2010a has a small Current Directory selection window near the top, with the Work folder specified initially. If other folders have been added, then another current directory setting can be selected from among those available. The main area has the Command window on the right and an upper and lower window on the left side. The upper left panel shows a Current Directory window which can be toggled with a Workspace window. The lower left panel shows a Command History window. There are also undocked informational windows that can be launched from `Help > MATLAB Help` and `Help > Demos`. There is an undocked `Figure` window that is launched whenever a command involving graphical display is executed.

The Current Directory Window

The Current Directory window displays the current directory with a listing of its contents. It is possible to reset the current directory to any directory among those set in the path. This window is useful for finding the location of particular files and scripts so that they can be edited, moved, renamed, deleted, etc. The default current directory is the `Work` subdirectory of the original MATLAB installation directory. By default, its contents are displayed in the upper left area of toggled windows when the application is first launched or when `Desktop > Desktop Layout > Default` is selected from the navigation bar.

The Workspace Window

The Workspace window provides an inventory of all the items in the workspace that are currently defined, either by assignment or calculation, in the Command window or by importation with a load or similar command from the MATLAB command line prompt. These items consist of the set of arrays (including 1×1 scalars) whose elements are variables or constants. They have been constructed or loaded during the current MATLAB session and have remained stored in memory. Those which have been cleared and no longer are in memory will not be included. The Workspace window shows the name of each variable, its value or array size and if numerical, the minimum and maximum values among constituent elements. Values of a variable or constant can be edited in an Array Editor which is launched by double clicking its icon in the Workspace window.

From the Workspace window, it is also possible to generate a graph of a multi-element vector or matrix variable. To create a graph, choose a variable, click the graph button on the Workspace window toolbar, and select the graph type from the pull down menu (Figure 2.3). The graph appears in a figure window. The button itself changes to reflect the currently selected style of graph. Alternately, you can use the right-click in Windows (or the equivalent button or keystroke operation for other operating systems) on the variable you want to graph. The type of graph desired can then be chosen from the context menu. It is also possible to select multiple variables to graph together. The values of a variable or values within a selected range of contiguous elements can also be displayed in graphic form after opening an Array Editor window. This will have a graphing button with a pull down menu for the different types of graph.

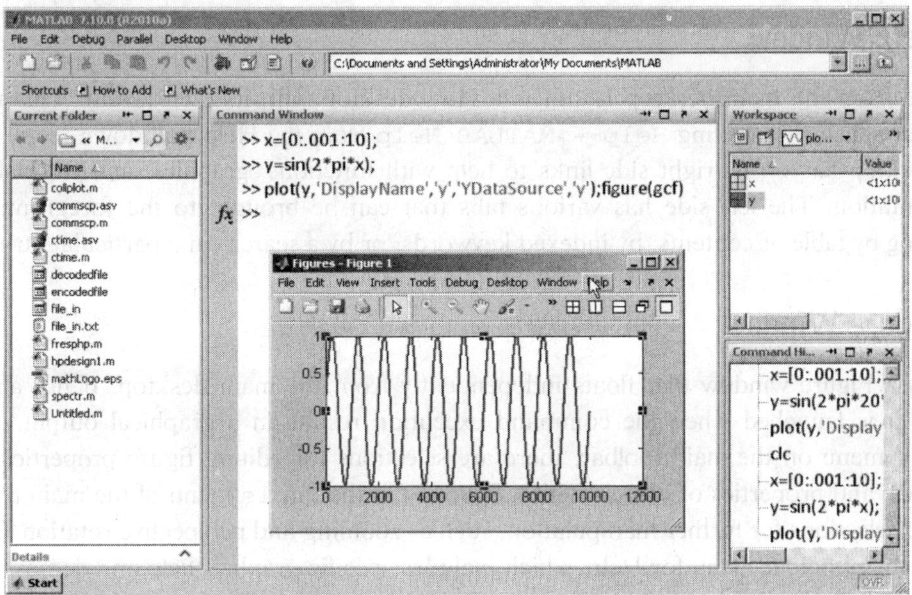

Figure 2.3 Plotting a variable in the workspace window using the graph icon

The Command History Window

The Command History window, at the lower left in the default desktop, contains a log of commands that have been executed within the Command window. This is a convenient feature for tracking when developing or debugging programs. It also helps to confirm that commands are executed in a particular sequence during a multi-step calculation from the command line.

The Command Window

The Command window is where the command line prompts for interactive commands is located. This is also the only window that appears if you execute the UNIX version of MATLAB outside of an X environment, e.g., on a *vt100* screen. Commands and scripts can be executed from a *vt100* window, but graphics and desktop tools will not be available. The MATLAB prompt on the command window consists of two adjacent right angle brackets, i.e., >>. Results of command operations will also be displayed in this window unless the command line is terminated by a semi-colon, in which case the display of results is suppressed. If a command or script specified on the command line is questionable or cannot be executed because of invalid syntax, undefined variables, etc., a diagnostic message will be displayed in the Command window. The current value of any saved variable is also displayed, if its name is entered at a prompt.

The Help Window

Separate from the main desktop layout is a Help desktop with its own layout. This utility can be launched by selecting `Help ->MATLAB Help` from the Help pull down menu. This Help desktop has on its right side links to help with functions, graphics, and tutorial type documentation. The left side has various tabs that can be brought to the foreground for navigating by table of contents, by indexed keywords, or by a search on a particular string.

The Figure Window

There is a Figure window that floats independently from the main desktop. If not already present, it is launched when the command execution results in a graphical output. From the `Edit` menu on the main toolbar, there are selections for editing figure properties, axis properties, and properties of objects within figures. On the `Tools` menu of the main toolbar there are selections for further manipulation, such as zooming and perspective rotation. There is also a main toolbar menu for Help, which includes specific graphics help and demos.

MATLAB Demos

Demonstrations are invaluable since they give an indication of MATLAB's capabilities. A comprehensive set of demonstrations are available by typing the command >> `demo`. The MATLAB Demos can also be run by double-clicking the demo menu at the MATLAB startup. In MATLAB 7.0 onwards, the command >> `demos` is used to evoke the demo.

2.3 Notation, Syntax, and Operations

Like other command driven applications, MATLAB requires information to presented in a certain manner in order to properly process it. It is a bit more rigid than some, for example, it is case sensitive to names of constants and variables, but a bit more flexible than others, for example, it provides many default values and interpretations for missing or incomplete arguments.

2.3.1 Variable names in MATLAB

The case sensitive names of variables and assigned constants can contain any of the 26 lower case and 26 upper case letters of the standard Latin alphabet along with the ten digits between 0 and 9 and the underscore. A name can be any sequence of 1 to 31 of these characters, but the first must be an upper or lower case letter and there cannot be any embedded blank spaces. Names longer than 31 characters are permitted but only the first 31 are used for unique identification. Constants and variables can be assigned values using the assignment operator, a single equal character (=), e.g., a = 3.

2.3.2 Numerical Conventions

MATLAB uses standard numerical notation. Numeric variables and constants are stored and displayed as sequences of base 10 digits. The radix point for fraction expansion is the period (.), and the lower case letter `e` is used to represent the floating point exponent. Note that this is not the natural logarithm base "*e*". The `e` must be immediately followed by a + or − sign and then an integer. The + is optional for positive exponents, and arbitrary preceding zeros are permitted. For example, the integer 2003 can be represented as 2.003e+003, 0.2003e3, 0002.003e0003, or even with a negative exponent as 20030e−1; and the fraction $\frac{1}{2000}$ can be represented as 0.0005, 5e−4, or 05.0000e−00004, or even with a positive exponent as 0.00005e001.

Complex Numbers

MATLAB accommodates complex-valued numbers of two-dimensional divisional algebra using the symbols `i` and `j` as default notations for $\sqrt{-1}$. These two symbols are initially identical, accommodating a historical notational difference between mathematical literature and engineering literature. They are not the separate roots of -1 in the classical **[i j k]** notation of higher dimensional divisional algebras such as the Hamiltonian quaternions. In fact **k** does not have an initial built-in assigned value. Once `i` or `j` has been assigned some value, the symbol must be immediately preceded by a numerical value in order to signify an imaginary part. If not, it will be interpreted as a separate entity. Thus, $(1+1i)$ is a single complex number with magnitude 1 for both real and imaginary parts; $(1+1*i)$ is a sum of the integer 1 and whatever value `i` happens to have at the time. Although `i` has an initial built-in value of $\sqrt{-1}$, it can be overwritten by assignment—it frequently is because this letter is used routinely to denote an index counter in loops.

Geometrical and Directional Conventions

Most of MATLAB's geometrical and directional conventions are common and should be familiar. The principal domain for multi-valued functions is symmetrically centred around zero, so that, for example, the inverse sine function `asin` has the principal domain $[-\pi/2, +\pi/2]$. When a branch cut is needed for analytic continuation in the complex plane, it typically extends from a point on the real axis to negative infinity along that axis. Angles in the complex plane or in polar coordinates are considered positive when measured in a counter-clockwise sense. Likewise the chirality of multi-dimensional coordinate systems is established by the counter-clockwise (right-hand thumb) rule: if the fingers of the right hand are curled from the positive nth axis toward the positive $(n+1)$th axis then the right thumb will point in the positive direction of the orthogonal $(n+2)$th axis. Of course, in terms of plotting and visualisation, dimensionality is limited to 3. For data analysis using matrix techniques, MATLAB interprets columns as variables with rows as observations.

Operator and Delimiter Symbolics

Basic MATLAB notation essential for computation includes symbols that distinguish between operations on elements within matrices and between matrices as a whole. The difference between all these stem from the fundamental definition of matrix multiplication which specifies that a product matrix element is the inner product of the corresponding row vector of the left-hand component with the column vector of the right-hand component.

The MATLAB notation for binary operations on matrices, vectors, and their elements are as follows:

- + for matrix or element addition
- − for matrix or element subtraction
- .* for element-wise multiplication
- * for matrix multiplication
- ./ for element division
- / for right matrix division (right multiplication by an inverse)
- \ for left matrix division (left multiplication by an inverse)

There are also MATLAB notations for a few unary operations:

- .^ for raising an element to a power
- ^ for raising a matrix to a power
- ' for converting the matrix to a complex conjugate transpose (single forward quote)

MATLAB also has specific notations and symbols for delimiters, separators, grouping, type assignment, and so forth. Essential among these are:

- [ ] for vector and matrix delimiter
- ( ) for grouping, vector and matrix element indices, function argument delimiter
- : for index range separator
- ; for matrix row separator
- blank space for matrix column element separator
- , comma for matrix index separator, function argument separator
- . period for radix expansion separator (American convention)
- ' ' single forward quotes for demarcation of character strings

MATLAB also has special interpretations for certain symbols related to positioning within a line of command instruction or code. Important and commonly used examples are:

- % anywhere in a line Ignore further text (when the comment for the rest of the line should remain uncomplied.)
- ; at the end of the line Suppress display
- ... (three periods) at the end of a line Continue on next line.

2.4 Importing and Exporting Information

Information can be imported into and exported from the MATLAB application by several different methods. Some of the more common procedures are discussed below.

2.4.1 Command Line Import

The most elementary method for importing external information is piece by piece directly from the command line by typing at the keyboard. For example: `>> earthradius = 6371;` will assign the numerical value 6371 to a variable `earthradius`. For extensive amounts of information, there are more efficient methods.

2.4.2 The Import Wizard

MATLAB provides an `Import Wizard` for convenient importation of data from external files. This tool can be activated by selecting `File > Import Data`, or by executing the `uiimport` command at a MATLAB command line prompt. This utility can be used for importing both text and numerical data contained within the same data file, but entries have to be in a matrix format with specified column separators. As an example, consider a small file, `planetsize.txt`, containing a few planets' names, radii, and masses with columns separated by tabs:

```
Planet Radius  Mass-kg*10^24
Earth  6371    5.97
Mars   3390    0.64
Venus  6052    4.87
```

This file can be imported directly with the command:

`>> uiimport planetsize.txt` or, the file can be specified from a browse tool button with `File > Import Data`. With either method, the contents of the file will be displayed in a floating Import Wizard window.

2.4.3 Other Import Functions

There are several other means to import data in MATLAB.

- `csvread` This function imports numeric data with comma-separated values (csv). For example, in the planetary data given above, suppose we have an external file `planets1.txt`, containing the kilometre radial distances and 10^{24} kg mass values for Earth, Mars and Venus:

  ```
  6371, 5.97
  3390, 0.64
  6052, 4.87
  ```

  The command `>> planets1 = csvread('planets1.txt')` would create a 3×2 matrix with the name `planets1` whose content is the same as that shown on the data tab generated previously by using the import wizard for the `planetsize.txt file`.
- `dlmread` This function is similar to `csvread` but is more flexible. It allows the delimiter to be specified by any character rather than restricting it to a comma.
- `load` This is similar to `csvread` and `dlmread` but the separators have to be blank spaces.
- `fscanf` This is a lower level import function, equivalent to the C language function of the same name but with the important difference that the result is vectorised. It requires extra manipulations for opening and closing the file, but is more versatile in allowing text and numbers to be read in together. For example, if we want to import the data from our file `planetsize.txt`, we could use the following sequence of commands to import the contents of the file in vectorised form:

  ```
  fid = fopen('planetsize.txt');
  planetsize = fscanf(fid,'%c');
  fclose(fid);
  ```

  where the "%c" argument for `fscanf` is identical to the one in C language, i.e., parsing as character strings. The variable `planetsize` is then actually an 80 element row vector of 21 characters (including blank spaces, tabs, and linefeeds) which have numerical ASCII character code values. Characterised data values need to be converted to numbers before mathematical manipulations will make sense.

- `textread` The `textread` function is similar to the primitive `fscanf` but will allow data variables to be defined as part of the import process. As an example, again suppose that the file `planetsize.txt` contains the information that we want to import into MATLAB. We can specify the number of header lines to skip before reaching the actual data (one such line in this example), and the individual data formats for each column of data. The file contains the character string planet names in the first column, the decimal integer planet radii in the second column and the floating point planet masses in the third column.

2.4.4 Export Functions

Now, let us explore the export functions in MATLAB.

- `diary` The simplest way to export data to an external file is to make use of the diary function. This is a utility for logging a transcript of the MATLAB command line input and screen output. The logging process starts subsequent to the command `>> diary filename` where "filename" is chosen, and terminates with the command `>> diary off`, thus creating an external file that can be edited with a text editor to remove extraneous material.

- `dlmwrite` The `dlmwrite` function allows one to write external data files in which the delimiter can be specified. Let us assume that we have the variables loaded into the workspace. We have defined the vector variables volumes and densities; and we want to write out a new file `planets2.txt` with the new volume and density data. We create a local array `planets2` in the Command Window by typing in the desired data, a column for each of the two vector variables

```
>> planets2(:,1) = volumes;
>> planets2(:,2) = densities;
```

The command `>> dlmwrite('planets2.txt',planets2, ';')` requests that the contents of the array `planets2` be written to an external file `planets2.txt` using a semicolon delimiter.

- `save` This utility is a primitive function that will save an array in an external file with columns separated by blank space. With no arguments at all, the `save` command will store the current values of all variables in a binary file `matlab.mat` from which they can be retrieved in a subsequent MATLAB session.

- `fprintf` This is another low level function that is equivalent to the C language function of the same name. It is useful for exporting information that contains both text and data in a specified format, using syntax similar to that of the C programming language.

2.5 Elements of MATLAB Programming

To enter a 3×3 matrix into a MATLAB workspace, we type the following:

```
a=[1 2 3;4 0 6;7 -2 9]
```

This will result in:

```
a =

     1     2     3
     4     0     6
     7   -12     9
```

If we add a semicolon (;) at the end of the command, values in matrix **a** will not be echoed. Now, let A=[1 −1; 2 4]; then if b=A+2, will get b= [3 1; 4 6]. If a=[1 2; 3 0]; and b=[1 −1; 0 2]; then c=2*a will get [2 4; 6 0] in c (scalar multiplication). c=a*b will get [1 3;3 −3] (matrix multiplication). Now, c=a.*b will result in element-wise multiplication and get [1 −2;0 0] in c.

The following classes of built-in (library) functions are supported in MATLAB:

1. Linear algebraic functions
2. Trigonometric functions
3. Hyperbolic functions
4. Logical functions
5. Exponential and logarithmic functions
6. Complex functions
7. Round-off functions
8. Matrix functions
9. Polynomial functions
10. String functions

2.5.1 Special Built-in Constants

In addition to the default assignment for i and j as the complex-valued $\sqrt{-1}$, MATLAB has several other built-in constants, some of which can be overwritten by assignment, but which are then restorable to the original default with a clearing command. Some commonly used ones with universal meaning are:

1. `pi` for the rational approximation of π.
2. `inf` for generic infinity (without regard to cardinality).
3. `NaN` for a numerically derived expression that is not a number, e.g., $\frac{0}{0}$.

One particular built-in constant is a defacto variable that is constantly overwritten: `ans` for the evaluation of the most recent input expression with no explicit assignment. Care needs to be taken that no variable is intentionally assigned the name `ans` because that variable name can be re-assigned a value without explicit instruction during the execution of a program. Thus, though *years* is a commonly used variable name in computational problems, its French equivalent *ans* should be avoided.

There are also some built-in constants that are characteristic of the particular computer on which calculations are being performed. They are again susceptible to being overwritten, such as

1. `realmin` for the smallest positive real number that can be used.
2. `realmax` for the largest positive real number that can be used.
3. `eps` for the smallest real positive number such that $(1 + eps)$ differs from 1.

2.5.2 Linear Algebra

MATLAB supports two kinds of division operators: / and \. Now, let P = 8 and Q = 5; then: `R=P/Q` will yield 1.6000. `R=P\Q` will get 0.6250=Q/P. If AX=B; then to get X, we write: `X=inv(A)*B`.

For example, if A=[6 −4 8;−5 −3 7;14 9 −5]; and B=[40 12 −22]'; then `X=inv(A)*B` will yield: X=[2 −5 1]'. The same result can be obtained by X = A\B. [2]

Operator Overloading

Let A=[1 0 2;2 4 1;0 6 4]. Then we have:

```
A^2 = A*A = [1 12 10;10 22 12;12 48 22].
```

This is true matrix multiplication.

```
A.^2 = A.*A = [1 0 4;4 16 1;0 36 16].
```

This is referred to as *element-wise* multiplication.

Some of the other important linear algebraic functions in MATLAB are illustrated below:

- `pinv(B)` computes the pseudo inverse of a matrix B.

[2] This requires the matrix A to be *non-singular*.

- `rank(A)` computes the rank of a matrix A.
- `det(A)` will get the determinant of a square matrix A.
- `eig(B)` will get the eigen values of B.
- `rref(B)` computes the reduced row echelon form of matrix B.
- `[U R]=eig(C)` calculates the eigen values and eigen vectors of C.

EXAMPLE `D = [3 -2 0;2 -2 0;0 1 1];` then `eig(D)` gets

```
ans =
  1
 -1
  2
```

- `eye(4)` gets a 4×4 "Identity" matrix.
- `ones(1,6)` gets [1 1 1 1 1 1].
- `zeros(4,1)` gets [0 0 0 0]'.
- `size(eye(2,3))` gets [2 3].
- `length([1 1 7 -4])` gets 4.
- `sum([1:6])` gets 21.
- `prod([1:6])` gets 6!=720.
- If A=[22 −3 0 15 7], `find (A>0)` gets [1 4 5].
  `A(A<0)` gets −3.
  `A(find(A~=0))` or `A(A~=0)` gets [22 −3 15 7].
  `A~=0` gets [1 1 0 1 1].

- Let A=[6 −4 8;−5 −3 7;14 9 −5]; B=[1 2 3]; then `C=[A;B]` will get [6 −4 8;−5 −3 7;14 9 −5;1 2 3] in C.% A row is appended. `%` is used to comment on a line. The MATLAB interpreter will ignore whatever follows a `%` symbol.
  Also `C=[A B']` gets [6 −4 8 1;−5 −3 7 2;14 9 −5 3] in C. % A column is appended.
  Now `C(2,:)=[];` deletes the second row of C.
  Also `C(:,3)=[];` deletes the third column of C.
- `rand(m,n)` % returns an $m \times n$ matrix of uniformly distributed random numbers, between 0 and 1.
- `randi(m,n)` % returns an $n \times n$ matrix containing pseudo-random integer values drawn from the discrete uniform distribution on [1: m]
- `randn(m,n)` % returns $m \times n$ matrix of normally (Gaussian) distributed random numbers with zero mean and unity variance.
- `diag(v)` % generates a diagonal matrix with the vector v on the diagonal.
- `diag(A)` % extracts the diagonal of matrix A as a column vector. This is another case of operator overloading.
- `diag(A,1)` % extracts the first upper off-diagonal vector of A.
- `rot90(A);` % rotates A by 90 degrees.

```
A= [6 -4 9; -5 -3 7;14 19 -5];
   rot90(A)
   ans=
         9  7 -5
        -4 -3 19
         6 -5 14
```

- `fliplr(A);` flips a matrix from left to right.
- `flipud(A);` flips a matrix from up to down.
- `tril(A);` extracts the lower triangular part of a matrix.
- `triu(A);` extracts the upper triangular part of a matrix.
- `reshape(B,4,2);` If B is a 2×4 matrix, it is reshaped as a 4×2 matrix.

Array Operators

- .* element-by-element multiplication.
- ./ element-by-element left-division.
- .\ element-by-element right-division.
- .^ element-by-element exponentiation.
- .' non-conjugated transpose.

Relational Operators

If x=[1 5 3 7] and y=[0 2 8 7]; then:

- < less than; `K=x<y` gets K=[0 0 1 0].
- <= less than or equal to; `K=(x<=y)` gets K=[0 0 1 1];
- > greater than; `K=x>y` gets K=[1 1 0 0];
- >= greater than or equal to; `K=(x>=y)` gets K=[1 1 0 1];
- == equal to; `K=(x==y)` gets K=[0 0 0 1];
- ~= not equal to; `K=(x~= y)` gets K=[1 1 1 0];

2.5.3 Trigonometric Functions

MATLAB supports the following trigonometric functions:

- `acos(x)` computes inverse cosine; arccos $(x) = \cos^{-1}(x)$
- `acot(x)` computes inverse cotangent; arccot $(x) = \cot^{-1}(x)$

- `acsc(x)` computes inverse cosecant; $\text{arccsc}(x) = \csc^{-1}(x)$
- `asec(x)` computes inverse secant; $\text{arcsec}(x) = \sec^{-1}(x)$
- `asin(x)` computes inverse sine; $a\sin(x) = \sin^{-1}(x)$
- `atan(x)` computes inverse tangent; $arc\tan(x) = \tan^{-1}(x)$
- `atan2(y,x)` computes the four-quadrant inverse tangent
- `cos(x)` computes cosine
- `cot(x)` computes cotangent
- `csc(x)` computes cosecant
- `sec(x)` computes secant
- `sin(x)` computes sine
- `tan(x)` computes tangent

2.5.4 Hyperbolic Functions

MATLAB supports the following hyperbolic functions:

- `acosh(x)` computes inverse hyperbolic cosine; $\cosh^{-1}(x)$
- `acoth(x)` computes inverse hyperbolic cotangent; $\coth^{-1}(x)$
- `acsch(x)` computes inverse hyperbolic cosecant; $\text{csch}^{-1}(x)$
- `asech(x)` computes inverse hyperbolic secant; $\text{sech}^{-1}(x)$
- `asinh(x)` computes inverse hyperbolic sine; $\sinh^{-1}(x)$
- `atanh(x)` computes inverse hyperbolic tangent; $\tanh^{-1}(x)$
- `cosh(x)` computes hyperbolic cosine
- `coth(x)` computes hyperbolic cotangent
- `csch(x)` computes hyperbolic cosecant
- `sec h(x)` computes hyperbolic secant
- `sinh(x)` computes hyperbolic sine
- `tanh(x)` computes hyperbolic tangent

2.5.5 Logical Functions

In MATLAB the following logical functions/operators are supported:

If A=[0 15 3 12] and B=[0 3 0 5];then:

- `&` logical AND; `C=A & B`=[0 1 0 1];
- `|` logical OR; `C = A|B`=[0 1 1 1];
- `~` logical complement (NOT); `C = ~A`=[1 0 0 0];
- `xor` exclusive OR; `C = xor(A,B)`=[0 0 1 0];

Built-in Logical Functions

- `all:` if B=[−1 − 8 − 5]; then `all(B<0)` returns 1.
- `any:` if B=[0 5 7]; then `any(B>5)` returns 1.
- `exist;` if matrix A exists in a workspace, then `exist('A')` returns 1.
- `isempty;` if B=[] then `isempty(B)` returns 1.
- `isinf;` returns 1 iff argument is infinity.
- `isfinite;` returns 1 iff argument is finite.
- `isnan;` returns 1 iff argument is not a number.
- `find;` If V=[−1 7 − 5]; then `find(V)`=[1 2 3].

2.5.6 Exponential and Logarithmic Functions

Examples of exponential and logarithmic functions are given below:

- If A=[0 1]; then `exp(A)=[1 e];`
- If A=[1 e]; then `log(A)=[0 1];`
- If B=[100 1000]; then `log10(B)=[2 3];`
- If C=[25 49 81]; then `sqrt(C)=[5 7 9];`

2.5.7 Complex Functions

MATLAB has the following functions that operate on complex entities.

- `abs;%` abs(3+4i) returns 5 and abs(−3) returns 3.
- `angle;%` angle(3+4i) gets 0.9273 rad.
- `conj;%` conj(3+4i) returns 3 − 4i.
- `imag;%` imag(8+7i) returns 7.
- `real;%` real(8+7i) returns 8.

2.5.8 Round-off Functions

- `fix%` rounds towards zero. fix([−2.133 2.828]) =[−2 2].
- `floor; %` rounds towards −infinity.`floor([-2.338 2.766])=[-3 2].`
- `ceil; %` rounds towards +infinity.`ceil([-2.334 2.889])=[-2 3].`
- `round; %` rounds towards the nearest integer. `round([-2.335 2.667])=[-2 3].`
- `rem; %` `rem(a,b)=a-fix(a./b).`
- `sign; %` signum function, `sign([-2.3 0 2.6])=[-1 0 1].`

2.5.9 Matrix Functions

These are special functions that accept a whole matrix as an argument.

- `expm(A);` % finds the exponential of the matrix A, exp(A).
- `logm(A);` % finds log(A) such that A = exp(log(A)).
- `sqrt(A);` % finds $\sqrt{A}$.

2.5.10 Polynomial Functions

MATLAB supports the following polynomial functions:

- `conv;` computes the product of two polynomials.
- `deconv;` computes the ratio of two polynomials.
- `eig;` computes the eigen values of a matrix.
- `poly;` computes the polynomial from the roots.
- `polyfit;` fits a polynomial to data.
- `polyval;` evaluates a polynomial.
- `roots;` computes the roots of a polynomial.

2.5.11 String Functions

MATLAB has a rich collection of functions that operate on strings.

- `char;` creates character arrays using automatic padding. Also converts ASCII numeric values to character arrays.
  EXAMPLE `Greetings=char('Hi','Raman','Howdi?');` results in:

  ```
  Greetings =
  Hi
  Raman
  Howdi?
  ```

  `char(66)` returns B.
- `abs;` % converts characters to their ASCII numerical values. abs("C") returns 67.
- `blanks(n);` % creates n blank characters.
- `deblank;` % removes the trailing blanks from a string.
- `eval;` % executes the string as a command, if they contain valid MATLAB commands. `eval('y=15*sin(x)')` does the same thing as `y=15*sin(x)`.
- `findstr;` finds a specified substring.

```
s = 'How much wood would a woodchuck chuck?';
        findstr(s,'a')      returns 21
        findstr('a',s)      returns 21
        findstr(s,'wood')   returns  [10 23]
        findstr(s,'Wood')   returns  []
        findstr(s,' ')      returns  [4 9 14 20 22 32]
```

- `int2str;` converts integers to string.
- `ischar;` true (=1) for character arrays.
- `isletter;` true (=1) for alphabetical characters.
- `isstr;` true if argument is a string; isstr('MATLAB') returns 1.
- `lower;` converts upper case to lower case.
- `upper;` converts lower case to upper case.
- `mat2str;` converts a matrix to a string.
- `num2str;` converts numbers to strings. (similar to `int2str`)
- `strcmp;` compares two strings, returns 1 if they are the same.

```
 s='abba';
>> p=fliplr(s);
>> strcmp(s,p)
ans =
     1
```

- `strncmp;` compares the first n characters in given strings. `strncmp(s,p,4)`=1, but `strncmp(s,p,10)`=0.
- `strcat;` concatenates strings ignoring trailing blanks..

```
P=strcat('The quick brown fox', 'jumps over the lazy dog.')
```

returns:

```
P=The quick brown fox jumps over the lazy dog.
```

- `strvcat;` similar to `char`, but ignores empty strings.

```
P=strvcat('The quick brown fox','', 'jumps over the lazy dog.')
```

returns:

```
P =
The quick brown fox
jumps over the lazy dog.
```

2.6 Plotting with MATLAB

MATLAB has a rich collection of plotting commands.

- `plot(x,y,'r');` results in a simple 2-D plot.
- `fplot('function',[xmin xmax]);` results in a function plotter. The usage of plot and `fplot` functions are illustrated in Figure 2.4.

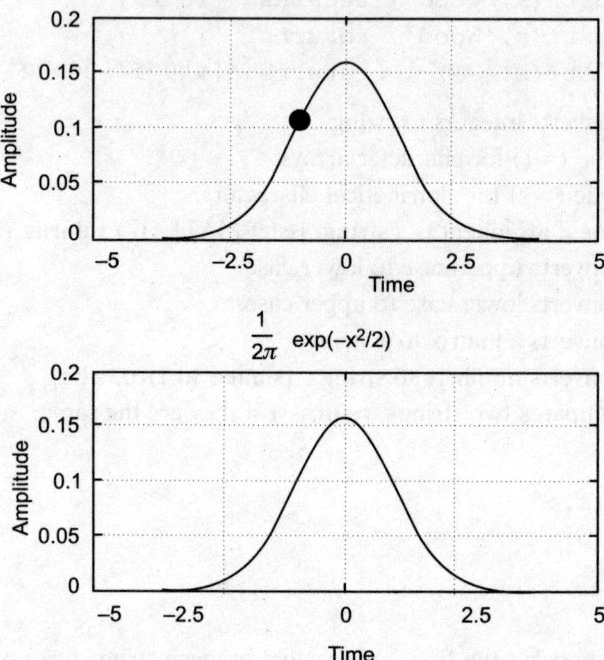

Figure 2.4 Plots obtained using `plot` and `fplot` commands

- `ezplot('function',[xmin xmax]);` easy function plotter.
- `stem(x,y);` plots a discrete signal. A typical plot obtained using `stem` command is illustrated in Figure 2.5.
- `ezpolar('function', [0 2*pi]);` polar version of ezplot.
- `plot3(x,y,z);` results in a 3-D plot.
- `ezplot3('f1','f2','f3', [0 2*pi]);` easy 3-D plotter.
- `contour(X,Y,Z);` contour plot.
- `ezcontour(Z);` easy contour plot.
- `ezcontourf(Z);`
- `surf(X,Y,Z);` surface plot.
- `ezsurf(Z);` eazy surface plot.
- `ezsurfc(z,[x,y]);`
- `ginput;` reads coordinates of the cursor position.
- `grid;` displays grid lines.
- `print;` prints plots or saves plots to a file.
- `title;` puts text at top of a plot.

- `xlabel;` adds text label to the x-axis.
- `ylabel;` adds text label to the y-axis.

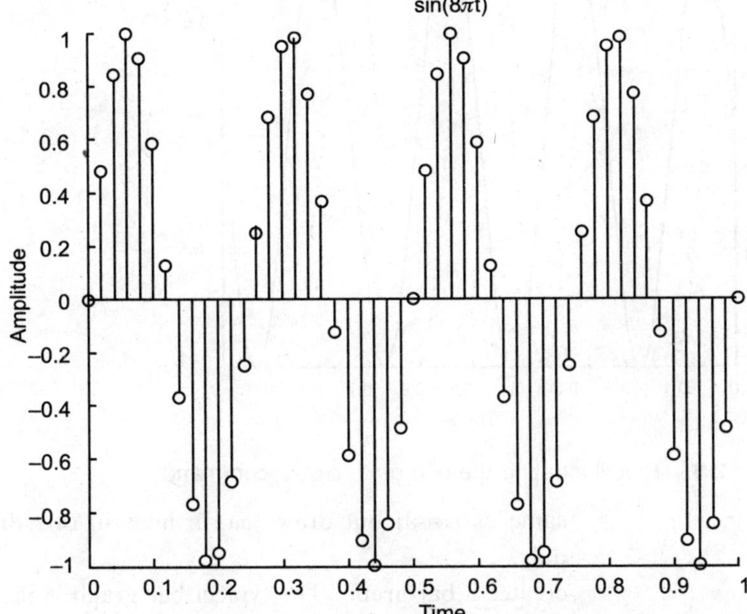

Figure 2.5 Plot obtained using `stem` command

2.6.1 Specialised Plotting

- `loglog;` creates a log-log plot.
- `plotyy;` enables plotting on the left and right axes. A typical plot obtained using the `plotyy` command is illustrated in Figure 2.6.
- `polar;` creates a polar plot.
- `semilogx;` creates a semilog plot (logarithmic abscissa).
- `semilogy;` creates a semilog plot (logarithmic ordinate).
- `stairs;` creates a stairs plot.
- `mesh(x,y,z);`
- `meshc(x,y,z);` same as `mesh`, but draws a contour plot under the surface.
- `meshz(x,y,z);` same as `mesh` but draws a series of vertical lines under the surface.
- `ezmesh(z);` easy `mesh`.
- `ezmeshc(z);` easy `meshc`.

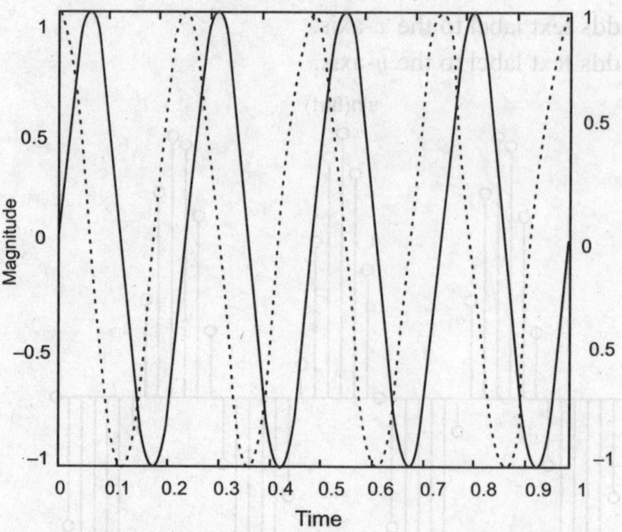

Figure 2.6 Plot illustrating the use of `plotyy` command

- `waterfall(x,y,z);` same as `mesh` but draws `mesh` lines in one direction only.
- `bar(n,x);` creates a bar graph. The typical bar graph is illustrated in Figure 2.7.
- `[x,y]=meshgrid(min:max);` creates the matrices x and y from the vector `[min:max]` which are the limits of x and y.

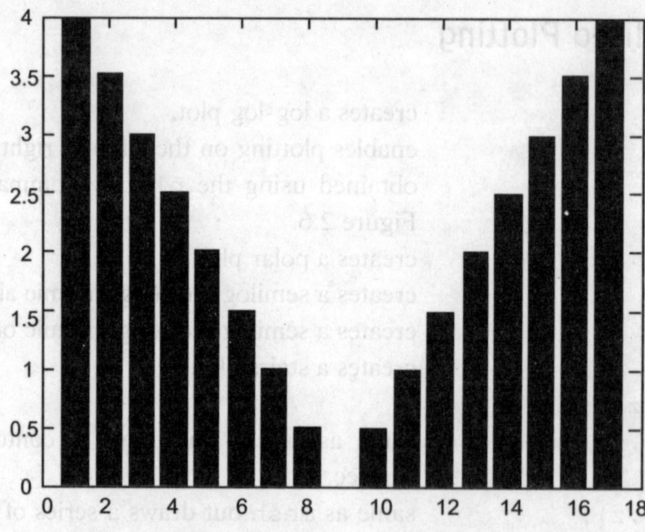

Figure 2.7 A typical bar plot

The plot of the jointly Gaussian random variable obtained by the MATLAB `surf(.)` command and the corresponding MATLAB code are shown in Figure 2.8.

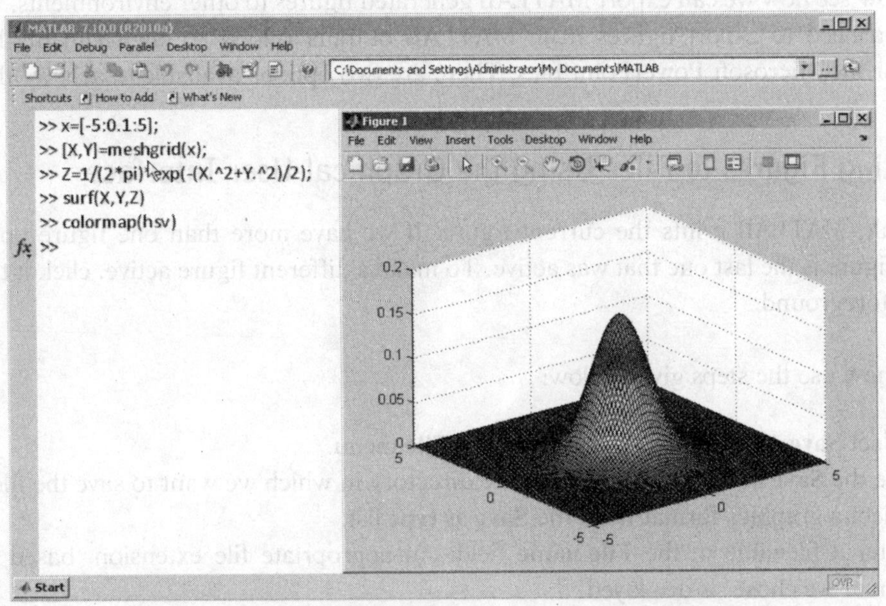

Figure 2.8 Plot of a jointly Gaussian random variable

2.6.2 Plot Enhancement Commands

The following commands enhances the plots in MATLAB:

- `axes;` creates axes object. `axes('equal')` sets the x- and y-axes to equal proportion. `axes('square')` does the same.
  `axes([xmin xmax ymin ymax])` sets the limits of the x- and y-axes.
- `gtext;` enables label placement using the mouse.
- `hold;` freezes current plot (a toggle command). `hold on` and `hold off` are used for this purpose.
- `legend;` legend placement using mouse.
- `refresh;` redraws the current figure window.
- `set;` specifies properties of objects such as axes.
- `subplot;` creates plots in sub-windows. `subplot(221), plot(x,y)` plots *y versus x* in the first sub-window of a 2×2 window space.
- `text ;` places string in the figure.

2.6.3 Exporting of MATLAB Figures to Files

Let us now see how we can export MATLAB generated figures to other environments. Usually there is a need to export figures from MATLAB outputs (plots) to environments like the LaTeX or the Microsoft PowerPoint files. There are two options available to achieve this.

Exporting Figures to Files Using the Graphical User Interface

By default, MATLAB prints the current figure. If we have more than one figure open, the current figure is the last one that was active. To make a different figure active, click it to bring it to the foreground.

We can now use the steps given below:

1. Select **Save As** from the figure window's **File** menu.
2. Use the **Save in** field to navigate to the directory in which we want to save the file.
3. Select a graphics format from the **Save as type** list.
4. Enter a filename in the **File name** field. An appropriate file extension, based on the format we chose, is displayed.
5. Click **Save** to export the figure.

Exporting Figures to Files Using MATLAB Commands

From the command line, we must specify the graphics format as an option. For example to export a figure to an EPS colour file, `myfig.eps`, in the current directory, we can use the command:

```
>> print -depsc myfig
```

When there are multiple figure objects, we can use the following command to export the first figure, say Figure 1 into a file, `myfig1.eps`:

```
>> print -f1 -deps myfig1
```

The qualifier `-f1` is the figure handle. To choose the second figure, say Figure 2, change it to `-f2`. MATLAB supports a number of file formats including postscript (.ps), encapsulated postscript (.eps), jpeg (.jpg), enhanced metafile (.emf), and bitmap (.bmp).

2.6.4 Exporting of MATLAB Figures to Clipboard

We can export a figure to the clipboard in graphics format when we want to paste it into Windows or any other application such as a word processor. There are two options for doing this.

Using the Graphical User Interface

For example, it is required to export a figure to the clipboard in enhanced metafile (EMF) format. The figure settings that would make the exported figure suitable for use in a Microsoft Word or PowerPoint slide are chosen. Note that changing the settings modifies the figure displayed on the screen.

1. Create a figure containing text.
2. Select **Preferences** from the **File** menu of either the figure or the main desktop window. Then select **Figure Copy Template** from the Preferences dialog box.
3. In the **Figure Copy Template Preferences** panel, click the **PowerPoint** button. The MATLAB suggested settings for PowerPoint are added to the template.
4. In the **Lines** panel, change the custom width to 4 points (to make thicker lines).
5. In the **Uicontrols and axes** panel, select **Keep axes limits and tick spacing** to prevent MATLAB from possibly rescaling tick marks and limits when we export.
6. Click **Apply to Figure**. The changes appear in the figure window. If we do not like the way the figure looks with the new settings, restore it to its original settings by clicking the **Restore Figure** button.
7. In the left pane of the Preferences dialog box, expand the **Figure Copy Template** topic. Select **Copy Options**.
8. In the **Copy Options** panel, select **Metafile** to tell MATLAB to export the figure in EMF format.
9. Check that the **Transparent background** is selected. This choice makes the figure background transparent and allows the slide background to frame the axes part of the figure.
10. Clear the **Match figure screen size** check box so that we can use our own figure size settings.
11. Click **OK**.
12. Select **Export Setup** from the figure window's **File** menu.
13. Select the **Size** properties, and set **Width** to 6 and **Height** to 4.5. Make sure that Units are set to inches.
14. Click **Close**.
15. Select **Copy Figure** from the **Edit** menu. The figure is now exported to the clipboard and can be pasted into another Windows application, such as PowerPoint.

Using MATLAB Commands

Use the print function and one of two clipboard formats (-dmeta, -dbitmap) to export a figure to the clipboard. *Do not specify a filename*. For example to export a figure to the clipboard in enhanced metafile (EMF) format, type:

```
>> print -dmeta
```

In order to export a figure to the clipboard in bitmap (BMP) 8-bit colour format type:[3]

```
>> print -dbitmap
```

2.7 Specific Features of MATLAB

In MATLAB, element-wise array operators are preceded by a period (.). A line can be continued by putting three consecutive periods (...) at the end of the line. Comma is the delimiter for elements of a vector, array or different arrays/vectors while semi-column is the statement delimiter. *Output will be echoed only if the semi-column is absent*. Please note that in MATLAB, unlike C/C++, the array index starts at 1. Zero cannot be the starting index. A comment can be entered by typing a % character, and the MATLAB interpreter ignores whatever succeeds it.

2.7.1 M-files

There are two types of M-files—script M-files and function M-files. M-files provide a very convenient way to handle large program scripts. We can create M-files using any standard editor or the MATLAB's own editor.

Script M-files

A script M-file is equivalent to a macro definition in C/C++. Parameter passing is not intended but a script M-file can share parameters already in the workspace. They are less efficient compared to function M-files.

Function M-files

The function M-file is equivalent to a function call. Nesting of functions is permitted. The comment lines given after the function definition line appears when help on that function is requested.

Function Definition Line

The general form of a function definition line is:

```
function   [output variable]=function_name(input variables);
```

The above function has to be saved as `function_name.m` . After the function definition line, any number of comment lines can be given, starting with a % character.

2.7.2 P-Code

The P-code stands for parsed-function codes in MATLAB. It is the parsed code generated by the MATLAB interpreter. To parse a function `project.m`, type: `>> pcode project,`

[3] When printing, the print -d option specifies a printer driver. When exporting, the print -d option specifies a graphics format. If we print a figure to a file, the file can only be printed. It cannot be imported into another application.

which generates the parsed function and is saved in `project.p`. When “project” is typed the next time, the interpreter executes the “`project.p`” file. If it is absent, only then will “`project.m`” be executed.

2.7.3 M-Book

The M-book is a feature supported by MATLAB version 6.0 onwards. The M-book feature is used to transfer data between MATLAB and Microsoft Word, a commonly used word processing utility. The M-book is a MS Word overlay feature available if the MS Word is installed in the system. To install M-book as a MS Word overlay, type:

```
>> notebook  -setup;
```

and follow the instructions. Once the installation of M-book is over, type `notebook` at the MATLAB command prompt to evoke the M-book. A word document with the file name `mbook.doc` will be opened, on which we can type MATLAB commands followed by “`Cntl-Enter`”, to get results identical to that obtained at the workspace. If we open the `mbook.doc` file from MS Word, MATLAB will be opened automatically. Thus MS Word acts as a front end for MATLAB. It is very useful in document preparation.

2.7.4 Control Flow

The following control constructs are available in MATLAB:

• `for-end` loop	`For` loops can be nested.
• `while-end` loop	These loops can be nested, but every `while` loop must have a matching end.
• `if-elseif-else-end` statement	These loops can also be nested.
• `switch-case-otherwise-end` statement.	
• `break`	This is used for terminating the `for` and `while` loops prematurely.
• `error`	The command `error` (“message”) inside a function will abort the function and display the `error` “message”.
• `return`	Returns the control to the invoking function.

2.7.5 Interactive Input

There are mainly four commands for interactive inputs.

Input

```
LOV=input('Length of the vector ')
Length of the vector 5
LOV =
        5
ms=input('More Simulations? (y/n) ','s')
More Simulations? (y/n) y
ms =
        y
```

Keyboard

On execution of the keyboard command, the command window prompt changes to `>>k`. The user can examine the status of the program variables up to that level by typing the appropriate variable name. After finishing, type `return` and press the `return` key to get back to the execution of the remaining part of the program.

Menu

The menu command creates an on-screen menu.

```
p=menu('plot','circle','polar','cartesian');
On pressing the cartesian option:
p=3
```

Pause

The pause temporarily halts the execution of the program. Pressing any key resumes execution. `Pause(n);` halts the program for *n* seconds.

2.8 Special MATLAB Functions

There are several special MATLAB functions useful for communications students. They are included in the Control System Toolbox and the Signal Processing Toolbox. Some general purpose functions are listed below.

2.8.1 Statistical Functions

The following functions are available in MATLAB for statistical computations:

- `primes(N);` lists all primes less than or equal to N.
- `isprime(N);` checks if N is a prime.
- `factor(N);` factors N into its prime factors.
- `std(A);` computes the standard deviation of the elements of vector A. If A is a matrix, then it computes the standard deviations of each column.

- `mean(A);` computes the mean of the elements of vector A. If A is a matrix, then it computes the mean of each column.
- `var(A);` similar to `std(.)`, but computes variance.
- `bar(A);` plots a bargraph using data from vector A.

2.8.2 Signal Processing Functions

The user may find the functions listed below useful for signal processing applications.

- `modulate(.);` modulator function.
- `conv(X,H);` obtains the linear convolution of sequences X and H.
- `xcorr(X,H);` obtains the cross-correlation between sequences X and H. `xcorr(X,X);` computes the auto-correlation of sequence X.
- `fft(X,N);` computes the N point fast Fourier transform (FFT) of sequence X.
- `ifft(X);` computes the inverse FFT.
- `dftmtx(N);` computes $N \times N$ DFT of Galois field vector.
- `fftfilt(h,x);` overlap-add method implementation of linear convolution.
- `zplane(zeros,poles);` z-plane plot of poles and zeros.
- `zp2sos(zeros,poles,k);` zero-poles to second order section conversion.
- `[r,p,k]=residue(num,den);` partial fraction expansion in s-domain.
- `[r,p,k]=residuez(num,den);` partial fraction expansion in z-domain.
- `[h,t]=impz(num,den);` inverse z-transform.
- `filter(num,den,X);` response of the LTI filter with numerator polynomial coefficients "num", and denominator coefficients "den" and the input sequence X.
- `[N,Wn]=buttord(Wp,Ws,Rp,Rs,'s');` computes the lowest order N of a Butterworth analog transfer function meeting the specifications given.
- `[num,den]=butter(N,Wn,'s');` analog Butterworth filter
- `[N,Wn]=cheby1ord(Wp,Ws,Rp,Rs,'s');` Type 1 Chebyshev filter order N.
- `[num,den]=cheby1(N,Rp,Wn,'s');` Chebyshev analog lowpass filter transfer function.
- `[N,Wn]=ellipord(Wp,Ws,Rp,Rs,'s');` Order N of an elliptical filter.
- `[num,den]=ellip(N,Rp,Rs,Wn,'s');` Elliptical analog lowpass transfer function.
- `[num,den]=besself(N,Wn);` Used to design Nth order Bessel filter.
- `[b,a]=lp2lp(num,den);` lowpass to lowpass conversion.
- `[b,a]=lp2hp(num,den);` lowpass to highpass conversion.
- `[b,a]=lp2bp(num,den,Wp1,Wp2);` lowpass to bandpass conversion.
- `[num,den]=bilinear(b,a,Ws);` bilinear transformation to get a digital filter equivalent.
- `fvtool(num,den);` filter visualisation tool, available only in MATLAB ver 7.0 onwards.

- `fdatool(num,den);` filter design and analysis tool.
- `sptool(.);` Signal processing tool. `sptool` is a graphical user interface (GUI). `sptool` opens the Signal Processing Tool window which allows you to import, analyse, and manipulate signals, filters, and spectra.
- `wintool;` window design and analysis tool for FIR filter design using *windows*. This is a GUI available in Filter Design Toolbox, for transforming IIR filters into FIR filters by means of suitable windowing functions.

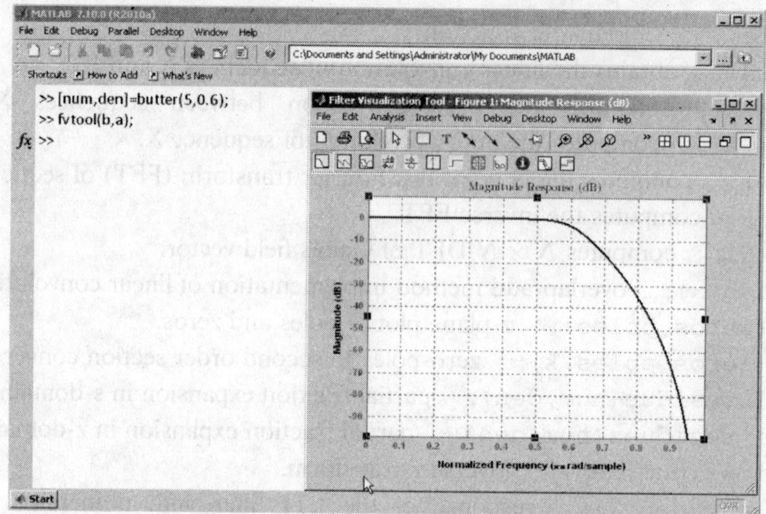

Figure 2.9 Filter visualisation tool window

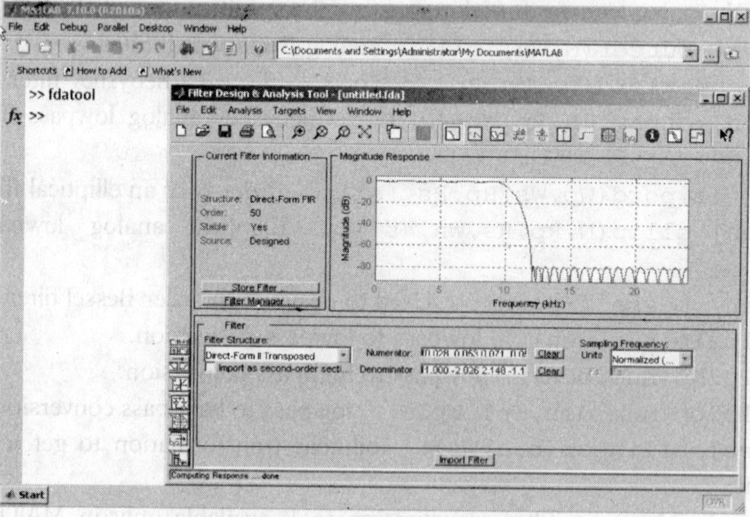

Figure 2.10 Filter design and analysis tool window

The screen shots of the *Filter Visualisation Tool (fvtool), Filter Design and Analysis Tool (fdatool), Signal Processing Tool (sptool),* and *Window Design and Analysis Tool (wintool)* are shown in Figures 2.9, 2.10, 2.11, and 2.12 respectively.

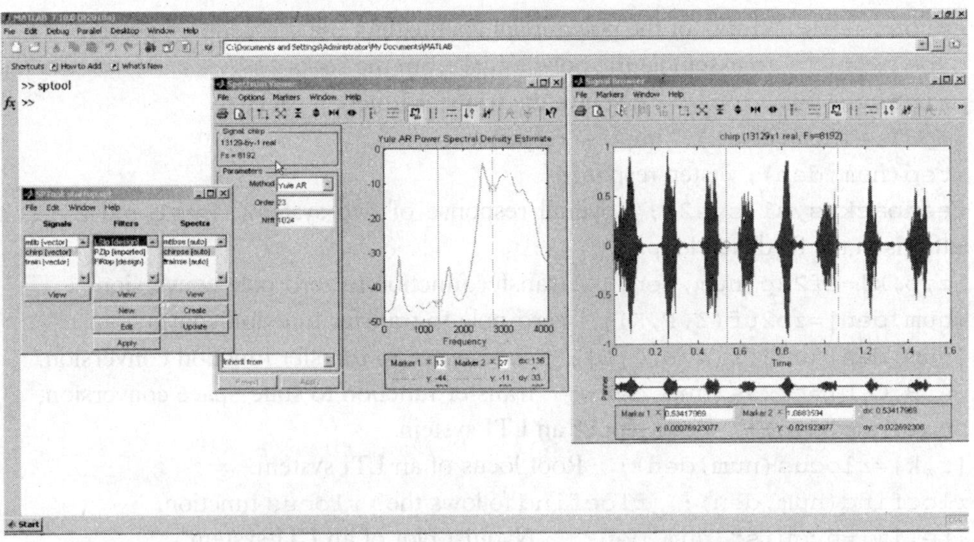

Figure 2.11 Signal processing tool window

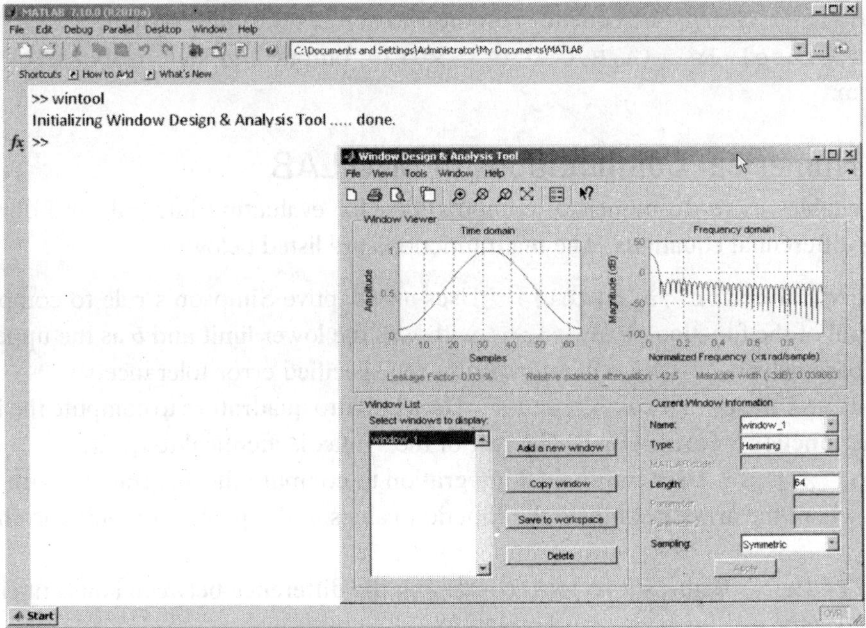

Figure 2.12 Window design and analysis tool window

2.8.3 Control System Functions

There are several special functions in the Control System Toolbox useful for control system design.

- `r=roots(p);` roots of the polynomial coefficients `p` in descending powers of `s`.
- `p=poly(r);` re-assemble the polynomial from the roots.
- `printsys(num,den);` displays the transfer function `H(s)`.
- `impulse(num,den);` impulse response.
- `step(num,den);` step response.
- `feedback(sys1,sys2);` overall response of two systems, `sys1` and `sys2`, the latter is in the feedback loop.
- `[z,p,k]=tf2zp(num,den);` transfer function to zero-pole conversion.
- `[num,den]=zp2tf(Z,P,K);` zero-pole to transfer function conversion.
- `[num,den]=ss2tf(A,B,C,D);` state-space to transfer function conversion.
- `[A,B,C,D]=tf2ss(num,den);` transfer function to state-space conversion.
- `bode(num,den);` Bode plot of an LTI system.
- `[r,k]=rlocus(num,den);` Root locus of an LTI system.
- `rlocfind(num,den);` `rlocfind` follows the `rlocus` function.
- `[re,im]=nyquist(num,den);` Nyquist plot of an LTI system.
- `[mag,phase,w]=nichols(num,den,w);` Nichols chart.
- `freqs(num,den);` frequency response (continuous time) of a system.
- `freqz(num,den);` frequency response (discrete time) of a system.
- `[out,state]=lsim(A,B,C,D,u,t,x0);` output and state response of an LTI system.

2.8.4 Numerical Computations in MATLAB

MATLAB enables us to do numerical computations for evaluating integrals and derivatives for solving differential equations. The main functions are listed below:

- `quad('function',a,b,tol);` Uses an adaptive Simpson's rule to compute the integral of the function `'function'` with *a* as the lower limit and *b* as the upper limit. The parameter *tol* is optional. *tol* indicates the specified error tolerance.
- `quadl('function',a,b,tol);` Uses Lobatto quadrature to compute the integral of the function `'function'`. The rest of the syntax is identical to `quad`.
- `trapz(x,y);` Uses trapezoidal integration to compute the integral of *y* with respect to *x*, where the array *y* contains the function values at the points contained in the array *x*.
- `d=diff(x);` Returns a vector *d* containing the difference between adjacent elements in the vector *x*.
- `b=polyder(p);` Returns a vector *b* containing the coefficients of the derivative of the polynomial represented by the vector *p*.

- `b=polyder(p1,p2);` Returns a vector b containing the coefficients of the polynomial that is the derivative of the *product* of the polynomials represented by p_1 and p_2.
- `[num,den]=polyder(p1,p2);` Returns the vectors *num* and *den* containing the coefficients of the numerator and denominator polynomials of the derivative of the *quotient* p_2/p_1, where p_1 and p_2 are polynomials.
- The MATLAB ODE Solvers `ode23` and `ode45;` These are simple ordinary differential equation solvers. There are several variants like *ode23, ode45, ode113, ode23s, ode23t, ode23tb*, and *ode15s*. The syntax and explanation is as follows:

```
[t,y]=ode23('ydot',tspan,y0);
```

  This solves the vector differential equation $\dot{y}$=f(t,y) specified in the function file `ydot`, whose inputs must be t and y and whose outputs must be a column vector representing dy/dt, that is f(t,y). The number of rows in this column vector must be equal to the order of the equation. The vector *tspan* contains the starting and ending values of the independent variable t, and optionally, any intermediate values of t where the solution is desired. The vector $y0$ contains $y(t_0)$. The function file must have two input arguments t and y even for equations where f(t,y) is not a function of t. The syntax is identical for other ode solvers.

2.8.5 MATLAB Symbolic Math Toolbox

The MATLAB Symbolic Math Toolbox enables us to do symbolic mathematics by which we get the results in the form of mathematical expressions. The main Symbolic Toolbox functions are listed below:

Symbolic Algebra

This includes functions for simplifying math expressions.

- `syms a b c real;` This command is used to specify that variables a, b and c are real. We can also use `sym` function to create *symbolic constants* by using a numerical value for the argument. For example:

```
>>pi=sym('pi');
```

- `syms x y;` Defines the symbolic variables x and y. Now we can use them in expressions like:

```
>> s= x + y;
>> t= sqrt(x^2+y^2);
```

- `findsym(Ex);` To find the symbols (pre-defined) in the expression, *Ex*.
- `collect(E);` Collects the coefficients of like powers in the expression *E*.
- `factor(E);` Factors the expression *E*.

- `simplify(E);` Simplifies the expression *E*.
- `simple(E);` Searches for the shortest form of the expression *E* in terms of number of characters.
- `expand(E);` Expands the expression *E*.
- `pretty(E);` Displays the expression *E* on the screen in a form that resembles typeset mathematics.
- `[num,den]=numden(E);` Returns two symbolic expressions that represent the numerator *num* and the denominator *den* for the rational representation of the expression *E*.
- `z=double(E);` Converts the expression *E* to a numeric form. The expression *E* must not contain any symbolic variables.
- `poly2sym(p,'x');` Converts a coefficient vector *p* to a symbolic polynomial in terms of the variable x.
- `sym2poly(E);` Converts the expression *E* to a polynomial coefficient vector.
- `F=subs(E,x,y);` Substitutes the symbolic variable *x* by symbolic variable *y* in expression *E* and gets the result as expression *F*.
- MATLAB does not have a symbolic factorial function, but we can use the *sym* and *subs* functions to access the *Maple* factorial function to compute $(n-1)!$ as follows:

```
>> kfact=sym('k!');
>> syms k n
>> E=subs(kfact,k,n-1)
E =
     (n-1)!
>> expand(E)
ans=
     n!/n
```

- `digits(d);` Changes the number of digits used to *d*.
- `vpa(E);` To compute the expression *E* to the number of digits specified by the default value of 32 or the current setting of *digits*.

Symbolic Math Toolbox in Solving Transcendental Equations

The Symbolic Math Toolbox can solve algebraic and transcendental equations as well as systems of such equations.[4]

- `solve(E);` Solves a symbolic expression or equation represented by the expression *E*. For example:

```
>> syms x y
>> y=solve(x+5)
```

[4] A *transcendental* equation is one that contains one or more transcendental functions such as $\sin\ x$, e^x, or $\log\ x$.

```
y=
  -5
```

Equations containing periodic functions can have an *infinite* number of solutions. In such cases the `solve` function restricts the solution search to solutions near 0. For example to solve the equation $\sin(2x) - \cos x = 0$, we write the following MATLAB code:

```
>> solve('sin(2*x)-cox(x)=0')
 ans=
        [1/2*pi]
        [-1/2*pi]
        [1/6*pi]
        [5/6*pi]
```

- `diff(X,x);` Differentiate expression *X*, which is a function of *x* with respect to *x*.
- `int(E,v);` Returns the integral of the expression *E* with respect to the variable *v*.
- `limit(E,v,a,'d');` Returns the limit of the expression *E* as the variable *v* goes to *a* from the direction specified by *d*, which may be *right* or *left*.
- `symsum(E);` Returns the symbolic summation of the expression *E*.

Solving Non-linear Differential Equations Using Symbolic Math Toolbox

Using the Symbolic Math Toolbox, many non-linear first order differential equations can be solved. For example, the first order non-linear differential equation:

$$\frac{dy}{dt} = 4 - y^2, \quad y(0) = 1$$

can be solved by the MATLAB code:

```
dsolve('Dy=4-y^2','y(0)=1')
ans=
   2*(exp(4*t-log(-1/3))+1)/(-1+exp(4*t-log(-1/3)))
  >> simple(ans)
ans=
    2*(3+exp(4*t)-1)/(1+3*exp(4*t))
```

Laplace Transform and Inverse Laplace Transform

The Laplace transform $\mathcal{L}[y(t)]$ of a function $y(t)$ is defined to be

$$\mathcal{L}[y(t)] = \int_{t=0}^{\infty} y(t)e^{-st}\, dt = F(s) \tag{2.1}$$

For example, to find the Laplace transform of the expressions t^3 and $\exp(-b * t)$, we can use the following MATLAB, code:

```
>> syms b t
>>> laplace(t^2)
ans=
   6/s^4
>> laplace(exp(-b*t))
ans=
     1/(s+b)
```

The inverse Laplace transform is defined to be

$$\mathcal{L}^{-1}[Y(s)] = \frac{1}{2\pi} \int_{s=0}^{\infty} F(s)e^{st}\, ds \tag{2.2}$$

To obtain the inverse Laplace transform of the expressions $\frac{1}{s^4}$ and $\frac{1}{(s+b)}$, we write the following MATLAB code:

```
>> syms b s
>> ilaplace(1/s^4)
ans=
     1/6*t^3
>> ilaplace(1/(s+b))
ans=
     exp(-b*t)
```

The *funtool* Function in Symbolic Math Toolbox

The *funtool* is a very compact data visualising tool in the Symbolic Math Toolbox of MATLAB. It can be evoked by typing:

```
>> funtool
```

The resulting figure windows are shown in Figure 2.13. Funtool is an interactive graphing calculator that manipulates functions of a single variable. At any given time, there are two functions displayed, $f(x)$ and $g(x)$. The result of most operations replaces $f(x)$. The controls labelled "$f =$" and "$g =$" are editable text that may be changed any time to install a new function. The control labelled "$x =$" may be changed to specify a new domain. The control labelled "$a =$" may be changed to specify a new value of a parameter.

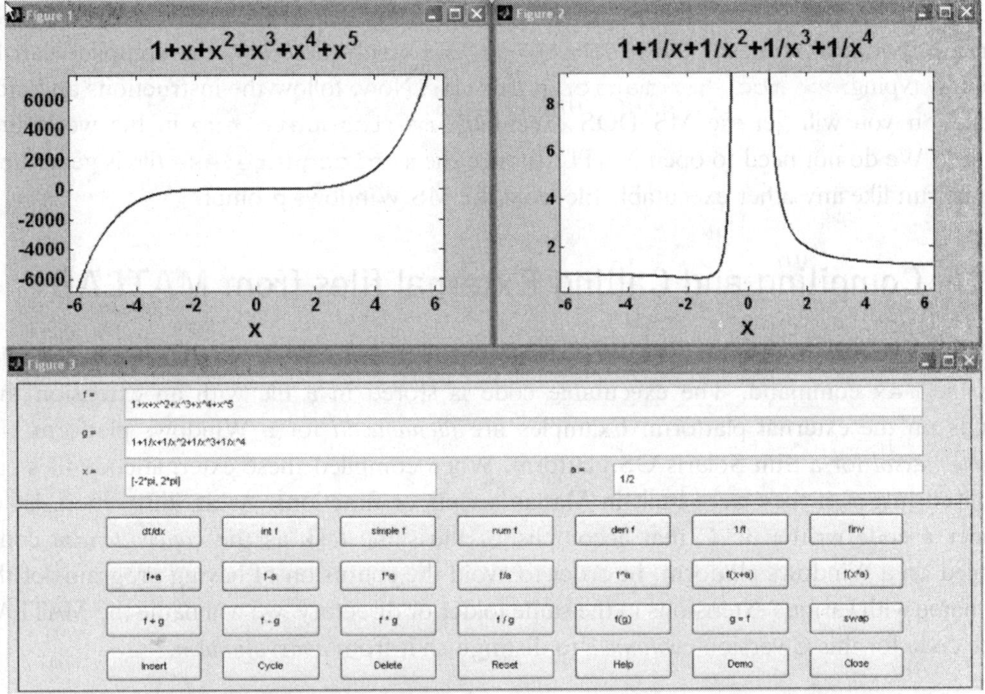

Figure 2.13 The figure windows of the funtool function

2.9 Getting MATLAB Help Online

To get online help on MATLAB topics, the following commands can be employed:

- `help topic.` (for online help on "topic.m") This command will list out all the *comments* (lines starting with a "%" character) given immediately after the function definition line. The comments that are placed elsewhere, that is *not just after* the function definition line, will not appear.
- `helpwin.` for listing out topics).
- `doc topic.` (for html documentation.) This is the most elaborate online help available in MATLAB.
- `lookfor topic.` (a sort of keyword search, takes more time than the other two). The `lookfor` command will list out all places where the string *topic* appears. It is an exhaustive search.

2.10 Generating Executable Files in MATLAB

It is possible to generate executable files from MATLAB script/function files by using the MATLAB Compiler available in the full MATLAB suite. Try the documentation:

`>> doc compiler;` for details on MATLAB Compiler. If you have, for example, the `magicsquare.m` file in the `/MATLAB7p1/work` sub-directory, the compiler can be evoked by typing: `>> mcc -mv magicsquare.m;`. Now, follow the instructions and after compilation you will get the MS DOS executable `magicsquare.exe` in the work sub-directory. We do not need to open MATLAB once the `magicsquare.exe` file is generated: it can be run like any other executable file from the MS Windows prompt.

2.11 Compiling and Calling External files from MATLAB

MATLAB can compile external FORTRAN and C code into MEX (Matlab EXternal) files using the `mex` command. The executable code is stored in a file with an extension that depends on the external platform. Examples are *filename.dll* for a Windows platform and *filename.mexsol* for a Sun Solaris OS platform. When compiled these external code files can be utilised just as if they were built-in Matlab scripts or functions. As an illustration, let us consider a code written in C that accomplishes the same task as the *conevolume.m* code, compiled on a Windows platform. In order to avoid the confusion of having programs of the same name with various extensions in the same folder or directory, we will name the MATLAB source code for this C version *cvolume.c* to distinguish it from *conevolume.m*.

```
function f = conevolume(r,h)
% volume of a cone with base radius r and height h
f = pi*(r^2)*h/3;
%%end of conevolume.m
/*=======================================================
  * CVOLUME.C volume of cone from base radius and height
  *   Calling syntax:        v = cvolume(r,h)
  *=====================================================*/
#include <math.h>
#include <mex.h>
/* Input Arguments */
#define    R_IN prhs[0]
#define     H_IN prhs[1]
/* Output Arguments */
#define    V_OUT      plhs[0]
#define PI 3.14159265
static void cvolume(
              double v[],
              double r[],
              double h[]
              )
```

```
{
    v[0] = PI*r[0]*r[0]*h[0]/3;
    return;
}
void mexFunction( int nlhs, mxArray *plhs[],
                  int nrhs, const mxArray *prhs[] )
{
  double *v;
  double *r,*h;
  V_OUT = mxCreateDoubleMatrix(1,1, mxREAL);
  /* Assign pointers to the various parameters */
  v = mxGetPr(V_OUT);
  r = mxGetPr(R_IN);
  h = mxGetPr(H_IN);
  /* Do the actual computation in a subroutine */
  cvolume(v,r,h);
  return;
}
%%%end of cvolume.c
```

We see that the C code is quite a bit longer and more complex, so normally we just use the MATLAB programming language to do simple calculations. However, there may be occasions when execution time can be improved by using the compiled code of another language. This situation can occur, for example, when the MATLAB code involves extensive looping or iterating. Also, other languages may have libraries available for specialised purposes or functions.

To compile this code, we will need to setup for MEX files if it has not been done so already. At the Command Window MATLAB prompt, type

```
>> mex -setup,
```

and we will subsequently be prompted for information about our computer's operating system and the compiler that we want to use. UNIX systems usually have FORTRAN and C compilers such as *f 77* or *gcc* installed, but Windows platforms may not come configured with any. To overcome these short comings, MATLAB has a bundled compiler, *Lcc,* which is used as the default C complier if no other is specified. Unfortunately, the current version of MATLAB does not have a bundled FORTRAN compiler. After finishing the setup, we should be ready to compile programs, at least ones written in C. The syntax for compiling is to give the file name and extension as the target for the mex command, e.g.

```
>> mex cvolume.c
```

to compile the C code given in the illustrative example. If we do this on a Windows platform, we will generate an executable file *cvolume.dll*.

Once we have compiled the code, we can use the command `cvolume` at a MATLAB prompt and get the same answer as we get using the command `conevolume` whose source is a MATLAB M-file. The volume of a cone which has a base radius 1 and a perpendicular height 1 is computed by these two codes as

```
>> volume_Matlab = conevolume(1,1)
  volume_Matlab =
        1.0472
>> volume_C = cvolume(1,1)
 volume_C =
     1.0472
```

2.12 Calling MATLAB Objects from External Programs

MATLAB has an engine with functions that allow it to act as a callable external function or sub-routine library in FORTRAN and C programs. The functions open the MATLAB engine, close it, get and send matrix arrays, and evaluate MATLAB strings. There is extensive information about these in the built-in MATLAB help utility, with examples of FORTRAN and C programs that call the MATLAB engine. External FORTRAN and C programs can also call binary MATLAB files such as those created by default with the save command. The save command with no format flag will save the current workspace information in a binary file format (MAT) with a default name *filename.mat*, or the default *matlab.mat* if no file name is supplied. MAT file information can be accessed by external programs with commands similar to those for the MATLAB engine. There is extensive information about the commands for exchanging data with external programs using MAT files in the built-in MATLAB help utility.

2.13 Using Java Classes in MATLAB

The desktop interface that is used for MATLAB was developed and written in Java. As a result, MATLAB has an integrated Java Virtual Machine (JVM) and Java classes can be used directly in MATLAB at the command line or within function M-files. Before using these classes, we must check whether there is a file with the name *classpath.txt* in the MATLAB search path. MATLAB has a default file located in the folder or directory *MATLAB_root -¿ toolbox -¿ local*. This can be copied to a directory in the MATLAB path and edited if the programmer has created classes other than those in the default list.

A class or a package of classes can be imported into the workspace with the import command. If this has not been done for a particular class, that class has to be referenced by its complete name. As an illustration, consider a simple example where the default *classpath.txt* file has already been copied to the current working directory. The Java *awt* class package has also been imported but the Java *lang* class package has not. In this case, we can use a class name from the imported package directly on the command line but must give the complete full name for a class in the package which has not been imported.

The *Dimension* class is recognised because its package has been imported, but the *String* class is not recognised as a Java class because its package has not been imported. However, if the complete name of the *String* class, i.e., *java.lang.String*, is used, then the MATLAB interpreter recognises it as a Java class.

2.14 The MATLAB GUIDE

GUIDE stands for graphical user interface design environment for MATLAB. The first step to evoke MATLAB GUIDE is to type "guide" in the MATLAB command window:

```
>> guide
```

Now, using the save options, save the blank GUI to "multiplier.fig". Then calling the guide again as `>> guide multiplier` will open up a window illustrated in Figure 2.14.

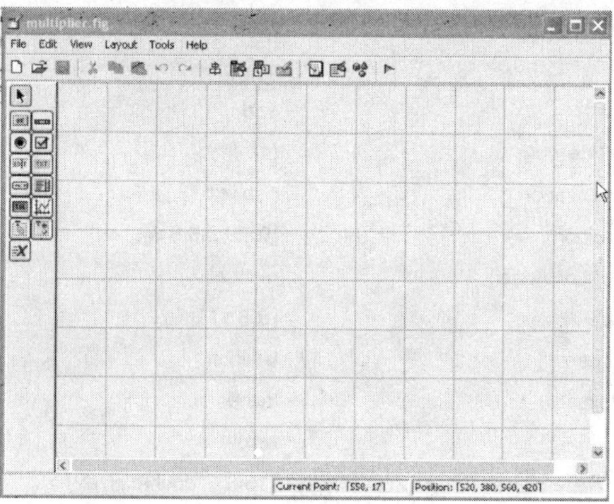

Figure 2.14 The GUIDE opening window

The user can now add as many code activating devices (i.e., buttons, edit boxes, popup menus, etc.) as he/she wishes. These items are located on the left panel of the GUIDE frame. To add a device, left-click on that device to select it and place it anywhere on the layout. This is where it will be displayed on the GUIDE once it is executed.

2.14.1 Editing a GUI

We will now explore how to edit the basic graphical user interface (GUI) in few simple steps.

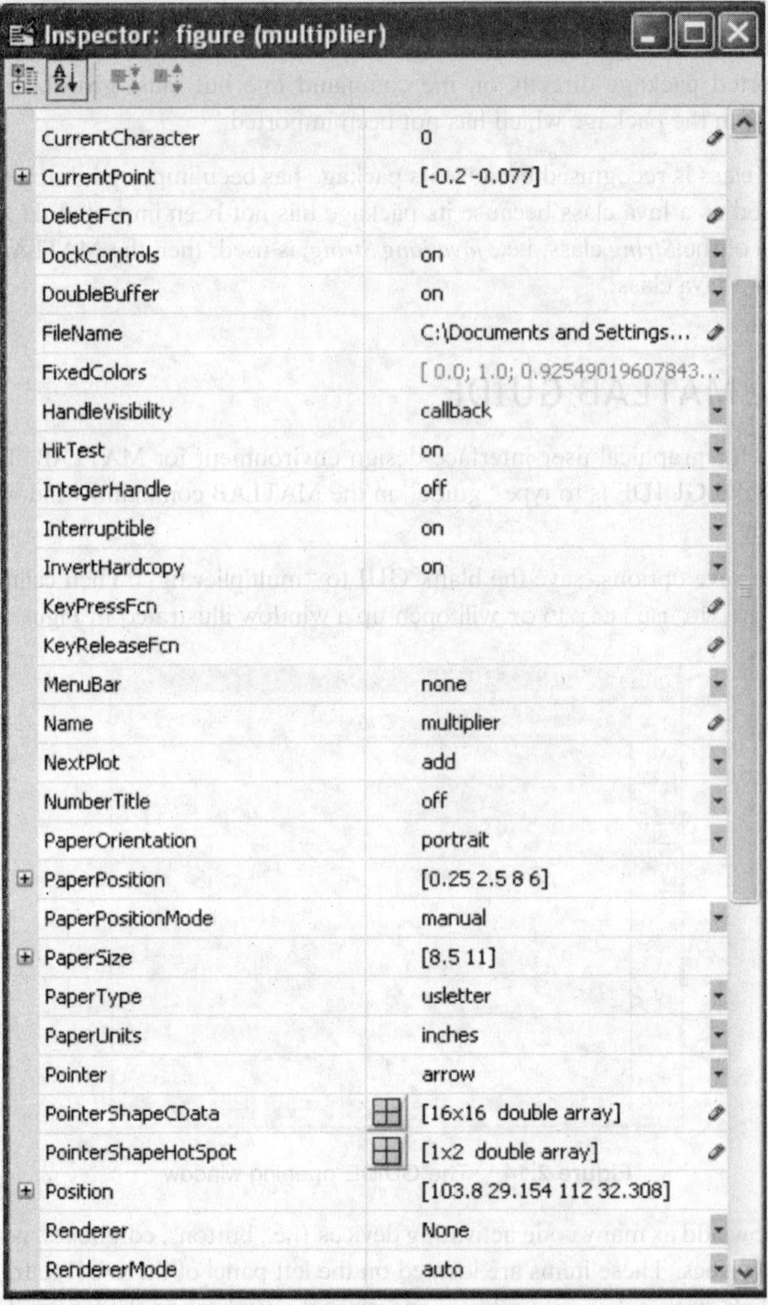

Figure 2.15 The Property Inspector of GUI

Property Inspector

If needed, the GUI designer can manipulate the size, colour, and label of the button. To change the size of the button, for example, simply click and hold any of the corners of the button using the cursor until the button reaches the desired size. Most of the property changes of the button will take place using the button's Property Inspector (Figure 2.15). Each component has its own Property Inspector that is activated by double-clicking on that device.

To change the colour of the button, the designer must first activate the Property Inspector and then double-click on the colour wheel icon. This will open a colour-editing window where changes can be made. To change the button's label, scroll down on the button's Property Inspector and type in the desired information next to "String". The designer will notice instant changes to the GUI layout.

Now, the designer can add as many components to the GUI layout as he/she wishes. In the example given in Figure 2.16, some more components were added: two edit boxes (white) and four static text boxes ("Simple Multiplier", "×", "--------" and the "Get Answer" box).

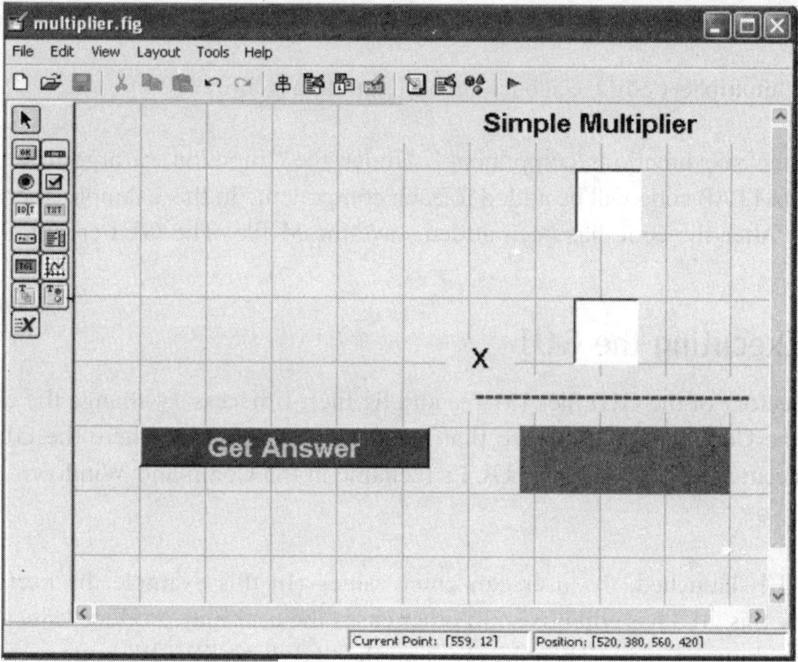

Figure 2.16 The Final Multiplier GUI

The components were manipulated using the Property Inspector. It is important to note that the static text boxes are components which will not have an applied function, therefore once the code-attaching process takes place, these devices will not receive any code.

2.14.2 Code Attachment Process

Once the GUI is "physically" designed, code will be attached to each component to complete the process. To get to the code-attachment section, the GUI must be saved. The saving process will produce two files; a .fig file (the recently designed GUI frame) and an M-file (newly created for code attachment). The M-file will pop up and it will contain as many sub-functions as the number of components (not including static text boxes and frames) on the GUI layout. Each sub-function in the M-file will begin with "function varargout = . . . ".

To verify that the code is added to the sub-function that corresponds to it, with the correct GUI component, activate the Property Inspector in the GUI figure file (layout frame) and view the Callback line of each device. Each component's Property Inspector should display the callback label in single quotes next to the line. For example:

M-file: "function varargout = edit2_Callback(hObject, eventdata, handles, varargin)"

matches with

.fig file: "multiplier('edit2_Callback',gcbo,[],guidata(gcbo))"

Add code to the sub-functions/components. Under the "function varargout = . . . " line is where the MATLAB code will be added to each component. In this example, there are three sub-functions. After the code has been added, save the M-file. The GUI creation process is now over.

2.14.3 Executing the GUI

Locate the directory of the GUI files (M-file and fig file). If necessary change the directory of MATLAB in the Command Window so that it reflects the directory where the GUI files are located. To execute the GUI, type the GUI's filename in the Command Window:

```
>>multiplier
```

Once the GUI is launched, the user can enter values (In this example the user can enter values, because this GUI has edit boxes. In other cases the user may produce values via popup windows, radial buttons, etc.). Then, by pressing the "GET ANSWER" button, the GUI will display the result as shown in Figure 2.17.

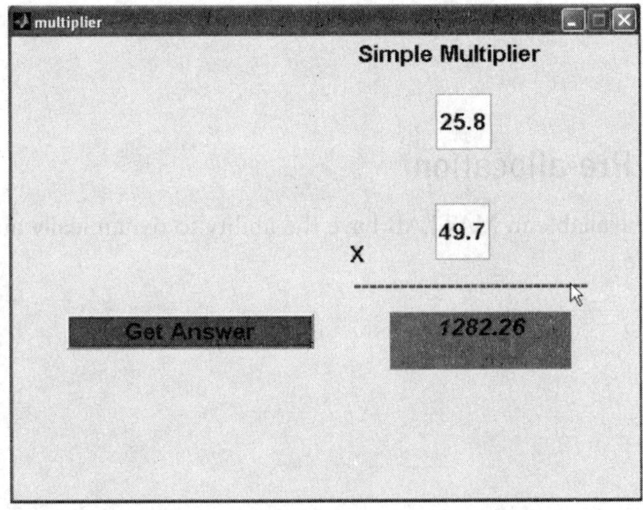

Figure 2.17 On executing the multiplier GUI

2.15 Writing Efficient MATLAB Code

MATLAB code is interpreted during runtime. Languages like C and Fortran are faster because they are first compiled into the computer's native language. Interpreting in real time enables better platform independence, greater language flexibility, and interactive debugging, but at the cost of slower speed, increased overhead, and limited low-level control.

In this section, we will discuss strategies for improving the speed of MATLAB code. Keep in mind that speed depends heavily on the computation platform and that the fastest method on one system is not necessarily the fastest on another. Secondly, MATLAB has gone through several versions and continues to evolve: a slow method may become fast in a newer version. We will consider methods that are generally fast.

2.15.1 The MATLAB Profiler

To evaluate the performance of functions, MATLAB version 5.0 onwards provides a tool called *profiler*. The profiler keeps track of the time spend on each line of the function (in units of 0.01s) as the function is executed. The profile report shows how much time was spent on which line. The profile output can also be seen graphically as a Pareto plot. The following commands will invoke the MATLAB profiler.

```
profile on
profile clear
File_name
profile report
```

```
profile plot
profile off
```

2.15.2 Array Pre-allocation

The matrix variables available in MATLAB have the ability to dynamically augment rows and columns. For example:

```
>> a = 5
a =
     5
>> a(2,5) = 2
a =
     5 0 0 0 0
     0 0 0 0 2
```

MATLAB automatically resizes the matrix. Internally, the matrix data memory must be reallocated with larger size. If a matrix is resized repeatedly—like within a loop—this overhead can be significant. To avoid frequent re-allocations, the matrix is pre-allocated with the zeros command. Pre-allocation can also be done with cell arrays, using the cell command to create the desired size. Using pre-allocation with a frequently resizing cell array is even more beneficial than with double arrays.

2.15.3 JIT Acceleration

MATLAB 6.5 (Release 13) and later versions feature the Just-In-Time (JIT) Accelerator which improve the speed of M-code functions and scripts, particularly self-contained loops. By becoming familiar with the accelerator, we can improve its performance. The JIT Accelerator is enabled by default. To disable it, type "feature accel off" in the console, and "feature accel on" to enable it again.

As of MATLAB 7.5 (R2007b), only a sub-set of the MATLAB language is supported for acceleration. When an unsupported feature is encountered, acceleration processing is interrupted to handle it using non-accelerated evaluation. The greatest acceleration improvements are gained when significant contiguous portions of code are supported. The following points may be kept in mind:

- Code must use supported data types for acceleration: Double (both *real* and *complex*), *logical, char, int8, uint8, int16, uint16, int32, uint32*. Code that uses other data types (for example, cell, struct, and function handles) is not accelerated. Sparse arrays are also not accelerated.

- Array shapes of any size with 3 or fewer dimensions are supported. Changing the shape or data type of an array interrupts acceleration.
- Only calls to built-in functions are accelerated. Calling M-files and MEX functions interrupts acceleration.
- The conditional statements *if, elseif, while,* and *switch* are supported if the conditional expression evaluates to a scalar. Loops are accelerated if all the code within the loop is supported. Additionally, *for* statements must have scalar loop indices.

In future releases, JIT Accelerator may support more of the language and reduce these restrictions.

Multi-threaded Computation

MATLAB 7.4 (R2007a) introduced multi-threaded computation for multi-core processors. Multi-threaded computation accelerates some per-element functions when applied to large arrays (for example, `.^`, `sin`, `exp`) and certain linear algebra functions in the BLAS library.

Multi-threaded computation is disabled by default. To enable it, we must select:

$$File \rightarrow Preferences \rightarrow General \rightarrow Multi\text{-}threading$$

and select "Enable multi-threaded computation". As of MATLAB 7.5 (R2007b), it seems that most MATLAB code gains no improvement from multi-threaded computation. In fact, some code is slightly slower when it is enabled. (When comparing, be aware that there is overhead when running code for the first time; run the test code twice and time the second run.) Hopefully, the multi-threaded computation feature will be developed further in future releases.

2.15.4 Vectorisation

A computation is vectorised by taking advantage of vector operations. A variety of programming situations can be vectorised, often improving speed to 10 times faster or even better. Vectorisation is one of the most general and effective techniques for writing fast M-code.

Vectorised Computations

Many standard MATLAB functions are "vectorised": they can operate on an array as if the function had been applied individually to every element. Some useful functions for vectorising computations are: `min`, `max`, `repmat`, `meshgrid`, `sum`, `cumsum`, `diff`, `prod`, `cumprod`, `accumarray`, `filter`.

Vectorised Logic

The previous section shows how to vectorise pure computation. Bottleneck code often involves conditional logic. Like computations, logic operators in MATLAB are also vectorised. Logic operations return "logical" arrays with binary values. This is made useful by employing powerful functions for operating on logical arrays: `find, any, all`.

2.15.5 Inlining Simple Functions

Every time an M-file function is called, the MATLAB interpreter incurs some overhead. Additionally, many M-file functions begin with conditional code that checks the input arguments for errors or determines the mode of operation. Of course, this overhead is negligible for a single function call. It becomes significant only when the function being called is an M-file, the function itself is "simple", that is, implemented with only a few lines, and called frequently from within a loop.

"Inlining a function" means to replace a call to a function with the function code itself. Note that inlining should not be confused with the "inline" function datatype of MATLAB. Studying median.m (type "edit median" on the console) reveals that most of the work is done using the built-in *sort* function. The median call can be inlined as:

```
% Apply the median filter of size 5 to signal x
y = zeros(size(x)); % Preallocate
for k = 3:length(x)
   tmp = sort(x(k:k+2));
                              % y(k) = median(x(k:k+2));
   y(k) = tmp(3);
end
```

By inlining median, it can be specifically tailored to evaluate 5-sample medians.

A surprisingly large number of MATLAB functions are implemented as M-files, of which many can be inlined in just a few lines. In MATLAB 5.3 (Release 11), the following functions are worth inlining:

```
conv,cross,fft2, fliplr,flipud,ifft,ifft2,ifftn,ind2sub,
ismember,linspace,logspace, mean,median,meshgrid,poly,
polyval,repmat,roots,rot90,setdiff, setxor,sortrows,
std,sub2ind,union,unique,var.
```

Use the which command or try "edit function name" to determine whether a function is implemented as an M-file. Also note that inlining functions is only beneficial when the function is simple and when it is called frequently. Doing it unnecessarily obfuscates the code.

2.15.6 Referencing Operations

Referencing in MATLAB is varied and powerful enough to deserve a section of discussion. A good understanding of referencing enables vectorising a broader range of programming situations.

Subscripts versus Indices

Subscripts are the most common method used to refer to matrix elements, for example, $A(3, 9)$ refers to row 3, column 9. Indices are an alternative referencing method. Consider a 10×10 matrix A. Internally, MATLAB stores the matrix data linearly as a one-dimensional, 100-element array of data in column-major order. An index refers to an element's position in this one-dimensional array. Using an index, $A(83)$ also refers to the element on row 3, column 9.

It is faster to scan down columns than over rows. The column-major order means that elements of a column are closer together in memory than elements of a row, which promotes cache efficiency. Conversion between subscripts and indices can be done with the *sub2ind* and *ind2sub* functions. However, because these are M-file functions rather than fast built-in operations, it is more efficient to compute conversions directly. For a two-dimensional matrix A of size $M \times N$, the conversions between subscript (i, j) and index $(index)$ are

$$
\begin{aligned}
A(i,j) &\leftrightarrow A(i + (j-1) * M) \\
A(index) &\leftrightarrow A(rem(index-1, M) + 1, floor((index-1)/M) + 1).
\end{aligned}
$$

Indexing extends to N-D matrices as well, with indices increasing first through the columns, then through the rows, through the third dimension, and so on. Subscript notation extends intuitively, $A(..., dim4, dim3, row, col)$.

Vectorised Subscripts

It is useful to work with sub-matrices rather than individual elements. This is done with a vector of indices or subscripts. If A is a two-dimensional matrix, a vector subscript reference has the syntax $A(rowv, colv)$, where $rowv$ is a vector of rows with M elements and $colv$ is a vector of columns with N elements. Both may be of any length and their elements may be in any order. If either is a matrix, it is reshaped to a vector. There is no difference between using row vectors or column vectors in vector subscripts.

Vector Indices

Multiple elements can also be referenced with vector indices, $A(indexv)$, where $indexv$ is an array of indices. On the right-hand side, a vector index reference returns a matrix the same size as $indexv$. For example, if $indexv$ is a 3×3 matrix, $A(indexv)$ is the 3×3 matrix

$$A(indexv) = \begin{bmatrix} A(indexv(1,1)) & A(indexv(1,2)) & A(indexv(1,3)) \\ A(indexv(2,1)) & A(indexv(2,2)) & A(indexv(2,3)) \\ A(indexv(3,1)) & A(indexv(3,2)) & A(indexv(3,3)) \end{bmatrix}$$

While vector subscripts are limited to referring to block-shaped sub-matrices, vector indices can refer to any shape.

If a vector index reference is on the left-hand side, the right-hand side must return a matrix of the same size as $indexv$ or a scalar. As with vector subscripts, ambiguous duplicate assignments use the value with the greater source index.

Reference Wildcards

Using the wildcard, :, in a subscript refers to an entire row or column. For example, A(:,1) refers to every row in column one or the entire first column. This can be combined with vector subscripts. $A([2,4],:)$ refers to the second and fourth rows.

When the wildcard is used in a vector index, the entire matrix is referenced. On the right-hand side, this always returns a column vector.

$$A(:) = columnvector$$

This is frequently useful; for example, if a function input must be a row vector, the user's input can be quickly reshaped into a row vector with $A(:)'$ (make it a column vector and transpose it to a row vector). $A(:)$ on the left-hand side assigns all the elements of A, but does not change its size. For example, $A(:) = 8$ changes all elements of matrix A to 8.

Logical Indexing

Given a logical array mask with the same size as A, $A(mask)$ refers to all the elements of A where the corresponding element of mask is 1 (true). It is equivalent to $A(find(mask))$. A common usage of logical indexing is to refer to elements based on a per-element condition, for example,

$$A(abs(A) < 1e - 3) = 0$$

sets all elements with magnitude less than 10^{-3} to zero. Logical indexing is also useful to select non-rectangular sets of elements, for example,

$$A(logical(eye(size(A))))$$

references the diagonal elements of A. Note that for a right-hand side reference, it is faster to use $diag(A)$ to get the diagonal of A.

Deleting Sub-matrices with [ ]

Elements in a matrix can be deleted by assigning them to an empty matrix. For example, $A([3,5]) = []$ deletes the third and fifth element from A. If this is done with index references, the matrix is reshaped into a row vector.

It is also possible to delete with subscripts if all but one subscript are the wildcard. $A(2,:) = []$ deletes the second row. Deletions like $A(2,1) = []$ or even $A(2,1:end) = []$ are illegal.

2.15.7 Numerical Integration

Numerical approximation of integrals is usually done with quadrature formulas which have the form

$$\int_a^b f(x)\,dx = \sum_k w_k f(x_k),$$

where the x_k are called the nodes or abscissas and w_k are the associated weights. Simpson's rule is

$$\int_a^b f(x)\,dx = \frac{h}{3}\left[f(a) + 4f(a+h) + f(b)\right], \quad h = \frac{b-a}{2}.$$

Simpson's rule is a quadrature formula with nodes $a, a+h, b$ and node weights $\frac{h}{3}, \frac{4h}{3}, \frac{h}{3}$.

MATLAB offers *quad* and *quadl* for quadrature in one dimension. These functions are robust and precise, however, they are not very efficient. Both use an adaptive refinement procedure to reduce the number of function calls. However, as *quad* and *quadl* are recursive M-file functions, the algorithmic overhead is significant. Furthermore, the adaptive algorithm gains little from vectorisation.

One-Dimensional Integration

$\int_a^b f(x)\,dx$ is approximated by composite Simpson's rule with

$$\begin{aligned} h &= (b-a)/(N-1); \\ x &= (a:h:b).'; \\ w &= ones(1,N); w(2:2:N-1) = 4; w(3:2:N-2) = 2; w = w * h/3; \\ I &= w * f(x); \end{aligned}$$

where N is an odd integer specifying the number of nodes. A good higher-order choice is the composite 4th-order Gauss–Lobatto quadrature, based on the approximation

$$\int_{-1}^{1} f(x)\,dx \approx \frac{1}{6}f(-1) + \frac{5}{6}f(-\frac{1}{\sqrt{5}}) + \frac{5}{6}f(\frac{1}{\sqrt{5}}) + \frac{1}{6}f(1).$$

```
N =  max(3*round((N-1)/3),3) + 1; % Adjust N to the closest
% valid choice...
h =   (b - a)/(N-1);
d =   (3/sqrt(5) - 1)*h/2;
x =   (a:h:b).'; x(2:3:N-2) = x(2:3:N-2) + d;
x(3:3:N-1) = x(3:3:N-1) + d; w = ones(1,N);
w(4:3:N-3) = 2; w([2:3:N-2,3:3:N-1]) = 5; w = w*h/4;
I =  w * f(x);      % Approximately evaluate the integral
```

The number of nodes N must be such that $(N-1)/3$ is an integer. If not, the first line adjusts N to the closest valid choice. It is usually more accurate than Simpson's rule when f has six continuous derivatives, $f \in C^6(a,b)$.

A disadvantage of this non-adaptive approach is that the accuracy of the result is only indirectly controlled by the parameter N. To guarantee a desired accuracy, we have to either use a generously large value for N or if possible determine the error bounds.

For most purposes, composite Simpson's rule is a sufficient default choice. Depending on the integrand, other choices can improve accuracy:

- Use higher-order quadrature formulas if the integrand has many continuous derivatives.
- Use lower-order quadrature if the integrand function is not smooth.
- Use the substitution $u = \frac{1}{1-x}$ or Gauss–Laguerre quadrature for infinite-domain integrals like $\int_0^\infty$.

Multi-dimensional Integration

An approach for evaluating double integrals of the form $\int_a^b \int_c^d f(x,y)\,dy\,dx$ is to apply one-dimensional quadrature to the outer integral $\int_a^b F(x)\,dx$ and then for each x use one-dimensional quadrature over the inner dimension to approximate $F(x) = \int_c^d f(x,y)\,dy$. The following MATLAB code does this with composite Simpson's rule with $Nx \times Ny$ nodes:

```
%%% Construct Simpson nodes and weights over x %%%
h = (b - a)/(Nx-1);
x = (a:h:b).';
wx = ones(1,Nx); wx(2:2:Nx-1) = 4; wx(3:2:Nx-2) = 2;
wx = w*h/3;
%%% Construct Simpson nodes and weights over y %%%
h = (d - c)/(Ny-1);
y = (c:h:d).';
wy = ones(1,Ny); wy(2:2:Ny-1) = 4; wy(3:2:Ny-2) = 2;
wy = w*h/3;
%%% Combine for two-dimensional integration %%%
[x,y] = meshgrid(x,y); x = x(:); y = y(:);
w = wy.'*wx; w = w(:).';
I = w * f(x,y);     % Approximately evaluate the integral
```

Similarly for three-dimensional integrals, the weights are combined with

```
[x,y,z] = meshgrid(x,y,z);x = x(:);y = y(:);z = z(:);
w = wy.'*wx;w = w(:)*wz;w = w(:).';
```

When the integration region is complicated or of high dimension, Monte Carlo integration techniques are appropriate.

2.15.8 Speeding Up Signal Processing

Even without the Signal Processing Toolbox, MATLAB is quite efficient in signal processing computations. This section lists code snippets to perform several common operations efficiently.

- *Locating zero-crossings and extrema* To obtain the indices where signal x crosses zero:

```
i = find(diff(sign(x)));
% The kth zero-crossing lies between x(i(k)) and x(i(k)+1)
```

Since local maximum and minimum points of a signal have zero derivative, their locations can be estimated from the zero-crossings of *diff(x)*, provided the signal is sampled with a sufficiently fine resolution.

- *Moving average filter* To compute an N-sample moving average of x with zero padding:

```
y = filter(ones(N,1)/N,1,x);
```

For large N, it is faster to use

```
y = cumsum(x)/N;
y(N+1:end) = y(N+1:end) - y(1:end-N);
```

- *FFT-based convolution* This line performs FFT-based circular convolution, equivalent to $y = filter(b, 1, x)$ except near the boundaries, provided that $length(b) < length(x)$:

```
y = ifft(fft(b,length(x)).*fft(x));
```

For FFT-based zero-padded convolution equivalent to $y = filter(b, 1, x)$,

```
N = length(x)+length(b)-1;
y = ifft(fft(b,N).*fft(x,N));
y = y(1:length(x));
```

In both the above code snippets, y will be complex-valued, even if x and b are both real. To force y to be real, follow the computation with $y = real(y)$. If the Signal Processing Toolbox is available, it is faster to use `fftfilt` for FFT-based, zero-padded filtering.

- *Non-causal filtering and other boundary extensions* For its intended use, the filter command is limited to causal filters, that is, filters that do not involve "future" values to the right of the current sample. Furthermore, the filter is limited to zero-padded boundary extensions; data beyond the array boundaries are assumed zero as if the data were padded with zeros. For two-tap filters, non-causal filtering and other boundary extensions are possible through the filter's fourth initial condition argument. Given a boundary extension value `padLeft` for $x(0)$, the filter $y_n = b_1 x_n + b_2 x_{n-1}$ may be implemented as

```
y = filter(b,1,x,padLeft*b(2));
```

Similarly, given a boundary extension value `padRight` for $x(end + 1)$, the filter $y_n = b_1 x_{n+1} + b_2 x_n$ is implemented as

```
y = filter(b,1,[x(2:end),padRight],x(1)*b(2));
```

It is in principle possible to use a similar approach for longer filters, but ironically, computing the initial conditions itself requires filtering. To implement non-causal filtering and filtering with other boundary handling, it is usually fastest to pad the input signal, apply filter, and then truncate the result.

- *Upsampling and downsampling* The following code upsamples x (insert zeros) by a factor p:

```
y = zeros(length(x)*p-p+1,1);
% For trailing zeros, use y = zeros(length(x)*p,1);
y(1:p:length(x)*p) = x;
```

To downsample x by a factor p, where $1 \le q \le p$, we use the following:

```
y = x(q:p:end);
```

- *Haar wavelet* This MATLAB code performs K stages of the Haar wavelet transform on the input data x to produce wavelet coefficients y. The input array x must have a length divisible by 2^K.

Forward transform:

```
y = x(:); N = length(y);

for k = 1:K
  tmp = y(1:2:N) + y(2:2:N);
  y([1:N/2,N/2+1:N]) = ...
  [tmp;y(1:2:N) - 0.5*tmp]/sqrt(2);
  N = N/2;
end
```

Inverse transform:

```
x = y(:); N = length(x)*pow2(-K);
for k = 1:K
   N = N*2;
   tmp = x(N/2+1:N) + 0.5*x(1:N/2);
   x([1:2:N,2:2:N]) = [tmp;x(1:N/2) - tmp]*sqrt(2);
end
```

- *Daubechies 4-tap wavelet* This MATLAB code implements the Daubechies 4-tap wavelet in a lifting scheme form. The input array x must have a length divisible by 2^K. Filtering is done with symmetric boundary handling.

Forward transform:

```
U = 0.25*[2-sqrt(3),-sqrt(3)];
ScaleS = (sqrt(3) - 1)/sqrt(2);
ScaleD = (sqrt(3) + 1)/sqrt(2);
y = x(:); N = length(y);
for k = 1:K
```

```
        N = N/2;

        y1 = y(1:2:2*N);
        y2 = y(2:2:2*N) + sqrt(3)*y1;
        y1 = y1 + filter(U,1,...
          y2([2:N,max(N-1,1)]),y2(1)*U(2));
        y(1:2*N) = [ScaleS*...
          (y2 - y1([min(2,N),1:N-1]));ScaleD*y1];
    end
```

Inverse transform:

```
U = 0.25*[2-sqrt(3),-sqrt(3)];
ScaleS = (sqrt(3) - 1)/sqrt(2);
ScaleD = (sqrt(3) + 1)/sqrt(2);
x = y(:); N = length(x)*pow2(-K);
for k = 1:K
    y1 = x(N+1:2*N)/ScaleD;
    y2 = x(1:N)/ScaleS + y1([min(2,N),1:N-1]);
    y1 = y1 - filter(U,1,...
        y2([2:N,max(N-1,1)]),y2(1)*U(2));
    x([1:2:2*N,2:2:2*N]) = [y1;y2 - sqrt(3)*y1];
    N = 2*N;
end
```

To use periodic boundary handling rather than symmetric boundary handling, change appearances of $[2:N, max(N-1,1)]$ to $[2:N,1]$ and $[min(2,N), 1:N-1]$ to $[N, 1:N-1]$.

2.15.9 Miscellaneous Tricks

You may also find the following tricks/tips useful.

- *Clip a value without using* if *statements* To clip (or clamp, bound, or saturate) a value to within a range, the straightforward implementation is

```
if x < lowerBound
   x= lowerBound;
      x > upperBound
elseif
   x= upperBound;
end
```

Unfortunately, this is slow. A faster method is to use the `min` and `max` functions:

```
x = max(x,lowerBound);
% Clip elements from below, force x >= lowerBound
x = min(x,upperBound);
% Clip elements from above, force x <= upperBound
```

Moreover, it works per element if x is a matrix of any size.

- *Convert any array into a column vector* It is often needed to convert an array to a column vector, for example, when writing a function expecting a column vector as an input. This simple trick will convert the input array of any shape and number of dimensions to a column vector, even if the input is already a column vector:

```
x = x(:);    % convert x to a column vector
```

By following this operation with a transpose `'`, it is possible to convert an array to a row vector.

- *Find the min/max of a matrix or N dimensional array* Given a matrix input (with no other inputs), the `min` and `max` functions operate along the columns, finding the extreme element in each column. One way to find the extreme element over the entire matrix for a two-dimensional matrix is `min(min(A))`. A better method that works regardless of the number of dimensions and determines the extreme element's location is

```
[MinValue, MinIndex] = min(A(:));
 % Find the minimum element in A
 % The minimum value is MinValue,
 % the index is MinIndex
MinSub = ind2sub(size(A), MinIndex);
 % Convert MinIndex to subscripts.
```

The minimum element is `A(MinIndex)` or `A(MinSub(1), MinSub(2), . . .)` as a subscript reference. (Similarly, replace `min` with `max` for maximum value.)

- *Flood filling* Flood filling, like the "bucket" tool in image editors, can be elegantly written as a recursive function. The following MATLAB code is faster:

```
function I = flood2(I,c,x,y)
% Flood fills image I from point (x,y) with color c.
LastFlood = zeros(size(I));
Flood = LastFlood;
Flood(y,x) = 1;
Mask = (I == I(y,x));
FloodFilter = [0,1,0; 1,1,1; 0,1,0];

while any(LastFlood(:) E = Flood(:))
   LastFlood = Flood;
```

```
    Flood = conv2(Flood,FloodFilter,'same') & Mask;
end
I(find(Flood)) = c;
```

The key is the *conv2* two-dimensional convolution function.

- *Vectorised use of sets on GUI objects* While not a speed improvement, a trick for cleaner code is the vectorised use of sets on GUI objects. A serious graphical user interface (GUI) can have dozens of objects like text labels, buttons, and sliders. Consider defining three edit boxes with white text background and left text alignment. A vectorised call to set reduces the definition to

```
h(1) = uicontrol('Units', 'normalized',...
'Position', [0.1,0.9,0.7,0.05]);
h(2) = uicontrol('Units', 'normalized',...
'Position', [0.1,0.8,0.7,0.05]);
h(3) = uicontrol('Units', 'normalized',...
'Position', [0.1,0.7,0.7,0.05]);
set(h, 'HorizontalAlignment', 'left',...
'Style', 'edit','BackgroundColor', [1,1,1]);
```

2.16 MATLAB Clones

Several programs similar to MATLAB are now available. Some of them are commercial software tools and some of them are available in the open software domain. Examples for commercial equivalents of MATLAB are:

- *Mathematica*
- *Mathcad*
- *Maple*
- *Macsyma*

Maple, developed by Maplesoft, is a very popular technical computing environment. Then there is Mathematica, developed by Wolfram Research. To get a rough idea of the popularity of the three software packages, the search results on CiteSeer for the number of citations and Google for the number of page hits, for these languages, is illustrated in Table 2.1.

Table 2.1 CiteSeer and Google searches

Math Package	CiteSeer	Google
MATLAB	2961	1860000
Maple	1678	Common Word
Mathematica	1710	1340000

The need to create an open source alternative to MATLAB arose with the advent of open source softwares. The major open source software alternatives to MATLAB are GNU Octave and Scilab. Scilab was developed by the French National Institute for Research in Computer Science and Control (INRIA) and the National School of Bridges and Roads (ENPC). Octave was developed by James Rawlings of the University of Wisconsin and John Eaton of the University of Texas. The latest version of GNU Octave is 3.0.0 and that of Scilab is 4.1.2. The major features of these software are:

- Scilab and Octave can be freely downloaded from the home pages *www.scilab.org* and *www.octave.org* respectively.
- They can be used in all prominent operating systems.
- The user is free to modify the source code which is also available in the same link.

A comparion between MATLAB and its open source competitors would be of advantage to the reader.

- MATLAB GUI is excellent comprising the command history, workspace, current directory, highly featured menus and all the required tools.
- Scilab GUI is not very highly interactive. When loaded in UNIX, the GUI is even less interactive.
- No command history, workspace, current directory windows are available in Scilab.
- Octave has only a character user interface.
- Help files are very detailed in MATLAB whereas it is not so detailed and explanatory in Scilab and Octave.
- Octave can be considered as a better MATLAB clone than Scilab.
- Scilab has a converter which converts MATLAB .m files to Scilab .sci files.
- To maintain better MATLAB compatibility, Octave is a better option than Scilab.
- Scicos is the Scilab equivalent for SIMULINK®.
- There is no Octave equivalent for SIMULINK, since Octave has only a command line interface (CLI).
- Communication and signal processing toolboxes are available in both Scilab and Octave.

We will now explore a recent development in the annals of MATLAB computing—parallel MATLAB, which we feel would reach a wider audience compared to even the commercial equivalents of MATLAB.

2.17 Parallel MATLAB

MATLAB is one of the most widely used mathematical computing environments in technical computing. It is an interactive environment that provides high-performance computational routines and an easy-to-use, C-like scripting language. It started out as an interactive interface to EISPACK and LINPACK and has remained a serial program. Yet, it has grown to be a feature-rich product utilising modern numerical libraries such as ATLAS and FFTW and with toolboxes in a number of application areas, for example, financial mathematics, neural networks, and control theory. It has a built-in interpreted language that is similar to Fortran 90, and the flexible matrix indexing makes it very suitable for programming matrix problems. Also, it provides hooks to Java classes and dynamically linked libraries, making integration with compiled code easy.

In 1995, Cleve B. Moler of MathWorks argued that there was no market at the time for a parallel MATLAB. His arguments could be summarised as follows.

- *Memory model* Distributed memory was the dominant model for parallel computers. But for linear algebra applications, scatter/gather of the matrix took too long to make parallel computation worthwhile.
- *Granularity* During regular use, MATLAB spends most of its time in the parser, interpreter and graphics routines where any parallelism is difficult to find. Also, to handle embarrassingly parallel applications, which only requires a collection of results at the end, MATLAB would require fundamental changes in its architecture.
- *Business situation* There were not enough customers with parallel computers to support the development.

It has been twelve years since the article was written, and we have seen tremendous changes in the computing world. These changes have invalidated the arguments that a parallel MATLAB is not necessary. We are seeing increasing interest in developing a parallel MATLAB, from both academic and commercial sectors. In a recent survey, 27 parallel MATLAB projects have been identified. The arguments justifying the development of a parallel MATLAB are:

- *Memory model* As modern scientific and engineering problems grow in complexity, the computation time and memory requirements are bound to skyrocket. The increase in processor speed and the amount of memory that can fit in a single machine can not catch up with the pace of computation requirements.
- *Granularity* Over the past twelve years, simple parallel MATLAB projects, some consisting of only 2 M-files, have shown that multiple MATLAB instances running on a parallel computer could be used to solve embarrassingly parallel problems, without any change to MATLAB itself. Also, increase in problem sizes and processor speed have reduced the portion of time spent in non-computation related routines.
- *Business situation* The past few years have seen the proliferation of Beowulf clusters. Beowulf clusters are parallel computers made from commodity off-the-shelf (COTS) hardware. They often consist of workstations connected together with Ethernet or other common, non-proprietary interconnect devices. Researchers prefer Beowulf clusters over traditional supercomputers because Beowulfs are quite easy to set up and maintain, and are inexpensive so that a researcher can get his or her "personal supercomputer."

There are several approaches in parallelising MATLAB. We explore a few of them.

2.17.1 Embarrassingly Parallel System

This approach makes use of multiple MATLAB processes running on different machines or a single machine with multiple processors. However no coordination between the MATLAB processes is provided. Instead, a parent process passes off data to the child processes. Then all processes work on its local data and return the result to the parent process. Examples for these types of software are: PLab, MultiMATLAB, Paralize, and Parmatlab.

2.17.2 Message Passing System

This approach provides message passing routines between MATLAB processes. It enables users to write their own parallel programs in MATLAB in a fashion similar to writing parallel programs with a compiled language using message passing interface (MPI). This approach is a super-set of the embarrassingly parallel approach. Software that makes use of this approach are: MultiMATLAB, CMTM, DPToolbox, MPITB/PVMTB, PMI, PTToolbox, MatlabMPI, pMATLAB, and MATLAB Parallelization Toolkit.

2.17.3 Back-End Support System

This approach uses MATLAB as a front end for a parallel computation engine. Computation is done on the engine, usually making use of high-performance numerical computation libraries like ScaLAPACK. Software that makes use of this approach are NetSolve, DLab, Matpar, PLAPACK, PARAMAT, and MATLAB $*$ P.

2.17.4 MATLAB Compilers

Software that makes use of this approach are: Otter, RT-Express, ParAL, FALCON, CONLAB, MATCH, and Menhir. These projects compile MATLAB scripts into an executable, sometimes translating the scripts into a compiled language as an intermediate step. This approach has the advantage that the compiled code runs without the overhead incurred by MATLAB. Also, an executable is usually easier to manage if it is to be run non-interactively regularly. In this approach, MATLAB is used as a development platform instead of a computing environment. This allows the produced parallel program to run on platforms which does not support MATLAB.

2.17.5 Shared Memory System

A software that make use of this approach is MATmarks. MATmarks, the only project in this category, allows multiple running instances of MATLAB to share the value of variables. It is based on Treadmarks, a distributed shared memory system developed at Rice University.

2.18 Conclusion

In the 1960s and 1970s before the appearance of personal computers, complex and large-scale calculations were done on large mainframes using code primarily developed with FORTRAN. As a number of related large sub-routines were developed for specific computational purposes, they were organised into public domain packages and distributed for free. MATLAB was originally created as a front end for one of these, the LINPACK package—a group of routines for working with matrices and linear algebra. The primary developer, Professor Cleve Moler at the University of New Mexico, eventually founded MathWorks, Inc., to further develop and market the product in a commercial setting. From the original MATLAB, a high powered suite of applications has evolved. The current generation release, the MATLAB R2010a suite, features the newest kernel, MATLAB 7.10.

In this introductory chapter on MATLAB programming, we have discussed in depth the salient features of the MATLAB programming philosophy, the major library functions available in various toolboxes of MATLAB, and the more recent developments in the evolution history of this high level language.

Today, the use of MATLAB and Simulink in the engineering curriculum is widespread. Many engineering textbooks offer MATLAB and Simulink exercises. The MathWorks' web site (www.mathworks.com) lists hundreds of engineering texts that feature MATLAB or Simulink examples and exercises. There is also extensive literature on the use of these tools to augment engineering courses. These references provide a representative sampling of the various approaches to exploit these tools in the curriculum. Two main approaches to the use of MATLAB and Simulink are evident in literature. The first approach is to use MATLAB and Simulink to develop custom software to allow students to experiment with important concepts. A second, more advanced approach to engineering course enhancement is to make the students do the programming themselves. This book is based on this approach. Simulink will be introduced in the next chapter. MATLAB has grown into a comprehensive programming environment suitable for a wide range of engineering problems. The language is rich with additional data constructs including a variety of data types (fixed point, single precision, etc) and constructs (cell arrays, multi-dimensional arrays).

MATLAB and Simulink provide a rich set of capabilities for producing graphical animations. Among these are primitive graphics using the MATLAB plotting commands, the Animation Toolbox (available through free download from the MathWorks' website), Virtual Reality Toolbox, and Dials and Gauges Toolbox.

Further Reading

1. *Getting Started with Communications Blockset*. The MathWorks. 2009.

2. *Getting Started with MATLAB 7*. The MathWorks. 2009.
3. *Getting Started with Signal Processing Toolbox*. The MathWorks. 2009.
4. *User's Guide, Communications Toolbox*. The MathWorks. 2009.
5. *User's Guide, Simulink*. The MathWorks. 2009.
6. *User's Guide, Statistics Toolbox*. The MathWorks. 2009.

Problems

1. For a given n, create a vector X with the elements, $X_i = (-1)^{i+1}/(2i-1)$, $i = 1, 2, \ldots, n$. What is the sum of the elements of the version of this vector that has 100 elements?
2. Write a MATLAB program to check whether a given string is a *palindrome*.
3. Find the sum of the first 10 terms in the series $5k^3$, $k = 1, 2, 3, \ldots, 10$.
4. Use MATLAB to find the product: $(10x^3 + 8x^2 - 12x + 4)(6x^3 - 4x^2 + 12x + 8)$.
5. Use MATLAB to obtain the quotient and remainder of $\dfrac{16x^3 - 9x^2 + 12}{5x^2 + 7x - 4}$.
6. Find the roots of $13x^3 + 182x^2 - 184x + 2503 = 0$, and use the `poly` function to verify the answer.
7. Create the matrix $M = \begin{bmatrix} 3 & 4 & 4 \\ 4 & 3 & 4 \\ 4 & 4 & 3 \end{bmatrix}$ without entering the elements one-by-one. [Hint: Use `ones(.)` and `diag(.)` functions.]
8. Write a function, `spread`, which will take a vector and spread it either across or down to produce a two-dimensional array, i.e., (1 3 2) becomes (1 3 2; 1 3 2; 1 3 2). [Hint: use a vector outer product.]
9. Write an M-file and a function file to solve the following system of ODEs.

$$\begin{aligned} \frac{dx}{dt} &= ax - bxy - cx^2 \\ \frac{dy}{dt} &= dxy - ey \end{aligned}$$

   where $a = 0.05$, $b = 0.0002$; $c = 0.00001$; $d = 0.0003$; $e = 0.06$. Solve for t between 0 and 300, with initial values of either $\begin{matrix} (1) & x = 300, & y = 100 \\ (2) & x = 0, & y = 100 \end{matrix}$. Create plots to show the behaviour of x and y with time. x and y may be interpreted as prey and predator populations, respectively.
10. Solve the equation for y given x over the range of 1 to 100:

$$1000 = y * (3 + x) * (1 + y)^4$$

   Plot the solution curve.

11. Use MATLAB to solve the following set of equations.

$$\begin{aligned} 7x + 14y - 6z &= 96 \\ 12x - 5y + 9z &= -50 \\ -5x + 7y + 15z &= 145 \end{aligned}$$

12. Use MATLAB to solve the following equations for x, y, and z as functions of the parameter c:

$$\begin{aligned} x - 5y - 2z &= 11c \\ 6x + 3y + z &= 13c \\ 7x + 3y - 5z &= 10c \end{aligned}$$

Plot the solutions for x, y, and z versus c on the same plot for $-10 \leq c \leq 10$.

13. Use MATLAB to solve the following problem:

$$\begin{aligned} x - 3y &= 2 \\ x + 5y &= 18 \\ 4x - 6y &= 20 \end{aligned}$$

14. If we set $p = poly(A)$, then the command $roots(p)$ calculates the roots of the characteristic polynomial of the matrix A. Use this sequence of commands to find the eigenvalues of the matrix $A = \begin{bmatrix} 1 & 2 & -2 \\ -2 & 5 & -2 \\ -6 & 6 & -3 \end{bmatrix}$.

15. Obtain the product of the *eigen values* of the matrix: $A = \begin{bmatrix} 1 & 0 & 0 \\ 0 & 3 & -1 \\ 0 & -1 & 3 \end{bmatrix}$

16. Show that the matrix A is diagonalisable. $A = \begin{bmatrix} 3 & 1 & -1 \\ -2 & 1 & 2 \\ 0 & 1 & 2 \end{bmatrix}$. Hence, obtain the matrix P such that $P^{-1}AP$ is a diagonal matrix.

17. For any given matrix A, use MATLAB to find the eigenvalues and corresponding eigenvectors of A, A^T, and A^{-1}. What is the observation?

18. For a symmetric matrix A, the MATLAB command $[P, D] = eig(A)$ will produce a diagonal matrix D containing the eigenvalues of A, and an orthogonal matrix P containing the corresponding eigenvectors. Use this procedure to orthogonally diagonalise the following symmetric matrix, $D = \begin{bmatrix} 2 & 3 \\ 3 & 4 \end{bmatrix}$.

19. Use MATLAB to find the coefficients of the quadratic polynomial $y = ax^2 + bx + c$ that passes through the three points: $(x, y) = (1, 4), (4, 73), (5, 120)$.

20. For several values of x in the range $0 \leq x \leq 2\pi$, verify that $\sin^{-1} x + \cos^{-1} x = \pi/2$.

21. Using MATLAB, plot various deterministic analog signals like sines and cosines. Change their amplitude and frequency and repeat the exercise.
22. Write a function $chon(x, y, z, w)$ for calculating the molecular weight of the fictitious compound $C_x\ H_y\ O_z\ N_w$.
23. Write a MATLAB program to generate an exponential waveform for $0 \leq t \leq 2$. Now modify the code so that N cycles of the waveform is generated and plotted.
24. Write a MATLAB program to plot a circle in two different ways. [Hint: (1) Use the $\text{plot}(\cos(x), \sin(x))$ command. (2) Use the $\text{plot}((i * x))$ command, where $x = [0 : \pi/100 : 2 * \pi]$].
25. Write a MATLAB program to generate the "Lissajous figures". Vary the vertical and horizontal signal frequencies and observe the variation in shape.
26. In Fraunhofer diffraction, the intensity of light is given by

$$I(x) = \left[\frac{\sin\ x}{x}\right]^2$$

where x depends on the viewing angle, the wave number of the light, and the width of the slit. The positions of minimum intensity are $x = n\pi,\ \ n = \pm1, \pm2, \pm3, \ldots$. The positions of maximum intensity are solutions of the following equation:

$$x \cos\ x - \sin\ x = 0$$

which can be derived by differentiating $I(x)$. Write a MATLAB program to find the locations and values of the first several peaks in the spectrum.
27. Write the MATLAB code to generate Figure 2.18.

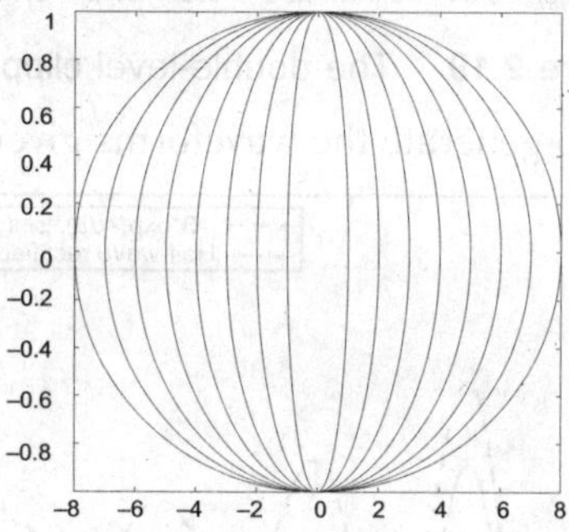

Figure 2.18 The longitudes

28. Plot a 1000 Hz sine wave and also plot its delayed version where the delay is $\pm\pi$. Now sum the two and plot. What do you observe?
29. Generate and plot a random signal using MATLAB. [Hint: Use `rand()` and `randn()` functions.]
30. Generate and plot a *Gaussian* distributed random signal vector with mean π and variance π^2.

31. Generate and plot a *uniform* distributed random signal vector with mean 0 and variance π^2.
32. Write a *script M-file* to plot 10 replicas of a random waveform. Use the `column (:)` operator.
33. Simulate the rolling of a *fair dice*. Show that for a large number of trials, the probability of getting the number 6 is $\frac{1}{6}$.
34. Simulate the tossing of a *fair coin* and show that for a large number of trials, the probability of getting a head is $\frac{1}{2}$.
35. Simulate ECG signals using MATLAB.
36. Simulate the operation of a clamping circuit.
37. Simulate the functioning of an asymmetrical double-level clipper circuit.
38. Write the MATLAB code to generate the waveform given in Figure 2.19 from a 50 Hz sine wave.

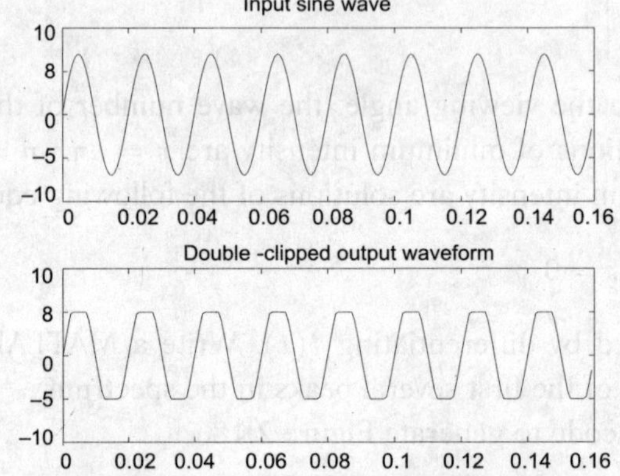

Figure 2.19 The double-level clipper

39. Write the MATLAB code to generate the waveforms given in Figure 2.20.

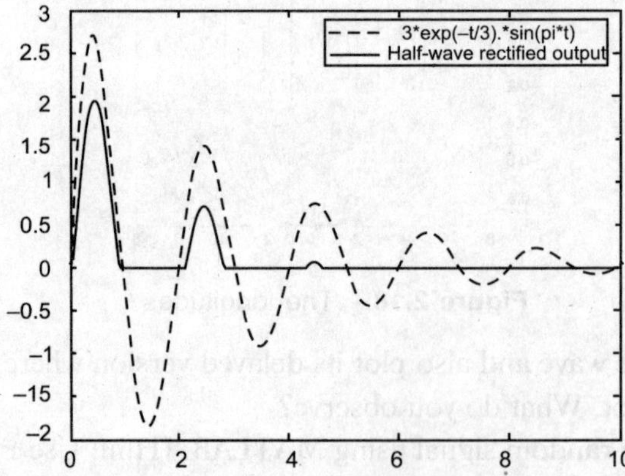

Figure 2.20 The signal clipper

40. Write the MATLAB code to generate the waveform given in Figure 2.21.

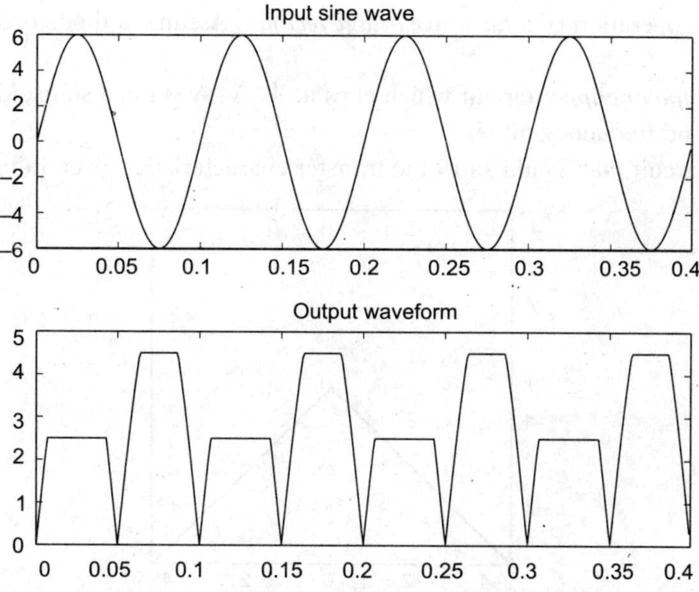

Figure 2.21 The asymmetrical double-level clipper

41. Simulate a circuit that would show the transfer characteristics shown in Figure 2.22.

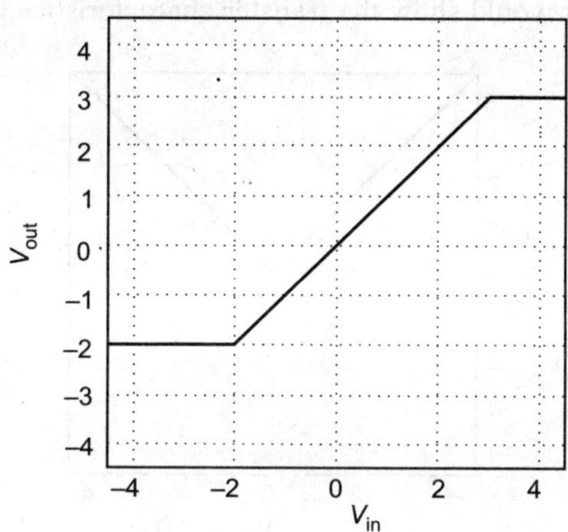

Figure 2.22 Transfer characteristics of a typical circuit

42. Plot the sampling function $Sa(t) = \frac{\sin\,t}{t}$ using MATLAB. Also plot $\left[\frac{\sin\,t}{t}\right]^2$ and $\frac{\sin\,t^2}{t^2}$.
43. If we add enough *sine* functions, together with appropriate phase, we can make a square wave. The formula is $Sq(x) = \sum\limits_{n=0}^{\infty} \frac{\sin\,(2n+1)x}{2n+1}$. We will need a *for* loop to calculate the sum. How many terms do we need to get a reasonable approximation?

44. Simulate the operation of a *full-wave bridge rectifier*. Assume a diode drop of 0.6 V per diode.
45. Simulate a *bipolar clipper* circuit which clips at ±5 V. Assume a sinusoidal input signal of $\pm 10V_{pp}$ and frequency 50 Hz.
46. Simulate a circuit that would show the transfer characteristics given in Figure 2.23.

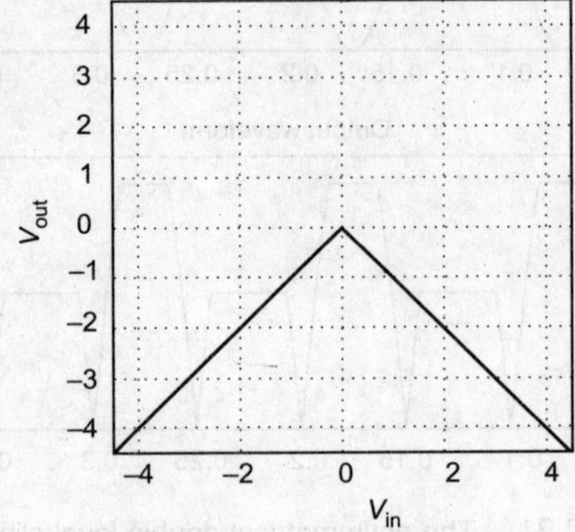

Figure 2.23 Transfer characteristics of a diode (negative) full-wave rectifier

47. Simulate a circuit that would show the transfer characteristics given in Figure 2.24.

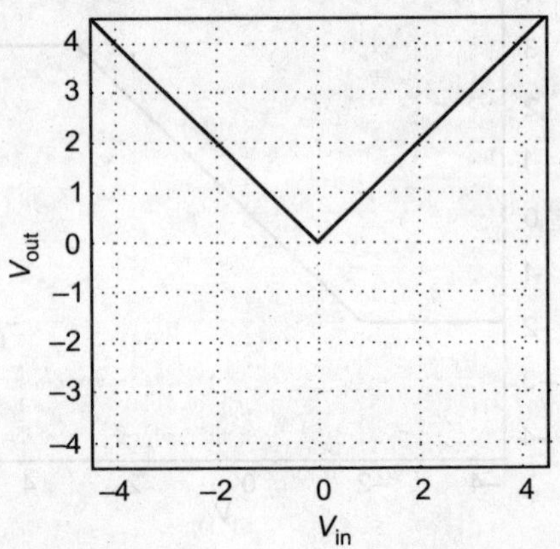

Figure 2.24 Transfer characteristics of a diode (positive) full-wave rectifier

48. Plot the $\sin c\, x = \frac{\sin \pi x}{\pi x}$ function for x in steps of 0.1 over the range $-2.2 \leq x \leq 2.2$.
49. One cycle of a periodic waveform is given by: $f(x) = \cos\, x$, for $0 < x < \pi$, and $-\cos\, x$, for $-\pi < x < 0$. Obtain the average value (DC) of the signal. [Hint: Use the *mean(.)* function in MATLAB.]

50. Simulate amplitude shift keying: when the data bit is "1", send $A_1 = 5\sin\,\omega_a\,t$ and when it is "0", send $A_0 = 2\sin\,\omega_a\,t$.Take $f_a = 1$ kHz.
51. Obtain the filtered output of a filter whose impulse response is $\{0, 0, \underset{\uparrow}{1}, 0, 0\}$ and the input sequence is $\{1, 2, \underset{\uparrow}{3}, 2, 1\}$. The correct time indices of output must also be obtained.
52. Compute the value of π using the following series

$$\frac{\pi^2 - 8}{16} = \sum_{n=0}^{\infty} \frac{1}{(2n-1)^2(2n+1)^2}$$

How many terms are needed to obtain an accuracy of $1e^{-12}$? How accurate is the sum of 100 terms of this series?
53. The Fibonacci numbers are computed according to the following relation:

$$F_n = F_{n-1} + F_{n-2}$$

with $F_0 = F_1 = 1$.
(a) Compute the first 10 Fibonacci numbers.
(b) For the first 50 Fibonacci numbers, compute the ratio F_n/F_{n-1}. It is claimed that this ratio approaches the value of the golden mean $\frac{1+\sqrt{5}}{2}$. What do the results show?
54. The Legendre polynomials $(P_n(x))$ are defined by the following recurrence relation:

$$(n+1)P_{n+1}(x) - (2n+1)P_n(x) + nP_{n-1}(x) = 0$$

with $P_0(x) = 1$, $P_1(x) = x$ and $P_2(x) = (3x^2 - 1)/2$. Compute the next three Legendre polynomials and plot all 6 over the interval [−1,1].
55. Write a function which computes the cumulative product of the elements in a vector. The cumulative product of the jth element of the vector x, x_j, is defined by

$$p_j = (x_1)(x_2)\ldots(x_j)$$

for j = 1: length of the vector x. Create two different versions of this function.
56. Write a script that asks for an integer (n) and then computes the following based on the value of the integer: *While the value of n is greater than 1, replace the integer with half of its value* $(n/2)$, *if the integer is even. Otherwise, replace the integer with three times its value, plus 1, that is* $(3*n+1)$. Make provision to count the number of values in (or the length of) the sequence that results. Make a plot of the length of the sequence that occurs as a function of the integers from 2 to 30. For example, when $n = 10$, the length is 6 while for $n = 15$, the length is 17. Is there any pattern? Try larger numbers to see if any pattern occurs. Is there any integer for which the sequence does not terminate?
57. Compute and plot the 100 roots (zeros!) of the of the numerator polynomial of the transfer function $H(s) = \frac{s^{100}+1}{X(s)}$ using MATLAB. The plot should have a "o" placed on the location where a zero is present. [Hint: w = [1, zeros(1,99), 1]; z = roots(w); plot(z, "o");)

58. Obtain the output of a filter whose impulse response is $h(n) = \{-2, 2, \underset{\uparrow}{1}, 1, 2, 2, 0\}$ to the input sequence $x(n) = \{0, 1, 1, 1, \underset{\uparrow}{1}, 0, 1, 0, 0\}$.
59. Find the impulse response and step response of a discrete time LTI system with transfer function $H(z) = \frac{2z^{-1}}{1+2z^{-1}+3z^{-2}}$.
60. Use the MATLAB function "modulate()" to generate and plot AMDSB-TC (A3E), frequency modulation (FM), phase modulation (PM), pulse width modulation (PWM), and pulse position modulation (PPM) waveforms.
61. Use MATLAB Symbolic Math Toolbox to simplify the following expression: $\sum_{k=1}^{10} 5x^3$.
62. Obtain the value of the triple integral $\int_0^2 \int_1^3 \int_1^2 xy^2 z\, dx\, dy\, dz$ using MATLAB Symbolic Math Toolbox.
63. Solve the equation $\cos\ 2x + \sin\ x - 1 = 0$ symbolically. Next, use *ezplot* to verify the result.
64. Solve the equation $\tan\ x + \sin\ x - 2 = 0$ symbolically. Next, determine the numerical values of the roots.
65. Design and simulate an RC bandpass filter with 1 kHz to 10 kHz passband and measure the midband gain and the roll-off in both the stopbands.
66. Design and simulate an RC highpass filter with half-power frequency of 5 kHz and a passband gain of 20 dB.
67. Given a random variable X and a random variable $Y = aX + b$, find μ_Y in terms of μ_X and $Var[Y]$ in terms of $Var[X]$.

3

Simulink

In this chapter we will introduce Simulink®. Simulink (simulation and link) is an extension of MATLAB® by The MathWorks™ Inc. It is a versatile software GUI tool that can be used for modelling, simulating, and analysing dynamic systems—systems that tend to vary their status from time to time. It can support both linear and nonlinear systems, modelled and simulated in continuous time, discrete time, as well as a mixture of the two. Simulink can also be used to model *multirate systems.*[1]

Simulink encourages one to try things out. One can easily build models from scratch, or take an existing model and add to it. It gives us instant access to all the analysis tools in MATLAB, so that we can analyse and visualise the results. Simulink was intended to give the user a sense of the fun of modelling and simulation, through an environment that encourages him/her to pose a question, model it, and see what happens. It is also very practical. With thousands of engineers around the world using it to model and solve real problems, knowledge of this tool will serve the model developer well throughout her/his professional career. Simulink interfaces well with MATLAB, allowing the user to define blocks with MATLAB functions and plot output using MATLAB tools. To summarise, the key features of Simulink are that:

- It is a graphical, interactive software tool for modelling, simulating, and analysing dynamic systems.
- It enables rapid construction of *virtual prototypes* to explore design concepts at any level of detail with minimal effort.
- It is ideally suited for linear, nonlinear, continuous time and discrete time systems.
- It is commonly used in control system design, DSP design, communication system design, and other simulation applications.
- It is a graphical plug-in for MATLAB, offering additional access to a range of non-graphical analysis and design tools.

[1] Multirate signals have different parts that are sampled or updated at different rates, in contrast to uniform sampling.

Traditional approaches to system design typically include building a prototype followed by extensive testing and revision. This method can be both time-consuming and expensive. As an effective and widely accepted alternative, simulation is now the preferred approach to engineering design. Simulink is a powerful simulation software tool that enables the user to build and test virtual prototypes fast, so that he/she can explore design concepts at any level of detail with minimal effort. By using Simulink to iterate and refine designs before building the first prototype, engineers can benefit from a faster, more efficient design process.

3.1 Simulink as a Tool for Model-Based Design

Simulink permits the systems designer to go beyond the idealised linear system models. The versatile modelling and simulation tool permits the system design engineer to explore more realistic nonlinear models such as frictional forces, air drag, gear slippage (gear backlash), hard stops and many other real world phenomena. Simulink turn the digital computer into a virtual laboratory, wherein one can model and analyse systems that would not have been possible by other means. Thus with Simulink, one can model a host of nonlinear systems such as the automotive clutch system, the flutter of an aircraft wing, the dynamics of a prey–predator model, or the impact of the monetary supply on the global economy.

Simulink provides a graphical user interface (GUI) for building models as block diagrams, using click-and-drag mouse operations. With this interface, we can draw models just as we would with pencil and paper (or as most textbooks depict them). Simulink is operationally far better than previous simulation packages that necessitates the user to develop a mathematical model and then write and solve lengthy differential equations for solving system dynamics. Simulink includes a comprehensive block library of sinks, sources, linear and nonlinear components, and connectors. Users can also customise and create their own blocks.

Models in Simulink are hierarchical, so we can build models using both top-down and bottom-up approaches. We can view the system at a high level, then double-click blocks to go down through the levels to see increasing levels of model detail. This approach provides insight into how a model is organised and how its parts interact with each other. After we define a model, we can simulate it, using a choice of integration methods, either from the Simulink menus or by entering commands in the MATLAB Command Window. The menus are particularly convenient for interactive work, while the command-line approach is very useful for running a batch of simulations (for example, if we are doing Monte Carlo simulations or want to sweep a parameter across a range of values). Using scopes and other display blocks, we can see the simulation results while the simulation is running. In addition, we can change many parameters and see what happens for "what if" explorations. The simulation results can be put in the MATLAB workspace for post-processing and visualisation.

Model analysis tools include linearisation and trimming tools, which can be accessed from the MATLAB command line, plus the many tools in MATLAB and its application toolboxes. Because MATLAB and Simulink are integrated, we can simulate, analyse, and revise our models in either environment at any point. As Simulink is an integral part of MATLAB, it is easy to switch back and forth during the analysis process and thus, the user can take full advantage of features offered in both environments. We can choose the simulation inputs ("simin") from and re-direct the simulation outputs ("simout") to MATLAB workspace. Apart from the available library of sources, system blocks and sinks, we can also build our own customised system building blocks by writing *S-functions*.

3.2 Invoking Simulink

Simulink is a program for simulating dynamic systems. It has two phases of use: model definition and model analysis. Model definition uses the metaphor of a block diagram—much like drawing a block diagram but instead of drawing the individual blocks, they are copied from libraries of blocks. After we define a model, we can analyse it either by choosing options from the Simulink menus or by entering commands in MATLAB's command window. The progress of a simulation can be viewed while the simulation is running, and the final results can be made available in the MATLAB workspace when the simulation is complete.

One can invoke Simulink by typing `simulink` at the MATLAB command window. Another way to invoke Simulink is to left-click the **Start** icon at the bottom left corner of the MATLAB command window and choose Simulink from the popped up menu. We can then select the **Library Browser** from the pull down menu. The Simulink window will then open up. A typical screen shot, when Simulink is evoked from Microsoft Windows platforms, is illustrated in Figure 3.1. Figure 3.2 illustrates a typical library window that will open up when Simulink is evoked from Linux platforms. It displays a new window containing icons for the sub-system blocks shown in Figure 3.1. Now, we can select **New** from the **File** menu on the menu bar to open a new empty window labelled **Untitled**, which we can re-name when we save it. The new window is where we will construct our system model by dragging blocks from their original location to the new window. Note that when we drag a block to a different window we drag only a copy of the block.

There are two levels of operation for Simulink: from the menu bar or from the command line. Simulation from the menu bar is interactive, simple to use, easy to learn and provides quick results. Simulation from the command line leads into MATLAB space, and built-in graphics tools.

A typical example is the command:

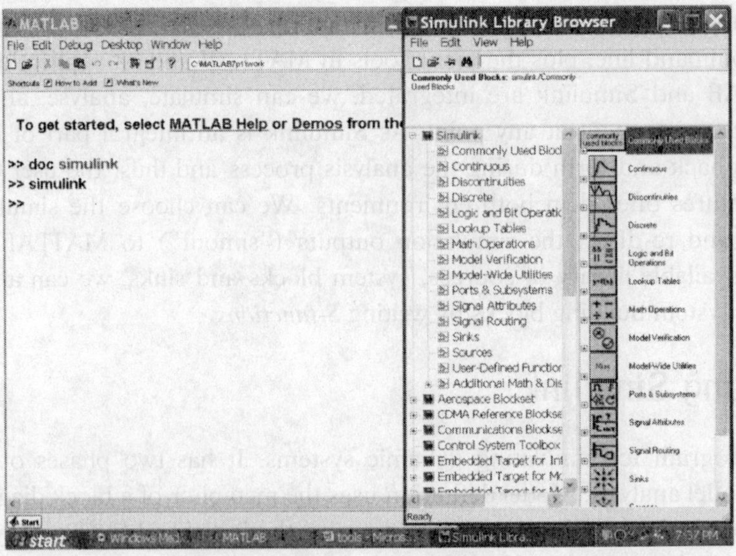

Figure 3.1 A typical screenshot of the Simulink opening window

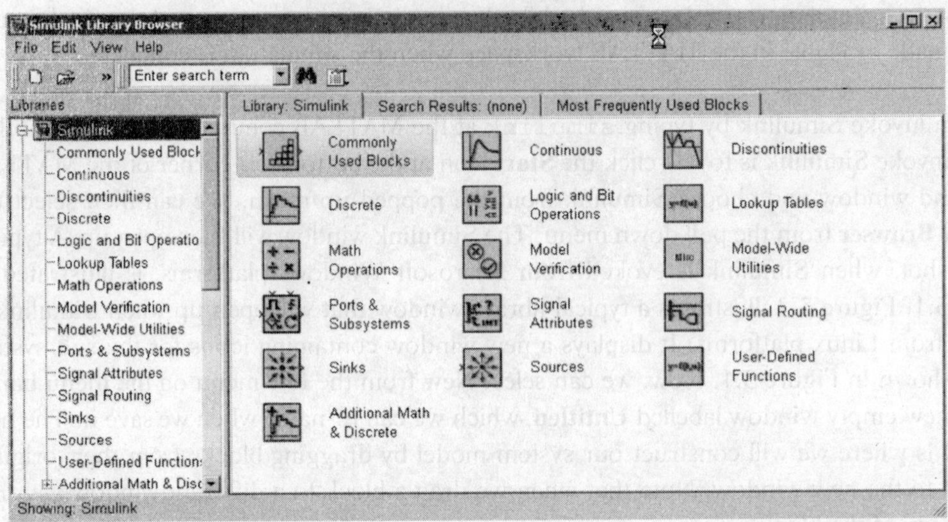

Figure 3.2 A typical Simulink library window

```
set_param('OBJ','PARAMETER1',VALUE1,'PARAMETER2',VALUE2,...).
```

In addition to the S-function, there are other ways to pass data from MATLAB to Simulink. They are

- *Initialising the variables in MATLAB* Instead of calling an M-function inside Simulink, we can type the variables at the MATLAB command line or run a program in MATLAB before running the model in Simulink. We can define any number of variables in the MATLAB workspace and just use the variable names in the Simulink model.

- *Using an M-file* We can also write a MATLAB M-file to define the variables that we want.
- *Using a sub-system and an M-file to initialise the variables* As the model increases in size and complexity, we can simplify it by grouping blocks into sub-systems.

3.3 Concept of Signal and Logic Flow

In Simulink, data or information from various blocks are sent to another block by lines connecting the relevant blocks. Signals can be *generated* and *fed* into blocks (dynamic or static). Data can be fed into functions and then dumped into *sinks,* which could be virtual oscilloscopes or displays. They could also be saved into a file. Data can be connected from one block to another, can be branched, multiplexed and so on. In simulation, data is processed and transferred only at *discrete* times, since all computers are by default discrete systems. Thus a *simulation* time step (otherwise called an *integration* time step) is essential, and the selection of that step is determined by the fastest dynamics in the simulated system.

3.3.1 Connecting Blocks

To connect blocks, *left-click* and drag the mouse from the output of one block to the input of another block.

3.3.2 Sources and Sinks

The *sources* library contains the sources of data or signals that one would use in a dynamic system simulation. One may want to use a *constant* input, a *sinusoidal* wave, a step, a repeating sequence such as *pulse train,* a ramp and so on. One may want to have *disturbance* effects. To do so, one can use the random signal generator to simulate *noise*. The clock may be used to create a time index for plotting purposes. *Ground* could be connected to any unused port to avoid warning messages indicating unconnected ports.

Sinks are blocks where signals are terminated or ultimately used. In most cases, we would want to store the resulting data in a file, or a matrix of variables. The data could be displayed or even stored in a file. The STOP block could be used to stop the simulation if the input to that block (the signal being sunk) is non-zero. Figure 3.3 show the available blocks in the sources and sinks libraries. Unused signals must be terminated to prevent warnings about unconnected signals.

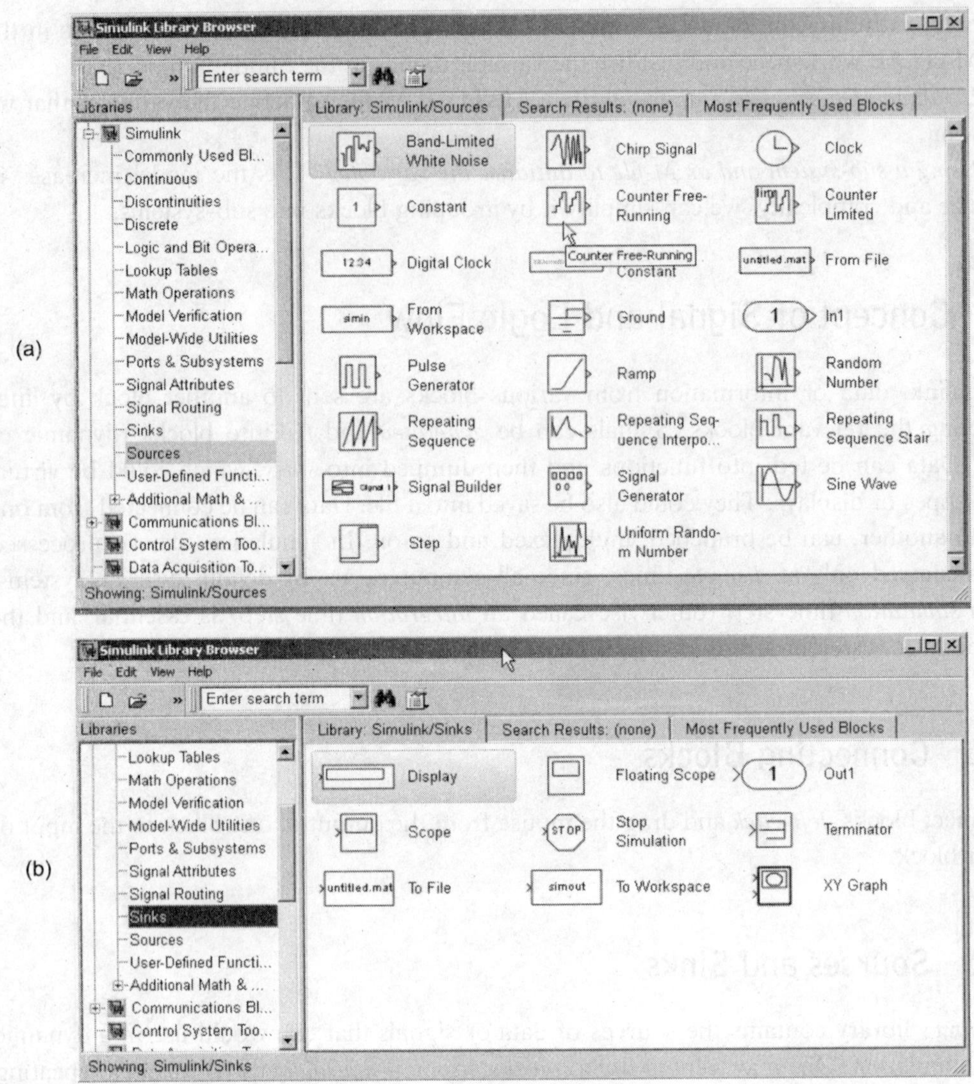

Figure 3.3 The sources and sinks in Simulink

3.3.3 Continuous and Discrete Systems

All dynamic systems can be analysed as continuous or discrete time systems. Simulink allows us to represent these systems using transfer functions, integration blocks, delay blocks and so on. Figure 3.4 shows the available dynamic systems blocks. Discrete systems can be designed in the z-plane to represent difference equations. Systems can be represented in state space forms which are useful in modern control system design.

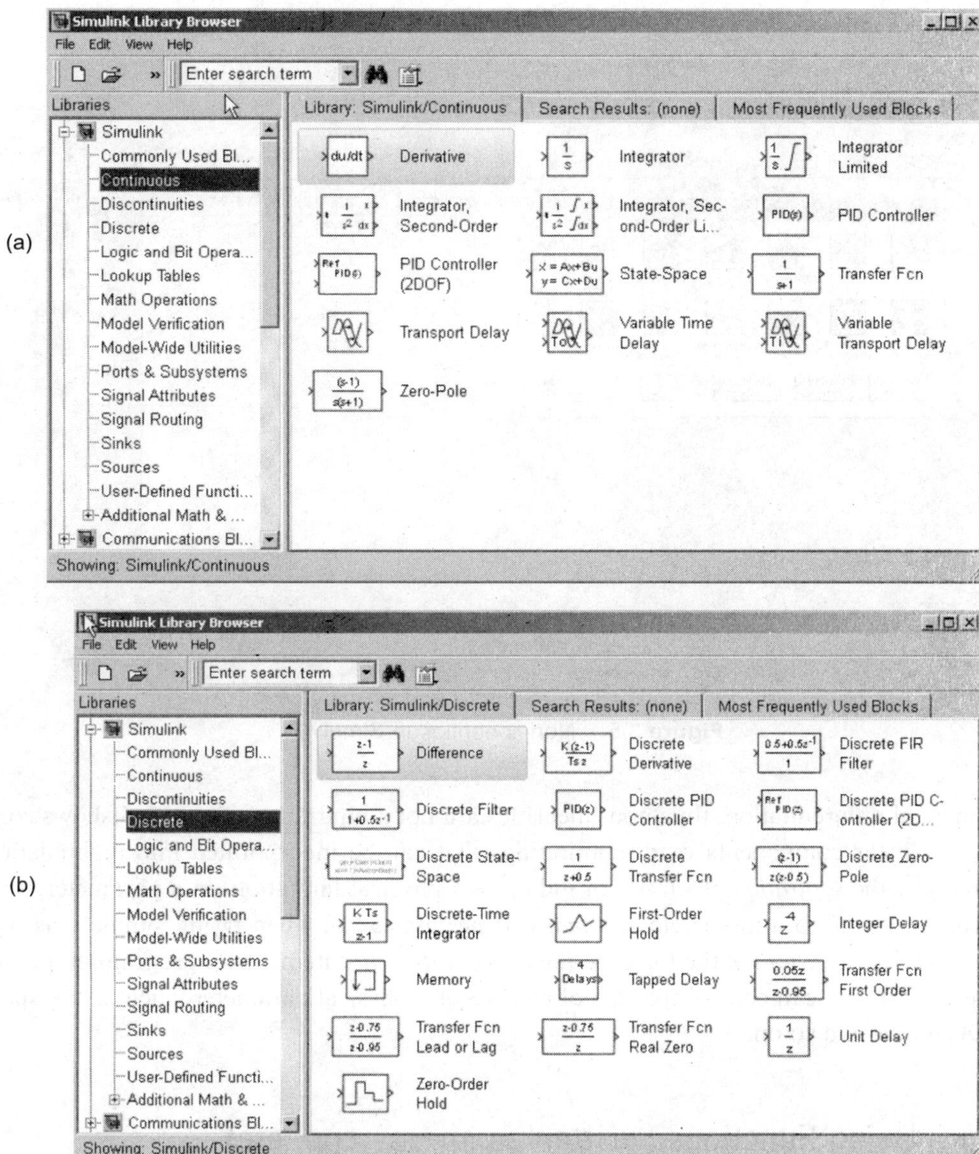

Figure 3.4 The continuous and discrete blocks in Simulink

3.3.4 Discontinuities in Simulink

One of the major advantages of using tools such as Simulink is the ability to simulate nonlinear systems and arrive at results without having to solve them analytically. It is virtually impossible to arrive at an analytical solution for a system having non-linearities such as saturation, signum function, limited slew rates and so on. In simulation, systems are analysed

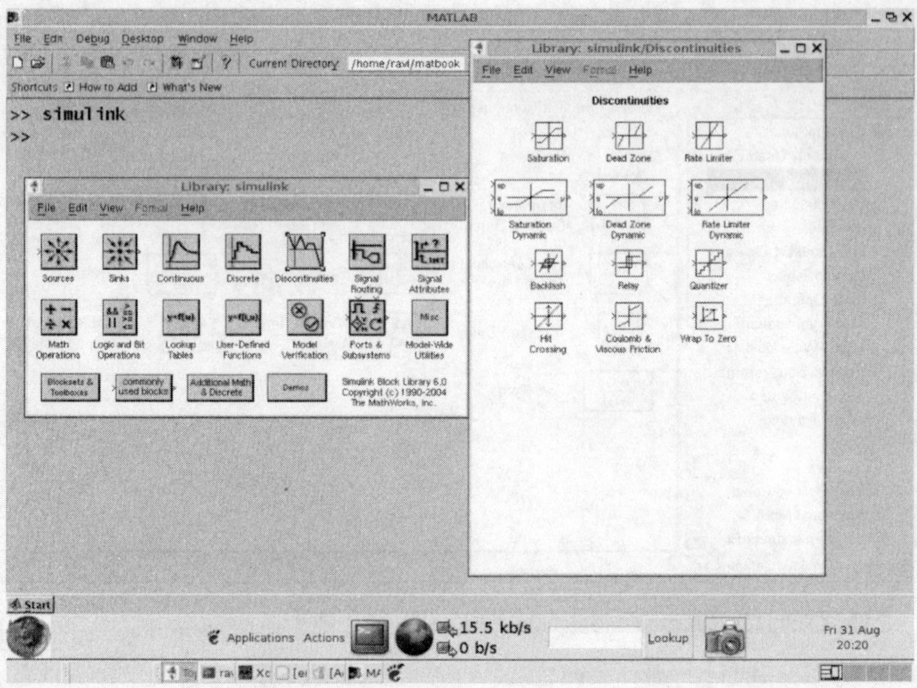

Figure 3.5 Non-linearities in Simulink

by numerical differentiation, thus non-linearities are not a hindrance. Figure 3.5 shows some of the nonlinear components or discontinuities that can be incorporated into a simulation, for example, the *saturation* block which indicates a physical limitation on a parameter, such as a voltage signal to a motor etc. *Manual switches* are useful when trying simulations with different cases. *Switches* are the logical equivalent of *if–then* statements in programming. *Slew rates* using limiters can control the rate of change of a physical parameter, such as the speed of a DC motor and so on.

3.3.5 Using Functions (written as .m, .c, .cpp, etc)

Functions written in MATLAB (such as an M-file) or any other language such as C or FORTRAN can be used in conjunction with Simulink to enhance the computing power of Simulink. Custom code written as M-files or C-programs, if included, are evaluated at every simulation step. S-functions are dynamic linked libraries (DLL) written in another language such as C, and then compiled using the MATLAB compiler "MEX". These functions are useful in large simulations, since a function written in C runs much faster than a comparably programmed M-file. Also for real time simulations, only S-functions can be used—the reason again being the high speed of processing.

Lookup tables are very useful in mapping different data points and functions. N-dimensional lookup tables are available in Simulink. Figure 3.6 shows various tables and functions used in Simulink. We will now see how Simulink can be used to simulate simple systems.

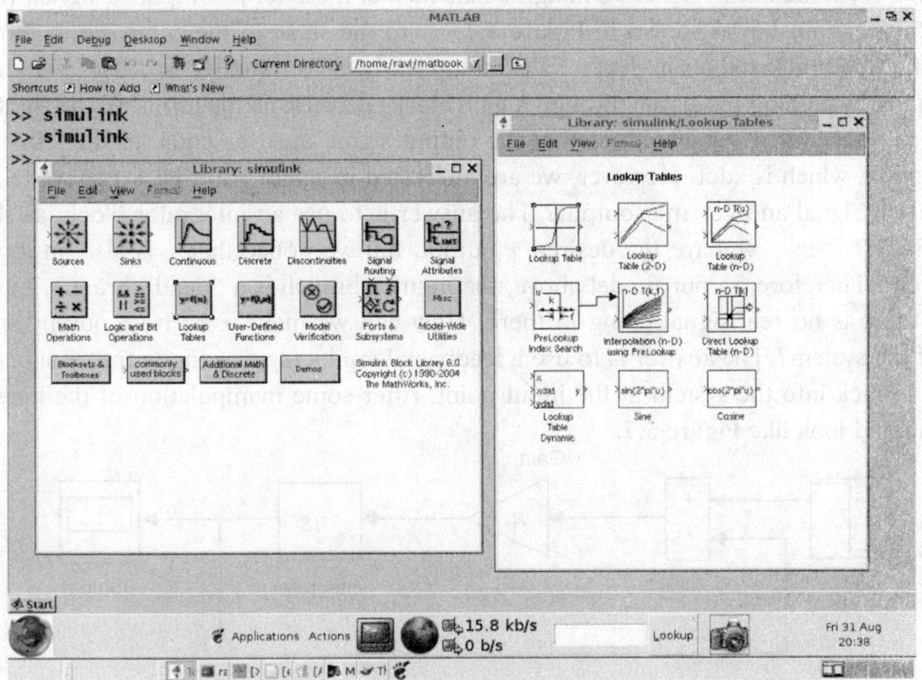

Figure 3.6 Lookup tables and functions in Simulink

3.3.6 Modelling a First Order System in Simulink

First and second order differential equations are commonly studied in dynamic systems courses, as they occur frequently in practice. Because of this, we will discuss the basics of modelling these equations in Simulink. The first example is a lowpass RC circuit that is often used as a filter. This is modelled using a first order differential equation. The second example is a mass–spring–dashpot system. This system is modelled with a second order differential equation (equation of motion). To better understand the dynamics of both these systems, we are going to build models using Simulink as discussed below. It is better to build both models first, then run them so that we can compare how each system responds to the same input. The first order RC lowpass filter is illustrated in Figure 3.7.

The differential equation for this is as shown in (3.1).

$$\dot{x} = \frac{1}{RC}\left[f(t) - x\right] \tag{3.1}$$

where $\dot{x}$ (xdot) is the time rate of change of the output voltage, R and C are constants, $f(t)$ is the forcing function (input voltage), and x is the output voltage. We are now going to analyse this circuit. First, we examine what is in the brackets and we notice that we are subtracting the term x from the term $f(t)$. If we imagine that each of these terms outputs a signal, we can model this relationship as shown in Figure 3.7, up to the stage of the comparator. Now we notice that the bracketed term $[f(t) - x]$ is multiplied by a constant, $K = 1/RC$. We do this in Simulink by passing the signal through a gain block. Because all the terms on the right-side of xdot are accounted for, we know that the output signal must be equal to the left side of the equation, which is xdot. However, we are interested in x, not xdot. How can we take the xdot output signal and get an x output? The answer is to use an integrator block, as shown in Figure 3.7. Now, we have the desired x output, but we notice that x is also an input of the system. Therefore, in our model above, the input x branch is a "dead" branch. In other words, there is no real signal going in there. How can we make x both an output and an input of the system? The answer is to use a feedback loop by tapping the output x signal and feeding it back into the system at the input point. After some manipulation of the lines, the model should look like Figure 3.7.

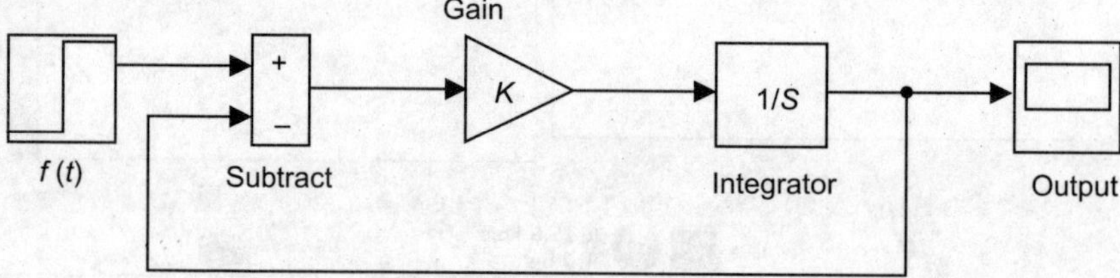

Figure 3.7 The first order RC circuit

Annotations

To add an annotation to our model, place the cursor at an unoccupied area in the model window and double-click (left button). A small rectangular area will appear with a cursor prompting for input.

To delete an annotation, hold down the SHIFT key while selecting the annotation, then press the DELETE or BACKSPACE key. We can also change the font type and colour from the FORMAT menu.

Printing a Simulink Block Diagram

One can print a block diagram by selecting Print from the File menu (on a Microsoft Windows system) or by using the print command in the MATLAB Command Window (on all platforms). The format of the Print command is:

```
>> print -ssys -device filename
```

where sys is the name of the system to be printed. The system name must be preceded by the s switch identifier and is the only required argument. sys must be open or must have been open during the current session. If the system name contains spaces or takes more than one line, one needs to specify the name as a string. device specifies a device type. filename is the Postscript file to which the output is saved. For example, to print the system named samplesys into a file sample.eps using the Encapsulated Postscript format, one can give the following command at MATLAB prompt:

```
>> print -ssamplesys -deps sample.eps
```

Running Simulation

Having completed the Simulink models for the first order system, it is now time to run a simple simulation and look at the results. Double-click on the integrator block and set the initial conditions to zero as shown in Figure 3.8. Leave the remaining fields as they are. Then, double click on the gain block and set the gain to the values shown in Figure 3.9. Now, open the step block to familiarise yourself with the parameters. Run the simulation and open the scope block. The results should be similar to what is shown in Figure 3.10. Notice how the response of the system lags the step input. This response is governed by the time constant of the system ($\tau = RC$).

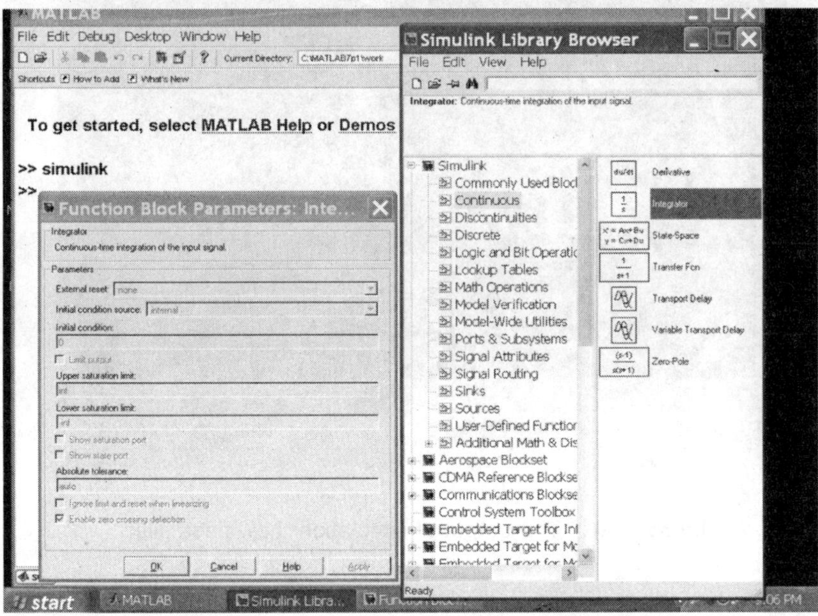

Figure 3.8 The integrator sub-system

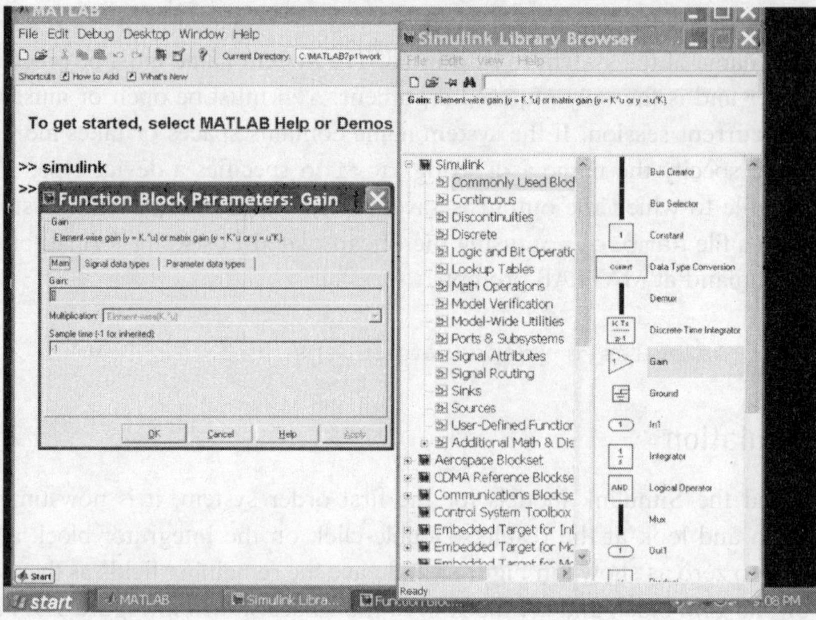

Figure 3.9 The gain sub-system

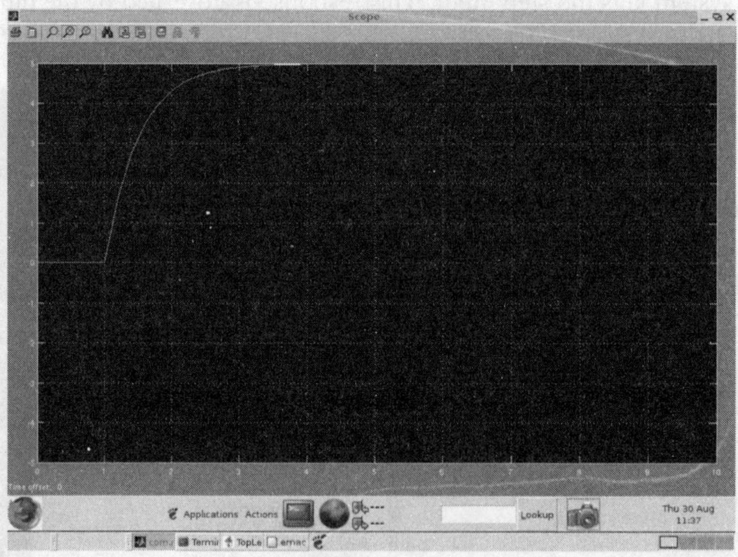

Figure 3.10 The output of simulation: Low pass filter

3.3.7 Modelling a Second Order System

The mass–spring–dashpot is a basic model used widely in mechanical engineering design to model real world mechanical systems. It is represented schematically as shown in Figure 3.11.

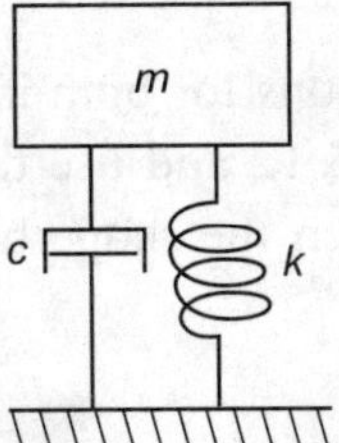

Figure 3.11 The single degree of freedom system (SDOF)

The response of this system is governed by the equation of motion which is the second order differential equation (3.2), where $\ddot{x}$ (xddot) is the acceleration of the mass m, $\dot{x}$ (xdot) is the velocity, x is the displacement, $f(t)$ is the forcing function (input force), c is the damping coefficient, and k is the spring constant.

$$\ddot{x} = \frac{1}{m}\left[f(t) - c\dot{x} - kx\right] \tag{3.2}$$

To model this system we start by looking at the terms in the bracket. There are three input signal lines: $f(t)$, xdot, and x. We also notice that both xdot and x are multiplied by constants. As in the case of the first order model, this can be done in Simulink by using a gain block. The signals are then summed together as shown in Figure 3.12. Now, we notice that the bracketed term $[f(t) - c\dot{x} - kx]$ is multiplied by the constant $1/m$. We do this by passing the signal through a gain block. Again, we are interested in the displacement x, not $\ddot{x}$. To get the x output signal, we integrate the $\ddot{x}$ output signal twice. We can see from the model that xdot and x are both outputs and inputs of the model. Therefore, we need to use a feedback loop for each of these signals as discussed in the first order model example. The resulting model should look like Figure 3.12.

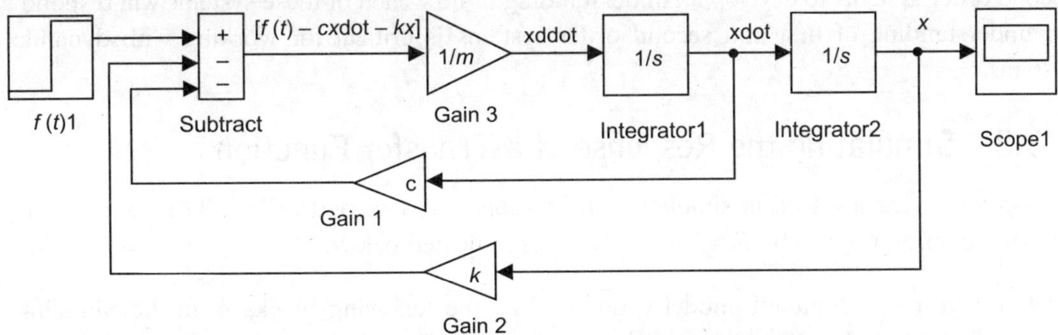

Figure 3.12 The finished Simulink model for a SDOF system

Before running the model, be sure to include a scope block for viewing the results. Now that the model is complete, we are ready to run the simulation and look at the results.

Running the Simulation

For the SDOF model, the initial conditions for both integrator blocks should be set to zero. As for the gain blocks, refer to Figure 3.12 and use the following values $m = 2, c = 2$, and $k = 4$. Now run the simulation and open the scope block. The results should be similar to what is shown in Figure 3.13.

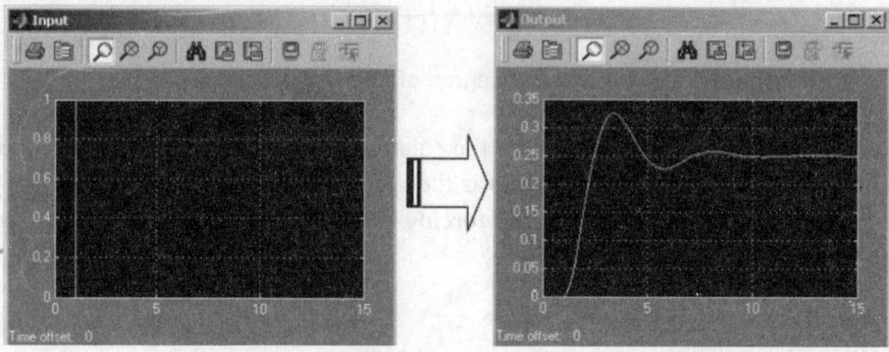

Figure 3.13 The simulated output of a SDOF system

As we can see, things get a little more interesting for this case because the system is capable of an oscillatory response. In fact, it can be seen in Figure 3.13. The system response in this case is "under-damped". It is important to note however, that with different values of m, c, and k, the response of the second order system can be made to mimic a first order response. When this is the case, the system is referred to as "critically-damped". Can the reader find out what values of m, c, and k will make this happen?

Finally, the readers are encouraged to play around with different values for both the first and second order systems to develop an understanding of how each of these systems will respond. An understanding of first and second order systems is critical for working with dynamic systems.

3.3.8 Simulating the Response of a Transfer Function

The various steps involved in simulating the response of a second order LTI system whose transfer function is given by $T(s) = \frac{1}{2s^2+0.7s+1}$ is indicated below:

STEP 1 : In a new Simulink model window, drag the following blocks from the Simulink library window: Step (from Sources), Transfer Function (from Continuous), Scope (from Sinks), and Save File to Workspace (from Sinks).

STEP 2 : Arrange the blocks as shown in Figure 3.14.[2]

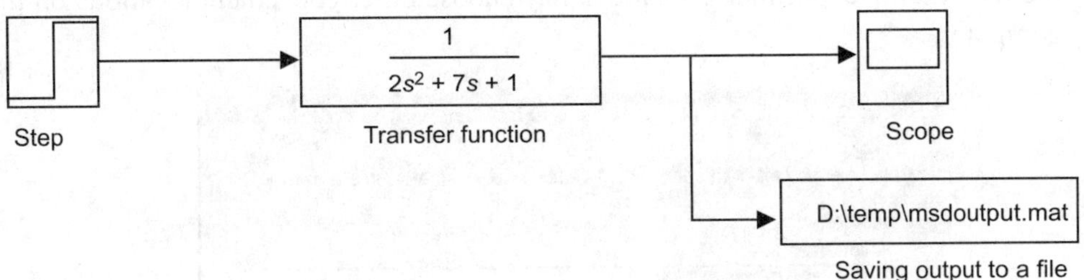

Figure 3.14 A second order LTI system

STEP 3 : Double-click on the transfer function to bring up the parameter dialog window and enter the values for the coefficients in the denominator as shown in Figure 3.15. Note that the transfer function block has a default form of first order in the denominator $(s + 1)$. We may specify a different order for the numerator and the denominator by entering the coefficients associated with the polynomials.

Block Parameters: Transfer Fcn

Transfer Fcn

Matrix expression for numerator, vector expression for denominator. Output width equals the number of rows in the numerator. Coefficients are for descending powers of s.

Parameters

Numerator:

[1]

Denominator:

[2 7 1]

OK Cancel Help Apply

Figure 3.15 The parameter setting

STEP 4 : Click OK to close the dialog. Double-click on the "Save output to a file" block to open the dialog window shown in Figure 3.16. In the Filename box specify the path and the name of the file we wish to save. The saved file will be in .mat format (yes, it is in binary format! So do not try to read it). We will be able to load this file onto a MATLAB workspace later on. Make sure to remember where we save the file to. In

[2]Block's background colour: We can change the colour of the block. Right-click on the block and select the colour from Background Colour menu.

this example, we have put the file in the D drive under "temp" directory and named the file "example3out.mat". Readers may choose other convenient locations on their computer.

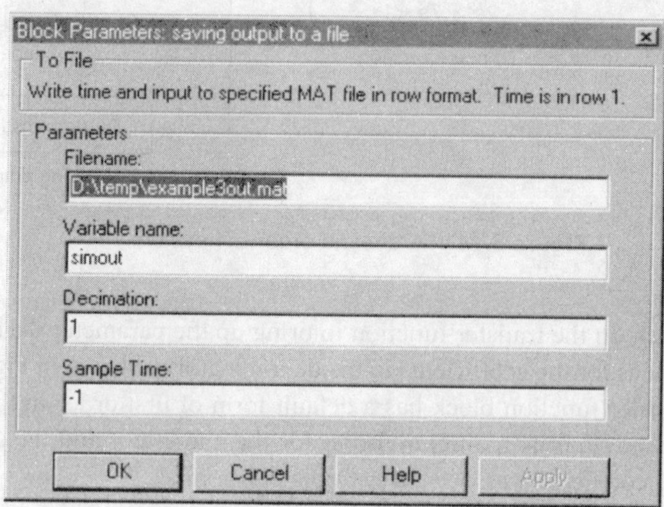

Figure 3.16 Saving the output of simulation

STEP 5 : Run the simulation by clicking on the button (alternately we may use the keyboard command CTRL+T). The screenshot of the output from the scope block is shown in Figure 3.17.

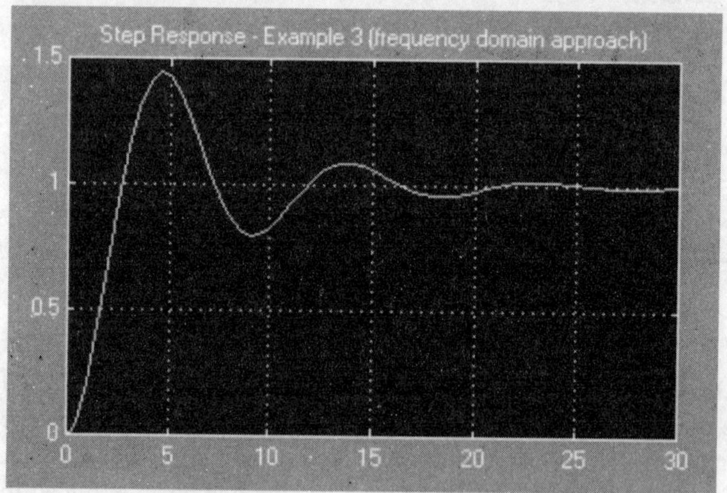

Figure 3.17 Step response of a second order system

Loading the .mat file

Use the load command to "import" the saved *.mat file generated from the simulation. In this example, we have set the path to the directory where the file "example3out.mat" is saved. If we do not set the path in MATLAB, we have to specify the full path in the load command, e.g., `>>load D:/temp/example3out.mat`. In the MATLAB command window, enter the following:

```
>> load example3out
```

If we want to verify the loading by asking MATLAB to list all the variables in the current workspace, we enter:

```
>> who
```

If the loading is successful, we should see the variable we specified earlier listed in the current workspace. "simout" is a $2 \times m$ matrix, where m is the number of columns reflecting the number of data points generated from the simulation. The first row contains the time array.

To generate a plot of the step input response from the simulation, simply use the plot command on the "simout" matrix. For this example, the following command produces the plot shown in Figure 3.18.

```
>> plot(simout(1,:),simout(2,:));grid
```

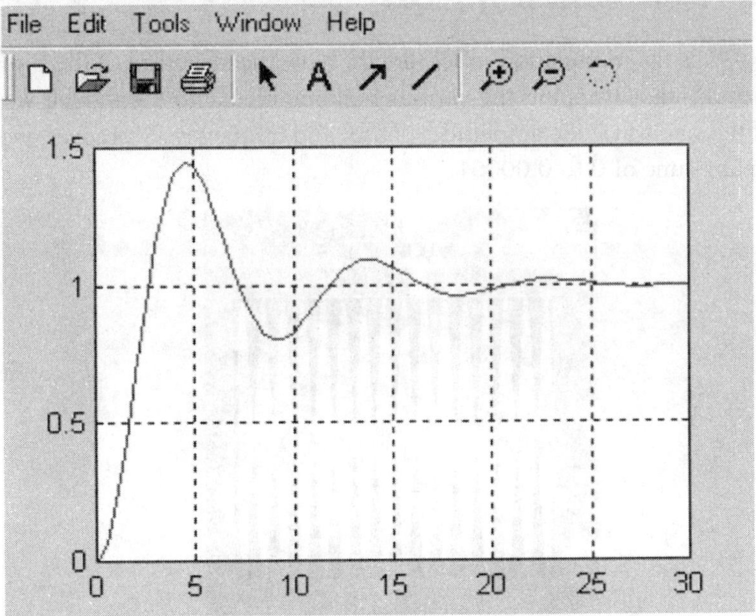

Figure 3.18 Plot of response of a second order system

3.3.9 Modelling an Amplitude Modulator in Simulink

We can simulate practically *anything* in Simulink. Figure 3.19 shows the building blocks of an amplitude modulator.

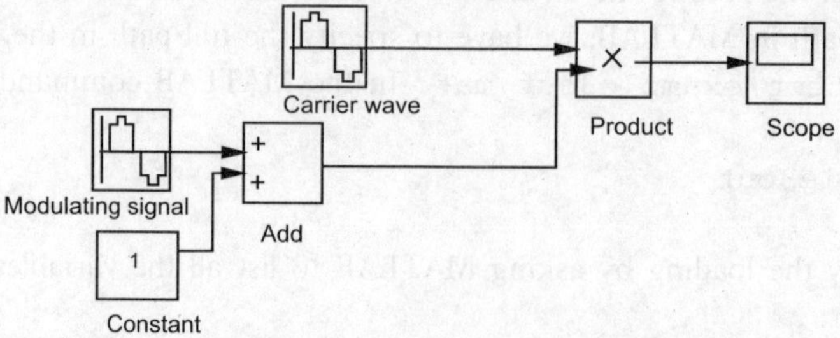

Figure 3.19 Amplitude modulator simulation using Simulink

Note that the *amplitude modulation depth*, m_a is kept as 80%. The output waveform is shown in Figure 3.20. One can change the modulation depth of the system by adjusting the *amplitude* of the modulating signal shown in Figure 3.19. Typically, the modulation depth is kept such that $0 \leq m_a \leq 1$. Therefore, the amplitude of the modulating signal is also maintained between 0 and 1. The Simulink block basically implements the amplitude modulation function given by:

$$\begin{aligned} AM_{\text{out}} &= (E_c + E_m \sin \omega_m t) \, . \sin \omega_c t \\ &= E_c \, (1 + m_a \sin \omega_m t) \, . \sin \omega_c t \end{aligned}$$

Note that $m_a = \frac{E_m}{E_c}$ is the modulation index/depth. Now the structure of the Simulink model is evident. After drag-and-dropping the various building blocks to the model, we can change the attributes of the sine wave like amplitude, phase, and frequency. Moreover, we can change the default sampling time of 0 to 0.00001.

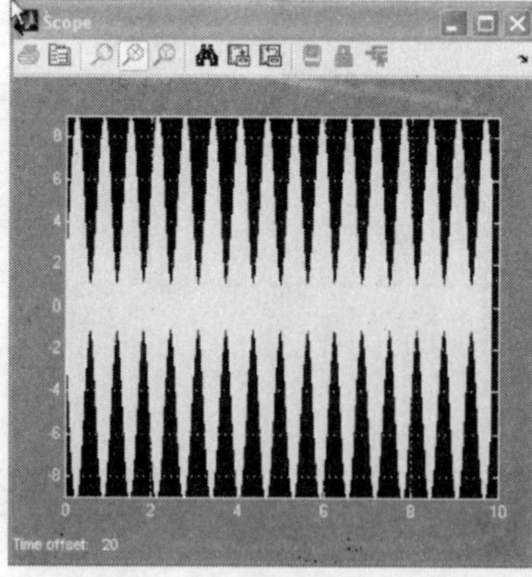

Figure 3.20 Simulated output waveform of amplitude modulator

3.3.10 Modelling a Zero-Crossing Detector in Simulink

A *zero-crossing detector* can be simulated in Simulink as shown in Figure 3.21. The zero-crossing detector (the relay block) switches its state when the sinusoid crosses the value $\pm eps$.

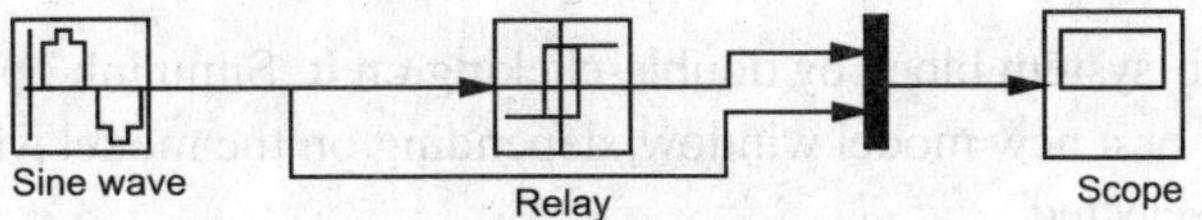

Figure 3.21 Block diagram of a zero-crossing detector

The output waveform obtained from the zero-crossing detector is shown in Figure 3.22.

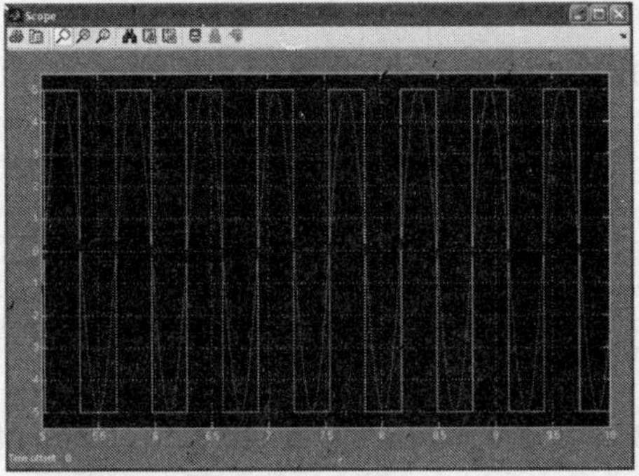

Figure 3.22 Simulated output waveform of a zero crossing detector

3.4 Creating Sub-systems in Simulink

As our model increases in size and complexity, we can simplify it by grouping blocks into sub-systems. Using sub-systems has the following advantages:

- It helps reduce the number of blocks displayed in our model window.
- It allows the user to keep functionally related blocks together.
- It enables us to establish a hierarchical block diagram, where a sub-system block is on one layer and the blocks that make up the sub-system are on another.

We can create a sub-system in two ways:

- Add a sub-system block to our model, then open that block and add the blocks it contains to the sub-system window.
- Add the blocks that make up the sub-system, then group those blocks into a sub-system.

3.4.1 Creating a Sub-system by Adding the Sub-system Block

To create a sub-system before adding the blocks it contains, add a sub-system block to the model, then add the blocks that make up the sub-system:

STEP 1 : Copy the sub-system block from the Signals & Systems library into our model.

STEP 2 : Open the sub-system block by double-clicking on it. Simulink opens the sub-system in the current or a new model window, depending on the model window re-use mode that we have selected.

STEP 3 : In the empty sub-system window, create the sub-system. Use inport blocks to represent input from outside the sub-system and outport blocks to represent external output.

For example, the sub-system shown in Figure 3.23 includes a Sum block and Inport and Outport blocks to represent input to and output from the sub-system.

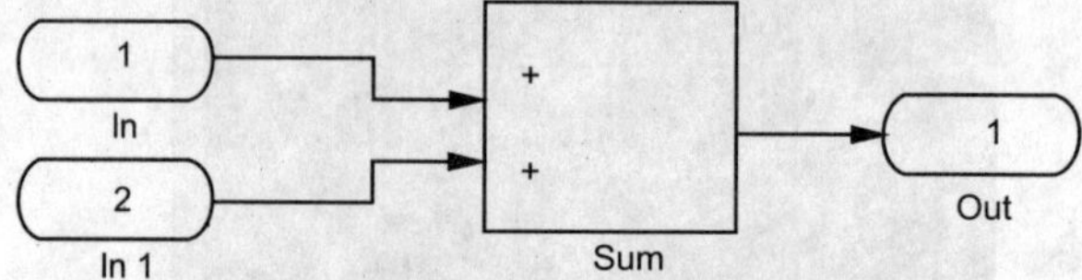

Figure 3.23 Creating a sub-system by adding blocks

3.4.2 Creating a Sub-system by Grouping Existing Blocks

If the model already contains the blocks we want to convert to a sub-system, we can create the sub-system by grouping those blocks. The following steps may be used to do so:

STEP 1 : Enclose the blocks and connecting lines that we want to include in the sub-system within a bounding box. We cannot specify the blocks to be grouped by selecting them individually or by using the Select All command. For more information, see "Selecting Multiple Objects Using a Bounding Box" available under the pull down menu, "Creating a sub-system by Grouping Existing Blocks". For example, Figure 3.24 shows a model that represents a counter. The sum and unit delay blocks are selected within a bounding box. When we release the mouse button, the two blocks and all the connecting lines are selected.

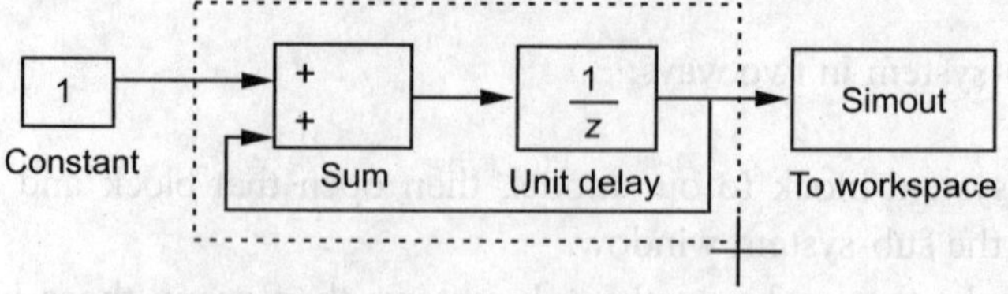

Figure 3.24 Creating a sub-system by grouping blocks

STEP 2 : Choose Create Sub-system from the Edit menu. Simulink replaces the selected blocks with a subsystem block.

Figure 3.25 shows the model after choosing the Create sub-system command (and resizing the sub-system block so that the port labels are readable).

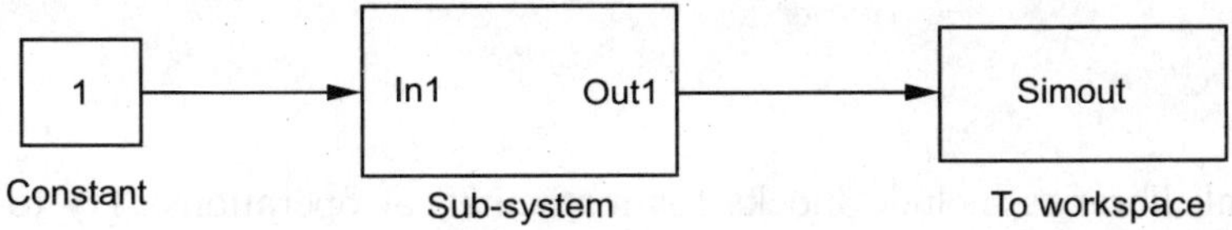

Figure 3.25 The sub-system created

If we open the sub-system block, Simulink displays the underlying system. Notice that Simulink adds inport and outport blocks to represent input from and output to blocks outside the sub-system. As with all blocks, we can change the name of the sub-system block. Also, we can customise the icon and dialog box for the block using the masking feature.

3.4.3 Undoing a Sub-system

To undo the creation of a sub-system by grouping blocks, select Undo from the Edit menu. We can also undo the creation of a sub-system that we have subsequently edited. However, the Undo command does not undo any non-graphical changes that we made to the blocks, such as changing the value of a block parameter or the name of a block. Simulink alerts us to this limitation by displaying a warning dialog box before undoing the creation of a modified sub-system.

3.5 Conclusion

This chapter gives the reader a tutorial introduction to Simulink. Simulink is a platform for multi-domain simulation and model-based design of dynamic systems. It has an interactive graphical environment and a customisable set of block libraries. We can design, simulate, implement, and test control signal processing, communications, and other time-varying systems using Simulink. Simulink can be used to explore the behaviour of a wide range of real world dynamic systems, including electrical circuits, shock absorbers, braking systems, and many other electrical, mechanical, and thermodynamic systems.

The Simulink tutorial begins with a review of block diagram notation. We then discussed solving ODEs using Simulink and simulated a number of simple systems like the amplitude modulator and the zero-crossing detector.

Further Reading

1. *Getting Started With MATLAB 7*. The MathWorks. 2009.
2. *Simulink*. The MathWorks. 2009.

Problems

1. Simulink libraries include blocks for mathematical operations. Try to find proper blocks and draw a graph of the following functions:

   (a) $f(x) = e^x, \ \forall x \in (0, 3)$.

   (b) $f(x) = 4x^2 - 2x + 1, \ \forall x \in (-2, 2)$.
2. Plot simultaneously a sine wave and a cosine wave of the following frequency and amplitude on the scope: 1 kHz, 10 V. Use an integrator to generate a cosine wave from a sine wave.
3. Simulate a sinusoidal oscillator using Simulink. The amplitude of the wave should be 10 V and frequency 1 kHz. [Hint: Use a step source signal and a transfer function block of the type, $T(s) = \frac{K_p}{s^2+\omega^2}$.]
4. Simulate a signal multiplier which will multiply a 1 kHz sinewave (of amplitude 5 V) with a ramp voltage of amplitude 10 V.
5. Simulate an ASK modulator in Simulink. Frequency of the carrier is 2 kHz. The amplitude should switch between 10 V and 2 V.
6. Simulate a *staircase generator* in Simulink. It should have a trigger input which effects the change in output.
7. Model the differential equation: $\dot{x}(t) = -2x(t) + u(t)$, where $u(t)$ is a square wave with an amplitude of 1, and a frequency of 1 rad/s, in two different ways.
8. Simulate a frequency modulator in Simulink. Choose suitable values for carrier and modulating frequencies and depth of modulation.
9. In Simulink it is possible to describe a dynamical system using its transfer function. Try to find the unit step response of a dynamical system using proper Simulink blocks. The transfer function of the dynamical system is:

$$F(s) = \frac{5}{s^2 + 2s + 25}$$

10. Obtain the transfer function of the system illustrated in Figure 3.26.
11. Obtain the *impulse response* and *step response* of the LTI system whose transfer function is $T(s) = \frac{s+2}{s^2+5s+4}$. Comment on the results.

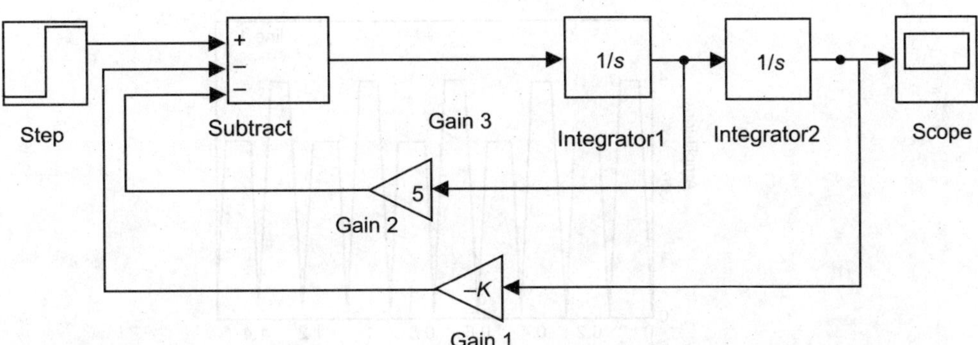

Figure 3.26 A type 1 system

12. The impulse response of an LTI system is given by $h(t) = \delta(n) + \delta(n-2) + \delta(n-4)$. Obtain:

    (a) The step response of the system using Simulink.

    (b) The response of the system to a sinusoidal input, $e(t) = \sin(2000\pi\, t)$.

13. The transfer function of a discrete time FIR system is given by $H(z) = 1 + z^{-1} + 2z^{-2} + 3z^{-3}$. Obtain, using Simulink,

    (a) The impulse response of the system.

    (b) The step response of the system.

14. Simulate a half-wave rectifier circuit in Simulink. Assume that the cut-in voltage of the rectifier diode is 0.6 V.
15. Simulate an *ideal* full-wave rectifier circuit using Simulink.
16. Simulate a *bipolar clipper* circuit which clips at ±5 V in Simulink. Assume a sinusoidal input signal of $\pm 10\text{V}_{pp}$ and frequency 50 Hz.
17. Generate the *Lissajous figure* using Simulink. Use a sine wave of frequency 4 kHz for the x-input and a sine wave of 16 kHz for the y-input. [Hint: In setting the block parameters of the sine waves, choose the default sample time as −1, and set the sample time of the xy-graph as low as 0.000001].
18. Simulate the operation of a *full-wave bridge rectifier*. Assume a diode drop of 0.6 V per diode.
19. Simulate a *bipolar clipper* circuit which clips at ±5 V. Assume a sinusoidal input signal of $\pm 10\text{V}_{pp}$ and frequency 50 Hz.
20. Simulate a circuit in Simulink that would generate the waveform shown in Figure 3.27.
21. Simulate the transient response of a simple RL circuit to an AC voltage energisation shown in Figure 3.28.

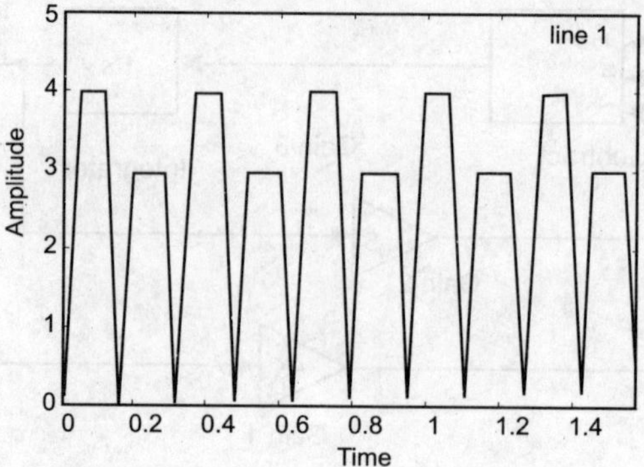

Figure 3.27 Asymmetrical double level clipper and rectifier waveform

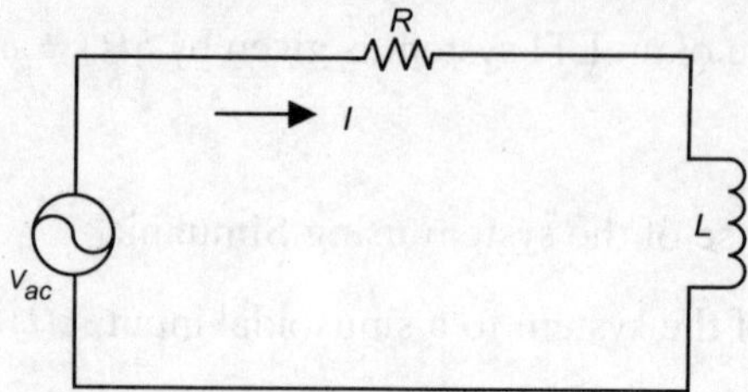

Figure 3.28 RL circuit with AC excitation

22. Create a block diagram and plot the following function over time using a scope from the Sinks menu in the Library Browser.

$$y(t) = 2t^2 + 3(\sqrt{t} + \sin t + 7.5) + 12.75\exp(t).$$

23. Figure 3.29 shows a simple electrical system. Simulate the behaviour of U_{out} when the input U_{in} is subjected to a step input from 0 to 10 V. The governing equations are:

$$\begin{aligned} U_{in} - U_{out} &= Ri. \\ U_{out} &= \frac{1}{C}\int i\,dt = \frac{1}{sC}i. \end{aligned}$$

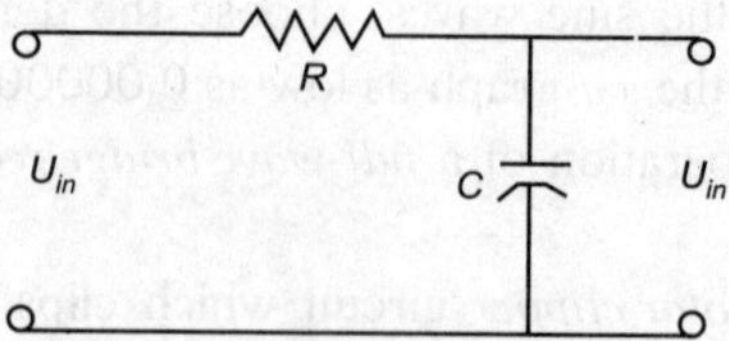

Figure 3.29 RC circuit with AC excitation

24. Calculate and plot the impulse response of the LTI system: $y(n) - y(n-1) + 0.9y(n-2) = x(n)$, using Simulink. Classify the system as IIR/FIR.

25. The *Bernard–Shaw attractor* is described by the following set of differential equations:

$$\dot{x}_1 = 10x_1(0.1 - x_2^2) + x_2.$$
$$\dot{x}_2 = -x_1 + 0.5\sin 2.15t.$$

Create the model and simulate it in Simulink. Maximum step should be set to 0.05 s and stop time set to 500 s.

26. The *Lorenz attractor* is a *chaotic map*, noted for its butterfly shape. The map shows how the state of a dynamical system (the three variables of a three-dimensional system) evolves over time in a complex, non-repeating pattern, often described as beautiful. The attractor itself, and the equations from which it is derived, were introduced by Edward Lorenz in 1963 who derived it from the simplified equations of convection rolls arising in the equations of the atmosphere. From a technical standpoint, the system is nonlinear, three-dimensional and deterministic. In 2001 it was proved by W. Tucker that for a certain set of parameters, the system exhibits chaotic behaviour and displays what is today called a *strange attractor*. The strange attractor in this case is a fractal of Hausdorff dimension between 2 and 3. Grassberger (1983) estimated the Hausdorff dimension to be 2.06 ± 0.01 and the correlation dimension to be 2.05 ± 0.01. The equations that govern the Lorenz attractor are:

$$\frac{dx}{dt} = \sigma(y - x).$$
$$\frac{dy}{dt} = x(r - z) - y.$$
$$\frac{dz}{dt} = xy - bz.$$

where σ is called the Prandtl number and r is called the Rayleigh number. All σ, r, $b > 0$, but usually $\sigma = 10$, $b = 8/3$ and r is varied. The system is stable for $r = 10$ and chaotic for $r = 28$. Try to simulate the problem. For computation time, choose 200s for a stable system and 15 s for a chaotic system. For maximal step, choose 0.005s. Initial conditions are $x_0 = 20$, $y_0 = 5$ and $z_0 = -5$. Export values of variables x, y and z to MATLAB workspace and plot a graph using `plot3` function.

4

Simulation of Signals and Systems

In this chapter, we will consider the modelling and simulation of signals and systems in general. The term "signal" has multiple interpretations. *It is used to represent a wide variety of physical phenomenon.* Although signals can be represented in many ways, in all cases, the information in a signal is contained in a pattern of variations of some form. Another definition of a signal is that it is the quantitative representation of a physical variable; which is a function of one or more independent variable(s). The signal can exist in the physical domain as physical parameter or can be observed as an electrical quantity using a *transducer*. A device or process that somehow receives a signal as its input and converts the input into one/more output signal(s) is termed as a system. In other words, *a system is any device or entity that can process a signal*. We begin our discussion with a typical classification of signals.

4.1 Continuous Time and Discrete Time Signals

Continuous time (CT) signals are those whose independent variable (usually time) and the dependent variable are both continuous entities.[1] Examples for continuous time signals are speech signals and the electrical signal obtained from a pressure or temperature transducer. The speech signal is a one-dimensional continuous time signal, where the independent variable is time. Figure 4.1 illustrates a portion of a typical speech signal.

In the case of continuous time signals, the independent variable is usually enclosed inside a parenthesis, for example $x(t)$.

Discrete time (DT) signals are those whose independent variable is discrete or discontinuous. Examples for discrete time signals are the daily stock market index or sampled electrical signals. In the case of discrete time signals, the independent variable is usually written within a pair of square brackets, as for example $x[n]$. In MATLAB®, we use the [`plot(.)`] and [`stem(.)`] commands to plot continuous time and discrete time signals respectively. This is illustrated in Figure 4.2. A discrete time signal is often referred to as a *sequence*. In MATLAB,

[1] Signals where the independent variable is time is often referred to as *temporal signals*.

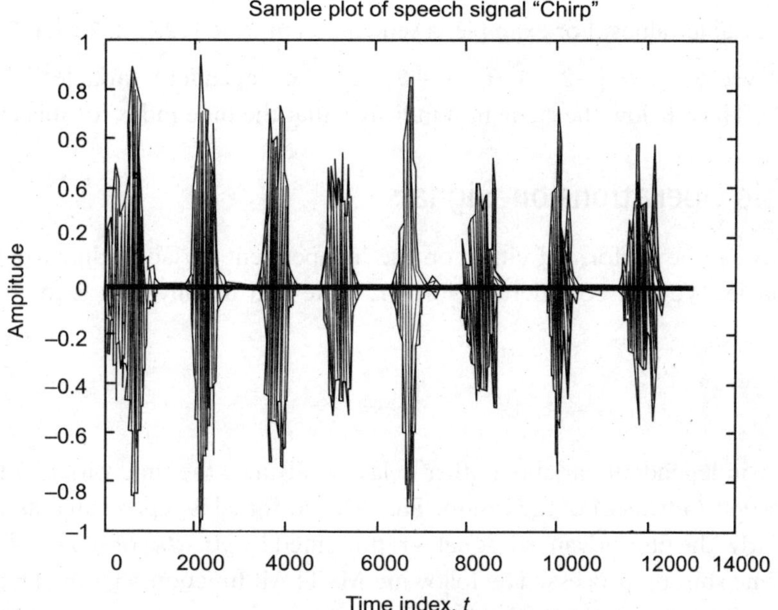

Figure 4.1 A sample of speech signal

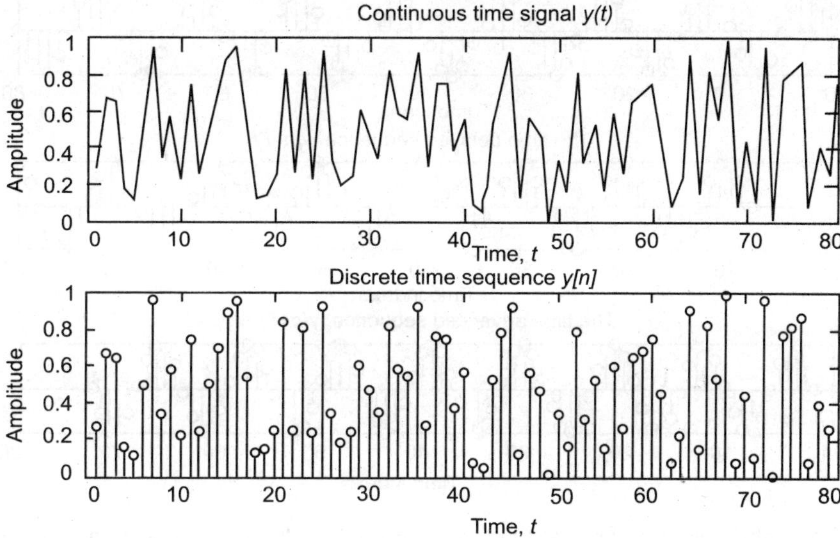

Figure 4.2 Plot of continuous time and discrete time signals

there is no difference between representing a continuous time signal and a discrete time sequence. The only thing to keep in mind is that continuous time representation needs much larger vector (matrix) sizes. We need two vectors (matrices) to represent a signal or sequence completely—one to hold the independent variable values (time indices) and the other to hold the dependent variable values. For example, a sequence $x[n] = \left\{1, 2, \underset{\uparrow}{3}, 4, 5\right\}$ has independent variables in the vector, $n = \{-2, -1, 0, +1, +2\}$ and the dependent variables in the vector, $x = [1, 2, 3, 4, 5]$. The ↑ below the element 3 indicates that the time index for this element is 0.

4.1.1 Basic Operations on Signals

Basic operations can be performed either on the independent variable (time axis) or on the dependent variable. We first consider the former. Note that usually time is the independent variable.

Time Shift

We can shift the independent variable (either delay or advance the time variable) to the right (delay) or to the left (advance) of the origin. The delayed signal is represented as $x(t - t_0)$ or $x[n - n_0]$. Similarly, the time advanced signal is represented by $y(t + t_0)$ or $y[n + n_0]$. Figure 4.3 illustrates the time shifting process. The following MATLAB function `sigshift(.)` shifts a given function to the left or right by an amount n_0.

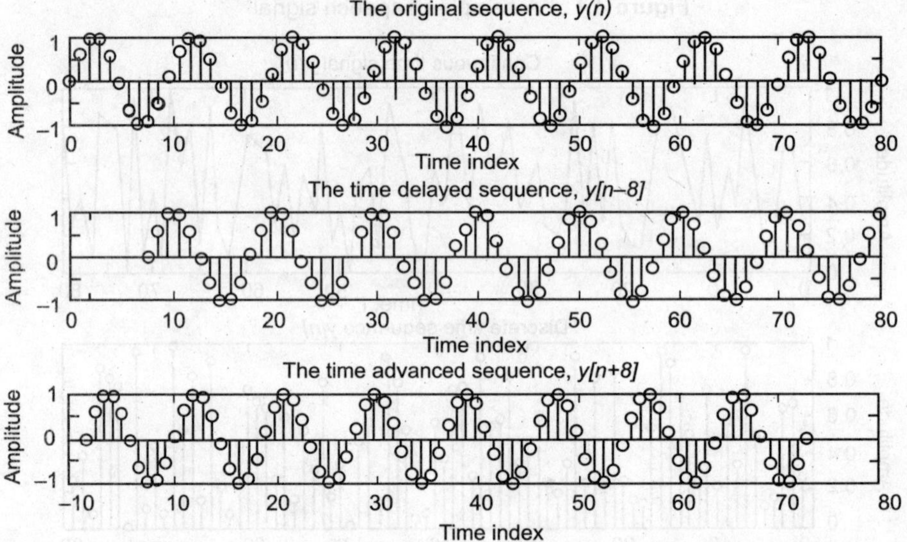

Figure 4.3 Illustration of time shift. (a) Original signal, $y(n)$. (b) Time delayed signal, $y(n-8)$. (c) Time advanced signal, $y(n+8)$.

```
function [y,ny]=sigshift(x,nx,n0)
% MATLAB function to shift a given signal (sequence)
% by n0. Implements y[n]=x[n-n0]..
y=x;
```

```
ny=nx+n0;
% end of sigshift(.)
```

Time Reversal/Signal Folding

The time reversed sequence $x[-n]$ is obtained from the original sequence $x[n]$ by a reflection about $n = 0$ (i.e., by reversing the signal). Similarly, signal $x(-t)$ is obtained from the signal $x(t)$ by a reflection about $t = 0$. Thus, if $x(t)$ represents an audio tape recording, then $x(-t)$ is the same tape recording played backward. The following MATLAB function `sigfold(.)` folds a given arbitrary sequence.

```
function [y,ny]=sigfold(x,nx)
% MATLAB function to fold (time reverse)
% a given signal (sequence).
% Implements y[n]=x[-n]..
y=fliplr(x);
ny=-fliplr(nx);
% end of sigfold(.)
```

Figure 4.4 illustrates the time reversing (signal folding) process.

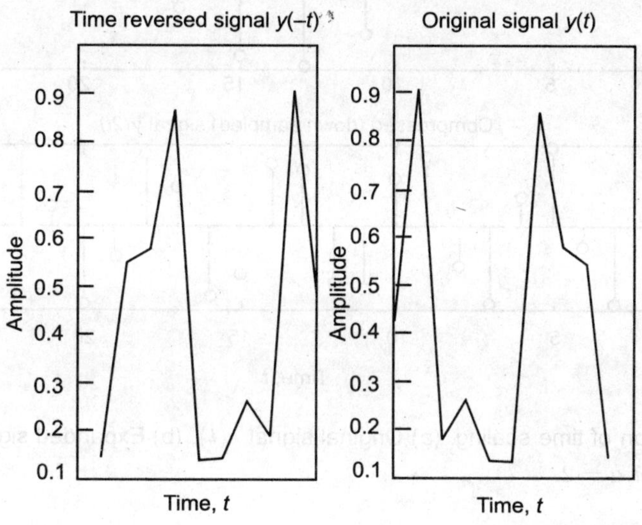

Figure 4.4 Illustration of time reversal. (a) Original signal, $y(t)$. (b) Time reversed signal, $y(-t)$.

Time Scaling

A linear scale change of the independent variable (time) is referred to as time scaling. Mathematically, time scaling can be represented by:

$$y(t) \;=\; x(at), \text{ or} \tag{4.1}$$

$$y[n] \;=\; x[an]. \tag{4.2}$$

Note that time scaling results in *signal compression* when $a > 1$ and *signal expansion* when $a < 1$ in equations (4.1) and (4.2). Signal compression is also called *down sampling* while signal expansion is also known as *up sampling*. Figure 4.5 illustrates the time scaling process. MATLAB functions for signal compression (down sampling) and signal expansion (up sampling) are given below.

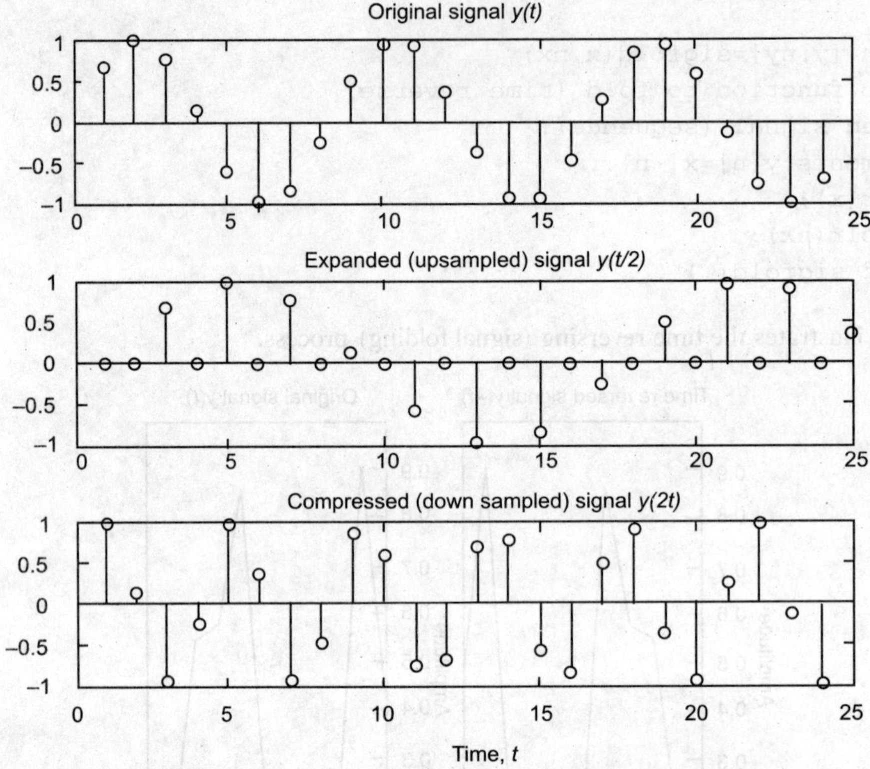

Figure 4.5 Illustration of time scaling. (a) Original signal $y(t)$. (b) Expanded signal for $a = \frac{1}{2}$. (c) Compressed signal for $a = 2$.

```
function [y,ny]=downsample(x,nx,a)
% MATLAB function to down sample
% a given sequence by an integer factor, a..
ny=[0:a*length(x)-1];
y=x([1:a:length(x)]);
%end of downsample.m
```

```
function [y,ny]=upsample(x,nx,a)
% MATLAB function to up sample
% a given sequence by an integer factor, a..
y=zeros(1,a*length(x));
y([1:a:length(x)])=x;
ny=[0:length(y)-1];
% end of upsample.m
```

When it is required to process a signal with more than one operator (say, time scaling, time shifting and time folding), the operations are to be done in the following order:

1. Time shifting (delay or advance) first.
2. Time scaling next.
3. Time folding last.

Operations on Dependent Variable

Level shifting and *amplitude scaling* are two possible operations that can be done on the dependent variable. Level shifting is mathematically represented as:

$$y(t) = x(t) + a$$

Similarly, amplitude scaling can be mathematically expressed as:

$$y(t) = a\,x(t)$$

4.2 Periodic Signals and Sequences

A periodic signal $x(t)$ has the property that there is a positive value of T for which we have:

$$x(t) = x(t+T)$$

for all values of t. In other words, *a periodic signal is unchanged by a time shift of T*. Now, the signal $x(t)$ is said to be periodic with period T. Similarly, a discrete time sequence $x[n]$ is periodic with period N if it satisfies the relation:

$$x[n] = x[n+N]$$

for all n, where N is a positive integer. Note that if:

$$\begin{aligned} x(t) &= x(t+T), \text{ then} \\ x(t) &= x(t+2T) = x(t+3T) = x(t+mT), \quad m \in \mathbb{Z} \end{aligned}$$

The lowest value of T is known as the *fundamental period*, T_0. A periodic sequence is illustrated in Figure 4.6. The MATLAB code to generate the sequence is given below:

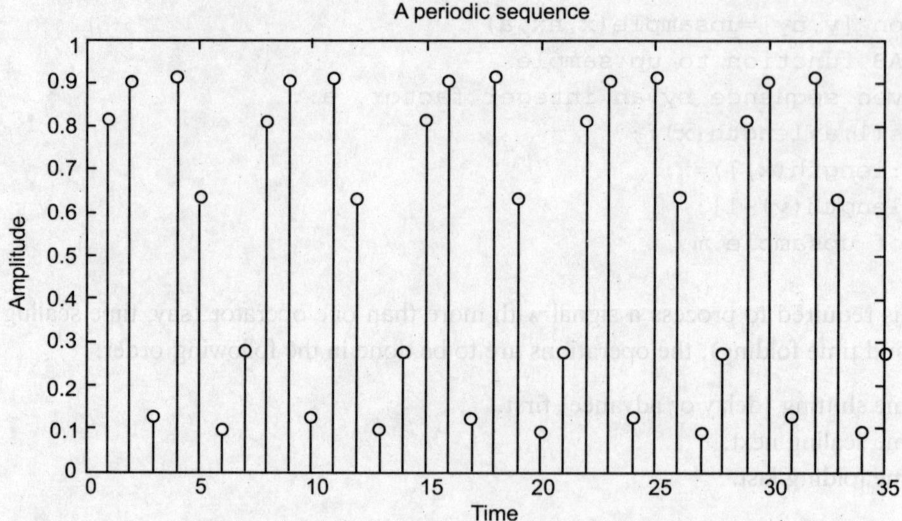

Figure 4.6 Illustration of a periodic sequence with fundamental period $N_0 = 7$.

```
% MATLAB script to generate and plot
% a periodic sequence..
r=rand(1,7);
p=[r,r,r,r,r];
stem(p,'r'),xlabel('Time'),ylabel('Amplitude');
title('A Periodic Sequence');
% end of MATLAB script..
```

4.3 Even and Odd Signals

A signal (sequence) is called an *even signal (sequence)* if it satisfies the condition:

$$x(-t) = x(t), \text{ or}$$

$$x[-n] = x[n]$$

Note that an even signal (sequence) is *symmetric* w.r.t. the y-$axis$. A signal (sequence) is called an *odd signal (sequence)* if it satisfies the condition:

$$x(-t) = -x(t), \text{ or}$$

$$x[-n] = -x[n]$$

Note that an odd signal (sequence) is *anti-symmetric* w.r.t. the y-$axis$. Even and odd signals are illustrated in Figure 4.7.

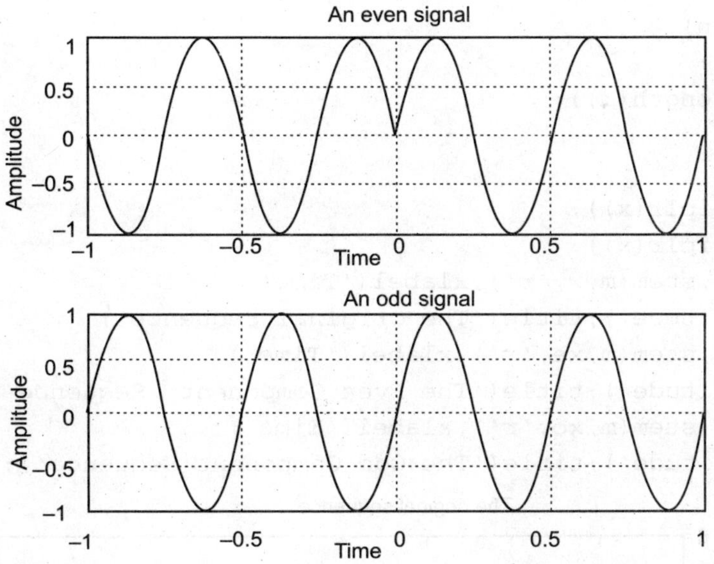

Figure 4.7 Illustration of even and odd signals. (a) Even signal. (b) Odd signal.

4.3.1 Signal Decomposition

An arbitrary signal (sequence) can be expressed as the sum of a pair of an even and odd signal (sequence), which are denoted by $\mathcal{EV}\{x(n)\}$ and $\mathcal{OD}\{x(n)\}$, respectively. Now, we have:

$$\begin{aligned} x(t) &= \mathcal{EV}\{x(n)\} + \mathcal{OD}\{x(n)\}, \text{ where} \\ \mathcal{EV}\{x(n)\} &= \frac{1}{2}\{x(n) + x(-n)\}, \text{ and} \\ \mathcal{OD}\{x(n)\} &= \frac{1}{2}\{x(n) - x(-n)\}. \end{aligned}$$

It is also interesting to note that the even part, $\mathcal{EV}\{x(n)\}$ of $x(n)$ is an even function of the time index n. Similarly, the odd part of $x(n)$, viz. $\mathcal{OD}\{x(n)\}$ is an odd function of the time index n. The reader is advised to prove this. Figure 4.8 illustrates the decomposition of an arbitrary sequence $x[n]$ into its even and odd components. The MATLAB script to generate the plot is given below.

```
% MATLAB script to decompose a real  arbitrary
% sequence into "even" and "odd" components..
x=5*rand(1,20);
n=[0:length(x)-1];
m=-fliplr(n);
m1=min([m,n]); m2=max([m,n]);
m=[m1:m2];
```

```
n1=1:length(n);
nx=n(1)-m(1);
x1=zeros(1,length(m));
x1(n1+nx)=x;
x=x1;
xe=0.5*(x+fliplr(x));
xo=0.5*(x-fliplr(x));
subplot(311),stem(m,x,'r'),xlabel('Time');
ylabel('Amplitude');title('The Original Sequence');
subplot(312),stem(m,xe,'r'),xlabel('Time');
ylabel('Amplitude');title('The Even Component  Sequence');
subplot(313),stem(m,xo,'r'),xlabel('Time');
ylabel('Amplitude');title('The Odd Component Sequence');
```

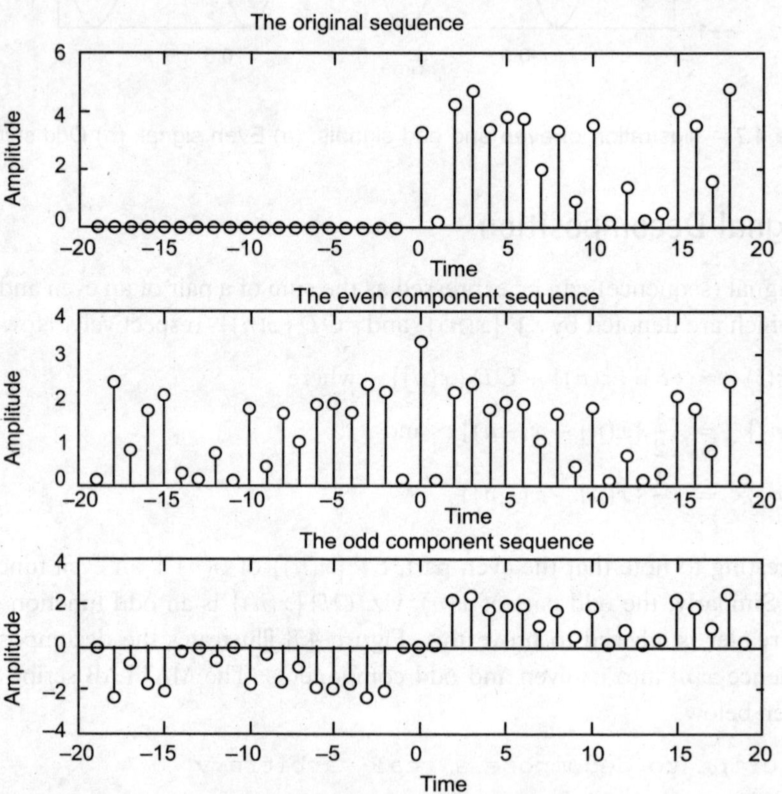

Figure 4.8 Illustration of sequence decomposition into even and odd components. (a) Original sequence. (b) Even component sequence. (c) Odd competent sequence.

4.4 Elementary Signals

In this section, we will introduce several continuous time and discrete time elementary signals (sequences). These signals (sequences) occur frequently and serve as basic building blocks from which we can construct many other signals (sequences).

4.4.1 Continuous Time Complex Exponential Signal

The continuous time *complex exponential signal* is of the form

$$x(t) = C\, e^{\alpha t} \tag{4.3}$$

where C and α are, in general, complex numbers. Depending on the values of these parameters, the complex exponential can have several different characteristics.

Real Exponential Signals

When C and α are real, we get a *real exponential signal* as illustrated in Figure 4.9. The MATLAB script to generate the waveform is given below:

```
% MATLAB script to generate and plot
% Real exponential signals..
clear all; close all; clf;
t=linspace(-5,5,400);
a=0.5;
c=2;
x=c*exp(a*t);.
y=c*exp(-a*t);
subplot(211),plot(t,x,'LineWidth',2); xlabel('Time');
ylabel('Amplitude');title('x(t) = c exp (at), a < 1');grid;
subplot(212),plot(t,y,'LineWidth',2); xlabel('Time');
ylabel('Amplitude');title('x(t) = c exp(-at), |a| < 1');grid;
% end of expsig.m
```

There are basically two types of behaviour: if α is positive, then as t increases, $x(t)$ is a *growing real exponential*, a form used in many physical processes including the chain reaction in atomic explosions and complex chemical reactions. If α is negative, then $x(t)$ is a *decaying real exponential*, a signal that is used to describe a wide variety of phenomena including the radio active decay and the response of RC circuits and damped mechanical systems. Also note that when $\alpha = 0$, $x(t)$ is a constant.

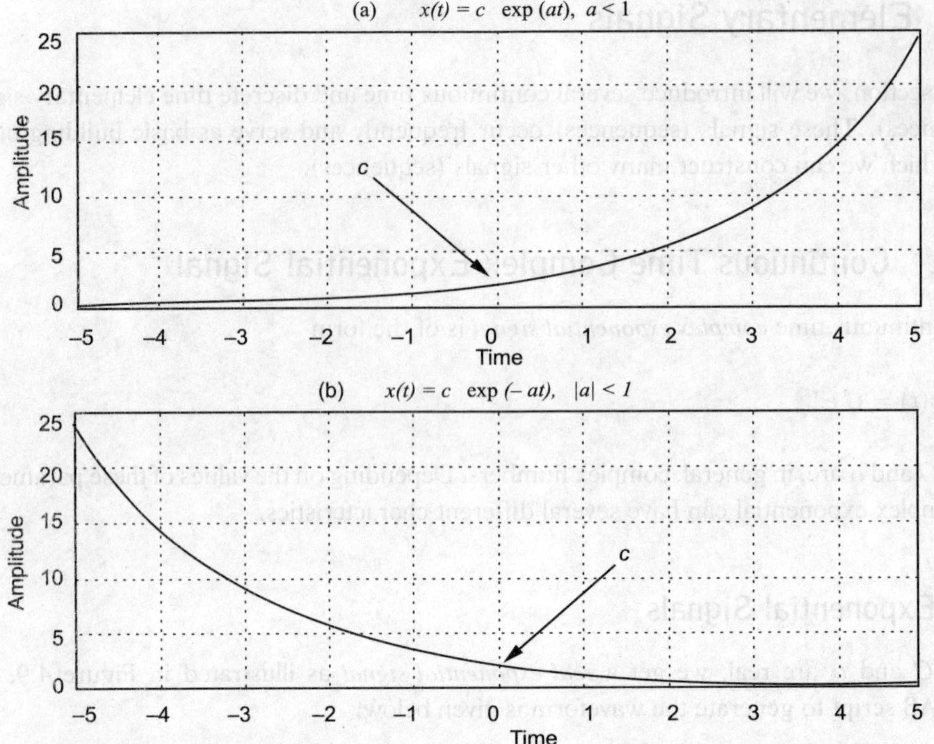

Figure 4.9 Illustration of a real exponential signal. (a) Growing real exponential. (b) Decaying real exponential.

Periodic Complex Exponential Signals

When α in equation (4.3) is purely imaginary and $C = 1$, we have

$$x(t) = e^{j\omega_0 t}$$

An important property of the above signal is that it is *periodic*. We will now derive the fundamental period.

$$\begin{aligned} e^{j\omega_0 t} &= e^{j\omega_0 (t+T)} \\ e^{j\omega_0 (t+T)} &= e^{j\omega_0 t} \cdot e^{j\omega_0 T} \end{aligned}$$

It follows that for periodicity, we must have

$$e^{j\omega_0 T} = 1 \tag{4.4}$$

If $\omega_0 = 0$, then $x(t) = 1$, which is periodic for all values of T. If $\omega_0 \neq 0$, then the fundamental period T_0 of $x(t)$—that is, the smallest positive value of T for which equation (4.4) holds—is

$$T_0 = m\left(\frac{2\pi}{|\omega_0|}\right), \quad m \in \mathbb{Z}. \tag{4.5}$$

Therefore, the signals $e^{j\omega_0 t}$ and $e^{-j\omega_0 t}$ have the same fundamental period.

Sinusoidal Signal

A signal closely related to the periodic complex exponential is the *sinusoidal signal*.

$$x(t) = A\,\cos(\omega_0 t + \phi) \tag{4.6}$$

The signal is illustrated in Figure 4.10.

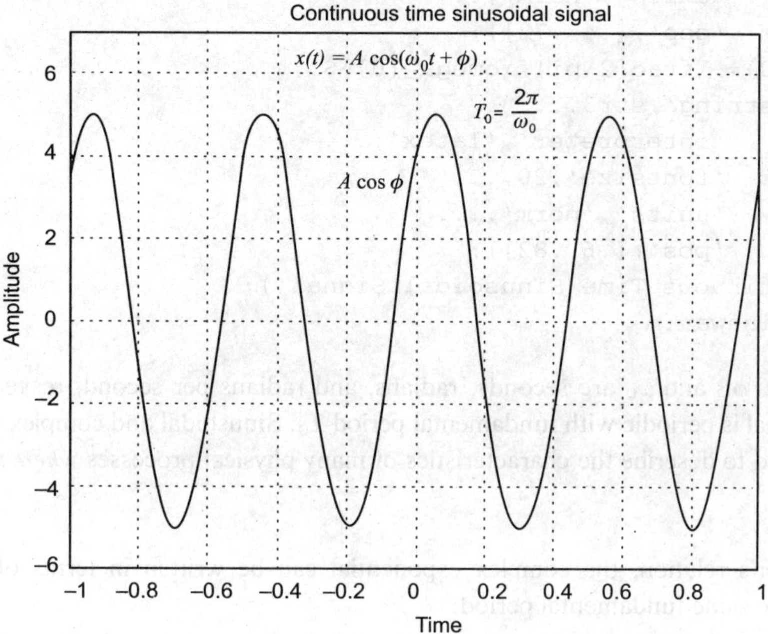

Figure 4.10 Illustration of a sinusoidal signal

The MATLAB script to generate and plot the sinusoidal signal is given below:

```
% MATLAB script to generate and plot
% a sinusoidal signal...
clear all; close all; clf;
t=linspace(-1,1,500);
A=5;
x=A*cos(2*pi*2*t-pi/4);
plot(t,x,'LineWidth',2), xlabel('Time');
ylabel('Amplitude');axis([-1 1 -6 7]); grid;
str1='$x(t)= A \cos(\omega_{0}t + \phi)$';
h = text('string',str1,...
```

```
               'interpreter','latex',...
               'fontsize',20,...
               'units','norm',...
               'pos',[.2 .92]);
str2='$A \cos \phi $';
h = text('string',str2,...
               'interpreter','latex',...
               'fontsize',16,...
               'units','norm',...
               'pos',[.4 .72]);
str3='$T_{0}= \frac{2\pi}{\omega_{0}}$';
h = text('string',str3,...
               'interpreter','latex',...
               'fontsize',20,...
               'units','norm',...
               'pos',[.6 .82]);
title('Continuous Time Sinusoidal Signal');
% end of sinewav.m
```

The units of t, ϕ, and ω_0 are seconds, radians, and radians per second, respectively. The sinusoidal signal is periodic with fundamental period T_0. Sinusoidal and complex exponential signals are used to describe the characteristics of many physical processes *where the energy is conserved.*

By using Euler's relation, the complex exponential can be written in terms of sinusoidal signals with the same fundamental period:

$$e^{j\omega_0 t} = \cos(\omega_0 t) + j\sin(\omega_0 t). \tag{4.7}$$

Similarly, the sinusoidal signal in equation (4.6) can be expressed in terms of periodic complex exponentials, again with the same fundamental period:

$$A\cos(\omega_0 t + \phi) = \frac{A}{2}e^{j\phi}e^{j\omega_0 t} + \frac{A}{2}e^{-j\phi}e^{-j\omega_0 t} \tag{4.8}$$

Note that the two exponentials in equation (4.8) have complex amplitudes. Alternatively, we can also express a sinusoidal signal in terms of a complex exponential signal as

$$A\cos(\omega_0 t + \phi) = A\Re e\left\{e^{j(\omega_0 t + \phi)}\right\} \tag{4.9}$$

where, if c is a complex number, $\Re e\{c\}$ denotes its real part. Similarly, we will use the notation $\Im m\{c\}$ for the imaginary part of c, so that:

$$A\sin(\omega_0 t + \phi) = A\Im m\left\{e^{j(\omega_0 t + \phi)}\right\} \tag{4.10}$$

Note that the fundamental period T_0 of a continuous time sinusoidal signal is or a periodic complex exponential is inversely proportional to $|\omega_0|$, which will be referred to as the *fundamental frequency*. When the magnitude of ω_0 is decreased, the rate of oscillation slows down and therefore the period increases. On the other hand, when the magnitude of ω_0 is increased, the exact opposite happens. In the case of $\omega_0 = 0$, as mentioned earlier, $x(t)$ is constant and hence it is periodic with period T for any positive value of T. Thus the fundamental period of a constant signal is *undefined*.

EXAMPLE 4.1

Plot the sum of two complex exponentials $x(t)$ as the product of a single complex exponential and a single sinusoidal signal. Given that:

$$x(t) = e^{j5t} + e^{j6t} \tag{4.11}$$

SOLUTION

We first factor out a complex exponential from the right side of equation (4.11). Doing this we get:

$$x(t) = e^{j5.5t}(e^{-j0.5t} + e^{j0.5t}) \tag{4.12}$$

which, using Euler's relation can be written as

$$x(t) = 2e^{j5.5t}\cos(0.5t) \tag{4.13}$$

Now the magnitude of $x(t)$ is:

$$|x(t)| = 2|\cos(0.5t)| \tag{4.14}$$

We have plotted the signal $|x(t)|$ in Figure 4.11. The MATLAB script to generate and plot the full-wave rectified sinusoidal waveform is given below:

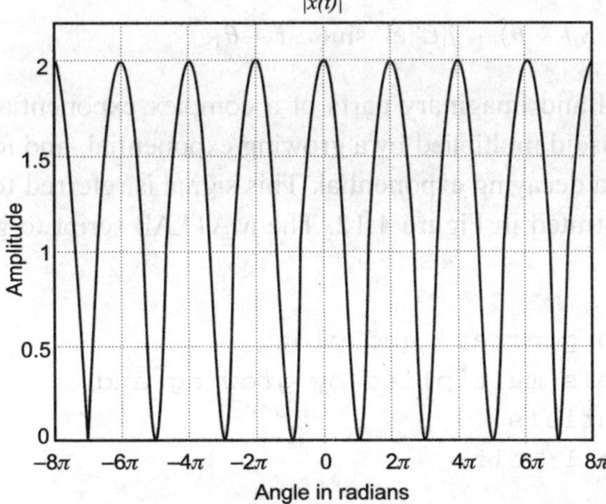

Figure 4.11 The full-wave rectified sinusoidal signal

```
% MATLAB script to generate and plot
% Full-Wave Rectifier Output Waveform.
clear all; close all; clf;
A=2;
t=[-2*pi:pi/256:2*pi];
x=A*cos(2*t);
x=abs(x);
plot(t,x,'LineWidth',2);
set(gca, 'FontName', 'Times','FontSize',14);
xlabel('Angle in Radians'); ylabel('Amplitude');
title('|x(t)|'); axis([-2*pi 2*pi 0 2.2]);
set(gca, 'FontName', 'Symbol','FontSize',16);
set(gca, 'XTick', (-2:0.5:2)*pi);
set(gca, 'XTickLabel', '-8p|-6p|-4p|-2p|0|2p|4p|6p|8p');grid;
% end of fwr.m
```

General Complex Exponential Signals

Consider a complex exponential $Ce^{\alpha t}$, where C is expressed in polar form and α in rectangular form.

$$\begin{aligned} C &= |C|e^{j\theta}, \text{ and} \\ \alpha &= r + j\omega_0 \end{aligned}$$

Then,

$$Ce^{\alpha t} = |C|e^{j\theta}e^{(r+j\omega_0)t} = |C|e^{rt}e^{j(\omega_0 t+\theta)} \tag{4.15}$$

By using Euler's relation, we can expand this as

$$Ce^{\alpha t} = |C|e^{rt}\cos(\omega_0 t + \theta) + j|C|e^{rt}\sin(\omega_0 t + \theta). \tag{4.16}$$

Now, for $r = 0$, the real and imaginary parts of a complex exponential are sinusoidal. For $r > 0$, the signal is a sinusoid multiplied by a growing exponential, and for $r < 0$, the signal is a sinusoid multiplied by a decaying exponential. This signal is referred to as *damped sinusoid*. Both the signals are illustrated in Figure 4.12. The MATLAB script to generate and plot the figure is given below:

```
% MATLAB script to generate and plot
% sinusoidal signals multiplied by growing and
% decaying exponentials..
clear all; close all; clf;
C=25;
w=2*pi*2;
```

```
th=pi/6;
t=linspace(-2,10,1000);
r=0.5;
x=C*exp(r*t).*cos(w*t+th);
subplot(211),plot(t,x,'r','LineWidth',2),...
xlabel('Time');ylabel('Amplitude'); grid;
str1='$x(t)= Ce^{rt}\!\cos(\omega_{0}t+\theta),\;r>0$';
h = text('string',str1,...
            'interpreter','latex',...
            'fontsize',16,...
            'units','norm',...
            'pos',[.1 .92]);
title('Growing Sinusoidal Signal');
x=C*exp(-r*t).*cos(w*t+th);
subplot(212),plot(t,x,'r','LineWidth',2),...
xlabel('Time');ylabel('Amplitude'); grid;
str2='$x(t)= Ce^{rt}\!\cos(\omega_{0}t+\theta),\;r<0$';
h = text('string',str2,...
            'interpreter','latex',...
            'fontsize',16,...
            'units','norm',...
            'pos',[.1 .92]);
title('Decaying Sinusoidal Signal');
%end of grds.m
```

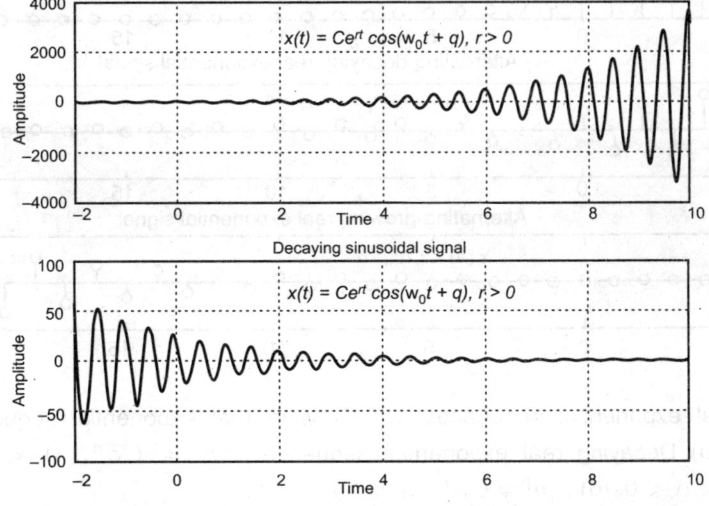

Figure 4.12 Complex exponential signals. (a) Growing sinusoidal signal $x(t) = Ce^{rt}\cos(\omega_0 t + \theta)$, $r > 0$. (b) Decaying sinusoidal signal $x(t) = Ce^{rt}\cos(\omega_0 t + \theta)$, $r < 0$.

4.4.2 Discrete Time Complex Exponential Sequences

A complex exponential sequence is expressed by

$$x[n] = C\alpha^n \tag{4.17}$$

where C and α are in general complex numbers. We can write the above equation as

$$x[n] = Ce^{\beta n} \tag{4.18}$$

where $\alpha = e^{\beta}$

Real Exponential Sequences

If C and α are real, we have a real exponential sequence in two possible forms, depending on the value of α. When $|\alpha| > 1$, the sequence grows exponentially with n, and when $0 < |\alpha| < 1$, the sequence decays with n. When $\alpha = -1$, $x[n]$ alternates between $+C$ and $-C$. The sequences are illustrated in Figure 4.13. The MATLAB script to generate and plot the figure is given below:

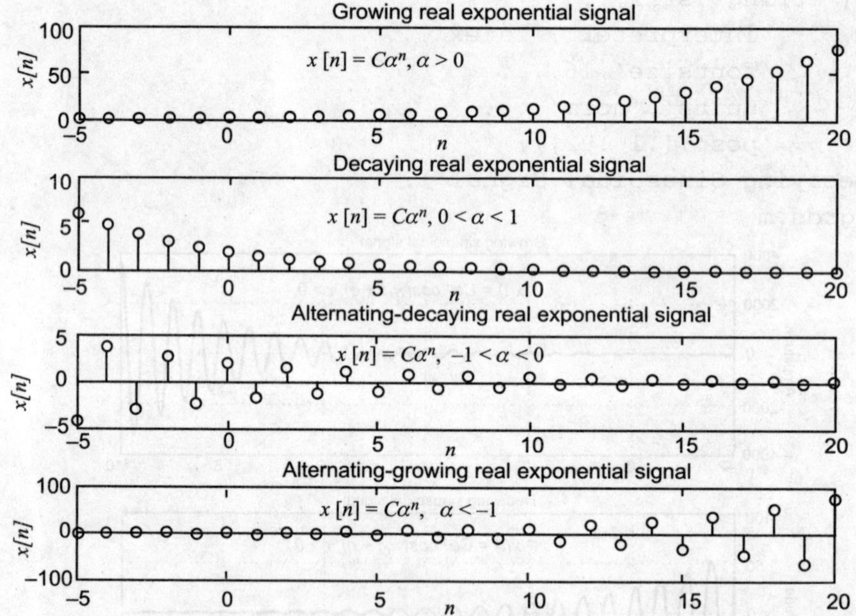

Figure 4.13 Real exponential sequences. (a) Growing real exponential sequence $x[n] = C\alpha^n$, $\alpha > 1$. (b) Decaying real exponential sequence $x[n] = C\alpha^n$, $0 < \alpha < 1$. (c) $x[n] = C\alpha^n$, $-1 < \alpha < 0$. (d) $x[n] = C\alpha^n$, $\alpha < -1$

```
% MATLAB script to generate and plot
```

```
% a real exponential sequence..
clear all; close all; clf;
c=2;
n=[-5:20];
a=1.2;
x=c*a.^n;
subplot(411),stem(n,x,'r','LineWidth',2),xlabel('n');
str1='$x[n]= C\alpha^{n},\;\alpha>0$';
h = text('string',str1,...
            'interpreter','latex',...
            'fontsize',14,...
            'units','norm',...
            'pos',[.3 .8]);
ylabel('x[n]');
title('Growing Real Exponential Signal');
a=0.8;
x=c*a.^n;
subplot(412),stem(n,x,'r','LineWidth',2),xlabel('n');
str2='$x[n]= C\alpha^{n},\; 0<\alpha<1$';
h = text('string',str2,...
            'interpreter','latex',...
            'fontsize',14,...
            'units','norm',...
            'pos',[.3 .8]);
ylabel('x[n]');
title('Decaying Real Exponential Signal');
a=-0.86;
x=c*a.^n;
subplot(413),stem(n,x,'r','LineWidth',2),xlabel('n');
str3='$x[n]= C\alpha^{n},\;-1<\alpha<0$';
h = text('string',str3,...
            'interpreter','latex',...
            'fontsize',14,...
            'units','norm',...
            'pos',[.3 .8]);
ylabel('x[n]');
title('Alternating Decaying Real Exponential Signal');
a=-1.2;
x=c*a.^n;
subplot(414),stem(n,x,'r','LineWidth',2),xlabel('n');
```

```
str4='$x[n]= C\alpha^{n},\; \alpha<-1$';
h = text('string',str4,...
         'interpreter','latex',...
         'fontsize',14,...
         'units','norm',...
         'pos',[.3 .8]);
ylabel('x[n]');
title('Alternating Growing Real Exponential Signal');
% end of rdse.m
```

Sinusoidal Sequences

When β is purely imaginary in equation (4.18) (so that $|\alpha| = 1$), we have the form:

$$x[n] = e^{j\omega_0 n}, \quad C = 1 \tag{4.19}$$

This sequence is closely related to the sinusoidal sequence

$$x[n] = A\cos(\omega_0 n + \phi) \tag{4.20}$$

where n is a mere number, and both ω_0 and ϕ have units of radians. Now using Euler's equation, we can relate complex exponential sequences and sinusoidal sequences.

$$e^{j\omega_0 n} = \cos(\omega_0 n) + j\sin(\omega_0 n), \text{ and} \tag{4.21}$$

$$A\cos(\omega_0 n + \phi) = \frac{A}{2}e^{j\phi}e^{j\omega_0 n} + \frac{A}{2}e^{-j\phi}e^{-j\omega_0 n}. \tag{4.22}$$

Discrete time sinusoidal sequences are illustrated in Figure 4.14. The MATLAB script to generate and plot the figure is given below:

```
% MATLAB script to generate and plot% sinusoidal sequences..
n=[-20:20];
x1=cos(4*pi*n/15);
x2=cos(n/8);
subplot(211),stem(n,x1,'r','LineWidth',2);
xlabel('n'); ylabel('x[n]');
title('x[n]=cos(4*pi*n/15)');
subplot(212),stem(n,x2,'r','LineWidth',2);
xlabel('n'); ylabel('x[n]');
title('x[n]=cos(n/8)');
% end of dtse.m
```

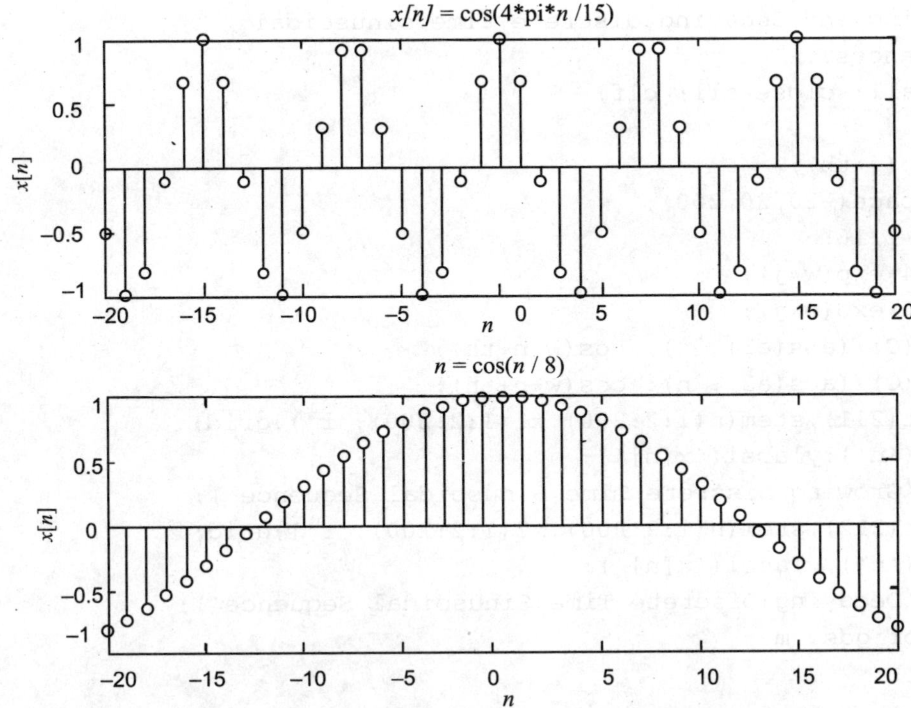

Figure 4.14 Discrete time sinusoidal sequences. (a) $x[n] = \cos(4\pi\, n/15)$. (b) $x[n] = \cos(n/8)$.

General Complex Exponential Sequences

The general complex exponential sequence can be written in terms of real exponential and sinusoidal sequences. If we write C and α in polar form:

$$\begin{aligned} C &= |C|e^{j\theta}, \text{ and} \\ \alpha &= |\alpha|e^{j\omega_0}, \text{ then,} \\ C\alpha^n &= |C||\alpha|^n \cos(\omega_0\, n + \theta) + j|C||\alpha|^n \sin(\omega_0\, n + \theta). \end{aligned} \tag{4.23}$$

Hence, for $|\alpha| = 1$, the real and imaginary parts of a complex exponential are sinusoidal. For $|\alpha| < 1$, they correspond to sinusoidal sequences multiplied by a decaying exponential, while for $|\alpha| > 1$, they correspond to a sinusoidal sequence multiplied by a growing exponential. These sequences are illustrated in Figure 4.15. The MATLAB script to generate and plot the figure is given below:

```
% MATLAB script to generate and plot
```

```
% Growing and Decaying discrete time sinusoidal
% sequences..
clear all; close all; clf;
th=0;
C=8*exp(j*th);
n=linspace(-20,20,200);
w=2*pi*1/16;
a1=1.04*exp(w*j);
a2=0.96*exp(w*j);
x1=abs(C)*(abs(a1).^n).*cos(w*n+th);
x2=abs(C)*(abs(a2).^n).*cos(w*n+th);
subplot(211),stem(n(1:2:200),x1(1:2:200),'r');grid;
xlabel('n');ylabel('x[n]');
title('Growing Discrete Time Sinusoidal Sequence');
subplot(212),stem(n(1:2:200),x2(1:2:200),'r');grid;
xlabel('n');ylabel('x[n]');
title('Decaying Discrete Time Sinusoidal Sequence');
% end of gdse.m
```

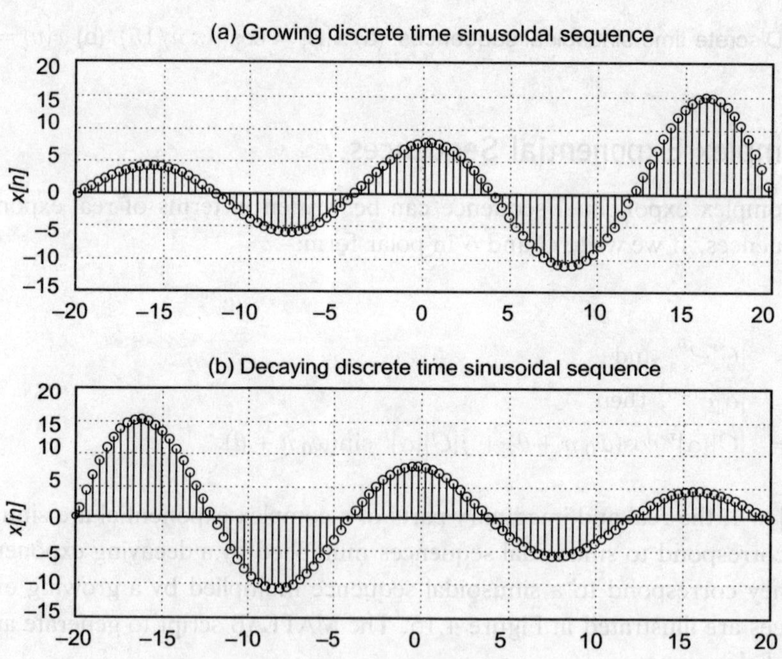

Figure 4.15 General complex exponential sequences. (a) Growing discrete time sinusoidal sequence. (b) Decaying discrete time sinusoidal sequence.

4.4.3 Periodicity of Discrete Time Complex Exponential Sequences

As in the case of continuous time signals, a discrete time sequence $e^{j\omega_0 n}$ is periodic with fundamental period, $N_0 = \left(\frac{2\pi}{\omega_0}\right)$. Note that when $\omega_0 = 0$, the discrete time sequence has a *fundamental frequency of zero*, and its fundamental period is *undefined*. Figure 4.16 illustrates many periodic sequences. The MATLAB script to generate and plot the figure is given below:

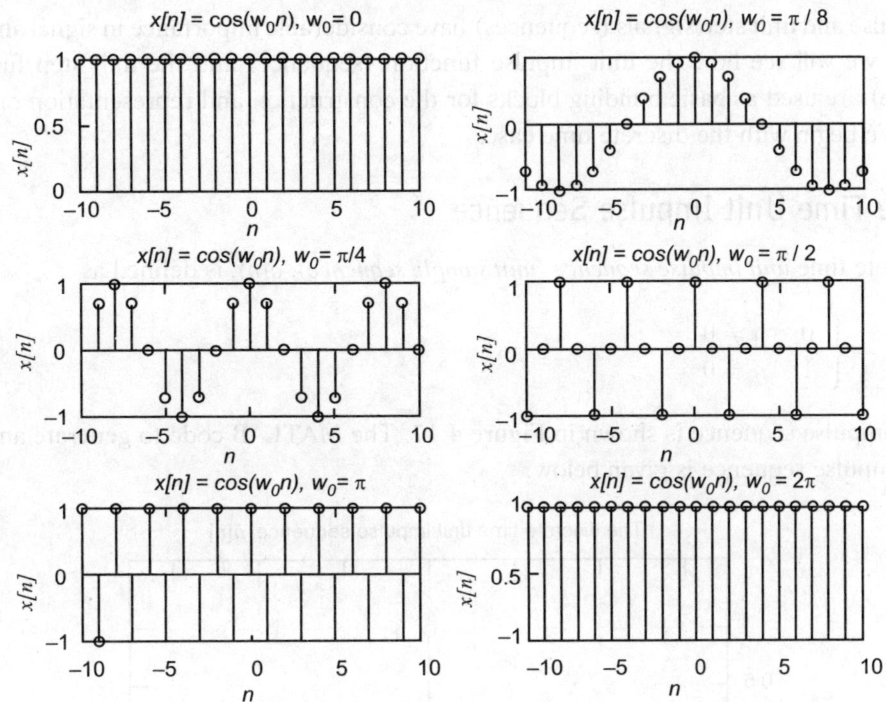

Figure 4.16 Discrete time sinusoidal sequences for different frequencies

```
% MATLAB script to generate and plot
% Discrete time sinusoidal sequences for
% various frequencies..
clear all; close all; clf;
n=linspace(-10,10,21);
w=[0,pi/8,pi/4,pi/2,pi,2*pi];
for k=1:6
    x(k,:)=cos(w(k)*n);
    subplot(3,2,k),stem(n,x(k,:));
    xlabel('n'), ylabel('x[n]');
    title(' x[n]=cos(w_{0}n), w_{0}=0');% This line will
    % be modified later using the "Figure Properties" and
```

```
    % "Axes Properties" controls from the Edit menu of
    % of the Figure Window...
end;
% end of mseq.m
```

4.4.4 Unit Impulse and Unit Step Functions and Sequences

Unit impulse and unit step signals (sequences) have considerable importance in signal analysis. Later on, we will see how the unit impulse function (sequence) and the unit step function (sequence) are used as basic building blocks for the construction and representation of other signals. We begin with the discrete time case.

Discrete Time Unit Impulse Sequence

The discrete time *unit impulse sequence (unit sample sequence)*, $\delta[n]$, is defined as

$$\delta[n] = \begin{cases} 0, & n \neq 0 \\ 1, & n = 0 \end{cases} \tag{4.24}$$

The unit impulse sequence is shown in Figure 4.17. The MATLAB code to generate and plot the unit impulse sequence is given below:

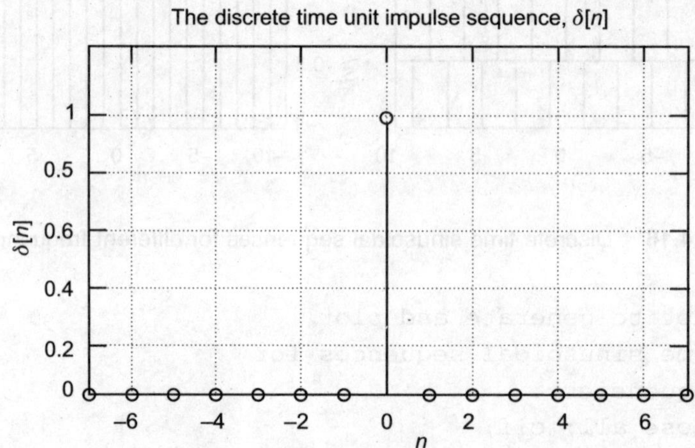

Figure 4.17 The discrete time unit impulse (unit sample) sequence

```
% MATLAB script to generate and plot
% a simple discrete time unit impulse sequence..
clear all; close all; clf;
x=[zeros(1,7),1,zeros(1,7)];
n=[-7:7];
```

```
stem(n,x,'r','LineWidth',2),axis([-7 7 0 1.2]);
xlabel('n'); ylabel('\delta[n]');grid;
title('The Discrete Time Unit Impulse Sequence, \delta[n]');
% end of uniti.m
```

Discrete Time Unit Step Sequences

The discrete time *unit step sequence*, $u[n]$ is defined as

$$u[n] = \begin{cases} 0, & n < 0 \\ 1, & n \geq 0 \end{cases} \tag{4.25}$$

The discrete time unit step sequence is shown in Figure 4.18(a). There is a close relation between the unit impulse and unit step sequences. The unit impulse sequence is the *first difference* of the discrete time unit step sequence.

$$\delta[n] = u[n] - u[n-1] \tag{4.26}$$

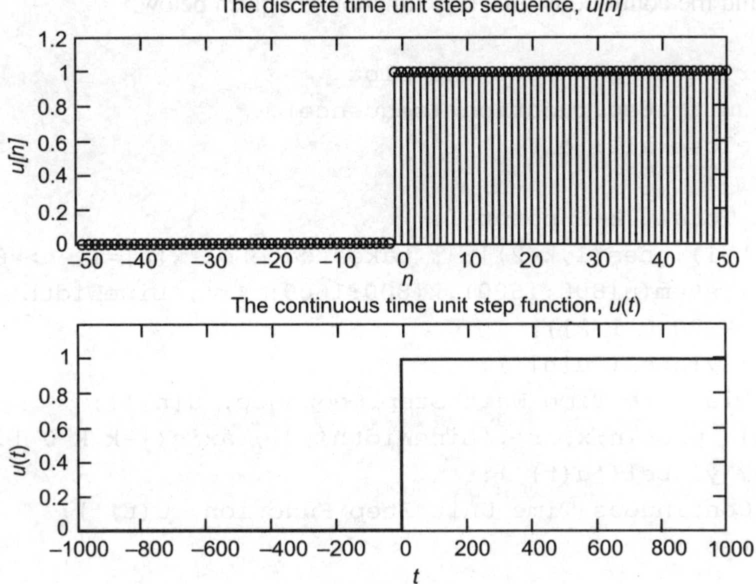

Figure 4.18 (a) The discrete time unit step sequence, $u[n]$. (b) The unit step function, $u(t)$.

Conversely, the discrete time unit step sequence is the *running sum* of the unit sample.

$$u[n] = \sum_{m=-\infty}^{n} \delta[m], \quad \text{and} \tag{4.27}$$

$$= \sum_{k=0}^{\infty} \delta[n-k] \tag{4.28}$$

The unit impulse can be used to sample the value of a signal at $n = 0$:

$$x[n]\delta[n] = x[0]\delta[n]$$

In general, we can take a delayed unit impulse (by an amount n_0) as $\delta[n - n_0]$ and hence:

$$x[n]\delta[n - n_0] = x[n_0]\delta[n - n_0] \tag{4.29}$$

Continuous Time Unit Step Function

The continuous time unit step function, $u(t)$ is defined as

$$u(t) = \begin{cases} 0, & t < 0 \\ 1, & t > 0 \end{cases} \tag{4.30}$$

Note that the unit step function has a discontinuity at $t = 0$. The contnuous time unit step is illustrated in Figure 4.18(b). The MATLAB script to generate and plot the discrete time unit step sequence and the continuous time step function are given below:

```
% MATLAB script to generate and plot
% a simple unit step function (sequence)..
clear all; close all; clf;
k=1000;
n=[-k:k]; % Total 2k+1 points..
x=[zeros(1,k-1),ones(1,k+2)]; % takes care of x[n]=1, n>=0.
subplot(211),stem(n(800:1600),x(800:1600),'r','LineWidth',2);
axis([-k/20 k/20 0 1.2]);
xlabel('n'); ylabel('u[n]');
title('The Discrete Time Unit Step Sequence, u[n]');
subplot(212), plot(n,x,'r','LineWidth',2); axis([-k k 0 1.2]);
xlabel('t'); ylabel('u(t)');
title('The Continuous Time Unit Step Function, u(t)');
% end of ustep.m
```

Continuous Time Unit Impulse Function

The continuous time unit impulse function $\delta(t)$ is related to the continuous time unit step function as:

$$u(t) = \int_{\tau=-\infty}^{t} \delta(\tau)\, d\tau \tag{4.31}$$

It follows from equation (4.31) that the unit impulse function can be thought of as the *first derivative of the unit step function*.

$$\delta(t) = \frac{du(t)}{dt} \tag{4.32}$$

However, since there exists a discontinuity in $u(t)$ at $t = 0$, there is a formal difficulty in equation (4.32). To work around this problem, we introduce an infinitesimally small delay, Δ at the origin, so that $u(t)$ rises to 1 from 0 in time Δ. Therefore, the new step function, $u_\Delta(t)$ is no longer discontinuous at $t = 0$. Now, we introduce a new delta function, $\delta_\Delta(t)$ as:

$$\delta_\Delta(t) = \frac{du_\Delta}{dt} \tag{4.33}$$

as shown in Figure 4.19. The MATLAB script to generate and plot the approximated unit step and unit impulse functions is given below:

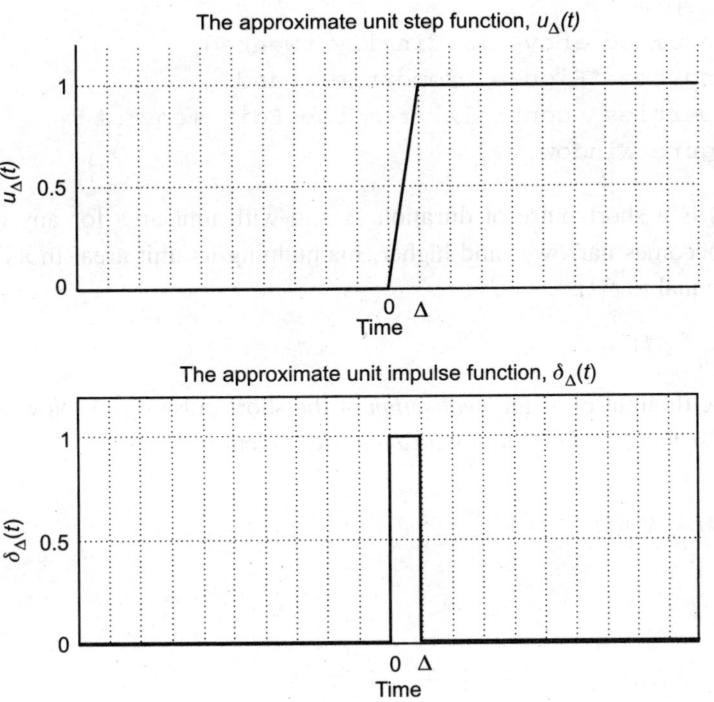

Figure 4.19 (a) Continuous time approximation of unit step, as $u_\Delta(t)$. (b) The derivative of $u_\Delta(t)$, termed as $\delta_\Delta(t)$.

```
% MATLAB script file to generate
% "approximate" unit step and unit impulse
% functions..
```

```
close all; clear all; clf;
k=10;
n=[-k:k];
x=[zeros(1,k+1),ones(1,k)];
subplot(211),plot(n,x,'r','LineWidth',3),grid;
axis([-k k 0 1.2]);
xlabel('Time');ylabel('u_{\Delta}(t)');
title('The approximate unit step function, u_{\Delta}(t)');
n1=linspace(-k,k,1000);
x1=[zeros(1,500),ones(1,50),zeros(1,450)];
subplot(212),plot(n1,x1,'r','LineWidth',3),grid;
axis([-k k 0 1.2]);
xlabel('Time');ylabel('\delta_{\Delta}(t)');
title('The approximate unit impulse function, \delta_{\Delta}(t)');
% end of astep.m
%The plot obtained above is finally tweaked ..
% later using the "Figure Properties" and
% "Axes Properties" controls from the Edit menu of
% of the Figure Window...
```

Note that $\delta_\Delta(t)$ is a short pulse of duration Δ and with unit area for any value of Δ. As $\Delta \to 0$, $\delta_\Delta(t)$ becomes narrower and higher, maintaining its unit area. In its limiting form, $\delta_\Delta(t)$ becomes equal to $\delta(t)$:

$$\delta(t) = \lim_{\Delta\to 0} \delta_\Delta(t) \tag{4.34}$$

Thus $\delta(t)$ can be thought of as an *idealisation* of the short pulse $\delta_\Delta(t)$. Now we can relate a *scaled unit impulse function*, $k\delta(t)$ to a *scaled unit step function*, $u(t)$ as:

$$\int_{-\infty}^{t} k\delta(\tau)\, d\tau = k\, u(t) \tag{4.35}$$

We also write:

$$u(t) = \int_{\sigma=0}^{\infty} \delta(t-\sigma)\, d\sigma \tag{4.36}$$

We can use the unit impulse function to *sample* arbitrary signals, $x(t)$ at $t = 0$, since:

$$x(t)\delta(t) = x(0)\delta(t)$$

Similarly, we also have:

$$x(t)\delta(t-t)0) = x(t_0)\delta(t-t_0) \tag{4.37}$$

4.4.5 Continuous Time and Discrete Time Systems

We can see that physical systems are the interconnection of various components, devices, or sub-systems. A system which processes one (or more) continuous time signal(s) is said to be a *continuous time system*. Similarly, a system which processes one (or more) discrete time signal(s) is called a *discrete time system*. Systems of both the above-mentioned types are shown in block diagram form in Figure 4.20.

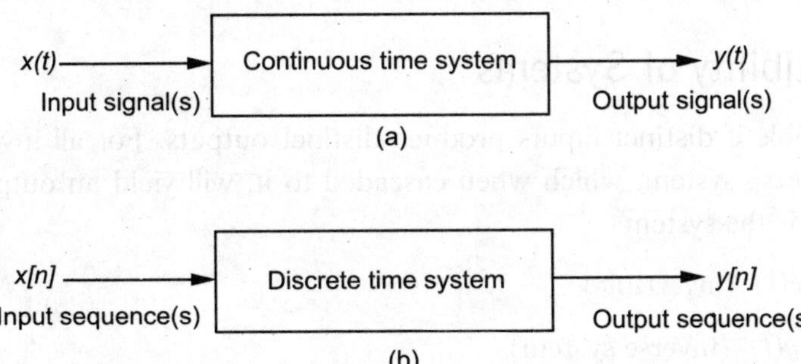

Figure 4.20 Continuous time and discrete time systems. (a) Continuous time system. (b) Discrete time system

A system that has both discrete and continuous time input(s) and/or output(s) is called a *hybrid system*.

4.5 Basic Properties of Systems

In this section, we will consider various basic properties of systems in general. These properties have significant physical interpretations. We give relatively simple mathematical descriptions for each property.

4.5.1 Memory

A system is said to be a *memory less (static)* system, if *the output for each value of independent variable at a given instant depends only on the input at that instant*. For example, the system expressed by the relation:

$$y[n] = \left(4x[n] - x^3[n]\right)^4 \tag{4.38}$$

is memory less (static) as the output, $y[n]$ at instant n, depends only on the value of $x[n]$ at that same instant. A contrary case is the system given by the equation:

$$y(t) = x(t) + \frac{1}{2}x(t - t_0) \tag{4.39}$$

An example of a discrete time system with memory is

$$y[n] = \sum_{k=-\infty}^{n} x[k] \tag{4.40}$$

A system with memory is also called a *dynamic system*. It should be noted that systems which can retain its state do have memory. For example, RC or LC circuits. For that matter, a simple resistive circuit (ignoring the parasitics) can be thought of as a memory less system.

4.5.2 Invertibility of Systems

A system is invertible if distinct inputs produce distinct outputs. For all invertible systems, there exists an inverse system, which when cascaded to it, will yield an output equal to the input. An example is the system:

$$\begin{aligned} y(t) &= 4x(t) \text{ (invertible)} && (4.41) \\ w(t) &= \frac{1}{4}y(t) \text{ (inverse system)} && (4.42) \end{aligned}$$

A system that is not invertible is the system given by:

$$y[n] = 3x^2[n] \tag{4.43}$$

as here two distinct inputs, say $x[n] = -1$ and $+1$, produce the same output, viz. 3. Invertible systems are important in the design of communication systems, as transmitter sub-systems like the *encoder* and the *encryptor* have to be invertible. Only then can the effect of these sub-systems be annulled at the receiver by including an inverse sub-system like the *decoder* and the *decryptor*.

The system represented by equation (4.40) is invertible, as we can rewrite the output as:

$$\begin{aligned} y[n] &= \sum_{k=-\infty}^{n} x[k] \\ &= \sum_{k=-\infty}^{n-1} x[k] + x[n] \\ &= y[n-1] + x[n] && (4.44) \end{aligned}$$

Now, note that the system, $w[n] = y[n] - y[n-1]$ is the true inverse of the system represented by equation (4.44), which is indeed, $x[n]$.

4.5.3 Causality of Systems

A system is *causal* if the output at any instant depends only on the values of the input at that instant and in the past. Such a system is often said to be *non-anticipative*, as *it cannot anticipate future values of inputs while calculating the output at any instance of time.* Therefore, if two inputs to a causal system are identical up to some point in time t_0 or n_0, then the corresponding outputs must also be equal up to this same time. RC circuits are causal. Similarly, the motion of an automotive is causal. Examples for a *non-causal systems* are

$$y[n] = 2x[n] + 5x[n+2], \text{ and} \tag{4.45}$$

$$w(t) = y(t+1). \tag{4.46}$$

The reader is encouraged to test the system

$$y[n] = x[-n] \tag{4.47}$$

for causality.[2] Note that all memory less systems are causal, since the output depends only on the current value of the input.

Causality is not often an essential constraint in applications where the independent variable is not time, such as in image processing. Moreover, if the processed data has been stored earlier as in the case of speech, geo-physical, and meteorological signals, we are not at all limited by causal processing.

4.5.4 Stability of Systems

Stability is an important system property. There are several kinds of stability. We will consider them in this section.

Asymptotical Stability

If a system is brought into any particular initial condition (or state) and its response decays continuously to the *zero state*, the system is said to be *asymptotically stable*. On the other hand, if the response grows without any limit, it is an *unstable system*. A gravity-driven pendulum is an example of a stable system, in the asymptotical sense.

Bounded Input Bounded Output (BIBO) Stability

If a system is excited with a bounded input, $x(t)$ such that:

$$|x(t)| \leq \delta_1 \leq \infty$$

and its output is also bounded, then it is *bounded input bounded output (BIBO) stable*. A linear time invariant (LTI) system, which is BIBO stable is also asymptotically stable and vice versa.

[2]The above system can be shown to be non-causal, for $n < 0$.

For example, the system denoted by:

$$y[n] = \sum_{k=-N_0}^{N_0} x[k]$$

is BIBO stable. The reader may verify this statement.

4.5.5 Time Invariance

A system is *time invariant* or *shift invariant* if the behaviour and characteristics of the system are fixed over time. That is, for a time (shift) invariant system, if

$$\begin{aligned} x(t) &\longrightarrow y(t), \text{ then} \\ x(t-t_0) &\longrightarrow y(t-t_0). \end{aligned}$$

The system represented by the relation, $y(t) = \sin[x(t)]$ is a time invariant system, whereas the systems $y[n] = n\,x[n]$ and $y(t) = x(2t)$ are *not time invariant.*

4.5.6 Linearity of Systems

A system possessing the *property of superposition* is said to be a linear system. Mathematically, if

$$\begin{aligned} x_1(t) &\longrightarrow y_1(t), \text{ and} \\ x_2(t) &\longrightarrow y_2(t), \text{ then iff} \\ a\,x_1(t) + b\,x_2(t) &\longrightarrow a\,y_1(t) + b\,y_2(t), \end{aligned}$$

then the system is linear. For example, the system $y(t) = t^2 x(t)$ is linear, whereas the system $y(t) = 4\,x^2(t)$ is non-linear.

4.6 Linear Time Invariant Systems

Linearity and time invariance properties play a key role in signal analysis. Many systems possess these two fundamental properties and they are called linear time invariant (LTI) systems. LTI systems are amenable to superposition and can be characterised by the *convolution integral* or the *convolution sum.*

4.6.1 Discrete Time LTI Systems and the Convolution Sum

The discrete time sequence can be visualised as a sum of discrete time (scaled and shifted) unit impulse sequences.

Representation of Discrete Time Signals in Terms of Impulses

This follows from equation (4.29):

$$\begin{aligned} x[n] &= \ldots + x[-3]\delta[n+3] + x[-2]\delta[n+2] + x[-1]\delta[n+1] + \\ &\quad x[0]\delta[n] + x[1]\delta[n-1] + x[2]\delta[n-2] + x[3]\delta[n-3] + \ldots \qquad (4.48) \\ x[n] &= \sum_{k=-\infty}^{+\infty} x[k]\delta[n-k] \qquad (4.49) \end{aligned}$$

Equation (4.49) corresponds to the representation of an arbitrary sequence $x[n]$ as a linear combination of shifted unit impulses $\delta[n-k]$, where the weights of the linear combination are $x[k]$. The equation is called the *sifting property* of the discrete time unit impulse.

Discrete Time Impulse Response

The importance of the sifting property is that it represents $x[n]$ as a superposition of scaled versions of a very simple set of elementary sequences, namely, shifted unit impulses $\delta[n-k]$, each of which is non-zero (with value 1) at a single point in time given by the variable k. *The response of a linear system to $x[n]$ will be the superposition of scaled responses of the system to each of these shifted impulses.* In addition, the property of time invariance states that the responses of a time invariant system to the time shifted unit impulses are simply time shifted versions of one another. The convolution sum representation of an LTI system results from these two basic facts.

Convolution Sum Representation of LTI Systems

If the response of an LTI system to a unit impulse sequence $\delta[n]$ is $h[n]$ (which is referred to as the *impulse response* of the system), the response of the same LTI system to an arbitrary input sequence, $x[n]$ is given by the convolution sum:

$$\begin{aligned} y[n] &= \sum_{k=-\infty}^{\infty} x[k]h[n-k] \\ y[n] &= x[n] * h[n] \end{aligned}$$

4.6.2 LTI Systems and the Convolution Integral

There is a similarity between discrete time and continuous time systems, in representing the outputs to arbitrary inputs. We first represent continuous time signals in terms of impulse signals.

Representation of Continuous Time Signals in Terms of Impulses

It follows from equation (4.37):

$$\hat{x}(t) = \ldots + x(-2\Delta)\delta_\Delta(t+2\Delta)\Delta + x(-\Delta)\delta_\Delta(t+\Delta)\Delta + x(0)\delta_\Delta(t)\Delta + x(\Delta)\delta_\Delta(t-\Delta)\Delta + x(2\Delta)\delta_\Delta(t-2\Delta)\Delta + \ldots \tag{4.50}$$

$$\hat{x}(t) = \sum_{k=-\infty}^{+\infty} x(k\Delta)\delta_\Delta(t-k\Delta)\Delta \tag{4.51}$$

As we let Δ approach 0, the approximation $\hat{x}(t)$ becomes better and better, and in the limit, it becomes equal to $x(t)$:

$$x(t) = \lim_{\Delta\to 0} \sum_{k=-\infty}^{+\infty} x(k\Delta)\delta_\Delta(t-k\Delta)\Delta \tag{4.52}$$

$$x(t) = \int_{\tau=-\infty}^{+\infty} x(\tau)\delta(t-\tau)\,d\tau \tag{4.53}$$

Continuous Time Impulse Response

As in the discrete time case, the response of an LTI system to a unit impulse signal is called impulse response of the system. The impulse response is usually denoted by $h(t)$.

Convolution Integral Representation of LTI Systems

The response of an LTI system to an arbitrary input signal $x(t)$ is given by the convolution integral:

$$y(t) = \int_{\tau=-\infty}^{+\infty} x(\tau)h(t-\tau)\,d\tau \tag{4.54}$$

$$y(t) = x(t) * h(t)$$

4.6.3 Properties of LTI Systems

We will now consider various properties of LTI systems. These properties are inherent in special cases of general linear systems.

Commutative Property

The commutative property states that the order in which the convolution sum is calculated is immaterial. Mathematically:

$$y(t) = x(t) * h(t) = h(t) * x(t) = \int_{\tau=-\infty}^{\infty} h(\tau)x(t-\tau)\, d\tau$$

$$y[n] = x[n] * h[n] = h[n] * x[n] = \sum_{k=-\infty}^{\infty} h[k]x[n-k]$$

The above results can easily be proved by a suitable change of variables.

Distributive Property

The distributive property is mathematically expressed as:

$$x[n] * (h_1[n] + h_2[n]) = x[n] * h_1[n] + x[n] * h_2[n]$$

$$x(t) * [h_1(t) + h_2(t)] = x(t) * h_1(t) + x(t) * h_2(t)$$

Associative Property

The associative property is mathematically expressed as:

$$x[n] * (h_1[n] * h_2[n]) = (x[n] * h_1[n]) * h_2[n]$$

$$x(t) * [h_1(t) * h_2(t)] = [x(t) * h_1(t)] * h_2(t)$$

LTI Systems with and without Memory

An LTI system is said to be without memory if its output at any time depends only on the value of the input at that same time. It follows that *an LTI system is memory less if its impulse response, $h[n]$ is zero for $n \neq 0$.* Hence for an LTI system without memory, the impulse response can be represented as

$$h[n] = K\,\delta[n]$$

$$h(t) = K\,\delta(t)$$

where $K = h[0]$ is a constant. Now the convolution sum becomes:

$$y[n] = K\,x[n]$$

$$y(t) = K\,x(t)$$

If a discrete time LTI system has an impulse response $h[n] \neq 0$ for $n \neq 0$, then the system has memory.

Invertibility of LTI Systems

For a discrete time LTI system with impulse response $h[n]$ to be invertible, there should be another system with impulse response $h_1[n]$ such that:

$$h[n] * h_1[n] = \delta[n]$$

A similar relation exists in the case of continuous time LTI systems.

EXAMPLE 4.2
Find the inverse system of the LTI system represented by

$$y(t) = x(t - t_0)$$

SOLUTION
The impulse response $h(t)$ of the system is the output of the system when the input is the unit impulse signal, $\delta(t)$. Hence,

$$h(t) = \delta(t - t_0)$$

Now, if the inverse system has an impulse response, $h_1(t)$ then:

$$\begin{aligned} h(t) * h_1(t) &= \delta(t) \\ &= \delta(t - t_0) * \delta(t + t_0) \end{aligned}$$

Hence, the inverse system can be represented as:

$$w(t) = y(t + t_0)$$

Causality of LTI Systems

For an LTI system to be causal, the condition is:

$$h[n] = 0, \quad \text{for } n < 0$$

Therefore, it follows that for *causal LTI systems*:

$$\begin{aligned} y[n] &= \sum_{k=0}^{\infty} h[k]x[n-k] = \sum_{k=-\infty}^{n} x[k]h[n-k] \\ y(t) &= \int_{\tau=0}^{\infty} h(\tau)x(t-\tau)\,d\tau = \int_{\tau=-\infty}^{t} x(\tau)h(t-\tau)\,d\tau \end{aligned}$$

Stability of LTI Systems

We will consider the BIBO stability condition for LTI systems. Assume that the input sequence to an LTI system $x[n]$ is bounded by B:

$$|x[n]| < B, \ \ \forall n.$$

Then,

$$\begin{aligned} |y[n]| &= |\sum_{k=-\infty}^{\infty} h[k]x[n-k]| \\ &\leq \sum_{k=-\infty}^{\infty} |h[k]||x[n-k]| \end{aligned}$$

Now,

$$|x[n-k]| < B, \ \ \forall k, \ \ \forall n$$

Therefore,

$$|y[n]| \leq B \leq \sum_{-\infty}^{\infty} |h[k]|, \ \ \forall n \tag{4.55}$$

That is, *if $h[n]$ is absolutely summable, i.e.* $\sum_{-\infty}^{\infty} |h[k]| < \infty$, *then $y[n]$ is bounded, and the system is stable.*

4.6.4 Unit Step Response of an LTI System

The response of the continuous time LTI system to a unit step sequence, $s(t)$ is an important output to be considered. If the LTI system impulse response is $h(t)$, then the step response is given by:

$$\begin{aligned} s(t) &= u(t) * h(t) \\ &= \int_{\tau=-\infty}^{t} h(\tau)\, d\tau = \int_{\tau=0}^{\infty} h(t-\tau)\, d\tau \end{aligned}$$

In the discrete time case, we have:

$$\begin{aligned} s[n] &= u[n] * h[n] \\ &= \sum_{k=-\infty}^{n} h[k] = \sum_{k=0}^{\infty} h[n-k] \end{aligned}$$

From the above equations, it follows that:

$$\begin{aligned} s[n] &= \sum_{k=-\infty}^{n} h[k] = \sum_{k=-\infty}^{n-1} h[k] + h[n] \\ &= s[n-1] + h[n] \\ \Rightarrow h[n] &= s[n] - s[n-1] \end{aligned}$$

That is, for a discrete time LTI system, *impulse response is the difference between step responses at instances n and $n-1$*. Similarly, for continuous time systems we have:

$$h(t) = \frac{d\,s(t)}{dt} = s'(t)$$

Therefore, for a continuous time LTI system, *the impulse response can be obtained from the step response by taking the first time derivative.*

4.6.5 Linear Differential/Difference Equations

An LTI system can be represented by means of a set of linear constant coefficient differential (difference) equations. These equations relate the input of the LTI system to its output. We will first consider the continuous time case.

Linear Constant Coefficient Differential Equations

A continuous time LTI system can, in general, be represented by an Nth order linear differential equation as:

$$\sum_{l=0}^{N} a_l \frac{d^l y(t)}{dt^l} = \sum_{k=0}^{M} b_k \frac{d^k x(t)}{dt^k} \tag{4.56}$$

In general, the above equation represents an LTI system that is *recursive*. When $l = 0$, we get:

$$y(t) = \sum_{k=0}^{M} \frac{b_k}{a_0} \frac{d^k x(t)}{dt^k} \tag{4.57}$$

Linear Constant Coefficient Difference Equations

Similarly, a discrete time LTI system of order N can be represented by:

$$\sum_{l=0}^{N} a_l y[n-l] = \sum_{k=0}^{M} b_k x[n-k] \tag{4.58}$$

Equation (4.58), in general, represents a *recursive LTI system*, the one with feedback from output to input. Note that a discrete time recursive system is also known as an *infinite impulse response (IIR)* system, as the *impulse response of the system is infinite in the time domain*. When $l = 0$ in equation (4.58), we get:

$$y[n] = \sum_{k=0}^{M} \frac{b_k}{a_0} x[n-k] \tag{4.59}$$

The LTI system represented by equation (4.59) is *non-recursive* as there is *no feedback from the output to the input*. A non-recursive system is also known as a *finite impulse response (FIR)* system, as its *impulse response is finite in the time domain*. The impulse response $h(n)$ of an FIR system can be represented as:

$$h(n) = \begin{cases} \dfrac{b_n}{a_0}, & 0 \le n \le M \\ 0, & \text{otherwise} \end{cases}$$

In the following section, we will consider an alternate representation of signals and LTI systems. The approach is based on representing signals (sequences) in the frequency domain rather than in the time domain.

4.7 The Fourier Series Representation

In this section, we will consider the representation of continuous time (discrete time) periodic signals (sequences) as Fourier series. Then we will extend the concept of a Fourier transform (FT) to represent a broad class of aperiodic, finite energy signals (sequences). Fourier series and the Fourier transform provide the most powerful and important sets of tools for analysing, designing, and understanding signals (sequences) and LTI systems.

4.7.1 A History of the Fourier Series and Transform

The idea of using "trigonometric sums" (sums of harmonically related sines and cosines) to represent periodic signals was known to the Babylonians. The modern history of trigonometric sums begins with L. Euler (Figure 4.21), a pioneering Swiss mathematician and physicist, who studied the motion of a vibrating string in 1748.

Figure 4.21 Leonhard Paul Euler (April 15, 1707–September 18, 1783)

Euler found that the "normal modes" in a vibrating string are harmonically related sinusoidal functions of the distance from the origin, x. Further, Euler showed that one could calculate the coefficients for the linear combination at a later time in a very straightforward manner from the coefficients observed at an earlier time.

In 1753, Daniel Bernoulli (Figure 4.22), a Dutch mathematician, showed that all physical motions of a string could be represented by linear combinations of normal modes. But his ideas were not widely accepted. [3] In 1759, J. L. Lagrange (Figure 4.23) argued that signals with discontinuities cannot be represented with trigonometric series.[4]

Figure 4.22 Daniel Bernoulli (February 8, 1700–March 17, 1782)

Figure 4.23 Joseph Louis Lagrange (January 25, 1736–April 10, 1813)

[3]Daniel Bernoulli's most important work considered the basic properties of fluid flow, pressure, density and velocity, and gave their fundamental relationship now known as Bernoulli's principle. Find out more at: http://www-history.mcs.st-andrews.ac.uk/history/ Mathematicians/Bernoulli_Daniel.html

[4]Joseph Louis Lagrange (January 25, 1736–April 10, 1813) was a mathematician and astronomer who made outstanding contributions to all fields of analysis, to number theory, and to classical and celestial mechanics. On the recommendation of Euler and D'Alembert, in 1766, Lagrange succeeded Euler as the director of mathematics at the Prussian Academy of Sciences in Berlin.

The physical motivation for Joseph Fourier's (Figure 4.24) work was the phenomenon of heat flow and diffusion in materials.[5] In 1807, Fourier was able to apply a series of harmonically related sinusoids to represent the temperature distribution through a body. In 1822, he published his *Theorie Analytique de la Chaleur*, in which he based his reasoning on Newton's law of cooling, namely, that the flow of heat between two adjacent molecules is proportional to the extremely small difference of their temperatures. In this work, Fourier claimed that any function of a variable, whether continuous or discontinuous, can be expanded into a series of sines of multiples of the variable. Though this result is not correct, Fourier's observation that some discontinuous functions are the sum of an infinite series was a breakthrough. It was Joham Dirichlet (Figure 4.25), a German mathematician, who provided the precise mathematical conditions under which a function can be represented by the Fourier series. In mathematics, the Dirichlet conditions are sufficient conditions for a periodic function $f(x)$ to have a Fourier series representation or to possess a Fourier transform. The conditions are:

1. $f(x)$ must have a finite number of extrema in any given interval.
2. $f(x)$ must have a finite number of discontinuities in any given interval.
3. $f(x)$ must be absolutely integrable over a period.

Figure 4.24 Jean Baptiste Joseph Fourier (March 21, 1768–May 16, 1830)

[5] Jean Baptiste Joseph (Baron) Fourier (1768–1830) was a remarkable French physicist who was also an outstanding mathematician. He was orphaned at eight, and educated in a military school run by the Benedictines who then gave him a lectureship in mathematics. He later moved to a chair at the Ecole Polytechnique in Paris, and later to Grenoble where he was appointed Prefect by Napoleon. In Grenoble, his experiments on heat conduction suggested by Newton's law of cooling, led him to propose his famous law of heat conduction (Fourier's law) and to the publication of his most important *Theorie Analytique de la Chaleur* in which he introduced the representation of an arbitrary function over an interval in terms of trigonometric functions, now called Fourier series. He was coronated as a Baron by Napoleon in 1808.

Figure 4.25 Johann Peter Gustav Lejeune Dirichlet (February 13, 1805–May 5, 1859)

4.7.2 Response of LTI Systems to Complex Exponentials

The importance of complex exponentials—i.e., signals of the form e^{st} in continuous time and z^n in discrete time, where s and z are complex variables—originate from the fact that *the response of an LTI system to a complex exponential input is the same complex exponential with only a change in amplitude*; that is:

$$\text{continuous time case}: \quad e^{st} \longrightarrow H(s)e^{st} \tag{4.60}$$

$$\text{discrete time case}: \quad z^n \longrightarrow H(z)z^n \tag{4.61}$$

where the complex amplitude factor[6] $H(s)$ or $H(z)$ will in general be a function of the complex variable s or z. To prove that complex exponentials are indeed eigen functions of LTI systems, assume that the input to the continuous time LTI system with impulse response $h(t)$ is $x(t) = e^{st}$. Then we have:

$$\begin{aligned} y(t) &= \int_{\tau=-\infty}^{+\infty} h(\tau)x(t-\tau)d\tau \\ &= \int_{\tau=-\infty}^{+\infty} h(\tau)e^{s(t-\tau)}d\tau = e^{st}\int_{\tau=-\infty}^{+\infty} h(\tau)e^{-s\tau}d\tau \end{aligned} \tag{4.62}$$

Assuming that the integral on the right-hand side of equation (4.62) converges, the response of the LTI system to input e^{st} will be of the form:

$$y(t) = H(s)e^{st} \tag{4.63}$$

[6] A signal for which the system response is a complex constant times the input is referred to as an *eigen function* of the system, and the amplitude factor is referred to as the system's *eigen value*.

where $H(s)$ is a complex constant whose value depends on s and which is related to the system impulse response by:

$$H(s) = \int_{\tau=-\infty}^{+\infty} h(\tau)e^{-s\tau}d\tau \tag{4.64}$$

The $H(s)$ is indeed the *Laplace transform* of the system impulse response and is termed as a *continuous system transfer function.*

In an analogous manner, we can show that complex exponential sequences are eigen functions of discrete time LTI systems. Assume that the input sequence $x[n] = z^n$, where z is complex number. The system response $y[n]$ is given by:

$$\begin{aligned} y[n] &= \sum_{k=-\infty}^{+\infty} h[k]x[n-k] \\ &= \sum_{k=-\infty}^{+\infty} h[k]z^{n-k} = z^n \sum_{k=-\infty}^{+\infty} h[k]z^{-k} \end{aligned} \tag{4.65}$$

Assuming that the summation on the right-side of equation (4.65) converges, the output of the discrete time LTI system is the same complex exponential multiplied by a constant that depends on the value of z. That is:

$$y[n] = H(z)z^n \tag{4.66}$$

where

$$H(z) = \sum_{k=-\infty}^{+\infty} h[k]z^{-k} \tag{4.67}$$

Here, $H(z)$ is indeed the *z-transform* of the discrete time system impulse response, which is called the *discrete system transfer function.*

Let $x(t) = \sum_k b_k e^{s_k t}$ (sum of several complex exponentials) be the input to a continuous time LTI system. Then it follows that the output of the system can be expressed as:

$$y(t) = \sum_k b_k H(s_k)e^{s_k t}$$

Similarly, for a discrete time LTI system, let $x[n] = \sum_k b_k z_k^n$ be the input to the system. Then the output of the system can be represented as:

$$y[n] = \sum_k b_k H(z_k)z_k^n$$

4.7.3 Fourier Series Representation of Continuous Time Periodic Signals

The Fourier series representation of a continuous time periodic function $f(x)$ over the interval $-\pi \leq x \leq \pi$ is an expression of the form:

$$\begin{aligned} f(x) &= a_0 + \sum_{n=1}^{\infty}(a_n \cos nx + b_n \sin nx) \\ &= a_0 + a_1 \cos x + b_1 \sin x + a_2 \cos 2x + b_2 \sin 2x + \ldots \end{aligned} \tag{4.68}$$

where the coefficients a_n and b_n are determined by the function $f(x)$. It is important to note that the Fourier series representation of $f(x)$ contains two infinite sums, one of even functions (the cosines) and the other of odd functions (the sines). Recall that a function $f(x)$ defined in the interval $-T \leq x \leq T$ is said to be an even function in the interval if $f(-x) = f(x)$ and to be an odd function if $f(-x) = -f(x)$. Most functions are neither even nor odd, but any function in an interval $-T \leq x \leq T$ can be expressed as the sum of an even function and an odd function defined over the interval, $-T \leq x \leq T$.

To arrive at a formula for the a_n in equation (4.68) corresponding to a given function $f(x)$, the equation is first multiplied term by term by $\cos nx$ and integrated over the interval $-\pi$ to π to obtain

$$\begin{aligned} \int_{x=-\pi}^{\pi} f(x) \cos nx \, dx &= a_0 \int_{x=-\pi}^{\pi} \cos nx \, dx + a_1 \int_{x=-\pi}^{\pi} \cos x \cos nx \, dx \\ &+ a_2 \int_{x=-\pi}^{\pi} \cos 2x \cos nx \, dx + a_3 \int_{x=-\pi}^{\pi} \cos 3x \cos nx \, dx + \ldots \\ &+ a_{n-1} \int_{x=-\pi}^{\pi} \cos (n-1)x \cos nx \, dx + a_n \int_{x=-\pi}^{\pi} \cos^2 nx \, dx + \ldots \\ &+ b_1 \int_{x=-\pi}^{\pi} \sin x \cos nx \, dx + b_2 \int_{x=-\pi}^{\pi} \sin 2x \cos nx \, dx + \ldots \end{aligned}$$

The orthogonality properties of the sine and cosine functions shows that all integrals on the right except the one with the integrand $\cos^2 nx$ vanish, giving rise to the result

$$\int_{x=-\pi}^{\pi} f(x) \cos nx \, dx = a_n \int_{x=-\pi}^{\pi} \cos^2 nx \, dx.$$

However, $\int\limits_{x=-\pi}^{\pi} \cos^2 nx\,dx = \pi$, for $n \neq 0$ and $\int\limits_{-\pi}^{\pi} 1\,dx = 2\pi$, for $n = 0$. Hence

$$a_0 = \frac{1}{2\pi}\int\limits_{x=-\pi}^{\pi} f(x)\,dx, \text{ and} \tag{4.69}$$

$$a_n = \frac{1}{\pi}\int\limits_{x=-\pi}^{\pi} f(x)\cos nx\,dx. \tag{4.70}$$

Similarly we can obtain b_n as

$$b_n = \frac{1}{\pi}\int\limits_{x=-\pi}^{\pi} f(x)\sin nx\,dx, \quad \text{for } n = 1, 2, 3, \ldots. \tag{4.71}$$

These results are the *Euler formulas* for the Fourier coefficients a_n and b_n.

The interval of integration $-\pi \leq x \leq \pi$ used when deriving the Euler formulas is called the *fundamental interval* of the Fourier series, and the Fourier coefficients will always be defined provided the integral $\int\limits_{-\pi}^{\pi} f(x)\,dx$ exists.[7]

Fourier Series Representation of $f(x)$ over the Interval $-T \leq x \leq T$

Let the function $f(t)$ be defined on the interval $-T \leq x \leq T$. Then the Fourier coefficients a_n and b_n in the Fourier series representation of $f(t)$,

$$f(t) = a_0 + \sum_{n=1}^{\infty}\left(a_n \cos\frac{2n\,\pi\,t}{T} + b_n \sin\frac{2n\,\pi\,t}{T}\right)$$

are given by the Euler formulas:

$$a_0 = \frac{1}{2T}\int\limits_{-T}^{T} f(t)\,dt \tag{4.72}$$

$$a_n = \frac{1}{T}\int\limits_{-T}^{T} f(t)\cos\frac{2n\,\pi\,t}{T}\,dt = \frac{1}{T}\int\limits_{-T}^{T} f(t)\cos(n\,\omega_0\,t)\,dt \tag{4.73}$$

$$b_n = \frac{1}{T}\int\limits_{-T}^{T} f(t)\sin\frac{2n\,\pi\,t}{T}\,dt = \frac{1}{T}\int\limits_{-T}^{T} f(t)\sin(n\,\omega_0\,t)\,dt, \quad \text{for } n = 1, 2, 3, \ldots \tag{4.74}$$

where $\omega_0 = \frac{2\pi}{T}$ is the *fundamental period* of the continuous time signal, $f(t)$.

---

[7] Although Fourier series comprise only even and odd functions, it can be used to represent arbitrary functions that are neither even nor odd.

Exponential Form of Fourier Series

The exponential form of the Fourier series of a continuous time signal is obtained as:

$$f(t) = \sum_{k=-\infty}^{\infty} a_k e^{jk\,\omega_0\,t} = \sum_{k=-\infty}^{\infty} a_k e^{jk\frac{2\pi}{T}t} \tag{4.75}$$

where the exponential Fourier series coefficients, a_k are given by:

$$a_k = \frac{1}{T}\int_T f(t)e^{-jk\,\omega_0\,t}dt = \frac{1}{T}\int_T f(t)e^{-jk\frac{2\pi}{T}t}dt \tag{4.76}$$

Gibb's Phenomenon

Quite often, we can approximate a continuous time periodic function by a sum of a *finite number* of terms. This is illustrated in Figure 4.26 for a square wave. We denote the finite series approximation of the continuous time periodic signal by:

$$x_N(t) = \sum_{k=-N}^{N} a_k e^{jk\,\omega_0\,t} \tag{4.77}$$

The MATLAB script file to generate the waveforms is given below:

```
%%% MATLAB script to demonstrate the
%%% Gibb's phenomenon..
clear all; close all; clf;
t=linspace(-2,2,2000);
u=linspace(-2,2,2000);
sq=[zeros(1,500),2*ones(1,1000),zeros(1,500)];
k=2;
N=[1,3,7,19,49,70];
for n=1:6;
an=[];
for  m=1:N(n)
    an=[an,2*k*sin(m*pi/2)/(m*pi)];
end;
fN=k/2;
for m=1:N(n)
    fN=fN+an(m)*cos(m*pi*t/2);
end;
nq=int2str(N(n));
subplot(3,2,n),plot(u,sq,'r','LineWidth',2);hold on;
```

```
plot(t,fN,'LineWidth',2); hold off; axis([-2 2 -0.5 2.5]);grid;
xlabel('Time'), ylabel('y_N(t)');title(['N= ',nq]);
end;
%%% End of gibb.m
```

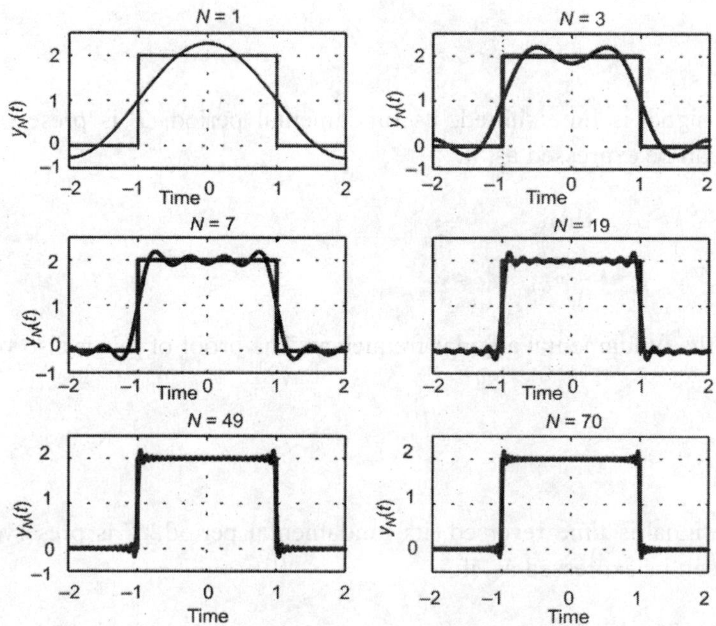

Figure 4.26 Illustration of Gibb's phenomenon. Finite sum approximation, $f_N(t)$ of a continuous time signal for different values of N.

4.7.4 Properties of Continuous Time Fourier Series

Throughout the following discussion we will use the notation given below to represent the function, $x(t)$ and its Fourier series coefficients, a_k:

$$x(t) \overset{\mathcal{FS}}{\longleftrightarrow} a_k$$

Linearity

Let $x(t)$ and $y(t)$ be two periodic signals with period T and having Fourier series coefficients a_k and b_k respectively. Then if:

$$\begin{aligned} x(t) &\overset{\mathcal{FS}}{\longleftrightarrow} a_k, \text{ and} \\ y(t) &\overset{\mathcal{FS}}{\longleftrightarrow} b_k, \text{ then} \\ Ax(t) + By(t) &\overset{\mathcal{FS}}{\longleftrightarrow} Aa_k + Bb_k. \end{aligned} \tag{4.78}$$

In short, the Fourier series coefficients obey the principle of superposition. The reader is encouraged to prove the *linearity* property.

Time Shifting

When a periodic signal is time shifted, its fundamental period, T is preserved. The time shifting property can be expressed as, if:

$$\begin{aligned} x(t) &\overset{\mathcal{FS}}{\longleftrightarrow} a_k, \text{ then} \\ x(t-t_0) &\overset{\mathcal{FS}}{\longleftrightarrow} e^{-jk\omega_0 t_0} a_k \end{aligned} \tag{4.79}$$

where $\omega_0 = \frac{2\pi}{T}$ is the fundamental angular frequency. The proof of this is also very trivial.

Time Reversal

When a periodic signal is time reversed, its fundamental period, T is preserved. The time reversal property can be expressed as, if:

$$\begin{aligned} x(t) &\overset{\mathcal{FS}}{\longleftrightarrow} a_k, \text{ then} \\ x(-t) &\overset{\mathcal{FS}}{\longleftrightarrow} a_{-k}. \end{aligned} \tag{4.80}$$

In essence, time reversal applied to a continuous time signal results in a time reversal of the corresponding sequence of Fourier series coefficients. It follows that for an even signal, for which $x(t) = x(-t)$, we have $a_{-k} = a_k$. Similarly, when $x(t)$ is *odd*, we have: $a_{-k} = -a_k$.

Time Scaling

If $x(t)$ is a periodic with fundamental period T and fundamental frequency $\omega_0 = 2\pi/T$, then $x(\alpha t)$, where α is a positive real number, is periodic with fundamental period T/α and fundamental frequency, $\alpha\omega_0$. Since *the time scaling applies directly to each of the harmonic components of $x(t)$, we may conclude that the Fourier series coefficients of these components remain the same*. In other words:

$$x(\alpha t) = \sum_{k=-\infty}^{\infty} a_k e^{jk(\alpha\omega_0)t} \tag{4.81}$$

Multiplicative Property

Let both $x(t)$ and $y(t)$ be periodic with period T, then the multiplicative property is stated as, if:

$$\begin{aligned} x(t) &\overset{\mathcal{FS}}{\longleftrightarrow} a_k, \text{ and} \\ y(t) &\overset{\mathcal{FS}}{\longleftrightarrow} b_k, \text{ then} \\ x(t).y(t) &\overset{\mathcal{FS}}{\longleftrightarrow} h_k = \sum_{l=-\infty}^{\infty} a_l b_{k-l}. \end{aligned} \tag{4.82}$$

Note that the product $x(t)y(t)$ is also periodic with period T.

Conjugative Property

Taking the complex conjugate of a periodic signal $x(t)$ has the same effect as complex conjugation and time reversal of the corresponding Fourier series coefficients. Thus we have:

$$\begin{aligned} x(t) &\overset{\mathcal{FS}}{\longleftrightarrow} a_k, \text{ then} \\ x^*(t) &\overset{\mathcal{FS}}{\longleftrightarrow} a^*_{-k}. \end{aligned} \tag{4.83}$$

Note that when $x(t)$ is *real*, i.e., $x(t) = x^*(t)$, the Fourier series coefficients are *conjugate symmetric.* That is:

$$\begin{aligned} a_{-k} &= a_k^* \\ |a_k| &= |a_{-k}| \\ \Re e\,(a_k) &= \Re e\,(a_{-k}) \\ \Im m\,(a_k) &= -\Im m\,(a_{-k}) \\ \angle a_k &= -\angle a_{-k} \end{aligned} \tag{4.84}$$

If $x(t)$ is *real and even*, then, $a_k = a_{-k}$, which implies that $a_k^* = a_{-k}$ so that $a_k = a_k^*$. That is *if $x(t)$ is real and even, so are its Fourier series coefficients.* Similarly, it can be shown that *if $x(t)$ is real and odd, then its Fourier series coefficients are purely imaginary and odd.* Thus $a_0 = 0$ if $x(t)$ is *real and odd.*

Parseval's Relation

Parseval's relation is:

$$\frac{1}{T}\int_T |x(t)|^2 dt = \sum_{k=-\infty}^{\infty} |a_k|^2 \tag{4.85}$$

where the a_ks are the Fourier series coefficients of $x(t)$ and T is the fundamental period of the signal. Note that the left-hand side of equation (4.85) is the *average power* (i.e., the energy per unit time) in one period of the periodic signal $x(t)$. Also note that:

$$\frac{1}{T}\int_T |a_k e^{jk\omega_0 t}|^2 dt = \frac{1}{T}\int_T |a_k| = |a_k|^2 \tag{4.86}$$

so that $|a_k|^2$ is the average power in the kth harmonic component of $x(t)$. Thus Parseval's relation states that *the total average power in a periodic signal equals the sum of the average powers in all of its harmonic components.*

The properties of continuous fourier series coefficients are summarised in Table 4.1.

Table 4.1 Properties of continuous time Fourier series

Property	Periodic signal	Fourier series coefficients
Linearity	$Ax(t) + By(t)$	$Aa_k + Bb_k$
Time shifting	$x(t - t_0)$	$e^{-jk(2\pi/T)t_0} a_k$
Time reversal	$x(-t)$	a_{-k}
Time scaling	$x(\alpha t)$, periodic with period T	periodic with period, $\frac{T}{\alpha}$
Multiplication	$x(t).y(t)$	$\sum\limits_{l=-\infty}^{\infty} a_l b_{k-l}$
Conjugate symmetry	$x(t)$, real	$\begin{cases} a_k = a^*_{-k} \\ \Re e\{a_k\} = \Re e\{a_{-k}\} \\ \Im m\{a_k\} = -\Im m\{a_{-k}\} \\ \lvert a_k\rvert = \lvert a_{-k}\rvert \\ \angle a_k = -\angle a_{-k} \end{cases}$
	$x(t)$ real and even	a_k real and even.
	$x(t)$ real and odd	a_k purely imaginary and odd.
Parseval's relation	$x(t)$	$\frac{1}{T}\int_T \lvert x(t)\rvert^2 dt = \sum\limits_{k=-\infty}^{\infty} \lvert a_k\rvert^2$

4.7.5 Fourier Series Representation of Discrete Time Periodic Sequences

The set of all discrete time complex exponential signals that are periodic with period N is given by

$$\Phi_k[n] = e^{jk\omega_0 n} = e^{jk(2\pi/N)n}, \quad k = 0, \pm 1, \pm 2, \ldots \tag{4.87}$$

All of these have fundamental frequencies that are multiples of $2\pi/N$ and thus harmonically related. Note that there are only N distinct signals in the set given by equation (4.87). This is due to the fact that

$$\Phi_k[n] = \Phi_{k+rN}[n] \tag{4.88}$$

Now, the Fourier series coefficients a_k are related to the discrete periodic sequence $x[n]$ as shown below:

$$x[n] = \sum_k a_k \Phi_k[n] = \sum_k a_k e^{jk\omega_0 n} = \sum_k a_k e^{jk(2\pi/N)n} \tag{4.89}$$

The summation on k, as k varies over a range of N successive integers, beginning with any value of k, is expressed by setting the limits of the summation as $k =< N >$. That is,

$$x[n] = \sum_{k=<N>} a_k \Phi_k[n] = \sum_{k=<N>} a_k e^{jk\omega_0 n} = \sum_{k=<N>} a_k e^{jk(2\pi/N)n} \tag{4.90}$$

The Fourier series coefficients a_k are given by

$$a_k = \frac{1}{N} \sum_{n=<N>} x[n] e^{-jk\omega_0 n} = \frac{1}{N} \sum_{n=<N>} x[n] e^{-jk(2\pi/N)n} \tag{4.91}$$

Equation (4.91) is known as the *analysis equation* and equation (4.90) is known as the *synthesis equation.*

4.7.6 Properties of Discrete Time Fourier Series

The properties of continuous time and discrete time Fourier series are quite similar. In fact, the linearity, time shifting, time reversal, multiplicative and conjugate symmetry properties are just the same. The properties are summarised in Table 4.2. We assume that $x[n]$ and $y[n]$ are periodic with fundamental period N.

4.8 Fourier Transform of Aperiodic Signals

Joseph Fourier reasoned that aperiodic signals can be viewed as a periodic signal with an *infinite period.* In the Fourier series representation of a periodic signal, as the period increases, the fundamental frequency $\omega_0 = 2\pi/T$ decreases and the harmonically related components become closer in frequency. As the period T becomes infinite, the frequency components form a *continuum* and the Fourier series becomes an integral. The forward Fourier transform is given by

$$X(j\omega) = \int_{-\infty}^{\infty} x(t) e^{-j\omega t} dt \tag{4.92}$$

Now the signal $x(t)$ can be obtained as

$$x(t) = \frac{1}{2\pi} \int_{-\infty}^{\infty} X(j\omega) e^{j\omega t} d\omega \tag{4.93}$$

Table 4.2 Properties of discrete time Fourier series

Property	Periodic sequence	Fourier series coefficients
Linearity	$Ax[n] + By[n]$	$Aa_k + Bb_k$
Time shifting	$x[n - n_0]$	$e^{-jk(2\pi/N)n_0}a_k$
Frequency shifting	$e^{jM(2\pi/N)n}x[n]$	a_k/M
Time reversal	$x[-n]$	a_{-k}
Time scaling	$x_{<m>}[n] = x[n/m]$, periodic with period mN	$\frac{1}{m}a_k$
Periodic convolution	$\sum_{r=<N>} x[r]y[n-r]$	Na_kb_k
Multiplication	$x[n].y[n]$	$\sum_{l=<N>} a_lb_{k-l}$
First difference	$x[n] - x[n-1]$	$\left(1 - e^{-jk(2\pi/N)}\right)a_k$
Running sum	$\sum_{k=-\infty}^{n} x[k]$	$\left(\frac{1}{1-e^{-jk(2\pi/N)}}\right)a_k$
Conjugate symmetry	$x[n]$, real	$\begin{cases} a_k = a^*_{-k} \\ \Re e\{a_k\} = \Re e\{a_{-k}\} \\ \Im m\{a_k\} = -\Im m\{a_{-k}\} \\ \lvert a_k\rvert = \lvert a_{-k}\rvert \\ \angle a_k = -\angle a_{-k} \end{cases}$
	$x[n]$ real and even	a_k real and even.
	$x[n]$ real and odd	a_k purely imaginary and odd.
Parseval's relation	$x[n]$	$\frac{1}{N}\sum_{n=<N>} \lvert x[n]\rvert^2 = \sum_{k=<N>} \lvert a_k\rvert^2$

4.8.1 Convergence of Fourier Transforms

The Dirichlet's conditions for the convergence of Fourier transforms are

1. The signal $x(t)$ must be *absolutely summable*. That is,

$$\int_{-\infty}^{\infty} |x(t)|dt < \infty$$

2. $x(t)$ must have a finite number of maxima and minima within any finite interval.

3. $x(t)$ must have a finite number of discontinuities within any finite interval; and each of this discontinuities must be finite.

Table 4.3 lists a number of signals and their respective Fourier transforms.

Table 4.3 Fourier transform pairs

Signal, $x(t)$	Fourier transform, $X(j\omega)$
$\delta(t)$	1
$\delta(t-t_0)$	$e^{-j\omega t_0}$
$x(t)=1$	$2\pi\,\delta(\omega)$
$u(t)$	$\frac{1}{j\omega}+\pi\delta(\omega)$
$tu(t)$	$\frac{1}{w^2}$
$e^{-at}u(t),\ a>0$	$\frac{1}{a+j\omega},\ a>0$
$e^{-a\|t\|}$	$\frac{2a}{a^2+\omega^2}$
$\sum_{k=-\infty}^{\infty} a_k e^{jk\omega_0 t}$	$2\pi \sum_{k=-\infty}^{\infty} a_k\delta(\omega-k\omega_0)$
$e^{j\omega_0 t}$	$2\pi\delta(\omega-\omega_0)$
$\sin(\omega_0 t)u(t)$	$\frac{\omega_0}{\omega_0^2-\omega^2}$
$\cos(\omega_0 t)u(t)$	$\frac{j\omega}{\omega_0^2-\omega^2}$
$\cos(\omega_0 t)$	$\pi[\delta(\omega-\omega_0)+\delta(\omega+\omega_0)]$
$\sin(\omega_0 t)$	$\frac{\pi}{j}[\delta(\omega-\omega_0)-\delta(\omega+\omega_0)]$
$\sum_{n=-\infty}^{\infty} \delta(t-nT)$	$\frac{2\pi}{T}\sum_{k=-\infty}^{\infty}\delta\left(\omega-\frac{2\pi k}{T}\right)$
$x(t)=\begin{cases}1, & \|t\|<T_1\\ 0, & \|t\|>T_1\end{cases}$	$\frac{2\sin(\omega T_1)}{\omega}=2T_1\text{sinc}\left(\frac{\omega T_1}{\pi}\right)$
$x(t)=\dfrac{\sin(Wt)}{\pi t}=\dfrac{W}{\pi}\text{sinc}\left(\dfrac{Wt}{\pi}\right)$	$X(j\omega)=\begin{cases}1, & \|\omega\|<W\\ 0, & \|\omega\|>W\end{cases}$

4.8.2 Properties of Fourier Transforms

We will now consider the properties of Fourier transforms.

Linearity

If

$$x(t) \overset{\mathcal{FT}}{\longleftrightarrow} X(j\omega)$$

and

$$y(t) \overset{\mathcal{FT}}{\longleftrightarrow} Y(j\omega),$$

then

$$ax(t)+by(t) \overset{\mathcal{FT}}{\longleftrightarrow} aX(j\omega)+bY(j\omega). \tag{4.94}$$

Thus the Fourier transforms satisfy the *principle of superposition*.

Time Shifting

If

$$x(t) \xleftrightarrow{\mathcal{FT}} X(j\omega),$$

then

$$x(t-t_0) \xleftrightarrow{\mathcal{FT}} e^{-j\omega t_0}X(j\omega). \tag{4.95}$$

Time Reversal

If

$$x(t) \xleftrightarrow{\mathcal{FT}} X(j\omega),$$

then

$$x(-t) \xleftrightarrow{\mathcal{FT}} X(-j\omega). \tag{4.96}$$

Conjugate Symmetry

If

$$x(t) \xleftrightarrow{\mathcal{FT}} X(j\omega),$$

then

$$x^*(t) \xleftrightarrow{\mathcal{FT}} X^*(-j\omega). \tag{4.97}$$

It follows that if $x(t)$ is real, then $X(j\omega)$ has *conjugate symmetry,* that is

$$X(-j\omega) = X^*(j\omega), \quad x(t) \text{ is real} \tag{4.98}$$

When $x(t)$ is real, so that $x^*(t) = x(t)$, then we have

$$X^*(-j\omega) = \int_{-\infty}^{\infty} x(t)e^{-j\omega t}dt = X(j\omega).$$

When $x(t)$ is both *real and even,* then $X(j\omega)$ is also *real and even*. That is, $X(-j\omega) = X(j\omega)$. This follows from

$$X(-j\omega) = \int_{-\infty}^{\infty} x(t)e^{j\omega t}dt = \int_{-\infty}^{\infty} x(-\tau)e^{-j\omega\tau}d\tau = \int_{-\infty}^{\infty} x(\tau)e^{-j\omega\tau}d\tau = X(j\omega), \quad as \ x(-\tau) = x(\tau)$$

Similarly, it can be shown that when $x(t)$ is *real and odd,* $X(j\omega)$ is purely *imaginary and odd.*

Differentiation and Integration

If

$$x(t) \stackrel{\mathcal{FT}}{\longleftrightarrow} X(j\omega),$$

then

$$\frac{d\,x(t)}{dt} = \frac{1}{2\pi}\int_{\infty}^{\infty} j\omega\, X(j\omega)e^{j\omega t}\,d\omega.$$

Hence

$$\frac{d\,x(t)}{dt} \stackrel{\mathcal{FT}}{\longleftrightarrow} j\omega X(j\omega) \tag{4.99}$$

Thus differentiation in the time domain is replaced by multiplication by $j\omega$ in the frequency domain. Therefore, it follows that

$$\int_{-\infty}^{t} x(\tau)d\tau \stackrel{\mathcal{FT}}{\longleftrightarrow} \frac{1}{j\omega}X(j\omega) + \pi X(0)\delta(\omega). \tag{4.100}$$

Differentiation in the Frequency Domain

If

$$x(t) \stackrel{\mathcal{FT}}{\longleftrightarrow} X(j\omega),$$

then

$$tx(t) \stackrel{\mathcal{FT}}{\longleftrightarrow} j\frac{d}{d\omega}X(j\omega). \tag{4.101}$$

Time and Frequency Scaling

If

$$x(t) \stackrel{\mathcal{FT}}{\longleftrightarrow} X(j\omega),$$

then

$$x(\alpha\, t) \stackrel{\mathcal{FT}}{\longleftrightarrow} \frac{1}{|\alpha|}X\left(\frac{j\omega}{\alpha}\right) \tag{4.102}$$

where α is a non-zero real number.

Duality

A signal $x(t)$ and its Fourier transform $X(j\omega)$ possess the *property of duality*. This is evident from Table 4.3.

Multiplication Property

If $y(t) = x(t).h(t)$ then $\mathcal{FT}\,[y(t)] = Y(j\omega)$ is given by

$$Y(j\omega) = \frac{1}{2\pi}\int_{-\infty}^{\infty} X(j\theta)H(j(\omega-\theta))d\theta \tag{4.103}$$

where $x(t) \overset{\mathcal{FT}}{\longleftrightarrow} X(j\omega)$ and $y(t) \overset{\mathcal{FT}}{\longleftrightarrow} Y(j\omega)$. Thus when two signals are multiplied, their Fourier transforms are convolved in the frequency domain. That is

$$x(t)y(t) \overset{\mathcal{FT}}{\longleftrightarrow} X(j\omega) * Y(j\omega)$$

Convolution Property

The convolution property of Fourier transforms follows from the multiplication property and the duality principle. That is, when two signals are convolved in the time domain, their Fourier transforms are multiplied in the frequency domain. Hence

$$y(t) = x(t) * h(t) \overset{\mathcal{FT}}{\longleftrightarrow} X(j\omega)H(j\omega) \tag{4.104}$$

Parseval's relation

If $x(t)$ and $X(j\omega)$ are a Fourier transform pair, then

$$\int_{-\infty}^{\infty} |x(t)|^2 dt = \frac{1}{2\pi}\int_{-\infty}^{\infty} |X(j\omega)|^2 d\omega \tag{4.105}$$

In Table 4.4 we list important properties of Fourier transforms.

Table 4.4 Properties of Fourier transforms

Property	Periodic signal	Fourier transform
Linearity	$ax(t) + by(t)$	$aX(j\omega) + bY(j\omega)$
Time shifting	$x(t - t_0)$	$e^{-j\omega t_0}X(j\omega)$
Time reversal	$x(-t)$	$X(-j\omega)$
Time and frequency scaling	$x(\alpha\, t)$	$\frac{1}{\vert\alpha\vert}X\left(\frac{j\omega}{\alpha}\right)$
Multiplication	$x(t).y(t)$	$X(j\omega) * Y(j\omega) = \frac{1}{2\pi}\int\limits_{-\infty}^{\infty} X(j\theta)Y(j(\omega-\theta))d\theta.$
Convolution	$x(t) * y(t)$	$X(j\omega)Y(j\omega)$
Differentiation	$\frac{d}{dt}x(t)$	$j\omega X(j\omega)$
Integration	$\int\limits_{-\infty}^{t} x(t)dt$	$\frac{1}{j\omega}X(j\omega) + \pi X(0)\delta(\omega)$
Differentiation in frequency	$tx(t)$	$j\frac{d}{d\omega}X(j\omega)$
Conjugate symmetry	$x(t)$ real	$\begin{cases} X(j\omega) & = & X^*(-j\omega) \\ \Re e\{X(j\omega)\} & = & \Re e\{X(-j\omega)\} \\ \Im m\{X(j\omega)\} & = & -\Im m\{X(-j\omega)\} \\ \vert X(j\omega)\vert & = & \vert X(-j\omega)\vert \\ \angle X(j\omega) & = & -\angle X(-j\omega) \end{cases}$
	$x(t)$ real and even	$X(j\omega)$ real and even.
	$x(t)$ real and odd	$X(j\omega)$ purely imaginary and odd.
Parseval's relation	$x(t)$	$\int\limits_{-\infty}^{\infty} \vert x(t)\vert^2 dt = \frac{1}{2\pi}\int\limits_{-\infty}^{\infty} \vert X(j\omega)\vert^2 d\omega$

4.8.3 Systems Characterised by Differential Equations

A very important and useful class of LTI systems is those for whom the input and the output satisfy a linear constant coefficient differential equation of the form

$$\sum_{l=0}^{N} a_l \frac{d^l y(t)}{dt^l} = \sum_{k=0}^{M} b_k \frac{d^k x(t)}{dt^k} \tag{4.106}$$

Consider an LTI system whose output $y(t)$ is the convolution of the input $x(t)$ and the system impulse response, $h(t)$. Then we have

$$y(t) = x(t) * h(t) = \int\limits_{\tau=-\infty}^{\infty} x(\tau)h(t-\tau)d\tau$$

Now from the convolution property we have

$$y(t) \stackrel{\mathcal{FT}}{\longleftrightarrow} Y(j\omega) = X(j\omega)H(j\omega)$$

Equivalently we can write

$$H(j\omega) = \frac{Y(j\omega)}{X(j\omega)} \tag{4.107}$$

Now applying the Fourier transform to both sides of equation (4.106), we have

$$\mathcal{FT}\left\{\sum_{l=0}^{N} a_l \frac{d^l y(t)}{dt^l}\right\} = \mathcal{FT}\left\{\sum_{k=0}^{M} b_k \frac{d^k x(t)}{dt^k}\right\} \tag{4.108}$$

From the linearity property, we have

$$\sum_{l=0}^{N} a_l\ \mathcal{FT}\left\{\frac{d^l y(t)}{dt^l}\right\} = \sum_{k=0}^{M} b_k\ \mathcal{FT}\left\{\frac{d^k x(t)}{dt^k}\right\} \tag{4.109}$$

From the differentiation property,

$$\begin{aligned} \sum_{l=0}^{N} a_l (j\omega)^l\, Y(j\omega) &= \sum_{k=0}^{M} b_k (j\omega)^k\ X(j\omega), \quad \text{that is} \\ Y(j\omega)\left[\sum_{l=0}^{N} a_l (j\omega)^l\right] &= X(j\omega)\left[\sum_{k=0}^{M} b_k (j\omega)^k\right] \end{aligned} \tag{4.110}$$

Now from equation (4.107)

$$H(j\omega) = \frac{Y(j\omega)}{X(j\omega)} = \frac{\sum_{k=0}^{M} b_k (j\omega)^k}{\sum_{l=0}^{N} a_l (j\omega)^l} \tag{4.111}$$

Note that $H(j\omega)$ is a rational function; that is, it is a ratio of polynomials in $j\omega$. The differential equation (4.106) is commonly known as the Nth order differential equation, as the equation contains derivatives of the output $y(t)$ up to the Nth derivative.

4.8.4 The Fourier Transform of Periodic Signals

We can construct the Fourier transform of a periodic signal directly from its Fourier series representation. The resulting transform consists of a *train of impulses* in the frequency domain, with the areas of the impulses proportional to the Fourier series coefficients. Consider a signal $x(t)$, whose Fourier transform $X(j\omega)$ is a single impulse of area 2π at $\omega = \omega_0$; that is

$$X(j\omega) = 2\pi\delta(\omega - \omega_0) \tag{4.112}$$

To obtain the signal $x(t)$, we apply the *inverse Fourier transform* equation

$$\begin{aligned} x(t) &= \frac{1}{2\pi}\int_{-\infty}^{\infty} 2\pi\delta(\omega - \omega_0)e^{j\omega t}d\omega \\ &= e^{j\omega_0 t} \end{aligned} \tag{4.113}$$

Therefore, in general if $X(j\omega)$ is of the form of a linear combination of impulses equally spaced in frequency, that is

$$X(j\omega) = \sum_{k=-\infty}^{\infty} 2\pi a_k \delta(\omega - k\omega_0) \tag{4.114}$$

then by applying the inverse Fourier transform formula

$$x(t) = \sum_{k=-\infty}^{\infty} a_k e^{jk\omega_0 t} \tag{4.115}$$

4.9 The Discrete Time Fourier Transform (DTFT)

Consider an arbitrary aperiodic sequence $x[n]$ that is of finite duration, which exists between $-N_1 \leq n \leq N_2$. The sequence is illustrated in Figure 4.27(a). The MATLAB script to generate Figure 4.27 is given below:

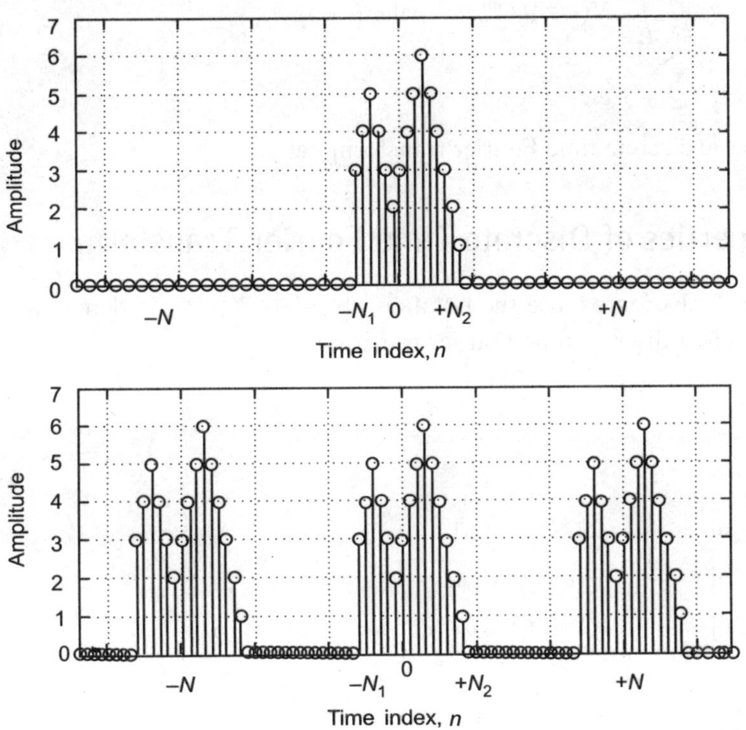

Figure 4.27 (a) An aperiodic sequence, $x[n]$. (b) Periodic sequence $\tilde{x}[n]$ constructed to be equal to $x[n]$ over one period.

```
%%% MATLAB script file to generate and
%%% plot an arbitrary aperiodic sequence, x[n]..
clear all; close all; clf;
y1=[zeros(1,8),3:5,4:-1:2,3:6,5:-1:1,zeros(1,7)];
n=[-14:15];
y=[y1,y1,y1];
x=[zeros(1,30), y1,zeros(1,30)];
m=[-44:45];
subplot(211),stem(m,x),axis([-44 45 0 7]);grid
xlabel('Time index, n}; ylabel('Amplitude');
subplot(212),stem(m,y);axis([-44 45 0 7]);grid
xlabel('Time index, n}; ylabel('Amplitude');
%%% end of fdur.m
```

From the aperiodic sequence $x[n]$, we can construct a periodic sequence $\tilde{x}[n]$ for which $x[n]$ is one period, as illustrated in Figure 4.27(b). We can show that as $N \rightarrow \infty$, $\tilde{x}[n] = x[n]$ and

$$x[n] = \frac{1}{2\pi} \int_{2\pi} X(e^{j\omega}) e^{j\omega n} d\omega, \text{ where} \tag{4.116}$$

$$X(e^{j\omega}) = \sum_{n=-\infty}^{\infty} x[n] e^{-j\omega n}. \tag{4.117}$$

Table 4.5 lists basic discrete time Fourier transform pairs.

4.9.1 Properties of Discrete Time Fourier Transform

In the following discussion we use the notation $x[n] \overset{\mathcal{FT}}{\longleftrightarrow} X(e^{j\omega})$ to denote a sequence $x[n]$ and its corresponding discrete time Fourier transform.

Linearity

If

$$\begin{aligned} x[n] &\overset{\mathcal{FT}}{\longleftrightarrow} X(e^{j\omega}), \text{ and} \\ y[n] &\overset{\mathcal{FT}}{\longleftrightarrow} Y(e^{j\omega}), \text{ then} \\ ax[n] + by[n] &\overset{\mathcal{FT}}{\longleftrightarrow} aX(e^{j\omega}) + bY(e^{j\omega}). \end{aligned} \tag{4.118}$$

Time Shifting

If

$$\begin{aligned} x[n] &\overset{\mathcal{FT}}{\longleftrightarrow} X(e^{j\omega}), \text{ then} \\ x[n-n_0] &\overset{\mathcal{FT}}{\longleftrightarrow} e^{-j\omega n_0} X(e^{j\omega}). \end{aligned} \tag{4.119}$$

Table 4.5 Basic discrete time fourier transform pairs

Sequence, $x[n]$	**Discrete Time Fourier Transform,** $X(e^{j\omega})$
$\delta[n]$	1
$\delta[n-n_0]$	$e^{-j\omega n_0}$
$x[n]=1$	$2\pi \sum_{k=-\infty}^{\infty} \delta(\omega-2\pi k)$
$\sum_{k=<N>} a_k e^{jk(2\pi/N)n}$	$2\pi \sum_{k=-\infty}^{\infty} a_k \delta\left(\omega-\frac{2\pi k}{N}\right)$
$e^{j\omega_0 n}$	$2\pi \sum_{k=-\infty}^{\infty} \delta(\omega-\omega_0-2\pi k)$
$\cos \omega_0 n$	$\pi \sum_{k=-\infty}^{\infty} \{\delta(\omega-\omega_0-2\pi k)+\delta(\omega+\omega_0-2\pi k)\}$
$\sin \omega_0 n$	$\frac{\pi}{j} \sum_{k=-\infty}^{\infty} \{\delta(\omega-\omega_0-2\pi k)-\delta(\omega+\omega_0-2\pi k)\}$
$x[n]=\begin{cases} 1, & \lvert n\rvert \le N_1, \\ 0, & N_1<\lvert n\rvert \le N/2, \\ and: & \\ x[n+N] & =x[n] \end{cases}$	$2\pi \sum_{k=-\infty}^{\infty} a_k\delta(\omega-\frac{2\pi k}{N})$
$\sum_{k=-\infty}^{\infty} \delta[\omega-kN]$	$\frac{2\pi}{N} \sum_{k=-\infty}^{\infty} \delta(\omega-\frac{2\pi k}{N})$
$a^n u[n]$	$\frac{1}{1-ae^{-j\omega}}$
$(n+1)a^n u[n],\ \lvert a\rvert<1$	$\frac{1}{(1-ae^{-j\omega})^2}$
$\frac{(n+r-1)!}{n!(r-1)!}a^n u[n],\ \lvert a\rvert<1$	$\frac{1}{(1-ae^{-j\omega})^r}$
$x[n]=\begin{cases} 1, & \lvert n\rvert \le N \\ 0, & \lvert n\rvert > N \end{cases}$	$\frac{\sin\{\omega(N+\frac{1}{2})\}}{\sin \omega/2}$
$x[n]=\frac{\sin Wn}{\pi n}=\frac{W}{\pi}\text{sinc}\left\{\frac{Wn}{\pi}\right\}$,	$X(e^{j\omega})=\begin{cases} 1, & 0\le\lvert\omega\rvert\le W \\ 0, & W<\lvert\omega\rvert\le\pi, \text{ and} \end{cases}$
$0<W<\pi.$	$X(e^{j\omega})$ *periodic with period* 2π.

Frequency Shifting

If

$$x[n] \overset{\mathcal{FT}}{\longleftrightarrow} X(e^{j\omega}), \text{ then}$$
$$e^{j\omega_0 n}x[n] \overset{\mathcal{FT}}{\longleftrightarrow} X(e^{j(\omega-\omega_0)}). \tag{4.120}$$

Conjugation and Conjugate Symmetry

If

$$x[n] \overset{\mathcal{FT}}{\longleftrightarrow} X(e^{j\omega}), \text{ then}$$
$$x^*[n] \overset{\mathcal{FT}}{\longleftrightarrow} X^*(e^{-j\omega}). \tag{4.121}$$

If $x[n]$ is real valued then $X(e^{j\omega})$ is conjugate symmetric. That is

$$X(e^{j\omega}) = X^*(e^{-j\omega}) \tag{4.122}$$

First Difference and Accumulation

We have

$$x[n] - x[n-1] \quad \overset{\mathcal{FT}}{\longleftrightarrow} \quad (1 - e^{-j\omega})X(e^{j\omega}) \ \text{ and} \tag{4.123}$$

$$\sum_{m=-\infty}^{n} x[m] \quad \overset{\mathcal{FT}}{\longleftrightarrow} \quad \frac{1}{1 - e^{-j\omega}} X(e^{j\omega}) + \pi X(e^{j0}) \sum_{k=-\infty}^{\infty} \delta(\omega - 2\pi k). \tag{4.124}$$

Time Reversal

If

$$\begin{aligned} x[n] &\overset{\mathcal{FT}}{\longleftrightarrow} X(e^{j\omega}), \text{ then} \\ x[-n] &\overset{\mathcal{FT}}{\longleftrightarrow} X(e^{-j\omega}). \end{aligned} \tag{4.125}$$

Time Expansion

If

$$x[n] \overset{\mathcal{FT}}{\longleftrightarrow} X(e^{j\omega}), \text{ then}$$

$$x_{<k>}[n] = \begin{cases} x[n/k], & \text{if } n \text{ is a multiple of } k \\ 0, & \text{if } n \text{ is not a multiple of } k \end{cases} \overset{\mathcal{FT}}{\longleftrightarrow} X(e^{jk\omega}). \tag{4.126}$$

Differentiation in Frequency

If

$$\begin{aligned} x[n] &\overset{\mathcal{FT}}{\longleftrightarrow} X(e^{j\omega}), \text{ then} \\ nx[n] &\overset{\mathcal{FT}}{\longleftrightarrow} j\frac{dX(e^{j\omega})}{d\omega}. \end{aligned} \tag{4.127}$$

Parseval's Relation

If $x[n]$ and $X(e^{j\omega})$ are a Fourier transform pair, then

$$\sum_{n=-\infty}^{\infty} |x[n]|^2 = \frac{1}{2\pi} \int_{2\pi} |X(e^{j\omega})|^2 d\omega. \tag{4.128}$$

Convolution Property

If

$$\begin{aligned} x[n] &\overset{\mathcal{FT}}{\longleftrightarrow} X(e^{j\omega}), \text{ and} \\ h[n] &\overset{\mathcal{FT}}{\longleftrightarrow} H(e^{j\omega}), \text{ then} \\ y[n] = x[n] * h[n] &\overset{\mathcal{FT}}{\longleftrightarrow} Y(e^{j\omega}) = X(e^{j\omega}).H(e^{j\omega}). \end{aligned} \tag{4.129}$$

Multiplication Property

If

$$\begin{aligned} x_1[n] &\overset{\mathcal{FT}}{\longleftrightarrow} X_1(e^{j\omega}), \text{ and} \\ x_2[n] &\overset{\mathcal{FT}}{\longleftrightarrow} X_2(e^{j\omega}), \text{ then} \\ y[n] = x_1[n].x_2[n] &\overset{\mathcal{FT}}{\longleftrightarrow} Y(e^{j\omega}) = X_1(e^{j\omega}) * X_2(e^{j\omega}) \\ X_1(e^{j\omega}) * X_2(e^{j\omega}) &= \frac{1}{2\pi}\int_{2\pi} X_1(e^{j\theta})X_2(e^{j(\omega-\theta)})d\theta. \end{aligned} \tag{4.130}$$

The important properties of discrete time Fourier transforms are listed in Table 4.6.

4.9.2 Systems Characterised by Difference Equations

A general linear constant coefficient difference equation is of the form

$$\sum_{l=0}^{N} a_l y[n-l] = \sum_{k=0}^{M} b_k x[n-k] \tag{4.131}$$

To obtain the frequency response of the LTI system represented by equation (4.131), we take Fourier transform of both sides

$$\sum_{l=0}^{N} a_l e^{-jl\omega} Y(e^{j\omega}) = \sum_{k=0}^{M} b_k e^{-jk\omega} X(e^{j\omega}), \text{ then}$$

$$H(e^{j\omega}) = \frac{Y(e^{j\omega})}{X(e^{j\omega})} = \frac{\sum_{k=0}^{M} b_k e^{-jk\omega}}{\sum_{l=0}^{N} a_l e^{-jl\omega}}. \tag{4.132}$$

4.10 Nyquist–Shannon Sampling Theorem

Sampling is the process of converting a continuous time signal into a discrete sequence of data. It is the starting point in any digital signal processing system. The Nyquist–Shannon sampling theorem depicts the rate at which an analog (continuous time) signal is to be sampled for optimum results. The theorem was first formulated by Harry Nyquist (Figure 4.28)

Table 4.6 Properties of discrete time Fourier transforms

Property	Sequence	Discrete time fourier transform
Linearity	$ax[n] + by[n]$	$aX(e^{j\omega}) + bY(e^{j\omega})$
Time shifting	$x[n - n_0]$	$e^{-j\omega n_0} X(e^{j\omega})$
Frequency shifting	$e^{j\omega_0 n} x[n]$	$X(e^{j(\omega - \omega_0)})$
Time reversal	$x[-n]$	$X(e^{-j\omega})$
Differencing in time	$x[n] - x[n-1]$	$(1 - e^{-j\omega})X(e^{j\omega})$
Differentiation in frequency	$nx[n]$	$j\frac{dX(e^{j\omega})}{d\omega}$
Accumulation	$\sum\limits_{m=-\infty}^{n} x[m]$	$\frac{1}{1-e^{-j\omega}} X(e^{j\omega}) + \pi X(e^{j0}) \sum\limits_{k=-\infty}^{\infty} \delta(\omega - 2\pi k)$
Time Expansion	$x_{<k>}[n] = \begin{cases} x[n/k], \\ if\ n = Mk \\ 0, \\ if\ n \neq Mk. \end{cases}$	$X(e^{jk\omega})$
Multiplication	$x[n].y[n]$	$X(e^{j\omega}) * Y(e^{j\omega}) = \frac{1}{2\pi} \int\limits_{-\infty}^{\infty} X(e^{j\theta})Y(e^{j(\omega-\theta)})d\theta.$
Convolution	$x[n] * y[n]$	$X(e^{j\omega})Y(e^{j\omega})$
Conjugate symmetry	$x[n]$ real	$\begin{cases} X(e^{j\omega}) & = & X^*(e^{-j\omega}) \\ \Re e\left\{X(e^{j\omega})\right\} & = & \\ \Re e\left\{X(e^{-j\omega})\right\} & & \\ \Im m\left\{X(e^{j\omega})\right\} & = & \\ -\Im m\left\{X(e^{-j\omega})\right\} & & \\ \lvert X(e^{j\omega})\rvert & = & \\ \lvert X(e^{-j\omega})\rvert & & \\ \angle X(e^{j\omega}) & = & \\ -\angle X(e^{-j\omega}) & & \end{cases}$
	$x[n]$ real and even	$X(e^{j\omega})$ real and even.
	$x[n]$ real and odd	$X(e^{j\omega})$ purely imaginary and odd.
Parseval's relation	$x[n]$	$\sum\limits_{n=-\infty}^{\infty} \lvert x[n]\rvert^2 = \frac{1}{2\pi} \int\limits_{2\pi} \lvert X(e^{j\omega})\rvert^2 d\omega$

in 1928[8] (in his paper "Certain topics in telegraph transmission theory"), but was only formally proven by Claude E. Shannon (Figure 4.29) in 1949 (in his paper "Communication

[8] Harry Nyquist was a gifted mathematician and electrical engineer. He is credited with three major achievements: explanation of the Johnson–Nyquist noise (thermal noise), the Nyquist frequency, and the Nyquist's stability criterion. Nyquist had 138 patents. He had the following awards/honours: the 1960 Stuart Ballantine Medal Franklin Institute, the 1960 IEEE Medal of Honour, the 1961 Melvin J Kelley Award, the 1969 Founders Medal NAE, the 1975 Rufus Oldenburger Medal ASME.

in the presence of noise"). Other major contributions were made by Kotelnikov in 1933, E.T. Whittaker in 1915, J.M.Whittaker in 1935, and Gabor in 1946. The sampling theorem is also known as the cardinal theorem of interpolation theory, the Whittaker–Kotelnikov–Shannon (WKS) sampling theorem, or simply the sampling theorem. The sampling theorem describes two processes in signal processing: a sampling process, in which a continuous time signal is converted to a discrete time signal, and a reconstruction process, in which the original continuous signal is recovered from the discrete time signal. The sampling process is performed by measuring the continuous signal's value every T units of time (or space), which is called the *sampling interval*. The theorem states that: *if a function $f(t)$ contains no frequencies higher than W cycles per second, it is completely determined by giving its ordinates at a series of points spaced $\frac{1}{2W}$ seconds apart.* The sampling theorem asserts that the uniformly spaced discrete samples are a complete representation of the signal if the bandwidth is less than half the sampling rate. This results in a sequence of numbers, called samples, to represent the original signal. Each sample value is associated with the instant in time when it was measured. The reciprocal of the sampling interval $(1/T)$ is the sampling frequency denoted by f_s, which is measured in samples per unit of time. If T is expressed in seconds, then f_s is expressed in Hz. The Nyquist–Shannon sampling theorem provides a prescription for the nominal sampling interval required to avoid aliasing.

Figure 4.28 Harry Nyquist (1889–1976)

THE MATHEMATICAL THEORY OF COMMUNICATION

"A mathematical theory of communication" is an influential 1948 article by mathematician, Claude E. Shannon. The article was one of the founding works in the field of information theory. Shannon expanded the ideas of this article in a 1963 book with Warren Weaver titled, *The Mathematical Theory of Communication (ISBN 0-25-272548-4).*

The Nyquist–Shannon Sampling Theorem

The sampling frequency should be greater than twice the highest frequency contained in the signal to enable perfect reconstruction of the original function from its samples.

Mathematically, we can write $f_s \geq 2f_c$, where f_s is the sampling frequency (how often samples are taken per unit of time or space), and f_c is the highest frequency contained in the signal. The frequency $f_N = f_s/2$ is often referred to as the Nyquist frequency or *critical frequency* in literature. The sampling theorem is really quite intuitive. Consider for example a signal composed of a single sine wave at a frequency of 1 Hz. If we sample this waveform at 2 Hz (as dictated by the Nyquist theorem), it is sufficient to capture each peak and trough of the signal. If we sample at a frequency higher than this, for example 4 Hz, then there are more than enough samples to capture the variations in the signal. However, it may be noted that if the sampling instances happen to be at the zero-crossings (assuming the sine wave has zero average value), all the samples will be zeros. This is a trivial situation, though.

If however we sample at a frequency lower than 2 Hz, for example at 1.5 Hz, then there are not enough samples to capture all the peaks and troughs in the signal. Note here that we are not only losing information; we are also getting the wrong information about the signal. The person receiving these samples, without any previous knowledge of the original signal, may well be mislead into thinking that the signal has quite a different form. From this example, we can see the reason for the term *aliasing*. That is, the signal now takes on a different *"persona,"* or a *false presentation*, due to being sampled at an insufficiently high frequency. This process is referred to as *aliasing*.

Now we consider the sampling of a complex signal composed of many frequency components. We know that any continuous time signal may be decomposed in terms of a sum of sines and cosines at different frequencies, which is the Fourier series expansion of the signal. For example, consider a complex waveform composed by adding together sine waves at frequencies of 1 Hz, 2 Hz, and 3 Hz. According to the Nyquist–Shannon sampling theorem, the signal must be sampled at twice the highest frequency contained in the signal. In this case, we have $f_c = 3$ Hz, and so the Nyquist theorem tells us that the sampling frequency, f_s must be at least 6 Hz. And sure enough, this appears to be sufficient.

Thus, when a signal contains not just one but many different frequencies added together, the minimal sampling rate needed to avoid aliasing is just twice the highest frequency present in the complex waveform, irrespective of how many other frequency components there are. The above sampling rate is known as the *Nyquist rate*.

In literature, the terms *Nyquist frequency* and *sampling frequency* appear, quite often, equivocally. However, there is subtle difference between the two. It may be noted that the Nyquist frequency invariably refers to the *highest frequency* in the signal; whereas sampling frequency refers to *twice the highest frequency*.

Figure 4.29 Claude Elwood Shannon (April 30, 1916–February 24, 2001)

CLAUDE ELWOOD SHANNON(1916–2001)

Claude E. Shannon was an American electrical engineer and mathematician. He is called the "father of information theory". Shannon is famous for having founded information theory and both digital computer and digital circuit design theory when he was 21 years old by way of a master's thesis published in 1937.

He was born in Petoskey, Michigan, on April 30, 1916. His father, Claude Sr., (1862–1934) was a businessman and his mother, Mabel Wolf Shannon (1880–1945), was Principal of Gaylord High School, Michigan. As a boy, Shannon showed an inclination toward things mechanical. His favourite subjects in school were science and mathematics, and at home he constructed devices like model planes, a radio-controlled model boat and a telegraph system.

In 1936 he obtained both a bachelor of science degree in electrical engineering and a bachelor of science degree in mathematics from the University of Michigan. This dual interest in mathematics and engineering continued throughout his career. In 1936 he accepted the position of a research assistant in the department of electrical engineering at the Massachusetts Institute of Technology. In his master's thesis he showed how Boolean algebra could be used in the analysis and synthesis of switching and computer circuits. It has been claimed that this was the most important master's thesis of all time.

The thesis, and his first published paper, aroused considerable interest when it appeared in 1938 in the A.I.E.E. Transactions. In 1940, it was awarded the Alfred Noble Prize of the combined engineering societies of the United States, an award given each year to a person not over thirty for a paper published in one of the journals of the participating societies. He spent the summer of 1939 at Cold Spring Harbor working under geneticist Dr. Barbara Burks, exploring the possibility of a similar mathematical application in genetics. It resulted in his dissertation "An algebra for theoretical genetics".

In the spring of 1940, Shannon received the S.M. degree in electrical engineering and the degree of doctor of philosophy in mathematics at the same commencement. He spent the next fifteen years at Bell Laboratories. During this period he worked in many areas, most notably in information theory, a development which was published in 1948 as "A mathematical theory of communication". In his paper "Communication theory of secrecy systems", Shannon related cryptography to communication in a noisy channel, the "noise" being the scrambling caused by the key of the cryptographic system. In 1956 Dr. Shannon was invited to be a visiting professor at M.I.T. and, in 1957–58, a fellow at the Centre for the Study of the Behavioural Sciences in Palo Alto, California. The following year he became a permanent member of the M.I.T. faculty as Donner Professor of Science, where he continued research in various areas of communication theory.

He held honorary doctorate degrees from ten universities. His awards include the Alfred Noble Prize (1940), the Morris Liebmann Memorial Award of the Institute of Radio Engineers (1949), the Stuart Ballantine Medal of the Franklin Institute (1955), the Research Corporation Award (1956), the Rice University Medal of Honour (1962), the Marvin J. Kelly Award (1962), the I.E.E.E.Medal of Honour (1966), the National Medal of Science (1966) presented by President Johnson, the Golden Plate Award (1967), the Harvey Prize, Technion, Haifa (1972) presented by the president of Israel, the Jacquard Award (1978), the Harold Pender Award (1978), the Audio Engineering Society Gold Medal (1985), the Kyoto Prize (1985) and the Eduard Rhein Prize (1991).

Outside his academic pursuits, Shannon was interested in juggling, unicycling, and chess. He also invented many devices, including rocket-powered flying discs, a motorised pogo stick, and a flame-throwing trumpet for a science exhibition. One of his more humorous devices was a box kept on his desk called the "ultimate machine" based on an idea by Marvin Minsky. The machine was a plain box with one switch on its side. When the switch was flipped, the top of the box opened, a mechanical hand came out, flipped off the switch then returned into the box.

Claude E. Shannon died on February 24, 2001, at the age of 84, after a long struggle with Alzheimer's disease.

4.10.1 Mathematical Proof of Sampling Theorem

Let $F(\omega)$ be the spectrum of the signal, $f(t)$. Then we have

$$\begin{aligned} f(t) &= \frac{1}{2\pi}\int_{-\infty}^{\infty} F(\omega)e^{j\omega t}d\omega \\ &= \frac{1}{2\pi}\int_{-2\pi W}^{2\pi W} F(\omega)e^{j\omega t}d\omega \end{aligned}$$

since $F(\omega)$ is assumed to be zero outside the band W. Now let $t = \frac{n}{2W}$, where n is any integer. Then, we obtain

$$f\left(\frac{n}{2W}\right) = \frac{1}{2\pi}\int_{-2\pi W}^{2\pi W} F(\omega)e^{j\omega \frac{n}{2W}}d\omega \tag{4.133}$$

On the left of equation (4.133) are values of $f(t)$ at the sampling points. The integral on the right will be recognised as essentially the nth coefficient in a Fourier series expansion of the function $F(\omega)$, taking the interval $-W$ to W as a fundamental period. This means that the values of the samples $f\,(n/2W)$ determine the Fourier coefficients in the series expansion of $F(\omega)$. Thus they determine $F(\omega)$, since $F(\omega)$ is zero for frequencies greater than W, and for lower frequencies, $F(\omega)$ is determined if its Fourier coefficients are determined. But $F(\omega)$ determines the original function $f(t)$ completely, since a function is determined if its spectrum is known. Therefore, the original samples determine the function $f(t)$ completely.

4.10.2 Aliasing

Aliasing arises when a signal is discretely sampled at a rate that is insufficient to capture the changes in the signal. Consider the following contexts in which signals are discretely sampled:

- Retinal images are sampled in space by photoreceptors.
- Film and video are sampled in time by discrete frames.
- Sound is commonly digitally sampled for recording and communications.

Aliasing may arise in all of these situations if sampling is done improperly. Because the effects of aliasing can be rather disastrous, it is important to understand why aliasing occurs, what its consequences are, and how it may be avoided.

4.10.3 Effects of Aliasing

Aliasing becomes evident in many different communication systems. We will consider a few representative cases in the following sections.

The Wagon Wheel Effect

One common situation in which aliasing occurs is in motion pictures. This is because continuously varying images are being discretely sampled at a rate of 24 frames/s. The Nyquist sampling theorem tells us that aliasing will occur if at any point in the image plane there are frequency components, or light–dark transitions that occur faster than $f_s/2$, which in this case is 12 frames/s. But in many situations the light–dark transitions may occur faster than this—such as a wagon wheel or propeller rotating at high speed.

Consider a wagon wheel with eight spokes turning at a rate of 3 revolutions per second (or 180 rpm) in the clockwise direction. In this case, the wagon wheel will move by one spoke per frame, since:

$$\left.\begin{array}{c}3\,\text{revolutions/s} \times 8\,\text{spokes/revolution}\\ (24\,\text{frames/s})\end{array}\right\} \equiv 1\,\text{spoke/frame}$$

Thus, the wagon wheel will appear to stand still! One rarely sees this happen though, because chances for the wheel to be turning at just this speed is very minimal. Now, consider what would happen if the wagon wheel was turning at a rate just below this, say at 2.5 revolutions/s. Now, the wheel will move by 83% of the spoke spacing at each frame. So, comparing two adjacent frames of the film we would see images, as depicted in Figure 4.30.

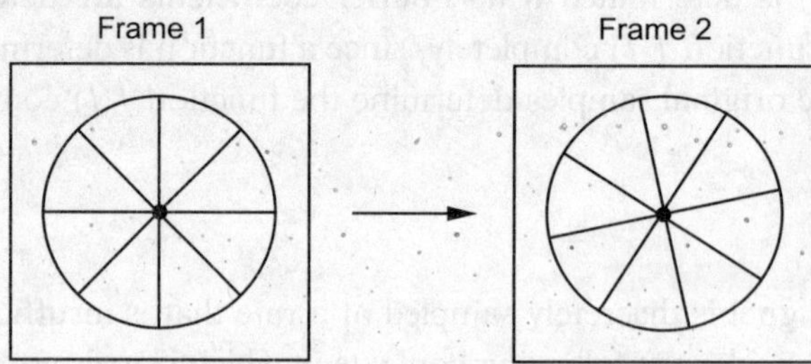

Figure 4.30 The wagon wheel effect in motion pictures

The problem the brain faces in viewing these frames in rapid succession, is that there are two interpretations. One interpretation is that the wheel has moved by 83% of the spoke interval in the clockwise direction. The alternative interpretation is that it has moved by 17% of the spoke interval in the counter-clockwise direction. It turns out that the brain prefers the latter interpretation, and so, as a result we perceive the wheel moving backwards (counter-clockwise) at a slower speed than it is actually moving.

Aliasing of Text Images on Web Pages

Another place aliasing is often seen is in images of text. This happens, for example, when people put an image on their web page that contains some text characters that has been improperly sub-sampled. The image contains half as many samples in each dimension (horizontal and vertical) when compared to the original, and as a result, it is now for all practical purposes illegible.

Aliasing in Images

Similar to one-dimensional discrete-time signals, images can also suffer from aliasing if the sampling resolution, or pixel density, is inadequate. For example, a digital photograph of a striped shirt with high frequencies (in other words, the distance between the stripes is small), can cause aliasing of the shirt when it is sampled by the camera's image sensor. The aliasing appears as a Moire pattern. The solution to this problem, i.e., to achieve higher sampling in the spatial domain for this case, would be to move closer to the shirt or use a higher resolution sensor.

4.10.4 Avoidance of Aliasing

The simple way to avoid aliasing of course is to always have enough samples to capture the spatial or temporal variations in a signal. But there are many situations in which the sample rate may be limited—for example, the motion picture film is limited to 24 frames/s, or we may be designing a web page where the images need to be a minimum number of pixels so that they download quickly. If the sampling rate f_s is fixed, then there is only one other parameter we can play with, and that is the highest frequency contained in the signal, f_c. This can be done by lowpass filtering, or in layman's terms, *smoothing*.

The easiest way to smooth a signal is to blur it. In film this is easily done by adjusting the lens so that the image is a bit out of focus. The more out of focus it is, the lower the spatial frequency content of the image becomes. And as the spatial-frequency content is lowered, the temporal frequency content is also lowered. Blurring is often used by film directors to eliminate aliasing from a scene. For example, when filming a shot where a car is racing by, it would be a mistake to keep the car in focus. The image of the car is usually purposefully de-focussed so as to eliminate the jerky appearance of motion, which breaks the illusion of reality in film. However, quite often, directors will not bother to eliminate aliasing in the form of backwards moving wheels, or they may even prefer to keep it for *"visual effect"*. Blurring may be easily accomplished on digital images by filtering (or convolving) with a mask that averages together the values of several neighbouring pixels. Such an operation is usually provided in image manipulation programmes such as Adobe Photoshop.

4.11 Signal Reconstruction

Reconstruction of the original signal is an interpolation process that mathematically defines a continuous time signal $x(t)$ from the discrete samples $x[n]$ and at times in between the sample instants nT.

4.11.1 The Exact Reconstruction Procedure

Each sample value $x(nT)$ is multiplied by the *sinc function* scaled so that the zero-crossings of the sinc function occur at the sampling instants and that the sinc function's central point is shifted to the time of that sample, nT. All of these shifted and scaled functions are then added together to recover the original signal. The scaled and time-shifted sinc functions are continuous, making the sum of these continuous too, so the result of this operation is a continuous signal. This procedure is based on the Whittaker–Shannon interpolation formula.

The signal obtained from this reconstruction procedure can have no frequencies higher than one-half the sampling frequency. According to the theorem, the reconstructed signal will match the original signal provided that the original signal contains no frequencies at or above this limit. This condition is called the *Nyquist criterion*, or the *Raabe Condition*.

The reconstruction or interpolation using sinc functions is not the only interpolation scheme. Indeed, it is impossible in practice because it requires summing an infinite number of terms. However, it is the interpolation method that in theory exactly reconstructs any given bandlimited signal $x(t)$, with any bandlimit $B < 1/2T$.

The reconstruction process that involves scaled and delayed sinc functions can be described as ideal. It cannot be realised in practice since it implies that each sample contributes to the reconstructed signal at almost all time points, requiring summing an infinite number of terms. Instead, some type of approximation of the sinc functions, finite in length, has to be used. The error that corresponds to the sinc–function approximation is referred to as *interpolation error*.

4.12 The Bilateral Laplace Transform

We have already considered the procedure for finding the response of a system by breaking the input $f(t)$ into impulses at regular intervals and then saving all the output components which constitute $y(t)$. The Laplace transform was named after the great French mathematician and astronomer Pierre Simon de Laplace (Figure 4.31), who first presented the transform and its application to differential equations in a paper published in 1779. [9] In the Laplace transform, we break up $f(t)$ into exponentials e^{st} (where s is a complex variable; $s = \sigma + j\omega$). Since the signal $f(t)$ is transformed into a continuous sum of exponentials e^{st}, we need to introduce the convergence factor $e^{-\sigma t}$ in the transformation from the time domain to the s-domain, which is called the Laplace transformation. For a signal $x(t)$, the *bilateral (two-sided) Laplace transform* is defined as

[9] Pierre Simon de Laplace was a French mathematician and astronomer, whose work was pivotal to the development of mathematical astronomy. He summarised and extended the work of his predecessors in his five volume *Mecanique Celeste* (*Celestial Mechanics*) (1799–1825).

Figure 4.31 Marquis Pierre Simon de Laplace (March 23, 1749–March 5, 1827)

$$X(s) = \int_{-\infty}^{\infty} x(t)e^{-st}dt \tag{4.134}$$

The signal $x(t)$ is said to be the *inverse Laplace transform* of $X(s)$. It can be shown that

$$x(t) = \frac{1}{2\pi j}\int_{c-j\infty}^{c+j\infty} X(s)e^{st}ds \tag{4.135}$$

where c is a constant chosen to ensure the convergence of the integral in equation (4.134). This pair of equations is known as the *bilateral Laplace transform pair*, where $X(s)$ is the direct Laplace transform of $x(t)$ and $x(t)$ is the inverse Laplace transform of $X(s)$. Symbolically,

$$X(s) = \mathcal{LT}\left[x(t)\right] \;\text{ and }\; x(t) = \mathcal{LT}^{-1}\left[X(s)\right] \tag{4.136}$$

Also note that

$$\mathcal{LT}^{-1}\{\mathcal{LT}\left[x(t)\right]\} = x(t) \;\text{ and }\; \mathcal{LT}\{\mathcal{LT}^{-1}\left[X(s)\right]\}$$

The Laplace transform pair is also indicated as shown below:

$$x(t) \overset{\mathcal{LT}}{\longleftrightarrow} X(s)$$

It is interesting to note that when $s = j\omega$, equation (4.134) becomes

$$X(j\omega) = \int_{-\infty}^{\infty} x(t)e^{-j\omega t}dt \tag{4.137}$$

which corresponds to the Fourier transform of $x(t)$; that is

$$X(s)|_{s=j\omega} = \mathcal{FT}\{x(t)\} \tag{4.138}$$

In general, $s = \sigma + j\omega$, and when $\sigma = 0$, the Laplace transform is equal to the Fourier transform.

4.12.1 Region of Convergence (ROC)

The *region of convergence* is also known as the *region of existence*. It is the set of values of s (the region in the complex plane) for which the integral in equation (4.134) converges.

EXAMPLE 4.3

For a signal $x(t) = e^{-at}u(t)$, find the Laplace transform and the ROC.

SOLUTION

By definition, $X(s) = \int_{-\infty}^{\infty} e^{-at}u(t)e^{-st}dt$. As $u(t) = 0$ for $t < 0$ and $u(t) = 1$ for $t \geq 0$, we have

$$X(s) = \int_0^{\infty} e^{-at}e^{-st}dt = \int_0^{\infty} e^{-(s+a)t}dt = -\frac{1}{s+a}\, e^{-(s+a)t}\Big|_0^{\infty} \tag{4.139}$$

Note that as s is complex, as $t \to \infty$, the term $e^{-(s+a)t}$ does not necessarily vanish. Now, we know that $s = \sigma + j\omega$ and $e^{-st} = e^{-\sigma t}e^{-j\omega t}$. But $\left|e^{-j\omega t}\right| = 1$ regardless of the value of ωt. Therefore, as $t \to \infty$, $e^{-st} \to 0$ only if $\sigma > 0$. Thus we have:

$$\lim_{t\to\infty} e^{-(s+a)t} = \begin{cases} 0 & \Re e(s+a) > 0 \\ \infty & \Re e(s+a) < 0 \end{cases}$$

Using this result in equation (4.139) yields

$$\begin{aligned} X(s) &= \frac{1}{s+a}, \quad \Re e(s+a) > 0, \text{ or} \\ e^{-at}u(t) &\overset{\mathcal{LT}}{\longleftrightarrow} \frac{1}{s+a}, \quad \Re e\ s > -a \text{ (which is the ROC)} \end{aligned}$$

4.12.2 Unilateral Laplace Transform

The unilateral Laplace transform is a special case of the bilateral Laplace transform in which all signals are restricted to being *causal*; consequently the limits of integration for the integral in equation (4.134) can be taken from 0 to ∞. Hence the unilateral Laplace transform $X(s)$ of a signal $x(t)$ is defined as

$$X(s) = \int_{0^-}^{\infty} x(t)e^{-st}dt \tag{4.140}$$

We choose 0^- (rather than 0^+) as the lower limit of integration to ensure the inclusion of the impulse function at $t = 0$. It also allows us to use initial conditions at 0^- (rather than at 0^+) in the solution of differential equations via the Laplace transform.

The unilateral Laplace transform simplifies the system analysis problem considerably because of its *uniqueness property*, which says that for a given $X(s)$, there is a unique inverse transform. But this simplification is attained at the cost of a limitation: we cannot analyse non-causal systems or use non-causal inputs. However, in most practical problems, this restriction is of little consequence. In practice, the term *Laplace transform* means the *unilateral Laplace transform*. A short table of unilateral Laplace transforms is given in Table 4.7.

Table 4.7 Unilateral Laplace transform pairs

Signal, $x(t)$	**Unilateral Laplace transform,** $X(s)$
$\delta(t)$	1
$\delta(t-t_0)$	e^{-st_0}
$u(t)$	$\frac{1}{s}$
$u(t-t_0)$	$\frac{e^{-st_0}}{s}$
$tu(t)$	$\frac{1}{s^2}$
$t^n u(t)$	$\frac{n!}{s^{n+1}}$
$e^{-at}u(t),\ a>0$	$\frac{1}{s+a},\ a>0$
$te^{at}u(t)$	$\frac{1}{(s-a)^2}$
$t^n e^{at}u(t)$	$\frac{n!}{(s-a)^{n+1}}$
$\cos(\omega_0 t)u(t)$	$\frac{s}{s^2+\omega_0^2}$
$\sin(\omega_0 t)u(t)$	$\frac{\omega_0}{s^2+\omega_0^2}$
$e^{-at}\cos(\omega_0 t)u(t)$	$\frac{s+a}{(s+a)^2+\omega_0^2}$
$e^{-at}\sin(\omega_0 t)u(t)$	$\frac{\omega_0}{(s+a)^2+\omega_0^2}$

4.12.3 Properties of Laplace Transform

We will now consider some important properties of Laplace transforms. They are useful not only in the derivation of the Laplace transform of functions but also in the solutions of linear integro-differential equations.

Linearity

If

$$\begin{aligned} x(t) &\overset{\mathcal{LT}}{\longleftrightarrow} X(s), \text{ and} \\ y(t) &\overset{\mathcal{LT}}{\longleftrightarrow} Y(s), \text{ then} \\ ax(t)+by(t) &\overset{\mathcal{LT}}{\longleftrightarrow} aX(s)+bY(s). \end{aligned} \tag{4.141}$$

Thus, the Laplace transforms obey the principle of superposition.

Time Shifting

The time shifting property states that if

$$\begin{aligned} x(t) &\stackrel{\mathcal{LT}}{\longleftrightarrow} X(s), \text{ then} \\ x(t-t_0) &\stackrel{\mathcal{LT}}{\longleftrightarrow} X(s)e^{-st_0}. \end{aligned} \tag{4.142}$$

This property of unilateral Laplace transform holds only for positive t_0 because if t_0 were negative, the signal $x(t-t_0)u(t-t_0)$ may not be causal.

Frequency Shifting

The frequency shifting property states that if

$$\begin{aligned} x(t) &\stackrel{\mathcal{LT}}{\longleftrightarrow} X(s), \text{ then} \\ e^{s_0 t} &\stackrel{\mathcal{LT}}{\longleftrightarrow} X(s-s_0). \end{aligned} \tag{4.143}$$

Time Scaling

The time scaling property states that if

$$\begin{aligned} x(t) &\stackrel{\mathcal{LT}}{\longleftrightarrow} X(s), \text{ then} \\ x(at),\ a \geq 0 &\stackrel{\mathcal{LT}}{\longleftrightarrow} \frac{1}{a}X\left(\frac{s}{a}\right). \end{aligned} \tag{4.144}$$

Differentiation in Time

The differentiation in time property states that if

$$\begin{aligned} x(t) &\stackrel{\mathcal{LT}}{\longleftrightarrow} X(s), \text{ then} \\ \frac{dx(t)}{dt} &\stackrel{\mathcal{LT}}{\longleftrightarrow} sX(s) - x(0^-). \end{aligned} \tag{4.145}$$

Integration

The time integration property states that if

$$x(t) \overset{\mathcal{LT}}{\longleftrightarrow} X(s), \text{ then}$$

$$\int_{0^-}^{t} x(\tau)d\tau \overset{\mathcal{LT}}{\longleftrightarrow} \frac{X(s)}{s}, \text{ and} \tag{4.146}$$

$$\int_{-\infty}^{t} x(\tau)d\tau \overset{\mathcal{LT}}{\longleftrightarrow} \frac{X(s)}{s} + \frac{\int_{-\infty}^{0^-} x(\tau)d\tau}{s}. \tag{4.147}$$

Convolution in Time

If

$$\begin{aligned} x_1(t) &\overset{\mathcal{LT}}{\longleftrightarrow} X_1(s), \text{ and} \\ x_2(t) &\overset{\mathcal{LT}}{\longleftrightarrow} X_2(s), \text{ then} \\ x_1(t) * x_2(t) &\overset{\mathcal{LT}}{\longleftrightarrow} X_1(s)X_2(s). \end{aligned} \tag{4.148}$$

Convolution in Frequency

If

$$\begin{aligned} x_1(t) &\overset{\mathcal{LT}}{\longleftrightarrow} X_1(s), \text{ and} \\ x_2(t) &\overset{\mathcal{LT}}{\longleftrightarrow} X_2(s), \text{ then} \\ x_1(t)x_2(t) &\overset{\mathcal{LT}}{\longleftrightarrow} \frac{1}{2\pi j}\left[X_1(s) * X_2(s)\right]. \end{aligned} \tag{4.149}$$

The important properties of unilateral Laplace transforms are tabulated in Table 4.8.

4.13 Analysis of LTI Systems Using Laplace Transforms

One of the major applications of Laplace transforms is in the analysis and characterisation of LTI systems. This follows from the convolution property of the Laplace transform. We know that the output signal, $y(t)$ of a continuous time system is the convolution of the system input signal, $x(t)$ and the impulse response of the system, $h(t)$. That is:

$$y(t) = x(t) * h(t) = h(t) * x(t)$$

Now in the Laplace transform domain, we have

$$Y(s) = X(s)H(s)$$

Table 4.8 Properties of unilateral Laplace transforms

Property	Signal, $x(t)$	Unilateral Laplace transform, $X(s)$
Linearity	$ax(t)+by(t)$	$aX(s)+bY(s)$
Time shifting	$x(t-t_0)u(t-t_0)$	$e^{-st_0}X(s)$
Frequency shifting	$e^{s_0t}x[n]$	$X(s-s_0)$
Differentiation in time	$\frac{dx(t)}{dt}$	$sX(s)-x(0^-)$
	$\frac{d^2x(t)}{dt^2}$	$s^2X(s)-sx(0^-)-\dot{x}(0^-)$
	$\frac{d^nx(t)}{dt^n}$	$s^nX(s)-\sum_{k=1}^{n} s^{n-k}x^{k-1}(0^-)$
Differentiation in frequency	$-tx(t)$	$\frac{dX(s)}{ds}$
Time integration	$\int_{0^-}^{t} x(\tau)d\tau$	$\frac{1}{s}X(s)$
	$\int_{-\infty}^{t} x(\tau)d\tau$	$\frac{1}{s}X(s)+\frac{1}{s}\int_{-\infty}^{0^-} x(t)dt$
Frequency integration	$\frac{x(t)}{t}$	$\int_{s}^{\infty} X(z)dz$
Time scaling	$x(at),\ a\geq 0$	$\frac{1}{a}X\left(\frac{s}{a}\right)$
Time convolution	$x(t)*y(t)$	$X(s)Y(s)$
Frequency convolution	$x(t)y(t)$	$\frac{1}{2\pi j}X(s)*Y(s)$
Initial value	$x(0^+)$	$\lim_{s\to\infty} sX(s)$
Final value	$x(\infty)$	$\lim_{s\to 0} sX(s)$, [poles of $sX(s)$ in LHP]
Parseval's relation	$x(t)$	$\int_{t=-\infty}^{\infty} \lvert x(t)\rvert^2dt=\frac{1}{2\pi j}\int_{2\pi j} \lvert X(s)\rvert^2ds$

Moreover, if the input to an LTI system is $x(t)=e^{st}$, with s in the ROC of $H(s)$, then the output will be $H(s)e^{st}$. That is, e^{st} is an *eigen function* of the system with *eigen value* equal to the Laplace transform of the impulse response.

If the ROC of $H(s)$ includes the imaginary axis, then for $s=j\omega$, $H(s)$ is the *frequency response* of the LTI system. In the broader sense, the Laplace transform of the impulse response, $H(s)$ is commonly referred to as the *system function* or the *transfer function*. Let us now examine some of the properties of the LTI systems in the light of the transfer function.

4.13.1 Causality of LTI Systems

For a causal LTI system, the impulse response is zero for $t<0$, and therefore it is right-sided. Consequently, we can see that:

THE ROC OF CAUSAL LTI SYSTEM FUNCTION

The ROC associated with a system function for a causal LTI system is a right half plane. However, it may be noted that the converse of this statement is not necessarily true.

ROC to the right of the rightmost pole does not ensure that a system is causal; it only guarantees that the impulse response is right-sided. However, if $H(s)$ is *rational*, we can find out whether the system is causal simply by checking to see if its ROC is a right half-plane. Therefore, we have:

CAUSALITY OF RATIONAL SYSTEM FUNCTION

For an LTI system with a rational system function, *causality* of the system is equivalent to the ROC being the right half-plane to the right of the rightmost pole.

EXAMPLE 4.4
For a system with impulse response $h(t) = e^{-at}u(t)$, obtain the ROC and show that it satisfies the above *dictum.*

SOLUTION
Since, $h(t) = 0$, for $t < 0$, this system is causal. The system function is given by:

$$H(s) = \frac{1}{s+a}, \quad \Re e\{s\} > -a.$$

In this case, the system function is rational and the ROC is to the right of the rightmost pole, which is consistent with the dictum.

EXAMPLE 4.5
For a system with impulse response $h(t) = e^{-a|t|}$, obtain the ROC and show that it is consistent.

SOLUTION
Since $h(t) \neq 0, \;\; t < 0$, the system is *not* causal. The system function is

$$h(t) \stackrel{\mathcal{LT}}{\longleftrightarrow} H(s) = \frac{1}{s+a} - \frac{1}{s-a} = \frac{-2a}{s^2 - a^2}, \quad -a < \Re e\{s\} < +a.$$

For this system, $H(s)$ is rational and has an ROC that is not to the right of the rightmost pole, which is consistent with the fact that the system is not causal.

EXAMPLE 4.6
For a system with system function $H(s) = \frac{e^s}{s+2}, \;\; \Re e\{s\} > -2$, obtain the impulse response $h(t)$ and show that it is consistent with the dictum.

SOLUTION

The system has the ROC to the right of the rightmost pole. Hence the impulse response must be right-sided. We know that

$$e^{-2t}u(t) \stackrel{\mathcal{LT}}{\longleftrightarrow} \frac{1}{s+2}, \quad \Re e\{s\} > -2.$$

Now using the time shifting property, we have

$$e^{-2(t+1)}u(t+1) \stackrel{\mathcal{LT}}{\longleftrightarrow} \frac{e^s}{s+2}, \quad \Re e\{s\} > -2.$$

Hence, the impulse response of the system is $h(t) = e^{-2(t+1)}u(t+1)$, which is non-zero for $-1 < t$, which in turn indicates that the system is not causal. This example shows that causality implies that the ROC is to the right of the rightmost pole, but the converse is not in general true.

4.13.2 Stability of an LTI System

The ROC of $H(s)$ can be related to the stability of the LTI system. The BIBO stability of a system implies that its impulse response is *absolutely integrable*, wherein the Fourier transform of the impulse response converges. As the Fourier transform of a signal is equal to the Laplace transform computed along the $j\omega$-axis, we have the following statement:

THE STABILITY OF LTI SYSTEMS IN TERMS OF ROC

An LTI system is stable *iff* the ROC associated with its system function $H(s)$ includes the entire $j\omega$-axis; that is, $\Re e\{s\} = 0$.

It is perfectly possible for a system to be stable or unstable and have a system function that is not rational. For instance, the system function $H(s) = \frac{e^s}{s+2}, \ \Re e\{s\} > -2$ is not rational, and its impulse response is absolutely integrable, and hence the system is stable.

For a causal LTI system with a rational system function $H(s)$, the ROC is to the right of the rightmost pole. Consequently, for this system to be stable (i.e., for the ROC to include the $j\omega$-axis), the rightmost pole of $H(s)$ must be to the *left* of the $j\omega$-axis, Thus we have:

THE STABILITY OF LTI SYSTEMS IN TERMS OF POLES

A causal system with rational system function $H(s)$ is stable *iff* all the poles of $H(s)$ lie in the left half of the s-plane—i.e., all the poles have only negative real parts.

4.14 The z-Transform

The z-transform is the discrete time counterpart of the Laplace transform. For a discrete time LTI system with impulse response $h[n]$, the response of the system to a complex exponential of the form z^n is given by

$$y[n] = H(z)z^n, \tag{4.150}$$

where

$$H(z) = \sum_{n=-\infty}^{\infty} h[n]z^{-n}. \tag{4.151}$$

If we set $z = e^{j\omega}$ with ω real (that is, $|z| = 1$), the summation in equation (4.151) corresponds to the discrete time Fourier transform of $h[n]$. The z-transform of a general discrete tie sequence $x[n]$ is given by

$$X(z) \triangleq \sum_{n=-\infty}^{\infty} x[n]z^{-n} \tag{4.152}$$

where z is a complex variable. Now we can represent the z-transform pair as

$$x[n] \overset{\mathcal{CT}}{\longleftrightarrow} X(z) \tag{4.153}$$

The complex variable z is expressed in polar form as

$$z = re^{j\omega}$$

where r is the magnitude and ω is the angle of z. Now we can rewrite equation (4.152) as

$$X\left(re^{j\omega}\right) = \sum_{n=-\infty}^{\infty} x[n](re^{j\omega})^{-n} = \sum_{n=-\infty}^{\infty} \left\{x[n]r^{-n}\right\} e^{-j\omega n} \tag{4.154}$$

Thus we can observe that $X\left(re^{j\omega}\right)$ is the Fourier transform of the sequence $x[n]$ multiplied by a real exponential r^{-n}; that is

$$X\left(re^{j\omega}\right) = \mathcal{FT}\left\{x[n]z^{-n}\right\} \tag{4.155}$$

We can also note that for $r = 1$ or equivalently $|z| = 1$, equation (4.152) reduces to the Fourier transform, that is:

$$X(z)|_{z=e^{j\omega}} = X(e^{j\omega}) = \mathcal{FT}\left\{x[n]\right\} \tag{4.156}$$

Thus the z-transform reduces to the Fourier transform when the magnitude of the transform variable z is *unity,* that is for $|z| = |e^{j\omega}| = 1$. Therefore, the z-transform reduces to the Fourier transform on the contour in the complex z-plane corresponding to a circle with a radius unity, as shown in Figure 4.32. This circle with unit radius is referred to as the *unit circle*.

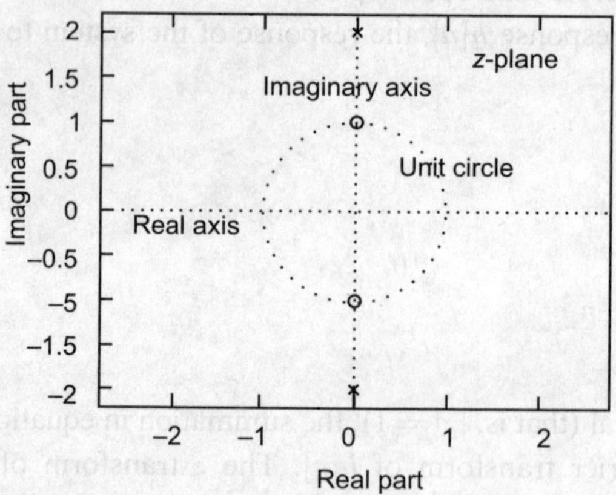

Figure 4.32 The complex z-plane

4.14.1 Region of Convergence

The complex z-*plane* is illustrated in Figure 4.32. We can note that for the convergence of z-transform, it is required that the Fourier transform of $x[n]r^{-n}$ converge. As in the case of the Laplace transform, the range of values of z over which the z-transform integral converges, is called the *region of convergence.* In other words, for any given sequence the set of values of z for which the z-transform converges is called the region of convergence.

EXAMPLE 4.7

Obtain the z-transform and the ROC of the sequence $x[n] = a^n u[n]$.

SOLUTION

The z-transform of $x[n]$ is given by:

$$\begin{aligned} X(z) &= \sum_{n=-\infty}^{\infty} x[n]z^{-n} \\ &= \sum_{n=0}^{\infty} a^n z^{-n} = \sum_{n=0}^{\infty} \frac{a^n}{z} \\ &= \frac{1}{1-a/z} = \frac{1}{1-az^{-1}}; \ |z| > |a| \\ &= \frac{z}{z-a}; \ |z| > |a| \end{aligned}$$

Thus the ROC for this case (for a right-sided causal sequence, $a^n u[n]$) is the exterior of a circle with radius a.

EXAMPLE 4.8
Obtain the z-transform and the ROC of the non-causal sequence $x[n] = -b^n u[-n-1]$.

SOLUTION
The z-transform of $x[n]$ is given by:

$$\begin{aligned} X(z) &= \sum_{n=-\infty}^{\infty} x[n] z^{-n} \\ &= \sum_{n=-\infty}^{-1} -b^n z^{-n} = \sum_{n=1}^{\infty} -b^{-n} z^n \\ &= \frac{1}{1-b/z} = \frac{1}{1-bz^{-1}}; \quad |z| < |b| \\ &= \frac{z}{z-b}; \quad |z| < |b| \end{aligned}$$

Thus the ROC for this case (for a left-sided non-causal sequence, $-b^n u[-n-1]$) is the interior of a circle with radius b.

EXAMPLE 4.9
Obtain the z-transform and the ROC of the real causal sequence $x[n] = 2\left(\frac{1}{5}\right)^n u[n] + 3\left(\frac{1}{7}\right)^n u[n]$.

SOLUTION
The z-transform of $x[n]$ is given by:

$$\begin{aligned} X_1(z) &= 2\sum_{n=0}^{\infty} \left(\frac{1}{5}\right)^n z^{-n} = \frac{2}{1-\frac{1}{5}z^{-1}}, \quad |z| > \frac{1}{5} \quad \text{and} \\ X_2(z) &= 3\sum_{n=0}^{\infty} \left(\frac{1}{7}\right)^n z^n = \frac{3}{1-\frac{1}{7}z^{-1}}, \quad |z| > \frac{1}{7} \quad \text{therefore,} \\ X(z) &= X_1(z) + X_2(z) = \frac{2}{1-\frac{1}{5}z^{-1}} + \frac{3}{1-\frac{1}{7}z^{-1}}, \quad |z| > \frac{1}{5}. \end{aligned}$$

The ROC is $|z| > \frac{1}{5}$ as shown above. We can arrive at the following properties for the ROC.

Properties of ROC of Z-Transforms

We can conclude that for an arbitrary sequence $x[n]$, the ROC of the z-transform has the following properties:

1. The ROC of $X(z)$ consists of a *ring* in the z-plane centred about the origin.

2. The ROC does not contain any poles.

3. If $x[n]$ is of finite duration, then the ROC is the entire z-plane, except possibly $z = 0$ and/or $z = \infty$.

4. If $x[n]$ is a right-sided sequence, and if the circle $|z| = a$ is the ROC, then all finite values of z for which $|z| > a$ will also be in the ROC.

5. If $x[n]$ is a left-sided sequence, and if the circle $|z| = a$ is the ROC, then all values of z for which $0 < |z| < a$ will also be in the ROC.

6. If $x[n]$ is two-sided, and if the circle $|z| = a$ is in the ROC, then the ROC will consist of a ring in the Z-plane that includes the circle $|z| = a$.

7. If the z-transform, $X(z)$ of $x[n]$ is rational, then its ROC is bounded by poles or extends to infinity.

8. If the z-transform, $X(z)$ of $x[n]$ is rational, and if $x[n]$ is right-sided, then its ROC is the region in the z-plane outside the outermost pole, i.e., outside the circle of radius equal to the largest magnitude of poles of $X(z)$. Furthermore, if $x[n]$ is also causal, the ROC also includes $z = \infty$.

9. If the z-transform, $X(z)$ of $x[n]$ is rational, and if $x[n]$ is left-sided, then its ROC is the region in the z-plane inside the innermost pole, i.e., inside the circle of radius equal to the smallest magnitude of poles of $X(z)$ other than any at $z = 0$ and extending inward to and possibly including $z = 0$. Particularly, if $x[n]$ is anti-causal, the ROC also includes $z = 0$.

Table 4.9 list out a number of z-transform pairs.

4.14.2 Inverse z-Transform

The *inverse z-transform* equation is used to get back the sequence $x[n]$ for which we have calculated the z-transform using the equation (4.152). It is expressed as

$$x[n] = \frac{1}{2\pi j} \oint X(z) z^{n-1} dz \tag{4.157}$$

where the $\oint$ denotes integration around a counter-clockwise closed contour centred at the origin and with radius r. The value of r can be chosen as any value for which $X(z)$ converges.

Table 4.9 z-transform pairs

Sequence, $x[n]$	**z-Transform, $X(z)$**	**ROC**
$\delta[n]$	1	All z.
$\delta[n-n_0]$	z^{-n_0}	All z, except 0 (if $n_0 > 0$) or ∞ (if $n_0 < 0$).
$u[n]$	$\frac{z}{z-1}$	$\|z\| > 1$
$-u[-n-1]$	$\frac{z}{z-1}$	$\|z\| < 1$
$a^n u[n]$	$\frac{z}{z-a}$	$\|z\| > \|a\|$
$-a^n u[-n-1]$	$\frac{z}{z-a}$	$\|z\| < \|a\|$
$na^n u[n]$	$\frac{az}{(z-a)^2}$	$\|z\| > \|a\|$
$-na^n u[-n-1]$	$\frac{az}{(z-a)^2}$	$\|z\| < \|a\|$
$\frac{(n+1)(n+2)...(2n-1)a^n}{(n-1)!}u[n]$	$\frac{z^n}{(z-a)^n}$; $z \geq 2$	$\|z\| > \|a\|$
$\frac{a^n}{n!}$	$\exp(a/z)$	$\|z\| > \|a\|$
$\cos\,\omega_0 n\, u[n]$	$\frac{z(z-\cos\,\omega_0)}{z^2-2z\cos\,\omega_0+1}$	$\|z\| > 1$
$b^n \cos\,\omega_0 n\, u[n]$	$\frac{z(z-\cos\,\omega_0)}{z^2-2bz\cos\,\omega_0+b^2}$	$\|z\| > b$
$\sin\,\omega_0 n\, u[n]$	$\frac{z\sin\,\omega_0}{z^2-2z\cos\,\omega_0+1}$	$\|z\| > 1$
$b^n \sin\,\omega_0 n\, u[n]$	$\frac{bz\sin\,\omega_0}{z^2-2bz\cos\,\omega_0+b^2}$	$\|z\| > b$

4.14.3 Properties of z-Transform

We will now consider some of the important properties of z-transforms.

Linearity

If

$$\begin{aligned} x[n] &\overset{\mathcal{ZT}}{\longleftrightarrow} X(z), \text{ with ROC} = R_1 \text{ and} \\ y[n] &\overset{\mathcal{ZT}}{\longleftrightarrow} Y(z), \text{ with ROC} = R_2 \text{ then} \\ ax[n]+by[n] &\overset{\mathcal{ZT}}{\longleftrightarrow} aX(z)+bY(z), \text{ with ROC} = R_1 \cap R_2. \end{aligned} \tag{4.158}$$

Time Shifting

If

$$\begin{aligned} x[n] &\overset{\mathcal{ZT}}{\longleftrightarrow} X(z), \text{ with ROC} = R \text{ then} \\ x[n-n_0] &\overset{\mathcal{ZT}}{\longleftrightarrow} z^{-n_0}X(z), \text{ with ROC} = R, \end{aligned} \tag{4.159}$$

except for addition/deletion of 0 and ∞.

Scaling in z-Domain

If

$$\begin{aligned} x[n] &\overset{\mathcal{ZT}}{\longleftrightarrow} X(z), \text{ with ROC} = R \text{ then} \\ z_0^n x[n] &\overset{\mathcal{ZT}}{\longleftrightarrow} X\left(\frac{z}{z_0}\right), \text{ with ROC} = |z_0|R. \end{aligned} \tag{4.160}$$

Time Reversal

If

$$\begin{aligned} x[n] &\overset{\mathcal{ZT}}{\longleftrightarrow} X(z), \text{ with ROC} = R \text{ then} \\ x[-n] &\overset{\mathcal{ZT}}{\longleftrightarrow} X\left(\frac{1}{z}\right), \text{ with ROC} = \frac{1}{R}. \end{aligned} \tag{4.161}$$

Time Expansion

If

$$\begin{aligned} x[n] &\overset{\mathcal{ZT}}{\longleftrightarrow} X(z), \text{ with ROC} = R \text{ then} \\ x_{<k>}[n] &\overset{\mathcal{ZT}}{\longleftrightarrow} X(z^k), \text{ with ROC} = R^{1/k}. \end{aligned} \tag{4.162}$$

Conjugation

If

$$\begin{aligned} x[n] &\overset{\mathcal{ZT}}{\longleftrightarrow} X(z), \text{ with ROC} = R \text{ then} \\ x^*[n] &\overset{\mathcal{ZT}}{\longleftrightarrow} X^*(z^*), \text{ with ROC} = R. \end{aligned} \tag{4.163}$$

Consequently, if $x[n]$ is real, then $X(z) = X^*(z^*)$.

Time Convolution

If

$$\begin{aligned} x[n] &\overset{\mathcal{ZT}}{\longleftrightarrow} X(z), \text{ with ROC} = R_1 \text{ and} \\ h[n] &\overset{\mathcal{ZT}}{\longleftrightarrow} H(z), \text{ with ROC} = R_2 \text{ then} \\ x[n] * h[n] &\overset{\mathcal{ZT}}{\longleftrightarrow} X(z)H(z), \text{ with ROC} = R_1 \cap R_2. \end{aligned}$$

Differentiation in z-Domain

If

$$\begin{aligned} x[n] &\overset{\mathcal{ZT}}{\longleftrightarrow} X(z), \text{ with ROC} = R \text{ then} \\ nx[n] &\overset{\mathcal{ZT}}{\longleftrightarrow} -z\frac{dX(z)}{dz}, \text{ with ROC} = R. \end{aligned} \tag{4.164}$$

The Initial Value Theorem

If $x[n] = 0,\ n < 0$ then

$$x[0] = \lim_{z\to\infty} X(z) \tag{4.165}$$

In Table 4.10 we summarise the properties of the z-transforms.

Table 4.10 Properties of z-transforms

Property	Sequence, $x[n]$	z-transform, $X(z)$
Linearity	$ax[n] + by[n]$	$aX(z) + bY(z)$
Time shifting	$x[n - n_0]$	$z^{-n_0}X(z)$
Scaling in z-domain	$e^{j\omega_0 n}x[n]$	$X(e^{-j\omega_0}z)$
	$z_0^n x[n]$	$X\left(\frac{z}{z_0}\right)$
	$a^n x[n]$	$X(a^{-1}z)$
Time reversal	$x[-n]$	$X(z^{-1})$
Time expansion	$x_{<k>}[n] = \begin{cases} x[k], & n = rk, \\ 0, & n \neq rk. \end{cases}$	$X(z^k)$
Differentiation in z-domain	$nx[n]$	$-z\frac{dX(z)}{dz}$
Conjugation	$x^*[n]$	$X^*(z^*)$
Convolution	$x[n] * h[n]$	$X(z)H(z)$
First difference	$x[n] - x[n-1]$	$(1 - z^{-1})X(z)$
Accumulation	$\sum_{k=-\infty}^{n} x[k]$	$\frac{1}{1-z^{-1}}X(z)$
Initial value	$x[0]$	$\lim_{z\to\infty} X(z)$
Final value	$x[\infty]$	$\lim_{z\to 1} \left[\frac{z-1}{z}X(z)\right]$
Parseval's relation	$x[n]$	$\sum_{n=-\infty}^{\infty} \lvert x[n]\rvert^2 = \frac{1}{2\pi j}\oint_{2\pi j} \lvert X(z)\rvert^2 dz$

4.15 Analysis of LTI Systems Using z-Transforms

From the convolution property of z-transforms, the z-transform of the output sequence is given by

$$Y(z) = X(z)H(z) \tag{4.166}$$

where $X(z)$ and $H(z)$ are the z-transforms of the input sequence and the system impulse response, respectively. Now, we can obtain the output sequence $y[n]$ by taking the inverse z-transform of $Y(z)$, as:

$$y[n] = \mathcal{Z}T^{-1}\{Y(z)\} = \frac{1}{2\pi j}\oint Y(z)z^{n-1}dz \tag{4.167}$$

We will now consider some of the important properties of LTI systems.

4.15.1 Causality

A causal LTI system has an impulse response $h[n]$ that is zero for $n < 0$, and hence right-sided. We know that the ROC of $H(z)$ will be the exterior of a circle in the z-plane. For discrete time causal systems, we can summarise that:

THE ROC OF CAUSAL LTI SYSTEMS

A discrete time LTI system is causal *if and only if* the ROC associated with its system function $H(z)$ is the exterior of a circle, including infinity.

The condition of the ROC of a discrete time LTI system with a rational system function can be stated as follows:

THE ROC OF AN LTI SYSTEM WITH A RATIONAL SYSTEM FUNCTION

A discrete time LTI system with a rational system function $H(z)$ is causal *if and only if* the ROC is the exterior of a circle outside the outermost pole, and with $H(z)$ expressed as a ratio of polynomials in z, the order of the numerator cannot be greater than that of the denominator.

EXAMPLE 4.10
Consider a system with system function as

$$H(z) = \frac{z^4 + 3z^3 - 4z^2 + 5z + 6}{3z^3 + z^2 - 5z + 6}$$

Determine whether the system is causal.

SOLUTION
Without even knowing the ROC for this system, we can conclude that the system is *not* causal as the order of the numerator polynomial is higher than that of the denominator.

4.15.2 Stability

The stability of a discrete time LTI system is equivalent to its impulse response being absolutely summable. Thus we have, for stability of a discrete time LTI system:

THE STABILITY OF AN LTI SYSTEM IN RELATION TO ROC

A discrete time LTI system is stable *if and only if* the ROC of its system function $H(z)$ includes the unit circle $|z| = 1$.

It can be shown that a system can be stable, while not *causal.* For a stable and causal system, we have following condition:

THE STABILITY OF A CAUSAL LTI SYSTEM WITH A RATIONAL SYSTEM FUNCTION

A causal discrete time LTI system with a rational system function $H(z)$ is stable *if and only if* all of the poles of $H(z)$ lie inside the unit circle—i.e., they must all have magnitude smaller than unity.

EXAMPLE 4.11

Find the *inverse system* of the system characterised by $y[n] = \alpha y[n-1] + x[n]$.

SOLUTION

Taking z-transform of both sides of the equation, we have:

$$Y(z) = \alpha z^{-1} Y(z) + X(z)$$

Therefore, $H(z) = \frac{Y(z)}{X(z)} = \frac{1}{1-\alpha z^{-1}}$. Now we have: $H(z)H^{-1}(z) = 1$. Hence, $H^{-1}(z) = 1 - \alpha z^{-1}$. It follows that for the *inverse system*, $\frac{X(z)}{Y(z)} = 1 - \alpha z^{-1}$. Cross-multiplying and taking *inverse z-transform*, we get:

$$x[n] = y[n] - \alpha y[n-1]$$

which is the system difference equation for the inverse system. Note that since the given system is *all pole*, its inverse is an *all zero* system.

4.15.3 Unilateral z-Transforms

The *unilateral z-transform* is particularly useful in analysing the characteristics of causal systems specified by linear constant coefficient difference equations with non-zero initial conditions. The unilateral z-transform of $x[n]$ is defined as

$$\mathcal{X}(z) = \sum_{n=0}^{\infty} x[n] z^{-n} \tag{4.168}$$

Usually the unilateral z-transform pair is represented as

$$x[n] \overset{\mathcal{UZT}}{\longleftrightarrow} \mathcal{X}(z) = \mathcal{UZT}\left\{x[n]\right\} \tag{4.169}$$

The unilateral z-transform differs from the bilateral z-transform in that the summation is carried out only over the non-negative values of n, immaterial of whether $x[n]$ is zero for $n < 0$. Thus, unilateral z-transform of $x[n]$ can be thought of as the bilateral z-transform of $x[n]u[n]$.

The important properties of unilateral z-transforms are summarised in Table 4.11.

Table 4.11 Properties of unilateral z-transforms

Property	Sequence, $x[n]$	z-transform, $\mathcal{X}(z)$
Linearity	$ax[n] + by[n]$	$a\mathcal{X}(z) + b\mathcal{Y}(z)$
Time delay	$x[n-1]$	$z^{-1}\mathcal{X}(z) + x[-1]$
Time advance	$x[n+1]$	$z\mathcal{X}(z) - zx[0]$
Scaling in z-domain	$e^{j\omega_0 n}x[n]$	$\mathcal{X}(e^{-j\omega_0}z)$
	$z_0^n x[n]$	$\mathcal{X}\left(\frac{z}{z_0}\right)$
	$a^n x[n]$	$\mathcal{X}(a^{-1}z)$
Time expansion	$x_{<k>}[n] = \begin{cases} x[k], & n = rk, \\ 0, & n \neq rk. \end{cases}$	$\mathcal{X}(z^k)$
Differentiation in z-domain	$nx[n]$	$-z\frac{d\mathcal{X}(z)}{dz}$
Conjugation	$x^*[n]$	$\mathcal{X}^*(z^*)$
Convolution	$x[n] * h[n]$	$\mathcal{X}(z)\mathcal{H}(z)$
First difference	$x[n] - x[n-1]$	$(1 - z^{-1})\mathcal{X}(z) - x[-1]$
Accumulation	$\sum_{k=-\infty}^{n} x[k]$	$\frac{1}{1-z^{-1}}\mathcal{X}(z)$
Initial value	$x[0]$	$\lim_{z\to\infty} \mathcal{X}(z)$

4.16 The Discrete Fourier Transform (DFT)

The discrete Fourier transform is a generalisation of a discrete function, $f(t) \to f(t_k)$, by letting $f_k \equiv f(t_k)$, where $t_k = k\Delta$, with $k = 0, 1, \ldots, N-1$. Thus we get:

$$F_n = \sum_{k=0}^{N-1} f_k e^{-2\pi jkn/N} \tag{4.170}$$

The inverse discrete Fourier transform (IDFT), f_k is defined as:

$$f_k = \frac{1}{N} \sum_{n=0}^{N-1} F_n e^{2\pi jkn/N} \tag{4.171}$$

Discrete Fourier transforms are extremely useful because they reveal periodicities in input data as well as the relative strengths of any periodic components. There are a few subtleties in the interpretation of discrete Fourier transforms, however. In general, the discrete Fourier transform of a real sequence of numbers will be a sequence of complex numbers of the same length. In particular, if f_k are real, then F_{N-n} and F_n are related by

$$F_{N-n} = F_n^*, \text{ for } n = 0, 1, \ldots, N-1. \tag{4.172}$$

where F_n^* is the complex conjugate of F_n. This means that the component F_0 is always real for real data. As a result of the above relation, a periodic function will contain transformed peaks in not one, but two places. This happens because the periods of the input data become split into "positive" and "negative" frequency complex components. We may also note that:

- The discrete Fourier transform is a special case of the z-transform.
- It can be computed efficiently using a fast Fourier transform.
- The transform can also be generalised to two and more dimensions.

The MATLAB functions `Y=fft(x)` and `y=ifft(X)` implement the transform and inverse transform pair given for vectors of length N by:

$$X(k) = \sum_{n=1}^{N} x(n)\omega_N^{(n-1)(k-1)} \tag{4.173}$$

$$x(n) = \frac{1}{N}\sum_{k=1}^{N} X(k)\omega_N^{-(n-1)(k-1)} \tag{4.174}$$

where $\omega_N = e^{(-2\pi j)/N}$, is an Nth root of unity.
`Y = fft(X)` returns the discrete Fourier transform (DFT) of vector X, computed with a fast Fourier transform (FFT) algorithm. If X is a matrix, `fft` returns the Fourier transform of each column of the matrix. If X is a multi-dimensional array, `fft` operates on the first non-singleton dimension.

EXAMPLE 4.12
Consider data sampled at 1000 Hz. Form a signal containing a 50 Hz sinusoid of amplitude 0.6 V and 120 Hz sinusoid of amplitude 1 V. Corrupt it with some zero-mean random noise. Find the frequency components of a signal buried in a noisy time domain signal.

SOLUTION
The MATLAB code to implement the above is listed below. Figure 4.33 illustrates the corresponding signal and the spectrum.

```
%%% MATLAB code to find the frequency components of a
%%% signal buried in a noisy time domain signal.
clear all; close all; clf;
Fs = 1000;                    % Sampling frequency
T = 1/Fs;                     % Sample time
L = 10000;                    % Length of signal
t = (0:L-1)*T;                % Time vector
% Sum of a 50 Hz sinusoid and a 120 Hz sinusoid
x = 0.6*sin(2*pi*50*t) + sin(2*pi*120*t);
y = x + 2*randn(size(t));     % Sinusoids plus noise
```

```
subplot(211),plot(Fs*t(1:50),y(1:50),'LineWidth',2)
title('Signal Corrupted with Zero-Mean Random Noise')
xlabel('time (milliseconds)');ylabel('Amplitude');grid;
NFFT = 2^nextpow2(L); % Next power of 2 from length of y
Y = fft(y,NFFT)/L;
f = Fs/2*linspace(0,1,NFFT/2+1);
% Plot single-sided amplitude spectrum.
subplot(212),plot(f,2*abs(Y(1:NFFT/2+1)),'LineWidth',2)
title('Single-Sided Amplitude Spectrum of y(t)')
xlabel('Frequency (Hz)')
ylabel('|Y(f)|');grid;
%%% end of dftcomp.m
```

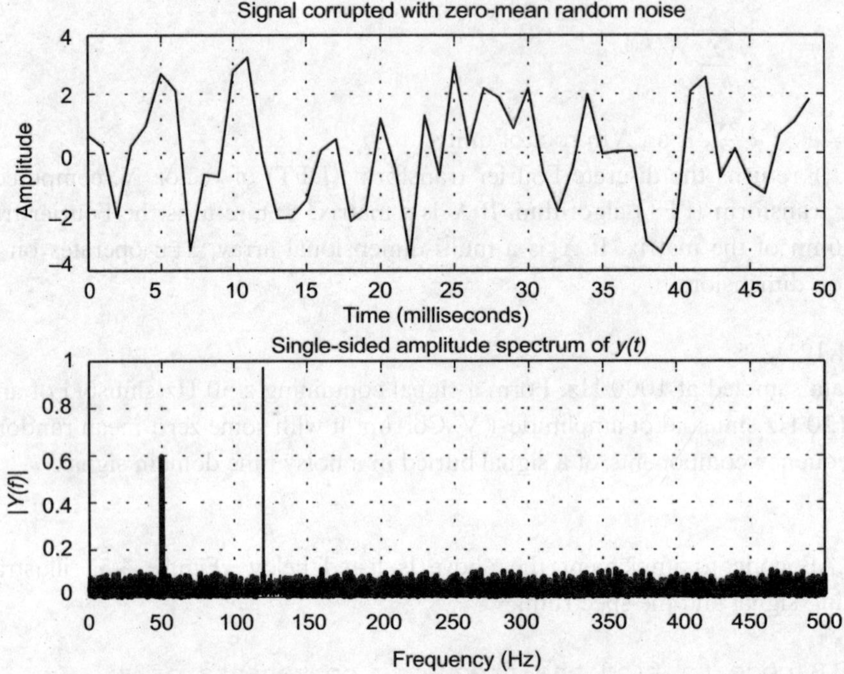

Figure 4.33 Illustration of application of `fft(.)` function. (a) Signal corrupted with zero-mean random Noise, $y(t)$. (b) Single-sided amplitude spectrum of $y(t)$.

4.17 Conclusion

In this chapter we considered the transform theory, which is a very prominent mathematical tool. We discussed the discrete time and continuous time signals separately and studied the Fourier series representation, the continuous time Fourier transform and the discrete time

Fourier transform. We also considered the Laplace transform of continuous time signals and studied the Fourier transform as a special case of the Laplace transform. Then we discussed the z-transform of discrete time signals, and the discrete Fourier transform (DFT) as a special case of the z-transform.

Further Reading

1. Cooley, J. W. and J. W. Tukey. An algorithm for the machine computation of the complex fourier series. *Mathematics of Computation*. 19: 297–30. April 1965.

2. *Getting Started with Communications Blockset*. The MathWorks. 2009.

3. *Getting Started with MATLAB 7*. The MathWorks. 2009.

4. *Getting Started with Signal Processing Toolbox*. The MathWorks. 2009.

5. Oppenheim, Alan V., Alan S. Willsky, and S. Hamid Nawas. *Signals and Systems*. 2nd Edition Pearson Education 2004.

6. Oppenheim, Alan V. and R. W. Schafer. *Discrete-Time Signal Processing*. Prentice-Hall, 1989.

7. *Simulink*. The MathWorks. 2009.

8. *User's Guide, Communications Toolbox*. The MathWorks. 2009.

Problems

1. Evaluate the convolution of the following two signals: $x(t) = \sin(2\pi f_0 t)$ and $h(t) = A$ for $t \in [0, \frac{2}{f_0}]$ and zero outside, using MATLAB.

2. Evaluate the convolution of the following two signals: $x(t) = \sin\left(\frac{\pi}{T}t\right)$ for $t \in [0, T]$, and zero outside, and $h(t) = A$ for $t \in [0, 2T]$, and zero outside, using MATLAB.

3. Evaluate the energy, average power, energy spectrum and power spectrum for the following signals using MATLAB:

   (a) $x(t) = A\cos(2\pi\, f_0 t + \phi_0)$.

   (b) $x(t) = A\cos^2(2\pi\, f_0 t + \phi_0)$.

   (c) $x(t) = A$, for $t \in [0, 2T]$ and zero outside.

   (d) $x(t) = A\exp(-b|t|)$, where b is a positive number. Over this signal, evaluate the 3 dB bandwidth as a function of the parameter b.

4. Plot the function $f(x) = \sin \frac{\pi}{2}x + \sin \frac{2}{5}\pi x$ over the interval $[0, 40]$.
   (a) How many peaks (relative maxima) does the graph have?
   (b) This function is periodic. How many periods are graphed in $[0, 40]$?
   (c) Estimate from the plot, the value of $f(10)$ to at least 1 decimal point.

5. Let $x = [1\ 2\ 3]$. Write MATLAB commands to compute:

$$f(x) = x - \frac{\cos\, x - \sin\, x}{\sin\, x + \cos\, x}$$

6. The impulse response of a system is

$$h(t) = \begin{cases} t^3\, e^{-t^2} & 0 < t \\ 0 & t < 0 \end{cases}$$

   Use the `conv(.)` function in MATLAB to find the response of the system to the pulse

$$x(t) = \begin{cases} A & 0 < t < T \\ 0 & \text{elsewhere} \end{cases}$$

   where A and T are real positive constants.

7. Show by an example that linear filters obey a superposition principle (i.e., the output obtained when two inputs are summed together, is the same as the sum of the outputs for individual inputs).

8. Show by an example that linear filtering in a cascade of two, three, or more separate filters gives the same answer regardless of the order in which they are applied.

9. Obtain the spectrum for a 3 V amplitude, with duration of 0.5 s rectangular pulse using the `fft()` function in MATLAB. Compare it with the theoretical spectrum.

10. Sketch, using MATLAB, a periodic function given by $f(x) = |\sin(x)|$ for $-\pi < x < \pi$. Determine whether it is odd or even function.

11. The signal $x(t)$ is given by: $x(t) = \sin c(100\, t) \cos(2\pi \times 200\, t)$. Plot the function and its magnitude spectrum using MATLAB.

12. Determine the Fourier series expansion of the *full-wave rectifier* signal:

$$x(t) = |\cos\, 2\pi f_0\, t|.$$

13. For a 3 V *half-wave rectified* sine wave with frequency 100 Hz, obtain the *Fourier series* coefficients.

14. Determine the spectrum of the above wave using the `fft()` function in MATLAB.

15. Find the output of an LTI system with impulse response $h(t)$ when driven by the input signal $x(t)$ when:

$$h(t) = \delta(t) + \delta^{'}(t)$$

16. Let $x(t)$ be an arbitrary signal and define $x_1(t) = \sum_{n=-\infty}^{\infty} x(t - nT_0)$.
(a) Show that $x_1(t)$ is periodic.
(b) How can we write $x_1(t)$ in terms of $x(t)$ and $\sum_{n=-\infty}^{\infty} \delta(t - nT_0)$?

17. Verify the convolution theorem using MATLAB to show that:

$$\text{sinc}\ t * \text{sinc}\ t = \text{sinc}\ t_0.$$

where $\text{sinc}\ x \triangleq \frac{\sin \pi x}{\pi x}$. If sinc t contains 1000 samples, how many samples will be there in sinc t_0?

18. Plot the functions (a) $\frac{\sin x}{x}$, and (b) $\frac{\sin x}{x} * \frac{\sin x}{x}$. What is your observation?

19. (a) Construct an array of discrete times

$$t = [0, \Delta t, \ldots, (N-1)\Delta t]$$

for some values of N and Δt.
(b) Using the above array of discrete times t_j, construct a discretely-sampled time series $x_j := x(t_j)$ representing the function

$$x(t) = \begin{cases} 0 & -\infty < t < 0 \\ e^{-t} & 0 \leq t < \infty \end{cases}$$

Plot x_j versus t_j for different choices of the sample period, total duration, etc.
(c) Repeat the above for

$$x(t) = \sin 2\pi f_0 t, \quad -\infty < t < \infty$$

where f_0 is some frequency (in Hz) that can be chosen. What is the sampling rate f_s and Nyquist frequency f_N in terms of the sampling period Δt? How must f_0 be related to the sampling rate and Nyquist frequencies in order that the sampled version of the sine wave "look" like a sine wave? Plot x_j versus t_j for several choices of f_0 relative to f_N.

20. Generate a square wave as a sum of several sinusoids. Write a MATLAB M-file that will do the job. Vary the number of harmonics and see the variation.

21. Obtain the *system differential equation* characterised by the following system, $H(j\omega) = \frac{3}{2+i\omega}$.

22. Let $X(e^{j\omega}) \longleftrightarrow (0.5)^n u[n] = x[n]$. Find the time signal corresponding to $Y(e^{j\omega}) = X(e^{j\omega}) * X(e^{j\omega})$.

23. Let $X(e^{j\omega}) = 1 + 3e^{-j2\omega} - 2e^{-j3\omega}$. Find $x[n]$.

24. The *step response* of an LTI system is given by $s[n] = u[n] - u[n-2]$. Obtain its *impulse response.*

25. Check whether the discrete time system characterised by the equation $y[n] - \frac{1}{6}y[n-1] - \frac{1}{6}y[n-2] = x[n]$ is *stable.*

26. Let $X(z) = \frac{z(z-2)}{(z-1)(z-0.5)}$. Find $x[0]$ and $\lim_{n\to\infty} x[n]$.

27. Obtain the system difference equation of the causal system characterised by $H(z) = \frac{3}{z+2}$.

28. Find the z-transform and its ROC for the following sequence, $x[n] = u[n+2] - u[n-2]$.

29. Consider the signal $x(t) = 10\cos(2\pi f_1 t) + 5\cos(4\pi f_1 t)$, where $f_1 = 2$ kHz. The signal is sent through an LTI system with impulse response $h(t) = 1$, for $t \in [0, 1\text{ms}]$ and zero outside. Let $y(t)$ be the output of the LTI system. Evaluate the following using MATLAB:

    (a) The Fourier transform of the signal $x(t)$.

    (b) The power spectrum of $x(t)$.

    (c) The average power of $x(t)$.

    (d) The transfer function of the linear system, drawing a qualitative plot.

    (e) The output signal $y(t)$.

    (f) The power of the output signal $y(t)$.

30. Consider the signal $y(t) = x(t)\cos(2\pi f_0 t)$, where the Fourier transform of $x(t)$ is equal to 1 in the interval $[-B, +B]$ and zero outside. The frequency f_0 is much greater than B. The signal $y(t)$ is sent to a non-linear device which generates the output $z(t) = Ay^2(t) + C$. The signal $z(t)$ is then sent to an ideal lowpass filter with bandwidth equal to 1.5 B. Estimate the spectrum of the output of this filter using MATLAB.

5

Simulation of Analog Modulation Systems

In this chapter we will discuss analog modulation schemes. We start with the analytical (mathematical) model of modulation schemes like amplitude modulation (AM) and simulate the output waveforms using MATLAB®. Note that amplitude modulation is treated as a *linear* modulation scheme. We will derive the frequency spectrum of the modulated wave using MATLAB. In a later section, we will also consider the noise performance of amplitude modulation schemes. Discussion of other analog modulation schemes like frequency modulation (FM) and phase modulation (PM) will be taken up in Chapter 6.

5.1 Introduction

Let us explore the need for modulation. For short range communication systems like the signal transmission in the telephone local loop or between the amplifier and the speakers of a sound system, the baseband signals are sent through wires. For longer distances, it is difficult to use wires as it needs more space and large quantities of expensive material (usually copper). Added to that, if transmission is *point-to-point*, one must specify the location of every terminal. Mobile communication by wire is almost impossible. Hence one resorts to radio communication, where it becomes quite simple to move around. The reasons for modulating (or varying in accordance with something else) attributes (like amplitude, frequency and phase) of a carrier wave are the following:

- Baseband has limited coverage.
- It is a less efficient means of transmission of information.
- Mobile communication is almost impossible with wired baseband systems.
- For efficiently radiating signals using an antenna, the spectrum has to be elevated to a higher level in order to reduce the antenna length.[1]
- Multiplexing in the frequency domain is possible with modulation.

[1] As a *rule of thumb*, for efficient radiation, the minimum antenna length should be one-tenth of the transmitted wavelength.

5.1.1 Amplitude Modulation (AM)

In amplitude modulation, the amplitude of a high frequency carrier wave is modulated (or varied) in accordance with the modulating signal. In practical systems, the carrier frequency should be 50 to 100 times the highest frequency present in the modulating signal. The carrier signal amplitude should be so chosen that it is always greater than the amplitude of the modulating signal. Generally, the modulating signal consists of several frequencies of varying amplitudes. Amplitude modulation has several variants like the double sideband with full carrier (DSBFC), double sideband suppressed carrier (DSBSC), single sideband (SSB) and so on.

5.1.2 Amplitude Generation and Demodulation

Switched modulation sums the carrier signal $c(t)$ and the modulating signal $m(t)$, and then passes the sum through a switch, which approximately multiplies it by a periodic square wave. This generates the desired signal plus extra terms that are filtered out. The spectrum of modulated signal is

$$S(f) = 0.5k_a A_c[M(f - f_c) + M(f + f_c)] + 0.5A_c[\delta(f - f_c) + \delta(f + f_c)].$$

The percentage modulation of the signal is defined as $\max\{100|k_a m(t)|\}$, where k_a is the index of modulation. AM waves can be demodulated using non-linear devices with some distortion. The envelope of the transmitted signal is

$$a(t) = A_c|1 + k_a m(t)|.$$

If $|k_a m(t)| \leq 1$ for all t, then $a(t)$ is always non-negative, which simplifies demodulation.

5.2 Mathematical Model of AM

In our analysis, we assume a sinusoidal carrier wave of amplitude A_c and frequency f_c. Hence the carrier is represented by:

$$e_c = A_c \sin(2\pi f_c t) \tag{5.1}$$

We then assume that the sinusoidal modulating signal consists of a single frequency, f_m with amplitude A_m. We will remove this restriction later on. Now, the instantaneous values of the modulating signal and the amplitude modulated output are given by:

$$\begin{aligned} e_m &= A_m \sin(2\pi f_m t) && (5.2)\\ e_{AM} &= [A_c + A_m \sin(2\pi f_m t)] \sin(2\pi f_c t) && (5.3)\\ &= A_c \left[1 + \frac{A_m}{A_c} \sin(2\pi f_m t)\right] \sin(2\pi f_c t) && (5.4)\\ &= A_c \left[1 + m_a \sin(2\pi f_m t)\right] \sin(2\pi f_c t), \text{ where } m_a = \frac{A_m}{A_c}. && (5.5) \end{aligned}$$

Note that $f_c >> f_m$. We call the ratio $m_a = \frac{A_m}{A_c}$ as *modulation index* or *modulation depth.* Now, expanding equation (5.5), we get:

$$\begin{aligned} e_{AM} &= A_c \sin(2\pi f_c t) + m_a A_c \sin(2\pi f_c t) \sin(2\pi f_m t) && (5.6)\\ &= A_c \sin(2\pi f_c t) + \frac{m_a A_c}{2} \cos\left[2\pi(f_c - f_m)t\right] \\ &\quad - \frac{m_a A_c}{2} \cos\left[2\pi(f_c + f_m)t\right] && (5.7) \end{aligned}$$

Equation (5.7) clearly shows that the amplitude modulated output waveform contains the carrier frequency as such. Apart from the carrier, it also contains two frequencies, $(f_c - f_m)$ and $(f_c + f_m)$, known as the *lower* and *upper* sidebands respectively.

5.2.1 Amplitude Modulation with Multiple Sinusoidal Signals

We will now consider modulation of a carrier wave having multiple sinusoidal signals with varying amplitudes and frequencies. Let there be N sinusoidal modulating signals denoted by $e_1, e_2, \ldots, e_N$. Now the resulting complex analog modulating signal is given by $e_1+e_2+\ldots+e_N$. Let us represent it as:

$$\begin{aligned} e_1 &= E_1 \sin(2\pi f_1 t)\\ e_2 &= E_2 \sin(2\pi f_2 t)\\ \vdots &= \vdots\\ e_N &= E_N \sin(2\pi f_N t) \end{aligned}$$

The amplitude modulator being a linear system, the principle of superposition can be applied. We then get the modulated output as:

$$\begin{aligned} e_{AM} &= A_c \sin(2\pi f_c t) + \frac{m_1 A_c}{2}\cos\left[2\pi(f_c - f_1)t\right] - \frac{m_1 A_c}{2}\cos\left[2\pi(f_c + f_1)t\right] + \\ & +\frac{m_2 A_c}{2}\cos\left[2\pi(f_c - f_2)t\right] - \frac{m_2 A_c}{2}\cos\left[2\pi(f_c + f_2)t\right] + \ldots + \ldots + \\ & +\frac{m_N A_c}{2}\cos\left[2\pi(f_c - f_N)t\right] - \frac{m_N A_c}{2}\cos\left[2\pi(f_c + f_N)t\right]. \end{aligned} \tag{5.8}$$

In the above equation, the modulation index of the ith component is given by $m_i = E_i/A_c$.

5.2.2 Power Contained in AM Components

We will now consider the power carried by the different components of an amplitude modulated output signal. The total power, when the load resistor is 1 Ω, can be obtained by:

$$\begin{aligned} P_{AM} &= \lim_{T\to\infty}\frac{1}{T}\int_{t=0}^{T} e_{AM}^2\,dt \\ &= \lim_{T\to\infty}\frac{1}{T}\Bigg[\int_{t=0}^{T} A_c^2\sin^2(2\pi f_c t)dt + \\ & + \left\{\int_{t=0}^{T}\frac{m_1^2 A_c^2}{4}\cos^2\left(2\pi[f_c - f_1]t\right) + \int_{t=0}^{T}\frac{m_1^2 A_c^2}{4}\cos^2\left(2\pi[f_c + f_1]t\right)\right\} + \\ & + \left\{\int_{t=0}^{T}\frac{m_2^2 A_c^2}{4}\cos^2\left(2\pi[f_c - f_2]t\right) + \int_{t=0}^{T}\frac{m_2^2 A_c^2}{4}\cos^2\left(2\pi[f_c + f_2]t\right)\right\} + \\ & \ldots + \ldots + \\ & + \left\{\int_{t=0}^{T}\frac{m_N^2 A_c^2}{4}\cos^2\left(2\pi[f_c - f_N]t\right) + \int_{t=0}^{T}\frac{m_N^2 A_c^2}{4}\cos^2\left(2\pi[f_c + f_N]t\right)\right\}\Bigg] \\ &= \frac{A_c^2}{2} + \frac{m_1^2 A_c^2}{4} + \frac{m_2^2 A_c^2}{4} + \ldots + \frac{m_N^2 A_c^2}{4} \\ &= \underbrace{\frac{A_c^2}{2}}_{\text{Power in carrier}} + \underbrace{\frac{m_1^2 A_c^2}{4}}_{\text{Power in sidebands due to } f_1} + \underbrace{\frac{m_2^2 A_c^2}{4}}_{\text{Power in sidebands due to } f_2} + \ldots + \\ & + \underbrace{\frac{m_N^2 A_c^2}{4}}_{\text{Power in sidebands due to } f_N} \end{aligned}$$

Hence it is evident that the total power is contained by the carrier and the sidebands. In other words:

$$P_{\text{total}} = P_c + \frac{m_1^2 P_c}{2} + \frac{m_2^2 P_c}{2} + \ldots + \frac{m_N^2 P_c}{2} \tag{5.9}$$

Note that the output power is a function of carrier power and the modulation depth.

Till now, we have considered modulation by sinusoidal waveforms. But in practical situations, there might be a need to modulate non-sinusoidal waveforms. In such cases, we can apply the *Fourier transform* method to obtain the *frequency spectrum.*

Effective Modulation Index

The *effective* modulation index, for modulating multiple sine waves, each having individual modulation indices $m_1, m_2, \ldots, m_N$ is given by:

$$m_{\text{eff}} = \sqrt{m_1^2 + m_2^2 + \ldots + m_N^2} \tag{5.10}$$

In terms of the effective modulation index, the total power contained when the load resistance is 1 Ω is:

$$\begin{aligned} P_{\text{total}} &= P_c + \frac{m_{\text{eff}}^2}{2} P_c \\ &= P_c \left[1 + \frac{m_{\text{eff}}^2}{2}\right] \end{aligned} \tag{5.11}$$

It follows that the *effective voltage* and *effective current* are given by:

$$E_{\text{eff}} = E_c \sqrt{1 + \frac{m_{\text{eff}}^2}{2}} \tag{5.12}$$

$$I_{\text{eff}} = I_c \sqrt{1 + \frac{m_{\text{eff}}^2}{2}} \tag{5.13}$$

where E_c and I_c are respectively the voltage and current without any modulating signal.

5.3 Simulation of Amplitude Modulation

We can simulate the generation of amplitude modulation in two different ways using MATLAB. The first technique involves explicitly implementing equation (5.5). The second approach is to use the `modulate(.)` function in MATLAB. There is another library function in MATLAB, viz. `ammod(.)` in the Communications Toolbox which can also generate amplitude modulation. We will consider all of them.

5.3.1 AM Generation—User Defined M-file

A simple set of MATLAB code to generate and plot an AM signal is given below along with the results in Figure 5.1. We assume that the carrier amplitude is 10 V and frequency 100 kHz. We use a single sinusoidal modulating signal with amplitude 8 V and frequency 1 kHz.

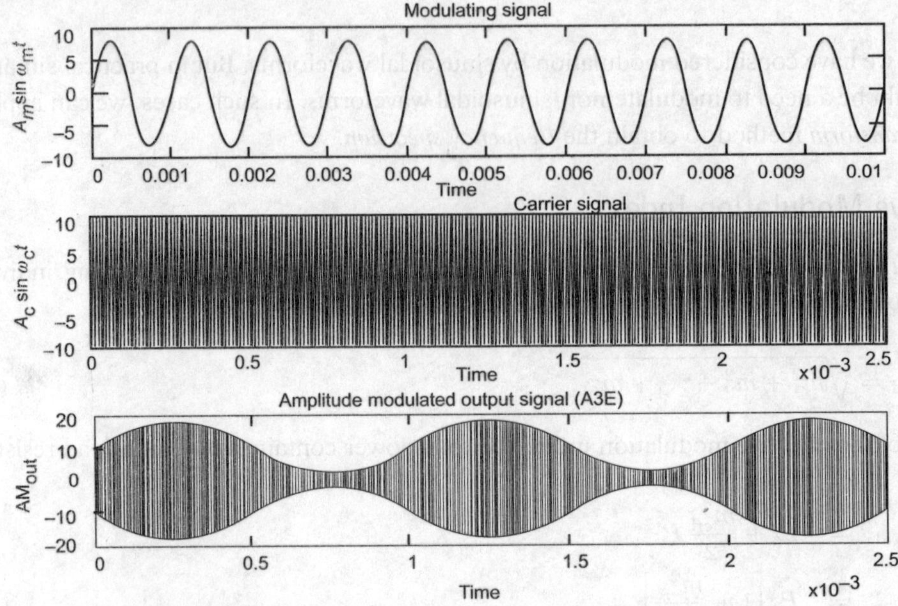

Figure 5.1 Amplitude modulation: Simulated waveforms I

```
%%% An M-file to generate and plot AM-DSBFC (A3E) signal.%%%
close all; clear all; clf;
t=linspace(0,.01,1000000);
fc=100000; % carrier frequency.
fm=1000;    % modulating frequency.
Ac=10;      % amplitude of carrier.
Am=8;       % amplitude of modulating signal.
ma=Am/Ac;   % modulation index..
wc=2*pi*fc*t;
wm=2*pi*fm*t;
ec=Ac*sin(wc);
em=Am*sin(wm);
y=Ac*(1+ma*sin(wm)).*sin(wc);
l=1000000;
subplot(311),plot(t(1:l),em(1:l)),...
```

```
xlabel('Time'),ylabel('A_m sin\omega_m t'),...
title('Modulating Signal');
subplot(312),plot(t(1:l/4),ec(1:l/4)),...
xlabel('Time'),ylabel('A_c sin\omega_c t'),...
title('Carrier  Signal');
subplot(313),plot(t(1:l/4),y(1:l/4)),...
xlabel('Time'), ylabel('AM_{out}'),...
title('Amplitude Modulated Output Signal (A3E)');
%% End of Program am.m %%%%
```

5.3.2 AM Generation—Using Library Functions

There are two functions, one in the Signal Processing Toolbox, `modulate(.)`, and the other in the Communications Toolbox, `ammod(.)`, respectively, which can be used to generate amplitude modulation. A short script for generating the AM with the above specifications of carrier and modulating signal, is given below. The simulated output waveform is illustrated in Figure 5.2.

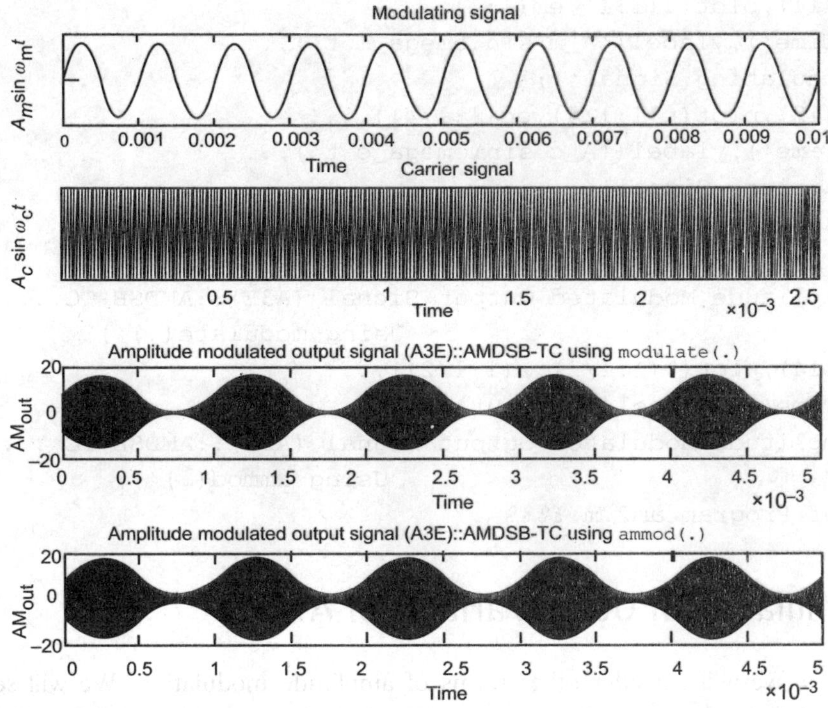

Figure 5.2 Amplitude modulation: Simulated waveforms II

```
%%% A script M-file to generate and plot AM-DSBFC (A3E) signal ...
```

```
%%% Using the modulate(.) and ammod(.) functions..
close all; clear all; clf;
t=linspace(0,.01,1000000);
fc=100000;  % carrier frequency.
fm=1000;    % modulating frequency.
fs=400000;  % sampling frequency.
Ac=10;      % amplitude of carrier.
Am=8;       % amplitude of modulating signal.
ma=Am/Ac;   % modulation index..
wc=2*pi*fc*t;
wm=2*pi*fm*t;
ec=Ac*sin(wc);
em=Am*sin(wm);
y=modulate(em,fc,fs,'amdsb-tc');% AM output using modulate(.)
                                % function..
z=ammod(em,fc,fs,0,Ac);% AM output using ammod(.) function..
l=1000000;
subplot(411),plot(t(1:l),em(1:l)),...
xlabel('Time'),ylabel('A_m sin\omega_m t'),...
title('Modulating Signal');
subplot(412),plot(t(1:l/4),ec(1:l/4)),...
xlabel('Time'),ylabel('A_c sin\omega_c t'),...
title('Carrier  Signal');
subplot(413),plot(t(1:l/2),y(1:l/2)),...
xlabel('Time'), ylabel('AM_{out}'),...
title('Amplitude Modulated Output Signal (A3E)::AMDSB-TC,...
                                 Using modulate(.)');
subplot(414),plot(t(1:l/2),z(1:l/2)),...
xlabel('Time'), ylabel('AM_{out}'),...
title('Amplitude Modulated Output Signal (A3E)::AMDSB-TC,...
                                  Using ammod(.)');
%%% End of Program am2.m %%%%
```

5.4 Simulation of Other Variants of AM

In this section, we will consider other forms of amplitude modulation. We will soon find that, as far as information transmission is concerned, the carrier and one of the sidebands in the spectrum of the modulated output signal are redundant. This gives rise to other variants of amplitude modulation, such as double sideband suppressed carrier (DSBSC) and single sideband (SSB). In DSBSC, the carrier is removed before transmission, thereby saving power and bandwidth. In SSB, the carrier and one of the sidebands is removed to save bandwidth and power. The demodulators for these two types of AM are comparatively more complex.

5.4.1 Simulation of DSBSC

We can conveniently make use of the `modulate(.)` and `ammod(.)` functions in the Signal Processing Toolbox of MATLAB to simulate a DSBSC. A typical code is given below. Figure 5.3 shows the simulated output waveform.

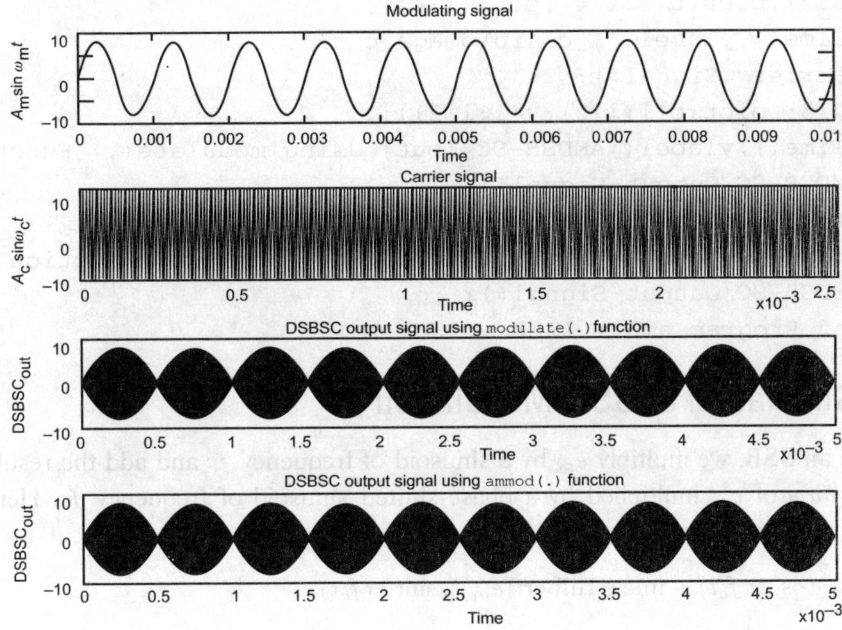

Figure 5.3 DSBSC: Simulated output waveform

```
%%% MATLAB Script to Simulate DSBSC..
close all; clear all; clf;
t=linspace(0,.01,1000000);
fc=100000;  % carrier frequency.
fm=1000;    % modulating frequency.
fs=400000;  % sampling frequency.
Ac=10;      % amplitude of carrier.
Am=8;       % amplitude of modulating signal.
ma=Am/Ac;   % modulation index..
wc=2*pi*fc*t;
wm=2*pi*fm*t;
ec=Ac*sin(wc);
```

```
em=Am*sin(wm);
y=modulate(em,fc,fs,'amdsb-sc');% AM-DSBSC output using
                                 % modulate(.) function..
z=ammod(em,fc,fs,0);% AM-DSBSC output using ammod(.) function..
l=1000000;
subplot(411),plot(t(1:l),em(1:l)),...
xlabel('Time'),ylabel('A_m sin\omega_m t'),...
title('Modulating Signal');
subplot(412),plot(t(1:l/4),ec(1:l/4)),...
xlabel('Time'),ylabel('A_c sin\omega_c t'),...
title('Carrier  Signal');
subplot(413),plot(t(1:l/2),y(1:l/2)),...
xlabel('Time'),ylabel('AMDSB-SC_{out} Using modulate(.) Function');
title('AMDSB-SC Output Signal');
subplot(414),plot(t(1:l/2),z(1:l/2)),...
xlabel('Time'),ylabel('AMDSB-SC_{out}Using ammod(.) Function');
title('AMDSB-SC Output Signal');
%%% End of Program am3.m %%%%
```

5.4.2 Simulation of SSB Modulation

To generate an SSB, we multiply e_m by a sinusoid of frequency f_c and add the result to the *Hilbert transform* of e_m multiplied by a phase-shifted sinusoid of frequency f_c. Hence, the SSB output signal is given by:

$$y = e_m.\cos(2\pi f_c t) + \text{imag}(\text{Hilbert}(e_m)).\sin(2\pi f_c t) \tag{5.14}$$

A simple MATLAB script file for this purpose is given below and the output waveform is illustrated in Figure 5.4.

```
%%% MATLAB Script to Simulate SSB Modulation...
close all; clear all; clf;
t=linspace(0,.01,1000000);
fc=100000;  % carrier frequency.
fm=1000;    % modulating frequency.
fs=400000;  % sampling frequency.
Ac=10;      % amplitude of carrier.
Am=8;       % amplitude of modulating signal.
wc=2*pi*fc*t;
wm=2*pi*fm*t;
ec=Ac*sin(wc);
em=Am*sin(wm);
```

```
y=modulate(em,fc,fs,'amssb');
l=1000000;
subplot(311),plot(t(1:l),em(1:l)),...
xlabel('Time'),ylabel('A_m sin\omega_m t'),...
title('Modulating Signal');
subplot(312),plot(t(1:l/4),ec(1:l/4)),...
xlabel('Time'),ylabel('A_c sin\omega_c t'),...
title('Carrier  Signal');
subplot(313),plot(t(1:l/2),y(1:l/2)),...
xlabel('Time'), ylabel('SSB_{out}'),...
title('SSB Output Signal');
%%% End of Program ssb.m %%%%
```

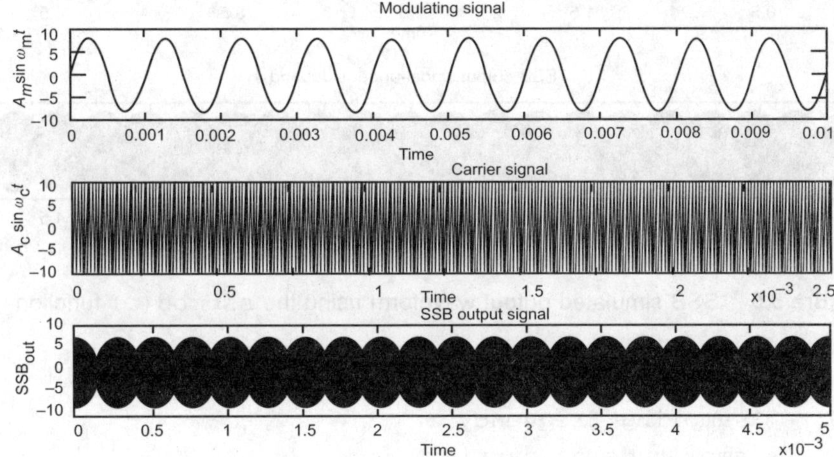

Figure 5.4 SSB: Simulated output waveform

Simulation of SSB Modulation Using `ssbmod(.)` Function

The `ssbmod(.)` function in the Communications Toolbox of MATLAB can also be used to generate SSB modulation very conveniently. A MATLAB script file using the `ssbmod(.)` function is given below. The output is illustrated in Figure 5.5.

```
%%% MATLAB Script file to generate SSB Modulation..
%%% Using ssbmod(.) Function in Communications Toolbox..
clear all; close all; clf;
l=1000000;
t=linspace(0,.01,l);
fc=100000;  % carrier frequency.
```

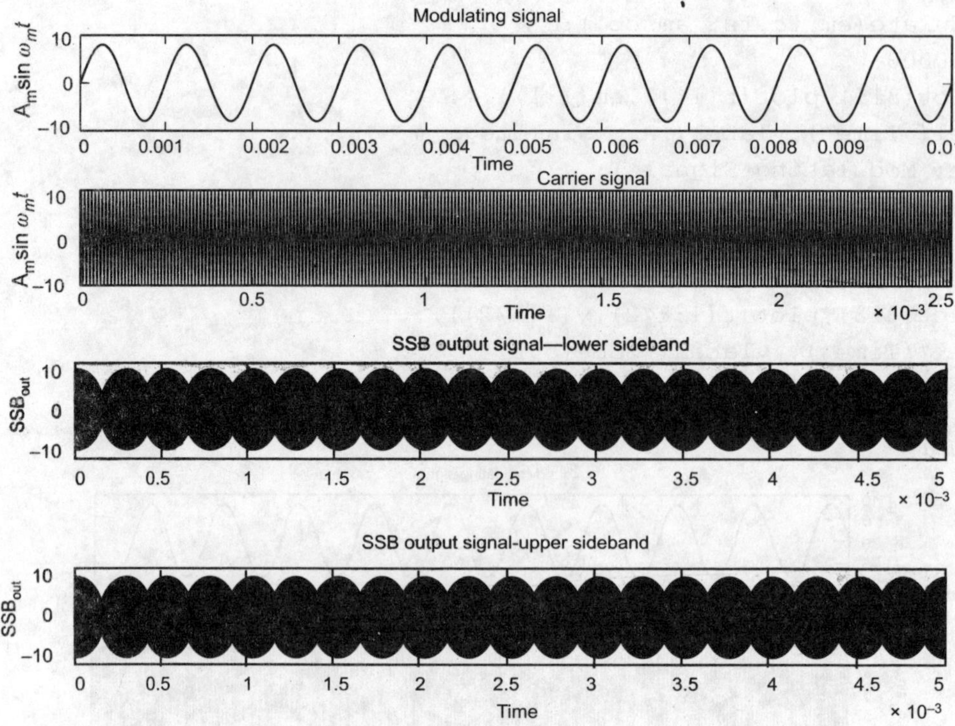

Figure 5.5 SSB simulated output waveform using the `ssbmod(.)` function

```
fm=1000;      % modulating frequency.
fs=400000;    % sampling frequency.
Ac=10;        % amplitude of carrier.
Am=8;         % amplitude of modulating signal.
wc=2*pi*fc*t;
wm=2*pi*fm*t;
ec=Ac*sin(wc);
em=Am*sin(wm);
y=ssbmod(em,fc,fs,0);
z=ssbmod(em,fc,fs,0,'upper');
subplot(411),plot(t(1:l),em(1:l)),...
xlabel('Time'),ylabel('A_m sin\omega_m t'),...
title('Modulating Signal');
subplot(412),plot(t(1:l/4),ec(1:l/4)),...
xlabel('Time'),ylabel('A_c sin\omega_c t'),...
title('Carrier  Signal');
subplot(413),plot(t(1:l/2),y(1:l/2)),...
xlabel('Time'), ylabel('SSB_{out}'),...
```

```
title('SSB Output Signal-- Lower Sideband');
subplot(414),plot(t(1:l/2),z(1:l/2)),...
xlabel('Time'), ylabel('SSB_{out}'),...
title('SSB Output Signal-- Upper Sideband');
%%% End of Program ssb2.m %%%%
```

5.5 Frequency Spectra

In this section, we will discuss the band of frequencies present in the output waveforms for different variants of amplitude modulation. As it is evident from equation (5.7), DSBTC output contains the carrier frequency and two sidebands. Apart from the analytical method, we can obtain the frequency spectra of different variants by using short MATLAB scripts. The script file given below computes and plots the frequency spectra of various AM output signals.

```
%%% Script file to compute and plot the ...
%%% Frequency spectra of various AM signals..
close all; clear all; clf;
fc=100000;  % carrier frequency.
fm=1000;    % modulating frequency.
fs=400000;  % sampling frequency.
Am=1;       % amplitude of modulating signal.
N=fc;       % Number of sampling elements for fft components..
t=linspace(0,1,N);
wm=2*pi*fm*t;
em=Am*sin(wm);
y1=modulate(em,fc,fs,'amdsb-tc');
y2=modulate(em,fc,fs,'amdsb-sc');
y3=modulate(em,fc,fs,'amssb');
NFFT = 2^nextpow2(N);% Next power of 2 from length of y
F1=fft(y1,NFFT)/N;
F2=fft(y2,NFFT)/N;
F3=fft(y3,NFFT)/N;
f = fs/2*linspace(0,1,NFFT/2+1);
subplot(311), stem(f,2*abs(F1(1:NFFT/2+1))),...
xlabel('Frequency'),ylabel('Amplitude of FFT');grid;
axis([0 fs/2 0 1.2]);title('FFT of AM Signal');
subplot(312), stem(f,2*abs(F2(1:NFFT/2+1))),...
xlabel('Frequency'),ylabel('Amplitude of FFT');grid;
axis([0 fs/2 0 1.2]);title('FFT of AM-DSBSC Signal');
subplot(313), stem(f,2*abs(F3(1:NFFT/2+1))),...
```

```
xlabel('Frequency'), ylabel('Amplitude of FFT');grid;
axis([0 fs/2 0 1.2]);title('FFT of SSB Signal');
%% End of Program fsp.m %%%%
```

The frequency spectra for the DSBTC, DSBSC and SSB are illustrated in Figure 5.6.

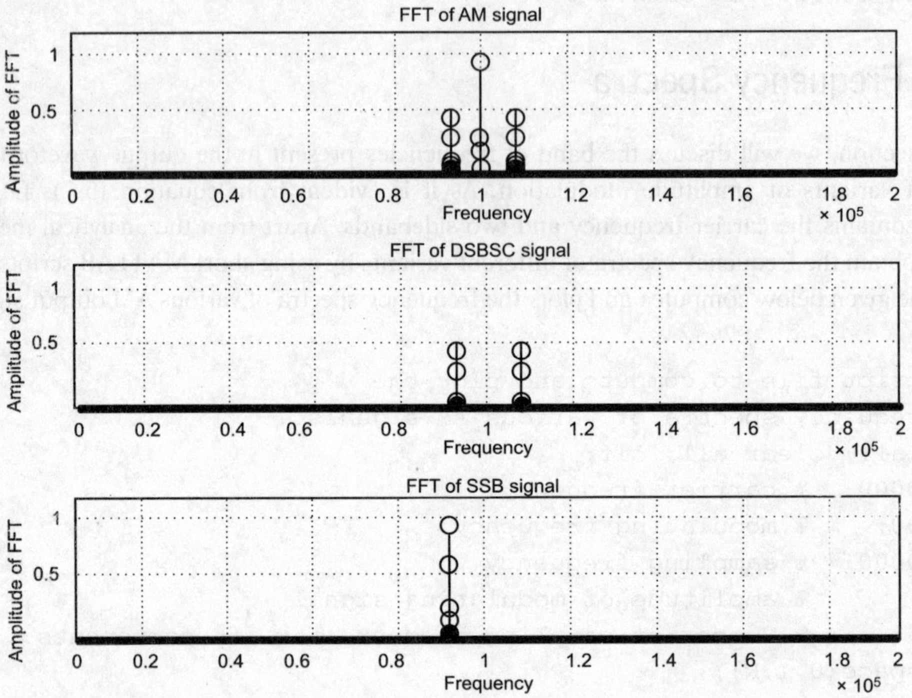

Figure 5.6 The frequency spectra

The following observations can be made from the plots:

- The spectra are symmetrical about the amplitude axis.
- For a standard amplitude modulation (DSBTC) with a single modulating frequency, a total of *three* frequencies are present at the output signal.
- For DSBSC, the carrier frequency is absent in the output spectra.
- For SSB with a single modulating frequency, there is only one frequency in the output spectra.

5.6 Demodulation of Amplitude Modulation

The `amdemod(.)` function in the Communications Toolbox of MATLAB can be used to simulate the demodulation of an amplitude modulated signal. The syntax is

- `y = amdemod(x,Fc,Fs);`
- `y = amdemod(x,Fc,Fs,ini_phase);`
- `y = amdemod(x,Fc,Fs,ini_phase,carramp);`
- `y = amdemod(x,Fc,Fs,ini_phase,carramp,num,den);`

`y = amdemod(x,Fc,Fs)` demodulates the amplitude modulated signal x from a carrier signal with frequency F_c (Hz). The carrier signal and x have a sample frequency of F_s (Hz). The modulated signal x has zero initial phase and zero carrier amplitude, so it represents a suppressed carrier modulation. The demodulation process uses the lowpass filter (by default) specified by

$$[\texttt{num}, \texttt{den}] = \texttt{butter}(5, \texttt{Fc} * 2/\texttt{Fs}).$$

Note that the F_c and F_s arguments must satisfy $F_s > 2(F_c + BW)$, where BW is the bandwidth of the original signal that was modulated.

The code given below illustrates the use of a 10th order Butterworth lowpass filter. The modulating signal and the demodulated output are illustrated in Figure 5.7

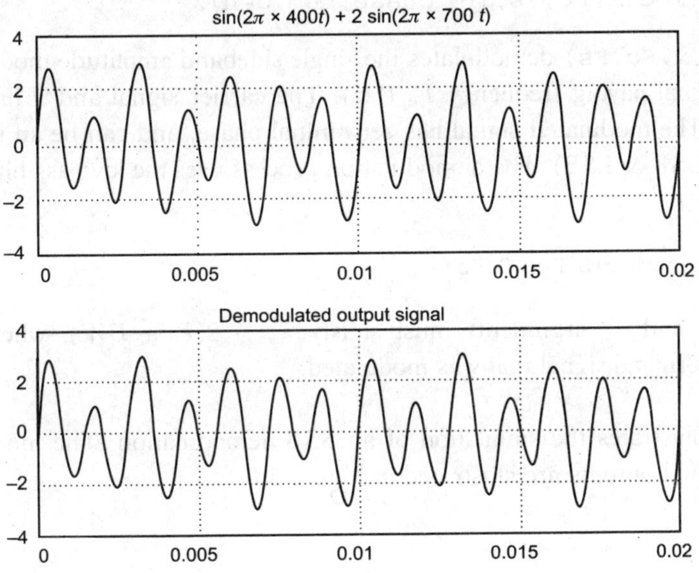

Figure 5.7 Simulation of an AM demodulation

```
clear all; close all; clf;
Fc = 20000; Fs = 80000;
t = [0:1/Fs:0.02];
```

```
s = sin(2*pi*400*t)+2*sin(2*pi*700*t);% Original signal
Ac=max(s);% Carrier amplitude.
[num,den] = butter(10,Fc*2/Fs); % Butterworth Lowpass filter
y = ammod(s,Fc,Fs,0,Ac); % Modulate.
s1 = amdemod(y,Fc,Fs,0,Ac,num,den); % Demodulate.
subplot(211),plot(t,s,'r','LineWidth',2),grid;
title('$\sin (2\pi \times 400 t) + 2\sin(2\pi \times 700 t)$');
subplot(212),plot(t,s1,'r','LineWidth',2),grid;
title('Demodulated Output Signal');
%%% end of amdem.m
```

5.6.1 Demodulation of an SSB Modulation

The `ssbdemod(.)` function in the Communications Toolbox of MATLAB is a convenient tool for demodulating SSB waveforms. The syntax of the function is

- `y = ssbdemod(x,Fc,Fs).`
- `y = ssbdemod(x,Fc,Fs,ini_phase).`
- `y = ssbdemod(x,Fc,Fs,ini_phase,num,den).`

`y = ssbdemod(x,Fc,Fs)` demodulates the single sideband amplitude modulated signal x from a carrier signal having frequency F_c (Hz). The carrier signal and x have a sampling rate of F_s (Hz). The modulated signal has zero initial phase, and can be an upper or lower sideband signal (USB or LSB). The demodulation process uses the lowpass filter specified by

$$[\texttt{num}, \texttt{den}] = \texttt{butter}(5, \texttt{Fc} * 2/\texttt{Fs}).$$

Note that the F_c and F_s arguments must satisfy $F_s > 2(F_c + BW)$, where BW is the bandwidth of the original signal that was modulated.

The code below illustrates the simulation of an SSB demodulation. The modulating signal and the demodulated outputs are illustrated in Figure 5.8

```
clear all; close all; clf;
Fc = 12000; Fs = 270000;
t = [0:1/Fs:0.02];
s = sin(2*pi*400*t)+2*sin(2*pi*700*t);
y1 = ssbmod(s,Fc,Fs,0); % Lower-sideband modulated signal
y2 = ssbmod(s,Fc,Fs,0,'upper'); % Upper-sideband modulated signal
s1 = ssbdemod(y1,Fc,Fs); % Demodulate lower sideband
```

```
s2 = ssbdemod(y2,Fc,Fs); % Demodulate upper sideband
subplot(311),plot(t,s,'Linewidth',2);grid;
title('Original Modulating Signal');
subplot(312),plot(t,s1,'Linewidth',2);grid;
title('Demodulation of upper sideband');
subplot(313),plot(t,s2,'Linewidth',2);grid;
title('Demodulation of lower sideband');
%%% end of ssbexp.m
```

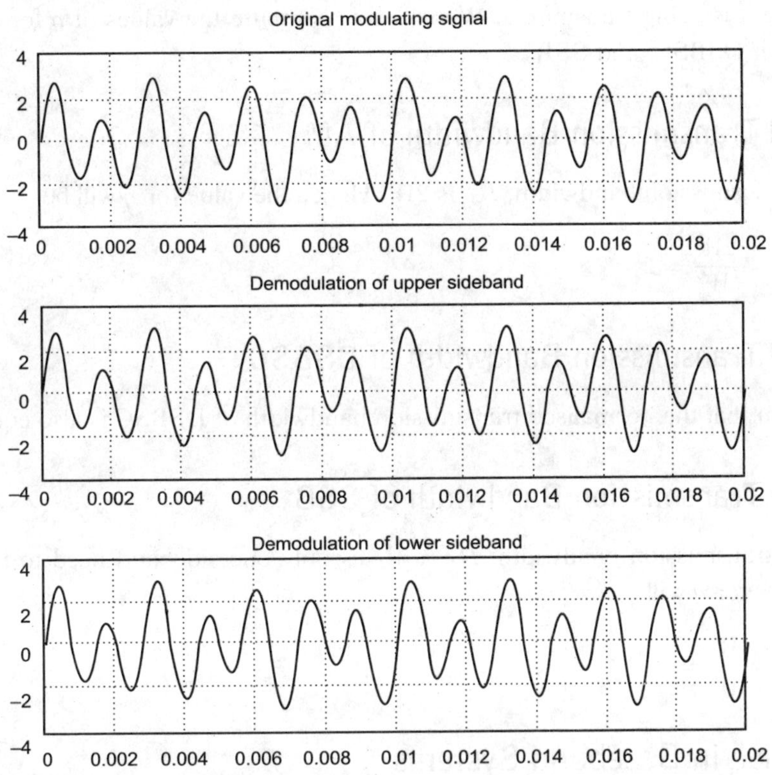

Figure 5.8 Simulation of an SSB demodulation

5.7 Noise Performance

In this section, we will consider the noise performance of various AM schemes. We begin with the concept of *normalised transmission bandwidth*.

5.7.1 Normalised Transmission Bandwidth

The normalised transmission bandwidth is defined by the equation:

$$\eta = \frac{B_T}{W} \tag{5.15}$$

where B_T is the transmission bandwidth of the modulated signal, and W is the message bandwidth. By message bandwidth, we mean the band of frequencies occupied by the message signal. The normalised transmission bandwidth points towards the amount the signal spectrum is spread while it is being transmitted. We will now compute the values of η for modulation schemes of AM, DSBSC, and SSB.

Normalised Transmission Bandwidth of AM

For AM, the transmission bandwidth, B_T is $2W$. Hence the value for η will be

$$\eta = \frac{B_T}{W} = \frac{2W}{W} = 2 \tag{5.16}$$

Normalised Transmission Bandwidth of DSBSC

It can be shown that the normalised transmission bandwidth of DSBSC is also equal to 2.

Normalised Transmission Bandwidth of SSB

For SSB, the transmission bandwidth, B_T is W as only one sideband need to be counted. Hence the value for η will be

$$\eta = \frac{B_T}{W} = \frac{W}{W} = 1 \tag{5.17}$$

5.7.2 Noise in Baseband Systems

In baseband systems, the signal is transmitted directly without any modulation—hence the name. This mode of communication is suitable over a pair of wires, optical fibre or coaxial cables. It is mainly used in short-haul (short distance) links. Baseband systems provide a basis against which other systems may be compared for their noise performance.

For a baseband system, the transmitter and receiver are ideal bandpass filters. See Figure 5.9 for details. The lowpass filter $H_p(f)$ at the transmitter limits the input signal spectrum to a given bandwidth. The lowpass filter $H_d(f)$ at the receiver eliminates out-of-band noise and other channel interference.

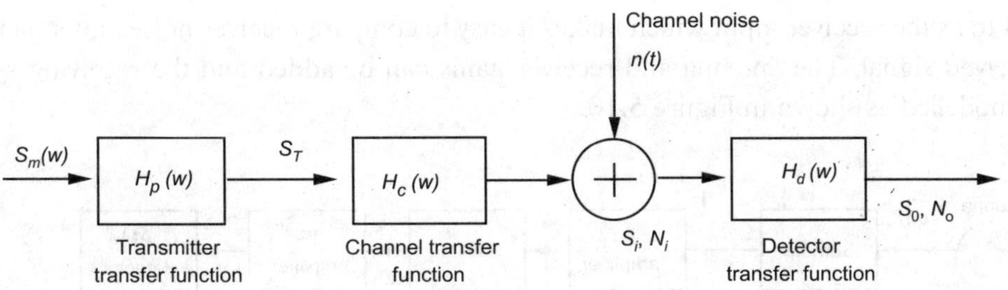

Figure 5.9 Noise model of a baseband system

The baseband signal is assumed to be a zero mean, wide-sense stationary random process bandlimited to B Hz. For a distortion-less channel,

$$S_o = S_i \tag{5.18}$$

and

$$N_o = 2\int_0^B S_n(f)\,df \tag{5.19}$$

where $S_n(f)$ is the power spectral density (PSD) of the channel noise. In the case of white noise, $S_n(f) = \frac{N}{2}$, and

$$N_o = 2\int_0^B \frac{N}{2}\,df = N.B \tag{5.20}$$

and,

$$\frac{S_o}{N_o} = \frac{S_i}{N.B} \tag{5.21}$$

We define a parameter γ as

$$\gamma = \frac{S_i}{N.B} = \frac{S_o}{N_o} \tag{5.22}$$

For voice signals, an SNR (signal-to-noise ratio) of 5 to 10 dB at the receiver implies a barely intelligible signal. Telephone quality signals have an SNR of 25 to 35 dB, whereas for television, an SNR of 45 to 55 dB is required.

5.7.3 Noise in AM Receivers

For AM receivers that carry analog type message signals, the signal-to-noise ratio is the most commonly used measure of performance. All the noise generated within the receiver can be referred to as the receiver input which makes it easy to compare receiver noise, antenna noise, and received signal. The antenna and receiver gains can be added and the receiving system can be modelled as shown in Figure 5.10.

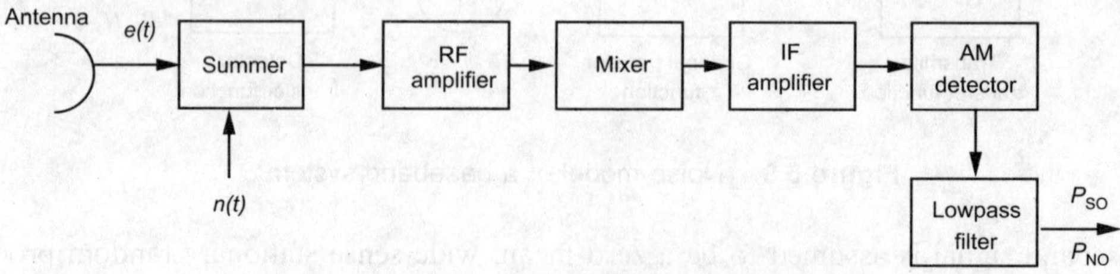

Figure 5.10 Noise model of an AM receiver

The bandwidth of the system is also required to determine the signal-to-noise ratio. From Figure 5.10, it is clear that between the antenna and the detector stage, there is a bandwidth of the RF (radio frequency) stages, followed by a bandwidth of the IF (intermediate frequency) stages. Normally, the bandwidth of the IF stages is very much smaller than that of the RF stages, and hence the IF bandwidth will decide the noise that is reaching the detector. From the detector onwards, the bandwidth will be that of the baseband. Let us denote the baseband bandwidth by W and the IF bandwidth by B_{IF}. For AM systems, it may be assumed that $B_{IF} \cong 2W$.

The noise output from a bandpass system is given by:

$$n_{IF}(t) = n_I(t)\ \cos\ 2\pi\, f_{IF}\, t\ -\ n_Q(t)\ \sin\ 2\pi\, f_{IF}\, t \tag{5.23}$$

where, $n_I(t)$ is the in-phase component and $n_Q(t)$ is the quadrature component of the noise signal.

The modulated carrier can be represented by:

$$\begin{aligned} e(t) &= E_{c\,\max}(1 + m\ \cos\ 2\pi\, f_m\, t) \cos\ 2\pi\, f_{IF}\, t \\ &= A_c(t)\ \cos\ 2\pi\, f_{IF}\, t \end{aligned} \tag{5.24}$$

The input to the detector is therefore:

$$\begin{aligned} e_{det}(t) &= e(t) + n_{IF}(t) \\ &= (A_c(t) + n_I(t)) \cos\ 2\pi\, f_{IF}\, t - n_Q(t) \sin\ 2\pi\, f_{IF}\, t \end{aligned} \tag{5.25}$$

Now, let $B(t) = \sqrt{[A_c(t) + n_I(t)]^2 + n_Q^2(t)}$, $\cos\ A = \frac{A_c(t)+n_I(t)}{B(t)}$, and $\sin\ A = \frac{n_Q(t)}{B(t)}$. Applying the trigonometric identity, we have:

$$e_{det}(t) = B(t).\cos(\ 2\pi\, f_{IF}\, t + \psi\,(t)) \tag{5.26}$$

where, $\psi(t) = \tan^{-1}\left[\frac{n_Q(t)}{A_c(t)+n_I(t)}\right]$.

The AM envelope detector recovers the envelope of the waveform, and therefore the waveform need to be expressed as shown in equation (5.26). The phase angle can be ignored, and the amplitude term B can be expressed as:

$$\begin{aligned} B(t) &= \sqrt{A_c^2(t) + 2A_c(t)n_I(t) + n_I^2(t) + n_Q^2(t)} \\ &\cong \sqrt{A_c^2(t) + 2A_c(t)n_I(t)} \end{aligned} \quad (5.27)$$

because the AM carrier amplitude is much higher than the noise. The expression for $B(t)$ can be further simplified as

$$\begin{aligned} B(t) &= \sqrt{A_c^2(t) + 2A_c(t)n_I(t)} \\ &= A_c(t)\left(1 + 2\frac{n_I(t)}{A_c(t)}\right)^{1/2} \\ &\cong A_c(t) + n_I(t) \quad (5.28) \\ &= E_{c\,\max} + mE_{c\,\max}\,\cos\,2\pi\,f_m\,t + n_I(t) \quad (5.29) \end{aligned}$$

The envelope consists of a DC term, the modulating signal voltage, and the noise voltage, $n_I(t)$. The available noise power output is given by:

$$P_{no} = 2kT_sW \quad (5.30)$$

where k is the Boltzmann constant, T_s is the absolute temperature in kelvins, and W is the bandwidth.

The peak signal voltage at the output is $mE_{c\,\max}$, and hence the rms voltage is mE_c, where E_c is the rms voltage of the unmodulated carrier at the receiver. Therefore, the available signal power at the output is:

$$P_{so} = \frac{m^2\,E_c^2}{4R_{\text{out}}} \quad (5.31)$$

The output SNR is

$$\begin{aligned} \left(\frac{S}{N}\right)_o &= \frac{P_{so}}{P_{no}} \\ &= \frac{m^2\,E_c^2}{8R_{\text{out}}kT_s\,W} \end{aligned} \quad (5.32)$$

The reference noise power at the detector is given by:

$$P_{n\,\mathrm{REF}} = kT_s W \tag{5.33}$$

The available signal power from a source with an internal resistance R_s is

$$P_R = \frac{E_c^2}{4R_s}\left(1 + \frac{m^2}{2}\right) \tag{5.34}$$

Therefore the signal-to-noise ratio is

$$\left(\frac{S}{N}\right)_{\mathrm{REF}} = \frac{P_R}{P_{n\,\mathrm{REF}}} \tag{5.35}$$

$$= \frac{E_c^2(1 + m^2/2)}{4R_s kT_s W} \tag{5.36}$$

The ratio of the above two SNRs is called the *figure of merit.*

$$\mathrm{FOM_{AM}} = \frac{(S/N)_o}{(S/N)_{\mathrm{REF}}}$$

$$= \frac{m^2}{2 + m^2}.\frac{R_s}{R_{\mathrm{out}}} \tag{5.37}$$

The higher the figure of merit, the better the system. Normally, $R_{\mathrm{out}} \cong R_s$ and hence the highest value of FOM is $\frac{1}{3}$, achieved at 100% modulation depth.

5.7.4 Noise in Coherent DSBSC Receivers

In the DSBSC, the received signal is of the form

$$e(t) = E_{\max}\ \cos\,\omega_m t\ \cos\,\omega_{IF} t \tag{5.38}$$

where $E_{\max}$ is the peak value of the received signal. The input to the detector is, therefore,

$$e_{\mathrm{det}}(t) = e(t) + n(t)$$

$$= (E_{\max}\ \cos\,\omega_m t + n_I(t)).\cos\,\omega_{IF} t - n_Q(t)\ \sin\,\omega_{IF} t$$

$$= A(t)\ \cos\,\omega_{IF} t - n_Q(t)\ \sin\,\omega_{IF} t \tag{5.39}$$

where $A(t) = E_{\max}\ \cos\,\omega_m t + n_I(t)$. To demodulate the DSBSC, we make use of a balanced mixer. The output of the balanced demodulator is

$$e_{\mathrm{out}}(t) = \beta\, e_{\mathrm{det}}(t)\cos\,\omega_{IF} t \tag{5.40}$$

where β is a constant of the multiplier circuit. Substituting the value of e_{det} from equation (5.39),

$$\begin{aligned} e_{\text{out}}(t) &= \frac{\beta}{2}A(t) + \frac{\beta}{2}A(t).\cos\, 2\omega_{IF}\,t - \frac{\beta}{2}n_Q(t).\sin\, 2\omega_{IF}\,t & (5.41)\\ &= \frac{\beta}{2}\left(E_{\max}\cos\omega_m\,t + n_I(t)\right) + \text{ higher order terms} & (5.42)\end{aligned}$$

The lowpass filter following the balanced demodulator removes the high frequency terms, leaving the baseband output.

$$e_B(t) = \frac{\beta}{2}\left(E_{\max}\cos\omega_m\,t + n_I(t)\right) \tag{5.43}$$

The $\frac{\beta}{2}$ factor is common for the signal and the noise, and can be ignored. Equation (5.32) is applicable to DSBSC too, with $\frac{E_{\max}}{\sqrt{2}}$ replacing $m\,E_c$.

$$\begin{aligned} \left(\frac{S}{N}\right)_o &= \frac{(E_{\max}/\sqrt{2})^2}{8R_{\text{out}}\,k\,T_s\,W}\\ &= \frac{E_{\max}^2}{16R_{\text{out}}\,k\,T_s\,W} & (5.44)\end{aligned}$$

The reference noise power is $P_{n\ \text{REF}} = kT_s\,W$. The rms value of the received DSBSC signal $E_{\max}\cos\omega_m t\,\cos\omega_{IF}\,t$ is $\frac{E_{\max}}{2}$. Hence the available signal power at the input is

$$\begin{aligned} P_R &= \frac{(E_{\max}/2)^2}{4R_s}\\ &= \frac{E_{\max}^2}{16R_s} & (5.45)\end{aligned}$$

The reference signal-to-noise ratio is therefore

$$\left(\frac{S}{N}\right)_o = \frac{E_{\max}^2}{16R_s\,k\,T_s\,W} \tag{5.46}$$

The *figure of merit* is therefore

$$\text{FOM}_{\text{DSBSC}} = \frac{(S/N)_o}{(S/N)_{\text{REF}}} = \frac{R_s}{R_{\text{out}}} \tag{5.47}$$

For $R_s = R_{\text{out}}$, the $\text{FOM}_{\text{DSBSC}}$ is unity, which is three time better than that for AM.

5.7.5 Noise in SSB Receivers

In SSB, only the upper or lower sideband of an AM wave is transmitted. SSB reduces the transmit signal bandwidth by a factor of 2. The transmitted signal can be written in terms of $m(t)$ and the Hilbert transform of $m(t)$ as

$$s(t) = A_c\left[m(t)\cos(2\pi f_c t) \pm m_h(t)\sin(2\pi f_c t)\right] \tag{5.48}$$

SSB uses the same demodulator as a DSBSC. It has half the SNR of DSBSC; but for half the transmit power. Hence there is no SNR gain. SSB can introduce significant distortion at DC where the sidebands meet. It is, therefore, not good for transmission of TV signals.

5.7.6 Vestigial Sideband (VSB) System

The key features of a vestigial sideband system are

- VSB is similar to SSB but it retains a small portion (a vestige) of the undesired sideband to reduce DC distortion.
- VSB signals are generated by using a standard AM or DSBSC modulation, and then passing the modulated signal through a sideband shaping filter.
- Demodulation uses either standard AM or DSBSC demodulation.
- VSB modulation with envelope detection is used to transmit the video in analog TV signals (sound is transmitted as an FM).

5.8 Measurement of Noise Performance

There are a number of ways in which the noise performance, and hence the sensitivity of a radio receiver can be measured. The most obvious method is to compare the signal and noise levels for a known signal level, i.e., the signal-to-noise (S/N) ratio or SNR. Obviously, the greater the difference between the signal and the unwanted noise, i.e., the greater the S/N ratio, the better the radio receiver sensitivity performance.

As with any sensitivity measurement, the performance of the overall radio receiver can also be determined by the performance of the front end RF amplifier stage. Any noise introduced by the first RF amplifier will be added to the signal and amplified by subsequent amplifiers in the receiver. As the noise introduced by the first RF amplifier will be amplified the most, this RF amplifier becomes the most critical in terms of radio receiver sensitivity performance. Thus, the first amplifier of any radio receiver should be a low noise amplifier.

5.8.1 Methods of Measuring Receiver Sensitivity

Although there are many ways of measuring the sensitivity performance of a radio receiver, the S/N ratio or SNR is one of the most straightforward and is used in a variety of applications. However, it has a number of limitations, and although it is widely used, other methods including noise figure are often used as well. Nevertheless the S/N ratio or SNR is an important specification, and it will be seen in many radio receiver specification sheets.

The SNR is normally expressed in decibels. As the signal input level obviously has an effect on this ratio, the input signal level must be given. This is usually expressed in microvolts. Typically, a certain input level is required to give a 10 dB signal-to-noise ratio.

Effect of bandwidth

Apart from the basic performance of the set, a number of other factors can affect the SNR specification. The first is the actual bandwidth of the receiver. As the noise spreads out over all frequencies it is found that the wider the bandwidth of the receiver, the greater the level of the noise. Accordingly, the receiver bandwidth needs to be stated.

Additionally, it is found that when using AM, the level of modulation has an effect on the SNR. The greater the level of modulation, the higher the audio output from the receiver. When measuring the noise performance, the audio output from the receiver is measured and therefore, the modulation level of the AM has an effect. Usually a modulation level of 30% is chosen for this measurement.

Typical figures

This method of measuring the performance is most commonly used for HF communications receivers. Typically in the case of SSB or Morse, one might expect to see a figure in the region of 0.5 μvolts for a 10 dB S/N in a 3 kHz bandwidth. For AM, a figure of 1.5 μvolts for a 10 dB S/N in a 6 kHz bandwidth at 30% modulation can be seen.

5.8.2 Points to Note while Measuring SNR

SNR is a very convenient method of quantifying the sensitivity of a receiver, but there are some points to note when measuring and interpreting the figures. To investigate these, it is necessary to look at the way the measurements of SNR are made. A calibrated RF signal generator is used as a signal source for the receiver. It must have an accurate method of setting the output level down to very low signal levels. Then at the output of the receiver a true RMS AC voltmeter is used to measure the output level.

S/N and (S+N)/N

When calculating the SNR, a 50 Ω match is given to the receiver with the generator signal switched off. The audio metre detects the noise generated by the receiver itself. This level is noted and the signal is turned on. Its level is adjusted until the audio level metre reads a level which is 10 dB higher than just the noise on its own. The level of the generator is that required to give the 10 dB signal-to-noise ratio.

Actually, the last statement is not strictly true. Whilst the first reading of the noise is quite accurate, the second reading of the signal includes some noise as well. In view of this, many manufacturers will specify a slightly different ratio: namely the signal plus noise-to-noise (S+N/N) ratio. In practice, the difference is not particularly large, but the S+N/N ratio is more correct.

5.9 Conclusion

In most communication media, only a fixed range of frequencies is available for transmission. One way to communicate a message signal whose frequency spectrum does not fall within that fixed frequency range, or one that is otherwise unsuitable for the channel, is to alter a transmittable signal according to the information in our message signal. This alteration is called modulation, and it is the modulated signal that we transmit. The receiver then recovers the original signal through a process called demodulation.

We will now summarise the key points discussed so far.

- Modulation is the process of encoding a message signal or bits into a carrier signal. To modulate, literally means, to vary in accordance with something.
- In amplitude modulation (AM), the amplitude of the carrier waveform is modulated with a message signal.
- A constant term is added to the message signal to simplify demodulation. This results in wastage of power and reduces the signal-to-noise ratio (SNR). In standard AM modulation, a constant term is added to the information signal to yield the transmitted signal $s(t) = A_c[1 + k_a m(t)]\cos(2\pi f_c t)$, where $m(t)$ is the modulating signal and k_a is the index of modulation. The constant term greatly simplifies demodulation but results in wastage of transmitted power.
- AM waves are typically generated using a non-linear device which gives the desired multiplication. Square law modulator sums the carrier $c(t)$ and information $m(t)$ signals, then squares them using a non-linear device. Unwanted terms are filtered out with a bandpass filter.
- The bandwidth of the modulated signal is twice that of the information signal.
- AM detection typically entails trade-offs between performance and complexity (cost). The square law detector squares the received signal which is then passed through a lowpass filter. This detection is simple but introduces an unwanted distortion term proportional to $m^2(t)$.
- Envelope detector is a simple circuit for AM detection consisting of resistors, a capacitor, and a diode. It only works when $|k_a m(t)| \leq 1,\ for\ all\ t$. It cannot detect sign changes. The $R_L C$ circuit must track the envelope but not the carrier ($f_c^{-1} \ll R_L C \ll B^{-1}$).

- Envelope detectors are simple, and cheap devices which can detect AM waves with no distortion. But they have poor SNR.

Further Reading

1. *Getting Started with Communications Blockset*. The MathWorks. 2009.
2. *Getting Started with MATLAB 7*. The MathWorks. 2009.
3. Roddy, Dennis and John Coolen. *Electronic Communications*. 4th Edition. Pearson Education (India) Ltd. 2008.
4. Roden, Martin S. *Analog and Digital Communication Systems*. 5th Edition. Discovery Press. 2002.
5. *Simulink*. The MathWorks. 2009.
6. *User's Guide, Communications Toolbox*. The MathWorks. 2009.

Problems

1. A 10 MHz carrier is simultaneously modulated with 800 kHz, 900 kHz and 1000 kHz audio sine wave signals. What will be the frequencies present at the output? [Answer: 10 MHz, 10 MHz $\pm$ 800 kHz, 10 MHz $\pm$ 900 kHz and 10 MHz $\pm$ 1000 kHz]
2. When the percentage modulation is 60, an AM transmitter generates 12 kW.
   (a) How much of this is the carrier power?
   (b) If the carrier and one of the sidebands were suppressed, what would be the percentage of power saving?
3. For a carrier power of 50 kW, plot the total transmitter power for a modulation index varying from 0 to 100%. Use MATLAB for coding.
4. Let $m(t)$ be a rectangular signal having an amplitude of 1 and a pulse-duration of 50 ms. The carrier signal frequency is 3 kHz. Assume that the phase of the carrier signal is zero and the amplitude of the carrier signal is 1.
   (a) Obtain the spectrum of the message signal, $M(f)$, using the MATLAB function `fft(.)`.
   (b) Obtain the spectrum of the DSBSC modulated signal, $U(f)$.
5. Let $m(t) = \sin c(400t)$ for $|t| < 50$ ms and 0 otherwise. Assume that the phase of the carrier signal is zero, the amplitude of the carrier signal is 1, and the carrier signal frequency is 10 kHz.

(a) Obtain the spectrum of the message signal, $M(f)$, using MATLAB function `fft(.)`.

(b) Obtain the DSBSC modulated signal both in the time domain and in the frequency domain, using MATLAB script.

6. Let $m(t) = \sin(2\pi f_m t)$, for $0 \le t \le 10$ ms and 0 otherwise, where f_m is 10 kHz. Carrier frequency is 400 kHz. Assume that the phase of the carrier signal is zero and the amplitude of the carrier signal is 1.

   (a) Obtain the spectrum of the message signal, $M(f)$.

   (b) Obtain the DSBSC modulated signal both in the time domain and in the frequency domain.

7. Let $m(t) = 2\sin(2\pi f_m t)$, for $0 \le t \le 10$ ms and 0 otherwise, where f_m is 400 Hz. Carrier frequency is 30 kHz. Assume that the phase of the carrier signal is zero and the amplitude of the carrier signal is 1.

   (a) Obtain the spectrum of the message signal, $M(f)$.

   (b) Obtain the envelope of the modulated signal and observe the *over-modulation*.

   (c) Obtain the USB-AM modulated signal both in the time domain and in the frequency domain.

   (d) Obtain the LSB-AM modulated signal both in the time domain and in the frequency domain.

8. Let $m(t) = \frac{1}{2}\sin(2\pi f_m t)$, for $0 \le t \le 10$ ms and 0 otherwise, where f_m is 200 Hz. Carrier frequency is 15 kHz. Assume that the phase of the carrier signal is zero and the amplitude of the carrier signal is 1.

   (a) Find the modulation index, m_a, analytically.

   (b) Show the conventional AM modulated signal both in the time domain and in the frequency domain using MATLAB script.

9. The information signal $x(t) = 2\sin 2000\pi t + \cos 4000\pi t$ is modulated by a DSB modulator operating at a carrier frequency of 100 kHz. Obtain the power spectral density of the output. Verify your answer by using MATLAB tools. [Answer: 4@100 kHz $\pm$ 1 kHz, 1@100 kHz $\pm$ 2 kHz]

10. Consider the block diagram shown in Figure 5.11 and a triangular pulse train with a period of 1.0 μs.

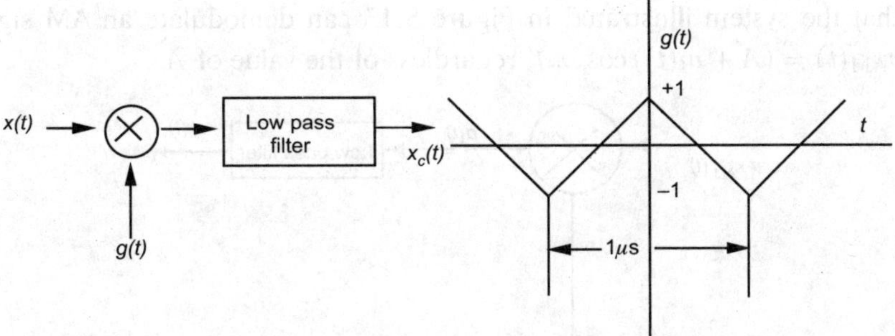

Figure 5.11 A simple AM modulator

(a) Show that this scheme will work well if the local carrier $g(t)$ has no DC component. The filter cut-off frequency is $f_c + f_x$, with f_c being the carrier frequency and f_x the bandwidth of the input.

(b) If the input is a single tone sinusoid $x(t) = 2\cos 1000\pi t$, find the required filter bandwidth.

(c) Write an expression for the output of the filter.

(d) How would you modify the system if the local carrier $g(t)$ had a DC bias of 2.0 volts?

11. The input to a *square law device* of the system illustrated in Figure 5.12 is given by:

$$x_c(t) = 10(1 + 0.4\cos 6000\pi t)$$

The input–output equation of the non-linear device is $y = (x+2)^2$ and the ideal lowpass filter has a cut-off frequency of 8.0 kHz.

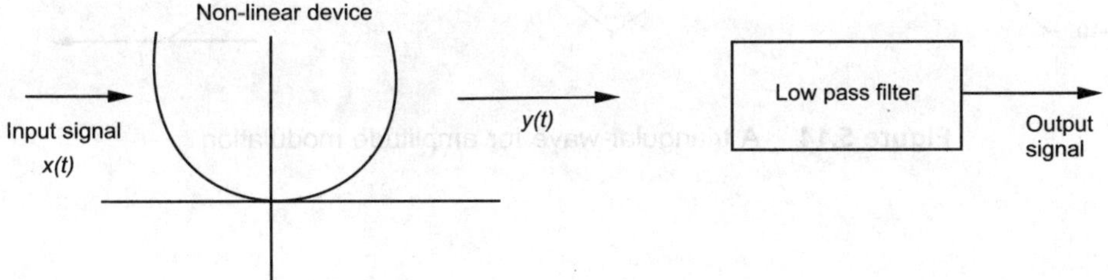

Figure 5.12 A non-linear device for AM generation

(a) Carefully sketch the amplitude spectrum of the filter and the spectrum of the output $y(t)$.

(b) Verify your answers using suitable MATLAB script.

12. Show that the system illustrated in Figure 5.13 can demodulate an AM signal of the form: $x_{\text{AM}}(t) = (A + m(t)) \cos \omega_c t$, regardless of the value of A.

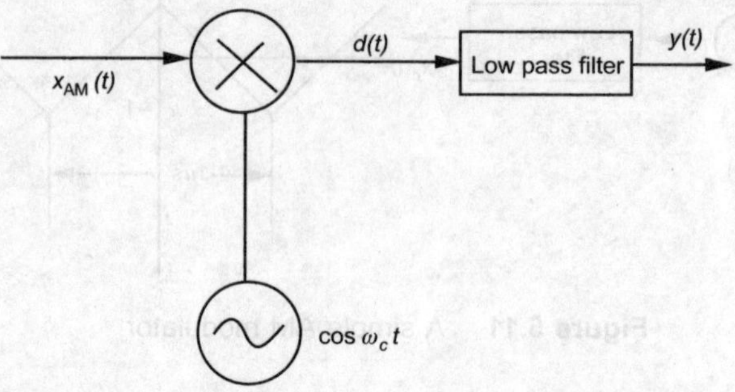

Figure 5.13 A generic AM demodulator

13. A signal $v_s = 30 \sin(2000\, \pi\, t)$ and a carrier signal $v_c = 10 \sin(4 \times 10^6\, \pi\, t)$ are applied to a non-linear device whose input voltage–output current characteristic can be approximated as $i_o = (5 + 2v_i - 0.5v_i^2)$ mA. Obtain the amplitude and frequencies of all the components present in the output current. Calculate the percentage modulation if the output current is passed through a tuned circuit such that only the components needed for AM are retained.

14. Sketch the AM signal $[A + m(t)]$ cos $\omega_c\, t$ for the periodic triangular wave $m(t)$ shown in Figure 5.14. corresponding to a modulation depth of (a) $m_a = 0.5$, (b) $m_a = 1.0$. Also plot, using MATLAB, the AM wave for the above two cases.

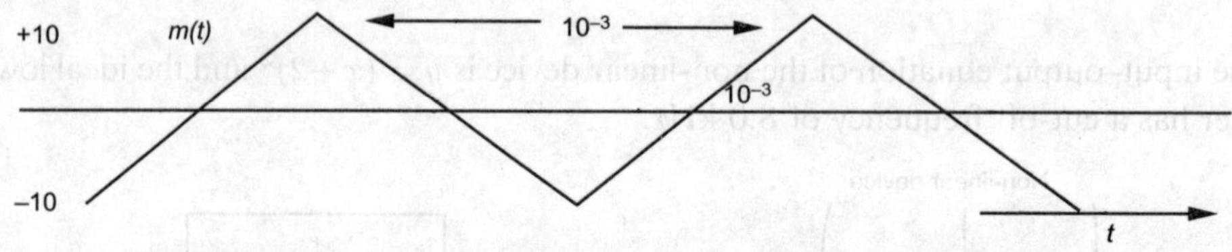

Figure 5.14 A triangular wave for amplitude modulation

6

Simulation of Angle Modulation Systems

In the previous chapter, we discussed amplitude modulation and its many variants. All of them can be classified as *linear modulation* schemes. This nomenclature was chosen to indicate that the overall modulated signal can be obtained by applying the *principle of superposition* on the modulating signals. In this chapter, we will look at another form of modulating the carrier—modulating its frequency rather than its amplitude. The resulting modulation is called *frequency modulation*. We can also modulate the phase of the carrier. The resulting modulation is termed as *phase modulation*. These two modulation schemes, viz., FM and PM, are collectively known as *angle modulation* schemes. Note that both of them are non-linear modulation schemes. Hence we cannot apply the *principle of superposition* to obtain the modulated signal from the modulating components. We begin our discussion with frequency modulation.

6.1 Frequency Modulation (FM)

Frequency modulation of a carrier wave occurs when its frequency is changed according to the instantaneous value of the modulating signal. In this process, the carrier amplitude remains constant. The amplitude of the modulating signal will cause the carrier frequency to deviate from its central frequency, (i.e., the frequency without any modulation) by a certain amount. According to the specifications of the Federal Communications Commission (FCC), the maximum frequency deviation allowed is 75 kHz. The FCC has allocated the 88–108 MHz band for FM radio broadcast. The shift in the carrier frequency from its resting point compared to the maximum frequency of the modulating voltage is called the *deviation ratio*. The maximum value stipulated by the FCC for deviation ratio is 5.

$$\text{Deviation ratio} = \frac{f_{\text{dev}}(\text{max})}{f_{\text{AF}}(\text{max})}$$

If the maximum frequency deviation of the carrier is $f_{\text{dev}}(\text{max})$ and the frequency of the corresponding modulating signal is f_{AF}, then the *modulation index* is defined as:

$$\text{Modulation index, } m_f = \beta = \frac{f_{\text{dev}}(\text{max})}{f_{\text{AF}}}$$

6.1.1 The Frequency Spectrum of FM

The frequency spectrum of the FM wave can be derived as given below.

Let us assume that the carrier wave in FM is represented by $e_c = E_c \cos \omega_c t$ and the modulating signal by $e_m = E_m \cos \omega_m t$. For simplicity, we assume that there is only one frequency component in the modulating signal. We will remove this restriction later on. The instantaneous value of the carrier frequency on modulation, f can be represented as:

$$f = f_c + kE_m \cos \omega_m t \tag{6.1}$$

where,

$$\begin{aligned} f_c &= \text{unmodulated carrier frequency} \\ k &= \text{proportionality constant} \\ E_m \cos \omega_m t &= \text{instantaneous modulating signal.} \end{aligned}$$

The maximum deviation for this particular carrier will occur when the cosine term has its maximum value, ± 1. Now, the instantaneous frequency of the modulated carrier will be given by equation (6.1). Hence the maximum deviation in frequency, δ will be given by:

$$\delta = \pm kE_m \tag{6.2}$$

The instantaneous amplitude of the FM signal is given by:

$$e = E_c \cos \theta \tag{6.3}$$

Now,

$$\begin{aligned} \omega &= 2\pi f = \omega_c + 2\pi kE_m \cos \omega_m t \\ \theta &= \int \omega dt = \int (\omega_c + 2\pi\, kE_m \cos \omega_m t) dt = \left(\omega_c t + \frac{2\pi kE_m \sin \omega_m t}{\omega_m} \right) \\ &= \omega_c t + \frac{kE_m \sin \omega_m t}{f_m} = \omega_c t + \frac{\delta}{f_m} \sin \omega_m t. \end{aligned} \tag{6.4}$$

Substituting the value of θ in equation (6.3), we get the instantaneous value of the FM signal. That is,

$$e = E_c \cos (\omega_c t + \frac{\delta}{f_m} \sin \omega_m t) \tag{6.5}$$

The *modulation index* for FM, β is defined as:

$$\beta = \frac{\text{Maximum frequency deviation}}{\text{Modulating frequency}} = \frac{\delta}{f_m} \tag{6.6}$$

Substituting the value of the modulation index in equation (6.5), we get:

$$e = E_c \cos (\omega_c t + \beta \sin \omega_m t) \tag{6.7}$$

It can be shown that for a sinusoidal modulating signal, assuming that e represents the instantaneous voltage impressed across a 1 Ω resistor, the average power over a cycle of the modulating frequency is given by:

$$\frac{1}{T}\int_{0}^{T} e^2\,dt = \frac{E_c^2}{T}\int_{0}^{T} \cos^2(\omega_c t + \beta \sin \omega_m t)\,dt \tag{6.8}$$

where $T = \frac{1}{f_m}$. This expression may be rewritten as

$$\frac{E_c^2}{T}\int_{0}^{T} \frac{1+\cos(2\omega_c t + 2\beta \sin \omega_m t)}{2}\,dt$$

The second part of the integral is zero since it is periodic in T. This assumes that $\omega_m = 2\pi/T \ll \omega_c$. The first term gives $\frac{E_c^2}{2}$. Although shown only for a sinusoidal modulating signal, the above result is true for any modulating signal whose highest frequency component B Hz is small compared to the carrier frequency f_c. The reader is advised to prove this statement.

We will now try to determine the frequency components and the amplitudes for the frequency modulated signal of arbitrary β and the sinusoidal modulating signal. Note that we can write equation (6.7) as:

$$e = E_c\,[\cos\,\omega_c t\,\cos\,(\beta\,\sin\,\omega_m t) - \sin\,\omega_c t\,\sin\,(\beta\,\sin\,\omega_m t)] \tag{6.9}$$

We can expand both $\cos\,(\beta\,\sin\,\omega_m t)$ and $\sin\,(\beta\,\sin\,\omega_m t)$ in their respective Fourier series. Both series may be found simultaneously by considering the periodic complex exponential:

$$v(t) = \exp(j\beta\,\sin\,\omega_m t), \quad -\frac{T}{2} < t < \frac{T}{2} \tag{6.10}$$

The real part of this function gives us our cosine function; the imaginary part, the sine function. If we expand this exponential in its Fourier series, we can expect to get a real part consisting of even harmonics of ω_m and an imaginary part consisting of the odd harmonics. By equating reals and imaginaries, we can then obtain the desired Fourier expansions for $\cos(\beta\,\omega_m t)$ and $\sin(\beta\,\omega_m t)$, respectively.

The Fourier coefficient of the complex Fourier series for the exponential of equation (6.10) is given by:

$$C_n = \int_{-T/2}^{T/2} \exp\left[j(\beta\,\sin\omega_m t - \omega_n t)\right]\,dt; \quad \omega_m = \frac{2\pi}{T}, \quad \omega_n = \frac{2\pi\,n}{T} = n\,\omega_m \tag{6.11}$$

Normalising this integral by letting $x = \omega_m t$, we get

$$\frac{C_n}{T} = \frac{1}{2\pi} \int_{-\pi}^{\pi} \exp\left[j(\beta \sin x - n\,x)\right]\, dx \tag{6.12}$$

This integral can only be evaluated as an infinite series. It is called the *Bessel function of the first kind* and is denoted by the symbol $J_n(\beta)$.

Specifically,

$$J_n(\beta) = \frac{1}{2\pi} \int_{-\pi}^{\pi} \exp\left[j(\beta \sin x - n\,x)\right]\, dx \tag{6.13}$$

so that $C_n = T\, J_n(\beta)$.

For $n = 0$, we get $C_0 = T\, J_0(\beta)$, the DC component of the Fourier series representation of the periodic complex exponential given in equation (6.10). Increasing values of n give the corresponding Fourier coefficients for the higher frequency terms of the Fourier series. The spectrum of the complex exponential of equation (6.10) (and ultimately that of the frequency modulated signal) will thus be given by the value of the Bessel function and will depend on the parameter β. Hence

$$\exp(j\beta \sin \omega_m t) = \frac{1}{T} \sum_{n=-\infty}^{\infty} C_n \exp(j\omega_n t) = \sum_{n=-\infty}^{\infty} J_n(\beta) \exp(j\omega_n t) \quad \omega_n = n\omega_m \tag{6.14}$$

This is for $-\frac{T}{2} < t < \frac{T}{2}$.

From equation (6.14), for the Fourier series expansion of the complex exponential, we can obtain the desired Fourier series for $\cos(\beta \sin \omega_m t)$ and $\sin(\beta \sin \omega_m t)$. It can be shown, either from the integral definition of $J_n(\beta)$ or from the power series expansion of $J_n(\beta)$, that

$$\begin{aligned} J_n(\beta) &= J_{-n}(\beta)\ ;\ n \text{ even} \\ \text{and } J_n(\beta) &= -J_{-n}(\beta)\ ;\ n \text{ odd} \end{aligned} \tag{6.15}$$

Now writing out the Fourier series term by term, and using equation (6.15) to combine the positive and negative terms of equal magnitude of n, we get

$$\begin{aligned} \exp(j\beta \sin \omega_m t) = J_0(\beta) &+ 2\left[J_2(\beta) \cos 2\omega_m t + J_4(\beta) \cos 4\omega_m t + \ldots\right] \\ &+ 2j\left[J_1(\beta) \sin \omega_m t + J_3(\beta) \sin 3\omega_m t + \ldots\right] \end{aligned} \tag{6.16}$$

But

$$\exp(j\beta \sin \omega_m t) = \cos(\beta \sin \omega_m t) + j \sin(\beta\, \omega_m t) \tag{6.17}$$

Equating the real and imaginary terms, we get:

$$\cos(\beta \sin \omega_m t) = J_0(\beta) + 2J_2(\beta) \cos 2\omega_m t + 2J_4(\beta) \cos 4\omega_m t + \ldots \quad (6.18)$$

$$\text{and} \quad \sin(\beta \sin \omega_m t) = 2J_1(\beta) \sin \omega_m t + 2J_3(\beta) \sin 3\omega_m t + \ldots \quad (6.19)$$

Now using the Fourier series expansions for the cosine and sine terms, and then utilising the trigonometric sum and difference formulae, we get:

$$\begin{aligned} e = E_c \quad \{ & \; J_0(\beta) \cos \omega_c t \\ + & \; J_1(\beta)[\cos(\omega_c + \omega_m)t - \cos(\omega_c - \omega_m)t] \\ + & \; J_2(\beta)[\cos(\omega_c + 2\omega_m)t + \cos(\omega_c - 2\omega_m)t] \\ + & \; J_3(\beta)[\cos(\omega_c + 3\omega_m)t - \cos(\omega_c - 3\omega_m)t] \\ + & \; J_4(\beta)[\cos(\omega_c + 4\omega_m)t + \cos(\omega_c - 4\omega_m)t] \ldots\} \end{aligned} \quad (6.20)$$

It can be seen that the FM output signal consists of a carrier and an apparently infinite number of sidebands, each preceded by the $J_n(\beta)$ coefficients. It can be shown that $J_n(\beta)$ is a solution of an equation of the form:

$$(\beta)^2 \frac{d^2 y}{d\beta^2} + \beta \frac{dy}{d\beta} + (\beta^2 - n^2)y = 0 \quad (6.21)$$

The solution, i.e., the formula for the Bessel function is:

$$J_n(\beta) = \left(\frac{\beta}{2}\right)^n \left[\frac{1}{n!} - \frac{(\beta/2)^2}{1!(n+1)!} + \frac{(\beta/2)^4}{2!(n+2)!} - \frac{(\beta/2)^6}{3!(n+3)!} + \ldots\right] \quad (6.22)$$

Yet another form of the Bessel function is:

$$J_n(\beta) = \beta^n \sum_{m=0}^{\infty} \frac{(-1)^m \beta^{2m}}{2^{2m+n} m!(n+m)!} \quad (6.23)$$

The MATLAB® function `bessfn.m` that generated the plots in Figure 6.1 is listed below:

```
function bessfn(n,mf)
% Computes and plots Bessel Functions of the
% First kind up to order n.
% Modulation Index varies from 0 to mf.
m=[0:.01:mf];
for i=1:n
```

```
    bf=besselj(i-1,m);
    plot(m,bf); hold on; grid on;
end;
hold off;
```

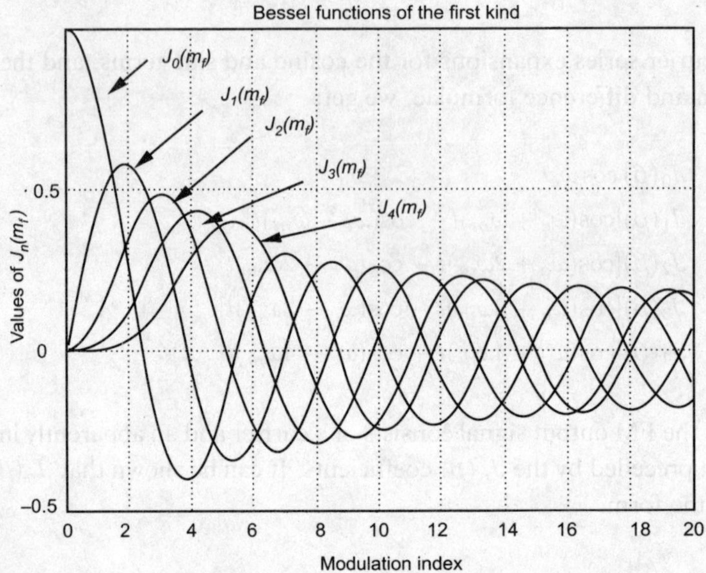

Figure 6.1 The Bessel functions

We can make the following observations about the FM signal:

1. Unlike the case of AM, *FM signal contains an infinite number of sidebands*, as well as the carrier. They are separated from the carrier by $\pm f_m$, $\pm 2f_m$, $\pm 3f_m$, ..., and thus have a recurrence frequency of f_m.

2. The $J_n(\beta)$ coefficients eventually decrease in value as n increases. As is seen from Figure 6.1, the value fluctuates on either side of zero, gradually diminishing.

3. The modulation index determines how many sideband components have a significant amplitude.

4. The sidebands at equal distance from f_c have equal amplitudes. The $J_n(\beta)$ coefficients have negative values occasionally, signifying a 180° phase change for that pair of sidebands.

5. In FM, the total transmitted power remains constant, but the required bandwidth is increased with increased depth of modulation.

6. Also, the amplitude of the carrier component does not remain constant. Its $J_n(\beta)$ coefficient is J_0, which is dependent on β.

7. It is possible for the carrier component to disappear completely. This happens for certain values of the modulation index as is evident from the plot for $J_0(\beta)$ in Figure 6.1, where it becomes zero when β is 2.4, 5.5, 8.6, 11.8 and so on. These values of the modulation index are called *eigen values*.

6.2 Simulation of Frequency Modulation Using MATLAB

The following MATLAB code can plot the FM wave along with the modulating signal, $e_m = 3\cos(1000\pi t)$. The carrier signal is represented by $e_c = 10\sin(20000\pi t)$ and we assume that the modulation index is 10.

```
% MATLAB code to plot an FM wave..
% fc= 10kHz and fm=500Hz
% mf=10
t=linspace(0,0.004,100000);
efm=10*sin(20000*pi*t+10*sin(1000*pi*t));
subplot(211),plot(t,3*cos(1000*pi*t)); axis([0 .004 -5 5]);
subplot(212),plot(t,efm);axis([0 .004 -10 10]);
%%
```

The plot of the FM wave is given in Figure 6.2.

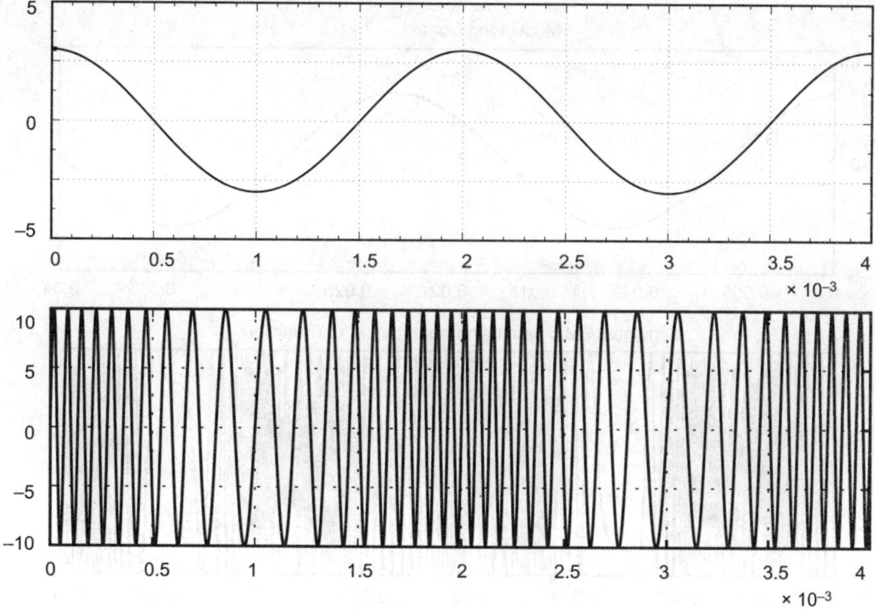

Figure 6.2 The frequency modulated waveform

6.2.1 Use of `modulate(.)` Function to Generate FM

An alternate code for generating the FM wave using the Signal Processing Toolbox function, `modulate(.)` is shown below:

```
% MATLAB code to generate and plot FM wave...
fc= 10000; % carrier frequency, 10KHz.
fs= 22000; % sampling frequency, 22000Hz. fs > 2*fc..
fm=500; % modulating signal frequency, 500Hz.
mf=10; % FM modulation index
t=linspace(0,.04,10000);
x=3*cos(1000*pi*t);
[y,t]=modulate(x,fc,fs,'fm');
subplot(211),plot(t,x);axis([0 .04 -5 5]);
title('Modulating Signal');
subplot(212),plot(t,5*y);axis([0 .04 -5 5]);
title('Simulated FM Output Using Modulate(.) Function');
%%
```

The simulated FM output waveform is shown in Figure 6.3. The inconsistency in the FM output waveform is due to the following reasons:

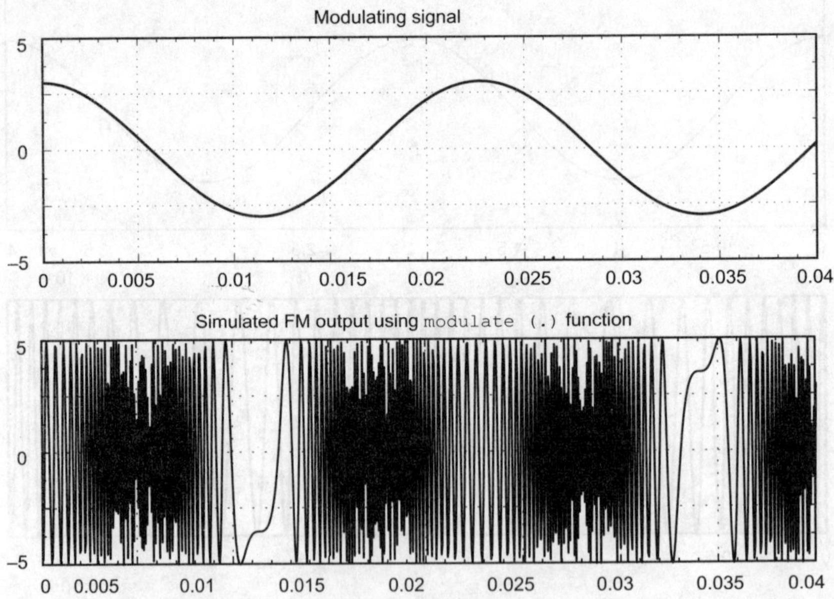

Figure 6.3 The simulated FM waveform using `modulate(.)` function

- The `modulate(x,fc,fs,'fm',opt)` function call implements the following line of code to generate FM:

  $$\mathtt{y} = \mathtt{cos}(2 * \mathtt{pi} * \mathtt{fc} * \mathtt{t} + \mathtt{opt} * \mathtt{cumsum}(\mathtt{x}))$$

  where `cumsum` is a rectangular approximation to the integral of x. The `modulate(.)` function uses `opt` as the constant of frequency modulation. If `opt` is not present, `modulate` uses a default value of

  ```
  opt = (fc/fs)*2*pi/max(max(x)))
  ```

  so that the maximum frequency excursion from f_c is f_c Hz.

- `cumsum` is a poor approximation of the time integral of x.

- If a better approximation for the time integral for x can be done, the output FM waveform becomes more smooth and realistic. The MATLAB `trapz(.)` is one such function which gives a better approximation.

6.2.2 Frequency Modulation and Demodulation Using Communications Toolbox

The Communications Toolbox of MATLAB contain two powerful functions for the modulation and demodulation of FM—the `fmmod(.)` and `fmdemod(.)` functions, respectively. The syntax of the `fmmod(.)` function is

- `y = fmmod(x,Fc,Fs,freqdev).`
- `y = fmmod(x,Fc,Fs,freqdev,ini\_phase).`

`y = fmmod(x,Fc,Fs,freqdev)` modulates the message signal x using frequency modulation. The carrier signal has frequency F_c (Hz) and sampling rate F_s (Hz), where F_s must be at least $2 \times F_c$. The `freqdev` argument is the frequency deviation constant (Hz) of the modulated signal.

`y = fmmod(x,Fc,Fs,freqdev,ini\_phase)` specifies the initial phase of the modulated signal in radians.

The code given below modulates a multichannel signal using `fmmod` and demodulates it using `fmdemod`.

```
clear all; close all; clf;
Fs = 8000; % Sampling rate of signal
Fc = 3000; % Carrier frequency
t = [0:Fs]'/Fs; % Sampling times
```

```
s1 = sin(2*pi*300*t)+2*sin(2*pi*600*t); % Channel 1
s2 = sin(2*pi*150*t)+2*sin(2*pi*900*t); % Channel 2
x = [s1,s2]; % Two-channel signal
dev = 50; % Frequency deviation in modulated signal.
y = fmmod(x,Fc,Fs,dev); % Modulate both channels.
z = fmdemod(y,Fc,Fs,dev); % Demodulate both..
z1=z(:,1); z2=z(:,2); % Separate out the Channels..
subplot(311),plot(t(100:600),s1(100:600),'b',...
    t(100:600),s2(100:600),'r','LineWidth',1);grid;
xlabel('Time'); ylabel('Amplitude');
axis([.015 .04 -3.5 3.5]); legend('Channel 1','Channel 2');
title('Original Channels');
subplot(312),plot(t(100:600),y(100:600),'b','LineWidth',1);grid;
xlabel('Time'); ylabel('Amplitude');
axis([.015 .04 -3.5 3.5]); title('FM Output');
subplot(313),plot(t(100:600),z1(100:600),'b',...
    t(100:600),z2(100:600),'r','LineWidth',1);grid;
xlabel('Time'); ylabel('Amplitude');
axis([.015 .04 -3.5 3.5]); legend('Channel 1','Channel 2');
title('FM Demodulated Outputs');
%%% end of fmexp.m
```

The simulated waveforms are illustrated in Figure 6.4.

6.2.3 The FM Radio Frequency Band

Since 1945, the range of frequencies from 88 MHz to 108 MHz have been kept reserved by the FCC for FM radio broadcasting. Each station in this band is allowed a ±75 kHz deviation (150 kHz carrier swing); a 25 kHz guardband is then added above and below the carrier frequency swing. Thus, a total bandwidth of 200 kHz is assigned to each station in this frequency band. There are a total of 100 such FM channels in the FM broadcast band. The FM channel numbering system starts at channel 201 and ends at channel 300. Channel 201 has a carrier centre (rest) frequency of 88.1 MHz and the next channel 202 has a carrier centre frequency of 88.3 MHz. The first 20 channels in this band are reserved for educational broadcasts (nonprofit), and the remaining 80 channels are for commercial broadcast services. Educational channels have a maximum *ERP* of 10 W.[1]

---

[1]The *effective radiated power (ERP)* is the product of the antenna input power and the antenna gain.

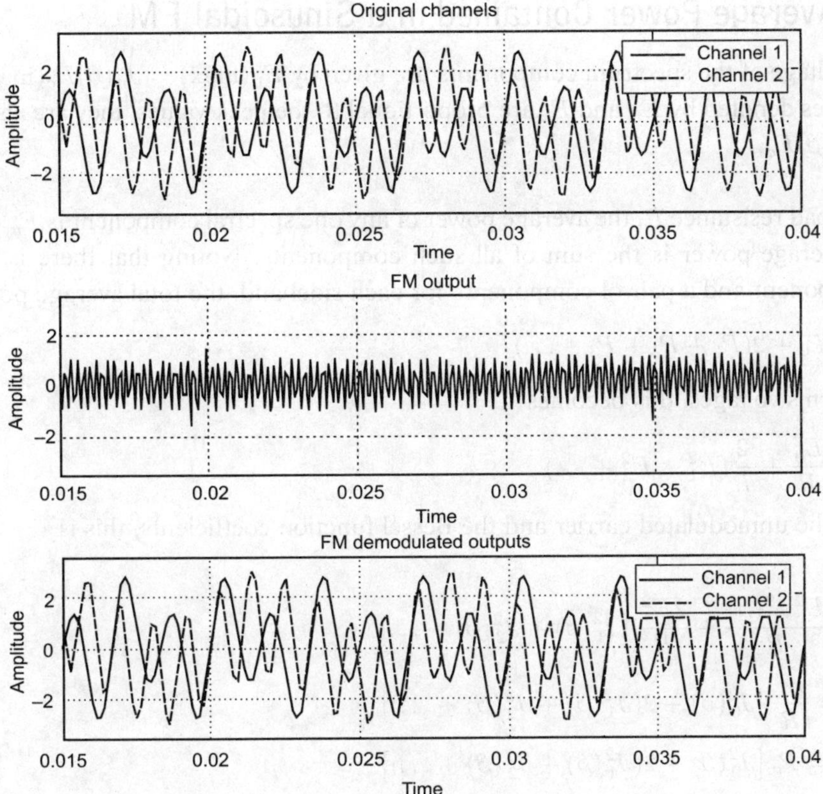

Figure 6.4 Simulation of frequency modulation and demodulation using Communications Toolbox functions.

6.2.4 Bandwidth Requirements for FM

It can be shown that as the modulation index increases, so does the bandwidth. Reduction in modulation frequency increases the number of sidebands, though not necessarily the bandwidth. Although the number of sideband components is theoretically *infinite*, in practice, a lot of sidebands have insignificant relative amplitudes. The exclusion of these sideband components will not distort the modulated wave unduly.

6.2.5 Carson's Rule on FM Bandwidth

Carson's rule states that the bandwidth required in an FM system is given by:

$$BW_{\mathrm{FM}} = 2 \times (\delta + f_{\max}) = 2 \times (\beta + 1) f_{\max} \tag{6.24}$$

where, δ is the deviation and $f_{\max}$ is the highest modulating frequency. The rule gives a fairly accurate result if the modulation index is above 6.

6.2.6 Average Power Contained in a Sinusoidal FM

The peak voltage of the spectrum components are given by $E_n(\max) = J_n(\beta)E_c(\max)$. Since the rms values denoted by E_n and E_c are proportional to the peak values, they are also related as $E_n = J_n(\beta)E_c$.

For a fixed load resistance R, the average power of any one spectral component is $P_n = E_n^2/R$. The total average power is the sum of all such components. Noting that there is only one carrier component and a pair of components for each sideband, the total average power is

$$P_T = P_0 + 2(P_1 + P_2 + P_3 + \ldots)$$

In terms of rms voltages, this becomes

$$P_T = \frac{E_0^2}{R} + \frac{2}{R}(E_1^2 + E_2^2 + \ldots) \tag{6.25}$$

In terms of the unmodulated carrier and the Bessel function coefficients, this is

$$\begin{aligned} P_T &= \frac{E_c^2 J_0^2(\beta)}{R} + \frac{2E_c^2}{R}\left[J_1^2(\beta) + J_2^2(\beta) + \ldots\right] \\ &= \frac{E_c^2}{R}\left[J_0^2(\beta) + 2(J_1^2(\beta) + J_2^2(\beta) + \ldots)\right] \\ &= P_c\left[J_0^2(\beta) + 2(J_1^2(\beta) + J_2^2(\beta) + \ldots)\right] \end{aligned} \tag{6.26}$$

Note that the unmodulated carrier power is $P_c = E_c^2/R$. A property of the Bessel functions is that the sum $J_0^2(\beta) + 2[J_1^2(\beta) + J_2^2(\beta) + \ldots] = 1$, so the total average power is equal to the unmodulated carrier power. This is in fact the expected result, as the envelope of the carrier does not change by frequency modulation. In effect, when modulation is applied, the total power that is originally present in the carrier is redistributed among all the components of the spectrum.

6.3 Phase Modulation (PM)

Phase modulation is closely related to frequency modulation. It is possible to obtain frequency modulation from phase modulation by the *Armstrong system*. PM is not used in practical analog modulation systems.

If the phase ϕ in the equation $e = A\sin(\omega_c t + \phi)$ is varied so that its magnitude is proportional to the instantaneous amplitude of the modulating voltage, the resulting wave is said to be phase-modulated. The expression for the PM wave is

$$e = A\sin(\omega_c t + \phi_m \sin\omega_m t) \tag{6.27}$$

where ϕ_m is the maximum value of phase change introduced by this particular modulating signal and is proportional to the maximum amplitude of this modulation. Now we can re-write equation (6.27) as:

$$e = A\sin(\omega_c t + m_p \sin\omega_m t) \tag{6.28}$$

where $m_p = \phi_m$, is the modulation index for phase modulation.

It may be noted that FM and PM are inseparable, and one can be generated from the other. This is evident from Figure 6.5, which shows the compatibility between the two systems.

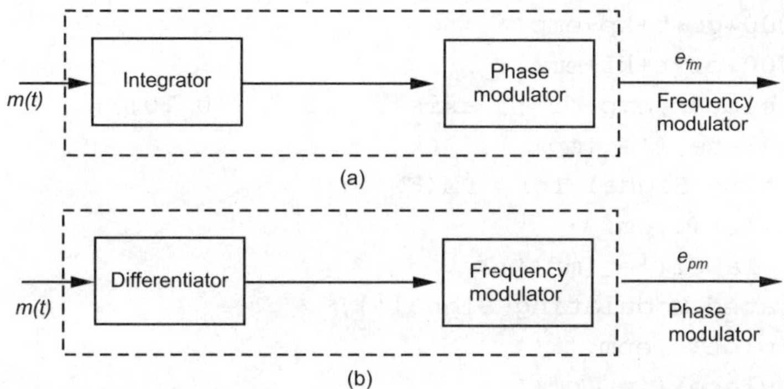

Figure 6.5 Compatibility between frequency and phase modulations

We can use the following MATLAB Signal Processing Toolbox function to generate phase modulated output by a signal $x(t)$:

```
[y,t]=modulate(x,fc,fs,'pm',opt);                    (6.29)
```

This function creates a sinusoid of frequency f_c whose phase varies with the message signal $x(t)$. Now, $y = \cos(2\pi f_c t + opt \times x)$. The function `modulate()` uses `opt` as the constant of phase modulation. If `opt` is not present, `modulate` uses a default value of `opt` $= \pi/(\max(\max(\mathrm{x})))$ so the maximum phase excursion is π radians.

6.3.1 Comparison of FM and PM Waveforms

To compare the shapes of FM and PM for a periodic modulating signal represented by $e_{mp} = 2\ square(2\pi\ f_m\ t)$, we resort to the following MATLAB simulation.

Let the period of the above square wave be 1 ms. The following MATLAB script file generates the PM and FM waves and plots them:

```
% MATLAB script to simulate the generation of FM and PM..
% The modulating signal is a square wave..
format long;
t=linspace(0,.002,10000); % time vector..
fm=1000;kp=4; % modulation index of PM.
tau=.0001; % time constant of the integrator..
emp=2*square(2*pi*fm*t); %
emf(1)=0; % first sample of integrated input..
kf=kp;
for l=2:length(emp)
    emf(l)=trapz(t(1:l),emp(1:l))/tau;% Trapezoidal integration
end;  % of input (modulating) signal..
epm=8*sin(40000*pi*t+kp*emp);
efm=8*sin(40000*pi*t+kf*emf);
subplot(411),plot(t,emp,'r'), axis([0 .002 -10 10]);
xlabel('t'), ylabel('e_{mp}');
title('Modulating Signal for  PM/FM');
subplot(412),plot(t,emf);
xlabel('t'), ylabel('e_{mf}');
title('Integrated Modulating Signal');
subplot(413),plot(t,epm,'r');
xlabel('t'), ylabel('e_{pm}');
title('PM_{out}for Square wave input');
subplot(414),plot(t,efm,'b');
xlabel('t'), ylabel('e_{fm}');
title('FM_{out}for Square wave input');
%%End of pmfmco.m
```

The resulting PM and FM waveforms are given in Figure 6.6.

Now we will try to simulate the PM and FM output waveforms for a triangular input signal. Note that this is the signal which is actually applied to a PM system (according to Figure 6.5) to generate an FM.

```
%% MATLAB  script file to generate and plot PM
% and  FM waveforms for a triangular input signal..
%
format long;
em=4*linspace(-1,1,1000); % One period of triangular wave
emp=em'*ones(1,10);
emp=emp(:)';
```

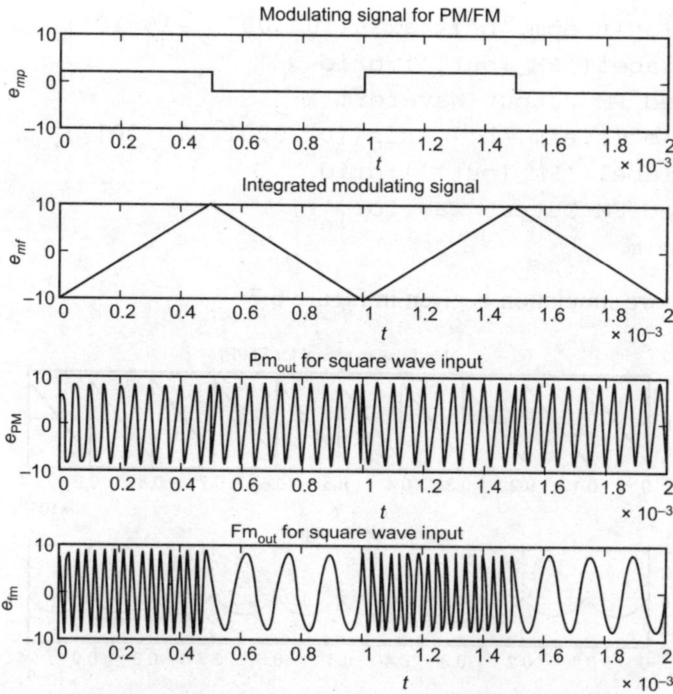

Figure 6.6 Comparison of PM and FM waveforms for a square wave input

```
t=linspace(0,.0001,length(emp));% Time vector for 10 cycles of
%% input wave.
fc=10^5;
kf=4000*pi; %FM modulation index.
kp=pi/2; %PM modulation index.
tau=kp/(2*kf); % Time constant of the integrator..
epm=8*sin(2*pi*fc*t+kp*emp);%PM out generated..
emf(1)=0;
for p=2:length(emp)
   emf(p)=trapz(t(1:p),emp(1:p))/tau; % Trapezoidal integration
end; % of input signal...
efm=8*sin(2*pi*fc*t+kp*emf);% FM out generated.
subplot(411),plot(t,emp,'r'), axis([0 .0001 -5 5]);
xlabel('t'); ylabel('e_{PM/FM}');grid
title('Modulating Signal for FM/PM');
subplot(412),plot(t,emf,'r'),axis([0 .0001 -.4 .4]);
xlabel('t'); ylabel('e_{FM}');grid
title('Integrated Input Signal');
```

```
subplot(413),plot(t,epm,'b'), axis([0 .0001 -10 10]);
xlabel('t'); ylabel('PM_{out}');grid
title('Modulated PM Output Waveform');
subplot(414),plot(t,efm,'b'),axis([0 .0001 -10 10]);
xlabel('t'); ylabel('FM_{out}');grid
title('Modulated FM Output Waveform');
%% end of pmtfm.m
```

The output of the above simulation is given in Figure 6.7.

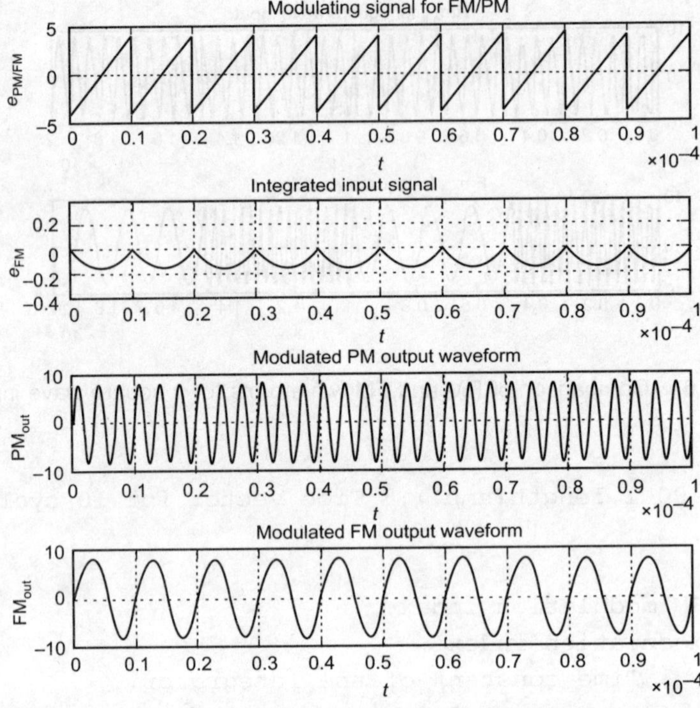

Figure 6.7 Simulated PM and FM waveforms for a triangular input

6.3.2 Simulation of Phase Modulation and Demodulation Using Communications Toolbox

The Communications Toolbox of MATLAB contains two powerful functions for the modulation and demodulation of PM—the `pmmod(.)` and `pmdemod(.)` functions, respectively. The syntax of the `pmmod(.)` function is

- `y = pmmod(x,Fc,Fs,phasedev).`
- `y = fmmod(x,Fc,Fs,phasedev,ini_phase).`

`y = pmmod(x,Fc,Fs,phasedev)` modulates the message signal x using phase modulation. The carrier signal has frequency F_c (hertz) and sampling rate F_s (hertz), where F_s must be at least $2 \times F_c$. The `phasedev` argument is the phase deviation of the modulated signal in radians.

`y = pmmod(x,Fc,Fs,phasedev,ini_phase)` specifies the initial phase of the modulated signal in radians. The example given below as MATLAB script `pmexp.m` samples an analog signal and phase modulates it. It then simulates an additive white Gaussian noise (AWGN) channel, demodulates the received signal, and plots the original, phase modulated and demodulated signals.

```
clear all; close all; clf;
% Prepare to sample a signal for two seconds,
% at a rate of 800 samples per second.
Fs = 800; % Sampling Frequency..
t = [0:2*Fs+1]/Fs; % Time points for sampling
% Create the signal, a sum of two sinusoids.
x = sin(2*pi*t) + sin(6*pi*t);
Fc = 50; % Carrier frequency in modulation
phasedev = pi/2; % Phase deviation for phase modulation
y1= pmmod(x,Fc,Fs,phasedev); % Modulate.
y = awgn(y1,10,'measured',199); % Add noise.
z = pmdemod(y,Fc,Fs,phasedev); % Demodulate.
% Plot the original, phase modulated  and demodulated signals..
subplot(311), plot(t,x,'LineWidth',1.5); grid;
axis([0 2 -2.5 2.5]); title('Original signal');
subplot(312), plot(t,y,'LineWidth',1.5); grid;
axis([0 2 -2.5 2.5]); title('Phase Modulated Signal');
subplot(313), plot(t,z,'LineWidth',1.5); grid;
axis([0 2 -2.5 2.5]); title('Demodulated Signal');
%%% end of pmexp.m
```

The simulated waveforms are illustrated in Figure 6.8.

6.3.3 Comparison Between Angle Modulations

From the theoretical point of view, the modulation index in FM and PM are defined differently. In phase modulation, the phase deviation is proportional to the amplitude of the modulating signal and independent of its frequency. Since the phase modulated vector sometimes leads and sometimes lags the reference carrier vector, its instantaneous angular velocity continually changes between the limits imposed by ϕ_m; thus some form of frequency change must

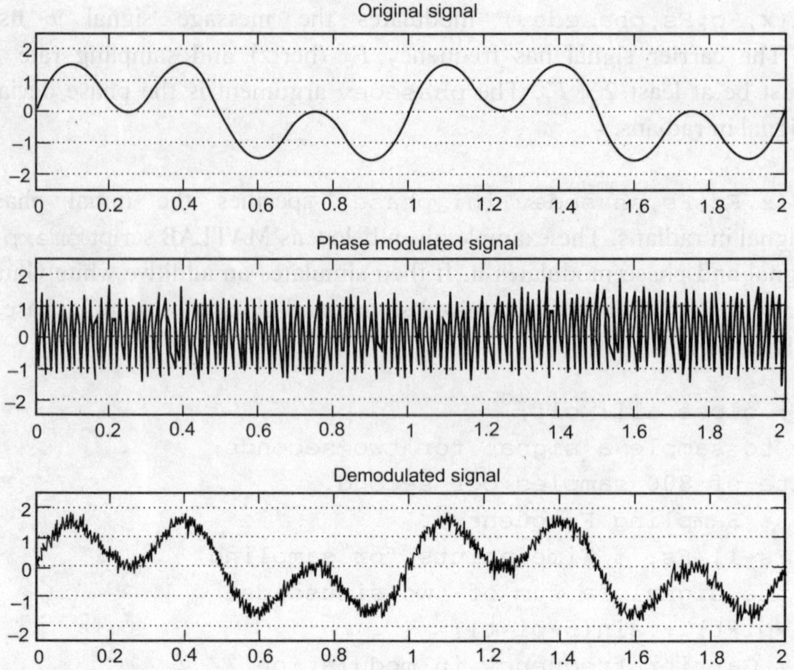

Figure 6.8 Simulation of phase modulation and demodulation

be taking place. In frequency modulation, the frequency deviation is proportional to the amplitude of the modulating voltage. Moreover, if we take a reference vector, rotating with a constant angular velocity which corresponds to the carrier frequency, the FM vector will have a phase lead or lag with respect to this reference, since its frequency oscillates between $f_c - \delta$ and $f_c + \delta$. Therefore, FM must be a form of PM. In FM, the larger the frequency deviation, larger is the phase deviation. So the latter depends at least to a certain extent on the amplitude of the modulation, just as in PM. But the modulation index of FM is also *inversely proportional to the modulating frequency.* This means that under identical conditions, *FM and PM are indistinguishable for a single modulating frequency.* When the modulating frequency is changed, the PM modulation index remains the same whereas the FM modulation index will increase as modulation frequency is reduced and vice versa. A numerical example will clearly illustrate this point.

EXAMPLE 6.1

A 40 MHz carrier is modulated by a 500 Hz audio sine wave. If the peak carrier voltage is 10 V and the maximum deviation is 15 kHz, write the equation of this modulated wave for: (a) FM and (b) PM. If the modulating frequency is now changed to 2.5 kHz, and everything else remains the same, write a new equation for: (c) FM and (d) PM.

SOLUTION

Calculating the angular frequencies, we have:

$$\omega_c = 2\pi \times 40 \times 10^6 = 2.5133 \times 10^8 \text{ rad/s}$$
$$\omega_m = 2\pi \times 500 = 3141.6 \text{ rad/s}.$$

The modulation index will be

$$m = \beta = m_p = \frac{\delta}{f_m} = \frac{15000}{500} = 30$$

This will give the equations for modulated waves as:

(a) $e = 10 \sin(2.5133 \times 10^8 t + 30 \sin 3141.6t)$ (FM)

(b) $e = 10 \sin(2.5133 \times 10^8 t + 30 \sin 3141.6t)$ (PM)

Note that, as expected, the two expressions are identical. Now when the modulating frequency is increased 5 times, the FM modulation index is reduced 5 fold, whereas the PM modulation index remains the same. Therefore,

(c) $e = 10 \sin(2.5133 \times 10^8 t + 6 \sin 3141.6t)$ (FM)

(d) $e = 10 \sin(2.5133 \times 10^8 t + 30 \sin 3141.6t)$ (PM)

The practical effect of all these considerations is that if an FM transmission were received on a PM receiver, the bass frequencies would have considerably more deviation of phase than a PM transmitter would have given them. Since the output of the PM receiver would be proportional to the phase deviation (or modulation index), the signal would appear unduly bass boosted. Phase modulation received by an FM receiver, on the other hand, would appear to be *lacking in bass.*

6.3.4 Bandwidth Requirements for PM

It is quite illuminating to look at the bandwidth requirements of the phase modulated wave. Note that Carson's rule is equally valid for all types of angle modulations, whereby we have:

$$B_c = 2(1+\beta)f_m = \begin{cases} 2(k_P.a+1)f_m, & \text{PM} \\ 2(\frac{k_f.a}{f_m}+1)f_m, & \text{FM} \end{cases} \tag{6.30}$$

where the modulating signal, $m(t) = a.\cos(2\pi f_m t)$, and β is the modulation index of PM/FM. Now, k_p is the phase deviation constant in radians/V and k_f is the frequency deviation constant in hertz/V.

6.3.5 Comparison Between FM and AM

FM and AM are two practical systems quite different from each other. FM has the following merits over AM:

- The envelope of the FM wave is constant. It is thus independent of the modulation depth, whereas in AM, modulation depth decides the transmitted power. Practically, this means that in FM transmitters, low-level modulation may be used. The subsequent amplifiers can be Class C, and therefore it is more efficient. Moreover, all the transmitted power in FM is useful, whereas in AM most of it is in the transmitted carrier which contains no useful information.

- FM receivers can be fitted with amplitude limiters to remove the amplitude variations caused by noise. This makes FM reception a great deal more immune to noise than AM.

- It is possible to reduce noise still further by increasing the deviation. AM does not have this feature. Increasing modulation index beyond 100% causes severe distortion in AM.

- The guard band allocation by the International Telecommunications Union (ITU) for FM stations ($\pm$ 25 kHz) provide good adjacent channel rejection.

- The FM broadcast band is in the upper VHF and UHF frequency ranges which happens to be less noisy than the MF and HF ranges occupied by the AM broadcast.

- At the FM broadcast frequencies, *space wave propagation* is used, so that the radius of operation is limited to slightly more than the *line of sight*. It is therefore possible to operate several independent transmitters on the same frequency with considerably less interference than would be possible with AM.

The following are some of the disadvantages of FM transmission:

- A much wider channel bandwidth is required for FM, up to 10 times as large as that required for AM. This is the most significant disadvantage of FM.

- FM transmitting and receiving equipments tend to be more complex, especially for modulation and demodulation.

- As the FM reception is limited to line of sight, the area of reception for FM is much smaller than for AM. This is a disadvantage for FM mobile communications.

6.4 FM Transmission and Noise

Frequency modulation is much more immune to noise than AM, and is significantly more immune than PM. In FM, the signal-to-noise ratio (SNR) improves as the modulating frequency is reduced. Under identical conditions, FM will be 4.75 dB better in SNR than PM. It can be shown that in FM, noise has a higher effect on the higher modulating frequencies than the lower modulating frequencies.

6.5 Noise in FM Receivers

In FM systems, amplitude limiters help to reduce impulse-type noise. Therefore, FM has an advantage over AM. Another advantage arises from the nature of the noise modulation process. The noise at the receiver input cannot directly modulate the frequency of the incoming carrier since its frequency is fixed by the remote transmitter, which may in fact be crystal controlled. An important advantage of the FM reception is that an improvement in SNR can be achieved by increasing the frequency deviation. This requires an increased bandwidth, but atleast there is an option for trading bandwidth for SNR.

The power spectral density (PSD) is kT_s, and therefore, the available noise power at the detector input for a bandwidth W is $P_{n\text{REF}} = kT_s W$. The rms signal voltage is $E_c = E_{c\,\max}/\sqrt{2}$, and hence the signal power at the detector input is $P_R = \frac{E_{c\,\max}^2}{8R_s}$. Therefore, the reference SNR for the FM system is

$$\left(\frac{S}{N}\right)_{\text{REF}} = \frac{P_R}{P_{n\,\text{REF}}} = \frac{E_{c\,\max}^2}{8R_s kT_s W} \tag{6.31}$$

It should be noted that though the reference SNR is decided at the input side of the detector, the bandwidth W is decided by the lowpass filter at the output side.

Consider the signal output from the bandpass filter when a sinusoidally modulated carrier is received in the absence of noise. The instantaneous frequency is given by

$$f_i = f_{IF} + \Delta f \cos \omega_m t \tag{6.32}$$

The FM discriminator converts this to a signal output given by

$$v_m(t) = \beta \Delta f \cos \omega_m t \tag{6.33}$$

where β is a constant, which is the frequency-to-voltage coefficient of the discriminator. The rms voltage at the output is $E_m = \frac{\beta \Delta f}{\sqrt{2}}$, and hence the available power output is

$$P_{so} = \frac{(\beta \Delta f)^2}{8R_{\text{out}}} \tag{6.34}$$

The noise output from a bandpass system is given by:

$$n_{IF}(t) = n_I(t)\ \cos\ 2\pi\, f_{IF}\, t\ -\ n_Q(t)\ \sin\ 2\pi\, f_{IF}\, t \tag{6.35}$$

Equation (6.35) can be written as:

$$n_{IF}(t) = n_I(t)\ \cos\ \omega_{IF}\, t\ -\ n_Q(t)\ \sin\ \omega_{IF}\, t \tag{6.36}$$

The incoming carrier in this case is frequency modulated and can be written as

$$e(t) = E_{c\ \max}\ \cos\ (\omega_{IF}\, t + \phi_m(t)) \tag{6.37}$$

where $\phi_m(t)$ is the equivalent phase modulation produced by the signal. The noise terms in the output resulting from the interaction of $\phi_m(t)$ and the noise modulation, lie outside the baseband. Therefore, the noise analysis can be done assuming that an unmodulated carrier is received. The input to the detector is

$$e_{\text{det}} = e_c(t) + n_{IF}(t) = (E_{c\ \max}\ + n_I(t))\ \cos\ \omega_{IF}\, t - n_Q(t)\ \sin\ \omega_{IF}\, t \tag{6.38}$$

We can express the above waveform in an equivalent form as $e_{\text{det}}(t) = B(t).\cos\ (\omega_{IF}\, t + \psi(t))$, where

$$B(t) = \sqrt{(E_{c\ \max} + n_I(t))^2 + n_Q^2(t)} \tag{6.39}$$

$$\psi(t) = \tan^{-1} \frac{n_Q(t)}{E_{c\ \max} + n_I(t)} \tag{6.40}$$

As the carrier amplitude is much greater than the noise voltage, the phase angle becomes

$$\psi(t) \cong \tan^{-1} \frac{n_Q(t)}{E_{c\ \max}} \cong \frac{n_Q(t)}{E_{c\ \max}} \tag{6.41}$$

The total carrier angle is $\theta(t) = \omega_{IF}\, t + \psi(t)$ and therefore the equivalent frequency modulation is

$$f_{ieq}(t) = f_{\text{IF}} + \frac{1}{2\pi}.\frac{d\psi(t)}{dt} = f_{IF} + \frac{\frac{dn_Q(t)}{dt}}{2\pi\, E_{c\ \max}} \tag{6.42}$$

The noise voltage at output is therefore

$$v_n(t) = \frac{\beta \frac{dn_Q(t)}{dt}}{2\pi\, E_{c\ \max}} \tag{6.43}$$

Fourier analysis shows that if a voltage waveform $v(t)$ has a power spectral density $G(f)$, then the PSD for $\frac{dv(t)}{dt}$ is $4\pi^2 f^2\, G(f)$. The PSD for $n_Q(t)$ is $2kT_s$ and hence the PSD for $\frac{dn_Q(t)}{dt}$ is $4\pi^2 f^2\, 2kT_s$. Therefore, we can show that the PSD of $v_n(t)$ is

$$G_v(f) = \frac{\beta^2 f^2 2kT_s}{E_{c\ \max}^2} \tag{6.44}$$

From the definition of PSD, the noise power at the output is

$$P_{no} = \int_0^W G_v(f)df = \frac{W^3\beta^2 2kT_s}{3E_{c\,\max}^2} \tag{6.45}$$

Therefore the SNR at the output is

$$\left(\frac{S}{N}\right)_o = \frac{P_{so}}{P_{no}} = \frac{3\Delta f^2 E_{c\,\max}^2}{16 R_{\text{out}} k T_s W^3} \tag{6.46}$$

Now the *figure of merit* of the FM system is

$$\text{FOM}_{\text{FM}} = \frac{(S/N)_o}{(S/N)_{\text{REF}}} = 1.5\left(\frac{\Delta f}{W}\right)^2 \frac{R_s}{R_{\text{out}}} = 1.5 m_f^2 \frac{R_s}{R_{\text{out}}} \tag{6.47}$$

where m_f is the modulation index calculated for the highest baseband frequency W. Note that this is different from the normal FM modulation index.

6.5.1 Carrier-to-Noise Ratio

The information obtained from the FM signal-to-noise ratio (SNR) is often expressed in another way, using the carrier-to-noise ratio (CNR) as the input parameter at the detector. The CNR is similar to the $(S/N)_{\text{REF}}$ except that the total IF bandwidth is used rather than W. So we have:

$$\left(\frac{C}{N}\right) = \frac{E_{c\,\max}^2}{8 R_s k T_s B_{\text{IF}}} \tag{6.48}$$

Applying Carson's rule, $B_{\text{IF}} = 2(m_f + 1)W$ gives (valid for $\beta > 6$):

$$\left(\frac{C}{N}\right) = \frac{E_{c\,\max}^2}{16 R_s k T_s (m_f + 1) W} \tag{6.49}$$

6.5.2 Processing Gain

The ratio of the output SNR to CNR is known as the *processing gain* and is given by

$$\text{PG} = \frac{(S/N)_o}{(C/N)} = 3 m_f^2 (m_f + 1) \frac{R_s}{R_{\text{out}}} \tag{6.50}$$

It should be noted well that the above result is valid only when the carrier is much larger than the noise, and that the deviation is for a sinusoidally modulated wave. When the carrier level is below the so-called *threshold level,* it is found that the output SNR becomes worse very rapidly.

6.6 Threshold Effect in FM Systems

The figure of merit of FM discussed above is valid only if the carrier-to-noise ratio (CNR) is high compared to unity. It has been found experimentally that as CNR is decreased below a threshold, each FM demodulator, either coherent or non-coherent, breaks down. At first, isolated clicks are heard. But if the CNR is decreased further, the clicks rapidly merge into a crackling sound. A qualitative explanation for the same, is as follows: if CNR is small, then the noise becomes dominant and the phasor representation and the decomposition of noise into a PM and AM are not valid any more. The phase of noise is a random variable and it may take any value. Recall that the FM demodulator is sensitive to the derivative of phase. When the phase of the demodulator input varies suddenly by 2π due to noise, then an impulse, i.e., a click appears at the receiver output.

6.6.1 FM Threshold Reduction

The threshold effect exists in every FM demodulator, either coherent or non-coherent. In certain applications such as space communication, the received signal level is very low. Consequently, the threshold has to be reduced in practice. It can be done by a PLL FM demodulator or a FM demodulator with a negative feedback (FMFB demodulator). Such circuits are referred to as *extended threshold demodulators*.

6.6.2 Comparison of Noise Performance in Continuous Wave Systems

The threshold problem is more serious in FM systems than in AM systems. The higher the modulation index, m_f, the better the FM noise performance. But the price to be paid is the wider transmission bandwidth. High fidelity (hi-fi) requirements may not be satisfied by AM in the presence of noise. The noise performance of various AM and FM systems are illustrated in Figure 6.9.

6.6.3 Pre-emphasis and De-emphasis

It can be shown that in FM, if the high frequencies are boosted before they are modulated (they are subsequently attenuated after demodulation at the receiver, to null the effect), there is an improvement in SNR. This boosting of high frequencies, in accordance with a pre-arranged curve is called *pre-emphasis*, and the compensation done at the receiver is called *de-emphasis*. Typical circuits are shown in Figure 6.10. The amount of pre-emphasis for FM broadcast in the US is 75 μs, whereas European and Australian TV transmission use 50 μs. Note that the pre-emphasis circuit is a *highpass filter* and the de-emphasis circuit is, therefore, a *lowpass filter.* A comparison of various carrier wave modulation systems is done in Tables 6.1 and 6.2.

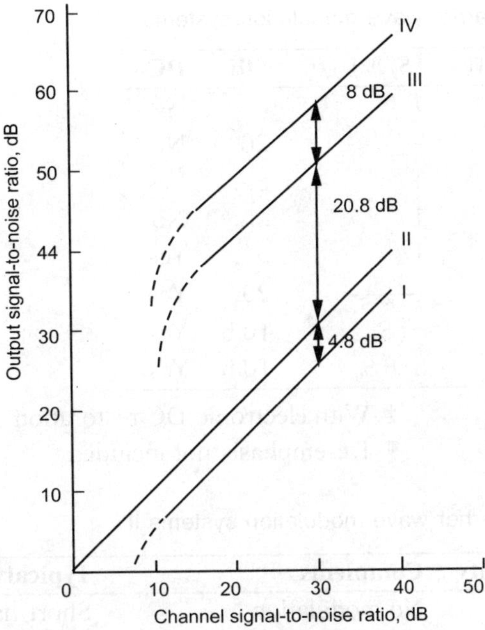

Figure 6.9 Noise performance of AM and FM. Curve I: DSB with envelope detector, $m_a = 1$; Curve II: DSBSC and SSB with a coherent detector; Curve III: FM with m_f = 2, 13 dB pre- and de-emphasis improvement is included; Curve IV: FM with m_f = 5, 13 dB pre- and de-emphasis improvement is included.

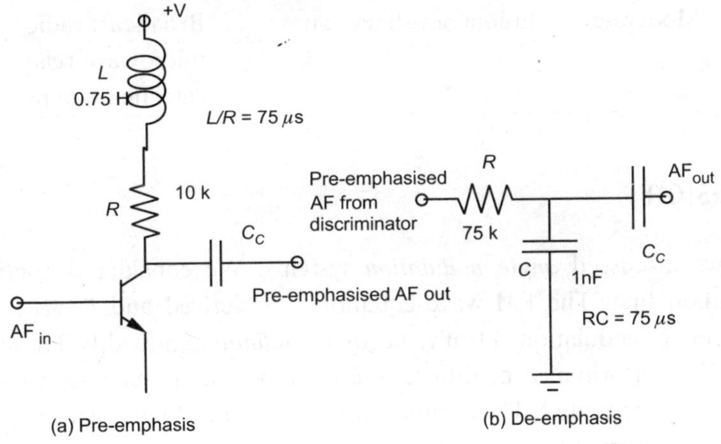

Figure 6.10 Pre-emphasis and de-emphasis circuits

Table 6.1 Comparison of carrier wave modulation systems I

Type of system	$b = B_T/W$	$(S/N)_D/\gamma$	γth	DC
Baseband	1	1	...	No†
AM	2	$\frac{\mu^2 S_x}{1+\mu^2 S_x}$	20	No
DSB	2	1	...	Yes
SSB	1	1	...	No
VSB	1+	1	...	Yes
VSB + C	1+	$\frac{\mu^2 S_x}{1+\mu^2 S_x}$	20	Yes‡
PM§	2M(ϕ_Λ)	$\phi_\Lambda^2 S_x$	10 b	Yes
FM§¶	2M(D)	$3D^2 S_x$	10 b	Yes

† Unless direct coupled ‡ With electronic DC restoration
§ $b \geq 2$ ¶ De-emphasis not included

Table 6.2 Comparison of carrier wave modulation systems II

Type of system	Complexity	Comments	Typical applications
Baseband	Minor	No modulation	Short-haul links
AM	Minor	Envelope detection, $\mu \leq 1$	Broadcast radio
DSB	Major	Synchronous detection	Analog data, multiplexing
SSB	Moderate	Synchronous detection	P2P voice, multiplexing
VSB	Major	Synchronous detection	Digital data
VSB + C	Moderate	Envelope detection, $\mu < 1$	Television video
PM	Moderate	Phase detection, $\phi_\Lambda \leq \pi$	Digital data
FM	Moderate	Frequency detection	Broadcast radio, microwave relay, satellite systems

6.7 Conclusion

In this chapter, we discussed *angle modulation* systems. We considered continuous wave frequency modulation first. The FM wave equation was derived and *Bessel functions* were introduced. Frequency modulation, ideally, needs an *infinite* bandwidth. Phase modulation was introduced. The performance of different angle modulation schemes were compared. Noise performance was evaluated. The *thresholding* problem in FM was considered. The need for pre-emphasis and de-emphasis in the case of FM was discussed.

Further Reading

1. *Getting Started with Communications Blockset*, The MathWorks, 2009.

2. *Getting Started with MATLAB 7*. The MathWorks. 2009.
3. Roddy and Coolen. *Electronic Communication Systems*. 4th Edition. Pearson Education (India) Ltd. 2008.
4. *Simulink*. The MathWorks. 2009.
5. *User's Guide, Communications Toolbox*. The MathWorks. 2009.

Problems

1. Create the *phasor diagram* for the signal $\sin(\omega_c t) + \cos(\omega_c t)$.
2. Determine the bandpass signal for the phasor diagram shown in Figure 6.11.

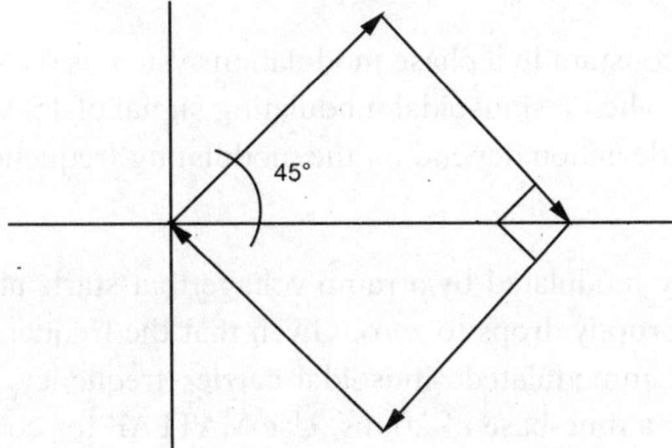

Figure 6.11 Phasor diagram of quadrature signals

3. What is the highest audio frequency allowed for use in commercial FM radio broadcasting? [Answer: 15 kHz.]
4. What will be the deviation, when the percentage of modulation in FM is 60%? [Answer: $0.6 \times \pm 75$ kHz= ± 45 kHz.]
5. What is the minimum distance in kilometres between two class C FM stations operating on the same frequency? [Answer: 289.67 km]
6. An FM broadcast carrier is deviated by ± 37.5 kHz. Find the percentage of modulation. [Answer: $\frac{37.5\ \text{kHz} \times 100}{75\ \text{kHz}} = 50\%$]
7. A carrier wave has an unmodulated frequency of 40 MHz. Sketch the instantaneous frequency–time curve when it is frequency modulated by a 4000 Hz sawtooth waveform, which varied 10 V peak-to-peak about zero DC value. The frequency deviation constant is 6 kHz per volt. Use MATLAB for coding.

8. A carrier is frequency modulated by a sinusoidal signal of 20 V peak and frequency 5 kHz, the frequency deviation constant being 4 kHz/volt. Calculate: (a) the peak frequency deviation, (b) the modulation index. [Answer: (a) 80 kHz, (b) 16.]

9. An FM carrier is limited to a maximum deviation of 75 kHz. Compare the bandwidths when the modulating signal is sinusoidal of frequency (a) 200 Hz, (b) 4 kHz and (c) 10 kHz, the carrier reaching maximum deviation in each case. State how you determine bandwidth limits. [Answer: (a) 150.4 kHz, (b) 158 kHz, (c) 170 kHz, in each case Carson's rule is applied, as $\beta > 6.0$]

10. A 2 kHz square wave is used to frequency modulate a carrier, producing a peak deviation of 75 kHz. Assuming that the harmonics of the square wave up to and including the eleventh need to be taken into account, calculate the deviation ratio and, using Carson's rule, the bandwidth. [Answer: $\frac{75}{2\times 11} = 3.41$, $2(75 + 22) = 194$ kHz.)

11. The phase deviation constant in a phase modulation system is 0.04 rad/V. Calculate the peak phase deviation when a sinusoidal modulating signal of 15 V peak is applied to it. Does the peak phase deviation depend on the modulating frequency? [Answer: 0.6 rad, No.]

12. A carrier is frequency modulated by a ramp voltage that starts at zero and rises to 10 V in 2 ms, when it abruptly drops to zero. Given that the frequency deviation constant is 5 kHz/V and the unmodulated sinusoidal carrier frequency is 400 kHz, plot the modulated angle over a time-base of 20 ms. Use MATLAB for coding.

13. A ramp voltage is used to phase modulate a 50 kHz carrier. The ramp rises linearly from zero to 5 V in 250 μs, when it abruptly drops to zero. Calculate the instantaneous frequency over the modulating period. The phase deviation constant is 2π rad/V. [Answer: $160\pi \times 10^6 + 50\pi \times 10^3$.]

14. A sinusoidal signal of 40 V peak is used to phase modulate a carrier, the phase deviation constant being 1 rad/V. Determine (a) the peak phase deviation and (b) the equivalent frequency deviation for a modulating frequency of 10 kHz. Repeat the calculations for the modulating frequency increased to 20 kHz, all other things remaining the same. [Answer: (a) 40 rad, (b) 400 kHz; 40 rad and 800 kHz.]

15. A 2000 Hz sinusoidal carrier signal with a 20 V peak is used to phase modulate a carrier, the phase deviation constant being 2 rad/V. Obtain the practical bandwidth required for the modulated signal. [Answer: 2(2+40) kHz = 84 kHz.]

16. A binary sequence 10101010 is used to phase modulate a carrier, the bit period being equal to 8 times the carrier period. Given that the modulated carrier amplitude is 5 V peak, accurately draw the modulated waveform showing the full modulating sequence.

17. A 100 kHz carrier is frequency modulated to produce a peak deviation of 1200 Hz. This FM is passed through a 4 × 4 × 3 frequency multiplier chain, the output of which is mixed with an oscillator signal and the difference frequency taken as the new output. Determine the frequency of the oscillator required to produce a 800 kHz FM output and the peak deviation of the output. [Answer: 4.0 MHz, 57.6 kHz.]

18. An Armstrong FM modulator uses a primary oscillator of 1 MHz, and the maximum phase deviation for good linearity is limited to 10^c rad with sinusoidal modulation. What is the corresponding peak frequency deviation at a modulating frequency of 1 kHz? If the transmitted signal is to have a maximum peak frequency deviation of 30 kHz at a carrier frequency of 120 MHz, specify the frequency multiplication factor needed, and suggest a chain of frequency doublers and triplers to accomplish this. For the above chain, specify the local oscillator frequency needed for the final frequency conversion. [Answer: 1×10^c kHz, 144, $2^4 \times 3^2$, 24 MHz.]

19. The message signal $m(t)$ shown in Figure 6.12 is sent to an FM modulator with peak frequency deviation f_d = 25 Hz/V. Plot the frequency deviation in hertz and the phase deviation in radians.

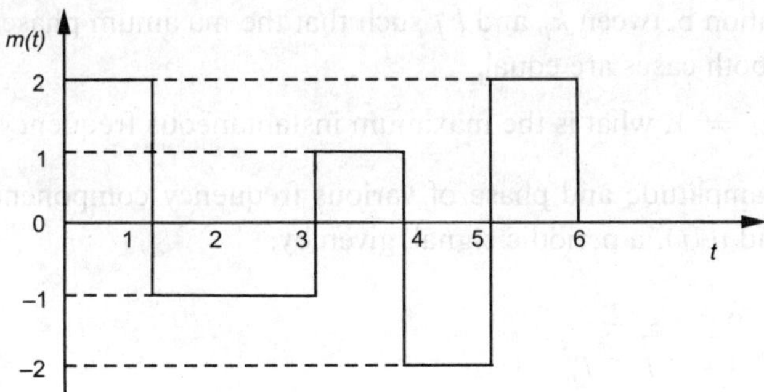

Figure 6.12 Quadrature level signal

20. An angle modulated signal is given by:

$$u(t) = 100 \cos[2\pi\, f_c t + 4 \sin 2\pi\, f_m t]$$

where f_c = 20 MHz and f_m = 2000 Hz.

(a) Assuming that this is an FM signal, determine the modulation index and the transmitted signal bandwidth.

(b) Repeat part (a) if f_m is doubled.

(c) Assuming that this is a PM signal, determine the modulation index and the transmitted signal bandwidth.

(d) Repeat part (c) if f_m is doubled.

[Answer: (a) 4, $2(1+4) \times 2$ kHz = 20 kHz, (b) 2, $2(1+2) \times 4$ kHz = 24 kHz, (c) 4, $2(1+4) \times 2$ kHz = 20kHz, (d) 4, $2(1+4) \times 4$ kHz = 40 kHz)

21. Signal $m(t)$ shown in Figure 6.13 is used to frequency modulate/phase modulate a carrier.

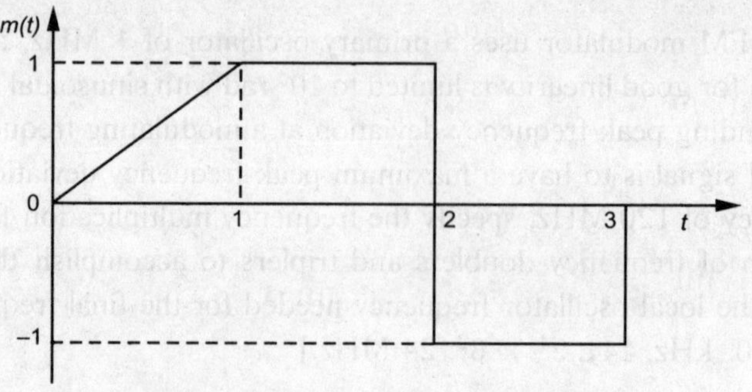

Figure 6.13 Multi-level signal

(a) Find a relation between k_p and k_f such that the maximum phase of the modulated signals in both cases are equal.

(b) If $k_p = f_d = 1$, what is the maximum instantaneous frequency in each case?

22. Determine the amplitude and phase of various frequency components of a PM signal with $k_p = 1$ and $m(t)$, a periodic signal, given by:

$$m(t) = \begin{cases} +1, & 0 \leq t \leq \frac{T_m}{2} \\ -1, & \frac{T_m}{2} \leq t \leq T_m. \end{cases}$$

for one period.

7

Simulation of Digital Modulation Systems

This chapter is devoted to a detailed discussion on various digital modulation schemes and their simulation studies. We begin with a brief introduction to digital modulation: their scope and relevance in modern communication systems. We then compare analog modulation schemes with digital modulation techniques. Digital modulation schemes offers several advantages over analog methods. A discussion on these advantages is followed by a detailed analysis of various digital baseband modulations of carrier waves—the keying techniques.

We will consider amplitude shift keying (ASK), and its variants like on–off keying (OOK) or binary amplitude shift keying (BASK), frequency shift keying (FSK) and its various forms like binary frequency shift keying (BFSK), M-ary frequency shift keying (MFSK), phase shift keying and its variants like binary phase shift keying (BPSK), quadrature phase shift keying (QPSK), differential quadrature phase shift keying (DQPSK), hybrid schemes like quadrature amplitude modulation (QAM) and its variants, minimum shift keying (MSK) and Gaussian minimum shift keying (GMSK). We then compare the performance of these modulation schemes with regard to bit error rate (BER). We also consider various applications scenarios.

In Section 7.4, we will consider digital modulation of a pulse carrier waveform. We will discuss pulse amplitude modulation (PAM), pulse width modulation (PWM), pulse position modulation (PPM), and pulse code modulation (PCM) and its variants like differential pulse code modulation (DPCM), adaptive differential PCM (ADPCM), delta modulation (DM), and adaptive delta modulation (ADM) techniques like sigma delta modulation (SDM) and continuously variable slope delta modulation (CVSD). We then compare the performance of these modulation schemes with regard to bit error rate (BER) and examine various application domains.

7.1 Introduction to Digital Modulation

The move to digital modulation provides more information capacity, compatibility with digital data services, higher data security, better quality communications, and quicker system availability. Developers of communications systems face these constraints:

1. available bandwidth,
2. permissible power and
3. inherent noise level of the system.

The RF spectrum must be shared, yet every day there are more users for this spectrum as demand for communications services increases. Digital modulation schemes have greater capacity to convey large amounts of information than analog modulation schemes.

7.1.1 Trading-off Simplicity and Bandwidth

There is a fundamental trade-off in communication systems. Simple hardware can be used in transmitters and receivers to communicate information. However, this uses a lot of spectrum which limits the number of users. Alternatively, more complex transmitters and receivers can be used to transmit the same information over less bandwidth. The transition to more and more spectrally efficient transmission techniques requires more and more complex hardware. Complex hardware is difficult to design, test, and build. This trade-off between simplicity and bandwidth exists whether communication is over air or wire, analog or digital.

The notion of the digital modulation can be thought of either as one having a discrete baseband (as is the case of the pulse modulation schemes) or one having a digital baseband (as in the case of keying techniques). Pulse modulation schemes like PAM, PPM, and PWM are not strictly "digital". The baseband (modulating) signal is usually analog. The pulse train whose parameters are modulated apparently serve as the carrier. The pulse stream as such is not discrete or digital; it is analog. This pulse is not differentiable (or continuous) everywhere (it is not differentiable at the edges), and this speciality makes it neither discrete nor digital.

In contrast to analog modulation, where both the baseband (modulating) signal and the carrier are analog, in digital modulation, either or both the carrier and the baseband signals are digital. Note that usually the message signal (also known as the baseband signal) is analog. We can discretise or digitise it by using an analog-to-digital converter (ADC). The discrete or digital baseband thus obtained can either modulate the carrier wave or a pulse train. When a digital baseband signal modulates a continuous carrier wave, it results in various keying techniques. On the other hand, when an analog baseband signal modulates a pulse train, we get various forms of pulse modulations.

It may be noted that the ADC actually effects *data conversion from analog to digital form.* We have to be careful here: The "digital" form is commonly effected through an encoder that identifies a binary number for the real value of the parameter of the function that has been sampled. This binary format, when represented as a waveform, takes the form of a pulse stream with an appropriate pulse width, period, and amplitudes (high or low in the binary case). This waveform is an analog function that acts as a modulating (baseband) signal. So in the strict sense, the modulation of a carrier using this "binary waveform" is analog. We call it digital modulation because the "binary waveform" represents the digits corresponding to the sample values of the function that has been sampled.

7.1.2 Comparison of Analog Modulation Schemes with Digital Modulation

In this section we will compare purely analog modulation schemes with digital modulation schemes.

- Analog modulation schemes need to use linear power amplifier stages. This results in reduced efficiencies.
- In the case of analog modulation systems, it is quite difficult to control the transmitted power effectively, and therefore, the range of communication is small.
- Digital communication is evolving into more than a necessity in many applications. The baseband is no more totally analog. The best example is communication involving computer data.
- By employing suitable data/signal compression and multiplexing techniques, digital transmission can be made spectrum efficient.

7.2 Quadrature Signals

Quadrature signals are based on the notion of complex numbers. Quadrature signal processing is used in many fields of science and engineering, and the signals are necessary to describe the processing and implementation that take place in modern digital communications systems.

Also called *complex* signals, they are used in many digital signal processing applications such as:

1. Digital communications systems,
2. Radar systems,
3. Time difference of arrival processing of radio-direction finding schemes,
4. Coherent pulse measurement systems,
5. Single sideband modulators.

These applications fall in the general category of *quadrature processing*, and they provide additional processing power through the coherent measurement of the phase of sinusoidal signals.

A quadrature signal is a two-dimensional signal whose value at any instant in time can be specified by a single *complex number* having two parts: the *real part (in-phase component)* and the *imaginary part (quadrature phase component)*. Multiplying any number on the real axis by j results in an imaginary product that lies on the imaginary axis, whose position is rotated 90° counter-clockwise from the real axis. In general, whenever any number is multiplied by j, the result is a counter-clockwise rotation of 90°. Conversely, multiplication by $-j$ results in a clockwise rotation of $-90°$ on the complex plane.

7.2.1 Representing Real Signals Using Complex Phasors

Consider a number whose magnitude is one, and whose phase angle increases with time. The complex number is $e^{j2\pi f_0 t}$. The $2\pi f_0$ terms is the frequency in radians/second, and it corresponds to a frequency of f_0 cycles/second, where f_0 is measured in Hertz. As time t gets larger, the complex number's phase angle increases and the number orbits the origin of the complex plane in a counter-clockwise manner. We can also think of another complex number $e^{-2\pi f_0 t}$ orbiting in a clockwise direction because its phase angle gets more negative as time increases.

The above two quadrature signals, $e^{j2\pi f_0 t}$ and $e^{-j2\pi f_0 t}$, can be considered as the tips of two phasors rotating in opposite directions. Note that the summation of these two phasors will *always* be a purely real number. This follows from Euler's equation:

$$\cos(2\pi f_0 t) = \frac{e^{j2\pi f_0 t} + e^{-j2\pi f_0 t}}{2} \tag{7.1}$$

Similarly, we also have:

$$\sin(2\pi f_0 t) = \frac{e^{-j2\pi f_0 t} - e^{j2\pi f_0 t}}{2} \tag{7.2}$$

Thus, we conclude that real signals, that can be transmitted over a coaxial cable or digitised or stored in a computer's memory, can be represented in complex number notation.

7.2.2 Representing Quadrature Signals in the Frequency Domain

We will represent a single complex exponential as a narrowband impulse located at the frequency specified in the exponent. Thus we can represent the in-phase component $\cos(2\pi f_0 t)$ by two impulses of amplitude $\frac{1}{2}$ placed at $-f_0$ and f_0, corresponding to the components $\frac{e^{-j2\pi f_0 t}}{2}$ and $\frac{e^{j2\pi f_0 t}}{2}$, respectively, in the frequency domain. Note that these two impulses are parallel (in-phase) to the real axis. Similarly, the quadrature component $\sin(2\pi f_0 t)$ can be represented by two impulses of amplitude $\pm\frac{1}{2}$ placed at $-f_0$ and f_0 parallel to the imaginary axis, corresponding to the components $j\frac{e^{-j2\pi f_0 t}}{2}$ and $-j\frac{e^{j2\pi f_0 t}}{2}$, respectively, in the frequency domain. The in-phase and quadrature components in the frequency domain are illustrated in Figure 7.1. The directions in which the spectral impulses point merely indicate the relative phases of the spectral components. The amplitude of these spectral impulses are 1/2.

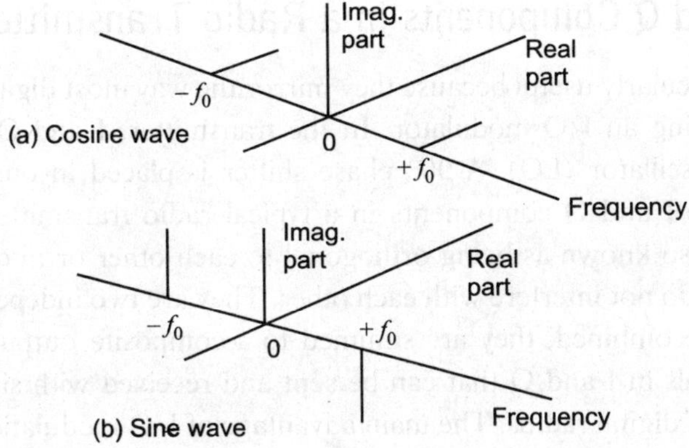

Figure 7.1 The complex frequency domain view of sine and cosine waves. (a) $\cos(2\pi f_0 t)$ (b) $\sin(2\pi f_0 t)$.

7.2.3 The I/Q Formats in Digital Communication

In digital communications, modulation is often expressed in terms of in-phase (I) and quadrature phase (Q) components. These components are a rectangular representation of the polar diagram. On a polar diagram, the I axis lies on the zero degree phase reference, and the Q axis is rotated by 90°, relative to this reference. The projection of the signal vector onto the I axis is its "I" component and the projection onto the Q axis is its "Q" component. The situation is illustrated in Figure 7.2.

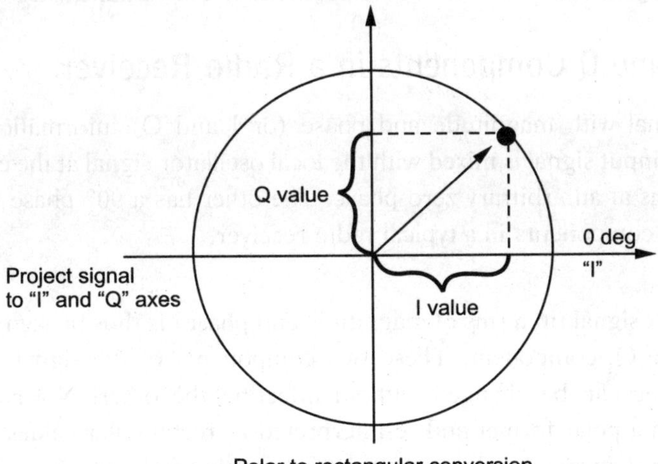

Figure 7.2 The I/Q format in digital communication

7.2.4 The I and Q Components in a Radio Transmitter

I/Q diagrams are particularly useful because they mirror the way most digital communications signals are created using an I/Q modulator. In the transmitter, I and Q signals are mixed with the same local oscillator (LO). A 90° phase shifter is placed in one of the LO paths. Figure 7.3 depicts the I and Q components in a typical radio transmitter. Signals that are separated by 90°are also known as being orthogonal to each other or in quadrature. Signals that are in quadrature do not interfere with each other. They are two independent components of the signal. When recombined, they are summed to a composite output signal. There are two independent signals in I and Q that can be sent and received with simple circuits. This simplifies the design of digital radios. The main advantage of I/Q modulation is the geometric ease of combining independent signal components into a single composite signal and later splitting such a composite signal into its independent component parts.

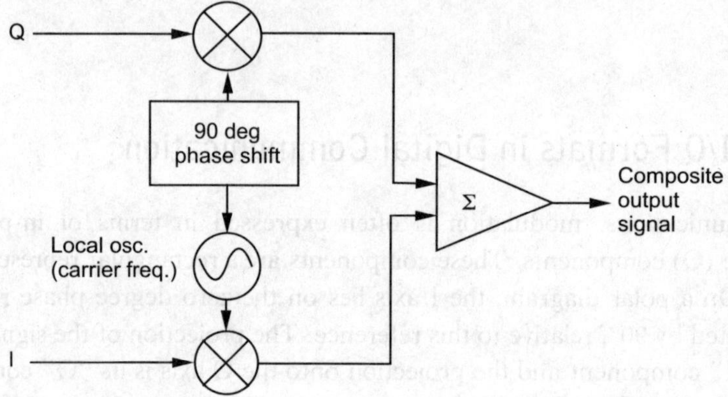

Figure 7.3 The I and Q components in a radio transmitter

7.2.5 The I and Q Components in a Radio Receiver

The composite signal with magnitude and phase (or I and Q) information arrives at the receiver input. The input signal is mixed with the local oscillator signal at the carrier frequency in two forms. One is at an arbitrary zero phase. The other has a 90° phase shift. Figure 7.4 depicts the I and Q components in a typical radio receiver.

The composite input signal (in terms of magnitude and phase) is thus broken into an in-phase I, and a quadrature Q, component. These two components of the signal are independent and orthogonal. One can be changed without affecting the other. Normally, information cannot be plotted in a polar format and re-interpreted as rectangular values without doing a polar-to-rectangular conversion. This conversion is exactly what is done by the in-phase and quadrature mixing processes in a digital radio. A local oscillator, phase shifter, and two mixers can perform the conversion accurately and efficiently.

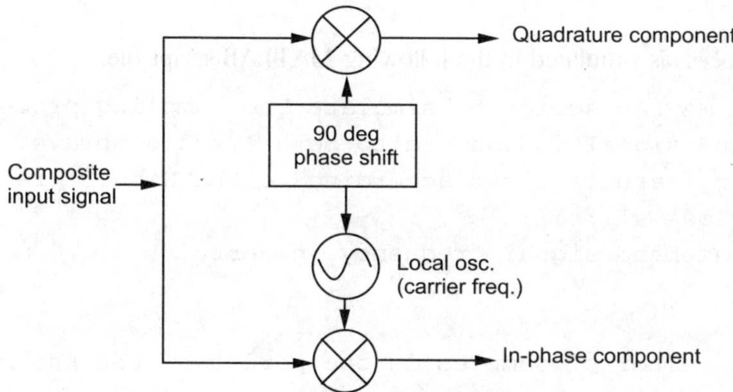

Figure 7.4 The I and Q components in a radio receiver

7.2.6 The Need for I/Q Components

Digital modulation is easy to accomplish with I/Q modulators. Most digital modulation maps the data to a number of discrete points on the I/Q plane. These are known as constellation points. As the signal moves from one point to another, it usually results in simultaneous amplitude and phase modulation. It is difficult and complex to accomplish this with an amplitude modulator and a phase modulator. It is also impossible with a conventional phase modulator. The signal may, in principal, circle the origin in one direction forever, necessitating infinite phase shifting capability. Alternatively, simultaneous AM and phase modulation is easy with an I/Q modulator. The I and Q control signals are bounded, but infinite phase wrap is possible by properly phasing the I and Q signals.

7.3 Digital Modulation of a Carrier Wave

In digital modulation of carrier waveforms, the analog baseband signals are first converted into a digital baseband by using an analog-to-digital converter (ADC). The analog signals are sampled at a rate termed as the Nyquist rate. The sampling frequency, as specified by the Nyquist rate, should be greater than *twice the highest frequency* in the analog baseband.

7.3.1 Introduction to Digital Basebands

There are two distinct sources of error in using a digital baseband. The first arises from the analog-to-digital conversion process where the sample values are rounded off. This produces a *round-off error* which is known as *quantisation noise.* Even when the transmission and reception of ones and zeros are perfect, we will still be left with quantisation noise. The second source of error is from the actual transmission process and the effects of distortion and additive noise. This causes *flipping of the bits* transmitted.

The sampling process is simulated in the following MATLAB script file.

```
%%% samp.m:: MATLAB script to simulate the sampling process..
% The baseband signal is assumed to be a 1 kHz sinewave..
% The sampling rate is fixed according to the Nyquist rate
clear all; close all;clf;
fb=1000; % baseband signal frequency in Hertz.
Tb=1/fb;
fs=40000;
Ns= fs/fb; % Number of samples in one period of the baseband signal...
t=linspace(0, .002, Ns);
sq=(1+square(t))/2;
asb=5*sin(2*pi*fb*t).*sq;
subplot(211), stem(t,sq); axis([0 .002 0 1]);
xlabel('Time in Seconds');
ylabel('Amplitude in Volts');
title('Square Wave output');
subplot(212),stem(t,asb);axis([0 .002 -5 5]);
xlabel('Time in Seconds');
ylabel('Amplitude in Volts');
title('Simulation of Sampling Process');
%%% end of samp.m
```

The resulting waveforms are illustrated in Figure 7.5.

7.3.2 Amplitude Shift Keying (ASK)

Amplitude shift keying (ASK) is a very popular modulation used in control applications. This is in partly due to its simplicity and low implementation costs. ASK modulation has the advantage of allowing the transmitter to idle during the transmission of a "zero", therefore conserving power. The disadvantage of ASK modulation arises in the presence of an undesired signal.[1]

In amplitude shift keying (ASK), as the name suggests, the amplitude of the carrier is changed in response to information. In other words, the amplitude of the carrier is switched between two (or more) levels according to the digital data. The information is assumed to be unipolar binary data. Bit 1 is transmitted by a carrier of particular amplitude. To transmit 0, we change the amplitude keeping the frequency constant. The ASK waveform can be represented by the

[1] The undesired part of the signal is usually the noise which causes the 1s to be interpreted as 0s and vice versa.

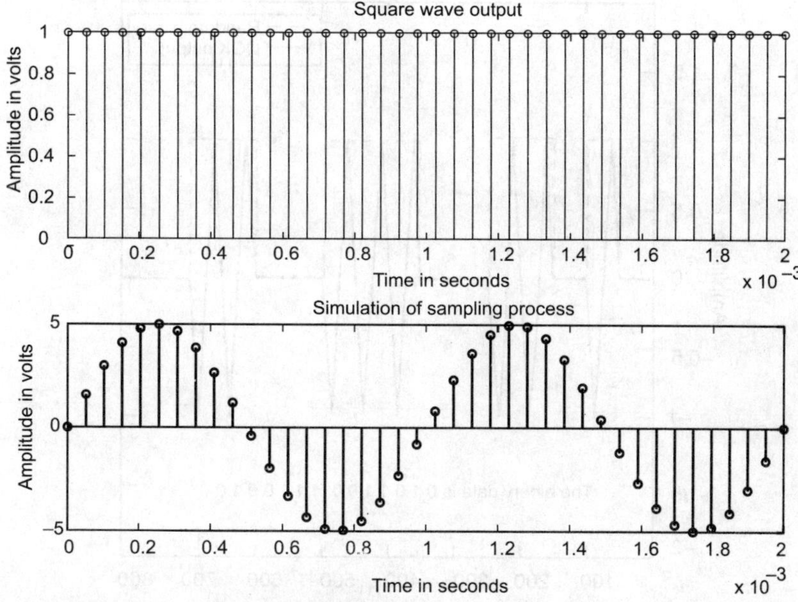

Figure 7.5 Simulation of sampling process: (a) The sampled form of a square pulse of width 2 ms and amplitude 1 V. (b) The sampled baseband signal.

following mathematical equation:

$$s(t) = m(t)\sin(2\pi f_c t) \tag{7.3}$$

where $s(t)$ is the ASK output signal, $m(t)$ is the binary message signal and f_c is the carrier frequency.

Binary ASK or On–Off Keying (OOK)

Binary amplitude shift keying (a.k.a. on–off keying) is a special case of ASK, where one of the amplitudes is zero as shown in Figure 7.6.

The corresponding MATLAB code is given below:

```
%%% MATLAB script to simulate OOK
clear all; close all; clf;
fc=4000;
t=linspace(0,1/4000,50);
ec=sin(2*pi*fc*t);
b=mod(randperm(16),2);
n=['The Binary Data is  ', num2str(b)];
```

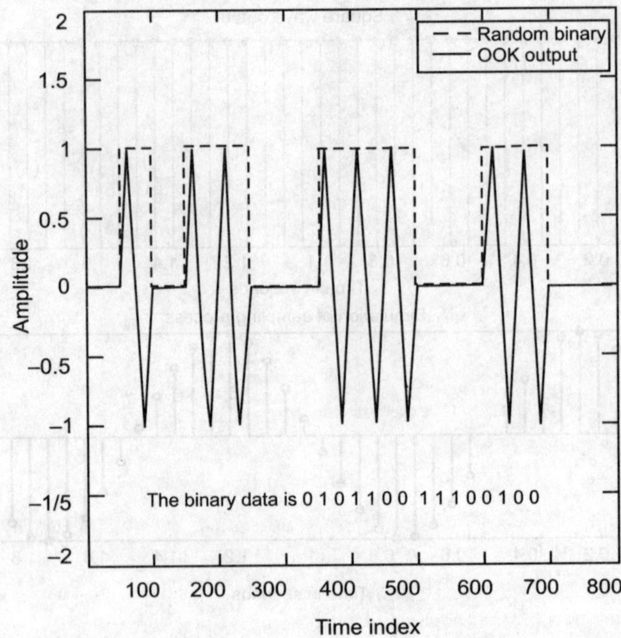

Figure 7.6 Simulation of on–off keying

```
ook=[];bin=[];
for i=1:length(b)
    ook=[ook,b(i)*ec];
    bin=[bin,b(i)*ones(1,50)];
end;
tm=[0:length(ook)-1];
plot(tm,bin,'b--');axis([0 length(bin) 0 2]);hold on;
plot(tm,ook,'r');axis([0 length(tm) -2 2]);hold off;
xlabel('Time index'); ylabel('Amplitude');
legend('Random binary', 'OOK output');
title('Simulation of On-Off Keying');
gtext(n); % Displays the random binary string..
%% end of onoffk.m
```

ASK techniques are most susceptible to the effects of non-linear devices which compress and distort the signal amplitude. To avoid such distortion, the system must be operated in the linear range, away from the point of maximum power where most of the non-linear behaviour occurs. Despite this problem in high frequency carrier systems, ASK is often used in wire-based radio signalling both with or without a carrier.

7.3.3 Frequency Shift Keying (FSK)

Frequency shift keying (FSK) is the most common form of digital modulation in the high-frequency radio spectrum, and has important applications in telephone circuits. In frequency shift keying (FSK), the instantaneous frequency of the carrier is switched between 2 or more levels according to the baseband digital data. Binary FSK (usually referred to simply as FSK) is a modulation scheme typically used to send digital information between digital equipment such as teleprinters and computers. One frequency is designated as the "mark" frequency and the other as the "space" frequency. The mark and space correspond to binary one and zero, respectively. By convention, mark corresponds to the higher radio frequency.

The minimum duration of a mark or space condition is called the *element length*. Typical values for element length are between 5 and 22 milliseconds, but element lengths of less than 1 microsecond and greater than 1 second have been used. Bandwidth constraints in telephone channels and signal propagation considerations in HF channels generally require the element length to be greater than 0.5 millisecond. An alternate way of specifying element length is in terms of the keying speed. The keying speed in *bauds* is equal to the inverse of the element length in seconds. For example, an element length of 20 milliseconds (.02 seconds) is equivalent to a 50-baud keying speed.

Coherent and Non-coherent FSK

FSK can be transmitted coherently or non-coherently. Coherency implies that the phase of each mark or space tone has a fixed phase relationship with respect to a reference. This is similar to generating an FSK signal by switching between two fixed frequency oscillators to produce the mark and space frequencies. While this method is sometimes used, the constraint that transitions from mark to space and vice versa must be phase continuous ("glitch" free) requires that the shift and keying rate be interrelated. A synchronous FSK signal which has a shift in Hertz equal to an exact integral multiple ($n = 1, 2, \ldots$) of the keying rate in bauds, is the most common form of coherent FSK. Coherent FSK is capable of superior error performance but non-coherent FSK is simpler to generate and is used in most FSK transmissions. Non-coherent FSK has no special phase relationship between consecutive elements, and, in general, the phase varies randomly.

Simulation of BFSK

In the binary frequency shift keying (BFSK), as mentioned, only two frequencies are involved. The BFSK signal can be represented by

$$s_0(t) = A_c \cos(2\pi f_0 t + \theta_0) \text{ for } m(t) = 0 \tag{7.4}$$

$$s_1(t) = A_c \cos(2\pi f_1 t + \theta_1) \text{ for } m(t) = 1 \tag{7.5}$$

where $s_0(t)$ and $s_1(t)$ are the FSK output signals corresponding to binary inputs 0 and 1 respectively. Note that frequencies f_0 and f_1 are chosen for 0 and 1, respectively. The equations given above will precisely correspond to a discontinuous phase FSK when $\theta_0 \neq \theta_1$. On the other hand, we will get a continuous phase FSK when $\theta_0 = \theta_1$. The MATLAB code to simulate continuous phase frequency shift keying (CPFSK) is given below. The simulated waveform is illustrated in Figure 7.7.

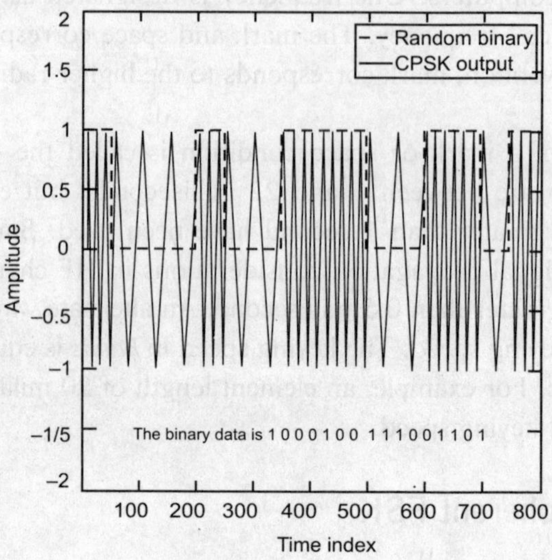

Figure 7.7 Simulated waveforms for continuous phase FSK

```
%%% cpfsk.m:: MATLAB script to generate continuous
% phase FSK..
clear all; close all; clf;
f0=1000; % frequency for "0" bits..
f1=3000; % frequency for "1" bits..
t=linspace(0,1/1000,50);
e0=cos(2*pi*f0*t); % theta0 =0;
e1=cos(2*pi*f1*t); % theta1 =1;
b=mod(randperm(16),2);
bnot=1-b;
n=['The Binary Data is  ', num2str(b)];
ask1=[];ask2=[];bin=[];
for i=1:length(b)
    ask1=[ask1,bnot(i)*e0];
    ask2=[ask2,b(i)*e1];
    bin=[bin,b(i)*ones(1,50)];
```

```
end;
fsk=ask1+ask2;
tm=[0:length(ask1)-1];
plot(tm,bin,'b--');axis([0 length(bin) 0 2]);hold on;
plot(tm,fsk,'r');axis([0 length(tm) -2 2]);hold off;
xlabel('Time index'); ylabel('Amplitude');
legend('Random binary', 'CPFSK output');
title('Simulation of Continuous Phase FSK');
gtext(n); % Displays the random binary string..
%%% end of cpfsk.m
```

M-ary Frequency Shift Keying (MFSK)

M-ary FSK is also known as multiple frequency shift keying. In MFSK, more than two frequencies are used. MFSK is more bandwidth efficient but also more susceptible to error than FSK. Mathematically, the MFSK signal can be represented by

$$
\begin{aligned}
s_i(t) &= \sqrt{2E/T}\cos(2\pi f_i t), \;\; 1 \le i \le M, \;\; \text{where} \qquad (7.6)\\
f_i &= f_c + (2i - 1 - M) f_d \\
f_c &= \text{the carrier frequency} \\
f_d &= \text{the difference frequency} \\
M &= \text{number of different symbols} = 2^L \\
L &= \text{number of bits per symbols}
\end{aligned}
$$

To match the data rate of the input bit stream, each output signal element is held for $T_s = LT$ seconds, where T is the bit period (data rate $= 1/T$). Hence, one signal element (symbol) encodes L bits. Note the following points for MFSK:

- Total bandwidth required $= 2Mf_d$.
- Minimum frequency separation required $= 2f_d = 1/T_s$.
- Therefore, the modulator requires a bandwidth of $W_d = 2^L/LT = M/T_s$.

The MATLAB code to simulate continuous phase multiple frequency shift keying (CPMFSK) is given below. The simulated waveform is illustrated in Figure 7.8.

```
%%% cpmfsk.m::: MATLAB script to generate continuous
%%% phase MFSK..
clear all; close all; clc;
L=input('The number of bits per symbol in message ');
```

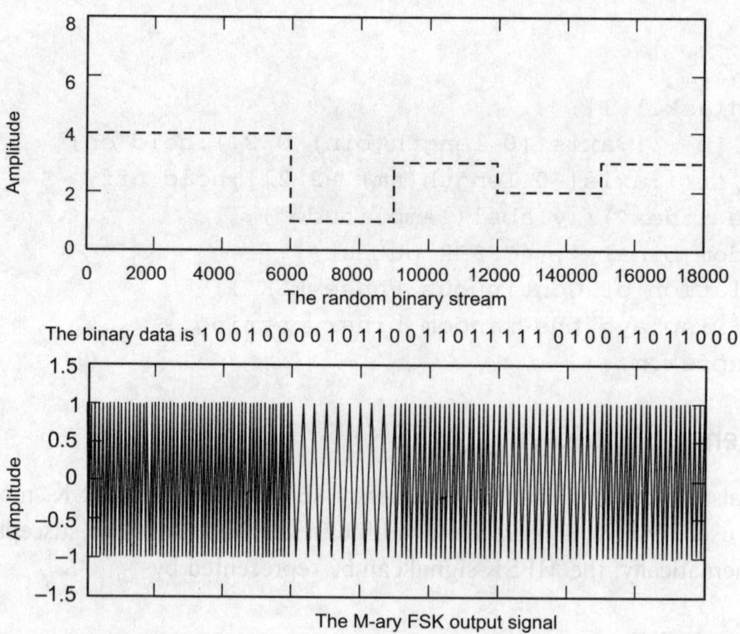

Figure 7.8 Simulated waveforms for M-ary FSK: (a) The random binary signal. (b) The 8-ary CPMFSK waveform. The number of bits per symbol in message = 3. The total number of symbols in message = 6.

```
N=input('The total number of symbols in message ');
M=2^L; % number of different symbols in message stream.
fc=4000; % carrier frequency.
fd=500; % difference frequency...
for i=1:M
    f(i)=fc+(2*i-1-M)*fd;
end;
samp=2*fd;
t=linspace(0,1/f(1),samp);
for j=1:M
    e(j,:)=cos(2*pi*f(j)*t);
end;
b=mod(randperm(2*N*L),2);
n=['The Binary Data is  ', num2str(b)];
mfsk=[];bin=[];
for k=1:L:2*N*L
    l=bin2int(b(k:k+L-1));
    mf=[];bn=[];
```

```
    for m=1:L
     mf=[mf, e(l+1,:)];
     bn=[bn,l*ones(1,samp)];
    end;
    mfsk=[mfsk, mf];
    bin=[bin,bn];
end;
tb=[0:length(bin)-1];
subplot(211),plot(tb,bin,'b--');axis([0 length(tb)*1/2  0 M]);
xlabel('The Random Binary Stream');ylabel('Amplitude');
title('Simulation of Continuous Phase MFSK');
subplot(212),plot(tb,mfsk,'r');axis([0 length(tb)*1/2 -1.5 1.5]);
gtext(n); % Displays the random binary string..
xlabel('The M-ary FSK Output Signal');ylabel('Amplitude');
%%% end of cpmfsk.m
%% bin2int.m function definition
function [y] = bin2int(b)
% function to convert binary numbers to integers.
y=0;
for i=1:length(b)
    y=y+b(i)*2^(length(b)-i);
end;
% end of bin2int.m
```

The Essence of FSK

The key points to remember regarding FSK are that

- they are less susceptible to error than ASK.
- they are used for high-frequency (3 to 30 MHz) radio transmission.
- they can be used at higher frequencies on local area networks (LANs) that employ coaxial cable.
- Amplitude of the carrier wave is constant, and therefore power efficient.

7.3.4 Binary Phase Shift Keying (PSK)

Phase shift keying (PSK) involves the switching of the instantaneous phase of the carrier between 2 or more levels according to the baseband digital data. In binary phase shift keying (BPSK), only two phases are involved. The BPSK signal can be represented by

$$s(t) = \begin{cases} \sqrt{2E/T}\cos(2\pi f_c t) & \text{binary} \quad 1 \\ \sqrt{2E/T}\cos(2\pi f_c t + \pi) & \text{binary} \quad 0 \end{cases} \tag{7.7}$$

$$= \begin{cases} \sqrt{2E/T}\cos(2\pi f_c t) & \text{binary} \quad 1 \\ -\sqrt{2E/T}\cos(2\pi f_c t) & \text{binary} \quad 0 \end{cases} \tag{7.8}$$

The MATLAB code to simulate binary phase shift keying (BPSK) is given below. The simulated waveform is illustrated in Figure 7.9.

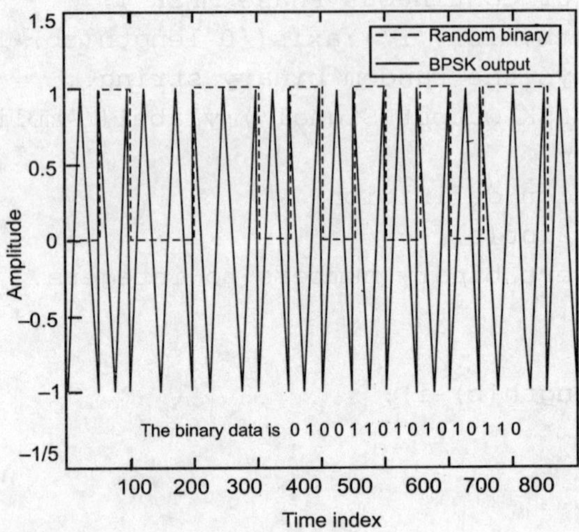

Figure 7.9 Simulated waveforms for binary phase shift keying

```
%%% bpsk.m::: MATLAB script to generate Binary PSK..
clear all; close all; clc;
fc=1000; % frequency for "0" bits..
t=linspace(0,1/1000,50);
e0=cos(2*pi*fc*t);% BPSK output for "1"..
e1=-cos(2*pi*fc*t);% BPSK output for "0".
b=mod(randperm(16),2);
bnot=1-b;
n=['The Binary Data is  ', num2str(b)];
bpsk1=[];bpsk2=[];bin=[];
for i=1:length(b)
   bpsk1=[bpsk1,b(i)*e0];
   bpsk2=[bpsk2,bnot(i)*e1];
```

```
    bin=[bin,b(i)*ones(1,50)];
end;
bpskout=bpsk1+bpsk2;
tm=[0:length(bpsk1)-1];
plot(tm,bin,'b--');axis([0 length(bin) 0 1.5]);hold on;
plot(tm,bpskout,'r');axis([0 length(tm) -1.5 1.5]);hold off;
xlabel('Time index'); ylabel('Amplitude');
legend('Random binary', 'BPSK output');
title('Simulation of Binary  Phase Shift Keying');
gtext(n); % Displays the random binary string.
%%% end of bpsk.m
```

7.3.5 Differential Phase Shift Keying (DPSK)

Differential phase shift keying (DPSK) is regarded as the non-coherent version of binary PSK. It might appear that quadrature phase shift keying (QPSK), a popular version of PSK which is explained in Section 7.3.6, offers advantages over both ASK, FSK and PSK. However, the demodulation of these signals requires various degrees of difficulty and hence are more expensive. The method of demodulation is an important factor in determining the selection of a modulation scheme. There are two types of demodulation which are distinguished by the need to provide knowledge of the phase of the carrier. Demodulation schemes requiring the carrier phase are termed *coherent.* Those that do not need the phase are termed *incoherent.* Incoherent demodulation can be applied to ASK and wideband FSK. It describes demodulation schemes that are sensitive only to the power in the signal. With ASK, the power is either present, or it is not. With wideband FSK, the power is either present at one frequency, or the other. Incoherent modulation is inexpensive but has poorer performance. Coherent demodulation requires more complex circuitry, but has better performance. In ASK incoherent demodulation, the signal is passed to an envelope detector. This is a device that outputs the "outline" of the signal. A decision is made as to whether the signal is present or not. Envelope detection is the simplest and cheapest method of demodulation.

Incoherent demodulation can be used for wideband FSK. Here the signals are passed to two circuits, each sensitive to one of the two carrier frequencies. Circuits whose output depends on the frequency of the input are called *discriminators* or *filters*. The outputs of the two discriminators are interrogated to determine the signal. Incoherent FSK demodulation is simple and cheap, but very wasteful of bandwidth. The signal must be wideband FSK to ensure that the two signals $f_1(t)$ and $f_2(t)$ are distinguished. Incoherent demodulation is used in circumstances where bandwidth is not the primary constraint.

The difficulty with coherent detection is the need to keep the phase of the replica signal, termed *local oscillator*, "locked" to the carrier. This is not easy to do. Oscillators are sensitive to (among other things) temperature, and a "free-running" oscillator will gradually drift in frequency and phase.

There are two methods to prevent such an occurrence. In one, a pilot carrier signal is sent in addition to the modulated carrier. This pilot carrier is used to synchronise the local oscillator phase. The alternative is to employ another form of modulation, differential phase shift keying (DSPK). Differential PSK is actually a simple form of coding. The modulating signal is not the binary code itself, but a code that records changes in the binary code. This way, the demodulator only needs to determine changes in the incoming signal phase. Because the drifts associated with local oscillators are slow, this is not difficult to arrange. The PSK signal is converted to a DPSK signal with two rules:

1. a 1 in the PSK signal is denoted by no change in the DPSK.
2. a 0 in the PSK signal is denoted by a change in the DPSK signal.

The sequence is initialised with a leading 1. An example of the pattern is thus:

PSK : 01001101

DPSK : 100100011

The DPSK generator can be implemented by using a *delay element* and an *EX-NOR* gate as shown in Figure 7.10.

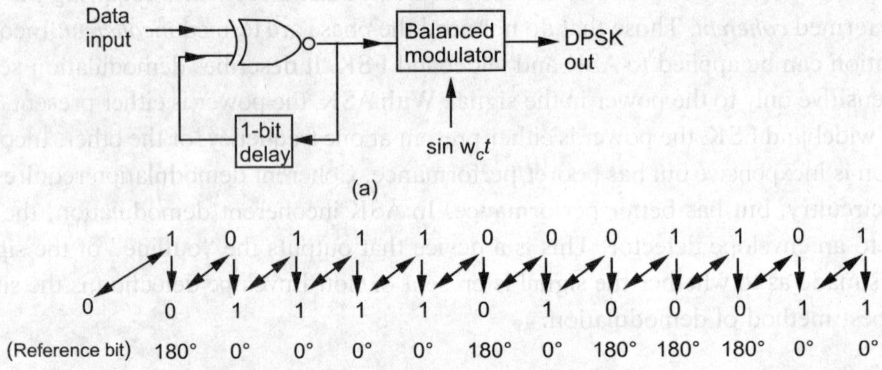

Figure 7.10 A simple DPSK generator

The MATLAB code to simulate differential phase shift keying (DPSK) is given below. The simulated waveform is illustrated in Figure 7.11.

```
%%% dpskgen.m::: MATLAB Script file to simulate
%%% dpsk generator..
%%% It comprises of a pre-processor block and a
```

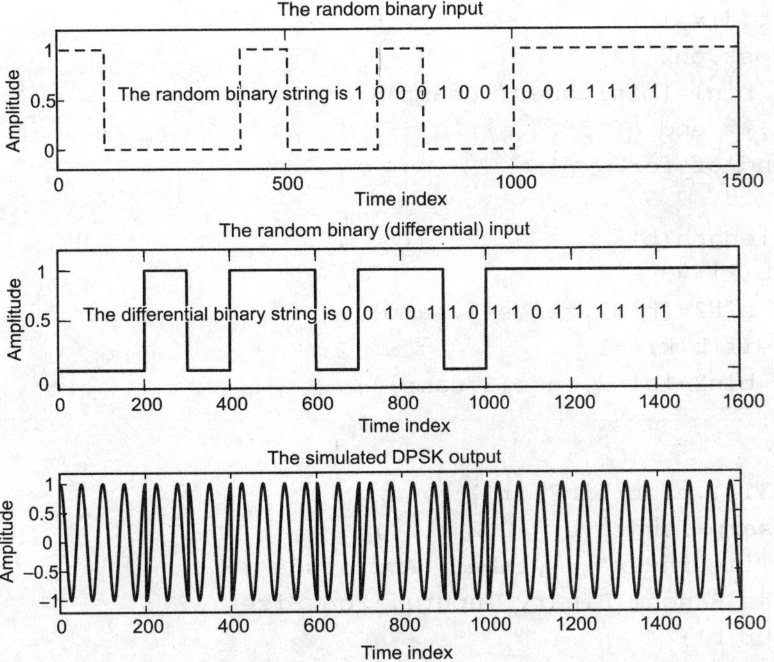

Figure 7.11 Simulated waveforms for differential phase shift keying

```
%%% PSK modulator..
clear all; close all; clc;
fc=2; % carrier frequency;
samp=100;
t=linspace(0,2*pi,samp);
ph1=cos(fc*t);
ph2=-cos(fc*t);
b=mod(randperm(15),2);% The random binary stream..
x=0;
nb(1)=not(xor(b(1),0));
for i=2:length(b)+1
    nb(i)=not(xor(b(i-1),x));
    x=nb(i);
end;
dpsk=[];bin1=[];bin2=[];
for j=1:length(nb)
    if nb(j)==0
        dpsk=[dpsk,ph1];
        bin1=[bin1,zeros(1,samp)];
```

```
elseif nb(j)==1
 dpsk=[dpsk,ph2];
          bin1=[bin1,ones(1,samp)];
     end;%% end of if..
end;%% end of for

for k=1:length(b)
     if b(k)==0
          bin2=[bin2,zeros(1,samp)];
     elseif b(k)==1
          bin2=[bin2,ones(1,samp)];
     end;
end;
subplot(311),plot(bin2,'r');
axis([0 samp*length(b) -0.2 1.2]);
xlabel('Time index'); ylabel('Amplitude');
title('The Random Binary Input','FontSize',12);
bn=num2str(b);
bx=['The Random Binary string is ',bn];
gtext(bx, 'FontSize',12);
subplot(312),plot(bin1,'LineWidth',1.5);
axis([0 samp*length(nb) -0.2 1.2]);hold on;
xlabel('Time index'); ylabel('Amplitude');
title('The Random Binary (differential) Input','FontSize',12);
bn=num2str(nb);
bx=['The Differential Binary string is ',bn];
gtext(bx,'FontSize',12);
subplot(313),plot(dpsk,'LineWidth',1.5);
axis([0 samp*length(nb) -1.2 1.2]);
xlabel('Time index'); ylabel('Amplitude');
title('The Simulated DPSK Output','FontSize',12);
%%% end of dpskgen.m
```

7.3.6 M-ary Phase Shift Keying (MPSK)

When the number of phases involved in PSK is more than 2 (i.e., $M > 2$), we get MPSK. We will study the following variants of MPSK:

1. Quadrature phase shift keying (QPSK)
2. Offset QPSK (staggered QPSK) (OQPSK/SQPSK)
3. $\pi/4$ differential QPSK (no carrier) ($\pi/4$ DQPSK)

4. $\pi/4$ differential QPSK (with carrier) ($\pi/4$ QPSK)
5. Differential MPSK (no carrier recovery) (DMPSK)

Quadrature Phase Shift Keying (QPSK)

The QPSK signal is an extension of the BPSK signal. Both of them are special cases of M-ary PSK signals. We can write the process that describes the digital phase modulated signal in a polar form as

$$s_i(t) = A_c\, p_s(t) \cos\left(2\pi\, f_c t + \frac{2\pi i}{M}\right); i = 0, 1, \ldots M - 1 \tag{7.9}$$

where $p_s(t)$ is the pulse shaping function. In digital phase modulation, the phase of the sinusoid is modified in response to a received bit. A sinusoid can go through a maximum phase change of 2π in one period. So the maximum phase we can change at any one time is 180°. We can use M quantised levels of 2π to create a variety of PSK modulation. The variable i is a number from 0 to $M - 1$. The allowed phases are given by

$$\text{Modulation angle } \theta_i = \frac{2\pi\, i}{M}$$

where M stands for the order of the digital phase modulation. $M = 2$ makes it a BPSK, $M = 4$ is QPSK, $M = 8$ is 8PSK and so on. Figure 7.12 shows three of these digital phase modulations in their "signal constellations". A rotation of the second signal constellation resulting in a third diagram does not change the modulation, its power or performance. These modulations are called *rotationally invariant.*

For baseband PSK signals, we use a square pulse. The pulse has an amplitude of A. The energy of this pulse is equal to the power of the signal times the duration, $T/2$ it lasts. The power is equal to A^2 with $R = 1\,\Omega$ and $T/2$ is the symbol time (duration). Now, we have $\epsilon = \frac{A^2 T}{2} = 1$, which is the energy of the pulse. This implies that $A = \sqrt{\frac{2}{T}}$. Thus the pulse has an amplitude of $\sqrt{\frac{2}{T}}$ over a period of $T/2$ seconds. Hence we have:

$$p_s(t) = \sqrt{\frac{2}{T}}, \quad 0 \leq t \leq T \tag{7.10}$$

Now, substituting equation (7.10) in equation (7.9), we get:

$$s_i(t) = A_c \sqrt{\frac{2}{T}} \cos\left(2\pi\, f_c t + \frac{2\pi i}{M}\right) \tag{7.11}$$

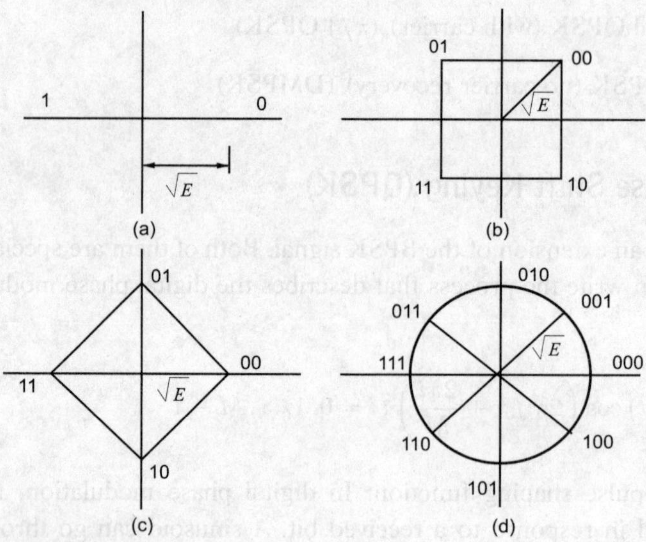

Figure 7.12 The signal constellations of various MPSK modulations: (a) BPSK; (b) QPSK; (c) also QPSK; (d) 8PSK

We now set the carrier amplitude A_c to $\sqrt{E_b}$ and get the *modulation equation of a general MPSK signal*.

$$s_i(t) = \underbrace{\sqrt{\frac{2E_b}{T}}}_{\text{Constant}} \cos\left(\underbrace{2\pi f_c t}_{\substack{\text{Changing}\\ \text{with time}}} + \underbrace{\frac{2\pi i}{M}}_{\substack{\text{Changing}\\ \text{with info.}}}\right) \quad i = 0, 1, \ldots, M-1. \tag{7.12}$$

QPSK is essentially a four-level phase shift keying technique. Each transmitted symbol represents two bits taken together. Mathematically, QPSK signal can be represented as:

$$s(t) = \begin{cases} \sqrt{2E_b/T}\cos(2\pi f_c t + \pi/4) & \text{for} \quad 11 \\ \sqrt{2E_b/T}\cos(2\pi f_c t + 3\pi/4) & \text{for} \quad 01 \\ \sqrt{2E_b/T}\cos(2\pi f_c t - 3\pi/4) & \text{for} \quad 00 \\ \sqrt{2E_b/T}\cos(2\pi f_c t - \pi/4) & \text{for} \quad 10 \end{cases} \tag{7.13}$$

Now expanding the above equation, we can express the QPSK signal as:

$$s(t) = \begin{cases} \sqrt{2E_b/T}\,[\cos(2\pi f_c t)\cos(\pi/4) - \sin(2\pi f_c t)\sin(\pi/4)] & \text{for} \quad 11 \\ \sqrt{2E_b/T}\,[\cos(2\pi f_c t)\cos(3\pi/4) - \sin(2\pi f_c t)\sin(3\pi/4)] & \text{for} \quad 01 \\ \sqrt{2E_b/T}\,[\cos(2\pi f_c t)\cos(3\pi/4) + \sin(2\pi f_c t)\sin(3\pi/4)] & \text{for} \quad 00 \\ \sqrt{2E_b/T}\,[\cos(2\pi f_c t)\cos(\pi/4) + \sin(2\pi f_c t)\sin(\pi/4)] & \text{for} \quad 10 \end{cases} \tag{7.14}$$

A typical QPSK modulator is illustrated in Figure 7.13.

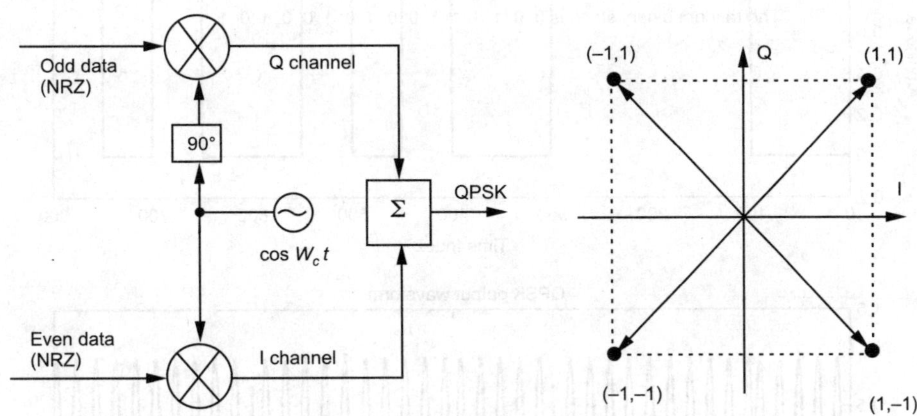

Figure 7.13 The block diagram of a QPSK modulator

The cosine term in equation (7.13) is known as the *in-phase component* and the sine term is known as the *quadrature component* of the QPSK output. Quadrature phase shift keying enables efficient utilisation of channel bandwidth. Note that there are two bits per symbol in a QPSK system, and the transmitted energy per symbol is twice the signal energy per bit.

The MATLAB code to simulate quadrature phase shift keying (QPSK) is given below. The simulated waveform is illustrated in Figure 7.14.

```
%%%qpskmod.m::: MATLAB script file to simulate..
%%% QPSK modulation of an arbitrary binary waveform..
clear all; close all; clc;
f=5; % Frequency of binary clock..
sam=100;
t=linspace(0,2*pi,sam);
b=mod(randperm(16),2);% Random binary waveform..
bn=num2str(b);
bx=['The Random Binary string is ',bn];
in=cos(f*t);
qd=sin(f*t);
cp=[];sp=[];
mod1=[];mod2=[];bit=[];
m=sqrt(1/2)*ones(1,sam);
for j=1:2:length(b)
```

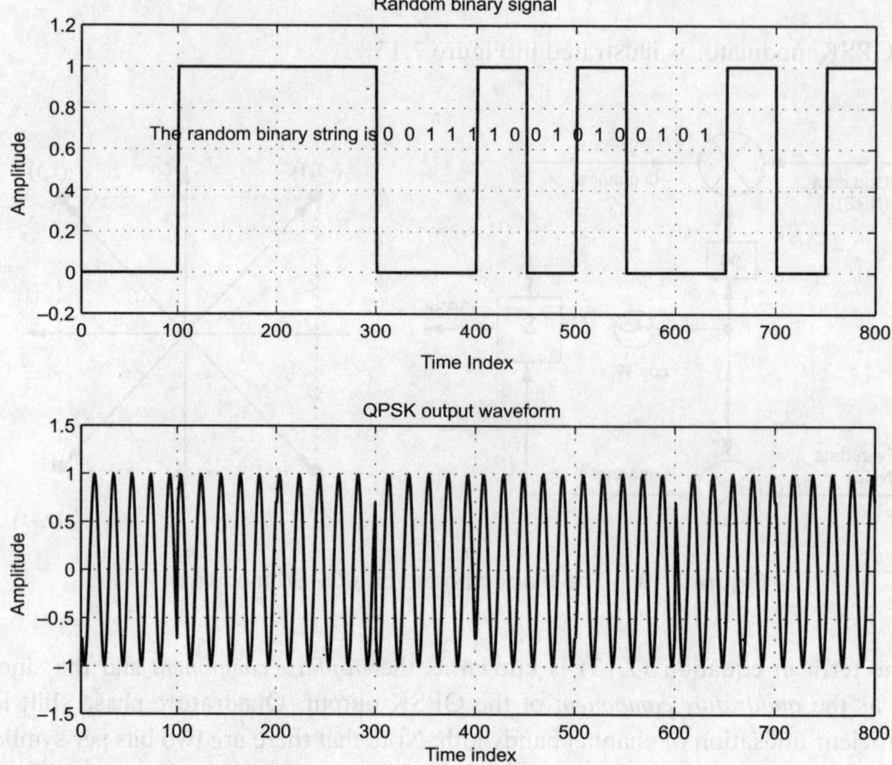

Figure 7.14 Simulated waveforms for quadrature phase shift keying

```
    eb=bin2int(b(j:j+1));
    switch eb
       case 0,
          m1=-m;
          m2=m1;
          se=zeros(1,sam);
     case 1,
          m1=m;
          m2=-m;
          se=[zeros(1,sam/2),ones(1,sam/2)];
     case 2,
          m1=-m;
          m2=m;
          se=[ones(1,sam/2),zeros(1,sam/2)];
     case 3,
          m1=m;
```

```
            m2=m;
            se=ones(1,sam);
         otherwise ;
      end; %% end of switch.
      cp=[cp,m1];
      sp=[sp,m2];
      mod1=[mod1,in];
      mod2=[mod2,qd];
      bit=[bit,se];
end;%%end of for..
qpsk=cp.*mod1+sp.*mod2;
subplot(211),plot(bit,'LineWidth',2);grid on;
title('Random Binary Signal');
gtext(bx,'FontSize',12);
axis([0 50*length(b) -.2 1.2]);
xlabel('Time index');ylabel('Amplitude');
subplot(212),plot(qpsk,'LineWidth',2);grid on;
title('QPSK Output Waveform');
axis([0 50*length(b) -1.5 1.5]);
xlabel('Time index');ylabel('Amplitude');
%%% end of qpskmod.m
```

Offset QPSK (Staggered QPSK) (OQPSK/SQPSK)

A variant of QPSK to be considered is offset quadrature shift keying (OQPSK), or the staggered QPSK (SQPSK). As previously mentioned, the potential for a 180° phase shift in QPSK results in the need for better linearity in the power amplifier stages and the potential for spectral re-growth due to 100% amplitude modulation. OQPSK reduces this tendency by adding a time delay of one-bit period (half a symbol) in the Q-arm (quadrature arm) of the modulator. The result is that the phase of the carrier is potentially modulated every bit (depending on the data), not every other bit as for QPSK. Hence the phase trajectory never approaches the origin. The ability of the modulated signal to demonstrate a phase shift of 180° is therefore removed.

As with the other phase modulation schemes considered, shaping of the phase trajectory between constellation points is typically implemented with a raised-cosine filter to improve the spectral efficiency. Due to the similarities between QPSK and OQPSK, similar signal spectra and probability of error are achieved. The OQPSK modulation is utilised in the North American IS-95 CDMA cellular system for the link from the mobile to the base station.

7.3.7 Quadrature Amplitude Modulation (QAM)

The modulation equation for quadrature amplitude modulation (QAM) is a variant of the one used for PSK. The QAM allows changing both the amplitude and the phase. In PSK, all points lie on a circle so that the I and Q values are related to each other. PSK signals therefore result in a constant envelope. If we allow the amplitude to change from symbol to symbol, we then get a modulation called QAM. It can be considered a linear combination of two DSBSC signals. So it is an AM and PM, simultaneously.

$$s(t) = \underbrace{\sqrt{\frac{2E_s}{T}}\cos\left(\theta(t)\right)\cos\left(2\pi f_c t\right)}_{\text{I}} - \underbrace{\sqrt{\frac{2E_s}{T}}\sin\left(\theta(t)\right)\sin\left(2\pi f_c t\right)}_{\text{Q}} \tag{7.15}$$

Equation (7.15) can be used to represent a hybrid modulation type of QAM. Assume that $M = 16$, so that we have 16 symbols, each representing a 4-bit word. This results in a 16-QAM. In QAM, the signal points lie in a rectangle, instead of a circle.

16-QAM

The signal constellation of a 16-QAM is illustrated in Figure 7.15.

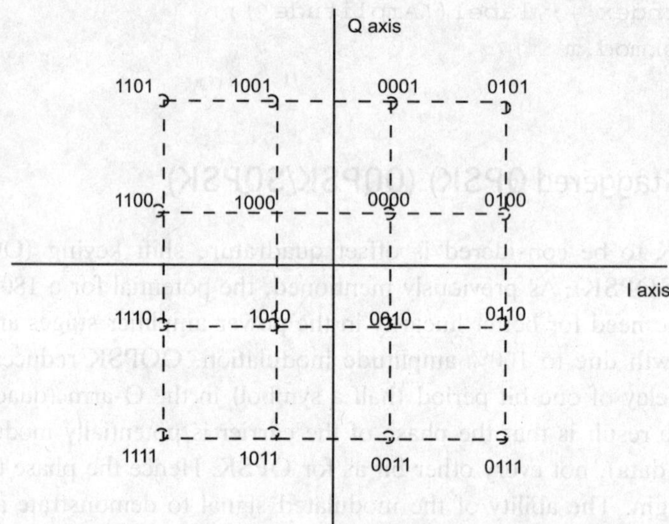

Figure 7.15 16-QAM signal constellation in the I-Q plane

In a 16-state quadrature amplitude modulation (16-QAM), there are four I values and four Q values. This results in a total of 16 possible states for the signal. It can transition from any state to any other state at every symbol time.

Note that this constellation has 16 points all spread out in the IQ plane, instead of 16 points all on the circle. It performs better in some situations. The points closer to the axes have lesser amplitudes and hence less energy than some others. We can compute the I and Q axis values of each of these points and depending on the total power we want, we can set the value for the amplitude a. Consider the case when $a = 1$. The 16-QAM signal mapping is shown in Table 7.1.

Table 7.1 16-QAM signal mapping

Symbol	Bits	Expression	Phase	I	Q
S1	0000	$s_1(t) = \sqrt{\frac{2E_s}{T}}\cos(2\pi f_c t + \pi/4)$	0°	1	1
S2	1000	$s_2(t) = \sqrt{\frac{2E_s}{T}}\cos(2\pi f_c t + 3\pi/4)$	90°	−1	1
S3	1010	$s_3(t) = \sqrt{\frac{2E_s}{T}}\cos(2\pi f_c t + 5\pi/4)$	180°	−1	−1
S4	0010	$s_4(t) = \sqrt{\frac{2E_s}{T}}\cos(2\pi f_c t - \pi/4)$	−90°	1	−1
S5	0100	$s_5(t) = \sqrt{\frac{20E_s}{T}}\cos(2\pi f_c t + 0.10242\pi)$	−26.565°	3	1
S6	1100	$s_6(t) = \sqrt{\frac{20E_s}{T}}\cos(2\pi f_c t + 0.85242\pi)$	116.56°	−3	1
S7	1110	$s_7(t) = \sqrt{\frac{20E_s}{T}}\cos(2\pi f_c t + 1.10242\pi)$	153.43°	−3	−1
S8	0110	$s_8(t) = \sqrt{\frac{20E_s}{T}}\cos(2\pi f_c t - 0.10242\pi)$	−63.435°	3	−1
S9	0001	$s_9(t) = \sqrt{\frac{20E_s}{T}}\cos(2\pi f_c t + 0.39758\pi)$	26.565°	1	3
S10	1001	$s_{10}(t) = \sqrt{\frac{20E_s}{T}}\cos(2\pi f_c t + 0.60242\pi)$	63.435°	−1	3
S11	1011	$s_{11}(t) = \sqrt{\frac{20E_s}{T}}\cos(2\pi f_c t + 1.3976\pi)$	206.57°	−1	−3
S12	0011	$s_{12}(t) = \sqrt{\frac{20E_s}{T}}\cos(2\pi f_c t + 1.60242\pi)$	243.43°	1	−3
S13	0101	$s_{13}(t) = \sqrt{\frac{36E_s}{T}}\cos(2\pi f_c t + \pi/4)$	0°	3	3
S14	1101	$s_{14}(t) = \sqrt{\frac{36E_s}{T}}\cos(2\pi f_c t + 3\pi/4)$	90°	−3	3
S15	1111	$s_{15}(t) = \sqrt{\frac{36E_s}{T}}\cos(2\pi f_c t + 5\pi/4)$	180°	−3	−3
S16	0111	$s_{16}(t) = \sqrt{\frac{36E_s}{T}}\cos(2\pi f_c t - \pi/4)$	−90°	3	−3

The symbol rate is one-fourth of the bit rate. So this modulation format produces a more spectrally efficient transmission. It is more efficient than BPSK, QPSK or 8PSK. Note that QPSK is the same as a 4-QAM.

64-QAM

The 64-QAM signal constellation has 64 points all spread out in the IQ plane. One can prepare a table similar to Table 7.1 for 64-QAM as well. The incoming serial bit stream is converted to a parallel stream, taking 6 bits at a time. Note that $2^6 = 64$.

256-QAM

The 256-QAM signal constellation has 256 points all spread out in the IQ plane. The parallel encoder takes 8 bits together. The current practical limits are approximately 256-QAM, though work is underway to extend the limits to 512 or 1024 QAM. A 256-QAM system uses 16 I values and 16 Q values, giving 256 possible states. Since $2^8 = 256$, each symbol can represent eight bits. A 256-QAM signal that can send eight bits per symbol is spectrally very efficient. However, the symbols are very close together and are thus more subject to errors due to noise and distortion. Such a signal may have to be transmitted with extra power (to effectively spread the symbols out more) and this reduces power efficiency as compared to simpler schemes.

1024-QAM

The 1024-QAM signal constellation (Figure 7.16) has 1024 points all spread out in the IQ plane. The parallel encoder takes 10 bits together. Low redundancy forward error correction (FEC) coded 1024-QAM modems, staggered 1024-QAM, and 256-QAM modems for spectrally efficient (up to 8.84 bits per second per Hertz) microwave and cable systems applications are reported in literature.

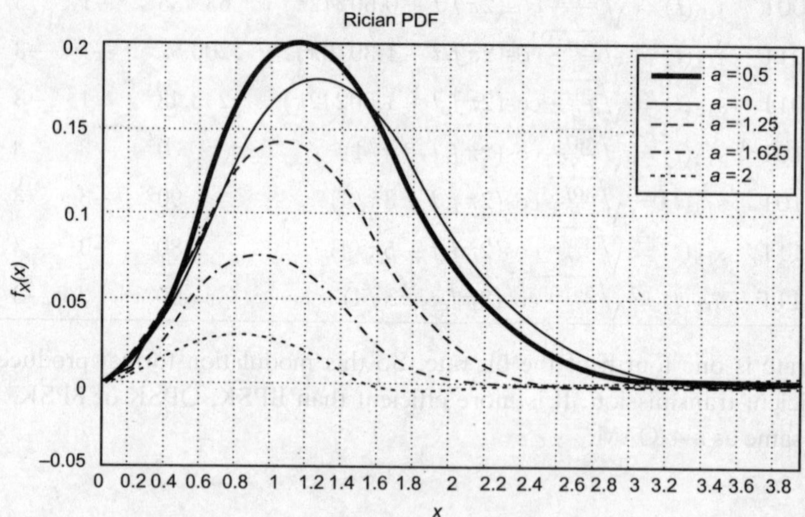

Figure 7.16 The signal constellation of 1024-QAM generated using Communications Toolbox of MATLAB

7.3.8 Minimum Shift Keying (MSK)

Coherent detection is also necessary for the correct demodulation of narrow band FSK. We have already noted that the form of the modulation signal gives rise to a bandwidth that is larger than that required by the Nyquist limit, and that has appreciable energy outside this bandwidth. This is in part due to the abrupt changes in the phase of the signal in FSK and PSK. By combining coherent detection with appropriate smoothing of the phase change, narrow band FSK can become very bandwidth efficient, approaching the Nyquist limit, and having low side-lobe levels. This form of modulation, which is a combination of FSK and PSK, is termed as *minimum shift keying (MSK)*, or *fast FSK (FFSK)*.

MSK is a continuous phase modulation (CPM) scheme where the modulated carrier contains no phase discontinuities and frequency changes occur at the carrier zero crossings. It is unique due to the relationship between the frequency of a logical zero and one: the difference between the frequency of a logical zero and a logical one is always equal to half the data rate. In other words, the modulation index is 0.5 for MSK, and is defined as:

$$m_{msk} = \Delta f \times T$$

where, $\Delta f = |f_{\text{logic 1}} - f_{\text{logic 0}}|$, and $T = 1/\text{bit rate}$. For example, a 1200 bit per second baseband MSK data signal could be composed of 1200 Hz and 1800 Hz frequencies for a logical one and zero respectively. Baseband MSK is a robust means of transmitting data in wireless systems where the data rate is relatively low compared to the channel bandwidth.

An alternative method for generating MSK modulation can be realised by directly injecting NRZ (non-return-to-zero) data into a frequency modulator with its modulation index set for 0.5 (see Figure 7.17). This approach is essentially equivalent to baseband MSK. However, in the direct approach, the VCO (voltage-controlled oscillator) is part of the RF/IF section, whereas in baseband MSK, the voltage-to-frequency conversion takes place at baseband.

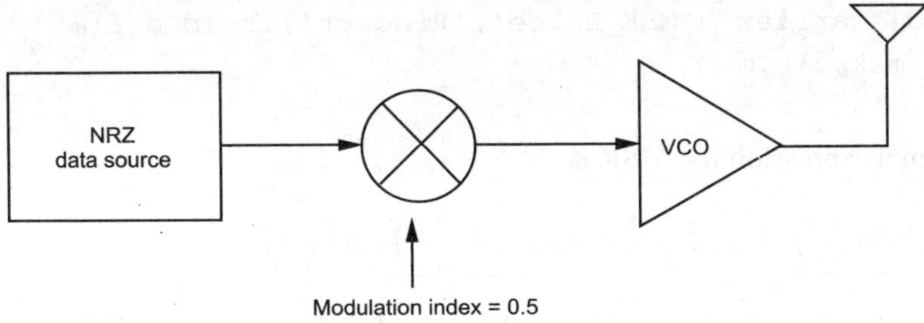

Figure 7.17 The block diagram of a direct MSK generator

7.3.9 Simulation of MSK Waveforms

Although MSK is often classified as an FM modulation, it is also related to offset-QPSK owing to the dual nature of FSK and PSK modulations. OQPSK is derived from a QPSK by delaying the Q channel by a half symbol from the I channel. This delay reduces the phase shifts the signal goes through at any one time and results in an *amplifier-friendly* signal.

MSK can be derived from OQPSK by making one further change: The I and Q channels of OQPSK use square root raised cosine pulses. For MSK, we have to change the pulse shape to a half-cycle sinusoid. Figure 7.18 shows a MSK pulse signal which is then multiplied by the carrier. In the figure, the carrier signal, the MSK pulse shape, and the multiplied signal of the pulse shape and the carrier are indicated separately. See the legend for details. The MATLAB code to generate Figure 7.18 is given below:

```
%%% MSK pulse simulation..
clear all; close all; clf;
t=linspace(0,1,100);
f=1;
x=cos(2*pi*f*t);
y=sin(2*pi*f/2*t);
z=x.*y;
x1=sin(2*pi*f*t);
y1=-y;
z1=x1.*y1;
subplot(121),plot(t,x,'--r','LineWidth',1.5);hold on;
plot(t,y,'b-.','LineWidth',2);plot(t,z,'black','LineWidth',2.5);
xlabel('Time index');ylabel('Amplitude');
grid;legend('Carrier','MSK Pulse','Product');hold off;
subplot(122),plot(t,x1,'--r','LineWidth',1.5);hold on;
plot(t,y1,'b-.','LineWidth',2); plot(t,z1,'black','LineWidth',2.5);
xlabel('Time index');ylabel('Amplitude');
grid;legend('Carrier','MSK Pulse','Product');hold off;
%%% end of mskpuls.m
```

The carrier signal expression for MSK is

$$c(t) = \underline{a(t)\sin\left(\frac{\pi}{2T}t\right)}\cos\left(\frac{\pi}{T}t\right) + \underline{a(t)\sin\left(\frac{\pi}{2T}t\right)}\sin\left(\frac{\pi}{T}t\right) \tag{7.16}$$

where the underlined portion gives the half-sinusoid pulse shape. In MSK, the shape is continuously changing, so there is no discrete jump in the modulated signal at the symbol edge as there is in QPSK. In Figure 7.19, the dashed lines are the I and Q channel symbols of

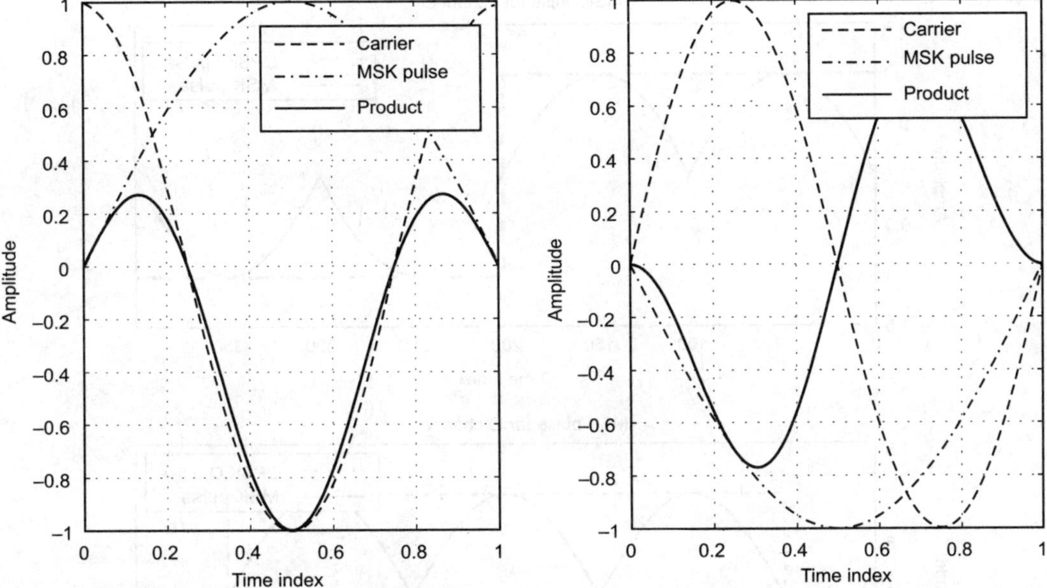

Figure 7.18 (a) MSK pulse and carrier for a 1 bit. (b) MSK pulse and carrier for 0 bit.

QPSK and the solid line shows how these have been shaped by the half-sine wave. The I and Q channels are computed by

$$\begin{aligned} MSKI(t) &= QPSKI(t)\left|\sin\left(\frac{\pi t}{2T}\right)\right| \\ MSKQ(t) &= QPSKQ(t)\left|\sin\left(\frac{\pi t}{2T}\right)\right| \end{aligned}$$

The MATLAB code to generate the plot in Figure 7.19 is given below:

```
%%% MSK pulse Carrier simulation..
close all; clear all; clf;
t=linspace(0,2,100);
t1=linspace(0,1,length(t)/2);
f=1;
x=sin(2*pi*f/4*t);%half wave sinusoid..
x1=[x,x,x,x];
y=[zeros(1,length(t)/2),x,x,x,sin(2*pi*f/4*t1)];
n=ones(1,length(t));
i=[n,n,-n,-n];
q=[zeros(1,length(t)/2),n,n,n,-ones(1,length(t)/2)];
ic=x1.*i;
qc=y.*q;
```

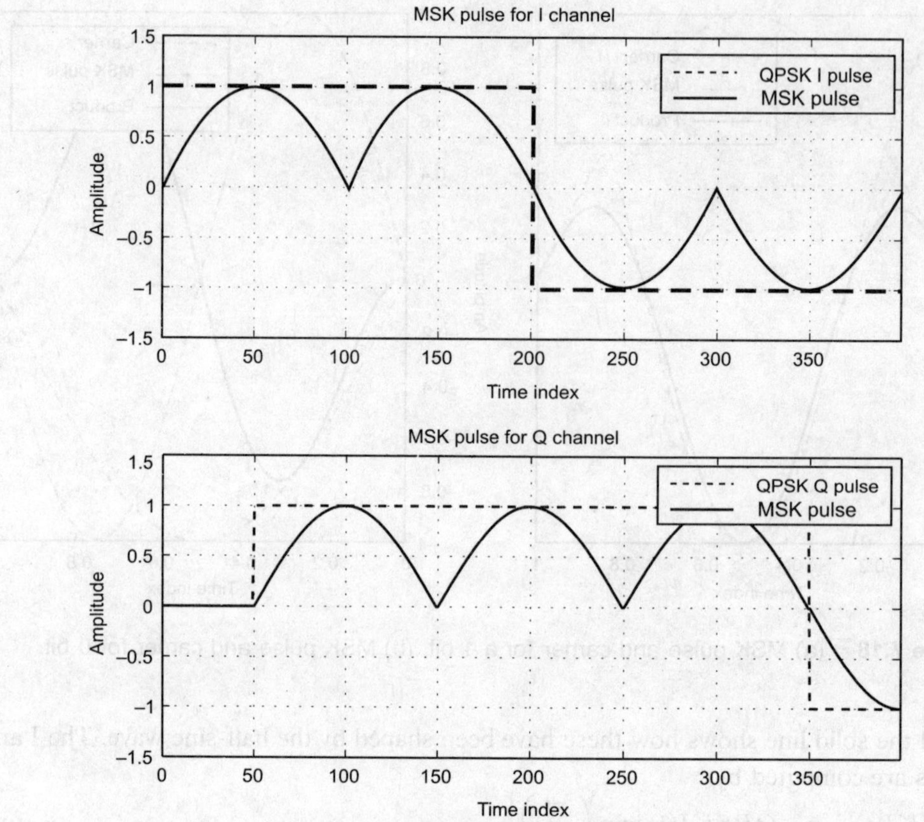

Figure 7.19 (a) MSK pulse for I channel. (b) MSK pulse for Q channel.

```
nx=[0:length(i)-1];
subplot(211),plot(nx,i,'b--','LineWidth',2);hold on;
plot(nx,ic,'r','LineWidth',2);hold off;
xlabel('Time index');ylabel('Amplitude');
axis([0 length(i)-1 -1.5 1.5]);grid;
title('MSK Pulse for I Channel');
legend('QPSK  I-Pulse','MSK Pulse');
subplot(212),plot(nx,q,'b--','LineWidth',2);hold on;
plot(nx,qc,'r','LineWidth',2);hold off;
xlabel('Time index');ylabel('Amplitude');
axis([0 length(i)-1 -1.5 1.5]);grid;
title('MSK Pulse for Q Channel');
legend('QPSK Q-Pulse','MSK Pulse');
%%% end of mskcar.m
```

The I and Q channels are then multiplied by the carrier, cosine for I channel, and sine for the Q channel. Note that the period of the pulse shape is twice that of the symbol rate.

$$\begin{aligned} \text{MSK}_{\text{carr}}I(t) &= \text{QPSKI}(t)\left|\sin\left(\frac{\pi t}{2T}\right)\right|\cos\left(\frac{\pi t}{T}\right) \\ \text{MSK}_{\text{carr}}Q(t) &= \text{QPSKQ}(t)\left|\sin\left(\frac{\pi t}{2T}\right)\right|\sin\left(\frac{\pi t}{T}\right) \end{aligned}$$

The FSK and MSK produce constant envelope carrier signals, which have no amplitude variations. This is a desirable characteristic for improving the power efficiency of transmitters. Amplitude variations can exercise non-linearities in an amplifier as an amplitude-transfer function, generating spectral re-growth, a component of the adjacent channels power. Therefore, more efficient amplifiers (which tend to be less linear) can be used with constant envelope signals, reducing power consumption.

MSK has a narrower spectrum than wider deviation forms of FSK. The width of the spectrum is also influenced by the waveforms causing the frequency shift. If those waveforms have fast transitions or a high slew rate, then the spectrum of the transmitter will be broad. In practice, waveforms are filtered with a Gaussian filter, resulting in a narrow spectrum. In addition, the Gaussian filter has no time-domain overshoot which would broaden the spectrum by increasing the peak deviation. MSK with a Gaussian filter is termed as GMSK (Gaussian MSK).

Limitations of MSK

The fundamental problem with MSK is that the spectrum is not compact enough to realise data rates approaching the RF channel bandwidth. A plot of the spectrum for MSK reveals side lobes extending well above the data rate. For wireless data transmission systems which require more efficient use of the RF channel bandwidth, it is necessary to reduce the energy of the MSK upper side lobes. Earlier, we stated that a straightforward means of reducing this energy is lowpass filtering the data stream prior to presenting it to the modulator (pre-modulation filtering). The pre-modulation lowpass filter must have a narrow bandwidth with a sharp cut-off frequency and very little overshoot in its impulse response. This is where the Gaussian filter characteristic comes in. It has an impulse response characterised by a classical Gaussian function (bell shaped curve), as shown in Figure 7.20. Notice the absence of overshoot or ringing. Figure 7.20 depicts the impulse response of a Gaussian filter for BT = 0.3 and 0.5. It may be noted that BT is the product of the bandwidth of the Gaussian filter and time interval between different bits (which is $\frac{1}{\text{Bit rate}}$). Thus, the BT is related to the filter's 3 dB bandwidth and data rate by

$$\text{BT} = \frac{f_{3\text{dB}}}{\text{Bit rate}} \tag{7.17}$$

Hence for a data rate of 9.6 kbps and a BT of 0.5, the filter's 3 dB cut-off frequency is 4800 Hz.

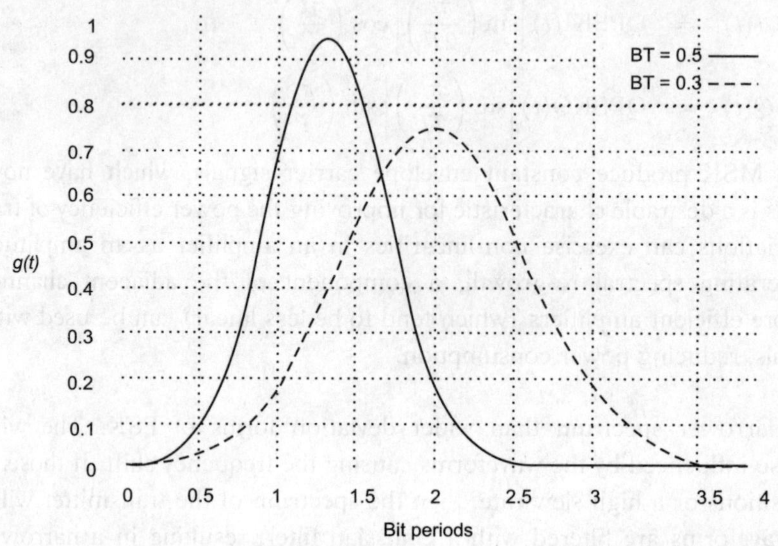

Figure 7.20 The Gaussian filter impulse response for BT = 0.3 and 0.5. BT $= \frac{f_{3\text{dB}}}{\text{Bit rate}}$

7.3.10 Gaussian Minimum Shift Keying (GMSK)

The proliferation of computers in today's society has increased the demand for transmission of data over wireless links. Binary data, composed of sharp "one to zero" and "zero to one" transitions, results in a spectrum rich in harmonic content that is not well suited to RF transmission. Hence, the field of digital modulation has been flourishing, in terms of bandwidth efficiency and power requirements. Recent standard systems such as the Cellular Digital Packet Data (CDPD) and Mobitex specify Gaussian filtered minimum shift keying (GMSK) for their modulation method.

GMSK is a simple yet effective approach to digital modulation for wireless data transmission. To provide a good understanding of GMSK, we will review the basics of MSK and GMSK, as well as how GMSK is implemented in CDPD and Mobitex systems. GMSK modems reduce system complexity, and in turn lower system cost. There are, however, some important implementation details to be considered.

The Working Principle of GMSK

If we look at a Fourier series expansion of a data signal, we will see harmonics extending to infinity. When these harmonics are summed, they give the data signal its sharp transitions. Hence, an unfiltered non-return-to-zero (NRZ) data stream used to modulate an RF carrier will produce an RF spectrum of considerable bandwidth. Of course, the FCC has strict regulations about spectrum usage and such a system is generally considered impractical. But if we remove the high frequency harmonics from the Fourier series (i.e., pass the data signal through a lowpass filter), the transitions in the data will become progressively less sharp. This suggests that pre-modulation filtering is an effective method of reducing the occupied spectrum for wireless data transmission. In addition to a compact spectrum, a wireless data modulation scheme must have good bit error rate (BER) performance under noisy conditions. Its performance should also be independent of power amplifier linearity to allow the use of class C power amplifiers.

It may also be noted that in general, for similar BER performance, schemes that rely on more than two levels (e.g. QAM, QPSK) require better signal-to-noise ratios (SNR) than two-level schemes. Additionally, in a wireless environment, multi-level schemes generally require greater power amplifier linearity than two-level schemes. The fact that GMSK uses a two-level continuous phase modulation (CPM) format has contributed to its popularity. Another point in its favour is that it allows the use of class C power amplifiers (relatively non-linear) and data rates approaching the channel bandwidth (dependent on filter bandwidth and channel spacing).

Demodulation of GMSK

Demodulation of a GMSK signal requires as much attention to the reservation of an unadulterated waveform as does modulation of the signal. A Gaussian shaped pre-modulation filter is chosen mainly for three reasons:

1. narrow bandwidth and sharp cut-off.
2. impulse response with low overshoot.
3. preservation of the filter output pulse area.

The first condition gives GMSK modulation its spectral efficiency. It also improves its noise immunity when the signal is demodulated. The second condition affords GMSK low phase distortion. This is a major concern when the receiver is demodulating the signal down to baseband, and care must be taken while designing the IF filtering to protect this characteristic. The third condition ensures the coherence of the signal. While this is quite strict and not realisable with a physical Gaussian filter, the phase response can be kept linear and therefore sufficient for coherent demodulation.

In most systems, the constraints on the above goals also include

- Data rate
- Transmitter filter bandwidth (BT)
- Channel spacing
- Allowable adjacent channel interference
- Peak carrier deviation
- Transmitter and receiver carrier frequency accuracy
- Modulator and demodulator linearity
- Receiver IF filter frequency and phase characteristics

These constraints are all part of the balance that must be struck to provide a robust GMSK system. The data rate, transmitter BT, peak carrier deviation, and carrier frequency accuracy between receiver and transmitter all contribute to the necessary width of the IF filter. The IF filter should have sufficient width to accommodate the maximum variations in the above parameters so that the received signal will not run into the skirts of the filter. The skirts of the IF filter can introduce excessive amounts of group delay (phase distortion) in the higher frequency components of the received data. The passband of the IF filter should have little or no group delay. The more group delay introduced, the more degraded the bit error rate (BER) performance of the receiver will become. Rules of thumb for group delay dictate that less than 10% of a bit time is tolerable. How satisfied we are with this level of performance is very dependent on the other factors that influence the BER of our system: BT, signal strength, fading, etc. Phase equalisation measures can also be taken to help reduce group delay, but if there is control over the IF filter's design, these steps can be avoided.

7.3.11 Theoretical Bandwidth Efficiency Limits

The bandwidth efficiency describes how efficiently the allocated bandwidth is utilised or the ability of a modulation scheme to accommodate data within a limited bandwidth. Table 7.2 shows the theoretical bandwidth efficiency limits for the main modulation types. Note that these figures cannot actually be achieved in practical radios since they require perfect modulators, demodulators, filter and transmission paths.

Table 7.2 Theoretical bandwidth efficiency limits

Modulation format	Theoretical bandwidth efficiency
BPSK	1 bit/second/Hz
QPSK	2 bits/second/Hz
8PSK	3 bits/second/Hz
MSK	1 bit/second/Hz
16-QAM	4 bits/second/Hz
256-QAM	8 bits/second/Hz
1024-QAM	10 bits/second/Hz

If the radio had a perfect (rectangular in the frequency domain) filter, then the occupied bandwidth could be made equal to the symbol rate.

Techniques for maximising spectral efficiency include the following:

1. Relate the data rate to the frequency shift, as in the Global System for Mobiles (GSM).
2. Use pre-modulation filtering to reduce the occupied bandwidth.
3. Raised cosine filters, as used in the North American Digital Cellular system (NADC), Pacific Digital Cellular system (PDC), and Personal Handyphone system (PHS) give the best spectral efficiency.
4. Restrict the types of transitions.

Spectral Efficiencies in Practical Radio Systems

The following examples illustrate the spectral efficiencies that are achieved in some practical radio systems.

The TDMA version of the North American Digital Cellular (NADC) system achieves a 48 kbits per second data rate over a 30 kHz bandwidth or 1.6 bits per second per Hz. It is a $\pi/4$ DQPSK based system and transmits two bits per symbol. The theoretical efficiency would be two bits per second per Hz, but in practice it is 1.6 bits per second per Hz.

Another example is a microwave digital radio using 16-QAM. This kind of signal is more susceptible to noise and distortion than something simpler such as a QPSK. This type of signal is usually sent over a direct line-of-sight microwave link or over a wire where there is very little noise and interference. In this microwave digital radio example, the bit rate is 140 Mbits per second over a very wide bandwidth of 52.5 MHz. The spectral efficiency is 2.7 bits per second per Hz. To implement this, it takes a very clear line-of-sight transmission path and a precise and optimised high-power transceiver.

7.3.12 Performance Comparison and Applications

In this section we compare the performance of the various modulation formats discussed so far. We first consider the definition of bit rate and symbol (baud) rate.

Bit Rate and Symbol Rate

To understand and compare different modulation format efficiencies, it is important to first understand the difference between bit rate and symbol rate. Bit rate defines the rate at which information is passed. Baud (or signalling) rate defines the number of symbols per second. Each symbol represents n bits, and has M signal states, where $M = 2^n$. This is called M-ary signalling. The signal bandwidth needed for communications channels depends on the symbol rate, not on the bit rate. Symbol rate is defined as:

$$\text{Symbol rate} = \frac{\text{Bit rate}}{\text{The number of bits transmitted with each symbol}} \tag{7.18}$$

Bit rate is the frequency of a system bit stream. Take for example, a radio with an 8-bit sampler, sampling at 10 kHz for voice. The bit rate, the basic bit stream rate in the radio, would be eight bits multiplied by 10 k samples per second, or 80 kbits per second. (For the moment we will ignore the extra bits required for synchronisation, error correction, etc.). The symbol rate is the bit rate divided by the number of bits that can be transmitted with each symbol. If one bit is transmitted per symbol, as in BPSK, then the symbol rate would be the same as the bit rate of 80 kbits per second. If two bits are transmitted per symbol, as in QPSK, then the symbol rate would be half of the bit rate or 40 kbits per second. Symbol rate is sometimes called *baud rate*. Note that the baud rate is not the same as the bit rate. These terms are often confused. If more bits can be sent with each symbol, then the same amount of data can be sent in a narrower spectrum. This is why modulation formats that are more complex and use a higher number of states can send the same information over a narrower piece of the RF spectrum.

The Maximum Data Rate

The maximum rate of information transfer through a baseband channel is given by:

$$\text{Channel capacity, } C = 2W \log_2 M \text{ bits per second} \tag{7.19}$$

where W = bandwidth of the modulating baseband signal.

The Shannon–Hartley Theorem on Channel Capacity

For error-free communication, it is possible to define the capacity which can be supported in an additive white Gaussian noise (AWGN) channel. The channel capacity is given by:

$$C = \log_2(1 + E_b f_b/\eta W) \tag{7.20}$$

where f_b = Capacity (bits per second)

W = bandwidth of the modulating baseband signal (Hz)

E_b = energy per bit

η = noise power density (watts/Hz).

Thus, $E_b f_b$ is the total signal power and ηW is the total noise power. The quantity f_b/W is known as the *bandwidth efficiency* (bits per second per Hertz). Equation (7.20) is referred to as the Shannon–Hartley theorem on channel capacity. A comparison of various modulation formats based on the logarithm of bandwidth efficiency (*to the base* 2), and error-free E_b/N_o ratio is given in Table 7.3.

Table 7.3 Comparison of various modulation formats

Modulation format	$\log_2$ (Bandwidth efficiency)	Error-free E_b/N_o
BFSK	0	13 dB
BPSK	0	10.6 dB
4-QAM	1	10.1 dB
4PSK	1	10.1 dB
8PSK	1.59	14.5 dB
16-QAM	2	15 dB
16PSK	2	18 dB

The Symbol Clock

The symbol clock represents the frequency and exact timing of the transmission of individual symbols. At symbol clock transitions, the transmitted carrier is at the correct I/Q (or magnitude/phase) value to represent a specific symbol (a specific point in the constellation). In any digital modulation system, if the input signal is distorted or severely attenuated, the receiver will eventually lose symbol lock completely. If the receiver can no longer recover the symbol clock, it cannot demodulate the signal or recover any information. With less degradation, the symbol clock can be recovered, but it is noisy. The symbol locations themselves are noisy. In some cases, a symbol will fall far enough away from its intended position so that it crosses over to an adjacent position. The I and Q level detectors used in the demodulator would misinterpret such a symbol as being in the wrong location, causing bit errors. QPSK is not as efficient as other methods, but the states are much farther apart and the system can tolerate a lot more noise before suffering symbol errors. QPSK has no intermediate states between the four corner symbol locations, so there is less opportunity for the demodulator to misinterpret symbols. QPSK requires less transmitter power than QAM to achieve the same bit error rate.

Applications of Various Modulation Formats

Table 7.4 covers the applications for different modulation formats in both wireless communications and video.

7.3.13 The Competing Goals of Spectral Efficiency and Power Consumption

As with any natural resource, it makes no sense to waste the RF spectrum by using channel bands that are too wide. Therefore, narrower filters are used to reduce the occupied bandwidth of the transmission. Narrower filters with sufficient accuracy and repeatability are more difficult to build.

Table 7.4 Applications of various modulation formats

Modulation format	Applications
MSK, GMSK	GSM, CDPD
BPSK	Deep space telemetry, cable modems
QPSK, $\pi/4$ DQPSK	Satellite, CDMA, NADC, TETRA, PHS, PDC, LMDS, DVB-S, cable modems
OQPSK	CDMA, satellite
FSK, GFSK	DECT, paging, RAM mobile data, AMPS, CT2, land mobile
8, 16 VSB	North American DTV, broadcast, cable
8PSK	Satellite, aircraft, telemetry
16-QAM	Microwave digital radio, modems, DVB-C, DVB-T
32-QAM	Terrestrial microwave, DVB-T
64-QAM	DVB-C, modems, MMDS
256-QAM	Modems, DVB-C (Europe), digital video (US)

7.3.14 Square-Root-Raised-Cosine Filter (SRRC)

In a digital communication system, a root-raised-cosine filter (RRC), sometimes known as square-root-raised-cosine filter (SRRC), is frequently used as the transmit and receive filter to perform matched filtering. The combined response of two such filters is that of the raised-cosine filter (RCF). It obtains its name from the fact that its frequency response, $H_{\text{rrc}}(f)$, is the square root of the frequency response of the raised-cosine filter, $H_{\text{rc}}(f)$:

$$H_{\text{rc}}(f) = H_{\text{rrc}}(f).H_{\text{rrc}}(f) \tag{7.21}$$

The impulse response of the root-raised-cosine filter is given by:

$$h(t) = \begin{cases} 1 - \beta + 4\dfrac{\beta}{\pi}; & t = 0 \\ \dfrac{\beta}{\sqrt{2}}\left[\left(1+\dfrac{2}{\pi}\right)\sin\left(\dfrac{\pi}{4\beta}\right) + \left(1-\dfrac{2}{\pi}\right)\cos\left(\dfrac{\pi}{4\beta}\right)\right]; & t = \pm\frac{T_s}{4\beta} \\ \dfrac{\sin\left[\pi\frac{t}{T_s}(1-\beta)\right] + 4\beta\frac{t}{T_s}\cos\left[\pi\frac{t}{T_s}(1+\beta)\right]}{\pi\frac{t}{T_s}\left[1-\left(4\beta\frac{t}{T_s}\right)^2\right]}; & \text{otherwise.} \end{cases} \tag{7.22}$$

It should be noted that unlike the raised-cosine filter, the impulse response is not zero at the intervals of $\pm T_s$. However, the combined transmit and receive filters form a raised-cosine filter which does have zero at the intervals of $\pm T_s$. The root raised-cosine have zeros at $\pm T_s$ only when $\beta = 0$.

7.3.15 The Raised-Cosine Filter (RCF)

The raised-cosine filter (RCF) is characterised by two factors: the roll-off factor β, and T_s, the reciprocal of the symbol rate. The impulse response of the raised-cosine filter is given by:

$$h(t) = \frac{\sin(\pi t/T_s}{\pi t} \cdot \frac{\cos(\pi t\beta/T_s)}{1 - 4\beta^2 t^2/T_s^2} \tag{7.23}$$

where t is the time, T_s is the symbol rate, and β is the *roll-off factor*. There are several other valid forms of the above equation. A plot of the impulse response of the raised-cosine filter is shown in Figure 7.21 and the MATLAB code to generate the same is appended below.

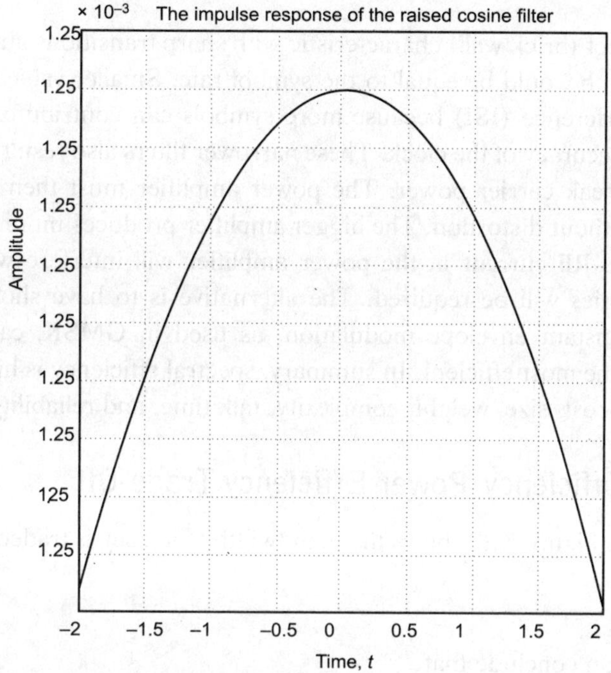

Figure 7.21 The impulse response of the raised-cosine filter

```
%%% Raised Cosine filter Impulse Response..
clear all; close all; clf;
t=[-2:.001:2];
Ts=800;
beta=0.8;
h=(sin(pi*t/Ts)./(pi*t)).*(cos(pi*t*beta/Ts)...
    ./(1-4*beta^2*t.^2/Ts^2));
```

```
plot(t,h,'Linewidth',2);grid
xlabel('Time, t'); ylabel('Amplitude');
title('The Impulse Response of the Raised Cosine Filter');
%%% end of rascos.m
```

The α Value of the Raised-Cosine Filter

The sharpness of a raised-cosine filter is described by its alpha (α). Alpha gives a direct measure of the occupied bandwidth of the system and is calculated as:

$$\text{Occupied bandwidth} = \text{symbol rate} \times (1 + \alpha). \tag{7.24}$$

If the filter had a perfect (brick wall) characteristic with sharp transitions and an alpha of zero, the occupied bandwidth would be equal to the symbol rate. Smaller values of alpha increase the inter-symbol interference (ISI) because more symbols can contribute. This tightens the requirements on the accuracy of the clock. These narrower filters also result in more overshoot and therefore more peak carrier power. The power amplifier must then accommodate the higher peak power without distortion. The bigger amplifier produces more heat and electrical interference since the RF current in the power amplifier will interfere with other circuits. Larger, heavier batteries will be required. The alternative is to have shorter talk time and smaller batteries. Constant envelope modulation, as used in GMSK, can employ class C amplifiers which are the most efficient. In summary, spectral efficiency is highly desirable, but there are penalties in cost, size, weight, complexity, talk time, and reliability.

The Bandwidth Efficiency–Power Efficiency Trade-Off

The graph depicted in Figure 7.22 shows that bandwidth efficiency is traded-off against power efficiency.

From the figure we can conclude that

- MFSK is power efficient, but not bandwidth efficient.
- MPSK and QAM are bandwidth efficient but not power efficient.
- Mobile radio systems are bandwidth limited and therefore PSK is more suited for them.

7.3.16 Eye Diagrams

An eye diagram is a useful tool for the qualitative analysis of the signals used in digital transmission. It provides an at-a-glance evaluation of system performance and can offer

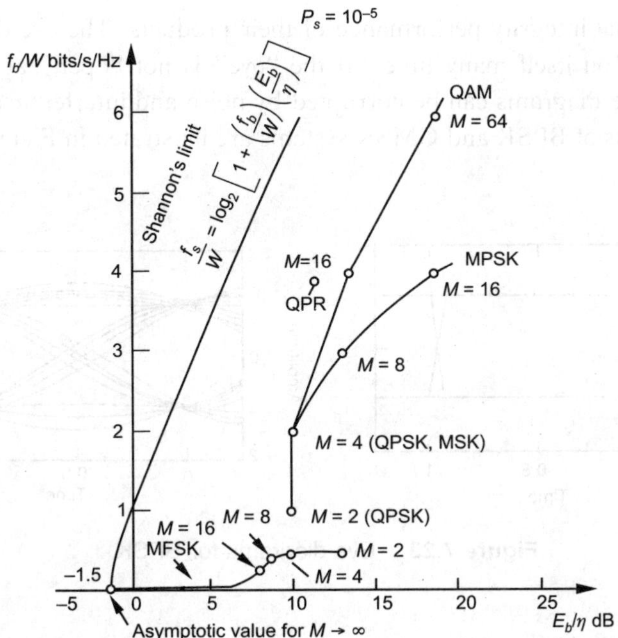

Figure 7.22 The trade-off between bandwidth efficiency and power efficiency

insight into the nature of channel imperfections. Careful analysis of this visual display can give the user a first-order approximation of the signal-to-noise ratio, clock timing jitter and skew.

The eye diagram is an oscilloscope display of a digital signal, repetitively sampled to get a good representation of its behaviour. In a radio system, the point of measurement may be prior to the modulator in a transmitter, or following the demodulator in a receiver, depending on which portion of the system needs to be examined. The eye diagram can also be used to examine signal integrity in a purely digital system such as fibre optic transmission, network cables or on a circuit board.

Impairments to the signal can occur in many places, from the pre-filtering stage in the transmitter, through the frequency conversion and amplifier chain, propagation path, receiver front-end, IF circuits, and baseband signal processing. Information from the eye diagram can help greatly with troubleshooting. Noise problems will most often be external to the equipment and timing issues can be isolated to the receiver or transmitter with tests on each. It is also important to record the eye diagram so it is available for comparison if new problems arise in the future.

The eye diagram is also a common indicator of performance in digital transmission systems. Makers of digital communications hardware often include eye diagrams in their literature to demonstrate the signal integrity performance of their products. The eye diagrams show the signal superimposed on itself many times. If the "eye" is not "open" at the sample point, errors will occur. Eye diagrams can be corrupted by noise and interference. Theoretical and practical eye diagrams of BPSK and GMSK systems are illustrated in Figures 7.23 and 7.24.

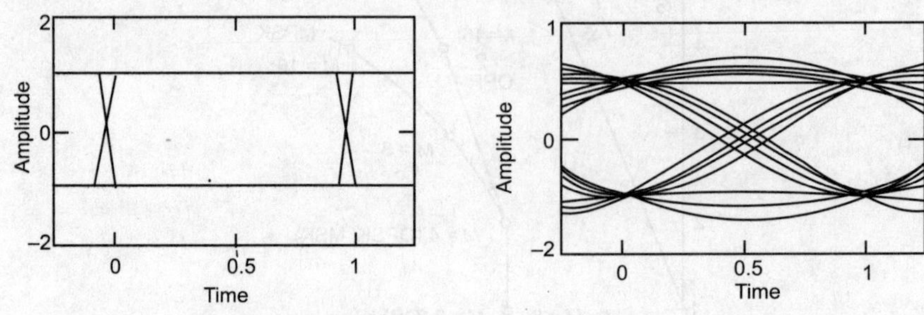

Figure 7.23 Eye diagrams for BPSK

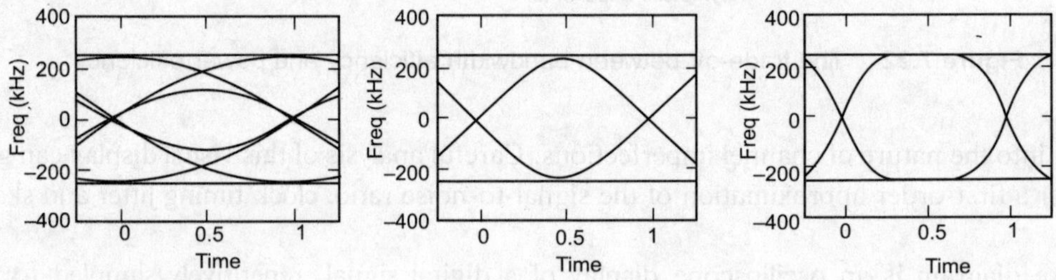

Figure 7.24 Eye diagrams for GMSK with $BT = 0.3$ (left), $BT = 0.5$ (centre) and $BT = 1.0$ (right).

A final note that applies primarily to high-speed digital signal analysis is the quality of the oscilloscope used to observe the eye diagram. The bandwidth of the instrument must be sufficient to accurately display the waveform. This usually means that the bandwidth must include the third, and preferably the fifth, harmonic of the bit rate frequency.

In summary, the eye diagram is a simple and useful tool for evaluating digital transmission circuitry and systems. It provides instant visual data to verify quality or demonstrate problems. Used in conjunction with other signal integrity measurements, it can help predict performance and identify the source of system impairments.

The Communications Toolbox of MATLAB contains a function, `eyediagram(.)` to generate and plot the eye diagram.

7.3.17 Probability of Bit Error

The probability of bit error (P_b) and symbol error (P_s) is related to power efficiency and bandwidth efficiency (spectral efficiency). They are two important performance metrics for qualitatively stating the reliability of a digital communication system. To begin with, it is known that the bit error rate (BER) of a system indicates the quality of the link and:

- a BER of 10^{-3} is the maximum rate acceptable for voice.
- a BER of 10^{-9} is the maximum rate acceptable for a data link.

The ratio of the signal strength to the noise level is called the signal-to-noise ratio (SNR). If SNR is high (ie., the signal power is much greater than the noise), few errors will occur and hence BER will be low. As the SNR reduces, the noise may cause errors.

Simulation of Probability of Error Rate

In this sub-section, we will consider the simulation of probability of error rate on communication links, implemented using different modulation techniques. The BER results in the following sections have been produced by performing computer-based simulation of the modulator, channel (AWGN), as well as bandpass filtering and demodulation. It is assumed that perfect carrier and bit synchronisation has been made. This is a very significant assumption and is unacceptable for a real system design, particularly at low to moderate BER. Ideally, the addition of carrier and bit synchronisation algorithms should be implemented in the simulator. Obviously, the performance of these will vary with physical realisation. A uniformly distributed random variable can be converted to a Gaussian distributed random variable by identifying a suitable function (or mapping) that acts on the uniformly distributed random variable.

In a real mobile communications system, the link between a moving (particularly vehicular) node and a base station will be subject to Rayleigh fading, resulting in fast phase shifts. This will have a significant effect on the resultant BER performance, depending on demodulator implementation and channel, possibly increasing the required carrier-to-noise ratio (CNR) for a specific BER by as much as 10–15 dB.

Considerable caution must be taken when comparing graphs of BER versus E_b/N_o. Additionally, the simulations have been performed with a relatively wideband input to the demodulator. Due to the varying spectral occupancy of different modulation schemes, it may be possible to employ narrower channel filtering for some schemes rather than others. For example, GMSK with a $BT = 0.3$ occupies less spectrum than MSK.

7.4 Pulse Modulation Schemes

When the modulating signal is *discrete,* it can be thought of as a sequence of real numbers representing the sample values of an analog waveform. Such type of modulating signals are known as *discrete baseband signals.* One way to send such a signal through a channel is to send a pulse waveform—one pulse is placed at each sampling instant. Such a modulation scheme is known as pulse modulation. There are three types of pulse modulations—pulse amplitude modulation (PAM), pulse width modulation (PWM), and pulse position modulation (PPM). We will consider them in greater detail.

7.4.1 Pulse Amplitude Modulation (PAM)

Pulse amplitude modulation (PAM) is the transmission of data by varying the amplitudes (voltage or power levels) of the individual pulses in a regularly timed sequence of electrical or electromagnetic pulses. It is the simplest form of pulse modulation. The number of possible pulse amplitudes can be infinite (in the case of analog PAM), but it is usually some power of two so that the resulting output signal can be digital.

In some PAM systems, the amplitude of each pulse is directly proportional to the instantaneous modulating signal amplitude at the time the pulse occurs. In other PAM systems, the amplitude of each pulse is inversely proportional to the instantaneous modulating signal amplitude at the time the pulse occurs. In still other systems, the intensity of each pulse depends on some characteristic of the modulating signal other than its strength, such as its instantaneous frequency or phase.

Generation of PAM

PAM is generated in much the same manner as an analog amplitude modulation. The timing pulses are applied to a pulse amplifier in which the gain is controlled by the modulating waveform. Since these variations in amplitude actually represent the signal, this type of modulation is basically a form of AM. The only difference is that the signal is now in the form of pulses. This means that PAM has the same built-in weaknesses that any other AM signal has: high susceptibility to noise and interference. The reason for susceptibility to noise is that any interference in the transmission path will either add to or subtract from any voltage already in the circuit (signal voltage). Thus, the amplitude of the signal will be changed. Since the amplitude of the voltage represents the signal, any unwanted change to the signal is considered a *signal distortion.* For this reason, PAM is not often used in practical telecommunication applications. PAM have been superseded by other techniques such as pulse position modulation (PPM) and pulse code modulation (PCM).

While newer technologies are fast making their presence known, it should be noted that pulse amplitude modulation is still useful in the popular Ethernet communication standard. For example, 100BASE-T2—operating at 100 Mb/s—Ethernet medium uses 5 level PAM modulations running at 25 mega pulses/s over four wires. Later developments include the 100BASE-T medium which raised the bar to 4 wire pairs, each running at 125 mega pulses/s in order to achieve 1000 Mbps data transfer rates, but still with the same PAM5 for each pair.

More recently, PAM-12 and PAM-8 have gained consideration in the newly proposed IEEE 802.3an standard for 10GBase-T—ten gigabyte Ethernet over copper wire.

Simulation of PAM in MATLAB

The MATLAB code to simulate the PAM generation is given below. The typical output obtained is shown in Figure 7.25.

```
%%% MATLAB script to simulate PAM...
clear all; Close all; clf;
fc=10000; % carrier frequency.
fm=200; % modulating frequency.
on=[zeros(1,2),ones(1,4),zeros(1,2)];
m=fc/fm;
t=linspace(0, 4,m*length(on));
x=5*sin(2*pi*fm*t); %modulating signal..
onx=[];
for i=1:m
    onx=[onx,on];
end;
pam=x.*onx;
subplot(211), plot(t,x,'LineWidth',2); axis([0 4 -5.5 5.5]);
xlabel('Time'); ylabel('Amplitude');
title('Modulating Signal');
subplot(212), plot(t,pam,'LineWidth',2); axis([0 4 -5.5 5.5]);
xlabel('Time'); ylabel('Amplitude');
title('PAM Output');
%%% end of pamsim.m
```

Demodulation of PAM

Demodulation of PAM is achieved by simply passing the PAM modulated signal through a lowpass filter. The cut-off frequency of the lowpass filter is chosen to be the maximum frequency of the modulating signal.

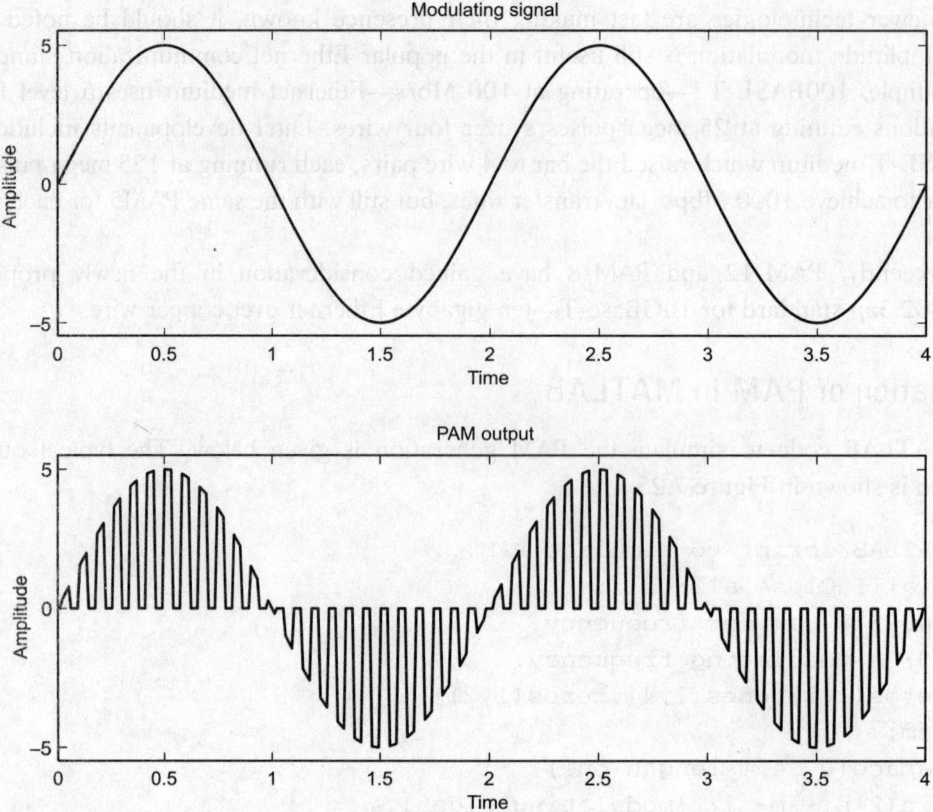

Figure 7.25 The simulated PAM output waveform

7.4.2 Pulse Width Modulation (PWM)

In pulse width modulation, the instantaneous width of a pulse carrier is varied in accordance with the modulating signal. Pulse width modulation is used when a digital system needs to control a system that expects an analog signal of varying amplitude. A typical example is a 12 V motor: the speed of the rotor can be regulated by changing the voltage from low (0 V) to high (12 V). At 12 V, the motor will go at full speed. The alternative is to pass 12 V to the rotor always, but in discrete pulses. If 20% of the time is filled by pulses (20% duty cycle), then the motor will receive small kicks that keep it running at a low percentage of full speed. The motor runs smoothly because of the inertia of the rotor and because the frequency of the pulses can be adjusted.

A PWM is, in some sense, a special purpose digital-to-analog converter. Most microcontrollers provide one or more PWM output lines. Pulse width modulation is also known as pulse duration modulation (PDM).

Sawtooth PWM

The simplest analog form of generating a fixed frequency PWM is a linear slope waveform such as a sawtooth. As seen in Figure 7.4.2, the output signal goes high when the sine wave is higher than the sawtooth. This is implemented using a comparator whose output voltage goes to a logic HIGH when the non-inverting input is greater than the other.

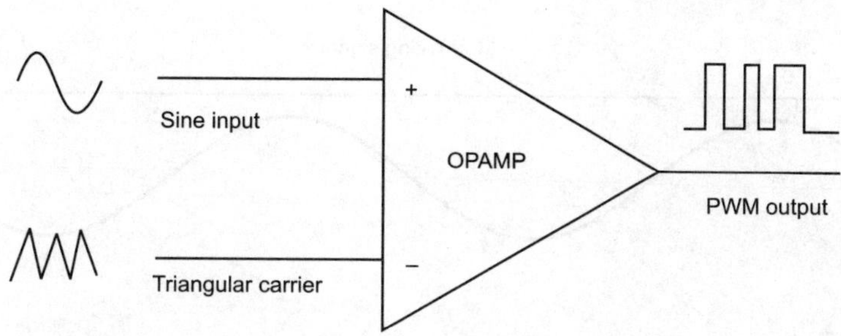

Figure 7.26 Sine sawtooth PWM generation

Three types of pulse width modulation (PWM) are possible:

- The pulse centre may be fixed in the centre of the time window and both edges moved to compress or expand the width.
- The lead edge can be held at the lead edge of the window and the tail edge modulated.
- The tail edge can be fixed and the lead edge modulated.

Simulation of PWM in MATLAB

The MATLAB script file to simulate PWM is given below. The output waveform is shown in Figure 7.27.

```
%%% MATLAB script to simulate PWM...
clear all; Close all; clf;
fc=4000; % carrier frequency.
fs=80000;%sampling frequency..
fm=400; % modulating frequency.
t1=linspace(0, 4,400);
x=(1+sin(2*pi*fm*t1)-eps)/2; %modulating signal..
[y,t]=modulate(x,fc,fs,'pwm','centered');
subplot(211), plot(t1(1:400),x(1:400),'LineWidth',2);
axis([0 2 -1.2 1.2]);
```

```
xlabel('Time'); ylabel('Amplitude');
title('Modulating Signal');
subplot(212), plot(t,y,'LineWidth',2);
axis([0 .004 -0.2 1.2]);
xlabel('Time'); ylabel('Amplitude');
title('PWM Output');
%%% end of pwmsim.m
```

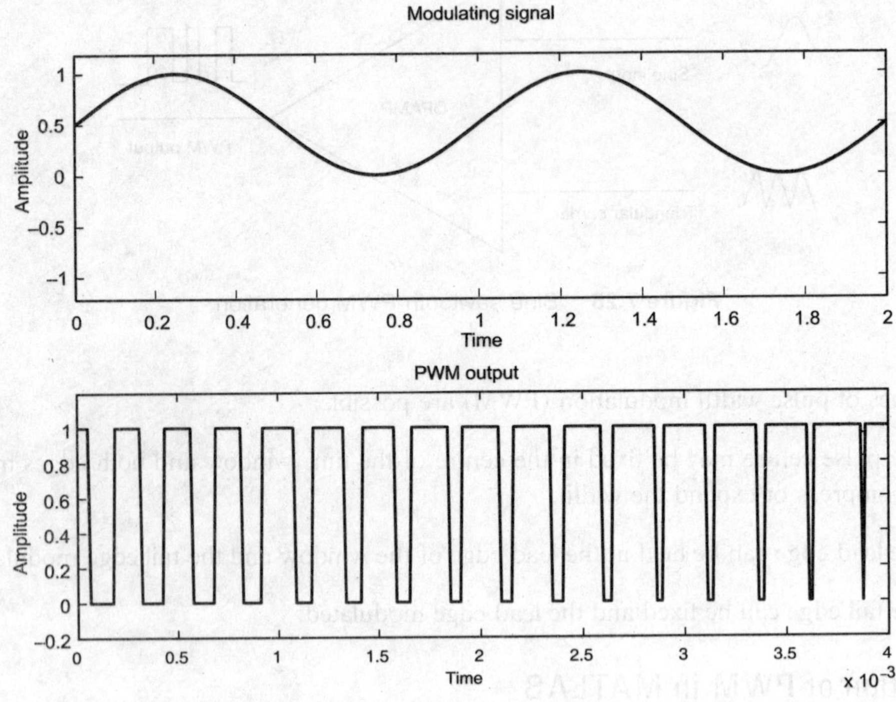

Figure 7.27 The simulated PWM output waveform

Demodulation of PWM

The demodulation of a PWM waveform is achieved by passing it through an integrator circuit. Note that the integrator output in this case will be proportional to the width of the pulses. So the PWM waveform is converted to a PAM waveform. Demodulation of a PAM waveform is as discussed before.

7.4.3 Pulse Position Modulation (PPM)

The amplitude and width of the pulse is kept constant in the system. The position of each pulse, in relation to the position of a recurrent reference pulse, is varied by each instantaneous sampled value of the modulating wave. PPM has the advantage of requiring constant transmitter power since the pulses are of constant amplitude and duration. It is widely used but has the disadvantage of depending on transmitter–receiver synchronisation.

Generation of PPM

PPM can be generated from a PWM. As illustrated in Figure 7.28, the PWM output is passed through a differentiator and a full-wave rectifier to obtain PPM.

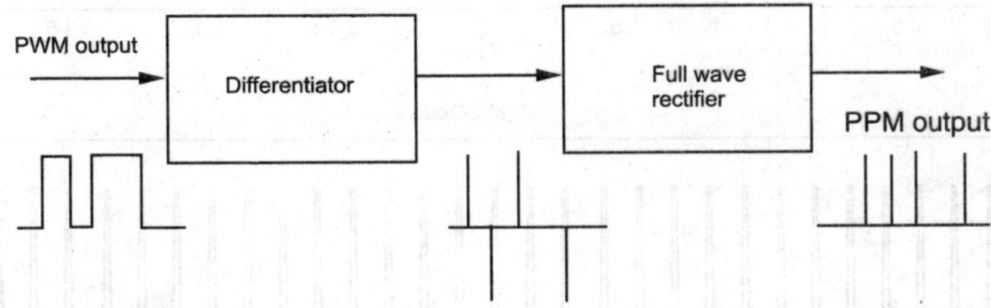

Figure 7.28 Generation of PPM from PWM

Simulation of PPM in MATLAB

The MATLAB script file to simulate PPM is given below. The output waveform is shown in Figure 7.29.

```
%%% MATLAB script to simulate PPM...
clear all; close all;clf;
fc=8000; % carrier frequency.
fs=80000;%sampling frequency..
fm=400; % modulating frequency.
t1=linspace(0,4,800);
x=(1+sin(2*pi*fm*t1))/2; %modulating signal..
[y,t]=modulate(x,fc,fs,'ppm',0.2);
subplot(211), plot(t1(1:800),x(1:800),'LineWidth',2);
axis([0 4 -0.2 1.2]);grid;
xlabel('Time'); ylabel('Amplitude');
title('Modulating Signal');
subplot(212), plot(t,y,'LineWidth',1.6);
axis([0 .004 -0.2 1.2]);grid;
xlabel('Time'); ylabel('Amplitude');
title('PPM Output');
%%% end of ppmsim.m
```

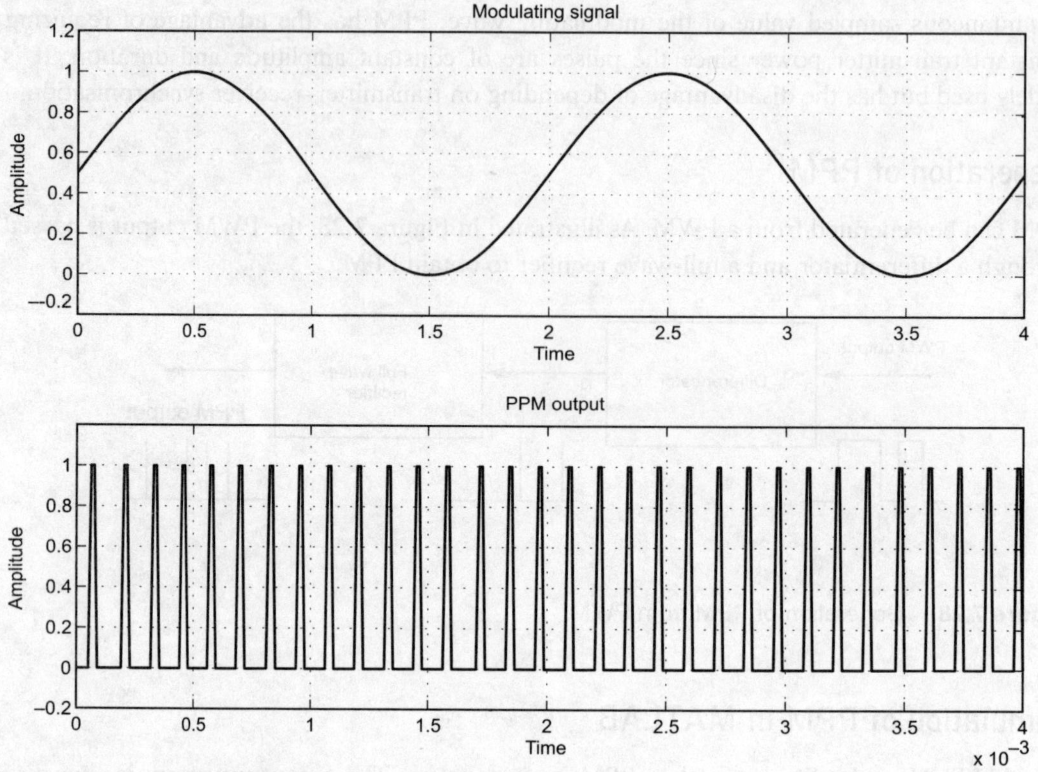

Figure 7.29 The simulated PPM output waveform

Demodulation of PPM

The PPM waveform can be demodulated by first converting it back to a PWM and then demodulating the PWM output. The conversion can be done by triggering a mono-stable multi-vibrator using the PPM pulses. The PWM can be demodulated by passing it through an integrator.

7.5 Pulse Code Modulation (PCM)

Pulse code modulation (PCM) is a digital scheme for transmitting analog data. The signals in PCM are binary; that is, there are only two possible states, represented by logic 1 (high) and logic 0 (low). This is true no matter how complex the analog waveform happens to be. Using PCM, it is possible to digitise all forms of analog data, including full motion video, voice, music, telemetry, and virtual reality (VR).

Pulse code modulation (PCM) is a direct application of the analog-to-digital converter.

Assume that the amplitude of each pulse in a PAM system is rounded off to one of several possible levels. This yields a stair-case type of waveform as shown in Figure 7.30.

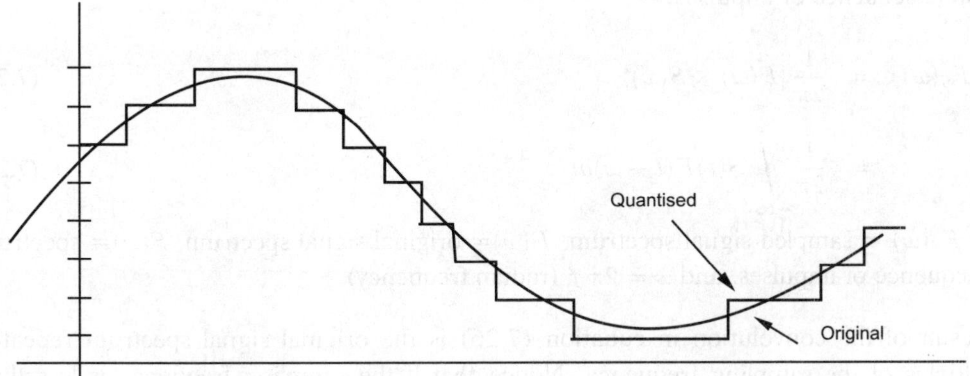

Figure 7.30 The PCM signal format

The *rounding-off* process is known as *quantisation* and it introduces an error known as *quantisation noise*. The sample values are now transmitted as a binary value.

To obtain PCM from an analog waveform at the source (transmitter end) of a communications circuit, the analog signal amplitude is sampled (measured) at regular time intervals. The sampling rate, or number of samples per second, is several times the maximum frequency of the analog waveform in cycles per second or hertz. The instantaneous amplitude of the analog signal at each sampling is rounded off to the nearest of several specific, predetermined levels. This process is called quantisation. The number of levels is always a power of 2— for example, 8, 16, 32, or 64. These numbers can be represented by three, four, five, or six binary digits (bits) respectively. The output of a pulse code modulator is thus a series of binary numbers, each represented by some power of 2 bits.

7.5.1 Sampling

Before a signal can be quantised it must first be sampled. Sampling is the process of instantaneously capturing the level of a continuous signal at some predetermined rate. This predetermined rate is called the *sampling frequency*. As the sampling rate increases, the sampled signal begins to approximate the original continuous signal. As the sampling frequency decreases, samples move further apart in time. Eventually the original signal cannot be reconstructed from the sampled version. The limit on how far apart these samples can be, without losing information, is the basis for *Shannon's sampling theorem*. Shannon's sampling theorem was originally stated as follows: "If a function $f(t)$ contains no frequencies higher than f cycles per second, it is completely determined by giving its ordinates at a series of points spaced $(1/2f)$ seconds apart." A mathematical version of this theorem can be obtained by convolving the Fourier transform of the signal to be sampled with the Fourier transform of an infinite sequence of impulses.

$$F_S(\omega) = \frac{1}{2\pi}[F(\omega) \times S(\omega)] \tag{7.25}$$

$$= \frac{1}{2\pi}\int_{-\infty}^{\infty} S(t)F(t-\omega)dt \tag{7.26}$$

where $F_S(\omega)$ = sampled signal spectrum, $F(\omega)$= original signal spectrum, $S(\omega)$= spectrum for a sequence of impulses, and $\omega = 2\pi f$ (radian frequency).

The result of the convolution in equation (7.26) is the original signal spectrum repeated at multiples of the sampling frequency. Notice that if the sampling frequency is less than twice the bandwidth of the original signal, the replicas centred at multiples of the sampling frequency will overlap and distort the original.

This undesirable phenomenon is *aliasing*. To avoid aliasing, it should be maintained that:

$$f_s > 2B \tag{7.27}$$

where f_s = sampling frequency in Hertz, B = bandwidth of the original signal in Hertz.

The Shannon's sampling theorem is mathematically accurate.[2] Although, in most cases it is not practical to sample a signal at exactly twice its highest frequency. Band-limiting is necessary to avoid aliasing. For $f_s = 2B$ the band-limiting filter must have a so-called "brick wall" roll-off at frequency B. A filter that matches this requirement is physically unrealisable. Several factors contribute to the actual sampling frequency used. Generally, there is a compromise between the complexity of the band-limiting filter versus the cost of the analog-to-digital converter (ADC). As f_s becomes closer to $2B$, the band-limiting filter requires more stages to give the desired roll-off. As f_s increases, the required conversion time necessitates a faster ADC. Cost for ADCs is inversely proportional to conversion time—as conversion time decreases, cost rises.

7.5.2 Linear/Uniform Quantisation

Figure 7.31 illustrates the transfer characteristic of a seven-level uniform quantiser.

[2]Consider sampling a sine wave of average value zero and frequency f_O at $2f_O$ with the sampling instants coinciding with the zero-crossing instants of the sine wave. Then, the result of sampling is a sequence of zeros. This is a *triviality*. To avoid such situations, we make $f_s > 2B$ and not $f_s \geq 2B$.

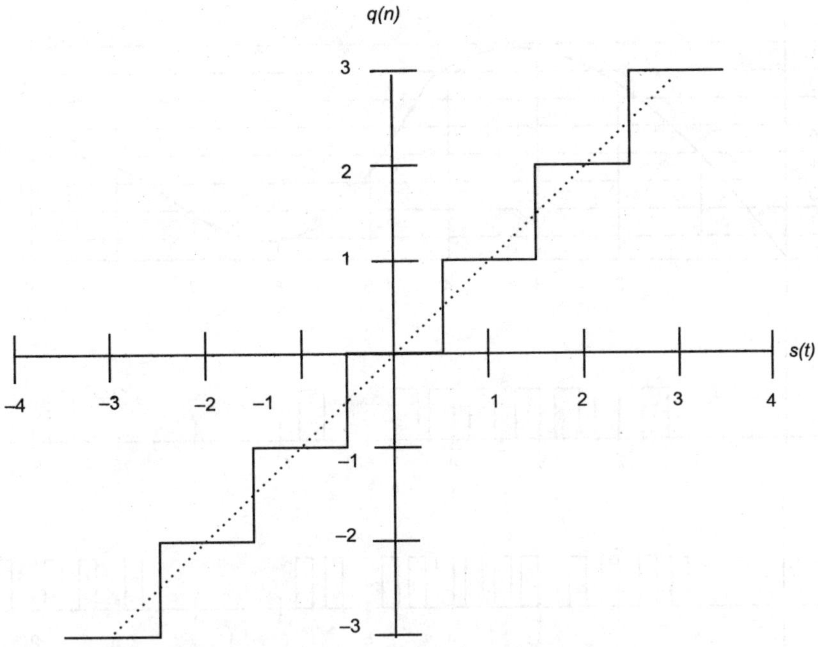

Figure 7.31 Linear quantiser transfer characteristics

To represent the quantised output $q(n)$ as a binary number would require 3 bits. Once a signal has been sampled, it is discrete in time. However, the amplitude remains continuous. The quantised version of a signal is obtained by applying the sampled signal to a binary encoder where the discrete voltage levels are assigned to the nearest binary numbers. The complete process, combining sampling and amplitude quantisation and encoding, is known as PCM.

In PCM, each analog sample is assigned a binary code. Typical binary codes for 2-bit and 3-bit PCM systems are illustrated in Figure 7.32.

The digital signal consists of a block of n bits, where each n-bit number is the amplitude of a PCM pulse. Note that the signal-to-noise ratio for quantisation noise is given by:

$$\mathrm{SNR_{dB}} = 20\log_{10} 2^n + 4.77\mathrm{dB} = 6.02n + 4.77\mathrm{dB} \tag{7.28}$$

Thus, each additional bit increases SNR by 6 dB, or a factor of 4.

Equation (7.28) is an objective measure of quality in systems employing uniform quantisation. It should be noted:

- the SNR calculated in equation (7.28) is a theoretical maximum. In practice, other factors (e.g., power supply noise) tend to reduce the final SNR.

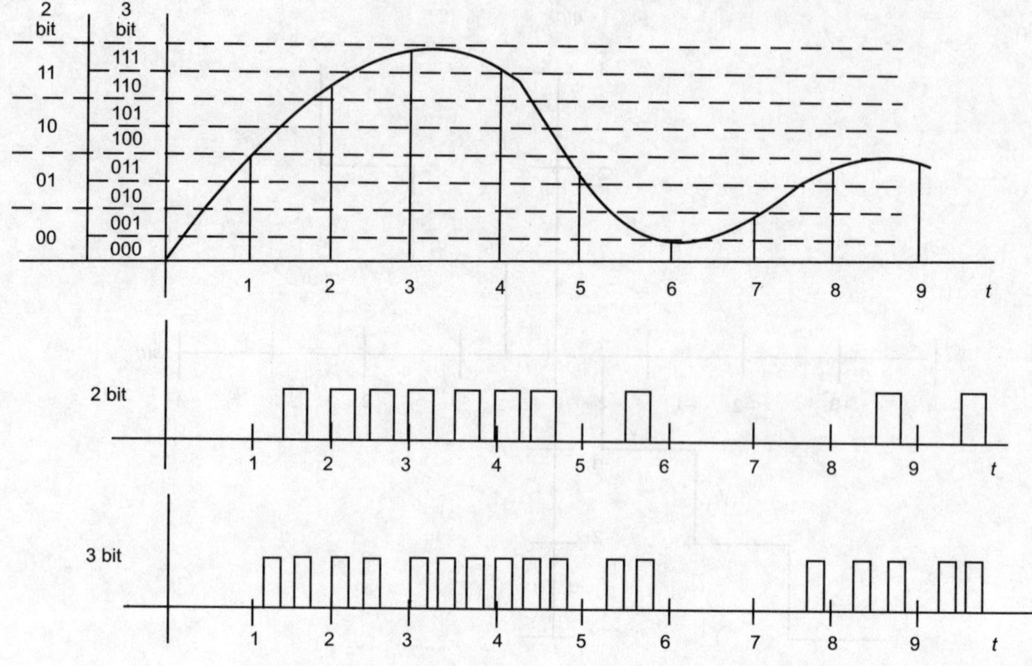

Figure 7.32 The linear PCM quantisation process

- Also, the human voice is considered to have about 40 dB of dynamic range. However, during most conversations, it is typically about 20 dB below maximum. In other words, we generally do not shout during normal conversation. Consequently, the average signal-to-noise ratio for uniformly quantised speech is about 20 dB less than what would be calculated using the above equation.

Dynamic Range

Another objective measure of quality which can be derived in a similar manner is dynamic range (DR). Dynamic range pertains to the resolution of a quantisation scheme. It is the ratio of the full scale amplitude to the smallest quantised amplitude change:

$$\mathrm{DR} = \frac{1}{2}\left(\frac{\alpha 2^n}{\alpha}\right) = 2^{n-1} \tag{7.29}$$

In dBs,

$$\mathrm{DR}_{\mathrm{dB}} = 20 \log 2^{n-1} = 6.02(n-1). \tag{7.30}$$

7.5.3 Non-Linear/Non-Uniform Quantisation

An alternative to linear quantisation is to make the finest resolution α, fine for low-level signals and coarse for high-level signals, introducing a non-uniform quantiser characteristic. This type of quantisation can result in an improved dynamic range for a given number of bits and effectively raise the SNR for lower level signals. The drawback of the non-linear quantisation process is a lower value for the maximum SNR that can be achieved. Equation (7.28) is not valid for non-uniform quantisation. Figure 7.33 shows a transfer characteristic for a seven-level non-uniform quantiser.

Notice that when compared to the uniform quantiser transfer characteristic shown in Figure 7.31, there are three quantisation levels for the input $s(t)$ between zero and one, whereas there is only one with the uniform quantiser.

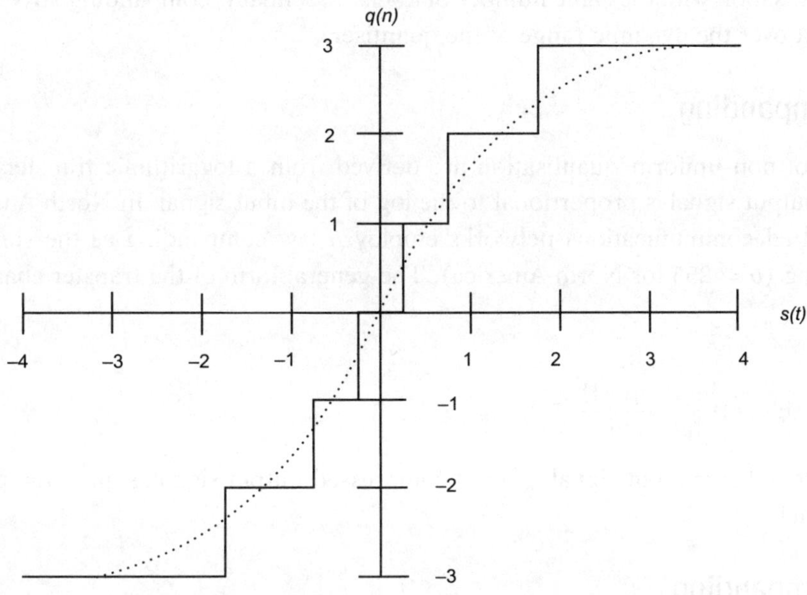

Figure 7.33 Non-linear quantiser transfer characteristics

7.5.4 Companding

A complete digital communication system, incorporating non-uniform speech coding, compresses the quantised signal at the transmitter and then expands the signal back to its linear form at the receiver. The compressed signal requires fewer bits and therefore consumes less bandwidth. Ideally, the expander transfer function is the exact inverse of the compressor and is able to reproduce the original uncoded analog signal. In literature pertaining to telecommunications, the words "compressor" and "expander" are generally combined into a single word; *compandor.*

Companding is one of the most popular forms of non-uniform quantisation. When compared to uniform quantisation, it allows for bandwidth compression without degradation in the dynamic range, at the expense of peak signal-to-noise ratio. For example, a signal uniformly quantised to 14 bits, would have a peak SNR and DR of approximately 89 dB and 78 dB respectively. If the same signal is non-uniformly quantised (compressed) using only 8 bits (256 levels), the minimum quantisation level can be set such that the DR of 78 dB can be retained, although the peak SNR will be degraded. Degradation in the peak SNR is due to the course quantisation levels used for large amplitude signals (where fine quantisation is not necessary). Low amplitude signals are quantised at finer resolution (more steps, where it is necessary). Consequently, the SNR at low signal levels is improved when compared to uniform quantisation with the same number of levels. Essentially, companding strives to make SNR constant over the dynamic range of the quantiser.

μ-Law Companding

Most forms of non-uniform quantisation are derived from a logarithmic transfer function. That is, the output signal is proportional to the log of the input signal. In North America and Japan, digital telecommunications networks employ μ-law companding as the standard for PCM encoding ($\mu = 255$ for North America). The general form of the transfer characteristic is:

$$y(x) = \text{sign}(x)\frac{\ln(1+\mu|x|)}{\ln(1+\mu)} \tag{7.31}$$

where $-1 \leq x \leq 1$ x = input signal, $y(x)$ = compressed output signal, sign (x) = polarity of the input signal.

A-Law Companding

The A-law is a standard companding algorithm used in European digital communications systems to optimise, i.e., modify, the dynamic range of an analog signal for digitising. It is similar to the μ-law algorithm.

For a given input x, the equation for an A-law encoding is as follows:

$$y(x) = \text{sign}(x)\frac{A|x|}{1+\ln(A)}, \quad |x| < \frac{1}{A} \tag{7.32}$$

$$= \text{sign}(x)\frac{1+\ln(A|x|)}{1+\ln(A)}, \quad \frac{1}{A} \leq |x| \leq 1. \tag{7.33}$$

where A is the compression parameter. In Europe, $A = 87.7$; the value 87.6 is also used. The A-law encoding effectively reduces the dynamic range of the signal, thereby increasing the coding efficiency and resulting in a signal-to-distortion ratio that is superior to that obtained by linear encoding for a given number of bits.

The A-law algorithm provides a slightly larger dynamic range than the μ-law at the cost of worse proportional distortion for small signals. A-law is used in Europe and the rest of the world (including India) and in all international routes.

At the destination (receiver end) of the communications circuit, a pulse code demodulator converts the binary numbers back into pulses having the same quantum levels as those in the modulator. These pulses are further processed to restore the original analog waveform.

7.5.5 Differential Pulse Code Modulation (DPCM)

Differential pulse code modulation (DPCM) is a procedure of converting an analog signal into a digital signal in which an analog signal is sampled and then the difference between the actual sample value and its predicted value (predicted value is based on previous sample or samples) is quantised and encoded forming a digital value.

The DPCM code words represent differences between samples unlike PCM where code words represented a sample value.

The basic concept of DPCM—coding a difference—is based on the fact that most source signals show significant correlation between successive samples so *encoding uses redundancy in sample values which implies lower bit rate*. The DPCM encoder and decoder are illustrated in Figure 7.34.

The realisation of the basic concept described above is based on a technique in which we have to predict the current sample value based upon previous samples (or sample) and encode the difference between actual values of sample and predicted values (the difference between samples can be interpreted as prediction error). Because it is necessary to predict sample value, DPCM is a form of *predictive coding*.

Applications of DPCM

In practice, DPCM is usually used with lossy compression techniques (techniques which discard some data in order to compress), for example coarser quantisation of differences which leads to shorter code words. This is used in JPEG and in adaptive DPCM (ADPCM), a common audio compression method. The ADPCM can be viewed as a superset of DPCM. The good side of the ADPCM method is minimal CPU load, but it has significant quantisation noise and only mediocre compression rates can be achieved (4:1).

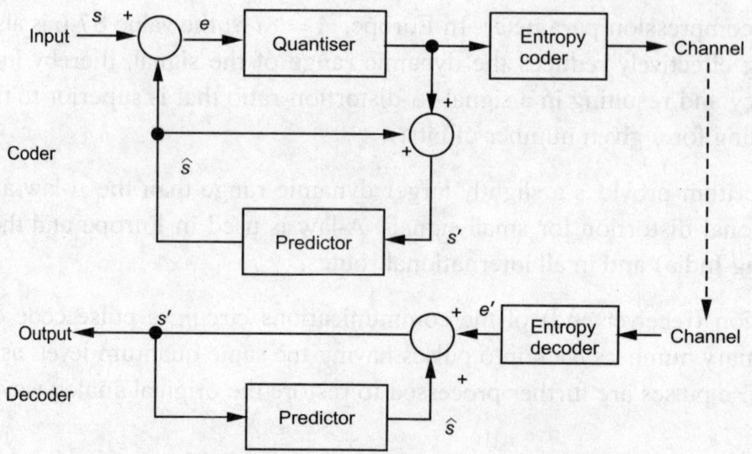

Figure 7.34 The DPCM encoder and decoder

7.5.6 Adaptive Differential PCM (ADPCM)

Adaptive differential pulse code modulation (ADPCM) is a technique for converting sound or analog information to binary information (a string of 0s and 1s) by taking frequent samples of sound and expressing the value of the sampled sound modulation in binary terms. ADPCM is used to send sound on fibre optic long-distance lines as well as to store sound along with text, images, and code on a CDROM. A typical ADPCM encoder and decoder is illustrated in Figures 7.35 and 7.36 respectively.

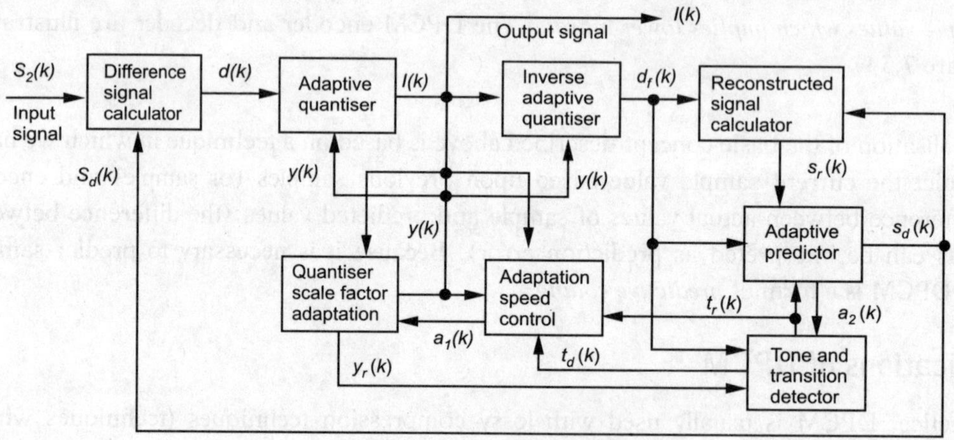

Figure 7.35 The ADPCM encoder

In ADPCM quantisation, the step size adapts to the current rate of change in the waveform which is being compressed. Different ADPCM implementations have been explored. The

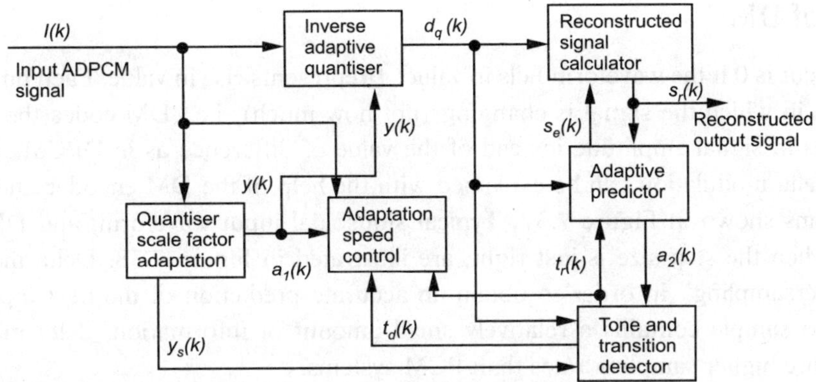

Figure 7.36 The ADPCM decoder

more popular is the International Multimedia Association (IMA) ADPCM. This ADPCM implementation is based on the algorithm proposed by the Interactive Multimedia Association (IMA). The IMA ADPCM standard specifies compression of PCM from 16 to 4 bits per sample.

IMA ADPCM

ADPCM is a lossy compression mechanism. There are a number of variants of ADPCM. The IMA ADPCM compresses data recorded at various sampling rates. Sound is encoded as a succession of 4-bit or 3-bit data packets. Each data packet represents the difference between the current sampled signal value and the previous value. The compression ratio obtained is relatively modest. As an example: a 16-bit data sample encoded as 4-bit differences result in a 4:1 compression format.

The IMA ADPCM is similar to Intel's DVI audio format. It is directly supported on most Windows implementations as a native format. Although the quality of IMA ADPCM voice files is not great, the files are portable. There is a real advantage in having compact files that can be played on most Windows PCs. Microsoft Windows supports IMA ADPCM ".wav" files in a 4-bit format only and at sample rates between 8 and 41 kHz.

7.5.7 Delta Modulation (DM)

Delta modulation (DM) is a sub-class of differential pulse code modulation. It can be viewed as a simplified variant of DPCM, in which a 1-bit quantiser is used with the fixed first order predictor, and developed for voice telephony applications.

Principle of DM

The DM output is 0 if the waveform falls in value. 1 represents rise in value. Each bit indicates the direction in which the signal is changing (not how much), i.e., DM codes the direction of differences in signal amplitude instead of the value of difference as in DPCM. The basic concept of delta modulation can be explained with the help of the DM encoder and decoder block diagrams shown in Figure 7.37. Typical sinusoidal input waveform, and DM output waveform, when the step size is just right, are illustrated in Figure 7.38. Delta modulation requires "oversampling" in order to obtain an accurate prediction of the next input. Since each encoded sample contains a relatively small amount of information, delta modulation systems require higher sampling rates than PCM systems.

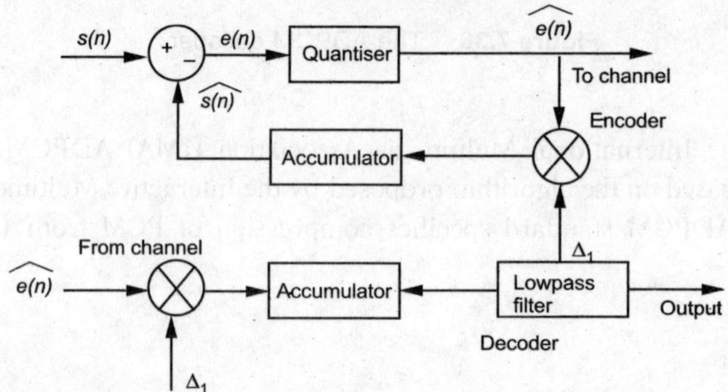

Figure 7.37 The DM encoder and decoder

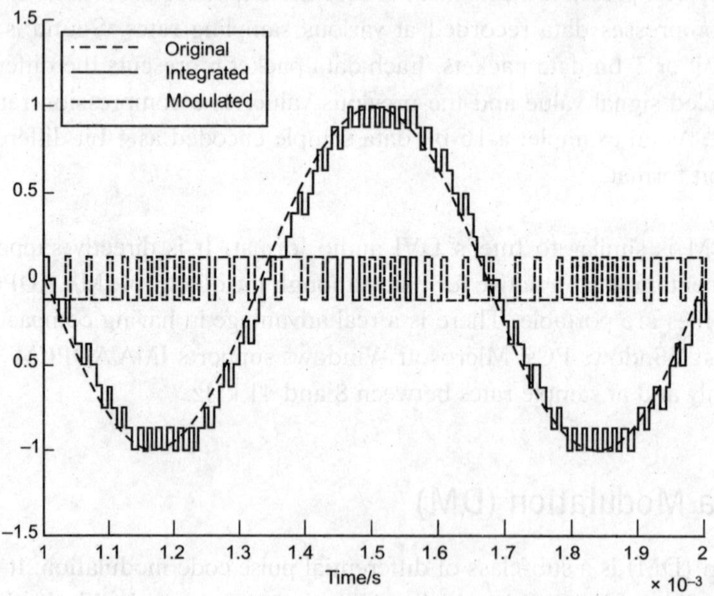

Figure 7.38 The delta modulator input and output waveforms

At any given sampling rate, two types of distortion, *slope overload distortion* and *granular noise,* limit the performance of the DM encoder. Granular noise and slope overload distortion are illustrated in Figures 7.39 and 7.40 respectively.

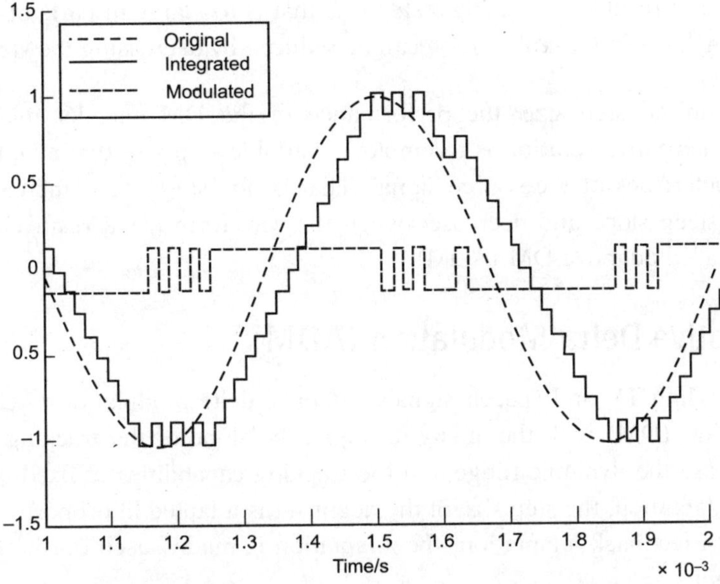

Figure 7.39 Delta modulation: Illustration of granular noise

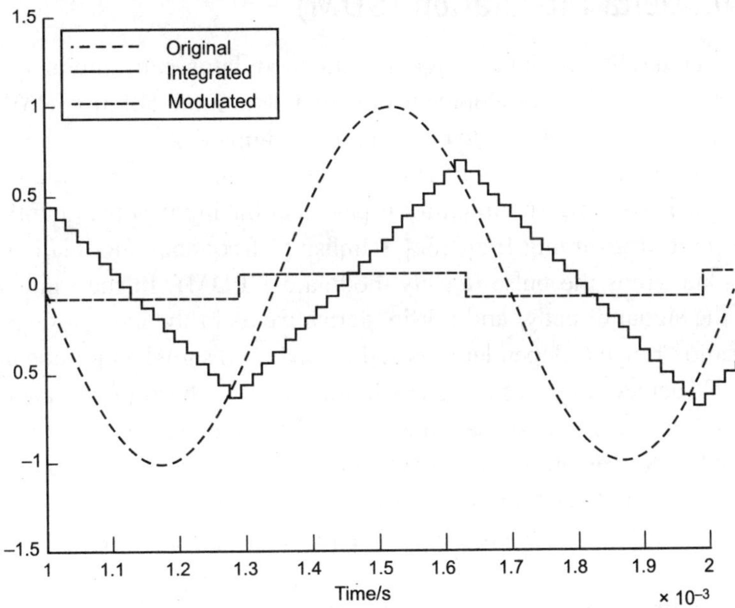

Figure 7.40 Delta modulation: Illustration of slope overload distortion

- Slope overload distortion is due to the use of a step size delta that is too small to follow portions of the waveform that have a steep slope. It can be reduced by increasing the step size.
- Granular noise results from using a step size that is too large in parts of the waveform having a small slope. Granular noise can be reduced by decreasing the step size.

Even for an optimised step size, the performance of the DM encoder may still be less satisfactory. An alternative solution is to employ a variable step size that adapts itself to the short-term characteristics of the source signal. That is, the step size is increased when the waveform has a steep slope and decreased when the waveform has a relatively small slope. This strategy is called adaptive DM (ADM).

7.5.8 Adaptive Delta Modulation (ADM)

Used widely in coding TV and speech signals, adaptive delta modulation (ADM) is similar to delta modulation (DM) with the ability to adjust the slope of the tracking signal. ADM attempts to increase the dynamic range and the tracking capabilities of fixed step-size DM. In feedforward adaptation, the step size of the quantiser is adapted in proportion to the input signal strength. In feedback adaptation, the adaptation is made based on the history of the quantiser as output.

7.5.9 Sigma Delta Modulation (SDM)

Modifying the delta modulator into a sigma delta modulator can eliminate the problems associated with the former. The development of sigma delta modulation (SDM) began in the 1960s, to overcome the limitations of delta simulation. Sigma delta systems quantise the delta (*D*, difference) between the current sigma and the sigma (sum) of the previous difference (it is a closed loop feedback system). An integrator is placed at the input of the quantiser; the signal amplitude is constant at a varying frequency (similar to frequency modulation, FM). Thus, the SDM is also known as the pulse density modulator (PDM). In the same way as PCM, SDM quantises the signal directly, and not its derivative as in the case of delta modulation. Thus the quantisation range is dependent upon the maximum signal amplitude and not on the signal spectrum. To achieve high resolution as in the PCM, high sampling rates are required. For instance, in CD players with a maximum allowable input signal of 20 kHz (44.1 kHz sampling rate) and 16X oversampling, the internal sampling frequency is at 705 kHz (44.1 kHz $\times$ 16). In this way quantisation noise is spread from DC (0 Hz) to 320 kHz (16 $\times$ 20 kHz). SDM adds noise shaping benefits as the integrator "kills" high frequency noise.

Figure 7.41 shows a first-order (single integrator) SDM encoder. The input to the quantiser is the integral of the difference between the input and the quantised output.

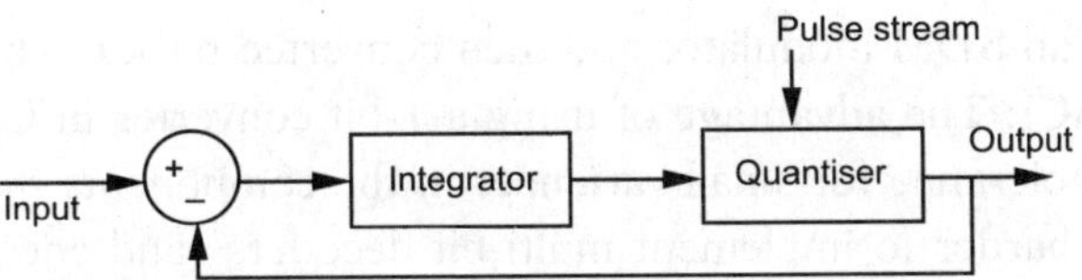

Figure 7.41 The sigma delta modulator

The difference between the input signal and the output signal approaches zero; the average value of the clocked output tracks the input. The integrator forms a lowpass filter on the difference signal thus providing low frequency feedback around the quantiser. The typical sinusoidal input waveform and the sigma delta modulated output waveform are illustrated in Figure 7.42. Another set of waveforms, when the slope of the input sinusoid tend to a limiting case, is illustrated in Figure 7.43. This feedback results in a reduction of quantisation noise at low (in-band) frequencies. Unlike PCM and DM, the noise is not white, but shaped by a first-order highpass characteristic. In practice, the in-band noise floor level is not satisfactory with first-order SDM.

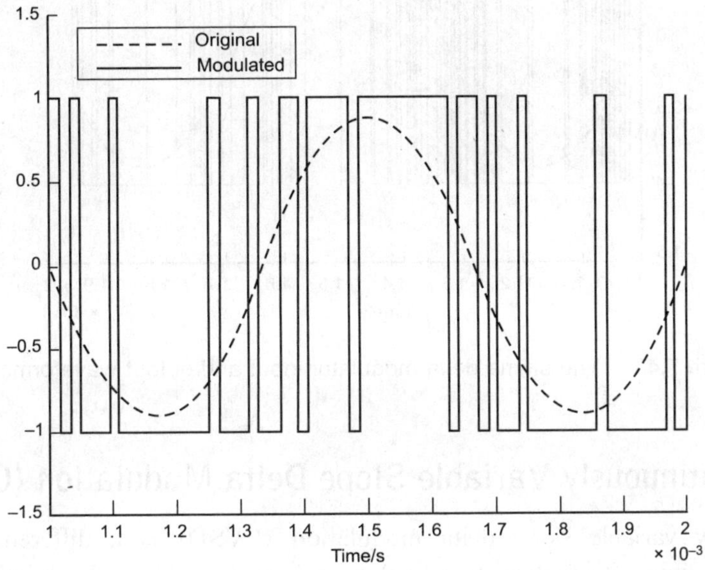

Figure 7.42 The sigma delta modulator input and output waveforms I

Using a high enough sampling rate low-bit conversion, the in-band noise can be better attenuated (or shaped out) from the audio frequency band that can exceed the noise immunity that the strict Nyquist rate sampling offers (PCM). The latest CD audio technology uses SDM DAC converters to convert the bits stored in a compact disc to an analog signal that we can then hear through a loudspeaker. The 44.1 kHz sampled data stored in a CD is re-quantised and oversampled with an SDM modulator and then converted back to an analog signal using an SDM decoder (DAC). The advantage of using a 1-bit converter in CD audio technology is that it offers better tolerance for small variances in the components that it uses compared to the more complex, harder to implement multi-bit decoders (and encoders) which have a complex inner structure of voltage references using a network of resistors as described earlier. Since there are so many components, the variance of the value of one component affects the other components (as they form a "chain"), thus affecting the overall performance and audio quality reproduction. Another matter of concern is the cost: 1-bit converters offer a better cost-to-performance ratio to multi-bit converters (they can even offer better performance at a lower cost!) that is of great concern in the competing audio and information industry.

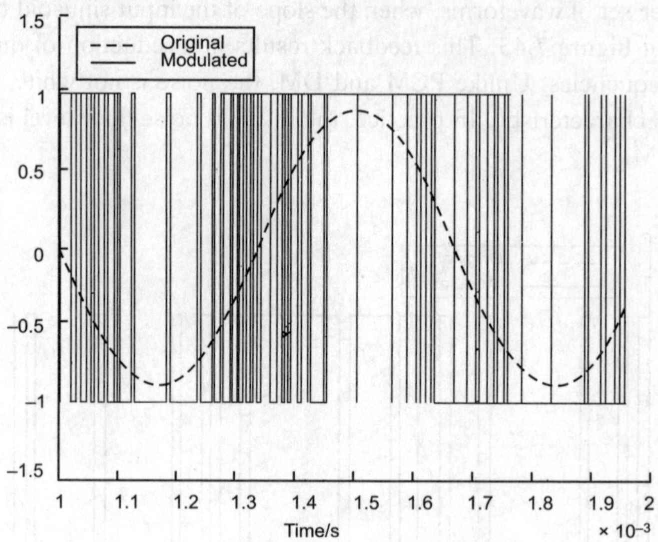

Figure 7.43 The sigma delta modulator input and output waveforms II

7.5.10 Continuously Variable Slope Delta Modulation (CVSD)

The continuously variable slope delta modulation (CVSD) is a differential waveform quantisation technique. It employs two level quantisers (one bit each). CVSD is basically a DM with an adaptive quantiser. Applying adaptive techniques to a DM quantiser allows for continuous step size adjustment. By adjusting the quantisation step size, the coder is able to represent low amplitude signals with greater accuracy (where it is needed) without sacrificing performance on large amplitude signals.

CVSD is used in tactical communications where communication quality is required without affecting the option for security. MIL-STD-188-113 (16 kb/s and 32 kb/s), and Federal

Standard 1023 (12 kb/s CVSD) are examples of a tactical communication systems using CVSD. With the tremendous worldwide growth in wireless technology, secure communication is becoming important to everyone. In addition to point-to-point communication, CVSD is commonly used in digital voice recording/messaging and audio delay lines. Note that DM and CVSD are equivalent to one-bit DPCM and ADPCM, respectively.

Issues with granularity and slope overload can be drastically reduced by making dynamic adjustments to the quantiser step size. Adaptive delta modulation (ADM) algorithms attempt to do this by making small Δ for slowly changing signals and large Δ for rapidly changing signals. The most publicised ADM algorithm is known as CVSD.

The CVSD algorithm was first proposed by Greefkes and Riemens in 1970. In their algorithm, adaptive changes in Δ are based on the past three or four sample outputs (i.e., $c(n), c(n-1), c(n-2), c(n-3)$). Figure 7.44 and Figure 7.45 show flow diagrams of the algorithms for the encoder and decoder respectively. Notice that only the last three samples of $c(n)$ are used here. The time constants for the integrator I2 and integrator I1 are typically 4 ms and 1 ms respectively. In CVSD literature, integrator I1 is referred to as the *principal integrator* and integrator I2 as the *syllabic integrator*. The so-called syllabic integrator derives its name from the length of a *syllable*. Actually a syllable is about 100 ms in duration, however, pitch changes are in the order of 10 ms. Consequently, 4 ms seems to work best for the CVSD syllabic (pitch) time constant. The block labelled L performs simple level conversion (i.e., for $c(n) = 1$, L outputs 1; $c(n) = 0$, L outputs -1). This CVSD algorithm is also known as a "digitally controlled DM".

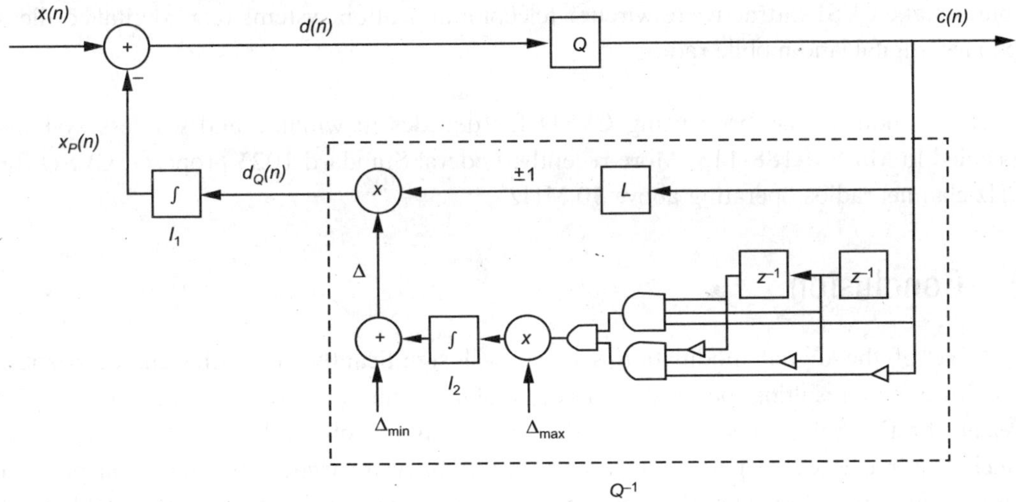

Figure 7.44 The CVSD encoder

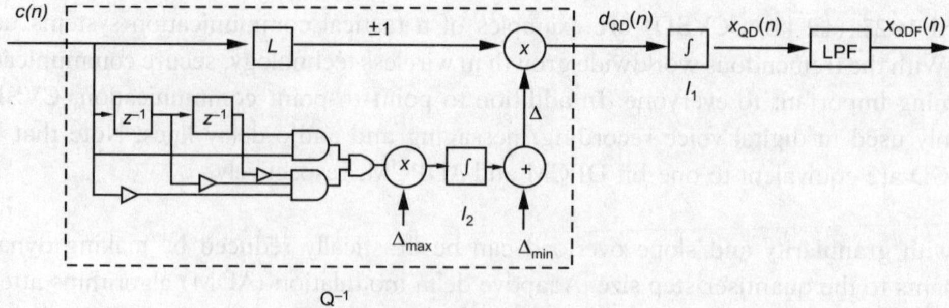

Figure 7.45 The CVSD decoder

7.5.11 Performance Comparison and Applications

CVSD has several attributes that make it well suited for digital coding of speech. One bit words eliminate the need for complex framing schemes. Robust performance in the presence of bit errors make error detection and correction hardware unnecessary. Other speech coding schemes may require a digital signal processing engine and external analog-to-digital/digital-to-analog converters to convert the analog signal into a form that can be processed digitally. The entire CVSD codec algorithm, including input and output filters, can be integrated on a single silicon substrate. Despite this simplicity, CVSD has enough flexibility to allow digital encryption for secure applications. Finally, CVSD can operate over a wide range of data rates. It has been successfully used from 9.6 kb/s to 64 kb/s. At 9.6 kb/s, audio quality is not particularly good, however, it is intelligible. At data rates of 24 kb/s to 48 kb/s, it is judged as quite acceptable. And above 48 kb/s, it is comparable to toll quality. All of these attributes make CVSD attractive to wireless telecommunication systems (e.g., digital cordless telephones, digital land mobile radio).

The defense industry has been using CVSD for decades in wireline and wireless systems as specified in Mil-Std-188-113. More recently, Federal Standard 1023 proposed CVSD for 25 kHz channel radios operating above 30 MHz.

7.6 Conclusion

The choice of the digital modulation scheme will significantly affect the characteristics, performance and resulting physical realisation of a communication system. There is no universal "best" choice of scheme, but depending on the physical characteristics of the channel, required levels of performance and target hardware trade-offs, some will prove a better fit than others. Consideration must be given to the required data rate, acceptable level of latency, available bandwidth, anticipated link budget and target hardware cost, size and current consumption. Typically, the physical characteristics of the channel, be it hardwired without the associated problems of fading, or a mobile communications system to a Formula One racing car with fast changing multipath, will significantly affect the choice of the optimum system.

Communication system design requires the simultaneous conservation of bandwidth, power, and cost. In the past, it was possible to make an inexpensive radio by sacrificing parameters such as power and bandwidth efficiency. But now, with more and more data needing to be transferred, it is not possible to let go of these parameters easily.

In the case of ASK, pulse shaping can be employed to remove spectral spreading. ASK demonstrates poor performance as it is heavily affected by noise and interference.

Bandwidth occupancy of FSK is dependent on the spacing of the two symbols. A frequency spacing of 0.5 times the symbol period is typically used. FSK can be expanded to a M-ary scheme, employing multiple frequencies as different states.

Binary phase shift keying (BPSK) demonstrates better performance than ASK and FSK. PSK can be expanded to a M-ary scheme, employing multiple phases and amplitudes as different states. Filtering can be employed to avoid spectral spreading.

Phase shift keying (PSK) is often used, as it provides a highly bandwidth efficient modulation scheme. QPSK modulation is very robust, but requires some form of linear amplification. Alternatives like offset QPSK and $\pi/4$-QPSK which reduce the envelope variations of the signal can be implemented. High level M-ary schemes (such as 64-QAM) are very bandwidth-efficient, but are more susceptible to noise and require linear amplification. Constant envelope schemes (such as GMSK) can be employed since an efficient, non-linear amplifier can be used. Coherent reception provides better performance than non-coherent (or differential) ones, but requires a more complex receiver.

The Nyquist bandwidth is the minimum bandwidth that can be used to represent a signal. It is important to limit the spectral occupancy of a signal, to improve bandwidth efficiency and remove adjacent channel interference. The raised-cosine filters allow an approximation to this minimum bandwidth.

Quadrature phase shift keying is effectively two independent BPSK systems (I and Q), and therefore exhibits the same performance as a BPSK but with twice the bandwidth efficiency. QPSK can be filtered using raised-cosine filters to achieve excellent out-of-band suppression. Large envelope variations occur during phase transitions, thus requiring linear amplification.

16-QAM has the largest distance between points, but requires very linear amplification. 16-PSK has less stringent linearity requirements, but has less spacing between constellation points, and is therefore more affected by noise. M-ary schemes are more bandwidth efficient, but more susceptible to noise.

Conventional QPSK has transitions through zero (i.e., 180° phase transition). A highly linear amplifier is required. In offset QPSK, the transitions on the I and Q channels are staggered. Phase transitions are therefore limited to 90°. In $\pi/4$-QPSK, the set of constellation points are toggled to each symbol, so transitions through zero cannot occur. This scheme produces the lowest envelope variations. All QPSK schemes require linear power amplifiers.

GMSK is a form of continuous phase FSK, in which the phase is changed between symbols to provide a constant envelope. The RF bandwidth is controlled by the Gaussian lowpass filter bandwidth. The degree of filtering is expressed by multiplying the filter 3 dB bandwidth by the bit period of the transmission, i.e., by BT. As bandwidth of this filter is lowered, the amount of inter-symbol interference introduced increases. GMSK allows efficient class C non-linear amplifiers to be used. However even with a low BT value, its bandwidth efficiency is less than filtered QPSK. GMSK generally achieves a bandwidth efficiency less than 0.7 bits per second per Hz (QPSK can be as high as 1.6 bits per second per Hz). It has a main lobe 1.5 times that of QPSK.

In MSK, the phase ramps up through 90 degrees for a binary one, and down 90 degrees for a binary zero. For GMSK transmission, a Gaussian pre-modulation baseband filter is used to suppress the high frequency components in the data. The degree of out-of-band suppression is controlled by the BT product.

In the case of pulse modulation schemes, pulse amplitude modulation is the simplest, compared to pulse width modulation and pulse position modulation. But it (PAM) is rarely used in practice. Both PWM and PPM provide greater *noise immunity* than PAM. In PAM, additive noise directly affects the reconstructed sample value. This disruption caused by noise is less severe in PWM and PPM, where the additive noise must affect the zero-crossings in order to cause an error. However, with multiplexing of channels, PWM and PPM necessitates greater care in spacing the different channels in the time domain. This is a disadvantage.

The answer to the question, which is better—PCM, DPCM or DM—depends on the criterion used for comparison and the type of message. If one needs a relatively simple, low-cost system, DM may be the best. On the other hand, to have a high output SNR, PCM is probably the best. Now, to interface existing equipment, or otherwise to have compatibility, PCM has the advantage.

Further Reading

1. *Getting Started with Communications Blockset*. The MathWorks. 2009.

2. *Getting Started with MATLAB 7*. The MathWorks. 2009.

3. Roddy, Dennis and John Coolen. *Electronic Communications*. 4th Edition. Pearson Education (India) Ltd. 2008.

4. Roden, Martin S. *Analog and Digital Communication Systems*. 5th Edition. Discovery Press. 2002.

5. *Simulink*. The MathWorks. 2009.

6. Tranter, William H., K. Sam Shanmugan, Theodore S. Rappaport, and Kurt L. Kosbar. *Principles of Communication Systems Simulation with Wireless Applications*. Pearson Education. 2004.

7. *User's Guide, Communications Toolbox*. The MathWorks. 2009.

8. *User's Guide, Signal Processing Toolbox*. The MathWorks. 2009.

Problems

1. A 10 Hz 1 volt p-p sine wave is used to Pulse Width Modulate a 1000 Hz pulse train. Simulate this experiment using MATLAB for a duration of 1 second. Plot the modulated wave form and its power spectrum.

   HINTS:

   (a) PWM can be generated by comparing the modulating signal with a biased saw tooth wave.

   (b) Think hard before choosing the sampling frequency. There are, in fact, two samplings happening here.

2. Simulate PPM modulation and demodulation in MATLAB.

   HINT: Use the `modulate(.)` command in the Signal Processing Toolbox in MATLAB for modulation.

3. Write MATLAB functions to simulate BPSK modulation and demodulation of a bit stream. The carrier frequency and symbol duration should be accepted as input parameters. The sampling frequency of the carrier (for simulation) should be estimated automatically.

   Required syntax : `x = bpsk_mod(b, fc, T)` and `b = bpsk_demod(x, fc, T)`.

   HINTS:

   (a) In the modulator, convert the $\{0, 1\}$ bit stream to a $\{-1, +1\}$ stream and take one bit at a time.

   (b) In the demodulator, use the correlation receiver followed by hard limiter.

4. Write MATLAB functions to simulate BFSK modulation and demodulation of a bit stream. The carrier frequency and symbol duration should be accepted as input parameters. The sampling frequency of the carrier (for simulation) should be estimated automatically.

   Required syntax :`x = bfsk_mod(b, fc, T)` and `b = bfsk_demod(x, fc, T)`.

5. Write MATLAB functions to quadrature phase shift modulate and demodulate a bit stream onto a carrier. The carrier frequency and symbol duration should be accepted as input parameters. The sampling frequency of the carrier (for simulation) should be estimated automatically.

   Required syntax : `x = qpsk_mod(b, fc, T)` and `b = qpsk_demod(x, fc, T)`.

   HINTS:

   (a) In the modulator, convert the $\{0, 1\}$ bit stream to a $\{-1, +1\}$ stream and take two bits at a time.
   (b) In the demodulator, use the correlation receiver followed by hard limiter.

6. Write MATLAB functions to quadrature amplitude modulate and demodulate a bit stream onto a carrier. The carrier frequency and symbol duration should be accepted as input parameters. The sampling frequency of the carrier (for simulation) should be estimated automatically.

   Required syntax : `x = qam_mod(b, fc, T)` and `b = qam_demod(x, fc, T)`.
   HINTS:

   (a) In the modulator, convert the $\{0, 1\}$ bit stream to a $\{-1, +1\}$ stream and take two bits at a time.
   (b) In the demodulator, use the correlation receiver followed by hard limiter.

7. Plot the constellation of the QAM modulated signal in the previous case.

8. Add a white Gaussian noise of small variance to the QAM modulated signal and then try to demodulate. Compute the bit error rate (BER).

9. Find the BER for different values of signal-to-noise ratio $\left(\frac{E_b}{N_0}\right)$ and plot the curve for the QAM.

10. Write the MATLAB script to simulate the pulse code modulation and demodulation of an arbitrary analog signal, $x(t)$.

11. Write the MATLAB script to simulate the delta modulation and demodulation of an arbitrary analog signal, $x(t)$.

12. Simulate ADPCM using MATLAB. HINT: Use Signal Processing Blockset in MATLAB.

8

Probability and Random Processes

This chapter is devoted to the study of random processes or stochastic processes. It is highly essential in the context of communication systems modelling and simulation. One main reason is that most practical signals encountered in systems theory are random, and non-deterministic in nature. For example, thermal noise and other types of noise encountered in communication systems analysis can only be represented by a random phenomenon. Several electrical behaviour also fall into this category. Random processes are studied on the basis of statistical variables. Probability is the most elementary concept in this study.

If the random process is *stationary*, a Fourier transform can simplify a random looking function into a collection of coefficients, thus transforming the process to the frequency domain. *Note that a random process does not have a predominant amplitude or frequency.*

When a signal is transmitted through a communication channel, there are two types of imperfections that cause the received signal to be different from the transmitted signal. One class of imperfections is deterministic in nature, such as linear and non-linear distortion, inter-symbol interference etc. The second class is non-deterministic such as addition of noise and multi-path fading etc.

We will start our discussion with a brief introduction to the basic statistical concepts.

8.1 Introduction

The study of probability, random variables, and random processes is fundamental to a wide range of disciplines. For example, many concepts of basic probability can be motivated by the *game of chance*. Foundations of the game of chance were, indeed, originally built on a foundation of probability. By nature, the outcomes of games of chance are random.

In an important application of probability theory, stock investors spend a great deal of time and effort trying to predict the random fluctuations in the market. Another business built on managing random occurrence is the insurance industry.

We will now introduce the basic concepts of probability theory.

Random Experiments

An *experiment* is a procedure we perform (quite often hypothetical) that produces a result. The outcome (or result) of a random experiment is random. Often we use the letter E to denote an experiment. For example, E_T may represent the tossing of a fair coin, and E_5 may denote the random experiment of tossing the coin five times in succession.

Outcome

An *outcome* is a possible result of an experiment. For example, getting a head (tail) in a coin tossing experiment. We use the Greek letter ξ to denote outcomes. In the tossing of the coin case, $\xi_1 = \{\text{head}\}$ and $\xi_2 = \{\text{tail}\}$.

Events

An *event* is a certain set of outcomes of an experiment. For example, the even C of an experiment E_5 of tossing a fair coin 5 times can be $C = \{$all outcomes consisting of an even number of heads$\}$.

Sample Space

The *sample space* is the collection or set of "all possible" distinct (collectively exhaustive and mutually exclusive) outcomes of an experiment. The letter S is used to denote the sample space of a random experiment, which is the *universal set* of outcomes of the experiment. A sample space is called discrete if it is a finite or a countably infinite set. It is called continuous or a continuum otherwise. In the case of the tossing of the coin experiment, we note that $S = \{\text{head, tail}\}$.

8.2 Axioms of Probability

The words *probability* and *probable* are quite commonly used in everyday language. In fact, there are several definitions for probability. The general notion of "probability" is that it is a *measure of the likelihood of various events.* Before we define probability, we will consider three axioms of probability that any method for assigning probabilities must satisfy:[1]

AXIOM 8.1:

For any event A, $P(A) \geq 0$ (That is, a negative probability does not make sense.).

[1] As the word "axiom" implies, these statements or dictums are taken for granted and do not need any proof.

AXIOM 8.2:

If S is the sample space for a given random experiment, then $P(S) = 1$ (The total probability of all events is unity.).

8.2.1 Mutually Exclusive Events

Two events A and B are said to *mutually exclusive* or *disjoint* if their corresponding sets have no common elements, that is, if and only if

$$A \cap B = \Phi \tag{8.1}$$

Several sets $A_1,\ A_2\ \ldots$ are mutually exclusive if and only if

$$A_i \cap A_j = \Phi, \text{ for every} i \text{and } j \neq i. \tag{8.2}$$

AXIOM 8.3A:

If two events, A and B are mutually exclusive, i.e., $A \cap B = \Phi$, then $P(A \cup B) = P(A) + P(B)$.

COROLLARY 8.3.1:

Consider N sets $A_1,\ A_2, \ldots, A_N$ that are mutually exclusive, i.e., $A_i \cap A_j = \Phi$ for all $i \neq j$, then

$$P\left(\bigcup_{i=1}^{N} A_i\right) = \sum_{i=1}^{N} P(A_i) \tag{8.3}$$

The above statement can be proved by *mathematical induction*.

AXIOM 8.3B:

For an infinite number of mutually exclusive sets, $A_i,\ i = 1, 2, 3, \ldots, \infty$, and $A_i \cap A_j = \Phi$ for all $i \neq j$, then

$$P\left(\bigcup_{i=1}^{\infty} A_i\right) = \sum_{i=1}^{\infty} P(A_i) \tag{8.4}$$

THEOREM 8.1:

For any two sets A and B (not necessarily mutually exclusive),

$$P(A \cup B) = P(A) + P(B) - P(A \cap B) \tag{8.5}$$

We can provide a *visual proof* for the above theorem using Venn diagrams.

THEOREM 8.2:

$P(\overline{A}) = 1 - P(A).$

PROOF:

$$\begin{aligned} 1 &= P(S) = P(A \cup \overline{A}) \quad \text{(by Axiom 8.2)} \\ &= P(A) + P(\overline{A}) \quad \text{(by Axiom 8.3a)} \end{aligned}$$

Hence, $P(\overline{A}) = 1 - P(A)$.

8.2.2 Definitions of Probability

We will now try to define probability. There are several definitions.

The Relative Frequency Definition

The relative frequency approach requires that the experiment is repeatable, and the probability of an event, A can be assigned by repeating the experiment a large number of times and observing how many times the event A actually occurs. If we let n be the number of times the experiment is repeated and n_A be the number of times the event A is observed, then the probability of the event A is defined as

$$P(A) = \lim_{n\to\infty} \frac{n_A}{n}. \tag{8.6}$$

The relative frequency definition is based on experimentation and hence has the practical flavour of it. The major limitation of the definition is that we have to *repeat the experiment an infinitely large number of times.*

EXAMPLE 8.1
Consider the random experiment of rolling a fair die, two times in succession. Obtain the sample space, and the probability of obtaining an even face in both attempts.

SOLUTION
The sample space, $S = \{(1,1),(1,2),(1,3),(1,4),(1,5),(1,6),(2,1),(2,2),\ldots,(6,6)\}$. An even numbered face would have turned up if the outcome of the experiment was: $\xi_{\text{Even}} = \{(2,2),(2,4),(2,6),(4,2),(4,4),(4,6),(6,2),(6,4),(6,6)\}$.
Hence, $P(\xi_{\text{Even}}) = \frac{9}{36} = \frac{1}{4}$.

The Axiomatic Definition

The axiomatic definition of probability is based on Axioms 8.1 to 8.3 discussed earlier. It might appear overly mathematical, however, this is not so.

The Classical Definition

For several centuries, the theory of probability was based on the classical definition. According to the classical definition, the probability $P(A)$ of an event A is determined a priori without actual experimentation. It is given by the ratio

$$P(A) = \frac{N_A}{N}. \tag{8.7}$$

where N is the number of possible outcomes and N_A is the number of outcomes that are *favourable* to the event A. The improved version of the classical definition is as follows:

The probability of an event equals the ratio of its favourable outcomes to the total number of outcomes, provided that all outcomes are equally likely.

The classical definition has many flaws. They are:

- The term *equally likely* means *equally probable,* which leads to problems in determining N and N_A.

- The classical definition can be applied to a limited class of problems. For example, in the case of a coin tossing experiment, the classical definition can be applied only if the *coin is fair.*

- The classical definition appears to be divorced from experience—in practice, the definition is not true.

- If the number of possible outcomes is infinite, then to apply the classical definition, we must use length, area, or some measure of infinity to determine the ratio N_A/N. This causes several, severe difficulties in practical problems.

8.2.3 Simulation of Random Experiments in MATLAB

We will now try to simulate a few random experiments in MATLAB®. There are several library functions in MATLAB that can be used to generate random numbers. The following MATLAB functions can be used to generate random entities: `randperm`, `randint`, `randi`, `rand` and `randn`. The `randperm(7)` command, for example, will list out all numbers up to 7 in a random order:

```
>> randperm(7)
>> ans =

5  4  3  7  6  1  2
```

Note that calling `randperm(7)` a second time will get a totally different permutation of the first seven numbers.

```
>> randperm(7)
>> ans =

 3  1  7  4  5  2  6
```

The `randint(m, n)` command generates an $m \times n$ binary matrix, each of whose entries independently takes the value 0 with probability 1/2. The `randi(imax,m,n)` command returns a uniformly distributed pseudo-random integer array of size $m \times n$, comprising of integers less than or equal to *imax*. For example, the command `randi(7,2,3)` gets

```
>> ans =

 5     6     5
 1     7     6
```

The command `rand(m,n)` generates a uniformly distributed random array of size $m \times n$, comprising of random numbers on the open interval (0,1). As an example, the command `rand(4,4)` gets

```
>>ans =

0.7431    0.7060    0.0971    0.9502
0.3922    0.0318    0.8235    0.0344
0.6555    0.2769    0.6948    0.4387
0.1712    0.0462    0.3171    0.3816
```

The command `randn(m,n)` generates a Gaussian (normal) distributed random array of size $m \times n$, comprising of random numbers with mean 0 and variance 1. For example, the command `randn(3,4)` gets

```
>>ans =

 0.3192   -0.0301    1.0933    0.0774
 0.3129   -0.1649    1.1093   -1.2141
-0.8649    0.6277   -0.8637   -1.1135
```

Simulation of Tossing of a Fair Coin

We will now develop the MATLAB script to simulate the tossing of a fair coin. As we all know, there are two possible outcomes in this random experiment: "getting a head" or "getting a tail". The MATLAB script for this purpose is given below. It is possible to repeat the random experiment any large number of times (it can even be infinitely large!) and arrive at the probabilities of a head (tail) turning up.

```
%%% MATLAB script to simulate a coin toss..
clear all; close all; clc;
N=input('The number of times the coin is to be tossed: ');
nh=0;nt=0;
for i=1:N
    p=randperm(2);
if p(1)==1
nt=nt+1;
else nh=nh+1;
end;
end;
Ph=nh/N;
Pt=nt/N;
fprintf('The probability of getting a tail is = %0.4f \n',Pt);
fprintf('The probability of getting a head is = %0.4f \n',Ph);
%%% end of cointoss.m
```

The results of tossing the coin 10 and 500000 times are given below:

```
>> cointoss
The number of times the coin is to be tossed: 10
The probability of getting a tail is = 0.4000
The probability of getting a head is = 0.6000
>> cointoss
The number of times the coin is to be tossed: 500000
The probability of getting a tail is = 0.4997
The probability of getting a head is = 0.5003
```

It is evident from the simulation that

$$P\{'head'\} = P\{'tail'\} = 0.5000, \ \ as \ N \to \infty$$

The Rolling of a Die

We will now develop the MATLAB script to simulate the rolling of a fair die. As we all know, there are six possible outcomes in this random experiment; therefore, the sample space, $S = \{1, 2, 3, 4, 5, 6\}$. The MATLAB script for this purpose is given below. It is possible to repeat the random experiment any large number of times (it can even be infinitely large!) and arrive at the probabilities of a face marked "1" turning up and so on.

```
%%% MATLAB script to simulate the rolling of a die..
clear all; close all; clc;
N=input('The number of times the die is to be rolled: ');
n=zeros(1,6);
for i=1:N
    p=randperm(6);
   switch p(1)
       case {1}
            n(1)=n(1)+1;
       case {2}
            n(2)=n(2)+1;
       case {3}
            n(3)=n(3)+1;
       case {4}
            n(4)=n(4)+1;
       case {5}
            n(5)=n(5)+1;
       otherwise
            n(6)=n(6)+1;
    end;
end;
P=n/N;
for i=1:6
    fprintf('The probability of getting a %2d is = %0.4f \n',i,P(i));
end;
%%% end of rolldie.m
```

The results of rolling the die 10 and 500000 times are given below:

```
>> rolldie
The number of times the die is to be rolled: 10
The probability of getting a  1 is = 0.1000
The probability of getting a  2 is = 0.0000
The probability of getting a  3 is = 0.1000
The probability of getting a  4 is = 0.3000
The probability of getting a  5 is = 0.2000
The probability of getting a  6 is = 0.3000
>> rolldie
The number of times the die is to be rolled: 500000
```

```
The probability of getting a  1 is = 0.1670
The probability of getting a  2 is = 0.1668
The probability of getting a  3 is = 0.1666
The probability of getting a  4 is = 0.1659
The probability of getting a  5 is = 0.1669
The probability of getting a  6 is = 0.1668
```

It may be noted that the above probabilities tend to $\frac{1}{6} = 0.1667$, for large N.

8.3 Probability Space

The most fundamental concept in any probabilistic model is the concept of a *random experiment*, which is any experiment whose outcome, for some reason or other, cannot be predicted with certainty. Flipping a coin, rolling a die, and drawing a card from a deck of cards are examples of random experiments. What is common in all these cases is that the result (or outcome) of the experiment is uncertain. A random experiment has certain *outcomes* that are elementary results of the experiment. In flipping a coin, "head" and "tail" are possible outcomes. The set of all possible outcomes is called the *sample space* and is denoted by Ω or S. Outcomes are denoted by ξs and certainly each ξ lies in Ω, i.e., $\xi \in \Omega$.

Events are sub-sets of the sample space for which a probability can be assigned. For discrete sample spaces, any sub-set of the sample space is an event, that is, a probability can be assigned to it. For example, for tossing a coin, events like "getting a head" or "getting a tail" can be considered. For a non-discrete sample space, not every sub-set of Ω can be assigned a probability without sacrificing some basic intuitive properties of probability. To overcome this difficulty, we define a σ-field $\mathcal{B}$ on the sample space as a collection of sub-sets of Ω such that the following conditions are satisfied:

1. $\Phi \in \mathcal{B}$.

2. If the sub-set (event) $E \in \mathcal{B}$, then $E^c \in \mathcal{B}$, where E^c denotes the complement of E.

3. If $E_i \in \mathcal{B}$ for all i, then $\bigcup_{i=1}^{\infty} E_i \in \mathcal{B}$.

We define a *probability measure* P on $\mathcal{B}$ as a set function assigning non-negative values to all events E in $\mathcal{B}$ such that the following conditions are satisfied:

1. $0 \leq P(E) \leq 1$ for all $E \in \mathcal{B}$.

2. $P(\Omega) = 1$.

3. For disjoint events, $E_1, E_2, E_3, \ldots$ (i.e., events for which $E_i \cap E_j = \Phi$ for all $i \neq j$,

where Φ is the null set), we have:

$$P\left(\bigcup_{i=1}^{\infty} E_i\right) = \sum_{i=1}^{\infty} P(E_i).$$

The triplet $(\Omega, \mathcal{B}, P)$ is called a *probability space.*

8.3.1 Joint Probability

The probability of the joint occurrence of two events A and B is referred to as the joint probability, $P(AB)$. Mathematically,

$$P(A \cap B) = P(AB) = \lim_{n\to\infty} \frac{n_{AB}}{n} \tag{8.8}$$

8.3.2 Equality of Events

Two events A and B are called *equal* if they consist of the same elements. They are called *equal with probability 1* if the set

$$(A \cup B)\,(\overline{AB}) = A\overline{B} \cup \overline{A}B$$

consisting of all outcomes that are in A or in B but not in AB, has zero probability.

8.3.3 Conditional Probability

The conditional probability of an event A assuming another event B, denoted by $P(A|B)$, is by definition, the ratio

$$P(A|B) = \frac{P(AB)}{P(B)} \tag{8.9}$$

where we assume that $P(B) \neq 0$. It follows that:

$$\text{If } B \subset A \text{ then } P(A|B) = 1 \tag{8.10}$$

because then $AB = B$. Similarly,

$$\text{If } A \subset B \text{ then } P(A|B) = \frac{P(A)}{P(B)} \geq P(A) \tag{8.11}$$

It follows from the definition of conditional probability that for events A and B,

$$P(AB) = P(A|B)P(B) = P(B|A)P(A) \tag{8.12}$$

This can be extended to more than two events. Thus for events A, B, and C,

$$P(ABC) = P(C|AB)P(AB) = P(C|AB)P(B|A)P(A) \tag{8.13}$$

In general, for N events, $A_1, A_2, \ldots, A_N$,

$$P(A_1A_2\ldots A_N) = P(A_N|A_1A_2\ldots A_{N-1})\times P(A_{N-1}|A_1A_2\ldots A_{N-2})\ldots\times P(A_2|A_1)P(A_1) \tag{8.14}$$

THEOREM 8.3:

For any events A and B such that $P(B) \neq 0$,

$$P(A|B) = \frac{P(B|A)P(A)}{P(B)} \tag{8.15}$$

PROOF:
From definition,

$$P(AB) = P(A|B)P(B) = P(B|A)P(A) \tag{8.16}$$

Theorem 8.3 follows directly by dividing the proceeding equations by $P(B)$.

THEOREM 8.4: THEOREM OF TOTAL PROBABILITY

Let $A_1, A_2, \ldots, A_N$ be a set of N mutually exclusive and exhaustive events. That is, $A_i \cap A_j = \Phi$ for all $i \neq j$ and

$$\bigcup_{i=1}^{N} A_i = S \Rightarrow \sum_{i=1}^{N} P(A_i) = 1 \tag{8.17}$$

Then

$$P(B) = \sum_{i=1}^{N} P(B|A_i)P(A_i) \tag{8.18}$$

PROOF:
A Venn diagram shown in Figure 8.1 is used here to visualise the result.

From the diagram, it can be seen that the event B can be written as

$$B = \{B\cap A_1\}\cup\{B\cap A_2\}\cup\ldots\cup\{B\cap A_N\} \tag{8.19}$$

$$\Rightarrow P(B) = P(\{B\cap A_1\}\cup\{B\cap A_2\}\cup\ldots\cup\{B\cap A_N\}) \tag{8.20}$$

Also, since the A_is are all mutually exclusive, the $\{B \cap A_i\}$s are also mutually exclusive, so that

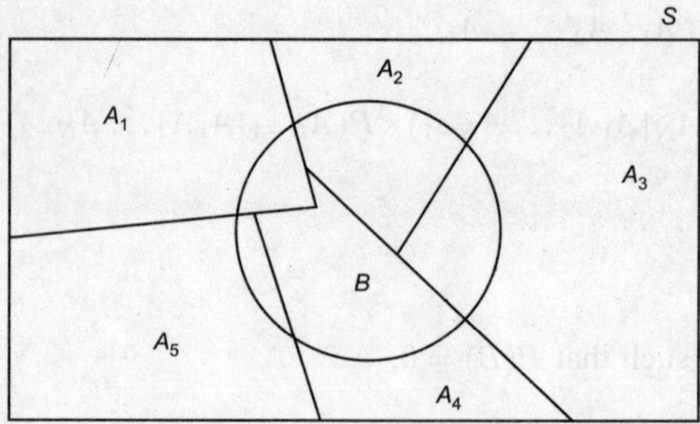

Figure 8.1 Venn diagram to prove the theorem of total probability

$$P(B) = \sum_{i=1}^{N} P(BA_i) \tag{8.21}$$

$$= \sum_{i=1}^{N} P(B|A_i)P(A_i) \tag{8.22}$$

Finally, combining the results of Theorems 8.3 and 8.4, we arrive at Bayes's theorem.

THEOREM 8.5: BAYES'S THEOREM

Let $A_1, A_2, \ldots, A_N$ be a set of N mutually exclusive and exhaustive events. Then,

$$P(A_i|B) = \frac{P(B|A_i)P(A_i)}{\sum\limits_{i=1}^{N} P(B|A_i)P(A_i)}. \tag{8.23}$$

The probability $P(A_i)$ is known as the *a priori*[2] probability of event A_i, whereas $P(A_i|B)$ is known as the *a posteriori*[3] probability of event A_i given B.

8.4 Statistical Independence of Events

Mathematically, two events A and B are *independent* if $P(A|B) = P(A)$.That is, *a priori* probability of event A is equal to the *a posteriori* probability of A given B. Note that if $P(A|B) = P(A)$, then the following two conditions also hold:

[2]The term *a priori* in Latin is translated as "from the former". In this context, it means probabilities that are formed from self-evident or pre-supposed models.

[3]The term *a posteriori* in Latin means "from the latter". In this context, it refers to probabilities that are derived or calculated after observing certain events.

$$P(B|A) = P(B) \tag{8.24}$$

$$P(AB) = P(A)P(B) \tag{8.25}$$

Furthermore, if $P(A|B) \neq P(A)$, then the other two conditions also do not hold.

THE STATISTICAL INDEPENDENCE OF EVENTS

Two events A and B are statistically independent if and only if $P(AB) = P(A)P(B)$.

8.5 Random Variables

Mathematically, a random variable is neither *random nor a variable*. It is a mapping from sample space into the real line ("real-valued" random variable) or the complex plane ("complex-valued" random variable). Suppose we have a probability space $\{S, \mathcal{R}, P\}$. Let $X : S \rightarrow \mathcal{R}$ be a function mapping the sample space S into the real line such that: for each $s \in S$, there exists a unique $X(s) \in \mathcal{R}$. Then X is called a random variable. Thus, a random variable associates the points in the sample space with real numbers.

8.6 The Discrete Random Variable

A *random variable* is a real-valued function of the elements of the sample space, S. Given an experiment, E, with sample space, S, the random variable X maps each possible outcome, $\xi \in S$, to a real number $X(\xi)$ as specified by some rule. If the mapping $X(\xi)$ is such that the random variable X takes on a finite or countably infinite number of values, then we call X as a *discrete random variable*, whereas, if the range of $X(\xi)$ is an uncountably infinite number of points, we refer to X as a *continuous random variable*. The range of values of x is usually denoted by $\{x_i\}$. A random variable X is called *discrete* if it takes values in some countable sub-set, $\{x_1, x_2, \ldots, x_n\}$, only, of the set of real numbers $\mathbb{R}$. In other words, a discrete random variable is a random variable whose sample space consists of integer values $n \in \{1, 2, 3, \ldots\}$.

Since $X = f(\xi)$ is a random variable whose numerical value depends on the outcome of a random experiment, we cannot describe the random variable by stating its value; rather we must give it a probabilistic description by stating the probabilities that the variable X takes on specific value or values (for example, $P(X = 3)$ or $P(X > 9)$).

8.6.1 The Probability Mass Function (PMF)

The *probability mass function*, $P_X(x)$, of a random variable, X, is a function that assigns a probability to each possible value of that random variable, X. The probability that the random variable X takes on the specific value x is the value of the probability mass function for x. Hence, we can write:

$$P_X(x) = P(X = x) \tag{8.26}$$

The convention is to use upper case letters for random variables, while lower case letters denote fixed values that the random variable can assume.

8.6.2 The Cumulative Distribution Function (CDF)

The *cumulative distribution function (CDF)* of a random variable X, denoted as $F_X(x)$, is defined as

$$F_X(x) = P(\xi \in S; X(\xi) \leq x) \tag{8.27}$$

which can be simply written as

$$F_X(x) = P(X \leq x) \tag{8.28}$$

The cumulative distribution function has the following important properties:

1. $0 \leq F_X(x) \leq 1$ (the cumulative distribution function is bounded by 0 and 1).
2. $\frac{dF_X(x)}{dx} \geq 0$ (that is, $F_X(x)$ is non-decreasing).
3. $\lim_{x \to -\infty} F_X(x) = 0$ and $\lim_{x \to +\infty} F_X(x) = 1$.
4. $F_X(x)$ is continuous from the right; i.e., $\lim_{\epsilon \to 0} F_X(x + \epsilon) = F_X(x)$.
5. $P(a < X \leq b) = F_X(b) - F_X(a)$.
6. $P(X = a) = F_X(a) - F_X(a^-)$.

For discrete random variables $F_X(x)$ is a staircase function, as illustrated in Figure 8.2.

The MATLAB script to generate the plot is given below.

```
%%% MATLAB script to plot CDF...
close all; clear all; clf;
t=[linspace(0,1,10),ones(1,8)];
subplot(311),stairs(t), axis([0 18 0 1.2]);
xlabel('x'); ylabel('P_{X}(x)');grid;
title('Cumulative Distribution Function (CDF)--Discrete.');
t=[linspace(0,1,80),ones(1,10)];
subplot(312),stairs(t), axis([0 90 0 1.2]);
xlabel('x'); ylabel('P_{X}(x)');grid;
```

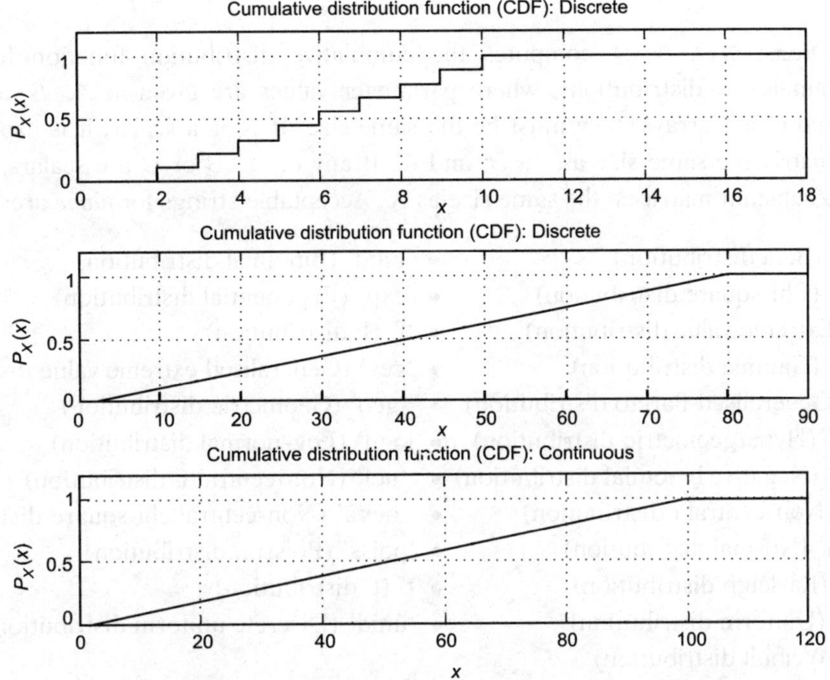

Figure 8.2 Cumulative distribution function (CDF)

```
title('Cumulative Distribution Function (CDF)--Discrete.');
t=[linspace(0,1,100),ones(1,20)];
subplot(313),plot(t), axis([0 120 0 1.2]);
xlabel('x'); ylabel('P_{X}(x)');grid;
title('Cumulative Distribution Function (CDF)--Continuous.');
%%% end of cdf.m
```

8.6.3 The `cdf(.)` Function in Statistics Toolbox

The Statistics Toolbox of MATLAB provides a very versatile function, `cdf(.)` to compute and plot various cumulative distribution functions.

`Y = cdf(name,X,A)` computes the cumulative distribution function for the one-parameter family of distributions specified by *name*. *A* contains parameter values for the distribution. The cumulative distribution function is evaluated at the values in *X* and its values are returned in *Y*.

`Y = cdf(name,X,A,B)` computes the cumulative distribution function for two-parameter families of distributions, where parameter values are given in *A* and *B*.

`Y = cdf(name,X,A,B,C)` computes the cumulative distribution function for three-parameter families of distributions, where parameter values are given in A, B, and C. If X, A, B, and C are arrays, they must be the same size. If X is a scalar, it is expanded to a constant matrix the same size as A, B, and C. If any of A, B or C are scalars, they are expanded to constant matrices, the same size as X. Acceptable strings for *name* are:

- 'beta' (Beta distribution)
- 'bino' (Binomial distribution)
- 'chi2' (Chi-square distribution)
- 'exp' (Exponential distribution)
- 'ev' (Extreme value distribution)
- 'f' (F distribution)
- 'gam' (Gamma distribution)
- 'gev' (Generalised extreme value distribution)
- 'gp' (Generalised Pareto distribution)
- 'geo' (Geometric distribution)
- 'hyge' (Hypergeometric distribution)
- 'logn' (Log-normal distribution)
- 'nbin' (Negative binomial distribution)
- 'ncf' (Non-central F distribution)
- 'nct' (Non-central t distribution)
- 'ncx2' (Non-central chi-square distribution)
- 'norm' (Normal distribution)
- 'poiss' (Poisson distribution)
- 'rayl' (Rayleigh distribution)
- 't' (t distribution)
- 'unif' (Uniform distribution)
- 'unid' (Discrete uniform distribution)
- 'wbl' (Weibull distribution)

8.7 The Continuous Random Variable

A random variable is called *continuous* if $F_X(x)$ is a continuous function. A random variable is called *mixed* if it is neither discrete nor continuous.

8.7.1 The Probability Density Function (PDF)

The *probability density function (PDF)* of a random variable X, denoted as $f_X(x)$, is defined as the first derivative of $F_X(x)$ with respect to x; i.e.,

$$f_X(x) \triangleq \frac{dF_X(x)}{dx} \tag{8.29}$$

In case of discrete or mixed random variables, the probability density function involves impulses. The most important and basic properties of probability density functions are listed below:

1. $f_X(x) \geq 0$ (that is, the probability density function is non-negative).
2. $\int\limits_{-\infty}^{\infty} f_X(x)dx = 1$.
3. $\int\limits_{a^+}^{b^+} f_X(x)dx = P(a < X \leq b)$.

4. In general, $P(X \in A) = \int\limits_A f_X(x)dx$.

5. $F_X(x) = \int\limits_{-\infty}^{x^+} f_X(u)du$.

For discrete random variables, we define the equivalent, *probability mass function (PMF)*, which is defined as $\{p_i\}$, where $p_i = P(X = x_i)$. Obviously for all i, we have $p_i \geq 0$ and $\sum\limits_i p_i = 1$.

8.7.2 The `pdf(.)` Function in Statistics Toolbox

The Statistics Toolbox of MATLAB provides another versatile function, `pdf(.)` to compute and plot various probability density functions.

`Y = pdf(name,X,A)` computes the probability density function for the one-parameter family of distributions specified by *name*. Parameter values for the distribution are given in A. Densities are evaluated at the values in X and returned in Y.

`Y = pdf(name,X,A,B)` computes the probability density function for two-parameter families of distributions, where parameter values are given in A and B.

`Y = pdf(name,X,A,B,C)` computes the probability density function for three-parameter families of distributions, where parameter values are given in A, B, and C. If X, A, B, and C are arrays, they must be the same size. If X is a scalar, it is expanded to a constant matrix, the same size as A, B, and C. If any of A, B or C are scalars, they are expanded to constant matrices, the same size as X. Acceptable strings for *name* are the same as for the `cdf(.)` function. Y is the common size of X, A, B, and C after necessary scalar expansion.

8.8 Some Discrete Random Variables

There are several commonly occurring discrete random variables used in the modelling and simulation of communication systems, as described below. The discrete random variables are generally specified by their respective probability mass functions and their cumulative distribution functions. The most important statistical parameters of random variables are their *mean* and *variance*.

8.8.1 The Bernoulli Random Variable

This a discrete random variable taking two values, *one* and *zero*, with probabilities p and $(1-p)$. A Bernoulli random variable is a good model for a binary data generator. It can also be used to model channel errors. The probability mass function (PMF) for the Bernoulli random variable is illustrated in Figure 8.3.

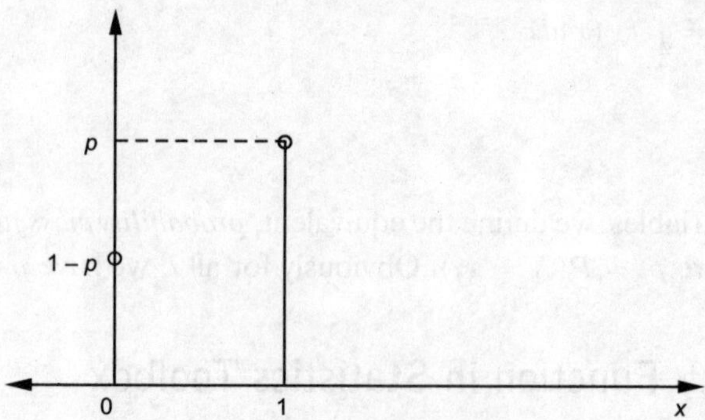

Figure 8.3 The PMF of a Bernoulli random variable

8.8.2 The Binomial Random Variable

This is a discrete random variable giving the number of 1s in a sequence of n independent Bernoulli trials. The probability mass function is given by

$$P(X=k)=\begin{cases}\begin{pmatrix} n \\ k \end{pmatrix} p^k(1-p)^{n-k}, & 0\leq k\leq n\\ 0, \text{otherwise.} & \end{cases} \tag{8.30}$$

This random variable models, for example, the total number of bits received in error when a sequence of n bits is transmitted over a channel with bit error probability of p. The PMF of a binomial random variable is illustrated in Figure 8.4. The MATLAB script M-file to generate the same is also given below.

```
%%% M-file to plot the PMF of Binomial Random Variable..
clear all; close all; clf;
n=12;
p=0.3;
for k=0:n
    P(k+1)=nchoosek(n,k)*p^k*(1-p)^(n-k);
end;
stem(P), xlabel('x'), ylabel('PMF');grid;
title('Probability Mass Function for Binomial Trials');
%%% end of bino.m
```

It can be shown that the binomial PMF is properly normalised. That is:

$$\sum_{k=0}^{n}\begin{pmatrix} n \\ k \end{pmatrix} p^k(1-p)^{n-k}=(p+1-p)^n=1 \tag{8.31}$$

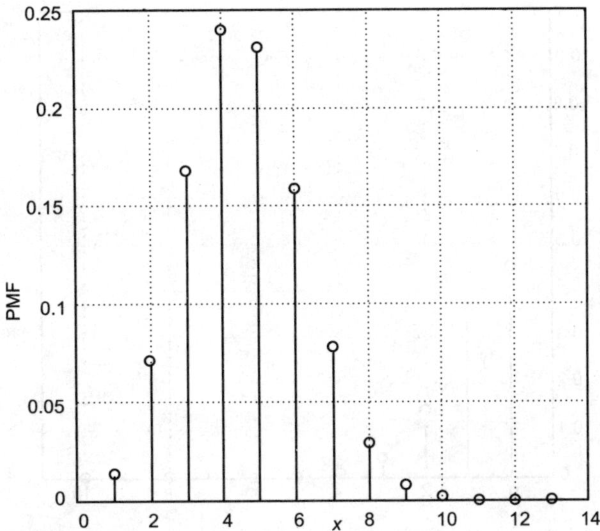

Figure 8.4 The PMF of a binomial random variable

8.8.3 The Poisson Random Variable

Consider a binomial random variable, X, where the number of repeated trials, n, is very large. In this case if the probability of success p is very small, then the binomial random variable can be approximated by the Poisson random variable. That is, the *Poisson random variable is a limiting case of the binomial random variable.* Mathematically, let n approach ∞ and p approach zero in a way that $\lim_{n\to\infty} np = \alpha$. Thus, the Poisson random variable is given by the probability mass function

$$P_X(x) = \frac{\alpha^m}{m!}e^{-\alpha} \tag{8.32}$$

We can show that the Poisson random variable is properly normalised by noting that

$$\sum_{m=0}^{\infty} \frac{\alpha^m}{m!}e^{-\alpha} = 1 \tag{8.33}$$

The PMF of the Poisson random variable is illustrated in Figure 8.5. The MATLAB script to generate the same is given below.

```
%%% MATLAB script to generate and
% plot Poisson probability mass function..
clear all; close all; clf;
a=0.8;
m=[0:10];
```

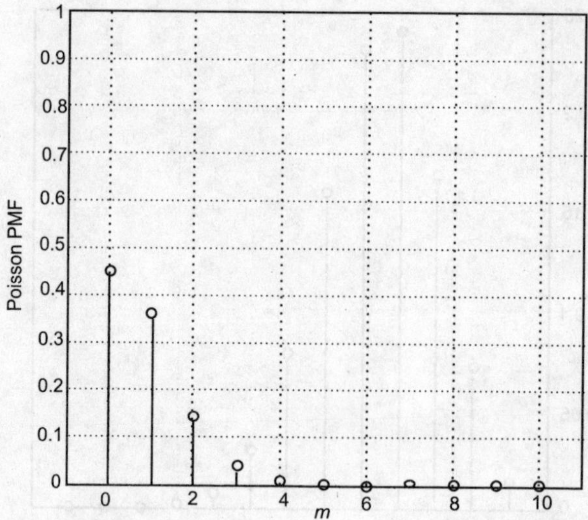

Figure 8.5 The PMF of a Poisson random variable

```
ppmf=(a.^m./factorial(m)).*exp(-a);
stem(m, ppmf, 'LineWidth', 2); xlabel('m');
ylabel('The Poisson PMF');grid;
title('The Poisson Probability Mass Function')
axis([-1 11 0 1]);
%%% end of poisson.m
```

The Poisson random variable is extremely important as it describes the behaviour of many physical phenomena. It is very commonly used in *queueing theory* and in communication networks. The number of telephone calls originating at a telephone exchange can be modelled as a Poisson random variable. Similarly, the number of customers arriving at a store during some time interval may be well modelled as a Poisson random variable. So is the case of the number of data packets arriving at a given node in a computer network.

8.8.4 The Geometric Random Variable

Consider repeating a Bernoulli trial until the first occurrence of the outcome ξ_0. If X represents the number of times the outcome ξ_1 occurs before the first occurrence of ξ_0, then X is a *geometric random variable*, whose probability mass function is given by

$$P_X(k) = (1-p)p^k, \quad k = 0, 1, 2, \ldots \tag{8.34}$$

Equation (8.34) can be derived as shown below. Suppose that the independent Bernoulli trials are performed at times $1, 2, \ldots$. Let τ_w be the time elapsed before the first success. We now call τ_w as the waiting time. Then, we have:

$$P(\tau_w > k) = (1-p)^k; p \in (0,1).$$

Thus we have:

$$P(\tau_w = k) = P(\tau_w > k-1) - P(\tau_w > k) = p(1-p)^{k-1}; k = 1, 2, \ldots \tag{8.35}$$

The PMF of the geometric random variable is illustrated in Figure 8.6.

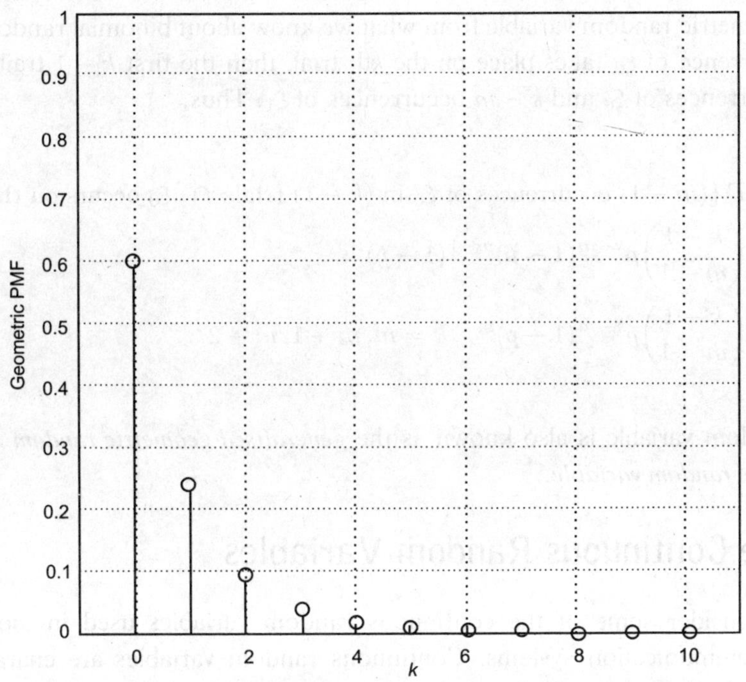

Figure 8.6 The PMF of a geometric random variable

The MATLAB script to generate and plot the geometric probability mass function is given below.

```
%%% MATLAB script to generate and
% plot Geometric PMF...
clear all; close all; clf;
p=0.4;
k=[0:10];
gpmf=(1-p).*p.^k;
stem(k,gpmf,'LineWidth',2);
```

```
xlabel('k'); ylabel('Geometric PMF');grid;
title('The Geometric Probability Mass Function');
axis([-1 11 0 1]);
%%% end of geome.m
```

8.8.5 The Pascal Random Variable

The geometric random variable can be generalised to the case where the outcome ξ_0 must occur exactly m times. We can derive the form of the probability mass function for the generalised geometric random variable from what we know about binomial random variables. If the mth occurrence of ξ_0 takes place on the kth trial, then the first $k-1$ trails must have had $m-1$ occurrences of ξ_0 and $k-m$ occurrences of ξ_1. Thus,

$$\begin{aligned} P_X(x) &= P\{(m-1) \text{ occurrences of } \xi_0 \text{ in } (k-1) \text{ trials} \cap \ \xi_0 \text{ occurs on the } k\text{th trial}\} \\ &= \binom{k-1}{m-1} p^{k-m}(1-p)^{m-1}(1-p) \\ &= \binom{k-1}{m-1} p^{k-m}(1-p)^{m}, \quad k = m, m+1, m+2, \ldots \end{aligned} \tag{8.36}$$

The Pascal random variable is also known as the *generalised geometric random variable* and *negative binomial random variable*.

8.9 Some Continuous Random Variables

We will now consider some of the continuous random variables used in modelling and simulation of communication systems. Continuous random variables are characterised by their respective cumulative distribution functions and probability density functions.

8.9.1 The Gaussian Random Variable

The Gaussian random variable is probably the most commonly used variable in communication systems and the most important. It is also known as the normal random variable. The *thermal noise* encountered in electronic circuits can be modelled as a Gaussian random variable. The probability density function of the Gaussian random variable is given by

$$f_X(x) = \frac{1}{\sqrt{2\pi\sigma^2}} \exp\left(-\frac{(x-\mu)^2}{2\sigma^2}\right) \tag{8.37}$$

The probability density function of a Gaussian random variable has two parameters, μ and σ, which are the *mean* and *standard deviation* of the random variable, X. The parameter

σ^2 is known as the *variance*. A plot of the Gaussian probability density function and the corresponding cumulative distribution function is shown in Figure 8.7. The MATLAB script to generate the same is given below.

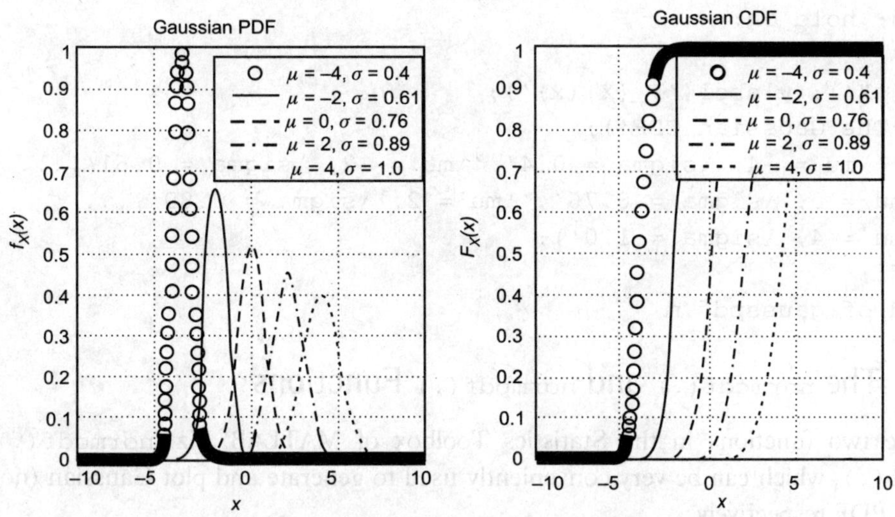

Figure 8.7 The Gaussian (normal) PDF and CDF

```
%%% MATLAB script to generate and
% plot Gaussian PDF and CDF..
close all; clear all; clf;
sig=sqrt(linspace(0.16,1,5));
m=linspace(-4,4,5);
clr=['o-','-.','+-','-o','-*'];
x=[-10:.05:10];
for i=1:length(sig)
fX=1/(sqrt(2*pi*sig(i)^2))*exp(-(x-m(i)).^2/(2*sig(i)^2));
subplot(121),plot(x,fX,clr(i),'LineWidth',2);
grid on;hold on;
end;
xlabel('X'); ylabel('f_{X}(x)');
title('The Gaussian PDF');
legend('\mu = -4, \sigma = 0.4','\mu = -2,\sigma = 0.61',...
    '\mu = 0, \sigma = 0.76','\mu = 2, \sigma = 0.89',...
    '\mu = 4, \sigma = 1.0');
for i=1:length(sig)
% FX=0.5*erfc(-x/sqrt(2));
```

```
FX=normcdf(x,m(i),sig(i));
% The normcdf(.) is available only in
% Statistics Toolbox of MATLAB....
subplot(122),plot(x,FX,clr(i),'LineWidth',2);
grid on; hold on;
end;
xlabel('X'); ylabel('F_{X}(x)');
title('The Gaussian CDF');
legend('\mu = -4, \sigma = 0.4','\mu = -2, \sigma = 0.61',...
    '\mu = 0, \sigma = 0.76','\mu = 2, \sigma = 0.89',...
    '\mu = 4, \sigma = 1.0');
hold off;
%%% end of gausspdf.m
```

8.9.2 The `normcdf(.)` and `normpdf(.)` Functions

There are two functions in the Statistics Toolbox of MATLAB, viz. `normcdf(.)` and `normpdf(.)`, which can be very conveniently used to generate and plot Gaussian (normal) CDF and PDF respectively.

`Y = normpdf(X,mu,sigma)` computes the PDF at each of the values in X using the normal distribution with mean μ and standard deviation σ. X, μ, and σ can be vectors, matrices, or multi-dimensional arrays that all have the same size. A scalar input is expanded to a constant array with the same dimensions as the other inputs. The parameters in σ must be positive.

In general, the Gaussian probability density function is centred about the point $x = \mu$ and has a width that is proportional to σ. Since the Gaussian random variable is so common, it is a standard practice to denote a Gaussian (normal) distributed random variable as $X \sim N(\mu, \sigma^2)$. This is read as "X distributed normally (or Gaussian) with mean μ and variance σ^2". The cumulative distribution function of the Gaussian random variable is given by

$$F_X(x) = \int_{-\infty}^{x} \frac{1}{\sqrt{2\pi\sigma^2}} \exp\left(-\frac{(y-\mu)^2}{2\sigma^2}\right) dy \tag{8.38}$$

It is impossible to express the above integral in a closed form. However, the required cumulative distribution function can be converted to one of the few commonly used standard forms. A few of them are listed below:

- error function integral, $\text{erf}(x) \triangleq \frac{2}{\sqrt{\pi}} \int_{0}^{x} \exp\left(-t^2\right) dt$.

- complimentary error function integral, $\text{erfc}(x) \triangleq 1 - \text{erf}(x) = \frac{2}{\sqrt{\pi}} \int_x^{\infty} \exp\left(-t^2\right) dt.$
- Φ function, $\Phi(x) \triangleq \frac{1}{\sqrt{2\pi}} \int_{-\infty}^{x} \exp\left(-\frac{t^2}{2}\right) dt.$
- Q function, $Q(x) \triangleq \frac{1}{\sqrt{2\pi}} \int_{x}^{\infty} \exp\left(-\frac{t^2}{2}\right) dt.$

We can show that the cumulative distribution function of a Gaussian random variable can be expressed as the Φ function, by making the transformation, $t = (y - \mu)/\sigma$.

$$
\begin{aligned}
F_X(x) &= \int_{-\infty}^{x} \frac{1}{\sqrt{2\pi\sigma^2}} \exp\left(-\frac{(y-\mu)^2}{2\sigma^2}\right) dy \\
&= \frac{1}{\sqrt{2\pi}} \int_{-\infty}^{\frac{x-\mu}{\sigma}} \exp\left(-\frac{t^2}{2}\right) dt \\
&= \Phi\left(\frac{x-\mu}{\sigma}\right)
\end{aligned}
$$

Thus to evaluate the cumulative distribution function of a Gaussian random variable, we only have to evaluate the Φ function at the points $(x - \mu)/\sigma$. Similarly, we can show that

$$P(X > x) = \frac{1}{\sqrt{2\pi}} \int_{\frac{x-\mu}{\sigma}}^{\infty} \exp\left(-\frac{t^2}{2}\right) dt = Q\left(\frac{x-\mu}{\sigma}\right) \tag{8.39}$$

Therefore, it is evident that $P(X > x) = 1 - P(X \leq x)$, which implies that

$$Q(x) = 1 - \Phi(x) \tag{8.40}$$

Thus, we infer that the cumulative distribution function of a Gaussian random variable is given by

$$F_X(x) = \Phi\left(\frac{x-\mu}{\sigma}\right) = 1 - Q\left(\frac{x-\mu}{\sigma}\right) \tag{8.41}$$

The `randn(.)` Function in MATLAB

The `randn(.)` function in MATLAB can be used to generate random vectors/matrices of any size. For example, `randn(1,N)` generates a row vector of N Gaussian (normal) distributed random vectors, between $-\infty$ and $+\infty$. The variance and mean of the random vector tends to 1 and 0 respectively, as $N \to \infty$.

The `y=randn(method,s)` causes `randn` to use the generator determined by *method*, and initialises the state of that generator using the value of s.

The value of s is dependent upon which method is selected. If *method* is set to "state" or "twister", then s must be either a scalar integer value from 0 to $2^{32}-1$ or the output of `randn(method)`. If method is set to "seed", then s must be either a scalar integer value from 0 to $2^{31}-2$ or the output of `randn(method)`.

8.9.3 The Log-normal Random Variable

A random variable Y has a log-normal distribution if $X = \ln(Y)$ has a normal distribution. Suppose that X has a normal distribution with mean μ and standard deviation, σ. The probability density function for X is

$$f_X(x) = \frac{1}{\sqrt{2\pi}\sigma} \exp\left(-\frac{(X-\mu)^2}{2\sigma^2}\right). \tag{8.42}$$

The probability density function for Y is therefore

$$f_Y(y) = \frac{1}{\sqrt{2\pi}\sigma Y} \exp\left(-\frac{[\ln Y-\mu]^2}{2\sigma^2}\right). \tag{8.43}$$

A plot of the log-normal probability density function and the corresponding cumulative distribution function is shown in Figure 8.8. The MATLAB script to generate the same is given below.

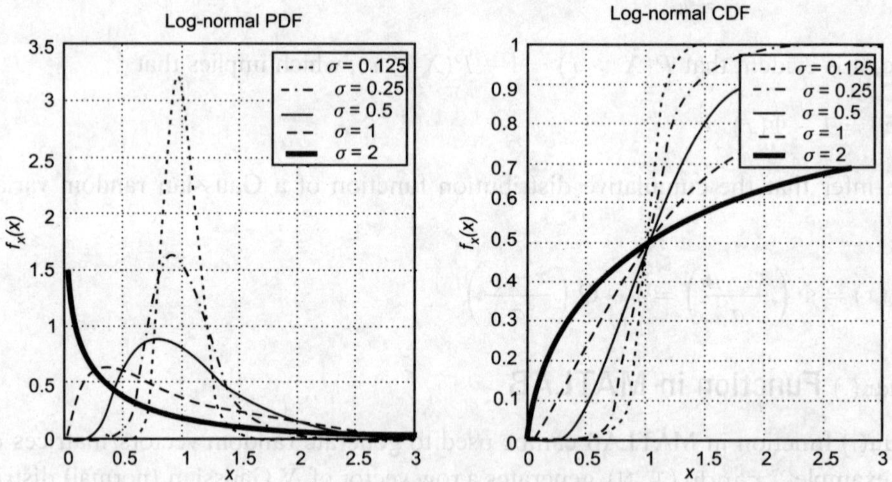

Figure 8.8 The PDF and CDF of a log-normal random variable

```
%%% MATLAB script to generate and
% plot Log-normal    PDF and CDF .
```

```
close all; clear all; clf;
mu=0;
sig=[0.125, 0.25, 0.5, 1, 2];
x=[0:.001:3];
clr=['-o-','-.-','-+-','--','-*-'];
for i=1:length(sig)
fX= 1./(x*sig(i)*sqrt(2*pi)).*exp(-(log(x)...
    -mu^2).^2/(2*sig(i)^2));
subplot(121),plot(x,fX,clr(i),'LineWidth',2);
grid on;hold on;
end;
xlabel('X'); ylabel('f_{X}(x)');
title('The Log-normal PDF');
legend('\sigma = 0.125', '\sigma = 0.25',...
    '\sigma = 0.5', '\sigma = 1','\sigma = 2');
for i=1:length(sig)
FX=0.5+0.5*erf( (log(x)-mu)/(sig(i)*sqrt(2)));
subplot(122),plot(x,FX,clr(i),'LineWidth',2);
grid on;hold on;
 end;
xlabel('X'); ylabel('F_{X}(x)');
title('The Log-normal CDF');
legend('\sigma = 0.125', '\sigma = 0.25',...
    '\sigma = 0.5', '\sigma = 1','\sigma = 2');
hold off;
%%% end of lognormal.m
```

In probability and statistics, the log-normal distribution is the single-tailed probability distribution of any random variable whose logarithm is normally distributed. If X is a random variable with a normal distribution, then $Y = \exp X$ has a log-normal distribution; likewise, if Y is log-normally distributed, then $\log Y$ is normally distributed. (The base of the logarithmic function does not matter: if $\log_a Y$ is normally distributed, then so is $\log_b Y$, for any two positive numbers $a, b \neq 1$.)

A random variable might be modelled as log-normal if it can be thought of as the multiplicative product of many small independent factors. For example, the long-term return rate on a stock investment can be considered to be the product of the daily return rates. In wireless communication, the attenuation caused by shadowing or slow fading from random objects is often assumed to be log-normally distributed.

8.9.4 The Uniform Random Variable

The *uniform* probability density function is *constant* over an interval $[a, b)$. The probability density function is given by

$$f_X(x) = \begin{cases} \frac{1}{b-a} & a \le x < b, \\ 0 & \text{elsewhere} \end{cases} \tag{8.44}$$

The cumulative distribution function of a uniform random variable is given by

$$F_X(x) = \begin{cases} 0 & x < a, \\ \frac{x-a}{b-a} & a \le x < b, \\ 1 & x \ge b. \end{cases} \tag{8.45}$$

The probability density function and cumulative distribution function of a uniform random variable are illustrated in Figure 8.9.

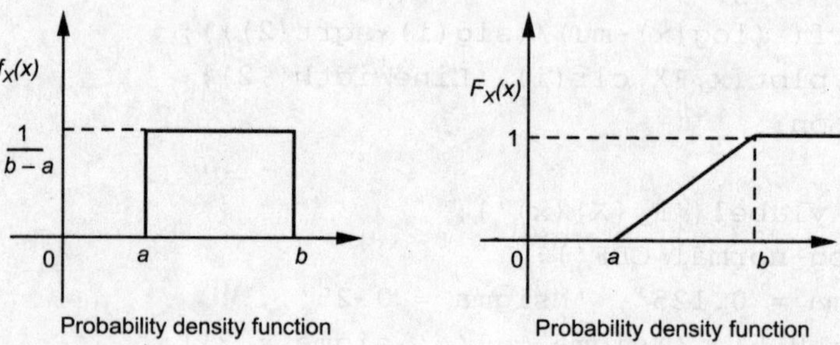

Figure 8.9 The probability density and cumulative distribution functions of a uniform random variable

An example of a uniformly distributed random variable is the *phase* of a radio frequency sinusoid in a communication system.

The `rand(.)` Function in MATLAB

The `rand(.)` function in MATLAB can be used to generate *uniformly distributed* random vectors/matrices of any size. For example, `rand(1,N)` generates a row vector of N uniformly distributed random numbers between 0 and 1. The variance of the random vector tends to $\frac{1}{12}$ and mean to 0.5, as $N \to \infty$.

`y=rand(method,s)` causes `randn` to use the generator determined by *method*, and initialises the state of that generator using the value of s

The value of s is dependent upon which method is selected. If *method* is set to "state", then s must be either a scalar integer value from 0 to $2^{32} - 1$ or the output of `rand(method)`. If method is set to "seed", then s must be either a scalar integer value from 0 to $2^{31} - 2$ or the output of `rand(method)`. To set the generator to its default initial state, set s equal to zero.

The `randn` and `rand` generators each maintain their own internal state information. Initialising the state of one has no effect on the other.

`s = randn(method)` returns in s the current internal state of the generator selected by *method*. It does not change the generator being used.

8.9.5 The Exponential Random Variable

The exponential random variable has a probability density function and cumulative distribution function given by (for $b > 0$)

$$f_X(x) = \frac{1}{b} \exp\left(-\frac{x}{b}\right) u(x) \tag{8.46}$$

$$F_X(x) = \left[1 - \exp\left(-\frac{x}{b}\right)\right] u(x) \tag{8.47}$$

A plot of the PDF and the CDF of an exponential random variable is illustrated in Figure 8.10. The MATLAB script to generate the same is given below.

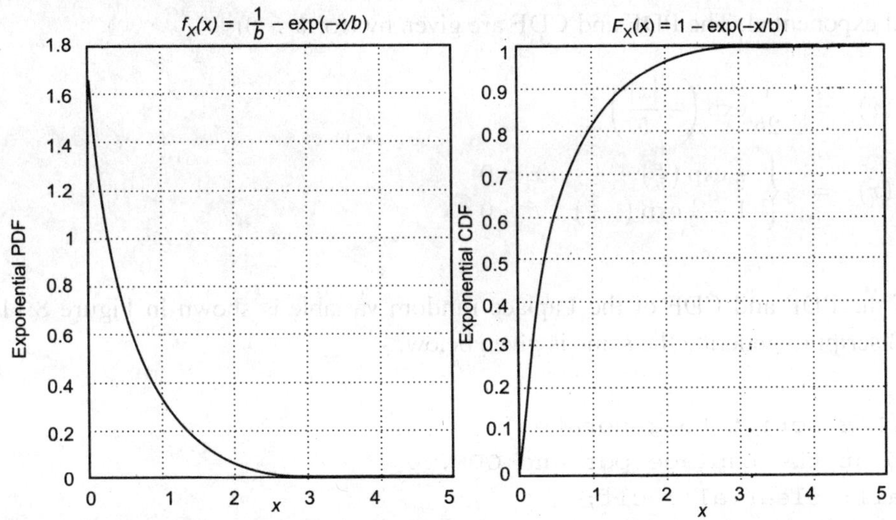

Figure 8.10 The PDF and CDF of an exponential random variable

```
%%% MATLAB script to generate
% and plot the exponential PDF and CDF...
close all; clear all; clf;
b=0.6;
x=linspace(0,5,100);
fX=1/b.*exp(-x/b);
FX=1-exp(-x/b);
subplot(121),plot(x,fX,'LineWidth',2);
xlabel('X'); ylabel('The Exponential PDF');
grid on;
title('$f_{X}(x)= \frac{1}{b}\exp(-x/b)$');
subplot(122),plot(x,FX,'LineWidth',2);
xlabel('X'); ylabel('The Exponential CDF');
grid on;
title('$F_{X}(x)=1-\exp(-x/b)$');
%%% end of exppdf.m
```

Exponential random variables are commonly encountered in the study of queueing systems. The time between arrivals (the inter-arrival time) of customers at a bank, for example, is commonly modelled as an exponential random variable. Similarly, the duration of voice calls in a telephone system can also be modelled as an exponential random variable.

8.9.6 The Laplace Random Variable

The Laplace random variable has a probability density function which takes the form of a two-sided exponential. The PDF and CDF are given by (for $b > 0$)

$$f_X(x) = \frac{1}{2b}\exp\left(-\frac{|x|}{b}\right) \tag{8.48}$$

$$F_X(x) = \begin{cases} \frac{1}{2}\exp\left(\frac{x}{b}\right) & x < 0 \\ 1 - \frac{1}{2}\exp\left(-\frac{x}{b}\right) & x \geq 0 \end{cases} \tag{8.49}$$

A plot of the PDF and CDF of the Laplace random variable is shown in Figure 8.11. The MATLAB script to generate the same is given below.

```
%%% MATLAB script to generate
% and plot the Laplace pdf and CDF...
close all; clear all; clf;
b=0.6;
x=linspace(-5,5,101);
```

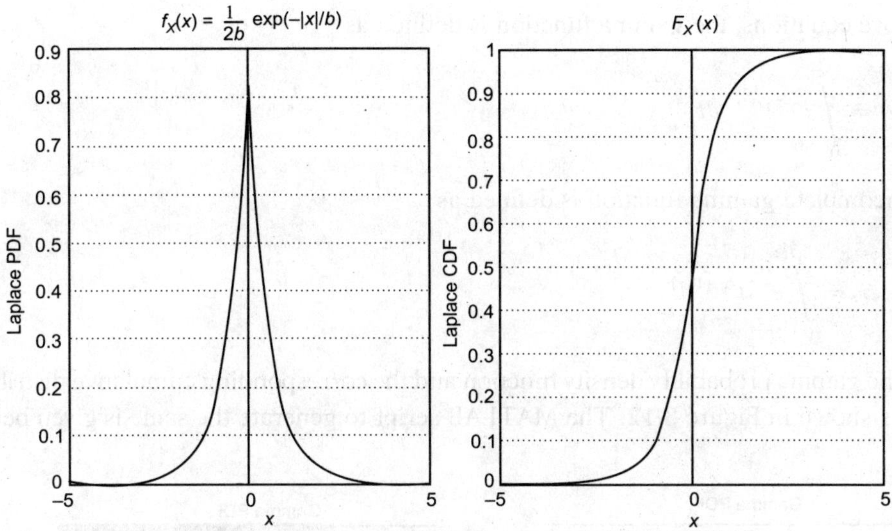

Figure 8.11 The PDF and CDF of a Laplace random variable

```
fX=1/(2*b).*exp(-abs(x)/b);
FX1=0.5*exp(x(1:50)/b);
FX2=1-0.5*exp(-x(51:101)/b);
FX=[FX1,FX2];
subplot(121),plot(x,fX,'LineWidth',2);
xlabel('X'); ylabel('The Laplace PDF');grid;
title('$f_{X}(x)= \frac{1}{2b}\exp(-|x|/b)$');
subplot(122),plot(x,FX,'LineWidth',2);
xlabel('X'); ylabel('The Laplace CDF');grid;
title('$F_{X}(x)$');
%%% end of laplap.m
```

The Laplace random variable is commonly used to model the speech signal.

8.9.7 The Gamma Random Variable

The gamma random variable has the PDF and CDF given by (for any $b > 0$ and any $c > 0$)

$$f_X(x) = \frac{\left(\frac{x}{b}\right)^{c-1}\exp\left(-\frac{x}{b}\right)}{b\Gamma(c)}u(x) \tag{8.50}$$

$$F_X(x) = \frac{\gamma(c, x/b)}{\Gamma(c)}u(x) \tag{8.51}$$

In the above equations, the gamma function is defined as

$$\Gamma(\alpha) = \int_0^\infty e^{-t}t^{\alpha-1}dt \tag{8.52}$$

and the incomplete gamma function is defined as

$$\gamma(\alpha, \beta) = \int_0^\beta e^{-t}t^{\alpha-1}dt \tag{8.53}$$

A plot of the gamma probability density function and the corresponding cumulative distribution function is shown in Figure 8.12. The MATLAB script to generate the same is given below.

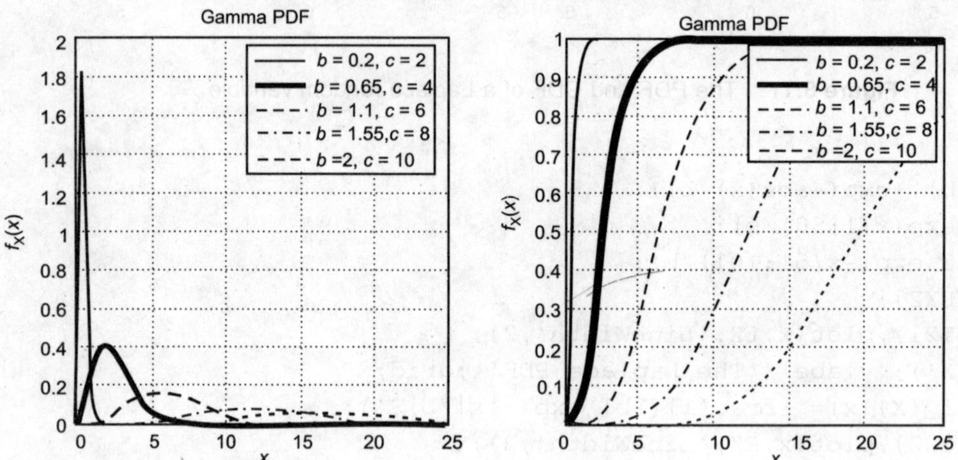

Figure 8.12 The gamma PDF and CDF

```
%%% MATLAB script to generate and
% plot Gamma   pdf and CDF..
close all; clear all; clf;
b=linspace(0.2,2,5);
c=linspace(2,10,5);
x=[0:.001:25];
clr=['-o-','-.-','-+-','--','-x-'];
for i=1:length(b)
fX=   (x/b(i)).^(c(i)-1).*exp(-x/b(i))/...
      (b(i)*gamma(c(i)));
subplot(121),plot(x,fX,clr(i),'LineWidth',2);
```

```
grid on;hold on;
end;
xlabel('X'); ylabel('f_{X}(x)');
title('The Gamma PDF');
legend('b = 0.2, c = 2', 'b = 0.65, c = 4',...
    'b = 1.1, c = 6', 'b = 1.55, c = 8', ...
    'b = 2, c = 10');
for i=1:length(b)
FX= gammainc(x/b(i),c(i));
subplot(122),plot(x,FX,clr(i),'LineWidth',2);
grid on;hold on;
 end;
xlabel('X'); ylabel('F_{X}(x)');
title('The Gamma CDF');
legend('b = 0.2, c = 2', 'b = 0.65, c = 4',...
    'b = 1.1, c = 6', 'b = 1.55, c = 8', ...
    'b = 2, c = 10');
hold off;
%%% end of gammapdf.m
```

The gamma random variable finds applications in queueing theory.

8.9.8 The Erlang Random Variable

If the parameter c in the gamma random variable is an integer, we get the *Erlang random variable*. The PDF and CDF are given below: (for positive integer n and any $b > 0$)

$$f_X(x) = \frac{\left(\frac{x}{b}\right)^{n-1}\exp\left(-\frac{x}{b}\right)}{b(n-1)!}u(x) \tag{8.54}$$

$$F_X(x) = \left[1 - \exp\left(-\frac{x}{b}\right)\sum_{m=0}^{n-1}\frac{(x/b)^m}{m!}\right]u(x). \tag{8.55}$$

A plot of the Erlang probability density function and the corresponding cumulative distribution function is shown in Figure 8.13. The MATLAB script to generate the same is given below.

```
%%% MATLAB script to generate and
% plot Erlang  PDF and CDF..
close all; clear all; clf;
b=linspace(0.2,2,5);
n=linspace(2,10,5);
x=[0:.001:25];
clr=['-o-','-.-','-+-','--','-x-'];
```

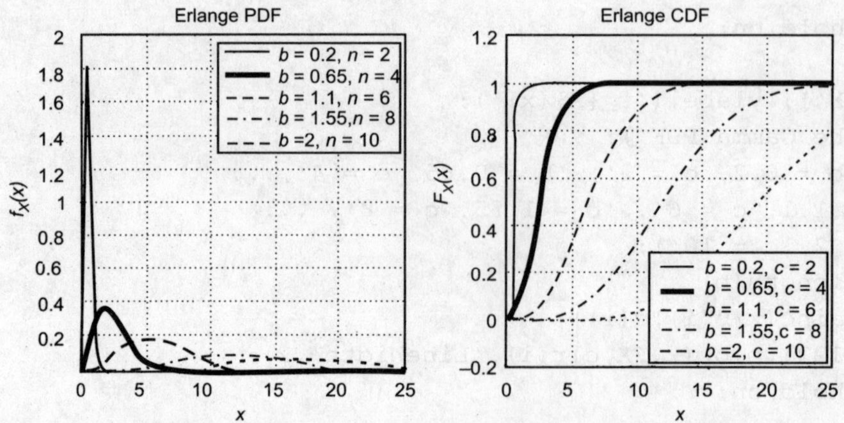

Figure 8.13 The Erlang PDF and CDF

```
for i=1:length(b)
fX=  (x/b(i)).^(n(i)-1).*exp(-x/b(i))/...
    (b(i)*factorial(n(i)-1));
subplot(121),plot(x,fX,clr(i),'LineWidth',2);
grid on;hold on;
end;
xlabel('X'); ylabel('f_{X}(x)');
title('The Erlang PDF');
legend('b = 0.2, n = 2', 'b = 0.65, n = 4',...
    'b = 1.1, n = 6', 'b = 1.55, n = 8', ...
    'b = 2, n = 10');
for i=1:length(b)
    s=ones(1,length(x));
    for m=1:n(i)-1
        s=s+(x/b(i)).^m/factorial(m);
    end;
    FX= 1-exp(-x/b(i)).*s;
subplot(122),plot(x,FX,clr(i),'LineWidth',2);
grid on;hold on;
 end;
xlabel('X'); ylabel('F_{X}(x)');
title('The Erlang CDF');
legend('b = 0.2, c = 2', 'b = 0.65, c = 4',...
    'b = 1.1, c = 6', 'b = 1.55, c = 8', ...
    'b = 2, c = 10');
hold off;
```

```
%%% end of erlangpd.m
```

The Erlang distribution plays a key role in the study of wireless communication networks. The amount of traffic in a trunked telephone network is measured in *Erlangs*.

8.9.9 The χ^2 Random Variable

In a gamma random variable, when the parameter $b = 2$ and c is a half integer, we get the χ^2*-random variable*. The PDF and CDF are as shown below:

$$fx(x) = \frac{x^{c-1}\exp\left(-\frac{x}{2}\right)}{2^c\Gamma(c)}u(x) \tag{8.56}$$

$$Fx(x) = \frac{\gamma(c, x/2)}{\Gamma(c)}u(x) \tag{8.57}$$

A plot of the χ^2 probability density function and the corresponding cumulative distribution function is shown in Figure 8.14. The MATLAB script to generate the same is given below.

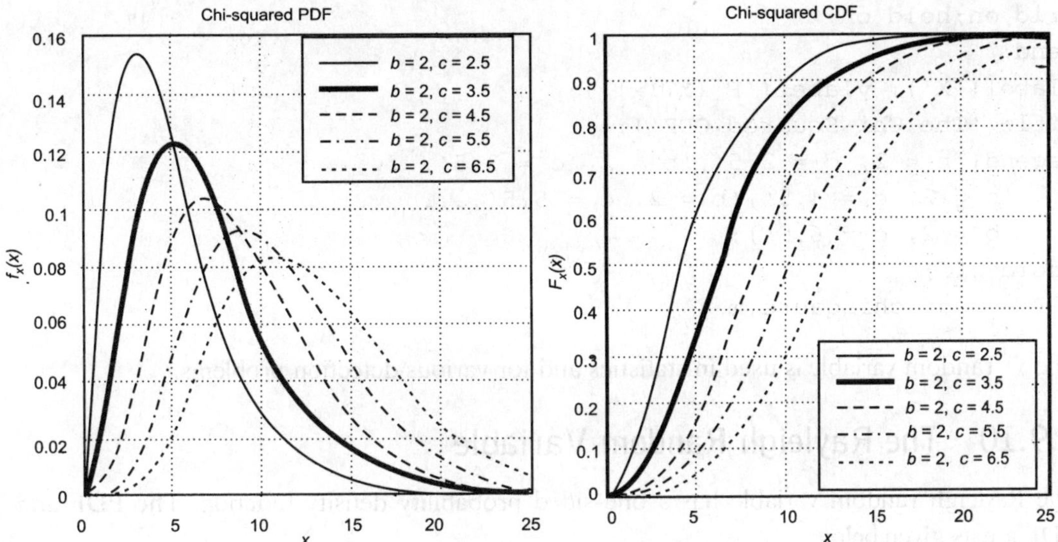

Figure 8.14 The χ^2 PDF and CDF

```
%%% MATLAB script to generate and
% plot Chi-squared  PDF and CDF..
close all; clear all; clf;
b= 2;%% For Chi-Squared PDF,
```

```
% b is set to 2 in Gamma PDF..
c=[2.5:6.5];
x=[0:.001:25];
clr=['-o-','-.-','-+-','--','-x-'];
for i=1:length(c)
fX=  x.^(c(i)-1).*exp(-x/2)/...
     (2^c(i)*gamma(c(i)));
subplot(121),plot(x,fX,clr(i),'LineWidth',2);
grid on;hold on;
end;
xlabel('X'); ylabel('f_{X}(x)');
title('The Chi-Squared PDF');
legend('b = 2, c = 2.5','b = 2, c = 3.5',...
     'b = 2, c = 4.5','b = 2, c = 5.5',...
     'b = 2, c = 6.5');
for i=1:length(c)
 FX=gammainc(x/2,c(i));
subplot(122),plot(x,FX,clr(i),'LineWidth',2);
grid on;hold on;
 end;
xlabel('X'); ylabel('F_{X}(x)');
title('The Chi-Squared CDF');
legend('b = 2, c = 2.5','b = 2, c = 3.5',...
     'b = 2, c = 4.5','b = 2, c = 5.5',...
     'b = 2, c = 6.5');
 hold off;
%%% end of chisqaure.m
```

The χ^2 random variable is used in statistics and for various detection problems.

8.9.10 The Rayleigh Random Variable

The Rayleigh random variable has a one-sided probability density function. The PDF and CDF are as given below:

$$f_X(x) = \frac{x}{\sigma^2}\exp\left(-\frac{x^2}{2\sigma^2}\right)u(x). \tag{8.58}$$

$$F_X(x) = \left[1-\exp\left(-\frac{x^2}{2\sigma^2}\right)\right]u(x). \tag{8.59}$$

A plot of the PDF and CDF are shown in Figure 8.15. The MATLAB script to generate the same is given below.

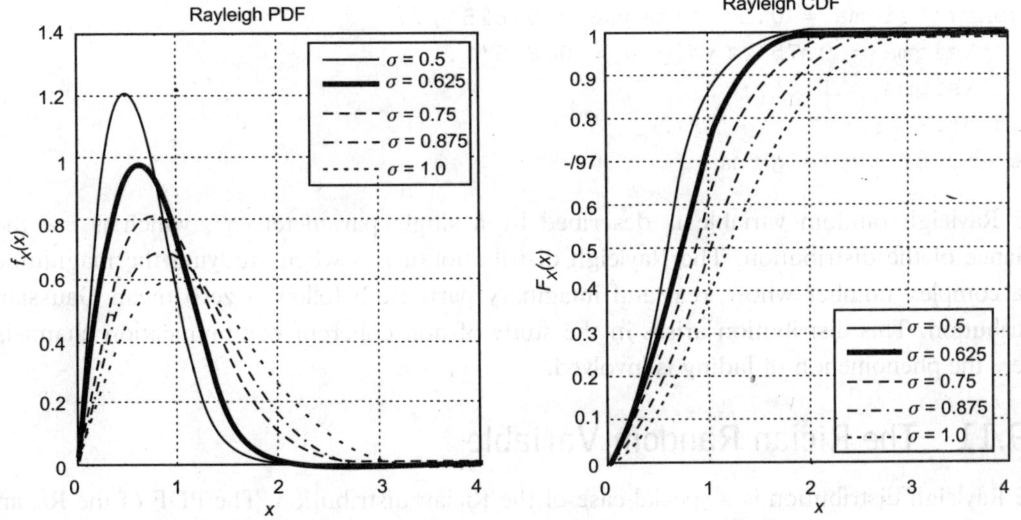

Figure 8.15 The PDF and CDF of a Rayleigh random variable

```
%%% MATLAB script to generate and
% plot Rayleigh  PDF and CDF..
close all; clear all; clf;
sig=linspace(0.5,1,5);
clr=['-o-','-.-','-+-','--','-x-'];
x=[0:.001:4];
for i=1:length(sig)
fX=x/sig(i)^2.*exp(-x.^2/(2*sig(i)^2));
subplot(121),plot(x,fX,clr(i),'LineWidth',2);
grid on; hold on;
end;
xlabel('X'); ylabel('f_{X}(x)');
title('The Rayleigh PDF');
legend('\sigma = 0.5','\sigma = 0.625',...
    '\sigma = 0.75','\sigma = 0.875',...
    '\sigma = 1.0');
for i=1:length(sig)
FX=1-exp(-x.^2/(2*sig(i)^2));
subplot(122),plot(x,FX,clr(i),'LineWidth',2);
grid on; hold on;
end;
xlabel('X'); ylabel('F_{X}(x)');
title('The Rayleigh CDF');
```

```
legend('\sigma = 0.5','\sigma = 0.625',...
    '\sigma = 0.75','\sigma = 0.875',...
    '\sigma = 1.0');
hold off;
%%% end of rayleigh.m
```

The Rayleigh random variable is described by a single parameter, σ^2, which is *not* the variance of the distribution. The Rayleigh distribution arises when studying the magnitude of a complex number whose real and imaginary parts both follow a zero mean Gaussian distribution. This distribution arises in the study of non-coherent communication channels where the phenomenon of fading is involved.

8.9.11 The Rician Random Variable

The Rayleigh distribution is a special case of the Rician distribution. The PDF of the Rician distribution is given by (for any $a > 0$ and any $\sigma > 0$)

$$f_X(x) = \frac{x}{\sigma^2} \exp\left(-\frac{x^2 + a^2}{2\sigma^2}\right) I_0\left(\frac{ax}{\sigma^2}\right) u(x) \tag{8.60}$$

In this expression, the function $I_0(x)$ is the modified Bessel function of the first kind of order *zero*, which is defined by

$$I_0(x) = \frac{1}{2\pi} \int_0^{2\pi} \exp(x \cos\theta) d\theta \tag{8.61}$$

The CDF of a Rician random variable cannot be written in the closed form. We define *Marcum's Q function* as

$$Q(\alpha, \beta) = \int_\beta^\infty z \exp\left(-\frac{z^2 + \alpha^2}{2}\right) I_0(\alpha z) dz \tag{8.62}$$

Now, the CDF of the Rician random variable is given by

$$F_X(x) = 1 - Q\left(\frac{a}{\sigma}, \frac{x}{\sigma}\right) \tag{8.63}$$

A plot of the Rician PDF is given in Figure 8.16. The MATLAB script to generate the same is given below.

```
%%% MATLAB script to generate and
% plot Rician  PDF...
close all; clear all; clf;
sig=0.9;
```

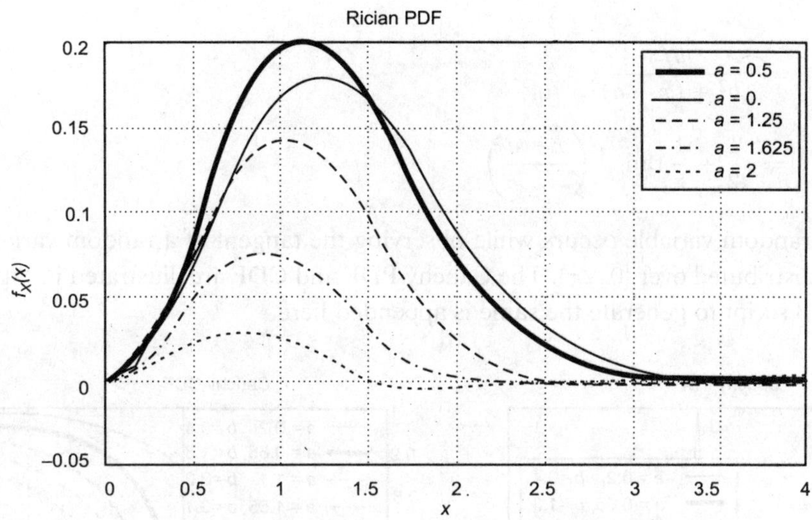

Figure 8.16 The Rician PDF

```
a=linspace(0.5,2,5);
x=[0:.001:4];
clr=['-o-','-.-','-+-','--','-x-'];
for i=1:length(a)
    fX=x/sig^2.*exp(-(x.^2+a(i)^2)/...
        (2*sig^2)).*besselj(1,a(i)*x/sig^2);
plot(x,fX,clr(i),'LineWidth',2);
grid on; hold on;
end;
xlabel('X'); ylabel('f_{X}(x)');
title('The Rician PDF');
legend('a = 0.5', 'a = 0.875',...
    'a = 1.25', 'a = 1.625', 'a = 2');
hold off;
%%% end of rician.m
```

The Rician distribution is used in the study of non-coherent communications systems and also in the study of satellite communication channels, where the fading is modelled using the Rician random variable. The Rician random variable is also known as the Nakagami-n random variable.

8.9.12 The Cauchy Random Variable

The Cauchy random variable has a PDF and CDF given by (for any a and any $b > 0$)

$$f_X(x) = \frac{b/\pi}{b^2 + (x-a)^2} \tag{8.64}$$

$$F_X(x) = \frac{1}{2} + \frac{1}{\pi}\tan^{-1}\left(\frac{x-a}{b}\right) \tag{8.65}$$

The Cauchy random variable occurs while observing the tangent of a random variable which is uniformly distributed over $[0, 2\pi)$. The Cauchy PDF and CDF are illustrated in Figure 8.17. The MATLAB script to generate the same is appended here.

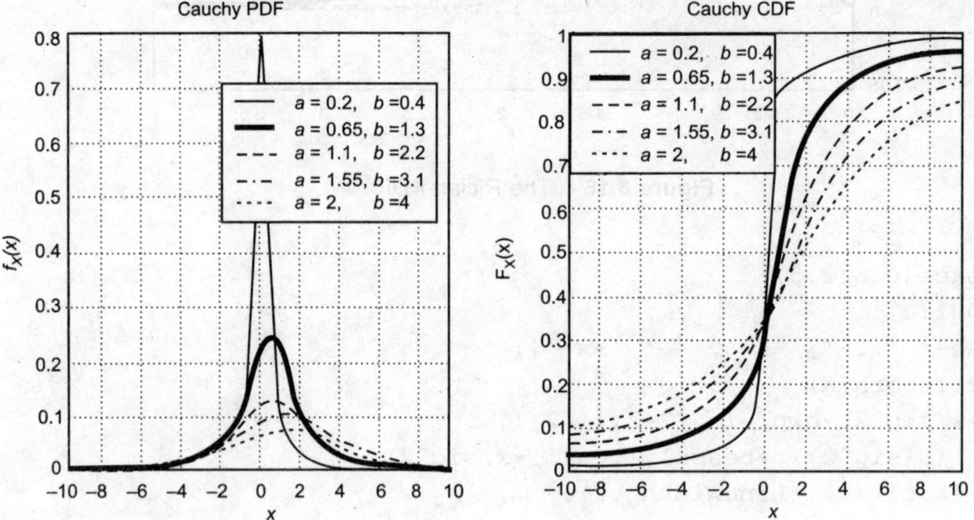

Figure 8.17 The PDF and CDF of Cauchy random variable

```
%%% MATLAB script to generate and
% plot Cauchy  PDF and CDF..
%%% MATLAB script to generate and
% plot Cauchy  PDF and CDF..
close all; clear all; clf;
a=linspace(0.2,2,5);
b=linspace(0.4,4,5);
clr=['-o-','-.-','-+-','--','-x-'];
x=[-10:.002:10];
for i=1:length(b)
fX=b(i)/pi./(b(i)^2+(x-a(i)).^2);
subplot(121),plot(x,fX,clr(i),'LineWidth',2);
grid on; hold on;
```

```
end;
xlabel('X'); ylabel('f_{X}(x)');
title('The Cauchy PDF');
legend('a = 0.2, b = 0.4', 'a = 0.65, b = 1.3',...
    'a = 1.1, b = 2.2', 'a = 1.55, b = 3.1', ...
    'a = 2, b = 4');
for i=1:length(b)
FX=0.5+1/pi*atan((x-a(i))/b(i));
subplot(122),plot(x,FX,clr(i),'LineWidth',2);
grid on; hold on;
end;
xlabel('X'); ylabel('F_{X}(x)');
title('The Cauchy CDF');
legend('a = 0.2, b = 0.4', 'a = 0.65, b = 1.3',...
    'a = 1.1, b = 2.2', 'a = 1.55, b = 3.1', ...
    'a = 2, b = 4');
hold off;
%%% end of cauch.m
```

8.9.13 The Weibull Random Variable

In probability theory and statistics, the Weibull distribution (named after Waloddi Weibull) is a continuous probability distribution. It is often called the Rosin–Rammler distribution when used to describe the size distribution of particles since it was introduced by P. Rosin and E. Rammler in 1933. The probability density function is

$$f_X(x) = \begin{cases} \frac{k}{\lambda}\left(\frac{x}{\lambda}\right)^{k-1} \exp(-\frac{x}{\lambda})^k, & x > 0 \\ 0, & x \leq 0. \end{cases} \tag{8.66}$$

where $k > 0$ is the shape parameter and $\lambda > 0$ is the scale parameter of the distribution. The cumulative distribution function of the Weibull random variable is given by

$$F_X(x) = 1 - \exp\left\{-(x/\lambda)^k\right\} \tag{8.67}$$

The Weibull distribution is often used in the field of life data analysis due to its flexibility—it can mimic the behaviour of other statistical distributions such as the normal and the exponential. If the failure rate decreases over time, then $k < 1$. If the failure rate is constant over time, then $k = 1$. If the failure rate increases over time, then $k > 1$.

An understanding of the failure rate may provide an insight into what is causing the failures:

- A decreasing failure rate would suggest "infant mortality". That is, defective items fail early and the failure rate decreases over time as they fall out of the population.
- A constant failure rate suggests that items are failing due to random events.
- An increasing failure rate suggests "wear out"—parts are more likely to fail as time goes on.

When $k = 1$, the Weibull distribution reduces to the exponential distribution. When $k = 3.4$, the Weibull distribution appears similar to the normal distribution.

A plot of the Weibull PDF and CDF is given in Figure 8.18. The MATLAB script to generate the same is given below.

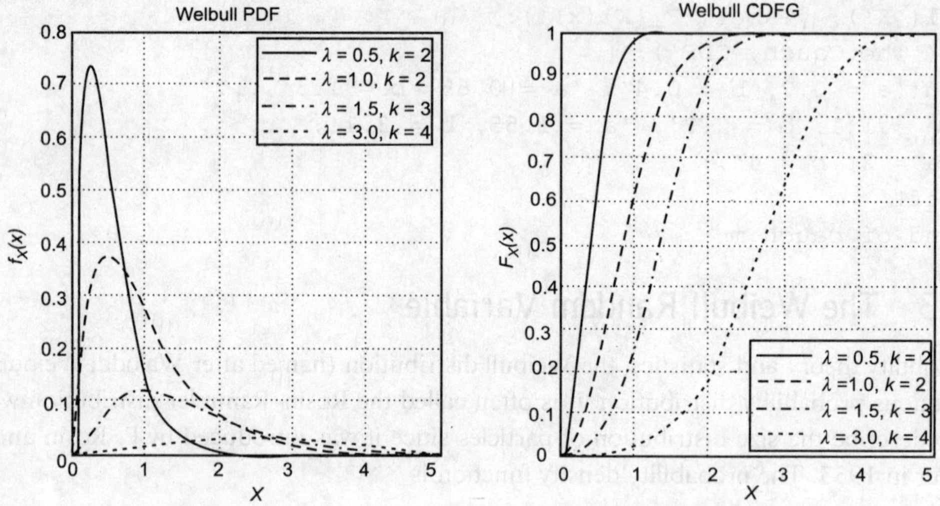

Figure 8.18 The PDF and CDF of a Weibull random variable

```
%%% MATLAB script to generate and
% plot Weibull  PDF and CDF..
close all; clear all; clf;
lam=[0.5,1,1.5,3];
k=[2,2,3,4];
x=[0:.001:5];
clr=['-o-','-.-','-+-','-x-'];
for i=1:length(k)
fX=k(i)/lam(i)*(x/lam(i)).^(k(i)-1).*exp(-(x/lam(i)).^k(i);
subplot(121),plot(x,fX,clr(i),'LineWidth',2);
grid on;hold on;
end;
```

```
xlabel('X'); ylabel('f_{X}(x)');
title('The Weibull  PDF');
legend('\lambda = 0.5, k=2', '\lambda = 1.0, k=2', ...
    '\lambda = 1.5, k=3', '\lambda = 3.0, k=4');
for i=1:length(k)
FX=1-exp(-(x/lam(i)).^k(i));
subplot(122),plot(x,FX,clr(i),'LineWidth',2);
grid on;hold on;
 end;
xlabel('X'); ylabel('F_{X}(x)');
title('The Weibull CDF');
legend('\lambda = 0.5, k=2', '\lambda = 1.0, k=2', ...
    '\lambda = 1.5, k=3', '\lambda = 3.0, k=4');
hold off;
%%% end of weibull.m
```

8.9.14 The Nakagami-m Random Variable

The Nakagami distribution or the Nakagami-m distribution is a probability distribution related to the gamma distribution. It has two parameters: a shape parameter μ and a second parameter controlling spread, ω. The Nakagami distribution is relatively new, being first proposed in 1960. It has been used to model attenuation of wireless signals traversing multiple paths, i.e., to model multi-path fading channels.

Nakagami-m distribution is a widely used statistical model for fading envelopes of signals due to its great versatility. With the parameter μ ranging from 0.5 to infinity, it can model different fading scenarios from severe to moderate. Rayleigh distribution is a special case when $\mu = 1$. There is no fading when $\mu = \infty$. Nakagami-m distribution fits certain urban path strength data better than Rayleigh, Rice or log-normal distributions.

Nakagami Fading

Mobile radio channels are subject to severe multi-path fading due to a combination of randomly delayed, reflected, scattered, and diffracted signal components. Fading leads to serious degradation in the link carrier-to-noise ratio (CNR), leading to higher bit error rate (BER). Rayleigh and Rician fading models have been widely used to simulate small-scale fading environments. M. Nakagami observed this fact and then formulated a parametric gamma function to describe his large-scale experiments on rapid fading in high frequency long distance propagation.

Nakagami fading occurs for multi-path scattering with relatively larger time delay spreads, with different clusters of reflected waves. Within any one cluster, the phases of individual reflected waves are random, but the time delays are approximately equal for the waves. As a result, the envelope of each cluster signal is Rayleigh distributed. The average time delay is assumed to differ between clusters. If the delay times significantly exceed the bit period of the digital link, the different clusters produce serious inter-symbol interference.

The Nakagami Fading Channel Model

The Nakagami fading model was initially proposed because it matched empirical results for short ionospheric propagation. The Nakagami distribution or the Nakagami-m distribution is a probability distribution related to the gamma distribution. This more general fading distribution was developed so that the parameters can be adjusted to fit a variety of empirical measurements. The Nakagami distribution describes the magnitude of the received envelope by the probability density function:

$$f_X(x) = \frac{2\mu^{\mu}x^{2\mu-1}}{\Gamma(\mu)\omega^{\mu}} \exp\left(-\frac{\mu}{\omega}x^2\right), \quad x \geq 0, \ \omega \geq 0, \ \mu \geq 5. \tag{8.68}$$

where $\omega = E(x^2)$ is the average received power or average CNR, $\Gamma(.)$ is the gamma function, and $\mu = \frac{E^2(x^2)}{var(x^2)}$ is the fading figure or the shape factor.

The probability density function is primarily known as first order characteristics. It is mainly used to obtain static metrics associated with the channel, i.e., bit error rate (BER). The cumulative distribution function of the Nakagami-m random variable is given by

$$F_X(x) = \frac{\gamma\left(\mu, \frac{\mu}{\omega}x^2\right)}{\Gamma(\mu)} \tag{8.69}$$

A plot of the Nakagami-m PDF and CDF is given in Figure 8.19. The MATLAB script to generate the same is given below.

```
%%% MATLAB script to generate and
% plot Nakagami-m  PDF and CDF..
%%% MATLAB script to generate and
% plot Nakagami-m  PDF and CDF..
close all; clear all; clf;
m=[0.5,1,1,1,2,2,5];
o=[2,1,2,3,1,2,1];
x=[0:.001:3];
clr=['-o-','-.-','-+-','-x-','.','+-'];
for i=1:length(m)
fX= 2*m(i)^m(i)/(gamma(m(i))*o(i)^m(i))...
    *x.^(2*m(i)-1).*exp(-(m(i)/o(i))*x.^2);
subplot(121),plot(x,fX,clr(i),'LineWidth',2);
```

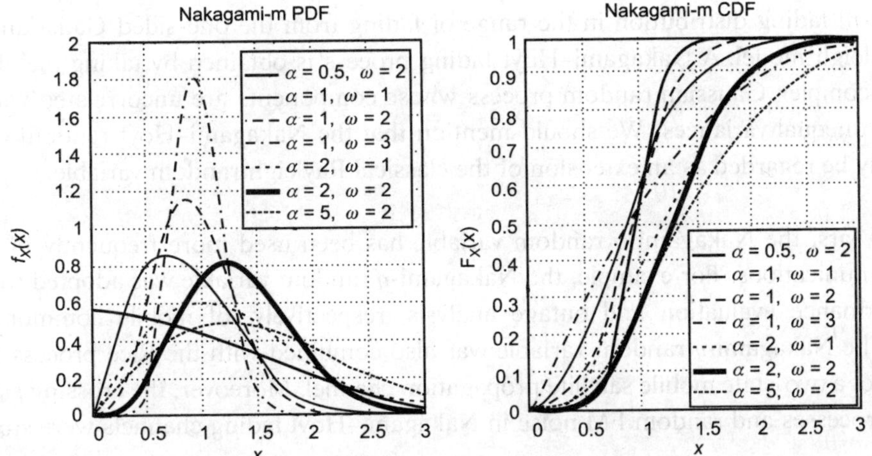

Figure 8.19 The PDF and CDF of a Nakagami-m random variable

```
grid on;hold on;
end;
xlabel('X'); ylabel('f_{X}(x)');
title('The Nakagami-m  PDF');
legend('\mu = 0.5, \omega=2', '\mu = 1, \omega=1',...
   '\mu = 1, \omega=2','\mu = 1, \omega=3',...
   '\mu = 2, \omega=1','\mu = 2, \omega=2',...
   '\mu = 5, \omega=1');
for i=1:length(m)
FX= gammainc((m(i)/o(i))*x.^2,m(i));
subplot(122),plot(x,FX,clr(i),'LineWidth',2);
grid on; hold on;
 end;
xlabel('X'); ylabel('F_{X}(x)');
title('The Nakagami-m  CDF');
legend('\mu = 0.5, \omega=2', '\mu = 1, \omega=1',...
   '\mu = 1, \omega=2','\mu = 1, \omega=3',...
   '\mu = 2, \omega=1','\mu = 2, \omega=2',...
   '\mu = 5, \omega=1');
 hold off;
%%% end of nakagamim.m
```

8.9.15 The Nakagami-q Random Variable

The Nakagami–Hoyt random variable (Nakagami-q random variable) was investigated independently by Hoyt and Nakagami. It was introduced as an approximation for the

Nakagami-m fading distribution in the range of fading from the one-sided Gaussian model to the Rayleigh model. A Nakagami–Hoyt fading process is obtained by taking the absolute value of a complex Gaussian random process whose components are uncorrelated with zero mean and unequal variances. We should mention that the Nakagami–Hoyt random variable can actually be regarded as an extension of the classical Rayleigh random variable.

In recent years, the Nakagami-q random variable has been used more frequently in mobile radio communications. For example, the Nakagami-q random variable was adopted for error rate performance evaluation and outage analysis, respectively, of mobile communication systems. The Nakagami-q random variable was also combined with the Rice process for the modelling of a two-state mobile satellite propagation channel. Moreover, the crossing statistics of phase processes and random FM noise in Nakagami–Hoyt fading channels were studied.

The instantaneous amplitude, $X(t)$, of the Nakagami-q fading process is obtained as the modulus of a complex Gaussian process, $\mu(t) = \mu_1(t) + j\mu_2(t)$. That is,

$$X(t) = |\mu_1(t) + j\mu_2(t)| = \sqrt{\mu_1^2(t) + \mu_2^2(t)} \tag{8.70}$$

where $\mu_1(t)$ and $\mu_2(t)$ are uncorrelated zero-mean lowpass Gaussian processes of variances σ_1^2 and σ_2^2, respectively. The probability density function (PDF) of the Nakagami-q process is given by

$$f_X(x) = \frac{x}{\sigma_1\sigma_2}\exp\left[-\frac{x^2}{4}(\frac{1}{\sigma_1^2}+\frac{1}{\sigma_2^2})\right] I_0\left[\frac{x^2}{4}(\frac{1}{\sigma_2^2}-\frac{1}{\sigma_1^2})\right], \quad x \geq 0. \tag{8.71}$$

where $I_0(.)$ designates the zeroth-order modified Bessel function of the first kind. Note that under the restriction that $\sigma_1 = \sigma_2$, the PDF of the process $X(t)$ reduces to the Rayleigh distribution.

A plot of the Nakagami-q probability density function for different combinations of σ_1 and σ_2 is given in Figure 8.20. The MATLAB script to generate the same is given below.

```
%%% MATLAB script to generate and
% plot Nakagami-q (Hoyt) PDF...
close all; clear all; clf;
s1=[0.1,0.2,0.4,0.8];
s2=[0.08,0.09,0.1,0.2];
x=[0:.001:1];
clr=['-o-','-.-','-+-','-x-'];
for i=1:length(s1)
fX= x/(s1(i)*s2(i)).*exp(-(x.^2)/4*...
    (1/s1(i)^2+1/s2(i)^2)).*...
```

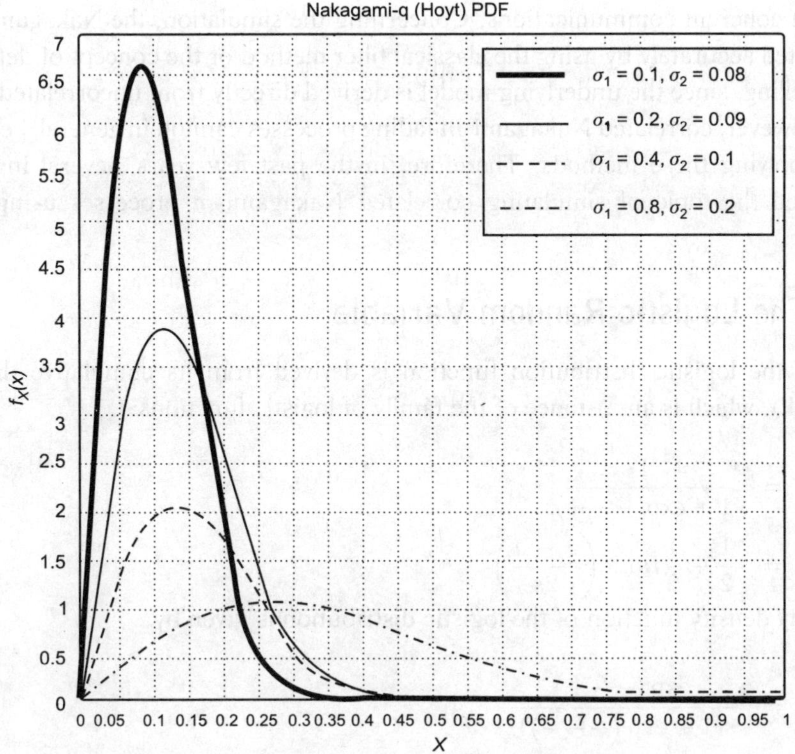

Figure 8.20 The PDF of Nakagami-q random variable

```
        besselj(0,x.^2/4*(1/s2(i)^2-1/s2(i)^2));
    plot(x,fX,clr(i),'LineWidth',2);
    hold on;
    end;
    xlabel('X'); ylabel('f_{X}(x)');
    title('The Nakagami-q (Hoyt) PDF');grid;
    legend('\sigma_{1} =0.1, \sigma_{2} = 0.08',...
      '\sigma_{1} =0.2, \sigma_{2} = 0.09',...
      '\sigma_{1} =0.4, \sigma_{2} = 0.1',...
      '\sigma_{1} =0.8, \sigma_{2} = 0.2');
    hold off;
    %%% end of nakagamiq.m
```

Since the Nakagami-m distribution approximates the Nakagami-q distribution and vice versa, it is worthwhile to present a brief comparison between the two models. It is well-known that while the Nakagami-m model offers features of analytical convenience with respect to the Nakagami-q model, it does not address the phase term statistics which is of great importance in coherent communications. Concerning the simulation, the Nakagami-q model can be simulated accurately by using the classical filter method or the concept of deterministic channel modelling, since the underlying model is derived directly from uncorrelated Gaussian processes. However, correlated Nakagami-m fading processes cannot, in general, be simulated directly by applying these methods. Therefore, in the past few years, several investigators have addressed the topic of simulating correlated Nakagami-m processes using different approaches.

8.9.16 The Logistic Random Variable

The name of the logistic distribution function is derived from its cumulative distribution function (CDF), which is an instance of the family of logistic functions:

$$F_X(x) = \frac{1}{1+\exp(-\frac{x-\mu}{s})} \quad (8.72)$$

$$= \frac{1}{2}+\frac{1}{2}\tanh\left(\frac{x-\mu}{2s}\right) \quad (8.73)$$

The probability density function of the logistic distribution is given by

$$f_X(x) = \frac{\exp\left(-\frac{x-\mu}{s}\right)}{s(1+\exp\left(-\frac{x-\mu}{s}\right))^2} \quad (8.74)$$

$$= \frac{1}{4s}\text{sech}^2\left(\frac{x-\mu}{2s}\right) \quad (8.75)$$

Because the PDF of logistic distribution can be expressed in terms of the square of the hyperbolic secant function "sech", it is sometimes referred to as the sech-square(d) distribution.

A plot of the logistic PDF and CDF is given in Figure 8.21. The MATLAB script to generate the same is given below.

```
%%% MATLAB script to generate and
% plot Logistic PDF and CDF..
close all; clear all; clf;
m=[5,9,9,6,2];
s=[2,3,4,2,1];
x=[-5:.001:30];
clr=['-o-','-.-','-+-','--','-x-'];
for i=1:length(m)
fX=  exp(-(x-m(i))/s(i))./(s(i)*(1+exp(-(x-m(i))/s(i))).^2);
subplot(121),plot(x,fX,clr(i),'LineWidth',2);
grid on;hold on;
```

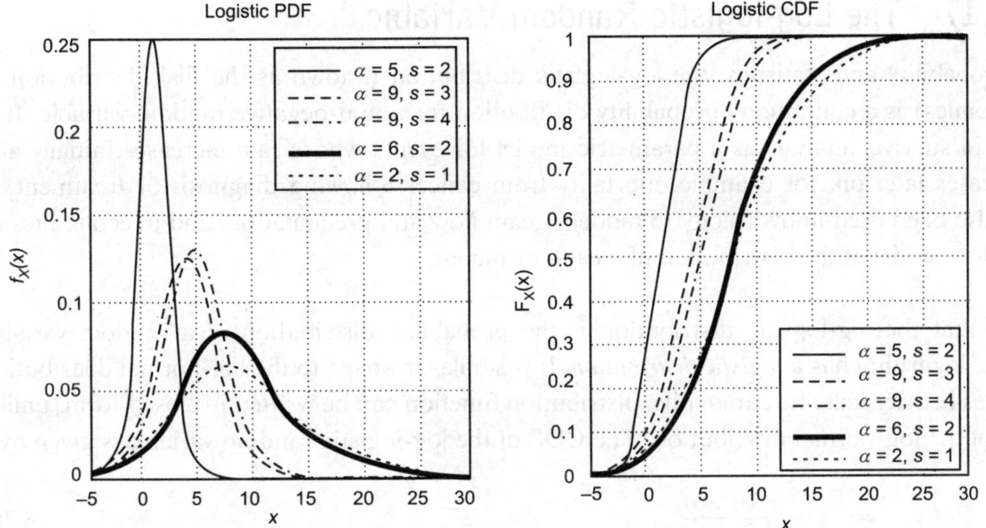

Figure 8.21 The PDF and CDF of a logistic random variable

```
end;
xlabel('X'); ylabel('f_{X}(x)');
title('The Logistic  PDF');
legend('\mu = 5, s=2','\mu = 9, s=3',...
    '\mu = 9, s=4','\mu = 6, s=2','\mu = 2, s=1');
for i=1:length(m)
FX=  1./(1+exp(-(x-m(i))/s(i)));
subplot(122),plot(x,FX,clr(i),'LineWidth',2);
grid on;hold on;
 end;
xlabel('X'); ylabel('F_{X}(x)');
title('The Logistic CDF');
legend('\mu = 5, s=2','\mu = 9, s=3',...
    '\mu = 9, s=4','\mu = 6, s=2','\mu = 2, s=1');
 hold off;
%%% end of logistic.m
```

The logistic distribution and the S-shaped pattern that results from it have been extensively used in many different areas, the most important of which include biology (to describe how species populations grow in competition), epidemiology (to describe the spreading of epidemics), psychology (to describe learning), technology (to describe how new technologies diffuse and become substitutes for each other), market (the diffusion of new product sales), and energy (the diffusion and substitution of primary energy sources).

8.9.17 The Log-logistic Random Variable

In probability and statistics, the log-logistic distribution (known as the Fisk distribution in economics) is a continuous probability distribution for a non-negative random variable. It is used in survival analysis as a parametric model for events whose rate increases initially and decreases later on, for example, mortality from cancer following diagnosis or treatment. It has also been used in hydrology to model stream flow and precipitation, and in economics as a simple model of the distribution of wealth or income.

Note that the log-logistic distribution is the probability distribution of a random variable whose logarithm has a *logistic distribution*. It is similar in shape to the log-normal distribution but has heavier tails. Its cumulative distribution function can be written in closed form, unlike that of the log-normal distribution. The CDF of the log-logistic random variable is given by

$$F_X(x) = \frac{1}{1+(x/\alpha)^{-\beta}} \tag{8.76}$$

$$= \frac{(x/\alpha)^{\beta}}{1+(x/\alpha)^{\beta}} \tag{8.77}$$

$$= \frac{x^{\beta}}{x^{\beta}+\alpha^{\beta}} \tag{8.78}$$

where $x > 0,\ \ \alpha > 0,\ \ \beta > 0$. The probability density function of the log-logistic random variable is given by

$$f_X(x) = \frac{(\beta/\alpha)(x/\alpha)^{-\beta-1}}{[1+(x/\alpha)^{-\beta}]^2} \tag{8.79}$$

A plot of the log-logistic PDF and CDF is given in Figure 8.22. The MATLAB script to generate the same is given below.

```
%%% MATLAB script to generate and
% plot Log-logistic PDF and CDF..
close all; clear all; clf;
a=1;
b=[1,2,4,8,16];
x=[0:.001:2];
clr=['-o-','-.-','-+-','--','-x-'];
for i=1:length(b)
fX=  b(i)*x.^(b(i)-1)./(1+x.^b(i)).^2;
subplot(121),plot(x,fX,clr(i),'LineWidth',2);
grid on;hold on;
end;
```

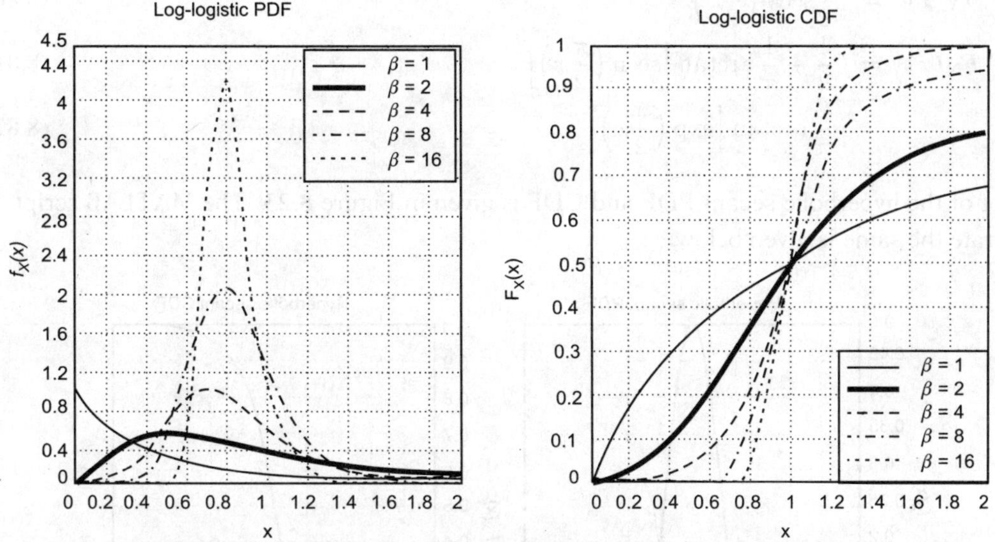

Figure 8.22 The PDF and CDF of log-logistic random variable

```
xlabel('X'); ylabel('f_{X}(x)');
title('The Log-logistic  PDF');
legend('\beta = 1','\beta = 2','\beta = 4',...
    '\beta = 8','\beta =16');
for i=1:length(b)
FX= x.^b(i)./(1+x.^(b(i)));
subplot(122),plot(x,FX,clr(i),'LineWidth',2);
grid on;hold on;
end;
xlabel('X'); ylabel('F_{X}(x)');
title('The Log-logistic CDF');
legend('\beta = 1','\beta = 2','\beta = 4',...
    '\beta = 8','\beta =16');
hold off;
%%%'end of loglogist.m
```

8.9.18 The Hyperbolic Secant Random Variable

The *hyperbolic secant distribution* is a continuous probability distribution whose probability density function and characteristic function are proportional to the hyperbolic secant function. The PDF and CDF of the hyperbolic secant distribution is given by

$$f_X(x) = \frac{1}{2}\text{sech}\left(\frac{\pi}{2}x\right) \tag{8.80}$$

$$F_X(x) = \frac{1}{2}+\frac{1}{\pi}\arctan\left[\text{sech}\left(\frac{\pi}{2}x\right)\right] \tag{8.81}$$

$$= \frac{2}{\pi}\arctan\left[\exp\left(\frac{\pi}{2}x\right)\right] \tag{8.82}$$

A plot of the hyperbolic secant PDF and CDF is given in Figure 8.23. The MATLAB script to generate the same is given below.

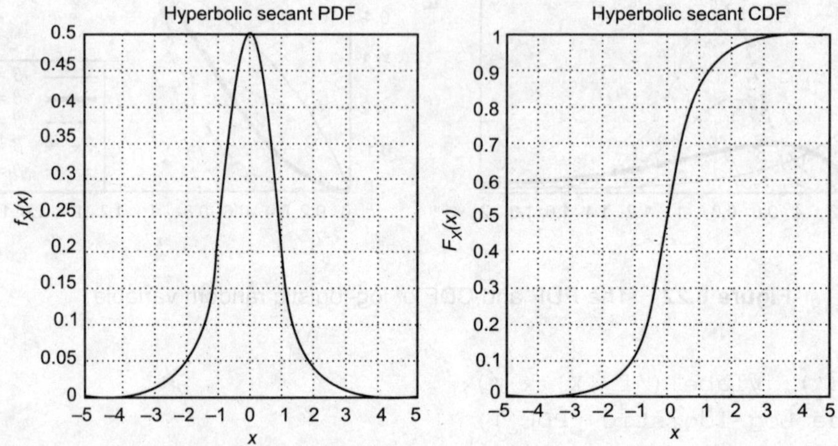

Figure 8.23 The PDF and CDF of a hyperbolic secant random variable

```
%%% MATLAB script to generate and
% plot Hyperbolic Secant PDF and CDF..
close all; clear all; clf;
x=[-5:.001:5];
fX= 0.5*sech(pi/2*x);
subplot(121),plot(x,fX, 'LineWidth',2);
xlabel('X'); ylabel('f_{X}(x)');
grid on;
title('The Hyperbolic Secant  PDF');
FX=2/pi*atan(exp(pi/2*x));
subplot(122),plot(x,FX, 'LineWidth',2);
xlabel('X'); ylabel('F_{X}(x)');
grid on;
title('The Hyperbolic Secant CDF');
%%% end of  hyperbol.m
```

The hyperbolic secant distribution shares many properties with the standard normal distribution: it is symmetric with unit variance and zero mean, median and mode, and its PDF is proportional to its characteristic function. However, the hyperbolic secant distribution is leptokurtic, that is, it has a more acute peak near its mean, compared with the standard normal distribution.

8.10 Random Number Generators

A large number of techniques in applied mathematics and statistics involve what is termed as Monte Carlo calculations. Such calculations depend on randomly occurring sequences of numbers which have particular probability distributions. The term "pseudo random" is often used to describe the random numbers which are obtained by computers. Random numbers are used for various purposes, such as to model and simulate complex phenomena, to generate data encryption keys and to select random samples from huge data sets. If we consider single numbers, a random number is one that is taken from a set of possible values, each of which is *equally probable or equally likely*—a random number is one that is taken from a set which possesses a *uniform distribution*. If we are considering a sequence of random numbers, each number taken must be *statistically independent* of the others selected.

Random numbers can be generated by a computer using two main methods: pseudo random number generators (PRNGs) and true random number generators (TRNGs). The two methods have different characteristics and each has its advantages and disadvantages.

8.10.1 Pseudo Random Number Generators (PRNGs)

Pseudo random numbers are not really random in the strict sense—that is why we use the word "pseudo". Basically, PRNGs are programs or algorithms that make use of mathematical formulae or pre-calculated tables to generate sequences of numbers that appear to be random. The *linear congruential method* is a good example of a PRNG. Over the years, pseudo random number theory has been well-researched. So much so, that pseudo random numbers generated by modern algorithms look like they were really random.

PRNGs can generate a large set of numbers in a very short time—thus they are *efficient*. If the starting point in a sequence is known, it can easily be reproduced at a later date—they are *deterministic*. If the application needs many numbers, the characteristic of being efficient is very useful. The deterministic nature of PRNGs is also helpful, especially if there is need to replay the same sequence of numbers again at a later stage. PRNGs also have the characteristic of being *periodic*—the sequence will eventually repeat itself. This is of course, not an advantage, but modern PRNGs have a period so large that they can be ignored for most practical purposes.

PRNGs efficiency and deterministic nature make it very apt for applications where a large set of numbers are required and where it is necessary to replay the same sequence easily. Common applications are simulation and modelling applications. PRNGs are not suitable in situation where the numbers must be really unpredictable, such as data encryption and gambling.

If we compare computer-generated random numbers to the results of the roll of a dice, we can understand the intrinsic difference between PRNGs and true random number generators (TRNGs). As mentioned before, PRNGs produce random numbers by using mathematical formulae or pre-calculated lists. This is similar to rolling a die a number of times and noting down the results—the die can only show the numbers 1 to 6. The numbers appear to be random, but they are really pre-determined. TRNGs, on the other hand, use a truly random physical phenomenon that can be easily connected to a computer.

8.10.2 True Random Number Generators (TRNGs)

TRNGs obtain randomness from a physical phenomena and send it to a computer. Generally, people use a physical phenomenon that is easy to connect to a computer like the little shifts in position of a computer's mouse or the variations in the amount of time between keystrokes. The choice of source of randomness has to be very carefully made. For instance, the computer's operating system might buffer the keystrokes—several keystrokes may be collected before they are sent to the program waiting for them. To the program, it might seem as though the keys were pressed simultaneously and there may not be a lot of randomness. But we can introduce true randomness into the digital computer through many other ways. For example, a *radioactive source* is a really good physical phenomenon to use. It is impossible to predict the points in time at which a radioactive source will decay though they can be easily detected and fed into a computer. An example of a random number generator that uses this technique is the HotBits service at Fourmilab in Switzerland. Another physical phenomenon that can be used is *atmospheric or galactic noise*. It is quite easy to pick up with a normal radio. The background noise from an office or laboratory, can also be used but we must be careful. For example, the background noise might contain the noise of the computer's fan rotating and the chances are that this might not be as random as atmospheric noise.

8.10.3 Algorithms for Pseudo Random Number Generation

Computer programs that generate "random" numbers use an algorithm. This means that if one knows the algorithm and the seed values, one can predict what numbers will result. Because we can predict the numbers, they are not truly random—they are pseudo random. For statistical purposes, "good" pseudo random number generators are good enough.

D. H. Lehmer proposed a good algorithm for generating random numbers in his paper,

"Mathematical methods in large-scale computing units". *Annals of Computer Lab, Harvard University.* pp. 141–146. 1951. The *multiplicative linear congruential algorithm* suggested by him is still being used today as it is can be very efficiently implemented. The randomness of its output have been tested by numerous emperical experiments, and its important theoretical properties analysed. The Lehmer's algorithm involves the careful choice of two fixed integer parameters:

- modulus: m which is a large prime number
- multiplier: a which is an integer in the range $2, 3, \ldots, m-1$.

If we assume that the *initial seed value* for the generation is z_0, the subsequent values are generated by the simple equation:

$$z_{n+1} = a * z_n \bmod m, \text{ for } n = 0, 1, 2, \ldots \tag{8.83}$$

The initial seed value z_0 is chosen from $1, 2, \ldots, m-1$. As an additional step, the sequence is conventionally normalised to the unit interval via division by the modulus to produce the real sequence $u_1, u_2, u_3, \ldots, u_n$, where

$$u_n = z_n/m \text{ for } n = 1, 2, \ldots \tag{8.84}$$

A random number generator based on this algorithm is also known as a *prime modulus multiplicative linear congruential generator (PMMLCG)*, or the *Lehmer generator*. One may note the following:

- Since m is prime, $z_{n+1} \pm 0$, for $n = 1, 2, \ldots, m-1$.
- The values $u = 0$ and $u = 1$, are impossible.
- $u \epsilon [1/m, 1 - 1/m]$.
- In general, all full period Lehmer generators produce a fixed virtual circular list defined by a permutation of the integers $1, 2, \ldots, m1$.
- The statistical properties are unaffected by the normalisation.

A typical implementation of the Lehmer's generator in MATLAB is appended below:

```
function [rand12_out] = rand12(seed)
% A random Number Generator using the
% Lehmer's Algorithm..
% seed is any integer in [1,12].
rand12_out=[];
a=6;
m=13;
```

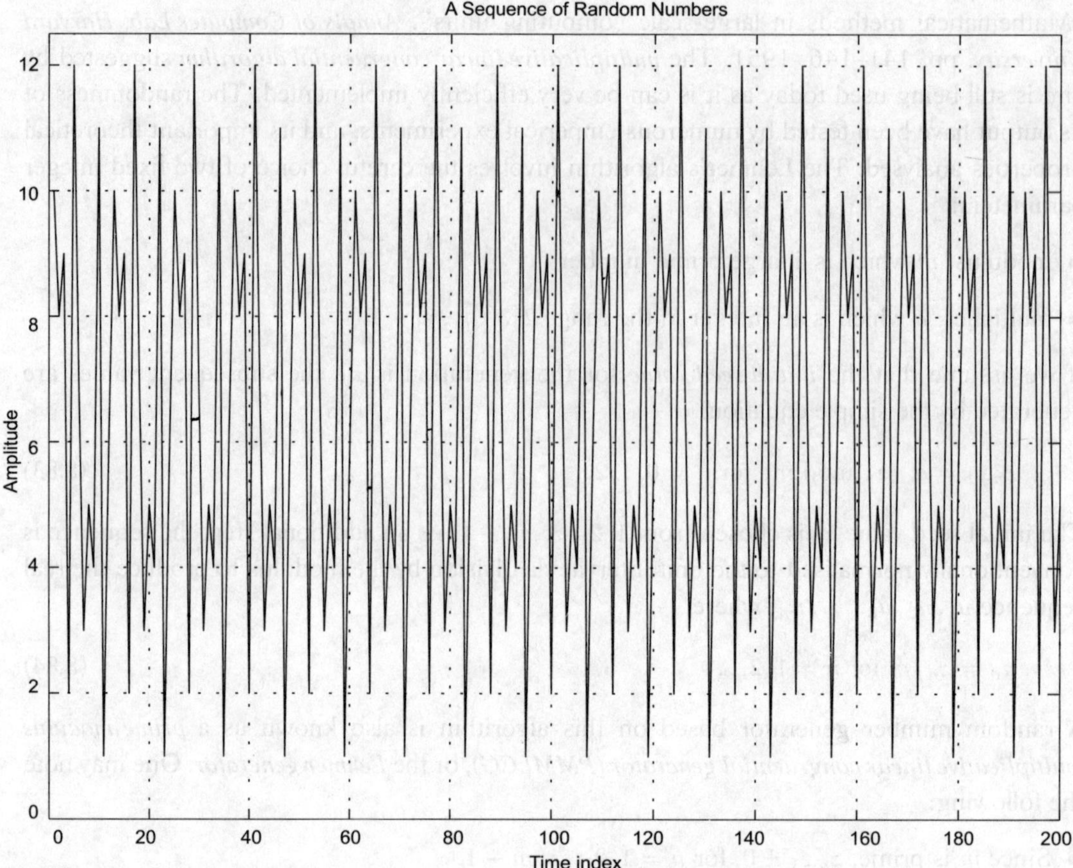

Figure 8.24 A plot of the sequence of random numbers generated by the `rand12(.)` function.

```
z=mod(a*seed,m);
for i=1:200
    z=mod(a*z,m);
    rand12_out=[rand12_out,z];
end;
end
```

A plot of the random numbers generated is shown in Figure 8.24.

A more recent implementation of the Schrage's algorithm which is also used to generate random numbers (by multiplying two 32-bit integers modulo a 32-bit constant without using any intermediates larger than 32-bits), removing the flaws of the previous one (overflow errors) is given below:

```
function [rand_out] = randsch(seed)
% A random Number Generator using the
% Schrage's Algorithm..
% seed is any integer in [1,2^31-2].
rand_out=[];
a=16807;
m=2^31-1;
q=floor(m/a);
r=mod(m,a);
for i=1:200
    hi=floor(seed/q);
    lo=mod(seed,q);
    test=a*lo-r*hi;
    if (test > 0)
        seed=test;
    else
        seed=test+m;
    end;
    rand_out=[rand_out,seed/m];
end;
end
```

A functionally equivalent algorithm to the real version of this implementation is also possible. In general, this is the version that must be used if *maxint* is smaller than $2^{31} - 1$.

```
function [rand_out] = randsch2(seed)
% A random Number Generator using the
% Schrage's Algorithm- Version 2.0
% seed is any integer in [1,2^31-2].
rand_out=[];
a=16807;
m=2^31-1;
q=floor(m/a);
r=mod(m,a);
for i=1:200
    hi=fix(seed/q);
    lo=seed-q*hi;
    test=a*lo-r*hi;
    if (test > 0)
        seed=test;
    else
```

```
        seed=test+m;
    end;
    rand_out=[rand_out,seed/m];
end;
end
```

The above algorithm is quite often referred to as the *minimal standard algorithm*.

Generalisations of multiplicative generators with generating functions of the form $f(z) = (a*z+c) \bmod m$, where the additive parameter c satisfies $c \bmod m \neq 0$ are called *mixed linear congruential generators*. By having one extra addition for each random number, the effect of c is to allow $z = 0$ as a possible value. Thus a full period sequence has length m rather than $m-1$. Theoretically, the modulus m can be any positive integer, prime or non-prime. However, practically, m is usually either a power of 2 or a power of 10. In 1978, P. Grogono defined a random number generator by:

$$z_{n+1} = (25173 * z_n + 13849) \bmod 2^{16}. \tag{8.85}$$

This generator of the mixed kind has a full period (of length 65536) and because the largest possible value of $25173z + 13849$ is approximately 1.54×2^{30}, it can be easily implemented correctly, provided *maxint* is $2^{31} - 1$ or larger. This generator is not good for scientific applications as it contains a relatively small period. Moreover, it has not yet been proved that the output of this generator is sufficiently random. In 1987, Konvalina and Wileman defined a mixed generator with $a = 93, c = 1$ and $m = 2^{13}$, by:

$$z_{n+1} = (93 * z_n + 1) \bmod 2^{13} \tag{8.86}$$

A comprehensive list of mixed linear congruent generators is given in Table 8.1.

Table 8.1 Summary of mixed linear congruent generators of the form $f(z) = (a*z+c)\,|m|$

Name	a	c	m	length
Grogono, 1978	25173	13849	2^{16}	2^{16}
Lamb, 1986	10924	11830	$2^{15}+1$	$2^{15}+1$
Konvalina and Wileman, 1987	93	1	2^{13}	2^{13}
Clocksin and Mellish, 1987	125	1	2^{12}	2^{12}
Savitch, 1984	40	3641 mod 723	729	729
Lamie, 1987	61	2323 mod 500	500	500
Collins, 1986	9806	1	$2^{17}-1$‡	$2^{17}-1$
RAND	1103515245	12345	2^{31}	2^{31}
Turbo Pascal	129	907633385	2^{32}	2^{32}

‡ The seed 37911 should not be used, as $f(37911) = 37911$.

8.10.4 Random Number Generation in MATLAB

There is a versatile function in the Statistics Toolbox of MATLAB to generate *random numbers* that have a particular probability distribution. The function is `random(.)`.

`Y = random(name,A)` returns random numbers Y from the one-parameter family of distributions specified by *name*. Parameter values for the distribution are given in A. Y is the same size as A.

`Y = random(name,A,B)` returns random numbers Y from a two-parameter family of distributions. Parameter values for the distribution are given in A and B.

`Y = random(name,A,B,C)` returns random numbers Y from a three-parameter family of distributions. Parameter values for the distribution are given in A, B, and C. If A, B, and C are arrays, they must be the same size. If any of A, B, or C are scalars, they are expanded to constant matrices of the same size. Acceptable strings for *name* are:

- 'beta' (Beta distribution)
- 'bino' (Binomial distribution)
- 'chi2' (Chi-square distribution)
- 'exp' (Exponential distribution)
- 'ev' (Extreme value distribution)
- 'f' (F distribution)
- 'gam' (Gamma distribution)
- 'gev' (Generalised extreme value distribution)
- 'gp' (Generalised Pareto distribution)
- 'geo' (Geometric distribution)
- 'hyge' (Hypergeometric distribution)
- 'logn' (Log-normal distribution)
- 'nbin' (Negative binomial distribution)
- 'ncf' (Non-central F distribution)
- 'nct' (Noncentral t distribution)
- 'ncx2' (Non-central chi-square distribution)
- 'norm' (Normal distribution)
- 'poiss' (Poisson distribution)
- 'rayl' (Rayleigh distribution)
- 't' (t distribution)
- 'unif' (Uniform distribution)
- 'unid' (Discrete uniform distribution)
- 'wbl' (Weibull distribution)

8.11 The Expected Value (Mean) of a Random Variable

We will first consider the discrete case. If X is a discrete random variable having a probability mass function $f(x)$, then the expected value of X is given by

$$E[X] = \sum_{x:f(x)>0} xf(x) \tag{8.87}$$

Thus, the expected value of X is a weighted average of the possible values that X can take on, each value being weighted by the probability that X assumes that value. In other words, it is the summation of $xf(x)$ over x such that $f(x) > 0$, whenever this sum is absolutely convergent.

EXAMPLE 8.1

Find $E[X]$, where X is the outcome of rolling a fair die.

SOLUTION

Since $p(1) = p(2) = p(3) = p(4) = p(5) = p(6) = \frac{1}{6}$, we get $E[X] = 1 \times \frac{1}{6} + 2 \times \frac{1}{6} + 3 \times \frac{1}{6} + 4 \times \frac{1}{6} + 5 \times \frac{1}{6} + 6 \times \frac{1}{6} = \frac{7}{2}$.

We will now consider the expected value of a continuous random variable. If X is a continuous random variable having a probability density function $f_X(x)$, then the expected value of X is given by

$$E[X] = \int_{-\infty}^{\infty} x f_X(x) dx \tag{8.88}$$

Table 8.2 lists the expected values of typical random variables.

Table 8.2 Expected values (means) and variances of random variables

Sl.No.	Name	Expected Value	Variance
1.	Normal	μ	σ^2
2.	Exponential	$\frac{1}{\lambda}$	$\frac{1}{\lambda^2}$
3.	Gamma $G(\alpha, \beta)$	$\alpha\beta$	$\alpha\beta^2$
4.	Chi-square $\chi^2(n)$	n	2n
5.	Weibull	$\left(\frac{\beta}{\alpha}\right)^{1/\beta} \Gamma\left(1 + \frac{1}{\beta}\right)$	$\left(\frac{\beta}{\alpha}\right)^{2/\beta} \left[\Gamma\left(1 + \frac{2}{\beta}\right) - \left(\Gamma\left(1 + \frac{1}{\beta}\right)\right)^2\right]$
6.	Rayleigh	$\sqrt{\frac{\pi}{2}}\sigma$	$(2 - \pi/2)\sigma^2$
7.	Nakagami-m	$\frac{\Gamma(m+1/2)}{\Gamma(m)}\sqrt{\frac{\Omega}{m}}$	$\Omega\left(1 - \frac{1}{m}\left(\frac{\Gamma(m+1/2)}{\Gamma(m)}\right)^2\right)$
8.	Uniform $U(a, b)$	$\frac{a+b}{2}$	$\frac{(b-a)^2}{12}$
9.	Beta $\beta(\alpha, \beta)$	$\frac{\alpha}{\alpha+\beta}$	$\frac{\alpha\beta}{(\alpha+\beta)^2(\alpha+\beta+1)}$
10.	Cauchy	—	∞
11.	Laplace	$\frac{1}{\alpha}$	$\frac{2-\alpha}{\alpha^3}$
12.	Maxwell	$2\alpha\sqrt{2/\pi}$	$(3 - \frac{8}{\pi})\alpha^2$
13.	Poisson	λ	λ
14.	Geometric	$\frac{1}{p}$	$\frac{1-p}{p^2}$
15.	Bernoulli	p	$p(1-p)$
16.	Binomial	np	$np(1-p)$
17.	Neg. binomial	$\frac{r}{p}$	$\frac{r(1-p)}{p^2}$
18.	Discrete uniform	$\frac{N+1}{2}$	$\frac{N^2-1}{12}$

8.11.1 Expected Values of Functions of Random Variables

Given a random variable X and its probability distribution, we can always obtain the expected value of a function of the random variable, $g(X)$. Since X is a random variable, $g(X)$ must also be a random variable. The expected value of the function of the random variable, $g(X)$, in the discrete case is given by

$$E[g(X)] = \sum_{x:f(x)>0} g(x)f(x) \tag{8.89}$$

where $f(x)$ is the probability mass function of the random variable X. Thus, it is the summation of $g(x)f(x)$ over x such that $f(x) > 0$, whenever this summation is absolutely convergent. Similarly, the expected value of the function of a continuous random variable, $g(X)$, is given by

$$E[g(X)] = \int_{-\infty}^{\infty} g(x)f_X(x)dx \tag{8.90}$$

EXAMPLE 8.2:

Let X have the probability mass function such that $f(0) = 0.2$, $f(1) = 0.5$, $f(2) = 0.3$. Calculate $E[X^3]$.

SOLUTION

Let $Y = X^3$. Now, Y can take on one of the three values, 0, 1, and 8. Then,

$$f_Y(0) = P(Y = 0^3) = 0.2$$
$$f_Y(1) = P(Y = 1^3) = 0.5$$
$$f_Y(2) = P(Y = 2^3) = 0.3$$

Therefore, $E[X^3] = E[Y] = 0(0.2) + 1(0.5) + 8(0.3) = 2.9$. It may be noted that $E[x^2] \neq [E(X)]^2$.

8.12 Conditional Distribution and Density Functions

We will consider the discrete case first. For any two events, A and B, the conditional probability of A given B is defined, as long as $P(B) > 0$, by

$$P(A|B) = \frac{P(AB)}{P(B)} \tag{8.91}$$

Therefore, if X and Y are discrete random variables, the *conditional probability mass function* of X given that $Y = y$ is given by

$$\begin{aligned} P_{X|Y}(x|y) &= P(X = x|Y = y) \\ &= \frac{P(X = x, Y = y)}{P(Y = y)} \\ &= \frac{p(x, y)}{p_Y(y)} \end{aligned} \tag{8.92}$$

for all values of y such that $P(Y = y) > 0$. The *conditional probability distribution function* of X given that $Y = y$ is defined, for all y such that $P(Y = y) > 0$, as

$$\begin{aligned} F_{X|Y}(x|y) &= P(X \leq x|Y = y) \\ &= \sum_{a \leq x} p_{X|Y}(a|y) \end{aligned} \tag{8.93}$$

We will now consider the continuous case. If two continuous random variables X and Y have a joint probability density function $f(x, y)$, then the *conditional probability density function* of X, given that $Y = y$, is defined for all values of y such that $f_Y(y) > 0$, as

$$f_{X|Y}(x|y) = \frac{f(x, y)}{f_Y(y)} \tag{8.94}$$

8.13 Conditional Expected Values

In the discrete case, the conditional expectation of random variable X given that random variable Y is

$$E(X|Y = y) = \sum_{x:f_{X|Y}>0} x f_{X|Y}(x|y) \tag{8.95}$$

In the case of continuous random variables, the conditional expectation is given as

$$E(X|Y = y) = \int_{-\infty}^{\infty} x f_{X|Y}(x|y) dx \tag{8.96}$$

8.13.1 Computing Expectations by Conditioning

Let us denote by $E(X|Y)$, a function of the random variable Y whose value at $Y = y$ is $E(X|Y = y)$. Note that $E(X|Y)$ itself is a random variable. An important property of conditional expectation is that for all random variables X and Y, we have

$$E(X) = E[E(X|Y)] \tag{8.97}$$

If Y is a discrete random variable, then equation (8.97) states that

$$E(X) = \sum_y E(X|Y = y)P(Y = y)$$

For the continuous case, we have

$$E(X) = \int_{-\infty}^{\infty} E(X|Y = y) f_Y(y) dy$$

The proof of equation (8.97), for the discrete case, is given below:

We must show that

$$E(X) = \sum_y E(X|Y = y)P(Y = y)$$

Now, we can write the right-hand side of the above equation as

$$\begin{aligned}
\sum_y E(X|Y = y)P(Y = y) &= \sum_y \sum_x xP(X = x|Y = y)P(Y = y) \\
&= \sum_y \sum_x x \frac{P(X = x, Y = y)}{P(Y = y)} P(Y = y) \\
&= \sum_y \sum_x xP(X = x, Y = y) \\
&= \sum_x x \sum_y P(X = x, Y = y) \\
&= \sum_x xP(X = x) \\
&= E(X)
\end{aligned}$$

and the result is proved.

8.14 The Variance and Standard Deviation

The *variance* of a discrete (continuous) random variable X is given by

$$\begin{aligned}
\text{Var}(X) &= E\left[(X - E(X))^2\right] &(8.98)\\
&= E\left[X^2 - 2XE(X) + E^2(X)\right] \\
&= E\left[X^2\right] - 2E[X]E[X] + E^2[X] \\
&= E\left[X^2\right] - E^2[X] &(8.99)
\end{aligned}$$

Thus the variance of X measures the expected square of the deviation of X from its expected (mean) value. We define the *standard deviation* of a random variable X as the square root of its variance.

8.14.1 Computing Variances by Conditioning

Conditional expectations can also be used to compute the variance of a random variable. We can use the basic variance relation as given by equation (8.99) and then use conditioning to obtain both $E[X]$ and $E[X^2]$.

The *conditional variance* of a random variable X given that $Y = y$ is defined as

$$\begin{aligned}
\text{Var}(X|Y = y) &= E\left[(X - E[X|Y = y])^2|Y = y\right] \qquad (8.100)\\
&= E[X^2|Y = y] - 2E[X|Y = y]E[X|Y = y] + (E[X|Y = y])^2\\
&= E[X^2|Y = y] - (E[X|Y = y])^2 \qquad (8.101)
\end{aligned}$$

Now, letting $\text{Var}(X|Y)$ denote the function of Y, whose value when $Y = y$ is $\text{var}(X|Y = y)$, we have the following relation:

$$\text{Var}(X) = E\left[\text{Var}(X|Y)\right] + \text{Var}(E[X|Y]) \qquad (8.102)$$

The proof of the above relation is as shown below.

$$\begin{aligned}
E\left[\text{Var}(X|Y)\right] &= E\left[E(X^2|Y) - (E(X|Y))^2\right]\\
&= E\left[E(X^2|Y)\right] - E\left[(E(X|Y))^2\right]\\
&= E[X^2] - E\left[(E(X|Y))^2\right] \qquad (8.103)
\end{aligned}$$

and,

$$\begin{aligned}
\text{Var}(E[X|Y]) &= E\left[(E[X|Y])^2\right] - (E\left[E(X|Y)\right])^2\\
&= E\left[(E[X|Y])^2\right] - (E[X])^2 \qquad (8.104)
\end{aligned}$$

Therefore,

$$E\left[\text{Var}(X|Y)\right] + \text{Var}(E[X|Y]) = E[X^2] - (E[X])^2$$

8.15 Operations on a Random Variable

We will now consider certain mathematical operations done on random variables. We begin our discussion with *moments* of random variables. Calculation of moments and *central moments* is an important operation done on random variables.

8.15.1 Moments

The *nth moment* of a continuous random variable X is defined as

$$E\left[X^n\right] = \int_{-\infty}^{\infty} x^n f_X(x)dx \qquad (8.105)$$

For a discrete random variable X, the definition is

$$E[X^n] = \sum_k x_k^n P_X(x_k) \tag{8.106}$$

The *zeroth* moment is simply the area under the probability density function and hence must be 1 for any random variable. The most commonly used moments are the first and second moments. The first moment is referred to as the *mean* and the second moment is the *mean squared value*.

8.15.2 Central Moments

Consider the case of a random variable Y which is the sum of a deterministic quantity and a random variable, expressed as $Y = a + X$. Further, suppose that the random part is very small compared to the deterministic (fixed) part. In this case, we may write $Y^n = (a+X)^n \approx a^n$. Here, the nth moment of Y is dominated by the fixed part. Thus, it is difficult to calculate the *randomness* in Y. To overcome this difficulty, we introduce the central moment.

Table 8.3 Expected values of various functions of random variables

Sl.No.	Name	Functions of X	Notation of expected value
1.	Mean, average, Expected value, expectation, first moment	$f(x) = x$	$\mu_X = \overline{X} = E[X]$
2.	mth moment	$f(x) = x^m$	$\overline{X^m} = E[X^m]$
3.	mth central moment	$f(x) = (x - \mu_X)^m$	$\overline{(X - \mu_X)} = E[X - \mu_X]$
4.	Variance	$f(x) = (x - \mu_X)^2$	$\sigma_X^2 = E\left[(X - \mu_X)^2\right]$
5.	Coefficient of skewness	$f(x) = \left(\frac{x-\mu_X}{\sigma_X}\right)^3$	$c_s = E\left[\left(\frac{X-\mu_X}{\sigma_X}\right)^3\right]$
6.	Coefficient of kurtosis	$f(x) = \left(\frac{x-\mu_X}{\sigma_X}\right)^4$	$c_k = E\left[\left(\frac{X-\mu_X}{\sigma_X}\right)^4\right]$
7.	Characteristic function	$f(x) = \exp(j\omega x)$	$\Phi_X(\omega) = E[\exp(j\omega X)]$
8.	Moment generating function	$f(x) = \exp(sx)$	$M_X(s) = E[\exp(sX)]$
9.	Probability generating function	$f(x) = z^x$	$H_X(z) = E\left[z^X\right]$

The nth central moment of a continuous random variable X is defined as

$$E[(X - \mu_X)^n] = \int_{-\infty}^{\infty} (x - \mu_X)^n f_X(x)dx \tag{8.107}$$

where, μ_X = mean$[X]$, is the mean (first moment). For discrete random variables, the corresponding relation is

$$E\left[(X-\mu_X)^n\right] = \sum_k (x_k - \mu_X)^n P_X(x_k) \tag{8.108}$$

In the case of central moments, the mean is subtracted from the variable before the moment is taken in order to remove the bias in the higher order moments due to the mean. Note that, like regular moments, the zeroth central moment is $E\left[(X-\mu_X)^0\right] = E[1] = 0$. Furthermore, the first central moment is $E\left[X-\mu_X\right] = E[X] - \mu_X = 0$. Hence, the lowest central moment of any real interest is the second central moment. This central moment is also known as the *variance* and is denoted as σ_X^2. It may also be noted that

$$\sigma_X^2 = E[X^2] - \mu_X^2 \tag{8.109}$$

Table 8.3 lists the expected values of various functions of random variables.

8.16 Transformations of Random Variables

Quite often, it is of interest, to find out the PDF and CDF of the output Y of a system, for which the PDF and CDF of the input random variable X is known. In this case, we say that the input random variable has undergone a *transformation*. We will first consider the case of a *monotonically increasing function*.

8.16.1 Monotonically Increasing Functions

Let us assume that the function is continuous, one-to-one, and monotonically increasing. Now, we have the mapping, $Y = g(X)$. Under the above conditions, the inverse function exists, and is given by

$$X = g^{-1}(Y) \tag{8.110}$$

To obtain the PDF of Y, we calculate its CDF. Recalling $F_Y(y) = P(Y \leq y)$, the CDF of Y can be written as

$$F_Y(y) = P(g(X) \leq y) = P(X \leq g^{-1}(y)) = F_X(g^{-1}(y)) \tag{8.111}$$

Note that this can also be written as

$$F_X(x) = F_Y(g(x)) \tag{8.112}$$

Differentiating equation (8.111) w.r.t. y produces

$$f_Y(y) = f_X\left(g^{-1}(y)\right)\frac{dg^{-1}(y)}{dy} = f_X(x)\left.\frac{dx}{dy}\right|_{x=g^{-1}(y)} \tag{8.113}$$

Differentiating equation (8.112) w.r.t. x produces

$$f_X(x) = f_Y\left(g(x)\right)\frac{dy}{dx} \Rightarrow f_Y(y) = \left.\frac{f_X(x)}{\frac{dy}{dx}}\right|_{x=g^{-1}(y)} \tag{8.114}$$

Any one of the above two equations can be used to compute the PDF of the new random variable.

8.16.2 Monotonically Decreasing Functions

Note that for monotonically decreasing functions, we have $X \geq g^{-1}(y)$. Then we have

$$F_Y(y) = P(Y \leq y) = P(X \geq g^{-1}(y)) = 1 - F_X\left(g^{-1}(y)\right) \tag{8.115}$$

Differentiating the above equation w.r.t. y gives

$$f_Y(y) = -f_X(x)\left.\frac{dx}{dy}\right|_{x=g^{-1}(y)} \tag{8.116}$$

Similarly, we have $F_Y(y) = 1 - F_X(x)$ and differentiating w.r.t. x results in

$$f_Y(y) = \left.\frac{-f_X(x)}{\frac{dy}{dx}}\right|_{x=g^{-1}(y)} \tag{8.117}$$

8.16.3 Non-monotonic Functions

In this case, we cannot associate the event $Y \leq y$ with the events of $X \leq g^{-1}(y)$ or $X \geq g^{-1}(y)$, because the transformation is not monotonic. Hence we calculate the PDF of Y directly. Consider an event of the form $y \leq Y < y + dy$ for an infinitesimal dy. The probability of this event is $P(y \leq Y < y + dy) = f_Y(y)dy$. To relate the PDF of Y to the PDF of X, we relate the event $y \leq Y < y + dy$ to events involving the random variable X. The roots of the equation $x = g^{-1}(y)$ is referred to as $x_1,\ x_2,\ x_3,\ \ldots, x_N$. Moreover, let X^+ be the sub-set of these roots at which the function $g(x)$ has a positive slope, and similarly let X^{-1} be the remaining roots for which the slope of the function is negative. Then we have

$$y \leq Y < y + dy = \left[\bigcup_{x_i \in X^+} x_i \leq X < x_i + dx_i\right] = \left[\bigcup_{x_i \in X^-} x_i + dx_i < X \leq x_i\right] \tag{8.118}$$

Since each of the events on the right-hand side is mutually exclusive, the probability of the union is simply the sum of the probabilities, so that

$$\begin{aligned} f_Y(y)dy &= \sum_{x_i \in X^+} P(x_i \leq X < x_i + dx_i) + P(x_i + dx_i < X \leq x_i) \\ &= \sum_{x_i \in X^+} f_X(x_i)dx_i + \sum_{x_i \in X^-} f_X(x_i)(-dx_i) \end{aligned} \tag{8.119}$$

Invoking absolute value signs to circumvent the need to have two separate sums and dividing by dy, we have

$$f_Y(y) = \sum_{x_i} f_X(x) \left| \frac{dx}{dy} \right| \Bigg|_{x_i = g^{-1}(y)} \tag{8.120}$$

The above equation can also be written as

$$f_Y(y) = \sum_{x_i} \frac{f_X(x)}{\left| \frac{dy}{dx} \right|} \Bigg|_{x_i = g^{-1}(y)} \tag{8.121}$$

EXAMPLE 8.3

Let X be a Gaussian random variable with zero mean and variance σ^2. Find the PDF of the random variable Y for the transformation $Y = X^2$.

SOLUTION

For any positive value of y, $y = x^2$ has two real roots, viz., $x = \pm\sqrt{y}$. For negative values of y, there are no real roots. Applying the equation for the PDF of Y

$$f_Y(y) = \left[\frac{f_X(+\sqrt{y})}{2|+\sqrt{y}|} + \frac{f_X(-\sqrt{y})}{2|-\sqrt{y}|} \right] u(y) = \frac{f_X(+\sqrt{y}) + f_X(-\sqrt{y})}{2\sqrt{y}} u(y)$$

where $u(y) = 1$, for $y > 0$, is the *unit step function*. For a zero mean Gaussian PDF, $f_X(x)$ is an even function so that $f_X(+\sqrt{y}) = f_X(-\sqrt{y})$. Hence,

$$f_Y(y) = \frac{1}{\sqrt{y}} f_X(\sqrt{y}) u(y) = \sqrt{\frac{1}{2\pi y \sigma^2}} \exp\left[-\frac{y}{2\sigma^2} \right] u(y)$$

8.17 Characteristic Functions

The *characteristic function* of a random variable is closely related to the Fourier transform of the PDF of the random variable. Therefore, the characteristic function provides a sort of "frequency domain" representation of a random variable. The characteristic function is quite useful in finding out the *moments* of a random variable. The characteristic function of a random variable X is given by

$$\Phi_X(\omega) = E\left[\exp(j\omega X)\right] = \int_{-\infty}^{\infty} \exp(j\omega x) f_X(x) dx \tag{8.122}$$

Since the Fourier transform of a function $f_X(x)$ is given by $\Phi(-\omega)$, we can obtain the PDF of a random variable from its inverse Fourier transform as given below

$$f_X(x) = \frac{1}{2\pi}\int_{-\infty}^{\infty} \exp(-j\omega x)\Phi_X(\omega)d\omega. \tag{8.123}$$

RELATION BETWEEN CHARACTERISTIC FUNCTION AND MEAN

For any random variable X whose characteristic function is differentiable at $\omega = 0$, we have $E[X] = -j\frac{d}{d\omega}\Phi_X(\omega)\big|_{\omega=0}$.

8.18 Probability Generating Functions (PGF)

For a discrete random variable with a probability mass function $f_X(x)$, defined on non-negative integers, $k = 0, 1, 2, \ldots$, the *probability generating function* $H_X(z)$ is defined as

$$H_X(z) = \sum_{k=0}^{\infty} f_X(k)z^k \tag{8.124}$$

where z is a complex variable such that $0 \leq |z| \leq 1$. Note that the probability generating function (PGF) is similar to the unilateral Z-transform of the probability mass function.

Since the probability mass function can be seen as the coefficients of the Taylor series expansion of $H_X(z)$, it should be apparent that the former can be obtained from the probability generating function through

$$f_X(k) = \frac{1}{k!}\frac{d^k}{dz^k}H_X(z)\bigg|_{z=0} \tag{8.125}$$

RELATION BETWEEN PROBABILITY GENERATING FUNCTION AND MEAN

For any discrete random variable X whose probability generating function (PGF) is $H_X(z)$, where z is a complex variable such that $|z| \leq 1$, and which is differentiable at $z = 1$, we have $E[X] = \frac{d}{dz}H_X(z)\big|_{z=1}$.

Probability generating functions have the following properties:

1. The values of $H_X(z)$ uniquely determine $\{p_k\}$, since $H^{(k)}(0)/k = p_k$ for $k = 0, 1, 2, \ldots$ In fact, we see that values of $H_X(z)$ for real s with $0 < s < 1$ are sufficient for this purpose since these values determine $H_X(1)$ as well as H_X and all of its derivatives at 0. Note that, in particular, $H_X(0) = p_0$ and $H_X(1) = \sum_{k=0}^{\infty} P_k = P(N < +\infty)$.

2. Probability generating functions obey all the rules of power series with non-negative coefficients.

3. For $|z| < 1, H_X^{'}(z) = \sum_{k=1}^{\infty} kz^{k-1}p_k$.

4. Similarly, for $n > 1$ and N finite-valued, we have:

$$H_X^{(n)}(1) = \lim_{s \uparrow 1} H_X^{(n)}(s) = E\left(N(N-1)\dots(N-n+1)\right).$$

5. If N and M are independent non-negative integer-valued random variables, with generating functions g_N and g_M respectively, then the generating function g_{N+M} of $N+M$ is given for $0 < s < 1$ by $g_{N+M}(s) = g_N(s).g_M(s)$.

6. Suppose $\{X_n\}$ are independent, identically distributed, finite non-negative integer-valued random variables which have a common generating function $g_X(s) = E\left(s^{X_1}\right)$. Let N be non-negative integer-valued, independent of the $\{X_n\}$, with generating function $g_N(s) = E\left(s^N\right)$. Define the random sum $S = \sum_{k=1}^{N} X_k$ to be 0 when $N = 0$ and to be $\sum_{k=1}^{N} X_k$ when $N = n \geq 1$. Then S has generating function g_S given by $g_S(s) = g_N\left(g_X(s)\right)$.

8.19 Moment Generating Functions

Moment generating functions are effective tools for analysing random variables which are inherently *non-negative*. The *moment generating function* $M_X(u)$ of a non-negative random variable X is defined as

$$M_X(u) = E\left[\exp(uX)\right] = \int_0^{\infty} f_X(x)\exp(ux)dx \tag{8.126}$$

Note the similarity between the moment generating function and the Laplace transform of the PDF. The PDF can be retrieved from the moment generating function through an operation similar to the inverse Laplace transformation.

$$f_X(x) = \frac{1}{2\pi j}\int_{c-j\infty}^{c+j\infty} M_X(u)\exp(-ux)du \tag{8.127}$$

As in the case of a characteristic function, the moments of the random variable can be found from the derivatives of the moment generating function (hence the name) as shown below:

$$E\left[X^k\right] = \left.\frac{d^k}{du^k}M_X(u)\right|_{u=0} \tag{8.128}$$

It can be noted that the moment generating function can be expanded as a *power series* of the form

$$M_X(x) = \sum_{k=0}^{\infty} m_k u^k \tag{8.129}$$

Then the moments of the random variable are given by $E\left[X^k\right] = k! m_k$.[4]

8.19.1 Markov's Inequality

Let X be a non-negative random variable (i.e., one whose PDF is non-zero only over the range $[0, \infty)$). Then

$$P(X \geq x_0) \leq \frac{E[X]}{x_0} \tag{8.130}$$

The proof of the above theorem is as follows. For non-negative random variables, the expected value is

$$\begin{aligned} E[X] &= \int_0^{\infty} x f_X(x) dx = \int_0^{x_0} x f_X(x) dx + \int_{x_0}^{\infty} x f_X(x) dx \geq \int_{x_0}^{\infty} x f_X(x) dx \\ &\geq x_0 \int_{x_0}^{\infty} f_X(x) dx = x_0 P(X \geq x_0) \end{aligned} \tag{8.131}$$

Dividing both sides by x_0 provides the necessary result.

Markov's inequality gives a bound on tail probability. The bound only needs knowledge of the mean of the random variable.

8.19.2 Chebyshev's Inequality

Let X be a random variable with mean μ_X and variance σ_X^2. The probability that the random variable takes on a value that is removed from the mean by more than x_0 is given by

$$P\left(|X - \mu_X| \geq x_0\right) \leq \frac{\sigma_X^2}{x_0^2} \tag{8.132}$$

Chebyshev's inequality is a direct result of Markov's inequality. Note that the event $\{|X - \mu_X| \geq x_0\}$ is equivalent to the event $\{|X - \mu_X|^2 \geq x_0^2\}$. Applying Markov's inequality to the later event results in

$$P\left[(X - \mu_X)^2 \geq x_0^2\right] \leq \frac{E\left[(X - \mu_X)^2\right]}{x_0^2} = \frac{\sigma_X^2}{x_0^2} \tag{8.133}$$

[4] In the case of random variables that are not necessarily non-negative, a two-sided Laplace transform is appropriate.

Note that Chebyshev's inequality gives a bound on two-sided tail probability, whereas Markov's inequality applies to one-sided tail probability. Chebyshev's inequality can be applied to any random variable, not just to those that are non-negative.

8.19.3 Chernoff Bound

Let X be a random variable whose moment generating function is $M_X(s)$. Then we have

$$P(X \geq x_0) \leq \min_{s \geq 0} \exp(-s x_0) M_X(s) \tag{8.134}$$

Note that

$$P(X \geq x_0) = \int_{x_0}^{\infty} f_X(x) dx = \int_{-\infty}^{\infty} f_X(x) u(x - x_0) dx \tag{8.135}$$

Now, the upper bound of the unit step function in the integrand is an exponential function of the form $u(x - x_0) \leq \exp(s(x - x_0))$. Note that the bound is valid for any real $s \geq 0$. The tail probability is then upper bounded by

$$P(X \geq x_0) \leq \exp(-s x_0) \int_{-\infty}^{\infty} f_X(x) \exp(sx) dx = \exp(-s x_0)\, M_X(s) \tag{8.136}$$

Since this bound is valid for any $s \geq 0$, it can be tightened by finding the value of s that minimises the right-hand side. In this expression, the two-sided Laplace transform must be used to obtain the moment generating function if the random variable is non-negative.

8.20 Joint Probability Distribution Functions

The *joint cumulative distribution function* of a pair of random variables $[X, Y]$ is $F_{X,Y}(x, y) = P(X \leq x, Y \leq y)$. That is, the joint CDF is the joint probability of the two events $\{X \leq x\}$ and $\{Y \leq y\}$. The joint cumulative distribution functions have the following properties:

- They must take a value between 0 and 1 (as it is a probability).
- $F_{X,Y}(x, y)$ evaluated at both $-\infty$ and ∞ must be zero.
- $F_{X,Y}(\infty, \infty)$ must be one.
- For $x_1 \leq x_2$ and $y_1 \leq y_2$, $[X \leq x_1] \cap [Y \leq y_1]$ is a sub-set of $[X \leq x_2] \cap [Y \leq y_2]$, so that $F_{X,Y}(x_1, y_1) \leq F_{X,Y}(x_2, y_2)$. That is, the CDF is a monotonic, non-decreasing function of both x and y.
- $F_{X,Y}(\infty, y) = F_Y(y)$ and $F_{X,Y}(x, \infty) = F_X(x)$.
- $P(x_1 < X_1 \leq x_2, y_1 < Y_1 \leq y_2) = F_{X,Y}(x_2, y_2) - F_{X,Y}(x_1, y_2) - F_{X,Y}(x_2, y_1) + F_{X,Y}(x_1, y_1) \geq 0$.

8.21 Joint Probability Density Functions

The *joint probability density function* of a pair of continuous random variables $[X, Y]$ evaluated at the point (x, y) is given by

$$f_{X,Y}(x,y) = \lim_{\varepsilon_x \to 0,\ \varepsilon_y \to 0} \frac{P\left[x \le X < x + \varepsilon_x,\ y \le Y < y + \varepsilon_y\right]}{\varepsilon_x \varepsilon_y} \tag{8.137}$$

RELATION BETWEEN JOINT CDF AND JOINT PDF

The joint PDF $f_{X,Y}(x, y)$ can be obtained from the joint CDF $F_{X,Y}(x, y)$ by taking a partial derivative with respect to each variable. That is, $f_{X,Y}(x,y) = \frac{\partial^2}{\partial x\, \partial y} F_{X,Y}(x,y)$.

The joint probability density function has the following properties:

- $f_{X,Y}(x, y) \ge 0$.
- $\int\limits_{-\infty}^{\infty}\int\limits_{-\infty}^{\infty} f_{X,Y}(x,y)dxdy = 1$.
- $F_{X,Y}(x,y) = \int\limits_{-\infty}^{y}\int\limits_{-\infty}^{x} f_{X,Y}(u,v)dudv$.
- $f_{X,Y}(x,y) = \frac{\partial^2}{\partial x\, \partial y} F_{X,Y}(x,y)$
- $f_X(x) = \int\limits_{-\infty}^{\infty} f_{X,Y}(x,y)dy,\ f_Y(y) = \int\limits_{-\infty}^{\infty} f_{X,Y}(x,y)dx$.
- $P\left[x_1 < X_1 \le x_2,\ y_1 < Y_1 \le y_2\right] = \int\limits_{y_1}^{y_2}\int\limits_{x_1}^{x_2} f_{X,Y}(x,y)dxdy$.

Given the joint probability density function, we can find out the conditional density function.

EXAMPLE 8.4

For random variables X and Y, the joint probability density function is given by

$$f_{X,Y}(x,y) = \frac{1+xy}{4},\ |x| \le 1,\ |y| \le 1.$$
$$= 0;\ \text{otherwise}$$

Find the marginal densities $f_X(x)$, $f_Y(y)$ and $f_{Y|X}(y|x)$. Are X and Y independent?

SOLUTION

$f_X(x) = \int\limits_{-1}^{1} \frac{1+xy}{4} dy = \frac{1}{2}$.

Similarly, $f_Y(y) = \frac{1}{2}$, $-1 \le y \le 1$, and

$$f_{Y|X}(y|x) = \frac{f_{X,Y}(x,y)}{f_X(x)} = \frac{1+xy}{2}, \ |x| \le 1, |y| \le 1$$
$$= 0, \text{ otherwise}$$

Hence, X and Y are not independent.

8.22 Joint Probability Mass Functions

The *joint probability mass function* of a pair of discrete random variables X and Y is given by

$$f_{X,Y}(x,y) = P[\{X = x\} \cap \{Y = y\}]$$

We now list the properties of joint probability mass functions:

- $0 \le f_{X,Y}(x_m, y_n) \le 1.$
- $\sum_{m=1}^{M} \sum_{n=1}^{N} f_{X,Y}(x_m, y_n) = 1.$
- $\sum_{n=1}^{N} f_{X,Y}(x_m, y_n) = f_X(x_m), \ \sum_{m=1}^{M} f_{X,Y}(x_m, y_n) = f_Y(y_n).$
- $P[(X,Y) \in A] = \sum\sum_{(x,y)\in A} f_{X,Y}(x,y).$

8.23 Independent Random Variables

A pair of random variables are said to be independent if and only if

$$P[X \le x, Y \le y] = P[X \le x]\, P[Y \le y] \Rightarrow F_{X,Y}(x,y) = F_X(x)F_Y(y) \tag{8.138}$$

The above statement can be extended to PDFs as well. Thus for two independent random variables X and Y,

$$f_{X,Y}(x,y) = f_X(x) f_Y(y) \tag{8.139}$$

The same statement is valid for probability mass functions as well. By dividing both sides of equation (8.139) by $f_X(x)$, we get

$$f_{Y|X}(y|x) = f_Y(y) \tag{8.140}$$

INDEPENDENCE OF FUNCTIONS OF TWO INDEPENDENT RANDOM VARIABLES

Let X and Y be two independent random variables and let two new random variables be defined by $U = g_1(X)$ and $V = g_2(Y)$. Then these two random variables U and V are also independent.

8.23.1 The Correlation Between Two Random Variables

The *correlation* between two random variables is given by

$$R_{XY} = E[XY] = \int_{-\infty}^{\infty}\int_{-\infty}^{\infty} xy f_{X,Y}(x,y)dxdy. \quad (8.141)$$

Two random variables that have a *zero* correlation are said to be *orthogonal*. Consider the expected value of $g(X,Y) = (X+Y)^2$. We have

$$E[X+Y]^2 = E[X^2 + 2XY + Y^2] = E[X^2] + E[Y^2] + 2E[XY]. \quad (8.142)$$

Therefore, the second moment of the sum is the sum of the second moments plus twice the correlation.

8.23.2 The Covariance

The *covariance* between two random variables is given by

$$\text{Cov}(X,Y) = E[(X-\mu_X)(Y-\mu_Y)] = \int_{-\infty}^{\infty}\int_{-\infty}^{\infty} (x-\mu_X)(y-\mu_Y) f_{X,Y}(x,y)dxdy. \quad (8.143)$$

If two random variables have a covariance of zero, they are said to be *uncorrelated*.

RELATION BETWEEN CORRELATION AND COVARIANCE OF RANDOM VARIABLES

The correlation and covariance of a pair of random variables are related as $\text{Cov}(X,Y) = R_{XY} - \mu_X\mu_Y$.

8.23.3 The Correlation Coefficient

The *correlation coefficient* of two random variables X and Y, ρ_{XY} is given by

$$\rho_{XY} = \frac{\text{Cov}(X,Y)}{\sqrt{\text{Var}(X)\text{Var}(Y)}} = \frac{E[(X-\mu_X)(Y-\mu_X)]}{\sigma_X\sigma_Y}. \quad (8.144)$$

The correlation coefficient is a quantitative measure of the correlation between two random variables.

8.23.4 The Joint Moment

The $(m,n)th$ *joint moment* of two random variables X and Y is given by

$$E[X^mY^n] = \int_{-\infty}^{\infty}\int_{-\infty}^{\infty} x^m y^n f_{X,Y}(x,y)dxdy. \quad (8.145)$$

8.23.5 The Joint Central Moment

The $(m, n)th$ *joint central moment* of two random variables X and Y is similarly given by

$$E\left[(X-\mu_X)^m(Y-\mu_Y)^n\right] = \int_{-\infty}^{\infty}\int_{-\infty}^{\infty}(x-\mu_X)^m(y-\mu_Y)^n f_{X,Y}(x,y)dxdy \tag{8.146}$$

CORRELATION COEFFICIENT/COVARIANCE OF INDEPENDENT RANDOM VARIABLES

If X and Y are two independent random variables, then $E[XY] = \mu_X\mu_Y$, $\text{Cov}(X,Y) = 0$, and $\rho_{XY} = 0$.

8.24 Jointly Gaussian Random Variables

A pair of random variables are said to be *jointly Gaussian* if they have a joint probability density function given by

$$f_{X,Y}(x,y) = \frac{1}{2\pi\sigma_X\sigma_Y\sqrt{1-\rho_{XY}^2}} \times$$

$$\exp\left(-\left[\frac{\left(\frac{x-\mu_X}{\sigma_X}\right)^2 - 2\rho_{XY}\left(\frac{x-\mu_X}{\sigma_X}\right)\left(\frac{y-\mu_Y}{\sigma_Y}\right) + \left(\frac{y-\mu_Y}{\sigma_Y}\right)^2}{2(1-\rho_{XY}^2)}\right]\right) \tag{8.147}$$

where μ_X and μ_Y are the means of X and Y respectively; σ_X and σ_Y are the standard deviations of X and Y, respectively; and ρ_{XY} is the correlation coefficient of X and Y. The jointly Gaussian PDF is illustrated in Figure 8.25. The MATLAB script to generate the same is also given below.

```
%%% MATLAB M-file to generate and plot
%%% a jointly Gaussian (Normal) PDF..
close all, clear all; clf;
sigx=1; sigy=1;
mux=0; muy=0;
rho=0;
x=linspace(-5,5,100);
y=x;
[x,y]=meshgrid(x,y);
fxy=1/(2*pi)*exp(-(x.^2+y.^2)/2);
% surfc(x,y,fxy);
mesh(x,y,fxy);
%%% end of jgausspdf.m
```

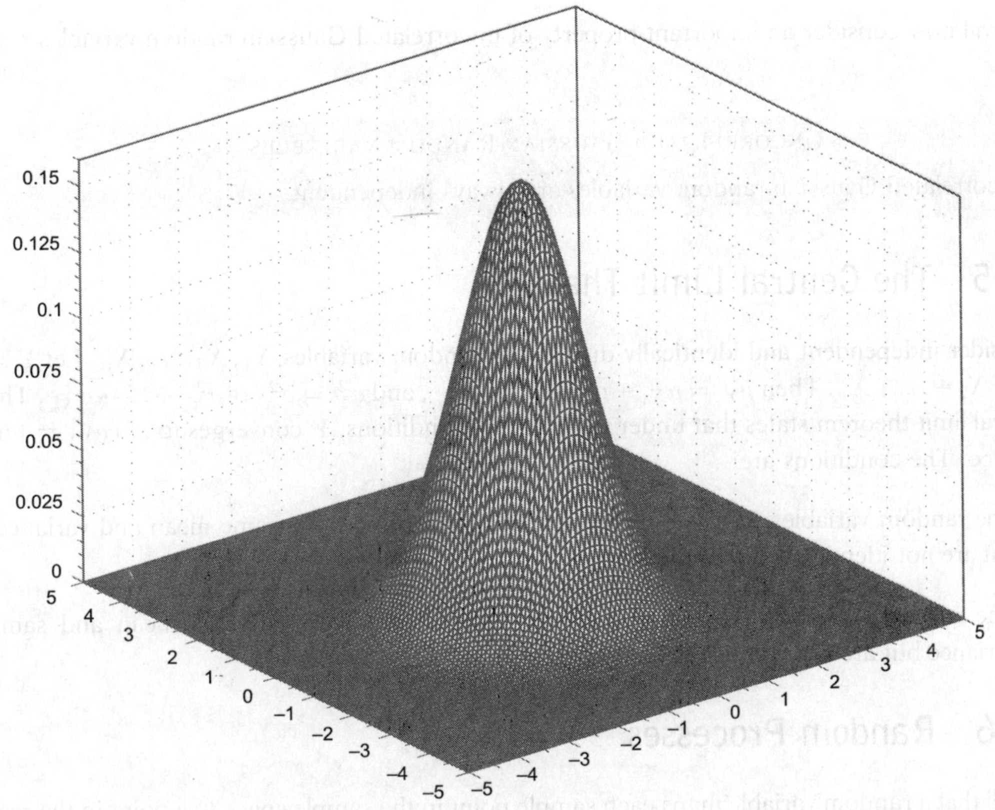

Figure 8.25 The jointly Gaussian PDF: $\sigma_X = \sigma_Y = 1,\ \mu_X = \mu_Y = 0,\ \rho_{XY} = 0$

8.24.1 Properties of Jointly Gaussian Random Variables

The jointly Gaussian random variables have the following important properties:

1. If X and Y are jointly Gaussian, then for any constants a and b, the random variable, Z, given by $Z = aX + bY$ is Gaussian with mean $\mu_Z = a\mu_X + b\mu_Y$ and variance $\sigma_Z^2 = a^2\sigma_X^2 + b^2\sigma_Y^2 + 2ab\sigma_X\sigma_Y\rho_{X,Y}$.

2. If two jointly Gaussian random variables are uncorrelated, i.e., if $\rho_{X,Y} = 0$, then they are statistically independent. $f_{X,Y}(x, y) = f_X(x)f_Y(y)$ in this case.

3. If $f_{X,Y}(x, y)$ is a jointly Gaussian distribution, then the marginal densities, $f_X(x),\ f_Y(y)$ are also Gaussian.

4. If X and Y are joint by Gaussian random variables, then the optimum non-linear estimator, $\hat{X}$ of X that minimises the mean square error $\xi = E\left[(X - \hat{X})^2\right]$ is a linear estimator $\hat{X} = aY$.

We will now consider an important property of uncorrelated Gaussian random variables.

UNCORRELATED GAUSSIAN RANDOM VARIABLES

Uncorrelated Gaussian random variables are always independent.

8.25 The Central Limit Theorem

Consider independent and identically distributed random variables $X_1, X_2, \ldots, X_n$. Let $Y = X_1 + X_2 + \ldots + X_n$. Then $\mu_Y = \mu_{X_1} + \mu_{X_2} + \ldots + \mu_{X_n}$, and $\sigma_Y^2 = \sigma_{X_1}^2 + \sigma_{X_2}^2 + \ldots + \sigma_{X_n}^2$. The central limit theorem states that under very general conditions, Y converges to $N\left(\mu_Y, \sigma_Y^2\right)$ as $n \to \infty$. The conditions are:

1. The random variables $X_1, X_2, \ldots, X_n$ are independent with the same mean and variance, but are not identically distributed.

2. The random variables $X_1, X_2, \ldots, X_n$ are independent with different mean and same variance but are not identically distributed.

8.26 Random Processes

Recall that a random variable maps each sample point in the sample space to a point in the real line. A random process maps each sample point to a waveform. It is defined as the ensemble (collection) of time functions together with a probability rule. Mathematically, $X(t, s)$ is a random process such that:

- It is an ensemble of all time functions together with a probability rule.
- $X(t; s_j)$ is a realisation or sample function of the random process.
- Probability rules assign probability to any meaningful event associated with an observation. An observation is a sample function of the random process.

The random process $X(t, \xi)$ is normally denoted by $X(t)$. We can define a discrete random process $X[n]$ on discrete points of time. Such a random process is more important in practical implementations. A typical random process, $X(t)$ is illustrated in Figure 8.26 and is described by the joint probability density functions of the random variables at different t.

8.26.1 Strict Sense Stationary Random Process

A random process is said to be stationary if its statistical characterisation is independent of the observation interval over which the process was initiated. A random process

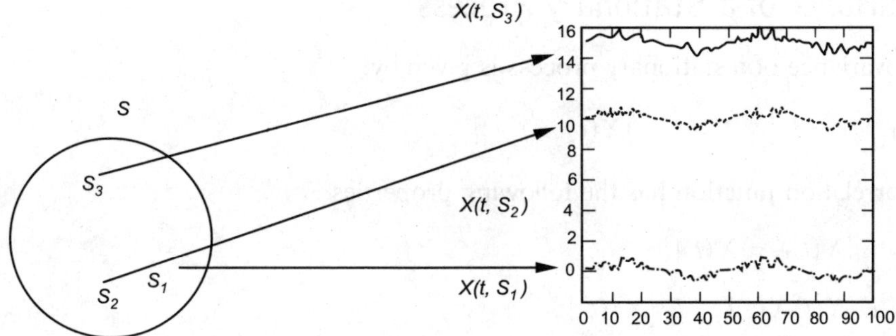

Figure 8.26 Illustration of a typical random process

$X(t)$ is called strict sense stationary if its probability structure is invariant with time. Mathematically,

$$f_{X(t_1+T)\ldots X(t_k+T)} = f_{X(t_1)\ldots X(t_k)}$$

The mean of a stationary random process is independent of the time of observation. Thus:

$$\mu_X(t) = E\left[X(t)\right] = \mu_X$$

8.26.2 Wide Sense Stationary Random Process

A random process $X(t)$ is called a wide sense stationary process (WSS) if $\mu_X(t) =$ constant and $R_X(t_1, t_2) = R_X(t_1 - t_2)$ is a function of time lag.

For a Gaussian random process, wide sense stationarity implies strict sense stationarity, because this process is completely described by the mean and the auto-correlation functions.

Auto-correlation of a Random Process

The auto-correlation of a random process is given by:

$$\begin{aligned} R_X(t_1, t_2) &= E\left[X(t_1), X(t_2)\right] \\ &= \int_{-\infty}^{\infty}\int_{-\infty}^{\infty} x_1 x_2 f_{X(t_1)X(t_2)}(x_1, x_2)dx_1 dx_2 \end{aligned} \tag{8.148}$$

For a stationary process, the auto-correlation is dependent only on the time shift and not on the time of observation.

Auto-covariance of a Stationary Process

The auto-covariance of a stationary process is given by:

$$C_X(t_1, t_2) = E\left[X(t_1 - \mu_X)X(t_2 - \mu_X)\right] \tag{8.149}$$

The auto-correlation function has the following properties:

1. $R_X(\tau) = E\left[X(t+\tau)X(t)\right]$.
2. $R_X(0) = E\left[X(t)X(t)\right] = E\left[X^2(t)\right]$.
3. The auto-correlation function is an even function i.e., $R_X(-\tau) = R_X(\tau)$.
4. The auto-correlation value is maximum for zero shift i.e., $R_X(\tau) \leq R_X(0)$.
5. If $R_X(\tau)$ drops quickly, then the signal samples are less correlated, which in turn means that the signal has lot of changes with respect to time. Such a signal has high frequency components. If $R_X(\tau)$ drops slowly, the signal samples are highly correlated and such a signal has less high frequency components.
6. $R_X(\tau)$ is directly related to the frequency domain representation of the WSS process.

Figure 8.27 illustrates the above concepts.

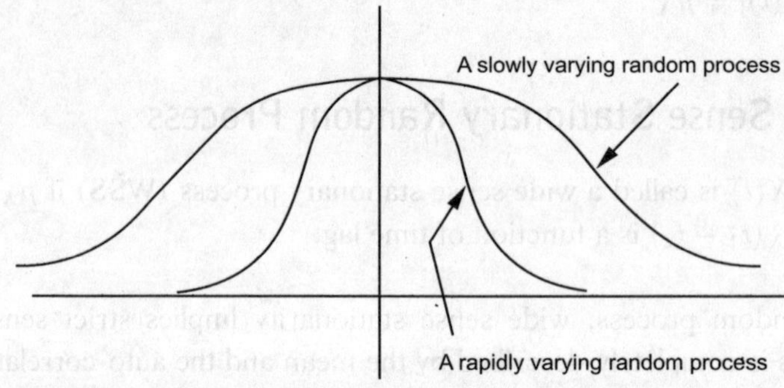

Figure 8.27 The auto-correlation function of a random process

8.27 Conclusion

In this chapter, we have discussed various probability density functions and cumulative distribution functions. Several library functions in the Statistics Toolbox of MATLAB were also introduced. Mathematical operations on random variables were discussed in detail. Probability generating functions and moment generating functions were introduced. We also considered jointly Gaussian random variables. A detailed discussion of random processes was also done.

Further Reading

1. Aiello W., S. Rajagopalan, and R. Venkatesan. Design of practical and provably good random number generators. *Journal of Algorithms* 29: 358–389. 1998.

2. Dagpunar J. *Principles of Random Variate Generation*. Clarendon. 1988.

3. *Getting Started with Communications Blockset*. The MathWorks. 2009.

4. *Getting Started with MATLAB 7*. The MathWorks. 2009.

5. Hull, T.E. and A.R. Dobell. Random number generators. *SIAM Review* 4(3): 230–254. July 1962.

6. Knuth, Donald E. *The Art of Computer Programming*. Vol. 2. Addison-Wesley. 1998.

7. Park, Stephen K. and Keith W. Miller. Random number generators: Good ones are hard to find. *Communications of the ACM* 31(10): 1192–1201. 1988.

8. Ross, Sheldon M. *Introduction to Probability Models*. 9th Edition. Academic Press. 2008.

9. *User's Guide, Statistics Toolbox*. The MathWorks. 2009.

Problems

1. Write the MATLAB code to randomly generate a number between $[0, 100]$ that is *equally likely*.

2. Write the MATLAB code to obtain a randomly generated number that follows the Bernoulli distribution for an arbitrary parameter, p.

3. Write the MATLAB code to obtain a randomly generated number that follows the binomial distribution for the arbitrary parameters, n, p.

4. Write the MATLAB code to simulate a random variable, X, whose probability mass function is given by $P_X(x) = 2^{-n}$, $n = 1, 2, 3, \ldots$

5. *Sterling's approximation* for the computation of the *factorial function* is given by

$$n! \approx \sqrt{2\pi}\left(n^{n+\frac{1}{2}}\right)\exp(-n)\left(1 - \frac{1}{12n}\right).$$

Develop a MATLAB program to compute $n!$ using Sterling's approximation formula. For what ranges of n is the approximation within 1% of the true value?

6. A communication system sends data in the form of *packets* of fixed length. Noise in the communication channel may result in a packet being received incorrectly—referred to as an *error in transmission*. In the case of an error, the packet(s) is/are re-transmitted. Let the probability that a packet is received incorrectly be q. Find the average number of transmissions that are necessary before a packet is received correctly. Model this system and simulate using MATLAB.

7. Let R be a random variable uniformly distributed over the interval $[0, 100]$. Form a new random variable R_1 by rounding R to the nearest integer. Finally, form the random rounding-off error as $\epsilon = R - R_1$.

   (a) Using the Statistics Toolbox of MATLAB, find the PDF of ϵ as well as the mean squared value, $E\left[\epsilon^2\right]$.

   (b) Using MATLAB, obtain a histogram for the probability densities for the random variable ϵ.

8. Let X be a random variable with $E[X] = 2$ and $\text{Var}(X) = 16$. Find the following:

   (a) $E[4X - 2]$.
   (b) $E[X]^2$.
   (c) $E[(4X - 2)^2]$.

9. The random variable X is *Gaussian distributed* with mean 4 and variance 1. We define another random variable, $Y = 4X + 6$. Find the mean (μ_Y), variance (σ_Y^2) and probability density function ($f_Y(y)$) of Y

10. Let X be a $(0, \sigma^2)$ Gaussian random variable. Given the transformation $Y = X^4$, find $f_Y(y)$.

11. Using MATLAB, generate a uniformly distributed random variable, A, over $(0, 1)$. Then create a new random variable according to the relation $B = -\log_e(X)$. From the sample of B, estimate and plot the PDF of B. Find an analytical model that will fit the estimate.

12. Using MATLAB, generate two Gaussian distributed random samples, X, and Y. Form a new random variable using the relation $Z = \sqrt{X^2 + Y^2}$. Using the samples of Z, estimate and plot its PDF. Also obtain an analytical solution for the PDF of Z.

13. Write a MATLAB code to implement the mixed linear congruent pseudo random number generators given in Table 8.1, and study their statistical properties.

14. Collect an extensive list of all pseudo random number generator algorithms known till date and implement them in MATLAB.

Index